Second Edition

INTRODUCTION TO FUTURES AND OPTIONS MARKETS

JOHN HULL
Faculty of Management
University of Toronto

Prentice Hall, Upper Saddle River, NJ 07458

Library of Congress Cataloging-in-Publication Data

Hull, John
Introduction to futures and options markets / John Hull, —2nd ed.
p. cm.
ISBN 0-13-122961-3
1. Futures market. 2. Options (Finance) 3. Futures market—Problems, exercises, etc. 4. Options (Finance)—Problems, exercises, etc. I. Title.
HG6024.A3H84 1995 94-17667
332.6415—dc20 CIP

Acquisitions editor: **Leah Jewell**
Production editor: **Maureen Wilson**
Cover designer: **Rosemarie Paccione**
Buyer: **Patrice Fraccio**
Editorial assistant: **Eileen Deguzman**

Printed in the United States of America

10 9 8 7 6 5 4

ISBN 0-13-122961-3

Prentice-Hall International (UK) Limited, *London*
Prentice-Hall of Australia Pty. Limited, *Sydney*
Prentice-Hall Canada Inc., *Toronto*
Prentice-Hall Hispanoamericana, S.A., *Mexico*
Prentice-Hall of India Private Limited, *New Delhi*
Prentice-Hall of Japan, Inc., *Tokyo*
Simon & Schuster Asia Pte. Ltd., *Singapore*
Editora Prentice Hall do Brasil, Ltda., *Rio de Janeiro*

To
My Family

CONTENTS

Appendix 4A

Chapter 5: Interest-Rate Futures 111

Chapter 6: Swaps 146

PART TWO: OPTIONS MARKETS

Chapter 7: Mechanics of Options Markets 172

PREFACE

I was persuaded to write this book by colleagues who liked my other book *Options, Futures, and Other Derivative Securities* but found the material a little too advanced for their students. *Introduction to Futures and Options Markets* covers some of the same ground as *Options, Futures, and Other Derivative Securities*—but in a way that readers who have had limited training in mathematics will find easier to understand. The book is appropriate for undergraduate and graduate elective courses in business and economics. Many practitioners who want to acquire a working knowledge of futures and options markets will also find the book useful. One important difference between this book and my other one is that there is no calculus in this book.

This edition can be used in a number of different ways. Instructors who like to focus on one- and two-step binomial trees when valuing options may wish to cover only the first ten chapters. Instructors who feel that swaps are adequately covered by other courses can choose to skip Chapter 6. Instructors who feel the material in Chapters 16 and 17 is too specialized can skip these chapters. Some instructors may choose to devote relatively more time to futures and swaps markets (Part One); others may choose to structure their course mostly around options markets (Part Two).

Chapter 1 provides an introduction to futures and options markets and outlines the different ways in which they can be used. Chapter 2 describes the mechanics of how futures and forward contracts work. Chapter 3 shows how forward and futures prices can be determined in a variety of different situations using pure arbitrage arguments. Chapter 4 discusses how futures contracts can be used for hedging. Chapter 5 deals with the special problems associated with interest-rate futures contracts. Chapter 6 covers swaps. Chapter 7 describes the mechanics of how options markets work. Chapter 8 develops some simple relationships that must hold in options market if there are to be no arbitrage opportunities. Chapter 9 outlines a number of different trading strategies involving options. Chapter 10 shows how options can be priced using one- and two-step binomial trees. Chapter 11 discusses the pricing of stock options using the Black-Scholes analysis. Chapter 12 extends the ideas in Chapter 11 to cover options on stock indices and currencies. Chapter 13 deals with futures options. Chapter 14 provides a detailed treatment of hedge parameters such as delta, gamma, and vega and discusses portfolio insurance. Chapter 15 explains the use of binomial trees to value American options. Chapter 16 describes and categorizes a number of alternatives to the Black-Scholes model for options pricing. It also provides a review of empirical research. Finally, Chapter 17 covers the difficult, but important, area of valuing interest-rate options.

At the end of each chapter there are seven quiz questions which students can use to test their understanding of the key concepts. The answers are at the end of the book. Additional questions and problems are provided at the end of each chapter.

CHANGES IN THIS EDITION

The changes in this edition reflect the feedback I have received from instructors who adopted the first edition. There is now much more emphasis on the use of binomial trees to value options. A new chapter, Chapter 10, shows how one- and two-step binomial trees can be analyzed using no-arbitrage and risk-neutral valuation arguments. New material on binomial trees has been included in Chapters 12 and 13. Chapter 15 provides a comprehensive treatment of numerical procedures based on binomial trees.

Wherever possible the presentation of the material has been improved. For example, the arbitrage arguments in Chapter 3 are now explained more simply. The material has also been updated where necessary and new material has been added. This edition has a new chapter, Chapter 13, devoted entirely to futures options.

ACKNOWLEDGMENTS

Many people have played a part in the production of this book. Colleagues who have made excellent and useful suggestions are: Giovanni Barone-Adesi, George Blazenko, Laurence Booth, Phelim Boyle, Peter Carr, Jerome Duncan, Steinar Ekern, Robert Eldridge, David Fowler, Louis Gagnon, Mark Garman, Jim Hilliard, Basil Kalymon, Elizabeth Maynes, Izzy Nelken, Paul Potvin, Gordon Roberts, Edward Robbins, Chris Robinson, John Rumsey, Klaus Schurger, Eduardo Schwartz,

Michael Selby, Piet Sercu, Stuart Turnbull, Yisong Tian, Zhanshun Wei, Bob Whaley, and Alan White.

I am particularly grateful to Jerome Duncan, John Rumsey, and Alan White. Jerome Duncan (Hofstra University) made many suggestions as to how the presentation could be improved, and corrected some of the institutional details in the first draft. John Rumsey (York University) read the early chapters very carefully and made many detailed suggestions for improvements.

Alan White is a colleague at the University of Toronto with whom I have been carrying out joint research in the options and futures area for about ten years. During that time we have spent many hours discussing different issues concerning options and futures markets. Many of the new ideas in this book, and many of the new ways used to explain old ideas, are as much Alan's as mine.

The development of my knowledge of options and futures markets has benefited considerably from the contacts I have had with practitioners. I would particularly like to thank Kannan Ayyar (Renaissance Software), Alex Bergier (Goldman Sachs), Emanuel Derman (Goldman Sachs), Don Goldman (Bankers Trust), Ian Hawkins (Kidder Peabody), Nico Meier (Citibank), Isaac Muskat (TMG), Bruce Rogers (Merrill Lynch), Armand Tatevossian (NationsBanc), and Cathy Willis (Société Générale). Ya-Ping Wang provided me with useful material on the accounting and tax treatment of futures and options in the United States.

I am grateful to the students in my MBA elective course on options and futures markets at the University of Toronto. They were taught from the first draft of this book and made many useful comments on how the book could be improved. I would particularly like to thank Aida Tammer who read the first draft of this book very carefully and made many suggestions on the presentation of material.

I would also like to thank the staff at Prentice Hall, particularly Scott Barr, Leah Jewell, and Maureen Wilson, for the interest they have shown in this project. They have been a continuing source of help and encouragement.

JOHN HULL
University of Toronto

1

INTRODUCTION

In recent years, futures and options markets have become increasingly important in the world of finance and investments. We have now reached the stage where it is essential that all finance professionals understand how these markets work, how they can be used, and what determines prices in them. This book addresses all these issues.

In this opening chapter, we take a first look at futures and options markets. We discuss their history and describe in general terms how they are used by hedgers, by speculators, and by arbitrageurs. In later chapters, we will give more details and elaborate on many of the points made here.

FUTURES CONTRACTS

A *futures contract* is an agreement to buy or sell an asset at a certain time in the future for a certain price. The two largest exchanges on which futures contracts trade are the Chicago Board of Trade (CBOT) and the Chicago Mercantile Exchange (CME). We will illustrate how a futures contract comes into existence by considering the corn futures that trade on the Chicago Board of Trade.

In March, an investor in New York might call his or her broker with instructions to buy 5,000 bushels of corn for July delivery. The broker would immediately pass these instructions on to a trader on the floor of the Chicago Board of Trade. At about the same time, another investor in Kansas might instruct his or her broker to sell 5,000 bushels of corn for July delivery. These instructions would also be passed on to a trader on the floor of the Chicago Board of Trade. The two floor traders would meet, agree on a price to be paid for the corn in July, and the deal would be done.

The investor in New York who has agreed to buy has what is termed a *long futures position;* the investor in Kansas who has agreed to sell has what is termed a *short futures position.* The price agreed to by the two traders on the floor of the exchange is known as the *futures price.* We will suppose the price is 170 cents per bushel. In essence, this price is determined by the laws of supply and demand in the same way as any other price. If at a particular time more floor traders wish to sell July corn than buy July corn, the price will go down. This will bring new buyers into the market so that a balance between buyers and sellers is maintained. If more floor traders wish to buy July corn than to sell July corn, the price goes up for similar reasons.

Issues such as margin requirements, daily settlement procedures, trading practices, commissions, bid-ask spreads, the role of the exchange clearinghouse, and so on will be discussed in later chapters. For the time being, we can consider that the end result of the events just described is that the investor in New York has agreed to buy 5,000 bushels of corn for 170 cents per bushel in July and the investor in Kansas has agreed to sell 5,000 bushels of corn for 170 cents per bushel in July. Both sides have entered into a binding contract.

HISTORY OF FUTURES MARKETS

Futures markets can be traced back to the Middle Ages. They were originally developed to meet the needs of farmers and merchants. Consider the position of a farmer in April of a certain year who will harvest grain in June. The farmer is uncertain as to the price he or she will receive for the grain. In years of scarcity, it might be possible to obtain relatively high prices—particularly if the farmer is not in a hurry to sell. On the other hand, in years of oversupply, the grain might have to be disposed of at fire-sale prices. The farmer and the farmer's family are clearly exposed to a great deal of risk.

Consider next a merchant who has an ongoing requirement for grain. The merchant is also exposed to price risk. In some years, an oversupply situation may create favorable prices; in other years, scarcity may cause the prices to be exorbitant. It clearly makes sense for the farmer and the merchant to get together in April (or even earlier) and agree on a price for the farmer's anticipated production of grain in June. In other words, it makes sense for them to negotiate a type of futures contract. The contract provides a way for each side to eliminate the risk it faces because of the uncertain future price of grain.

One might ask what happens to the merchant's requirements for grain during the rest of the year. Once the harvest season is over, the grain must be stored until the next season. If the merchant undertakes this storage, he or she does not bear any price risk but does incur the costs of storage. If the farmer or some other party stores the grain, the merchant and the storer both face risks associated with the future grain price, and again, there is a clear role for futures contracts.

The Chicago Board of Trade

The Chicago Board of Trade (CBOT) was established in 1848 to bring farmers and merchants together. Initially, its main task was to standardize the quantities and qualities of the grains that were traded. Within a few years, the first futures-type contract was developed. It was known as a *to-arrive contract*. Speculators soon became interested in the contract and found trading the contract to be an attractive alternative to trading the grain itself. The Chicago Board of Trade now offers futures contracts on many different underlying assets, including corn, oats, soybeans, soybean meal, soybean oil, wheat, silver, treasury bonds, treasury notes, and the Major Market Stock Index.

The Chicago Mercantile Exchange

In 1874, the Chicago Produce Exchange was established. This provided a market for butter, eggs, poultry, and other perishable agricultural products. In 1898, the butter and egg dealers withdrew from this exchange to form the Chicago Butter and Egg Board. In 1919, this was renamed the Chicago Mercantile Exchange (CME) and was reorganized for futures trading. Since then, the exchange has provided a futures market for many commodities including pork bellies (1961), live cattle (1964), live hogs (1966), and feeder cattle (1971). In 1982, it introduced a futures contract on the S&P 500 Stock Index.

The International Monetary Market (IMM) was formed as a division of the Chicago Mercantile Exchange in 1972 for futures trading in foreign currencies. The currency futures traded on the IMM now include the British pound, the Canadian dollar, the Japanese yen, the Swiss franc, the German mark, and the Australian dollar. The IMM also trades a gold futures contract, a treasury bill futures contract, and a Eurodollar futures contract.

Other Exchanges

Many other exchanges throughout the world now trade futures contracts. Among them are the Chicago Rice and Cotton Exchange (CRCE), the New York Futures Exchange (NYFE), the London International Financial Futures Exchange (LIFFE), the Toronto Futures Exchange (TFE), and the Singapore International Monetary Exchange (SIMEX). Most of the contracts that are traded on the various exchanges throughout the world can be categorized as either *commodity futures contracts* (where the underlying asset is a commodity) or *financial futures contracts* (where the underlying asset is a financial asset such as a bond or a portfolio of stocks). New contracts are being proposed all the time. There can be little doubt that futures markets are one of the most successful financial innovations ever.

OPTIONS CONTRACTS

Options contracts have been traded on exchanges for a far shorter period of time than futures contracts. Nevertheless, they too have been remarkably popular with investors. There are two basic types of options: calls and puts. A *call option* gives the holder the right to buy an asset by a certain date for a certain price. A *put option* gives the holder the right to sell an asset by a certain date for a certain price. The price in the contract is known as the *exercise price* or the *strike price*; the date in the contract is known as the *expiration date*, the *exercise date*, or the *maturity*. A *European* option can be exercised only on the maturity date; an *American* option can be exercised at any time during its life.

It should be emphasized that an option gives the holder the right to do something. The holder does not have to exercise this right. This fact distinguishes options from futures contracts. The holder of a long futures contract has committed himself or herself to buying an asset at a certain price at a certain time in the future. By contrast, the holder of a call option has a choice as to whether he or she buys the asset at a certain price at a certain time in the future. It costs nothing (except for margin requirements which will be discussed in Chapter 2) to enter into a futures contract. By contrast, an investor must pay an up-front fee or price for an options contract.

The largest exchange for trading stock options is the Chicago Board Options Exchange (CBOE). To illustrate how an options contract gets initiated, we suppose an investor instructs his or her broker to buy one call option contract on IBM stock with a strike price of $50 and an exercise date of October. The broker will relay these instructions to a trader on the floor of the CBOE. This trader will then find another trader who wants to sell one October call contract on IBM with a strike price of $50. A price will be agreed upon and the deal will be done. Suppose the agreed upon price is $6. This is the price for an option to buy one share. In the United States, one stock option contract is a contract to buy or sell 100 shares. Therefore, the investor must arrange for $600 to be remitted to the exchange through his or her broker. The exchange will then arrange for this to be passed on to the party on the other side of the transaction. Note that the stock price does not have to equal the exercise price. The price of IBM stock in this example could be, say, $52 at the time the deal is done.

In our example, the investor has obtained at a cost of $600 the right to buy 100 IBM shares for $50 each. The party on the other side of the transaction has received $600 and has agreed to sell 100 shares for $50 per share if the investor chooses to exercise the option. There are four types of participants in options markets:

1. Buyers of calls
2. Sellers of calls
3. Buyers of puts
4. Sellers of puts

Buyers are referred to as having *long positions*; sellers are referred to as having *short positions*. Selling an option is also known as *writing the option*.

HISTORY OF OPTIONS MARKETS

The first trading in puts and calls began in Europe and in the United States as early as the eighteenth century. In the early years, the market got a bad name because of certain corrupt practices. One of these involved brokers being given options on a certain stock as an inducement for them to recommend the stock to their clients.

Put and Call Brokers and Dealers Association

In the early 1900s, a group of firms set up what was known as the Put and Call Brokers and Dealers Association. The aim of this association was to provide a mechanism for bringing buyers and sellers together. If someone wanted to buy an option, he or she would contact one of the member firms. This firm would attempt to find a seller or writer of the option from either its own clients or those of other member firms. If no seller could be found, the firm would undertake to write the option itself in return for what was deemed to be an appropriate price. A market created in this way is known as an *over-the-counter market,* since traders do not physically meet on the floor of an exchange.

The options market of the Put and Call Brokers and Dealers Association suffered from two deficiencies. First, there was no secondary market. The buyer of an option did not have the right to sell it to another party prior to expiration. Second, there was no mechanism to guarantee that the writer of the option would honor the contract. If the writer did not fulfill his or her part of the bargain when the option was exercised, the buyer had to resort to costly lawsuits.

The Formation of Options Exchanges

In April 1973, the Chicago Board of Trade set up a new exchange, the Chicago Board Options Exchange, specifically for the purpose of trading stock options. Since then options markets have become increasingly popular with investors. The American Stock Exchange (AMEX) and the Philadelphia Stock Exchange (PHLX) began trading options in 1975. The Pacific Stock Exchange (PSE) did the same in 1976. By the early 1980s, the volume of trading had grown so rapidly that the number of shares underlying the option contracts sold each day exceeded the daily volume of shares traded on the New York Stock Exchange.

In the 1980s, markets developed for options in foreign exchange, options on stock indices, and options on futures contracts. The Philadelphia Stock Exchange is the premier exchange for trading foreign exchange options. The Chicago Board Options Exchange trades options on the S&P 100 and the S&P 500 stock indices while the American Stock Exchange trades options on the Major Market Stock Index, and the New York Stock Exchange trades options on the NYSE Index. Most exchanges offering futures contracts now also offer options on these futures contracts. Thus, the Chicago Board of Trade offers options on corn futures, the

Chicago Mercantile Exchange offers options on live cattle futures, the International Monetary Markets offers options on foreign currency futures, and so on.

Both options and futures markets have been outstandingly successful. One of the reasons for this is that they have attracted many different types of traders. Three broad categories of traders can be identified: hedgers, speculators, and arbitrageurs. In the next few sections, we consider the activities of each of these.

HEDGERS

As has already been mentioned, futures markets were originally set up to meet the needs of hedgers. Farmers wanted to lock in an assured price for their produce. Merchants wanted to lock in a price they would pay for this produce. Futures contracts enabled both sides to achieve their objectives.

An Example of Hedging Using Futures

Commodity futures are still widely used by producers and users of commodities for hedging. Financial futures can also be used for hedging purposes. Suppose that it is now July and company A, based in the United States, knows that it will have to pay £1 million in September for goods it has purchased from a British supplier. The current exchange rate is 1.6920 and the September futures price for IMM contracts on the British pound is 1.6850. This means that, ignoring commissions and other transactions costs, the exchange rate for immediate delivery is

$$\$1.6920 = £1$$

and the exchange rate for delivery in September is

$$\$1.6850 = £1$$

Company A could hedge its foreign exchange risk by taking a long position in £1 million worth of September futures contracts. (Each contract traded on the IMM is for the delivery of £62,500 so that a total of 16 contracts would have to be purchased.) Ignoring commissions and other transactions costs, the contracts have the effect of fixing the price to be paid to the British exporter at $1,685,000.

Consider next another U.S. company, which we will refer to as company B. This company is exporting goods to the United Kingdom and in July knows that it will receive £3 million in September. Company B can hedge its foreign exchange risk by shorting September futures. (In this case, 48 contracts would be required so that the company's total short position would be 48 × £62,500 or £3 million.) The company would have fixed the U.S. dollars to be realized for the sterling as $5,055,000 (= 3 × $1,685,000).

Table 1.1 summarizes the hedging strategies for company A and company B. Note that if the companies choose not to hedge, they might do better than if

Table 1.1 Use of Futures for Hedging

From the Trader's Desk—July

Company A—must pay £1 million in September for imports from Britain
Company B—will receive £3 million in September from exports to Britain
Quotes:

Current exchange rate	1.6920
September futures price	1.6850

Size of futures contract:
£62,500

Company A's Hedging Strategy

Long position in 16 futures contracts. This locks in an exchange rate of 1.6850 for the £1 million it will pay.

Company B's Hedging Strategy

Short position in 48 futures contracts. This locks in an exchange rate of 1.6850 for the £3 million it will receive.

they do hedge. Alternatively, they might do worse. Consider company A. If the exchange rate is 1.6600 in September and the company has not hedged, the £1 million that it has to pay will cost \$1,660,000—which is less than \$1,685,000. On the other hand, if the exchange rate is 1.7100, the £1 million will cost \$1,710,000—and the company will wish it had hedged! The position of company B if it does not hedge is the reverse. If the exchange rate in September proves to be less than 1.6850, company B will wish it had hedged; if it is greater than 1.6850, it will be pleased it has not done so.

This illustrates a key aspect of hedging using futures contracts. The cost of, or price received for, the underlying asset is assured. However, there is no assurance that the outcome with hedging will be better than the outcome without hedging.

Table 1.2 Hedging Strategies Using Options

From the Trader's Desk—August

An investor owns 500 IBM shares and wants protection against a possible decline in the share price over the next two months.

Quotes:

Current IBM share price	\$52
IBM October 50 put	\$4

The Investor's Strategy

The investor buys five put option contracts for a total of $5 \times 100 \times \$4 = \$2{,}000$.

The Outcome

Investor has the right to sell the shares for at least $500 \times \$50 = \$25{,}000$.

An Example of Hedging Using Options

Options can also be used for hedging. Consider an investor who in August owns 500 IBM shares. The current share price is $52 per share. The investor is concerned that the share price may decline sharply in the next two months and wishes to protect himself or herself. The investor could buy on the Chicago Board Options Exchange October put options to sell 500 shares for a strike price of $50. Since each contract on the CBOE is for the sale of 100 shares, a total of five contracts would be purchased. If the quoted option price is $4, this means that each option contract would cost 100 × $4 = $400 and the total cost of the hedging strategy would be 5 × $400 = $2,000.

This strategy is summarized in Table 1.2. The strategy costs $2,000 but guarantees that the shares can be sold for at least $50 per share during the life of the option. If the market price of IBM stock falls below $50, the options can be exercised so that $25,000 is realized for the whole holding. When the cost of the options is taken into account, the amount realized is $23,000. If the market price stays above $50, the options are not exercised and expire worthless. However, in this case the value of the holding is always above $25,000 (or above $23,000 when the cost of the options is taken into account).

A Comparison

A comparison of Tables 1.1 and 1.2 reveals a fundamental difference between the use of futures and options for hedging. Futures contracts are designed to neutralize risk by fixing the price that the hedger will pay or receive for the underlying asset. Options contracts by contrast provide insurance. They provide a way in which investors can protect themselves against adverse price movements in the future while still allowing them to benefit from favorable price movements. Unlike futures, options involve the payment of an up-front fee.

SPECULATORS

We now move on to consider how futures and options markets can be used by speculators. Whereas hedgers want to avoid an exposure to adverse movements in the price of an asset, speculators wish to take a position in the market. Either they are betting that the price will go up or they are betting that it will go down.

An Example of Speculation Using Futures

Consider a U.S. speculator who in February thinks that the pound sterling will strengthen relative to the U.S. dollar over the next two months and is prepared to back his or her hunch to the tune of £250,000. One thing the speculator can do is simply purchase £250,000 in the hope that it can be sold later at a profit. The

Table 1.3 Speculation Using Futures

From the Trader's Desk—February

An investor feels that sterling with strengthen relative to the U.S. dollar over the next two months and would like to take a speculative position.

Quotes:

Current exchange rate	1.6470
April futures price	1.6410

Alternative Strategies

1. Buy £250,000 for $411,750, deposit the sterling in an interest-earning account for two months, and hope that it can be sold for a profit at the end of the two months.
2. Take a long position in four April futures contracts. This will require the investor to buy £250,000 for $410,250 in April. If the exchange rate in April proves to be above 1.6410, the investor will realize a profit.

Possible Outcomes

1. Exchange rate is 1.7000 in two months. The investor makes $13,250 using the first strategy and $14,750 using the second strategy.
2. Exchange rate is 1.6000 in two months. The investor has a loss of $11,750 using the first strategy and $10,250 using the second strategy.

sterling once purchased would be kept in an interest-bearing account. Another possibility is to take a long position in four IMM April futures contracts on sterling. (Each futures contract is for the purchase of £62,500.) Table 1.3 summarizes the two alternatives on the assumption that the current exchange rate is 1.6470 and the April futures price is 1.6410. If the exchange rate turns out to be 1.7000 in April, the futures contract alternative enables the speculator to buy in April for $1.6410 an asset worth $1.7000 so that a profit of $(1.7000 - 1.6410) \times 250{,}000 =$ $14,750 is realized. The cash market alternative leads to an asset being purchased for 1.6470 in February and sold for 1.7000 in April so that a profit of $(1.7000 - 1.6470) \times 250{,}000 =$ $13,250 is made. If the exchange rate falls to 1.6000, the futures contract gives rise to a $(1.6410 - 1.6000) \times 250{,}000 =$ $10,250 loss, while the cash market alternative gives rise to a loss of $(1.6470 - 1.6000) \times 250{,}000 =$ $11,750. The alternatives appear to give rise to slightly different profits/losses. But these calculations do not reflect the interest that is earned or paid. It will be shown in Chapter 3 that when the interest earned in sterling and the interest paid in dollars are taken into account, the profit or loss from the two alternatives is the same.

What then is the difference between the two alternatives? The first alternative of buying sterling requires an up-front investment of $411,750. By contrast, the second alternative requires only a small margin—perhaps $25,000—to be deposited by the speculator. The futures market in effect allows the speculator to obtain leverage. With a relatively small initial outlay, he or she is able to take a large speculative position.

An Example of Speculation Using Options

We consider next an example of how a speculator could use options. Suppose that in September, a speculator wants to go long in Exxon stock. In other words, the speculator wants to take a position where he or she will gain if the stock price increases. Suppose that the stock price is currently \$78 and that a December call with an \$80 strike price is currently selling for \$3. Table 1.4 illustrates two alternatives open to the speculator assuming that he or she is willing to invest \$7,800. The first alternative involves the straight purchase of 100 shares. The second involves the purchase of 2,600 options (i.e., 26 option contracts) on Exxon.

Suppose that the speculator's hunch is correct and the price of Exxon's shares rises to \$90 by December. The first alternative of buying the stock yields a profit of

$$100 \times (\$90 - \$78) = \$1{,}200$$

However, the second alternative is far more profitable. A call option on Exxon with a strike price of \$80 gives a profit of \$10, since the option enables something worth \$90 to be bought for \$80. The total value of all the options that have been purchased is

$$2{,}600 \times \$10 = \$26{,}000$$

Subtracting the original cost of the options, the net profit is

$$\$26{,}000 - \$7{,}800 = \$18{,}200$$

The options strategy is, therefore, over 15 times more profitable than the strategy of buying the stock.

Table 1.4 Speculation Using Options

From the Trader's Desk—September

A speculator with \$7,800 to invest thinks that the price of Exxon will increase in the next three months and has obtained the following quotes:

Current stock price	\$78
Exxon December call with an \$80 strike price	\$3

The speculator has \$7,800 to invest.

Alternative Strategies

1. Buy 100 shares of Exxon
2. Buy 2,600 December call options (or 26 December contracts) on Exxon with an \$80 strike price.

The cost of both alternatives is \$7,800.

Possible Outcomes

1. Exxon rises to \$90 by December. The investor makes a profit of \$1,200 using the first strategy and \$18,200 using the second strategy.
2. Exxon falls to \$70 by December. The investor loses \$800 with the first strategy and \$7,800 with the second strategy.

Table 1.5 Comparison of Profits (Losses) from Two Alternative Strategies for Using $7,800 to Speculate on Exxon Stock

INVESTOR'S STRATEGY	*DECEMBER STOCK PRICE*	
	$70	*$90*
Buy shares	($800)	$1,200
Buy call options	($7,800)	$18,200

Of course, options also give rise to a greater potential loss. Suppose the stock price falls to $70 by December. The first alternative of buying stock yields a loss of

$$100 \times (\$78 - \$70) = \$800$$

Since the call options expire without being exercised, the options strategy would lead to a loss of $7,800—the original amount paid for the options. These results are summarized in Table 1.5.

It will be clear from Table 1.5 that options like futures provide a form of leverage. For a given investment, the use of options magnifies the financial consequences. Good outcomes become very good, while bad outcomes become very bad!

A Comparison

Futures and options are similar instruments for speculators in that they both provide a way in which a type of leverage can be obtained. However, there is an important difference between the two. In the futures example in Table 1.3, the speculator's potential loss as well as the potential gain is very large. In the options example in Table 1.4, no matter how bad things get, the speculator's loss is limited to the $7,800 paid for the options.

ARBITRAGEURS

Arbitrageurs are a third important group of participants in futures and options markets. Arbitrage involves locking in a riskless profit by simultaneously entering into transactions in two or more markets. In later chapters, we will show how arbitrage is sometimes possible when the futures price of an asset gets out of line with its cash price. We will also discuss how arbitrage can be used in options

Table 1.6 Arbitrage

From the Trader's Desk

A stock is traded on both the New York Stock Exchange and the London Stock Exchange. The following quotes have been obtained:

New York Stock Exchange	\$172 per share
London Stock Exchange	£100 per share
Value of £1	\$1.7500

The Trader's Arbitrage Strategy

1. Buy 100 shares in New York.
2. Sell the shares in London.
3. Convert the sale proceeds from pounds to dollars.

The Profit

$$100 \times (\$1.75 \times 100 - 172) = \$300$$

markets. In this section, we illustrate the concept of arbitrage with a very simple example.

Consider a stock that is traded on both the New York Stock Exchange and the London Stock Exchange. Suppose that the stock price is \$172 in New York and £100 in London at a time when the exchange rate is \$1.7500 per pound. An arbitrageur could simultaneously buy 100 shares of the stock in New York and sell them in London to obtain a risk-free profit of

$$100 \times (\$1.75 \times 100 - \$172)$$

or \$300 in the absence of transactions costs. The strategy is summarized in Table 1.6. Transactions costs would probably eliminate the profit for a small investor. However, a large investment house faces very low transactions costs in both the stock market and the foreign exchange market. It would find the arbitrage opportunity very attractive and would try to take as much advantage of it as possible.

Arbitrage opportunities such as the one that has just been described cannot last for long. As arbitrageurs buy the stock in New York, the forces of supply and demand will cause the dollar price to rise. Similarly, as they sell the stock in London, the sterling price will be driven down. Very quickly, the two prices will become equivalent at the current exchange rate. Indeed, the existence of profit-hungry arbitrageurs makes it unlikely that a major disparity between the sterling price and the dollar price could ever exist in the first place. Generalizing from this example, we can say that the very existence of arbitrageurs means that in practice only very small arbitrage opportunities are observed in the prices that are quoted in most financial markets. In this book, most of our arguments concerning futures prices and the values of option contracts will be based on the assumption that there are no arbitrage opportunities.

DERIVATIVES

Options and futures contracts are examples of what are termed *derivatives*. These are instruments whose values depend on the values of other more basic variables. An IBM stock option is a derivative because its value depends on the price of IBM stock, a wheat futures contract is a derivative because its value depends on the price of wheat, and so on.

In recent years, investment banks have been very imaginative in designing new derivatives to meet the needs of clients. Often these are not traded on exchanges. Instead, they are sold over the counter by financial institutions to their corporate clients, or they are added to bond or stock issues to make these issues more attractive to investors. Some of these derivatives are similar to the futures and options contracts traded on exchanges. Others are far more complex. The possibilities for designing new interesting derivatives seems to be virtually limitless. In this section, we give a few examples of nonexchange-traded derivatives.

Interest-Rate Caps

An interest-rate cap is a very popular derivative that is traded over the counter. When it is sold by financial institutions to corporate borrowers, it provides protection against the rate of interest on a floating-rate loan going above some level. This level is known as the *cap rate*. If the rate of interest on the loan does go above the cap rate, the seller of the cap provides the difference between the interest on the loan and the interest that would be required if the cap rate applied. Suppose the loan is for $10 million, the cap rate is 12 percent per annum, and that for a particular three-month period during the life of the cap, the floating rate applicable to the loan turns out to be 14 percent per annum. The seller of the cap would provide $50,000 (= ¼ of 2 percent of $10 million) at the end of the three months to bring interest payments for the three-month period down to 12 percent. Caps provide corporate borrowers with a guarantee that the rate on a loan will not go above a certain level. Occasionally they are structured to guarantee that the average rate paid during the life of the loan (rather than the rate at any particular time) will not go above the level. Caps will be discussed further in Chapter 17.

Standard Oil's Bond Issue

An example of a derivative added to a bond issue is provided by Standard Oil's issue of zero-coupon bonds in 1986. Some of these bonds matured in 1990. In addition to the bond's $1,000 maturity value, the company promised to pay an amount based on the price of oil at maturity of the bond. This additional amount was equal to the product of 170 and the excess (if any) of the price of a barrel of oil at maturity over $25. However, the maximum additional amount paid was restricted to $2,550 (which corresponds to a price of $40 per barrel). The bonds provided holders with a stake in a commodity that was critically important to the fortunes of the company. If the price of the commodity went up, the company was in a good position to provide the bondholder with the additional payment.

Other Examples

As mentioned earlier, there is virtually no limit to the innovations that are possible in the derivatives area. Up to now, the variables underlying derivatives have usually been stock prices, stock indices, interest rates, exchange rates, and commodity prices. However, other variables can be and are occasionally used. For example, ski slope operators have been known to issue bonds where the payoff depends on the total snow falling at a certain resort, and banks have been known to create deposit instruments where the interest paid depends on the performance of the local football team.

SUMMARY

In this chapter, we have taken a first look at futures and options markets. A futures contract involves an obligation to buy or sell an asset at a certain time in the future for a certain price. There are two types of options: calls and puts. A call option gives the holder the right to buy an asset by a certain date for a certain price. A put option gives the holder the right to sell an asset by a certain date for a certain price. Futures and options are now traded on a wide range of different assets.

Options and futures markets have been very successful innovations. Three main types of participants in the markets can be identified: hedgers, speculators, and arbitrageurs. Hedgers are in the position where they face risk associated with the price of an asset. They use futures or options markets to reduce or eliminate this risk. Speculators wish to bet on future movements in the price of an asset. Futures and options contracts can give them extra leverage; that is, they can increase both the potential gains and potential losses in a speculative venture. Arbitrageurs are in business to take advantage of a discrepancy between prices in two different markets. If, for example, they see the futures price of an asset getting out of line with the cash price, they will take offsetting positions in the two markets to lock in a profit.

Options and futures are examples of derivatives. These are instruments whose prices depend on the values of other more basic underlying variables. The price of a stock option depends on the value of the underlying stock, a commodity futures price depends on the value of the underlying commodity, and so on. Investment bankers have become increasingly imaginative in devising new derivatives in recent years. Most of these securities are not traded on exchanges. Either they are sold by financial institutions to their corporate clients or they are added to new issues of bonds and stocks in order to make the latter more attractive to investors.

Quiz

1. What is the difference between a long futures position and a short futures position?
2. Explain carefully the difference between (a) hedging, (b) speculation, and (c) arbitrage.
3. What is the difference between (a) entering into a long futures contract when the futures price is \$50 and (b) taking a long position in a call option with a strike price of \$50?
4. An investor enters into a short cotton futures contract when the futures price is 50 cents per pound. One contract is for the delivery of 50,000 pounds. How much does the investor gain or lose if the cotton price at the end of the contract is (a) 48.20 cents per pound and (b) 51.30 cents per pound?
5. Suppose that you write a put contract on IBM with a strike price of \$40 and expiration date in three months. The current price of IBM stock is \$41. What have you committed yourself to? How much could you gain or lose?
6. You would like to speculate on a rise in the price of a certain stock. The current stock price is \$29 and a three-month call with a strike of \$30 costs \$2.90. You have \$5,800 to invest. Identify two alternative strategies. Briefly outline the advantages and disadvantages of each.
7. Suppose you own 5,000 shares worth \$25 each. How can put options be used to provide you with insurance against a decline in the value of your holding over the next four months?

Questions and Problems

1.1. A stock when it is first issued provides funds for a company. Is the same true of a stock option? Discuss.

1.2. Explain why a futures contract can be used for either speculation or hedging.

1.3. A pig farmer expects to have 90,000 pounds of live hogs to sell in three months. The live hogs futures contract on the Chicago Mercantile Exchange is for the delivery of 30,000 pounds of hogs. How can the farmer use this for hedging? From the farmer's viewpoint, what are the pros and cons of hedging?

1.4. It is now July 1993. A mining company has just discovered a small deposit of gold. It will take six months to construct the mine. The gold will then be extracted on a more or less continuous basis for one year. Futures contracts on gold are available on the New York Commodity Exchange. The delivery months range from August 1993 to April 1995 and are at two-month intervals. Each contract is for the delivery of 100 ounces. Discuss how the mining company might use futures markets for hedging.

1.5. Suppose that a March call option with a strike price of \$50 costs \$2.50 and is held until March. Under what circumstances will the holder of the option make a gain? Under what circumstances will the option be exercised?

1.6. Suppose that a June put option with a strike price of \$60 costs \$4.00 and is held until June. Under what circumstances will the holder of the option make a gain? Under what circumstances will the option be exercised?

1.7. An investor writes a September call option with a strike price of \$20. It is now May, the stock price is \$18, and the option price is \$2. Describe the investor's cash flows if the option is held until September and the stock price is \$25 at this time.

1.8. An investor writes a December put option with a strike price of \$30. The price of the option is \$4. Under what circumstances does the investor make a gain?

1.9. Interest-rate caps are described in the section on derivatives. Is a cap on the average rate of interest during the life of a loan worth more or less than a cap on the rate at any given time? Explain your answer.

1.10. Show that the Standard Oil bond described in the section on derivatives is a combination of a regular bond, a long position in call options on oil with a strike price of \$25, and a short position in call options on oil with a strike price of \$40.

1.11. Discuss how foreign currency options can be used for hedging in the situation described in Table 1.1.

1.12. The price of gold is currently \$500 per ounce. The futures price for delivery in one year is \$700. An arbitrageur can borrow money at 10 percent per annum. What should the arbitrageur do? Assume that the cost of storing gold is zero.

1.13. The Chicago Board of Trade offers a futures contract on long-term treasury bonds. Characterize the investors likely to use this contract.

1.14. An airline executive has argued: "There is no point in our using oil futures. There is just as much chance that the price of oil in the future will be less than the futures price as there is that it will be greater than this price." Discuss this viewpoint.

1.15. The current price of a stock is \$94 and three-month call options with a strike price of \$95 currently sell for \$4.70. An investor who feels that the price of the stock will increase is trying to decide between buying 100 shares and buying 2,000 call options (= 20 contracts). Both strategies involve an investment of \$9,400. What advice would you give? How high does the stock price have to rise for the option strategy to be more profitable?

1.16. "Options and futures are zero-sum games." What do you think is meant by this statement?

2

MECHANICS OF FUTURES AND FORWARD MARKETS

In this chapter, we cover the details of how futures markets work. We discuss issues such as the specification of contracts, the operation of margin accounts, the organization of exchanges, the regulation of markets, the way in which quotes are made, and the treatment of futures transactions for accounting and tax purposes. We also discuss forward contracts. Forward contracts are in some respects similar to futures contracts. They involve an agreement to buy or sell an asset on a certain date for a certain price. However, there are important differences between the two types of contracts. Futures contracts are traded on an organized exchange, and the terms of the contract are standardized by the exchange. By contrast, forward contracts are private agreements between two financial institutions or between a financial institution and one of its corporate clients.

CLOSING OUT POSITIONS

As discussed in Chapter 1, a futures contract is an agreement to buy or sell an asset for a certain price at a certain time in the future. The reader may be surprised to learn that the vast majority of the futures contracts that are initiated do not lead to delivery. This is because most investors choose to close out their positions prior to the delivery period specified in the contract. Making or taking delivery under the terms of a futures contract is often inconvenient and, in some instances, quite expensive. This is true even for a hedger who wants to buy or sell the asset underlying the futures contract. Such a hedger usually prefers to close out the futures position and then buy or sell the asset in the usual way.

Closing out a position involves entering into an opposite trade to the original one. For example, if an investor buys five July corn futures contracts on May 6, he or she can close out the position on June 20 by selling (i.e., shorting) five July corn futures contracts. If an investor sells (i.e., shorts) five July contracts on May 6, he or she can close out the position on June 20 by buying five July contracts. In each case, the investor's total gain or loss is determined by the change in the futures price between May 6 and June 20.

In spite of the fact that delivery is so unusual, we will spend part of this chapter talking in some detail about the precise specification of futures contracts and the delivery arrangements. This is because it is the possibility of final delivery that ties the futures price to the cash price. An understanding of delivery procedures is, therefore, essential to a full understanding of the relationship between cash and futures prices.

THE SPECIFICATION OF THE FUTURES CONTRACT

The exchanges in the United States that trade futures contracts are listed in Table 2.1. When developing a new contract, the exchange must specify in some detail the exact nature of the agreement between the two parties. In particular, it must specify the asset, the contract size (that is, exactly how much of the asset will be delivered under one contract), where delivery will be made, and when delivery will be made. Sometimes alternatives are specified for the asset that will be delivered or for the delivery arrangements. As a general rule, it is the party with the short position (i.e., the party that has agreed to sell the asset) that chooses between these alternatives.

The Asset

When the asset is a commodity, there may be quite a variation in the quality of what is available in the marketplace. When specifying the asset, it is therefore important that the exchange stipulate the grade or grades of the commodity that are acceptable. The New York Cotton Exchange has specified the asset in its orange juice futures contract as

> US Grade A, with Brix value of not less than 57 degrees, having a Brix value to acid ratio of not less than 13 to 1 nor more than 19 to 1, with factors of color and flavor each scoring 37 points or higher and 19 for defects, with a minimum score 94.

The Chicago Mercantile Exchange in its random-length lumber futures contract has specified that

> Each delivery unit shall consist of nominal 2x4s of random lengths from 8 feet to 20 feet, grade-stamped Construction and Standard, Standard and better, or #1 and #2;

Table 2.1 U.S. Exchanges That Trade Futures

Chicago Board of Trade (CBOT)
141 W. Jackson Boulevard
Chicago, IL 60604
312-435-3500
Grains and oilseeds, metals, financials

Chicago Mercantile Exchange (CME)
30 S. Wacker Drive
Chicago, IL 60606
312-930-1000
Divisions: International Monetary Market (IMM), Index and Option Market (IOM)
Livestock, meat, financials, wood

Coffee, Sugar, and Cocoa Exchange (CSCE)
4 World Trade Center
New York, NY 10048
212-938-2800
Food and fiber, financials

Commodity Exchange, Inc. (COMEX)
4 World Trade Center
New York, NY 10048
212-938-2900
Metals, financials

New York Futures Exchange (NYFE)
4 World Trade Center
New York, NY 10048
212-656-4949
Financials

New York Mercantile Exchange (NYMEX)
4 World Trade Center
New York, NY 10048
212-938-2222
Metals, petroleum, food and fiber

Kansas City Board of Trade (KCBT)
4800 Main Street, Suite 303
Kansas City, MO 64112
816-753-7500
Grains, financials

MidAmerica Commodity Exchange (MidAm)
444 W. Jackson Boulevard
Chicago, IL 60604
312-341-3000
Grains and oilseeds, livestock, meat, metals, financials

Minneapolis Grain Exchange (MGE)
400 S. Fourth Street
Minneapolis, MN 55415
612-338-6212
Grains

New York Cotton Exchange (CTN)
4 World Trade Center
New York, NY 10048
212-938-2650
Divisions: Financial Instruments Exchange (FINEX)
Food and fiber, financials

Chicago Rice and Cotton Exchange (CRCE)
444 West Jackson Boulevard
Chicago, IL 60604
312-341-3078
Food and fiber

Philadelphia Board of Trade (PBOT)
1900 Market Street
Philadelphia, PA 19103
215-496-5165
Financials

> however, in no case may the quantity of Standard grade or #2 exceed 50 percent. Each delivery unit shall be manufactured in California, Idaho, Montana, Nevada, Oregon, Washington, Wyoming, or Alberta or British Columbia, Canada, and contain lumber produced from and grade-stamped Alpine fir, Englemann spruce, hem-fir, lodgepole pine and/or spruce pine fir.

In the case of some commodities, a range of grades can be delivered but the price received is adjusted depending on the grade chosen. For example, in the Chicago Board of Trade corn futures contract, the standard grade is "No. 2 Yellow," but substitutions are allowed at differentials established by the exchange.

The financial assets in futures contracts are generally well defined and unambiguous. For example, there is no need to specify the grade of a Japanese yen.

However, there are some interesting features of the treasury bond and treasury note futures contracts traded on the Chicago Board of Trade. The underlying asset in the treasury bond contract is any long-term U.S. treasury bond which has a maturity of greater than 15 years and is not callable within 15 years. In the treasury note futures contract, the underlying asset is any long-term treasury note with a maturity no less than 6.5 years and not greater than 10 years from the date of delivery. In both of these cases, the exchange has a formula for adjusting the price received according to the coupon and maturity date of the bond delivered. This will be discussed in Chapter 5.

The Contract Size

The contract size specifies the amount of the asset that has to be delivered under one contract. This is an important decision for the exchange. If the contract size is too large, many investors who wish to hedge relatively small exposures or who wish to take relatively small speculative positions will be unable to use the exchange. On the other hand, if the contract size is too small, trading may be expensive since there is a cost associated with each contract traded.

The correct size for a contract clearly depends on the likely user. Whereas the value of what is delivered under a futures contract on an agricultural product might be $10,000 to $20,000, it is much higher for some financial futures. For example, under the treasury bond futures contract traded on the Chicago Board of Trade, instruments with face value of $100,000 are delivered.

Delivery Arrangements

The place where delivery will be made must be specified by the exchange. This is particularly important for commodities where there may be significant transportation costs. In the case of the Chicago Mercantile Exchange random-length lumber contract, the delivery location is specified as

> On track and shall either be unitized in double-door boxcars or, at no additional cost to the buyer, each unit shall be individually paper-wrapped and loaded on flatcars. Par delivery of hem-fir in California, Idaho, Montana, Nevada, Oregon, and Washington, and in the province of British Columbia.

When alternative delivery locations are specified, the price received by the party with the short position is sometimes adjusted according to the location chosen by that party. For example, in the case of the corn futures contract traded by the Chicago Board of Trade, delivery can be made at Chicago, Burns Habor, Toledo, or St. Louis. However, deliveries at Toledo and St. Louis are made at a discount of 4 cents per bushel from the Chicago contract price.

A futures contract is referred to by its delivery month. The exchange must specify the precise period during the month when delivery can be made. For many futures contracts, the delivery period is the whole month.

Delivery Months

The delivery months vary from contract to contract and are chosen by the exchange to meet the needs of market participants. For example, currency futures on the International Monetary Exchange have delivery months of March, June, September, and December; corn futures traded on the Chicago Board of Trade have delivery months of March, May, July, September, and December. At any given time, contracts trade for the closest delivery month and a number of subsequent delivery months. The exchange specifies when trading in a particular month's contract will begin. The exchange also specifies the last day on which trading can take place for a given contract. This is generally a few days before the last day on which delivery can be made.

Price Quotes

The futures price is quoted in a way that is convenient and easy to understand. For example, crude oil futures prices on the New York Mercantile Exchange are quoted in dollars per barrel to two decimal places (i.e., to the nearest cent). Treasury bond and treasury note futures prices on the Chicago Board of Trade are quoted in dollars and thirty-seconds of a dollar. The minimum price movement that can occur in trading is consistent with the way in which the price is quoted. Thus, it is $0.01 (or 1 cent per barrel) for the oil futures and one thirty-second of a dollar for the treasury bond and treasury note futures.

Daily Price Movement Limits

For most contracts, daily price movement limits are specified by the exchange. For example, at the time of writing the daily price movement limit for oil futures is $1. If the price moves down by an amount equal to the daily price limit, the contract is said to be *limit down*. If it moves up by the limit, it is said to be *limit up*. A *limit move* is a move in either direction equal to the daily price limit. Normally, trading ceases for the day once the contract is limit up or limit down. However, in some instances, the exchange has the authority to step in and change the limits.

The purpose of daily price limits is to prevent large price movements from occurring because of speculative excesses. However, they can become an artificial barrier to trading when the price of the underlying commodity is advancing or declining rapidly. Whether price limits are, on balance, good for futures markets is controversial.

Position Limits

Position limits are the maximum number of contracts that a speculator may hold. In the Chicago Mercantile Exchange random-length lumber contract, for example, the position limit is 1,000 contracts with no more than 300 in any one delivery month. Bona fide hedgers are not affected by position limits. The purpose of the limits is to prevent speculators from exercising undue influence on the market.

CONVERGENCE OF FUTURES PRICE TO SPOT PRICE

As the delivery month of a futures contract is approached, the futures price converges to the spot price of the underlying asset. When the delivery period is reached, the futures price equals—or is very close to—the spot price.

To show why this is so, we first suppose that the futures price is above the spot price during the delivery period. This gives rise to a clear arbitrage opportunity for traders:

1. Short a futures contract.
2. Buy the asset.
3. Make delivery.

This is certain to lead to a profit equal to the amount by which the futures price exceeds the spot price. As traders exploit this arbitrage opportunity, the futures price will fall. We next suppose that the futures price is below the spot price during the delivery period. Companies interested in acquiring the asset will find it attractive to enter into a long futures contract and then wait for delivery to be made. As they do this, the futures price will tend to rise.

The result of all this is that the futures price is very close to the spot price during the delivery period. Figure 2.1 illustrates the convergence of the futures price to the spot price. In Figure 2.1a the futures price is above the spot price prior to the delivery month. In Figure 2.1b the futures price is below the spot price prior to the delivery month. The circumstances under which these two patterns are observed will be discussed later in this chapter and in Chapter 3.

THE OPERATION OF MARGINS

If two investors get in touch with each other directly and agree to trade an asset in the future for a certain price, there are obvious risks. One of the investors may regret the deal and try to back out. Alternatively, the investor simply may not have the financial resources to honor the agreement. One of the key roles of the exchange is to organize trading so that contract defaults are minimized. This is where margins come in.

Marking to Market

To illustrate how margins work, consider an investor who contacts his or her broker on Thursday, June 3, 1993, to buy two December 1993 gold futures contracts on the New York Commodity Exchange (COMEX). We suppose that the

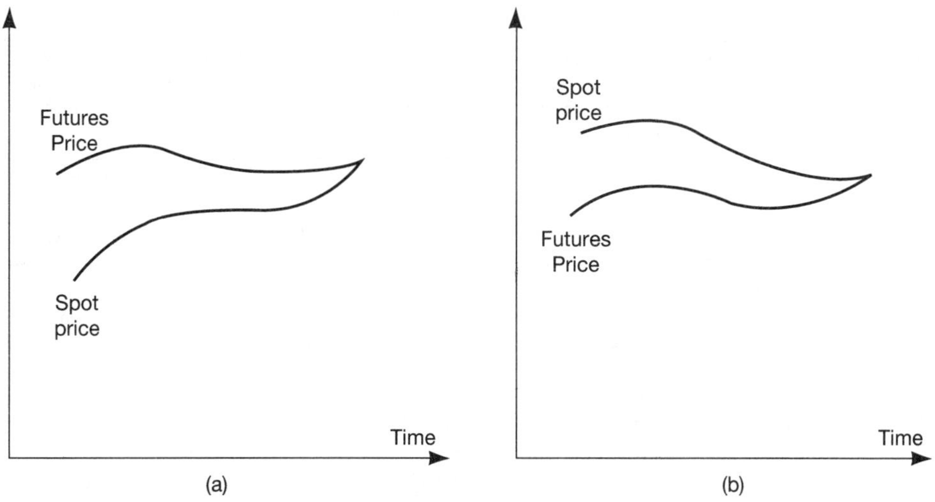

Figure 2.1 Relationship between futures price and spot price as the delivery month is approached. (a) Futures price above spot price; (b) futures price below spot price.

current futures price is \$400 per ounce. Since the contract size is 100 ounces, the investor has contracted to buy a total of 200 ounces at this price. The broker will require the investor to deposit funds in what is termed a *margin account*. The amount that must be deposited at the time the contract is first entered into is known as the *initial margin*. We suppose this is \$2,000 per contract or \$4,000 in total. At the end of each trading day, the margin account is adjusted to reflect the investor's gain or loss. This is known as *marking to market* the account.

Suppose, for example, that by the end of June 3, the futures price has dropped from \$400 to \$397. The investor has a loss of 200 × \$3 or \$600. This is because the 200 ounces of December gold, which he or she contracted to buy at \$400, can now only be sold for \$397. The balance in the margin account would, therefore, be reduced by \$600 to \$3,400. Similarly, if the price of December gold rose to \$403 by the end of the first day, the balance in the margin account would be increased by \$600 to \$4,600. A trade is first marked to market at the close of the day on which it takes place. It is then marked to market at the close of trading on each subsequent day.

Note that marking to market is not merely an arrangement between broker and client. When there is a \$600 decrease in the futures price so that the margin account of an investor with a long position is reduced by \$600, the investor's broker has to pay the exchange \$600 and the exchange passes the money on to the broker of an investor with a short position. Similarly, when there is an increase in the futures price, brokers for parties with short positions pay money to the exchange and brokers for parties with long positions receive money from the exchange. We will give more details of the mechanism by which this happens later.

The investor is entitled to withdraw any balance in the margin account in

Table 2.2 Operation of Margins for a Long Position in Two Gold Futures Contracts

The initial margin is $2,000 per contract or $4,000 in total and the maintenance margin is $1,500 per contract or $3,000 in total. The contract is entered into on June 3 at $400 and closed out on June 24 at $392.30. The numbers in column 2, except the first and the last, are the futures price at the close of trading.

DAY	*FUTURES PRICE ($)*	*DAILY GAIN (LOSS) ($)*	*CUMULATIVE GAIN (LOSS) ($)*	*MARGIN ACCOUNT BALANCE ($)*	*MARGIN CALL ($)*
	400.00			4,000	
June 3	397.00	(600)	(600)	3,400	
June 4	396.10	(180)	(780)	3,220	
June 7	398.20	420	(360)	3,640	
June 8	397.10	(220)	(580)	3,420	
June 9	396.70	(80)	(660)	3,340	
June 10	395.40	(260)	(920)	3,080	
June 11	393.30	(420)	(1,340)	2,660	1,340
June 14	393.60	60	(1,280)	4,060	
June 15	391.80	(360)	(1,640)	3,700	
June 16	392.70	180	(1,460)	3,880	
June 17	387.00	(1,140)	(2,600)	2,740	1,260
June 18	387.00	0	(2,600)	4,000	
June 21	388.10	220	(2,380)	4,220	
June 22	388.70	120	(2,260)	4,340	
June 23	391.00	460	(1,800)	4,800	
June 24	392.30	260	(1,540)	5,060	

excess of the initial margin. To ensure that the balance in the margin account never becomes negative a *maintenance margin,* which is somewhat lower than the initial margin, is set. If the balance in the margin account falls below the maintenance margin, the investor receives a *margin call* and is expected to top up the margin account to the initial margin level the next day. The extra funds deposited are known as a *variation margin*. If the investor does not provide the variation margin, the broker closes out the position by selling the contract. In the case of the investor considered earlier closing out the position would involve neutralizing the existing contract by selling 200 ounces of gold for delivery in December.

Table 2.2 illustrates the operation of the margin account for one possible sequence of futures prices in the case of the investor considered earlier. The maintenance margin is assumed for the purpose of the illustration to be $1,500 per contract or $3,000 in total.

On June 11, the balance in the margin account falls $340 below the maintenance margin level. This triggers a margin call from the broker for additional margin of $1,340. Table 2.2 assumes that the investor does in fact provide this margin by close of trading on June 14. On June 17, the balance in the margin account again falls below the maintenance margin level and a margin call for $1,260 is sent out. The investor provides this margin by close of trading on June 18. On June 24, the investor decides to close out the position by shorting two contracts. The futures price on that day is $392.30 and the investor has a cumulative loss of $1,540. Note that the investor has excess margin on June 14, 21, 22, and 23. Table 2.2 assumes that this is not withdrawn.

Further Details

Some brokers allow an investor to earn interest on the balance in his or her margin account. The balance in the account does not, therefore, represent a true cost, providing the interest rate is competitive with that which could be earned elsewhere. To satisfy the initial margin requirements (but not subsequent margin calls), an investor can sometimes deposit securities with the broker. Treasury bills are usually accepted in lieu of cash at about 90 percent of their face value. Shares are also sometimes accepted in lieu of cash—but at about 50 percent of their face value.

The effect of the marking to market is that a futures contract is settled daily rather than all at the end of its life. At the end of each day, the investor's gain (loss) is added to (subtracted from) the margin account. This brings the value of the contract back to zero. A futures contract is in effect closed out and rewritten at a new price each day.

Minimum levels for initial and maintenance margins are set by the exchange. Individual brokers may require greater margins from their clients than those specified by the exchange. However, they cannot require lower margins than those specified by the exchange. Margin levels are determined by the variability of the price of the underlying asset. The higher this variability, the higher the margin levels. The maintenance margin is usually about 75 percent of the initial margin.

Margin requirements may depend on the objectives of the trader. A bona fide hedger, such as a company that produces the commodity on which the futures contract is written, is often subject to lower margin requirements than a speculator. This is because there is deemed to be less risk of default. Day trades and spread transactions often give rise to lower margin requirements than hedge transactions. A *day trade* is a trade where the trader announces to the broker that he or she plans to close out the position in the same day. Thus, if the trader has taken a long position, the plan is to take an offsetting short position later in the day; if the trader has taken a short position, the plan is to take an offsetting long position later in the day. A *spread transaction* is one where the trader simultaneously takes a long position in the contract corresponding to one month and a short position in a contract corresponding to another month.

Note that margin requirements are the same on short futures positions as they are on long futures positions. It is just as easy to take a short futures position as it is to take a long futures position. The cash market does not have this symmetry. Taking a long position in the cash market involves buying the asset and presents no problems. Taking a short position involves selling an asset that you do not own. This is a more complex transaction that may or may not be possible in a particular market. It will be discussed further in the next chapter.

The Clearinghouse and Clearing Margins

The *exchange clearinghouse* is an adjunct of the exchange and acts as an intermediary or middleman in futures transactions. It guarantees the performance of the parties to each transaction. The clearinghouse has a number of members all of which have offices close to the clearinghouse. Brokers who are not clearinghouse members themselves must channel their business through a member. The main task of the clearinghouse is to keep track of all the transactions that take place during a day so that it can calculate the net position of each of its members.

Just as an investor is required to maintain a margin account with his or her broker, a clearinghouse member is required to maintain a margin account with the clearinghouse. This is known as a *clearing margin*. The margin accounts for clearinghouse members are adjusted for gains and losses at the end of each trading day in the same way as the margin accounts of investors. However, in the case of the clearinghouse member, there is an original margin but no maintenance margin. Every day, the account balance for each contract must be maintained at an amount equal to the original margin times the number of contracts outstanding. Thus, depending on transactions during the day and price movements, the clearinghouse member may have to add funds to its margin account at the end of the day. Alternatively, it may find it can remove funds from the account at this time. Brokers who are not clearinghouse members must maintain a margin account with a clearinghouse member.

In the calculation of clearing margins, the exchange clearinghouse calculates the number of contracts outstanding on either a gross or a net basis. The *gross basis* simply adds the total of all long positions entered into by clients to the total of all the short positions entered into by clients. The *net basis* allows these to be offset against each other. Suppose a clearinghouse member has two clients, one with a long position in 20 contracts, the other with a short position in 15 contracts. Gross margining would calculate the clearing margin on the basis of 35 contracts; net margining would calculate the clearing margin on the basis of five contracts. Most exchanges currently use net margining.

It should be stressed that the whole purpose of the margining system is to reduce the possibility of market participants sustaining losses because of defaults. Overall, the system has been very successful. Losses arising from defaults in contracts at major exchanges have been almost nonexistent.

NEWSPAPER QUOTES

Many newspapers carry futures quotations. In *The Wall Street Journal* futures quotations can currently be found in the Money and Investing section. Table 2.3 shows the quotations for commodities as they appeared in *The Wall Street Journal* of

Table 2.3 Commodity Futures Quotes from *The Wall Street Journal* on August 12, 1993

FUTURES PRICES

Wednesday, August 11, 1993.

Open Interest Reflects Previous Trading Day.

GRAINS AND OILSEEDS

CORN (CBT) 5,000 bu.; cents per bu.

	Open	High	Low	Settle	Change	Lifetime High	Lifetime Low	Open Interest
Sept	238½	241¼	237¾	240¾	+ 2	271½	217¾	54,216
Dec	245¼	247¾	244½	247¼	+ 1½	268½	225¼	158,743
Mr94	253	255	251¾	254¾	+ 1¾	266½	232¾	23,221
May	257¼	259½	257¼	259¼	+ 1¾	270½	238½	8,098
July	259	261½	258¾	261½	+ 1¾	270½	241	9,128
Sept	253	253	252	252	– ½	259	240½	1,010
Dec	245	245½	244	244½	– ¾	255	236½	8,728

Est vol 40,000; vol Tues 34,847; open int 263,144, –1,596.

OATS (CBT) 5,000 bu.; cents per bu.

	Open	High	Low	Settle	Change	Lifetime High	Lifetime Low	Open Interest
Sept	139¾	143¼	139	143	+ 3¼	160½	129¾	4,474
Dec	144	148¾	143¼	148¼	+ 4¼	161	134	6,048
Mr94	148	152¾	148	152¾	+ 4¾	163½	138¾	250
May	151	153½	151	154½	+ 4½	164	141	497

Est vol 2,000; vol Tues 610; open int 11,281, –50.

SOYBEANS (CBT) 5,000 bu.; cents per bu.

	Open	High	Low	Settle	Change	Lifetime High	Lifetime Low	Open Interest
Aug	669	681	668½	679¼	+ 12¾	754½	551	1,383
Sept	670½	584	669	681½	+ 11¾	756½	554	24,038
Nov	675	686	672	683¼	+ 10	757½	555½	110,937
Ja94	678½	689½	677	686½	+ 9	756	576½	13,913
Mar	681½	692	680	689	+ 8½	754	589¾	7,627
May	681½	693½	680½	692	+ 10½	751	592½	11,544
July	683½	694½	682½	691¾	+ 9½	750	592½	8,989
Aug	676½	686	676½	686	+ 10	735	639	827
Sept	646½	646½	643	646½	+ 1½	676	649	399
Nov	624	624	618½	622¼	– 1½	650	581½	5,256

Est vol 50,000; vol Tues 42,189; open int 184,913, –1,793.

SOYBEAN MEAL (CBT) 100 tons; $ per ton.

	Open	High	Low	Settle	Change	Lifetime High	Lifetime Low	Open Interest
Aug	216.00	220.00	215.50	219.40	+ 4.00	241.50	180.10	4,657
Sept	214.00	218.20	213.50	216.90	+ 3.20	239.20	181.00	16,310
Oct	213.20	217.00	212.20	217.00	+ 4.30	239.20	181.70	7,079
Dec	213.40	216.80	212.00	215.70	+ 3.40	240.00	183.40	28,846
Ja94	211.80	216.00	211.50	215.00	+ 3.50	239.50	184.60	4,708
Mar	212.00	215.00	211.50	213.70	+ 2.20	237.50	184.60	5,119
May	211.00	213.00	210.50	212.20	+ 1.80	232.00	185.50	3,868
July	210.00	211.00	209.60	210.20	+ 1.70	230.00	197.50	1,050
Aug	209.00	209.00	208.50	206.00	– 2.50	225.00	191.50	124
Sept	206.50	206.50	206.50	205.50	+ .50	210.00	204.00	107

Est vol 22,000; vol Tues 16,441; open int 71,887, –2,205.

SOYBEAN OIL (CBT) 60,000 lbs.; cents per lb.

	Open	High	Low	Settle	Change	Lifetime High	Lifetime Low	Open Interest
Aug	23.75	23.90	23.68	23.90	+ .25	25.78	19.29	3,241
Sept	23.75	23.99	23.75	23.93	+ .19	25.94	19.40	21,269
Oct	23.95	24.13	23.90	24.06	+ .21	26.05	19.55	8,215
Dec	24.15	24.35	24.12	24.30	+ .21	26.20	19.76	30,295
Ja94	24.25	24.45	24.20	24.41	+ .26	25.95	20.90	3,524
Mar	24.38	24.58	24.30	24.55	+ .27	26.10	21.13	4,573
May	24.45	24.60	24.45	24.59	+ .29	26.00	21.30	2,446
July	24.50	24.60	24.45	24.60	+ .33	25.95	21.55	1,792
Sept	24.00	24.30	24.00	24.30	+ .31	25.15	23.65	117

Est vol 17,000; vol Tues 12,990; open int 75,612, –1,382.

WHEAT (CBT) 5,000 bu.; cents per bu.

	Open	High	Low	Settle	Change	Lifetime High	Lifetime Low	Open Interest
Sept	310¾	317	310	313½	+ 2¾	353	282¼	16,191
Dec	317½	323	316¾	321	+ 3	360	294	31,292
Mr94	320	326	319¼	323¼	+ 3	353	300	12,607
May	314	319	315	316½	+ 2½	330	300	1,265
July	304	305	301¾	303	– ¼	327	299½	3,171

Est vol 10,000; vol Tues 6,075; open int 64,529, +351.

WHEAT (KC) 5,000 bu.; cents per bu.

	Open	High	Low	Settle	Change	Lifetime High	Lifetime Low	Open Interest
Sept	307½	311¼	306¼	309¾	+ 2½	339	283	10,835
Dec	314½	318¼	313	316½	+ 1¾	341½	293¼	15,141
Mr94	317½	320¼	317	318¾	+ 1½	329½	298	6,866
May	311¼	312	311¼	312	+ ¾	325	298	657
July	303	303½	303	303½	– ½	316	297	875

Est vol 3,059; vol Tues 2,375; open int 34,422, –4.

WHEAT (MPLS) 5,000 bu.; cents per bu.

	Open	High	Low	Settle	Change	Lifetime High	Lifetime Low	Open Interest
Sept	314½	318½	314	317	+ 2½	343¼	280	5,727
Dec	318½	321½	317½	320¾	+ 2½	342	290	7,056
Mr94	325½	325	325	325	+ 2	343	297½	866

Est vol 1,813; vol Tues 2,012; open int 13,625, –110.

BARLEY (WPG) 20 metric tons; Can. $ per ton

	Open	High	Low	Settle	Change	Lifetime High	Lifetime Low	Open Interest
Oct	92.50	93.00	92.50	93.00	+ 1.00	102.40	80.00	1,553
Dec	96.00	97.00	96.00	96.20	+ 1.70	97.00	83.00	193

Est vol 200; vol Tues 35; open int 1,781, +9.

FLAXSEED (WPG) 20 metric tons; Can. $ per ton

	Open	High	Low	Settle	Change	Lifetime High	Lifetime Low	Open Interest
Oct	249.00	253.00	249.00	252.50	+ 5.50	301.80	244.20	2,790
Dec	252.50	257.00	252.50	257.00	+ 6.00	300.50	248.40	2,566
Mr94		....	....	262.90	+ 3.40	282.30	256.00	456

Est vol 425; vol Tues 136; open int 5,812, +60.

CANOLA (WPG) 20 metric tons; Can. $ per ton

	Open	High	Low	Settle	Change	Lifetime High	Lifetime Low	Open Interest
Sept	331.00	335.00	331.00	334.00	+ 4.30	351.50	283.50	4,734
Nov	334.70	338.00	333.80	337.00	+ 4.60	354.60	281.00	20,126
Ja94	340.80	341.90	338.60	341.00	+ 4.30	358.50	304.70	8,209
Mar	344.80	344.80	342.50	343.50	+ 2.70	362.90	307.50	5,769
June	346.50	349.50	346.40	349.50	+ 4.40	367.80	319.00	3,108
Aug	346.50	348.50	346.00	348.50	+ 3.00	371.90	333.00	477
Sept	329.50	331.50	328.00	330.80	+ 4.30	358.50	325.10	846
Nov	330.50	332.50	329.00	332.00	+ 3.30	332.50	326.50	220

Est vol 3,525; vol Tues 2,403; open int 43,489, +121.

WHEAT (WPG) 20 metric tons; Can. $ per ton

	Open	High	Low	Settle	Change	Lifetime High	Lifetime Low	Open Interest
Oct	95.00	95.70	94.30	94.40	– .50	108.80	90.10	5,891
Dec	96.70	97.00	95.20	95.50	– 1.00	108.30	92.00	2,870
Mr94	100,50	101.00	99.20	99.20	– 1.30	111.00	96.00	1,328
May		....	....	102.20	– 1.10	109.70	99.50	308

Est vol 1,465; vol Tues 537; open int 10,397, –90.

LIVESTOCK AND MEAT

CATTLE–FEEDER (CME) 50,000 lbs.; cents per lb.

	Open	High	Low	Settle	Change	Lifetime High	Lifetime Low	Open Interest
Aug	89.10	89.15	88.80	88.87	– .27	89.50	76.60	4,883
Sept	87.65	87.75	87.35	87.40	– .30	88.35	75.70	2,390
Oct	86.80	86.95	86.60	86.67	– .12	87.50	75.90	3,633
Nov	87.50	87.52	87.25	87.35	– .22	87.90	77.45	2,769
Ja94	86.65	86.65	86.40	86.50	– .15	86.85	79.90	572
Mar	84.87	84.95	84.80	84.80	– .10	85.35	81.20	378
Apr	84.30	84.45	84.30	84.40	– .10	85.00	82.05	135

Est vol 1,111; vol Tues 1,265; open int 14,824, –10.

col. continues on p. 28

	Open	High	Low	Settle	Change	Lifetime High	Lifetime Low	Open Interest
Ja94	21.78	21.79	21.75	21.75	– .04	21.92	21.35	1,607
Mar	21.78	21.79	21.75	21.75	– .05	21.89	21.35	2,373
May	21.85	21.92	21.90	21.90	– .03	22.00	21.35	1,634
July	21.97	21.97	21.97	21.97	– .03	22.06	21.55	1,459
Sept		....	....	22.01	....	22.07	21.80	1,307
Nov		....	....	22.00	+ .01	22.00	21.82	261

Est vol 232; vol Tues 39; open int 12,178, –474.

COTTON (CTN) – 50,000 lbs.; cents per lb.

	Open	High	Low	Settle	Change	Lifetime High	Lifetime Low	Open Interest
Oct	56.70	56.70	55.51	55.63	– 1.00	64.40	54.40	4,557
Dec	57.65	57.75	56.66	56.76	– .84	64.25	54.60	18,786
Mr94	59.05	59.10	58.10	58.27	– .67	64.20	55.62	4,999
May	59.65	59.50	59.00	58.92	– .64	64.85	58.00	1,627
July	60.20	59.75	59.75	59.55	– .75	65.00	58.75	798
Dec		....	....	60.25	– .43	62.90	59.95	835

Est vol 4,500; vol Tues 3,212; open int 31,680, –566.

ORANGE JUICE (CTN) – 15,000 lbs.; cents per lb.

	Open	High	Low	Settle	Change	Lifetime High	Lifetime Low	Open Interest
Sept	119.00	119.30	115.60	115.65	– 1.90	127.70	75.10	10,631
Nov	122.00	122.25	118.80	118.90	– 1.95	131.00	78.50	2,881
Ja94	123.90	123.90	120.60	120.60	– 1.90	131.80	82.15	2,798
Mar	124.50	123.50	122.25	122.25	– 1.75	133.50	84.50	1,010
May	125.65	125.65	123.25	123.25	– 2.20	133.00	116.50	636
July	125.00	122.25	122.25	122.25	– 3.20	133.50	116.50	290

Est vol 1,700; vol Tues 1,360; open int 18,256, –86.

METALS AND PETROLEUM

COPPER-HIGH (CMX) – 25,000 lbs.; cents per lb.

	Open	High	Low	Settle	Change	Lifetime High	Lifetime Low	Open Interest
Aug	83.45	83.45	83.45	83.45	+ .45	106.70	79.00	383
Sept	83.60	84.10	83.05	83.70	+ .35	110.10	78.00	26,138
Oct	84.00	84.00	83.55	83.80	+ .30	104.30	80.00	1,150
Nov		....	....	83.90	+ .25	104.35	80.75	431
Dec	84.20	84.50	83.70	84.00	+ .20	109.20	79.00	17,696
Ja94		....	....	84.25	+ .20	104.40	81.00	542
Feb	84.70	84.70	84.70	84.45	+ .20	99.20	81.65	310
Mar	84.80	85.10	84.70	84.70	+ .20	107.50	80.00	3,614
May	85.15	85.20	85.10	85.10	+ .25	102.20	80.60	2,222
June		....	....	85.30	+ .30	89.50	87.00	106
July		....	....	85.50	+ .30	102.95	81.60	1,428
Sept		....	....	85.85	+ .30	103.30	82.10	1,218
Dec	86.60	86.60	86.60	86.35	+ .30	101.90	82.80	1,283

Est vol 11,000; vol Tues 11,917; open int 56,676, +954.

GOLD (CMX) – 100 troy oz.; $ per troy oz.

	Open	High	Low	Settle	Change	Lifetime High	Lifetime Low	Open Interest
Aug	377.50	379.00	374.00	375.30	– 5.60	409.00	328.50	1,307
Oct	382.70	383.80	375.00	376.80	– 5.70	411.50	330.80	11,010
Dec	384.70	385.80	377.00	378.70	– 5.70	414.00	331.70	112,339
Fb94	386.70	387.50	379.50	380.70	– 5.70	415.70	333.80	14,727
Apr	383.40	383.70	381.80	382.50	– 5.70	418.50	335.20	5,694
June	384.00	385.20	384.00	384.40	– 5.70	417.20	339.40	7,380
Aug	388.00	388.00	386.50	386.20	– 5.70	415.00	341.50	3,608
Oct	391.00	391.00	388.70	388.10	– 5.70	417.00	344.00	2,573
Dec	390.50	391.00	388.80	390.10	– 5.70	426.50	343.00	9,617
Fb95	386.70	392.00	392.00	392.20	– 5.70	411.00	368.00	2,270
Apr		....	....	394.40	– 5.70	425.00	390.20	798
June	400.00	400.00	396.00	396.60	– 5.70	430.00	351.00	2,276
Dec		....	....	404.10	– 5.70	439.50	358.00	1,470
Ju96		....	....	412.40	– 5.70	447.00	370.90	699
Dec		....	....	421.50	– 5.70	443.00	379.60	594
De97		....	....	441.80	– 5.70	477.00	406.00	469

Est vol 60,000; vol Tues 31,000; open int 176,847, –2,651.

PLATINUM (NYM) – 50 troy oz.; $ per troy oz.

	Open	High	Low	Settle	Change	Lifetime High	Lifetime Low	Open Interest
Oct	na	396.90	389.00	391.30	– 4.60	427.50	336.00	13,262
Ja94	397.00	397.00	391.00	392.10	– 4.80	427.00	335.50	4,612
Apr	na	394.00	394.00	393.10	– 4.30	428.50	335.00	1,634

Est vol 2,392; vol Tues 2,238; open int 19,594, –580.

PALLADIUM (NYM) 100 troy oz.; $ per troy oz.

	Open	High	Low	Settle	Change	Lifetime High	Lifetime Low	Open Interest
Sept	140.90	141.50	139.50	140.15	– .85	145.00	93.70	1,538
Dec	141.00	141.00	138.50	139.15	– .85	142.50	91.85	3,365
Mr94	136.00	136.00	136.00	136.65	– 1.35	139.50	99.00	332
June		....	....	134.15	– 1.85	134.00	121.60	162

Est vol 142; vol Tues 872; open int 5,399, +271.

SILVER (CMX) – 5,000 troy oz.; cents per troy oz.

	Open	High	Low	Settle	Change	Lifetime High	Lifetime Low	Open Interest
Aug		....	....	467.0	– 8.1	540.0	427.0	122
Sept	478.0	479.5	465.0	467.8	– 8.2	547.0	358.0	36,426
Dec	482.5	484.5	470.0	472.5	-8.2	553.0	362.0	45,161
Mr94	488.0	489.0	476.0	477.6	– 8.2	556.5	366.0	11,140
May	485.0	485.0	480.0	481.2	– 8.2	555.5	371.0	7,090
July	485.0	488.5	484.0	484.5	– 8.2	565.0	372.5	3,198
Sept	494.5	494.5	492.0	488.2	– 8.2	561.5	376.5	541
Dec	495.0	498.0	488.0	493.6	– 8.2	572.0	380.0	3,395
Mr95		....	....	499.4	– 8.2	572.0	457.0	536

Est vol 28,000; vol Tues24,584; open int 107,703, –2,233.

SILVER (CBT) – 1,000 troy oz.; cents per troy oz.

	Open	High	Low	Settle	Change	Lifetime High	Lifetime Low	Open Interest
Aug	468.0	468.0	468.0	468.0	– 8.0	543.0	355.0	7
Dec	484.0	484.0	469.0	470.0	– 9.5	551.0	361.0	4,783
Fb94	477.0	477.0	475.0	475.0	– 8.0	555.0	364.5	108
June	495.0	495.0	480.0	482.0	– 9.0	562.0	375.0	649

Est vol 200 ; vol Tues 273; open int 5,722, +20.

CRUDE OIL, Light Sweet (NYM) 1,000 bbls.; $ per bbl.

	Open	High	Low	Settle	Change	Lifetime High	Lifetime Low	Open Interest
Sept	17.53	17.92	17.51	17.88	+ .36	21.18	17.06	109,406
Oct	17.96	18.28	17.93	18.25	+ .35	21.15	17.29	79,181
Nov	na	18.52	18.27	18.49	+ .34	21.15	17.50	37,572
Dec	na	18.68	18.44	18.66	+ .32	23.00	17.75	49,368
Ja94	na	18.74	18.60	18.81	+ .31	21.15	17.92	22,877
Feb	18.75	18.82	18.74	18.92	+ .30	20.81	18.10	15,811
Mar	18.85	18.96	18.82	19.01	+ .29	21.10	18.10	10,950
Apr	18.90	19.00	18.90	19.09	+ .28	20.88	18.27	8,870
May	19.00	19.03	19.00	19.17	+ .27	21.07	18.37	8,239
June	19.05	19.15	19.05	19.24	+ .27	21.35	18.45	15,247
July	19.15	19.15	19.15	19.30	+ .27	20.78	18.50	11,384
Aug	19.20	19.20	19.20	19.35	+ .27	20.78	18.70	8,124
Sept	19.30	19.32	19.30	19.38	+ .27	20.78	18.86	7,713
Oct		....	....	19.40	+ .27	20.73	18.88	3,655
Nov		....	....	19.42	+ .27	20.69	18.90	5,254
Dec	19.28	19.28	19.26	19.44	+ .27	21.25	18.92	17,351
Ja95		....	....	19.46	+ .26	20.78	19.13	1,195
Feb		....	....	19.48	+ .25	19.21	19.20	205
Mar		....	....	19.49	+ .23	20.66	19.05	4,008
June	19.45	19.49	19.45	19.50	+ .22	21.21	19.00	16,240
Dec		....	....	19.58	+ .21	20.80	19.10	10,057
Ju96	19.55	19.62	19.53	19.66	+ .21	20.26	19.00	9,164

Est vol 111,851; vol Tues 96,691; open int 451,871, +10,595.

col. continues on p. 28

	Open	High	Low	Settle	Change	Lifetime High	Lifetime Low	Open Interest
May	2.180	2.190	2.180	2.165	– .010	2.300	1.540	3,263
June	2.185	2.195	2.185	2.170	– .010	2.300	1.560	3,868
July	2.210	2.210	2.195	2.180	– .010	2.315	1.590	4,269
Aug	na	2.235	2.230	2.215	– .010	2.335	1.715	4,011
Sept	na	2.275	2.260	2.245	– .010	2.375	1.850	3,673
Oct	2.375	2.375	2.357	2.360	– .010	2.470	1.995	2,600
Nov	2.495	2.505	2.495	2.480	– .010	2.580	2.285	5,132
Dec	2.640	2.655	2.640	2.630	– .010	2.730	2.410	3,359
Ja95	2.640	2.640	2.640	2.625	– .010	2.720	2.585	1,194
Feb	2.460	2.460	2.460	2.428	– .007	2.460	2.380	397

Est vol 13,499; vol Tues 11,592; open int 125,533, +1,926.

BRENT CRUDE (IPE) 1,000 net bbls.; $ per bbl.

	Open	High	Low	Settle	Change	Lifetime High	Lifetime Low	Open Interest
Sept	16.66	16.92	16.60	16.91	+ .35	19.58	15.90	49,759
Oct	16.80	17.07	16.76	17.05	+ .33	19.58	16.06	47,457
Nov	16.93	17.24	16.93	17.22	+ .33	19.44	16.34	10,248
Dec	17.19	17.39	17.13	17.38	+ .35	19.38	16.54	7,712
Ja94	17.28	17.50	17.27	17.50	+ .35	19.35	16.85	7,495
Feb	17.39	17.43	17.39	17.57	+ .29	19.30	17.11	1,761
Mar	17.43	17.43	17.42	17.68	+ .44	18.97	17.19	3,412
Apr	17.56	17.50	17.50	17.80	+ .35	18.04	17.26	630
May		....	....	17.90	+ .35	17.55	17.35	200

Est vol 42,334; vol Tues 39,290; open int 128,674, +2,756.

GAS OIL (IPE) 100 metric tons; $ per ton

	Open	High	Low	Settle	Change	Lifetime High	Lifetime Low	Open Interest
Aug	157.75	157.75	157.00	157.50	+ .75	183.25	151.50	10,761
Sept	158.50	159.50	158.25	159.00	+ 1.25	182.25	152.75	25,383
Oct	160.75	161.75	160.50	161.75	+ 2.00	184.00	155.75	15,958
Nov	162.75	163.75	162.75	163.75	+ 1.75	186.00	158.25	8,699
Dec	164.75	166.00	164.75	165.75	+ 1.75	186.00	161.25	9,688
Ja94	166.50	167.50	166.50	167.25	+ 1.50	187.00	162.75	9,971
Feb	167.50	167.50	167.50	167.25	+ 1.25	181.50	163.00	3,236
Mar	165.00	165.25	165.00	165.75	+ 1.25	182.50	162.25	1,599
Apr		....	....	163.75	+ 1.25	176.50	164.50	508
May		....	....	162.75	+ 1.25	172.75	163.00	450
June	162.00	162.00	162.00	162.00	+ 1.25	174.50	160.75	4,825
July		....	....	164.00	+ 1.25	165.75	163.50	464
Sept		....	....	164.00	+ 1.25	178.25	162.25	525

Est vol 16,351; vol Tues 13,261; open int 92,067, +966.

OTHER FUTURES

Settlement prices of selected contracts. Actual volume (from previous session) and open interest of all contract months.

	Vol.	High	Low	Close	Net Change	Lifetime High	Lifetime Low	Open Interest
ANHYDROUS AMMONIA (CBT) 100 tons; $ per ton								
Sep	16	96.50	96.00	96.50	....	102.60	93.30	649
BRITISH POUND (MCE) 12,500 pounds; $ per pound								
Sep	406	1.4756	1.4636	1.4676	+ .0060	1.5778	1.4080	387
CANADIAN DOLLAR (MCE) 50,000 Can. $; $ per Can. $								
Sep	25	.7698	.7650	.7659	– .0069	.7818	.7650	86
CATTLE-LIVE (MCE) 20,000 lb.; ¢ per lb.								
Oct	121	75.77	75.27	75.37	– .25	76.90	67.55	137
CORN (MCE) 1,000 bu.; cents per bu.								
Sep	1,318	241¼	237¾	240¾	+ 2	271½	217¾	7,217
COTTON-WORLD (CTN) 50,000 lbs.; cents per lbs.								
Oct	0	....	....	55.15	– .75	63.20	53.50	318
CRB INDEX (NYFE) – 500 times Index								
Sep	382	215.80	214.60	215.00	– .30	224.00	201.60	2,419
The Index: High 215.29; Low 214.25; Close 214.73 –.37								
DEUTSCHEMARK (MCE) 62,500 marks; $ per mark								
Sep	271	.5823	.5779	.5788	– .0016	.6431	.5753	2,023
DEUTSCHEMARK (PBOT) 125,000 marks; ¢ per mark								
Sep	16	.5783	.5783	.5788	– .0022	.6100	.5718	626
DIAMMONIUM PHOSPHATE (CBT 100 tons; $ per ton								
Sep	140	109.20	108.10	108.90	– .05	128.00	106.50	1,570
EURODOLLAR (MCE) $500,000; pts. of 100%								
Sep	8	96.67	96.66	96.67	....	96.75	95.28	147
EUROMARK (CME) DM 1,000,000; pts. of 100%								
Sep	562	93.55	93.55	93.55	+ .06	93.77	93.14	2,754
EUROTOP 100 INDEX (CMX) – $100 times index								
Sep	107	1113.2	1106.6	1112.8	+ 8.80	1113.2	987.0	809
The Index: High 1099.97; Low 1092.60; Close 1099.46 +8.11								
GSCI (CME) $250 X GSCI nearby index;								
Oct	555	176.20	174.70	176.00	+ 1.60	185.90	173.10	2,274
The Index: High 175.73; Low 174.07; Close 175.62 +1.97								
GOLD-NY (MCE) 33.2 fine troy oz.; cents per troy oz.								
Sep	31	....	....	375.90	– 5.70	407.30	371.00	992
GOLD-KILO (CBT) 32.15 troy oz.; $ per troy oz.								
Oct	82	383.00	376.80	376.80	– 5.80	412.00	343.70	747
HOGS (MCE) 20,000 lb.; ¢ per lb.								
Oct	103	45.40	44.80	44.92	+ .10	46.47	39.70	313
JAPANESE YEN (MCE) 6.25 million yen; $ per yen (.00)								
Sep	179	.9666	.9626	.9662	+ .0114	.9666	.8482	1,381
KC MINI VALUE LINE (KC) – 100 times index								
Sep	61	426.80	425.60	426.45	+ .85	424.00	398.20	447
KC VALUE LINE INDEX (KC) – 500 times index								
Sep	49	426.50	425.60	426.45	+ .85	424.10	370.45	1,063
The Index: High 424.97; Low 424.14; Close 424.96 +.82								
LUMBER (CME) 160,000 bd .ft., $ per 1,000 bd.ft.								
Sep	512	287.5	273.3	273.5	– 9.80	439.00	220.00	2,208
MILK-NONFAT DRY (CSCE) 44,000 lbs.; ¢ per lb.								
Nov	4	104.80	104.80	104.85	– .05	109.50	106.00	183
OATS (MCE) 1,000 bu.; ¢ per bu.								
Sep	20	....	....	143	+ 3¼	160	129¾	119
OATS (MPLS) 5,000 bu.; ¢ per bu.								
Sep	0	....	....	135	+ 3¼	153	122	165
PLATINUM (MCE) 25 troy oz.; cents per troy oz.								
Oct	0	....	....	391.30	– 4.60	424.70	340.00	206
PROPANE (NYM) 42,000 gal.; ¢ per gal.								
Sep	182	30.75	30.50	30.75	+ .05	35.45	30.25	2,548
RICE-ROUGH (MCE) 2000 cwt; $ per cwt								
Sep	316	5.860	5.800	5.840	– .040	7.350	5.080	2,120
RUSSELL 2000 INDEX (CME) $500 times index								
Sep	46	240.80	240.50	240.80	+ .30	240.80	229.45	9,729
SHRIMP (MPLS) 5,000 lbs.; ¢ per lb.								
Sep	9	328	327	329	+ 1½	355	327	97
SILVER (MCE) 1,000 troy oz.; cents per troy oz.								
Sep	19	479.5	465.0	467.8	– 8.2	542.5	358.0	2,202
SILVER (CBT) 5,000 troy oz.; cents per troy oz.								
Dec	0	....	....	468.0	– 8.0	551.0	385.0	225

col. continues on p. 28

Table 2.3 *(continued)*

CATTLE–LIVE (CME) 40,000 lbs.; cents per lb.

Aug	76.25	76.27	75.80	75.92	– .20	76.85	66.10	7,007
Oct	75.72	75.77	75.27	75.37	– .25	76.70	67.55	23,866
Dec	75.55	75.75	75.37	75.47	....	76.65	68.10	14,827
Fb94	76.00	76.20	75.85	75.87	– .05	76.50	70.90	9,962
Apr	77.10	77.27	76.85	76.95	– .15	77.55	73.20	4,959
June	73.82	73.90	73.60	73.60	– .12	74.27	71.25	3,743
Aug	72.40	72.60	72.22	72.22	+ .02	73.25	71.65	2,673

Est vol 8,471; vol Tues 10,227; open int 67,017, +76.

HOGS (CME) 40,000 lbs.; cents per lb.

Aug	48.20	48.75	48.07	48.45	+ .15	52.05	42.70	3,119
Oct	44.85	45.40	44.80	44.92	+ .10	47.15	39.70	9,262
Dec	44.60	45.07	44.42	44.67	+ .17	47.07	40.07	6,228
Fb94	44.32	44.85	44.30	44.50	+ .22	46.67	40.20	1,757
Apr	43.35	43.70	43.25	43.40	+ .20	45.37	39.57	717
June	48.70	49.02	48.60	48.60	+ .30	50.50	45.27	267
Jly	47.85	48.05	47.75	47.90	+ .40	49.60	45.30	103

Est vol 3,467; vol Tues 7,201; open int 21,455, –424.

PORK BELLIES (CME) 40,000 lbs.; cents per lb.

Aug	41.40	41.95	41.05	41.67	+ .27	53.95	31.80	715
Fb94	47.40	48.22	47.40	47.90	+ .82	55.45	39.10	4,088
Mar	47.30	47.75	47.20	47.30	+ .77	54.82	38.60	376

Est vol 1,926; vol Tues 3,245; open int 5.247, –387.

FOOD AND FIBER

COCOA (CSCE)–10 metric tons; $ per ton.

Sept	910	921	910	917	+ 12	1,536	878	14,783
Dec	957	968	957	965	+ 14	1,506	919	27,376
Mr94	994	1,001	991	997	+ 13	1,345	953	18,304
May	1,011	1,013	1,011	1,015	+ 13	1,368	978	6,251
July	1,025	1,035	1,035	1,035	+ 13	1,270	999	2,123
Sept		....	....	1,055	+ 13	1,280	1,020	4,460
Dec	1,070	1,075	1,075	1,083	+ 13	1,185	1,045	5,092
Mr95	1,093	1,101	1,100	1,106	+ 13	1,185	1,077	3,807
May		....	....	1,124	+ 13	1,180	1,125	753

Est vol 8,003; vol Tues 10,797; open int 82,949, –841.

COFFEE (CSCE)–37,500 lbs.; cents per lb.

Sept	74.65	75.25	69.10	70.10	– 4.85	89.75	56.05	25,068
Dec	77.80	77.85	71.80	73.00	– 4.80	91.00	59.00	19,031
Mr94	79.90	80.10	74.55	74.90	– 4.95	90.75	61.50	4,703
May	81.25	81.25	75.50	76.20	– 5.05	90.50	63.25	1,597
July	82.00	81.00	77.25	77.65	– 4.85	85.60	64.90	272
Sept	84.25	79.00	79.00	78.50	– 5.25	86.50	58.50	102

Est vol 26,147; vol Tues 9,475; open int 50,817, –50.

SUGAR–WORLD (CSCE)–112,000 lbs.; cents per lb.

Oct	9.87	9.93	9.65	9.69	– .15	12.85	8.35	46,473
Mr94	9.98	9.99	9.80	9.80	– .16	11.84	8.50	32,740
May	10.02	10.02	9.90	9.90	– .11	11.68	8.65	7,558
July	10.10	10.03	9.99	9.96	– .15	11.55	9.15	4,617
Oct	10.15	10.15	10.00	10.00	– .10	10.41	9.70	2,387

Est vol 10,677; vol Tues 15,939; open int 93,775, –9.

SUGAR–DOMESTIC (CSCE)–112,000 lbs.; cents per lb.

Nov	21.84	21.84	21.80	21.80	– .06	21.95	21.25	3,537

cont. 2nd col. fr. p. 27

HEATING OIL NO. 2 (NYM) 42,000 gal.; $ per gal.

Sept	.5000	.5170	.4990	.5157	+ .0156	.6200	.4885	39,800
Oct	na	.5270	.5145	.5262	+ .0138	.6070	.5010	21,800
Nov	na	.5380	.5275	.5377	+ .0133	.6125	.5140	13,016
Dec	na	.5485	.5380	.5487	+ .0128	.6200	.5250	22,825
Ja94	na	.5580	.5480	.5572	+ .0123	.6225	.5350	15,066
Feb	na	.5640	.5550	.5622	+ .0118	.6200	.5390	6,114
Mar	na	.5500	.5495	.5562	+ .0108	.6050	.5340	4,577
Apr	na	.5450	.5400	.5462	+ .0098	.5875	.5315	2,982
May		....	....	.5387	+ .0093	.5750	.5250	1,468
June		....	....	.5342	+ .0088	.5800	.5200	2,650
July		....	....	.5372	+ .0083	.5710	.5210	6,288
Aug		....	....	.5437	+ .0083	.5617	.5300	619
Sept		....	....	.5537	+ .0083	.5717	.5400	185
Oct		....	....	.5637	+ .0083	.5730	.5500	161
Nov		....	....	.5737	+ .0083	.5830	.5600	110
Dec		....	....	.5837	+ .0083	.5900	.5700	1,034

Est vol 36,437; vol Tues 25,209; open int 138,695, +5,576.

GASOLINE-NY Unleaded (NYM) 42,000 gal.; $ per gal.

Sept	na	.5590	.5365	.5578	+ .0215	.6100	.5035	50,599
Oct	.5315	.5320	.5190	.5312	+ .0128	.5860	.4950	25,220
Nov	.5075	.5200	.5125	.5189	+ .0105	.5770	.4925	10,697
Dec	.5130	.5150	.5095	.5145	+ .0091	.5690	.4890	8,900
Ja94	.5025	.5130	.5090	.5145	+ .0086	.5670	.4910	3,459
Feb		....	....	.5210	+ .0086	.5705	.5095	1,251
Mar		....	....	.5325	+ .0086	.5800	.5250	713
Apr		....	....	.5685	+ .0086	.6250	.5500	738
May		....	....	.5765	+ .0086	.6130	.5550	548
June		....	....	.5780	+ .0086	.6100	.5880	49
Aug		....	....	.5690	+ .0086	.6000	.5870	453

Est vol 51,324; vol Tues 31,743; open int 102,709, +2,965.

NATURAL GAS, (NYM) 10,000 MMBtu.; $ per MMBtu's

Sept	2.225	2.260	2.210	2.253	+ .035	2.465	1.470	18,096
Oct	2.285	2.305	2.275	2.294	+ .022	2.490	1.630	13,255
Nov	2.405	2.420	2.395	2.414	+ .014	2.582	1.765	11,465
Dec	2.560	2.570	2.545	2.560	+ .010	2.710	2.000	16,378
Ja94	2.550	2.570	2.540	2.545	+ .005	2.685	1.857	14,069
Feb	2.365	2.375	2.365	2.365	– .005	2.465	1.800	8,272
Mar	2.235	2.245	2.235	2.225	– .010	2.335	1.627	7,635
Apr	2.185	2.190	2.175	2.160	– .010	2.285	1.565	4,598

EXCHANGE ABBREVIATIONS
(for commodity futures and futures options)

CBT-Chicago Board of Trade; CME-Chicago Mercantile Exchange; CMX-Commodity Exchange, New York; CTN-New York Cotton Exchange; CSCE-Coffee, Sugar & Cocoa Exchange, New York; FNX-Finex, New York; IPE-International Petroleum Exchange; KC-Kansas City Board of Trade; LIFFE-Londion International Financial Futures Exchange; MCE-MidAmerica Commodity Exchange; MPLS-Minneapolis Grain Exchange; NYM-New York Mercantile Exchange; PBOT-Philadelphia Board of Trade; WPG-Winnipeg Commodity Exchange.

cont. 3rd col. fr. p. 27

SOYBEANS (MCE) 1,000 bu.; cents per bu.

Sep	3,546	684	669	681½	+ 1¾	756½	554	22,065

SOYBEAN MEAL (MCE) 20 tons; cents per ton

Sep	15	218.20	213.50	216.90	+ 3.20	239.20	181.00	529

SWISS FRANC (MCE) 62,500 francs; $ per franc

Sep	306	.6560	.6503	.6514	– .0021	.7850	.6433	472

10–YEAR T.NOTES (MCE) 50,000; pts. 32nds of 100%

Sep	18	113-17	113-08	113-15	+ 4	113-24	110-26	484

WHEAT (MCE) 1,000 bu.; cents per bu.

Sep	255	317	310	313½	+ 2¾	355	282½	1,906

WHITE WHEAT (MPLS) 5,000 bu.; cents per bu.

Sep	108	345	341½	345	– 1	394	325	549

Thursday, August 12, 1993. These refer to the trading that took place on the previous day (i.e., Wednesday, August 11, 1993). The quotations for index futures and currency futures are given in Chapter 3. The quotations for interest-rate futures are given in Chapter 5.

The asset underlying the futures contract, the exchange it is traded on, the contract size, and how the price is quoted are all shown at the top of each section. The first asset is corn, traded on the Chicago Board of Trade. The contract size is 5,000 bushels and the price is quoted in cents per bushel. The months in which particular contracts are traded are shown in the first column. Corn contracts with maturities in September 1993, December 1993, March 1994, May 1994, July 1994, September 1994, and December 1994 were traded on August 11, 1993.

Prices

The first three numbers in each row show the opening price, the highest price achieved in trading during the day, and the lowest price achieved in trading during the day. The opening price is representative of the prices at which contracts were trading immediately after the opening bell. For September corn on August

11, 1993, the opening price was 238½ cents per bushel and during the day, the price traded between 241¼ cents and 237¾ cents.

Settlement Price

The fourth number is the *settlement price*. This is the average of the prices at which the contract traded immediately before the bell signaling the end of trading for the day. The fifth number is the change in the settlement price from the previous day. In the case of the September 1993 corn futures contract, the settlement price was 240¾ cents on August 11, 1993, up 2 cents from August 10, 1993.

The settlement price is important because it is used for calculating daily gains and losses, and margin requirements. In the case of the September 1993 corn futures, an investor with a long position in one contract would find that his or her margin account balance increased by \$100 (= 5,000 × 2 cents) between August 10, 1993 and August 11, 1993. Similarly, an investor with a short position in one contract would find that the margin balance decreased by \$100 between August 10, 1993 and August 11, 1993.

Lifetime Highs and Lows

The sixth and seventh numbers show the highest futures price and the lowest futures price achieved in the trading of the particular contract. The September 1993 corn contract had traded for about 15 months on August 11, 1993. During this period, the highest and lowest prices achieved were 271½ cents and 217¾ cents.

Open Interest and Volume of Trading

The final column in Table 2.3 shows the *open interest* for each contract. This is the total number of the contracts outstanding. It is the sum of all the long positions or, equivalently, it is the sum of all the short positions. Because of the problems in compiling the data, the open interest information is one trading day older than the price information. Thus, in *The Wall Street Journal* of August 12, 1993, the open interest is for the close of trading on August 10, 1993. In the case of the September 1993 corn futures contract, the open interest was 54,216 contracts.

At the end of each section, Table 2.3 shows the estimated volume of trading in contracts of all maturities on August 11, 1993 and the actual volume of trading in these contracts on August 10, 1993. It also shows the total open interest for all contracts on August 10, 1993 and the change in this open interest from August 9. For all corn futures contracts, the estimated trading volume was 40,000 contracts on August 11, 1993 and the actual trading volume was 34,847 contracts on August 10, 1993. The open interest for all contracts was 263,144 on August 10, 1993, down 1,596 from August 9, 1993.

It sometimes happens that the volume of trading in a day is greater than the open interest at the end of the day. This is indicative of a large number of day trades.

Patterns of Futures Prices

A number of different patterns of futures prices can be picked out from Table 2.3. The futures price of gold on the New York Commodity Exchange and the futures price of oats on the Chicago Board of Trade increase as the time to maturity increases. This is known as a *normal market*. By contrast, the futures price of palladium on the New York Commodity Exchange is a decreasing function of the time to maturity. This is known as an *inverted market*. For live cattle, the pattern is mixed. The futures price first decreases, then increases, and then decreases again as the time to maturity increases.

KEYNES AND HICKS

As the maturity of the futures contract is approached, the futures price of an asset converges toward its spot price. An interesting question is whether the futures price is above or below the expected future spot price. If the futures price is above the expected future spot price, there is an expectation that the futures price will decline. Similarly, if the futures price is below the expected future spot price, there is an expectation that the futures price will rise. John Maynard Keynes and John Hicks argued that if hedgers tend to hold short positions and speculators tend to hold long positions, the futures price will be below the expected future spot price. This is because speculators require compensation for the risks they are bearing. They will only trade if there is an expectation that the futures price will rise over time. If hedgers tend to hold long positions while speculators hold short positions, Keynes and Hicks argue that the futures price must be above the expected future spot price. The reason is similar. To compensate speculators for the risks they are bearing, there must be an expectation that the futures prices will decline over time.

The situation where the futures price is below the expected future spot price is known as *normal backwardation*; the situation where the futures price is above the expected future spot price is known as *contango*. In the next chapter we will discuss both the determinants of futures prices and the relationship between futures prices and expected future spot prices in more detail.

DELIVERY

As mentioned earlier in this chapter, very few of the futures contracts that are entered into lead to delivery of the underlying asset. The rest are closed out early. Nevertheless, it is the possibility of eventual delivery that determines the futures price. An understanding of delivery procedures is therefore important.

The period during which delivery can be made is defined by the exchange and varies from contract to contract. The decision on when to deliver is made by the party with the short position, whom we shall refer to as investor A. When investor A decides to deliver, investor A's broker issues a *notice of intention to deliver* to the exchange clearinghouse. This states how many contracts will be delivered and, in the case of commodities, also specifies where delivery will be made and what grade will be delivered. The exchange then chooses a party with a long position to accept delivery.

Suppose that the party on the other side of investor A's futures contract when it was negotiated on the floor of the exchange was investor B. It is important to realize that there is no reason to expect that it will be investor B who takes delivery. Investor B may well have closed out his or her position by taking a short position in a contract with investor C, investor C may have closed out his or her position by taking a short position in a contract with investor D, and so on. The usual rule chosen by the exchange is to pass the notice of intention to deliver on to the party with the oldest outstanding long position. Parties with long positions must accept delivery notices. However, if the notices are transferable, they have a short period of time, usually half an hour, to find another party with a long position that is prepared to accept the notice from them.

In the case of a commodity, taking delivery usually means accepting a warehouse receipt in return for immediate payment. The party taking delivery is then responsible for all warehousing costs. In the case of livestock futures, there may be costs associated with feeding and looking after the animals. In the case of financial futures, delivery is usually made by wire transfer. For all contracts, the price paid is usually based on the previous day's settlement price adjusted for grade, the location of the delivery, and so on. The whole delivery procedure from the issuance of the notice of intention to deliver to the delivery itself generally takes two to three days.

There are three critical days for a contract. These are the first notice day, the last notice day, and the last trading day. The *first notice day* is the first day on which a notice of intention to make delivery can be submitted to the exchange. The *last notice day* is the last such day. The *last trading day* is generally a few days before the last notice day. To avoid the risk of having to take delivery, an investor with a long position should close out his or her contracts prior to the first notice day. Table 2.4 provides examples of how the first notice day, last notice day, and last trading day are set for a number of different contracts.

Cash Settlement

Some financial futures such as those on stock indices are settled in cash. This is because it is inconvenient or impossible to deliver the underlying asset. In the case of the futures contract on the S&P 500, for example, delivering the underlying asset would involve delivering a portfolio of 500 stocks. When a contract is settled in cash, it is simply marked to market at the end of the last trading day and all positions are declared closed. The settlement price on the last trading day is the

Table 2.4 First Notice Day, Last Notice Day and Last Trading Day for a Number of Different Contracts

EXCHANGE	*ASSET*	*FIRST NOTICE DAY*	*LAST NOTICE DAY*	*LAST TRADING DAY*
CBOT	Corn	Last business day prior to delivery month	Second-to-last business day of delivery month	Eighth-to-last business day of delivery month
CME	Cattle (live)	Sixth calendar day of delivery month	Second-to-last business day of delivery month	Twentieth calendar day of delivery month
CSCE	Cocoa	Seven business days prior to first business day of delivery month	Last trading day	Eighth-to-last business day of delivery month
COMEX	Gold	Second-to-last business day of month prior to delivery month	Second-to-last business day of delivery month	Third-to-last day of delivery month

closing spot price of the underlying asset. This ensures that the futures price converges to the spot price.

One exception to the rule that the settlement price on the last trading day equals the closing spot price is the S&P 500 futures contract. This bases the final settlement price on the opening price of the index the morning after the last trading day. This procedure is designed to avoid some of the problems connected with the fact that stock index futures, stock index options, and options on stock index futures all expire on the same day. Arbitrageurs often take large offsetting positions in these three contracts and there may be chaotic trading and significant price movements toward the end of an expiration day as they attempt to close out their positions. The media has coined the term *triple witching hour* to describe trading during the last hour of an expiration day.

THE TRADING PIT

Futures trading usually takes place in what are termed *trading pits*. These are polygonal-shaped rings with steps descending to the center. Each pit is generally dedicated to the trading of a particular asset. The traders interested in trading a certain contract month tend to meet at a particular place in the pit. Trading currently takes place by what is known as *open outcry auction*. A trader announcing a *bid* (i.e., a proposal to buy) will shout "*n* at *p*" where *n*. is the number of contracts and *p* is the price. A trader announcing an *offer* (i.e., a proposal to sell) will shout "*p* for *n*." The price is usually abbreviated. Thus, a trader wanting to buy four contracts of December gold at $403.20 might shout "4 at 20." The 20 would refer to 20 cents with $403 being understood. A complicated system of hand signals is also used to signal bids and offers.

A trader who announces a bid or offer must trade with the first trader who signals acceptance. The two traders then record the number of contracts, the contract type, the delivery date, the price, the name of the clearing firm on the other side of the transaction, and the initials of the trader on the other side.

Recently, there has been a great deal of discussion of the viability of automated futures trading systems. Under an automated system, buyer and seller would be matched by a computer. A potential buyer would sit at a computer terminal and indicate the price at which he or she is willing to buy. This price would be relayed throughout the system. Another trader, also sitting at a computer terminal and logged into the system, could signal a willingness to sell at the buyer's price by pressing the appropriate keys. Some of the major North American exchanges currently use this type of system outside normal trading hours and some European exchanges use it for all trading. It is possible that all exchanges will eventually eliminate the open outcry auction.

Pit Reporting

Reporters, who are employees of the exchange, record the times and prices of bids and offers. These are usually displayed on a large board above the trading floor. They are also communicated via ticker tape and in other ways to investors who are not on the floor of the exchange. Within a matter of seconds, the prices on a U.S. futures exchange are known throughout the world.

For each contract month, the board shows

1. The range of opening prices
2. The highest price (trade or bid) achieved during the day
3. The lowest price (trade or offer) achieved during the day
4. The estimated trading volume
5. The most recent seven prices before the last recorded price with an indication as to whether they are bids, offers, or trades
6. The last recorded price with an indication as to whether it is a bid, offer, or trade
7. The difference between the last price and the previous trading day's settlement price
8. The previous trading day's settlement price
9. The high for the year
10. The low for the year

Types of Traders

There are two main types of traders on the floor of the exchange: commission brokers and locals. *Commission brokers* execute trades for other people and charge a commission for doing so. *Locals* are individuals who add liquidity to the market by trading on their own accounts.

When an investor places an order with his or her broker, the broker relays the order by telephone to its trading desk on the floor of the exchange. The order is then sent by messenger to the commission broker for action. When the order has been filled, this information is sent back to the trading desk and a confirmation of the trade eventually reaches the investor. The total commission, charged when a contract is initiated, is usually a round-trip commission that covers both the purchase and sale of the contract. The same commission is charged regardless of whether the contract is ultimately closed out or not. Commissions vary significantly. One investor might pay only $25 per contract, while another pays $200 per contract.

Participants in futures markets, whether locals or those away from the floor of the exchange, can be categorized as hedgers, speculators, or arbitrageurs, as discussed in Chapter 1. Speculators can be classified as scalpers, day traders, or position traders. *Scalpers* are watching for very-short-term trends and attempt to profit from small changes in the contract price. They usually hold their positions for only a few minutes. *Day traders* hold their positions for less than one trading day. They are unwilling to take the risk that adverse news will occur overnight. *Position traders* hold their positions for much longer periods of time. They hope to make significant profits from major movements in the markets.

Seats on Exchanges

To trade on the floor of the exchange, an individual must buy or rent a seat on the exchange. Seats are being continually bought and sold, and their price depends on the volume of trading activity. Seats on the Chicago Board of Trade, the Chicago Mercantile Exchange, and the International Monetary Markets cost several hundred thousand dollars, while those on smaller exchanges are significantly less expensive. Owners of seats are exchange members. However, not all exchange members are clearinghouse members. An exchange member must maintain an account with a clearinghouse member for the purpose of clearing trades.

Types of Orders

The simplest type of order for an individual to place with his or her broker is a *market order*. This requests that a trade be carried out immediately at the best price available in the market. However, there are many other types of orders. We will consider those that are more commonly used.

A *limit order* specifies a particular price. The order can only be executed at this price or at one more favorable to the investor. Thus, if the limit price is $30 for an investor wanting to take a long position, the order will only be executed at a price of $30 or less. There is, of course, no guarantee that the order will be executed at all, since the limit price may never be reached.

A *stop order* or a *stop-loss order* also specifies a particular price. The order is executed at the best available price once there is a bid or offer at this particular price or a less favorable price. Suppose a stop order to sell at $30 is issued when the market price is $35. This becomes an order to sell when and if the price falls to $30. In effect, a stop order becomes a market order as soon as the specified price has been hit. The purpose of a stop order is usually to close out a position if unfavorable price movements take place. It limits the loss that can be incurred.

A *stop-limit order* is a combination of a stop order and a limit order. The order becomes a limit order as soon as there is a bid or offer at a price equal to or less favorable than the stop price. Two prices must be specified in a stop-limit order: the stop price and the limit price. Suppose that at the time the market price is $35, a stop-limit order to buy is issued with a stop price of $40 and a limit price of $41. As soon as there is a bid or offer at $40, this becomes a limit order at $41. If the stop price and the limit price are the same, the order is sometimes called a *stop-and-limit order*.

A *market-if-touched order* (MIT) is executed at the best available price after a trade occurs at a specified price or at a price more favorable than the specified price. In effect, an MIT becomes a market order once the specified price has been hit. An MIT is also known as a *board order*. Consider an investor who has a long position in a futures contract and is issuing instructions that would lead to the contract being closed out. A stop order is designed to place a limit on the loss that can occur in the event of unfavorable price movements. By contrast, a market-if-touched order is designed to ensure that profits are taken if sufficiently favorable price movements occur.

A *discretionary order* or a *market-not-held order* is traded as a market order except that execution may be delayed at the broker's discretion in an attempt to get a better price.

Some orders specify time conditions. Unless otherwise stated, an order is a day order and expires at the end of the trading day. A *time-of-day order* specifies a particular period of time during the day when the order can be executed. An *open order* or a *good-till-canceled order* is in effect until executed or until the end of trading in the particular contract. A *fill-or-kill order*, as its name implies, must be executed immediately when received or not at all.

REGULATION

Futures markets in the United States are currently regulated federally by the Commodity Futures Trading Commission (CFTC), which was established in 1974. This body is responsible for licensing futures exchanges and approving contracts. All new contracts and changes to existing contracts must be approved by the CFTC. To be approved, the contract must have some useful economic purpose. Usually this means that it must serve the needs of hedgers as well as speculators.

The CFTC looks after the public interest. It is responsible for ensuring that prices are communicated to the public and that futures traders report their outstanding positions if they are above certain levels. The CFTC also licenses all individuals who offer their services to the public in the futures area. The background of these individuals are investigated and there are minimum capital requirements. The CFTC deals with complaints brought by the public and ensures that disciplinary action is taken against individuals when this is appropriate. It has the authority to force exchanges to take disciplinary action against members who are in violation of exchange rules.

In 1982, the National Futures Association (NFA) was formed. This led to some of responsibilities of the CFTC being shifted to the futures industry itself. The NFA is an organization of individuals who participate in the futures industry. Its objective is to prevent fraud and ensure that the market operates in the best interests of the general public. The NFA requires its members to pass an exam. It is authorized to monitor trading and take disciplinary action where appropriate. It has set up an efficient system for arbitrating disputes between individuals and its members.

From time to time other bodies such as the Securities and Exchange Commission (SEC), the Federal Reserve Board, and the U.S. Treasury Department have claimed jurisdictional rights over some aspects of futures trading. These bodies are concerned about the effects of futures trading on the spot markets for securities such as stocks, treasury bills, and treasury bonds. The SEC currently has an effective veto over the approval of new stock or bond index futures contracts. However, the basic responsibility for all futures and options on futures rests with the CFTC. There has been speculation that the responsibilities of the CFTC will at some stage be taken over by the SEC.

Trading Irregularities

Most of the time futures markets operate efficiently and in the public interest. However, from time to time, trading irregularities do come to light. One type of trading irregularity occurs when an investor group tries to "corner the market."[1] The investor group takes a huge long futures position and also tries to exercise some control over the supply of the underlying commodity. As the maturity of the futures contracts is approached, the investor group does not close out its position and the number of outstanding futures contracts may exceed the amount of the commodity available for delivery. The holders of short positions realize that they will find it difficult to deliver and become desperate to close out their positions. The result is a large rise in both futures and spot prices. Regulators usually deal with this type of abuse of the market by increasing margin requirements, imposing stricter position limits, prohibiting trades that increase a speculator's open position, and forcing market participants to close out their positions.

Other types of trading irregularities can involve the traders on the floor of the exchange. These received some publicity early in 1989 when it was announced that the FBI had carried out a two-year investigation, using undercover agents, of trading on the Chicago Board of Trade and the Chicago Mercantile Exchange. The investigation was initiated because complaints were filed by a large agricultural concern. The alleged offenses included overcharging customers, not paying customers the full proceeds of sales, and traders using their knowledge of customer orders to trade first for themselves. The investigation led to a number of regular traders being subpoenaed to appear before a federal grand jury.

[1] Possibly the best known example of this is provided by the activities of the Hunt brothers in the silver market in 1979–1980. Between the middle of 1979 and the beginning of 1980, their activities led to a price rise from $9 per ounce to $50 per ounce.

ACCOUNTING AND TAX

The full details of the accounting and tax treatment of futures contracts are beyond the scope of this book. An investor who wants detailed information on this should consult experts.

FASB Statement No. 52, Foreign Currency Translation, established accounting standards in the United States for foreign currency futures. FASB Statement No. 80, Accounting for Futures Contracts, established accounting standards in the United States for all other contracts. The two statements require changes in market value to be recognized when they occur unless the contract qualifies as a hedge. If the contract does qualify as a hedge, gains or losses are generally recognized for accounting purposes in the same period in which the gains or losses from the item being hedged are recognized.

For tax purposes in the United States, the gain or loss on a foreign currency futures transaction is regarded as ordinary income. On other futures, the gain/loss is considered to be 60 percent a long-term capital gain/loss and 40 percent a short-term capital gain/loss. In foreign currency futures transactions that qualify as hedges, the gain or loss is generally recognized in the same period that the gain or loss on the item being hedged is recognized. In other futures transactions that qualify as hedges, the gain or loss is recognized when the contract is closed out or when delivery is made. All transactions that do not qualify as hedges are marked to market at the year end for tax purposes.

Consider an investor who, in September 1993, takes a long position in a March 1994 corn futures contract and closes out the position at the end of February 1994. Suppose that the futures prices are 150 cents per bushel when the contract is entered into, 170 cents per bushel at the end of 1993, and 180 cents per bushel when the contract is closed out. One contract is for the delivery of 5,000 bushels. If the investor is a speculator, the gains for accounting and tax purposes would be

$$5{,}000 \times \$0.20 = \$1{,}000$$

in 1993 and

$$5{,}000 \times \$0.10 = \$500$$

in 1994. If the investor is hedging the purchase of 5,000 bushels of corn in 1994, the whole gain of $1,500 is realized in 1994 for accounting and tax purposes.

This example is shown in Table 2.5. The treatment of hedging gains and losses is sensible. If the investor in our example is a company that is hedging the purchase of 5,000 bushels of corn at the end of February 1994, the effect of the futures contract is to ensure that the price paid is close to 150 cents per bushel.

Table 2.5 Accounting and Tax Treatment of a Futures Transaction

From the Trader's Desk—February 1994

September 1993:	Investor takes a long position in one March 1994 futures contract to buy 5,000 bushels of corn. Futures price is 150 cents per bushel.
End of 1993:	Futures price is 170 cents per bushel.
February 1994:	The contract is closed out. Futures price is 180 cents per bushel.

If Investory Is a Speculator

Accounting/tax gain in 1993 = 5,000 × 20 cents = $1,000
Accounting/tax gain in 1994 = 5,000 × 10 cents = $500

If Investor Is Hedging a Purchase of Corn in 1994

Accounting/tax gain in 1994 = 5,000 × 30 cents = $1,500

The accounting and tax treatment reflects that this price is paid in 1994. The 1993 accounting and tax calculations are unaffected by the futures transaction.

FORWARD CONTRACTS

Forward contracts are similar to futures contracts in that they are agreements to buy or sell an asset at a certain time in the future for a certain price. However, unlike futures contracts, they are not traded on an exchange. They are private agreements between two financial institutions or between a financial institution and one of its corporate clients.

One of the parties to a forward contract assumes a *long position* and agrees to buy the asset at a certain specified date for a certain price. The other party assumes a *short position* and agrees to sell the asset on the same date for the same price. Forward contracts do not have to conform to the standards of a particular exchange. The delivery date in the contract can be any date mutually convenient to the two parties. Usually, in forward contracts, a single delivery date is specified, whereas in futures contracts, there is a range of possible delivery dates.

Forward contracts are not marked to market daily like futures contracts. The two parties contract to settle up on the specified delivery date. Whereas most futures contracts are closed out prior to delivery, most forward contracts do lead to delivery of the physical asset or to final settlement in cash. Table 2.6 summarizes the main differences between forward and futures contracts.

Delivery Price

The specified price in a forward contract will be referred to as the *delivery price*. At the time the contract is entered into this is chosen so that the value of the contract to both parties is zero. This means that it costs nothing to take a long or a short position. We can think of the delivery price as being determined by

Table 2.6 Comparison of Forward and Futures Contracts

FORWARDS	*FUTURES*
Private contract between two parties	Traded on an exchange
Not standardized	Standardized contract
Usually one specified delivery date	Range of delivery dates
Settled at end of contract	Settled daily
Delivery or final cash settlement usually takes place	Contract usually closed out prior to maturity

supply and demand considerations. However, as we will show in the next chapter, for assets on which forward contracts are normally negotiated, there is a way of calculating the "correct" delivery price from the current spot price of the asset, the delivery date, and other observable variables.

Forward Price

The *forward price* for a forward contract is similar in general concept to the futures price for a futures contract. A contract's current forward price is the delivery price that would apply if the contract were negotiated today. More formally, we can say that the forward price for a certain contract is defined as the delivery price which would make that contract have zero value. The forward price and the delivery price are by definition equal at the time the contract is entered into. However, as time passes, the forward price is liable to change while the delivery price, of course, remains the same. The two are not therefore equal, except by chance, at any time after the start of the contract. Generally, the forward price at any given time varies with the maturity of the contract being considered. For example, the forward price for a contract to buy or sell in three months will typically be different from that for a contract to buy or sell in six months.

Forward Contracts on Foreign Exchange

Forward contracts on foreign exchange are very popular. Most large banks have a "forward desk" within their foreign exchange trading room. This is devoted to the trading of forward contracts. Forward foreign exchange rates are frequently quoted alongside spot rates. Consider the following quotes on the sterling–U.S. dollar exchange rate:

Spot	1.8470
30-day forward	1.8442
90-day forward	1.8381
180-day forward	1.8291

The first quote indicates that, ignoring commissions and other transactions costs, sterling can be bought or sold in the spot market (i.e., for virtually immediate delivery) at the rate of $1.8470 per pound; the second quote indicates that the forward price for a contract to buy or sell sterling in 30 days is $1.8442 per pound; the third quote indicates that the forward price for a contract to buy or sell sterling in 90 days is $1.8381 per pound; and so on.

Foreign Exchange Quotes

Futures prices are always quoted as the number of U.S. dollars per unit of the foreign currency or as the number of U.S. cents per unit of the foreign currency. Forward prices are always quoted in the same way as spot prices. This means that for the British pound, the forward quotes show the number of U.S. dollars per unit of the foreign currency and are directly comparable with futures quotes. For most other countries, forward quotes show the number of units of the foreign currency per U.S. dollar. Thus, in the forward market, a futures price of 0.6050 dollars per Swiss franc would be expressed as 1.6529 francs per dollar. This is because 1.6529 = 1/0.6050.

Forward-Rate Agreements

Forward contracts are frequently arranged on domestic interest-rate-bearing instruments as well as on foreign currencies. For example, two companies might agree that a 7 percent per annum rate of interest will apply to a one-year deposit in six months' time. If the actual rate proves to be different from 7 percent per annum, one company pays and the other receives the present value of the difference between two sets of interest cash flows. This is known as a *forward-rate agreement* (FRA).

Hedging

Like futures contracts, forward contracts can be used for hedging. Suppose a U.S. corporation knows that it is due to pay £1,000,000 in 90 days and the 90-day forward rate is 1.8381. It can choose at no cost to enter into a long forward contract to buy £1,000,000 in 90 days for $1,838,100. In this way, it hedges its foreign exchange risk by locking in the exchange rate that will apply to the sterling it requires. Similarly, a U.S. corporation that knows it is due to receive £1,000,000 in 90 days can at no cost enter into a short forward contract to sell £1,000,000 in 90 days for $1,838,100. In this way, it hedges its foreign exchange risk by locking in the price that will apply to the sterling it receives.

Speculation

Forward contracts can be used for speculation as well as hedging. An investor who thinks that sterling will increase in value relative to the U.S. dollar can speculate by taking a long position in a forward contract on sterling. Similarly, an investor who feels that sterling will fall in value can speculate by taking a short position in a forward contract on sterling. Let us again assume that the sterling

90-day forward rate is 1.8381. Suppose that the actual spot sterling exchange rate in 90 days proves to be 1.8600. An investor who has a long position in a 90-day forward contract will be able to purchase pounds for \$1.8381 when they are worth \$1.8600. He or she will realize a gain of \$0.0219 per pound. Similarly, an investor with a short position in three-month sterling will realize a loss of \$0.0219 per pound.

Speculators may well be required to deposit a margin up front. However, this is generally a relatively small proportion of the value of the assets underlying the forward contract. A forward contract, like a futures contract, therefore, provides speculators with a high degree of leverage.

The value at maturity or *terminal value* of a long position in a forward contract on one unit of an asset is

$$S_T - K$$

where K is the delivery price and S_T is the spot price of the asset at maturity of the contract. Similarly, the terminal value of a short position in a forward contract on one unit of an asset is

$$K - S_T$$

In the case of the example that has just been given, $S_T = 1.8600$, $K = 1.8381$, so that $S_T - K = +0.0219$ and $K - S_T = -0.0219$. Since it costs nothing to enter into a forward contract, the terminal value of the contract is also the speculator's total profit from the contract. The profits from a forward contract are illustrated in Figure 2.2.

Figure 2.2 Profit to speculator from a forward contract. (a) Long position, (b) short position; delivery price = K, price of asset at maturity = S_T.

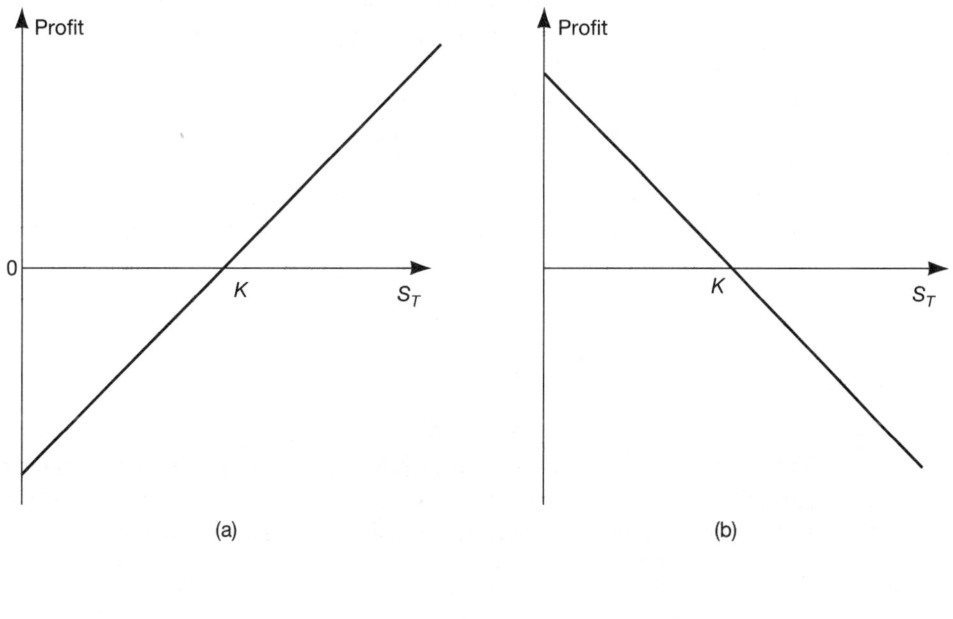

Table 2.7 The Payoffs from Futures and Forward Contracts

From the Trader's Desk

Investor A takes a long position in a 90-day forward contract on £1 million. Forward price is 1.8381.

Investor B takes a long position in 90-day futures contracts on £1 million. Futures price is 1.8381.

At the end of the 90 days, the sterling exchange rate proves to be 1.8600.

Outcome

Investors A and B each make a total gain equal to

$$(1.8600 - 1.8381) \times 1{,}000{,}000 = \$21{,}900$$

Investor A's gain is made entirely on the ninetieth day, while investor B's gain is realized day by day over the 90-day period. On some days, investor B may realize a loss while on other days, he or she will realize gains.

Profits from Forward and Futures Contracts

Suppose that the sterling exchange rate for a 90-day forward contract is 1.8381 and that this is also the futures price for a contract that will be delivered in exactly 90 days. What is the difference between the gains and losses under the two contracts?

Under the forward contract, the whole gain or loss is realized at the end of the life of the contract. Under the futures contract, the gain or loss is realized day by day because of the daily settlement procedures. Suppose that investor A is long £1 million in a 90-day forward contract and investor B is long £1 million in 90-day futures contracts. (Since each futures contract is for the purchase or sale of £62,500, investor B must purchase a total of 16 contracts.) Assume that the spot exchange rate in 90 days proves to be 1.8600. Investor A makes a gain of \$21,900 on the ninetieth day. Investor B makes the same gain—but spread out over the 90-day period. On some days, investor B may realize a loss, while on other days, he or she makes a gain. However, in total, when losses are netted against gains, there is a gain of \$21,900 over the 90-day period. This example is shown in Table 2.7.

SUMMARY

In this chapter, we have looked at how futures and forward markets operate. In futures markets, contracts are traded on an exchange, and it is necessary for the exchange to define carefully the precise nature of what it is that is traded, the procedures that will be followed, and the regulations that will govern the market. Forward contracts are negotiated directly over the telephone by two relatively sophisticated individuals. As a result, there is no need to standardize the product, and an extensive set of rules and procedures is not required.

A very high proportion of the futures contracts that are traded do not lead to the delivery of the underlying asset. They are closed out prior to the delivery period being reached. However, it is the possibility of final delivery that drives the determination of the futures price. For each futures contract, there is a range of days during which delivery can be made and a well-defined delivery procedure. Some contracts such as those on stock indices are settled in cash rather than by delivery of the underlying asset.

The specification of contracts is an important activity for a futures exchange. The two sides to any contract must know what can be delivered, where delivery can take place, and when delivery can take place. They also need to know such details as the trading hours, how prices will be quoted, maximum daily price movements, and so on. New contracts must be approved by the Commodity Futures Trading Commission before trading starts.

Margins are an important aspect of futures markets. An investor keeps a margin account with his or her broker. This is adjusted daily to reflect gains or losses, and the broker may require the account to be topped up from time to time if adverse price movements have taken place. The broker must either be a clearinghouse member or must maintain a margin account with a clearinghouse member. Each clearinghouse member maintains a margin account with the exchange clearinghouse. The balance in the account is adjusted daily to reflect gains and losses on the business for which the clearinghouse member is responsible.

The exchange ensures that information on prices is collected in a systematic way and relayed within a matter of seconds to investors throughout the world. Many newspapers such as *The Wall Street Journal* carry each day a summary of the previous day's trading.

The trading pit, to an uninformed observer, appears to be a mass of highly excited individuals shouting and signaling to each other. However, the individuals are following well-defined procedures for making and recording trades. There are two main types of traders: locals and commission brokers. Locals are trading on their own account while commission brokers are fulfilling a trade on behalf of someone else.

Forward contracts differ from futures contracts in a number of ways. Forward contracts are private arrangements between two parties, whereas futures contracts are traded on exchanges. There is generally a single delivery date in a forward contract, whereas futures contracts frequently involve a range of such dates. Since they are not traded on exchanges, the standardization of forward contracts is unnecessary. A forward contract is not usually settled until the end of its life, and most contracts do in fact lead to the delivery of the underlying asset or a cash settlement at this time.

In the next few chapters, we will discuss how forward and futures prices are determined. We will also describe in more detail the ways in which forward and futures contracts can be used for hedging.

Suggestions for Further Reading

CHANCE, D., *An Introduction to Options and Futures*. Orlando, FL: Dryden Press, 1989.
CHICAGO BOARD OF TRADE, *Commodity Trading Manual*. Chicago, 1989.
DUFFIE, D., *Futures Markets*. Englewood Cliffs, NJ: Prentice Hall, 1989.
HICKS, J. R., *Value and Capital*. Oxford: Clarendon Press, 1939.
HORN, F. F., *Trading in Commodity Futures*. New York: New York Institute of Finance, 1984.
KEYNES, J. M., *A Treatise on Money*. London: Macmillan, 1930.
KOLB, R., *Understanding Futures Markets*. Glenview, IL: Scott, Foresman, 1985.
SCHWARZ, E. W., J. M. HILL, and T. SCHNEEWEIS, *Financial Futures*. Homewood, IL: Richard D. Irwin, 1986.
TEWELES, R. J. and F. J. JONES, *The Futures Game*. New York: McGraw-Hill, 1987.

Quiz

1. Distinguish between the terms *open interest* and *trading volume*.
2. What is the difference between a *local* and a *commission broker*?
3. Suppose that you enter into a short futures contract to sell July silver for $5.20 per ounce on the New York Commodity Exchange. The size of the contract is 5,000 ounces. The initial margin is $4,000 and the maintenance margin is $3,000. What change in the futures price will lead to a margin call? What happens if you do not meet the margin call?
4. Suppose that in September 1993 you take a long position in a contract on May 1994 crude oil futures. You close out your position in March 1994. The futures price (per barrel) is $18.30 when you enter into your contract, $20.50 when you close out your position, and $19.10 at the end of December 1993. One contract is for the delivery of 1,000 barrels. What is your total profit? When is it realized? How is it taxed if you are (a) a hedger and (b) a speculator?
5. What does a stop order to sell at $2.00 mean? When might it be used? What does a limit order to sell at $2.00 mean? When might it be used?
6. What is the difference between the operation of the margin accounts administered by the clearinghouse and those administered by a broker?
7. What is the difference between the way in which prices are quoted in the foreign exchange futures market, the foreign exchange spot market, and the foreign exchange forward market?

Questions and Problems

2.1. The party with a short position in a futures contract sometimes has options as to the precise asset that will be delivered, where delivery will take place, when delivery will take place, and so on. Do these options increase or decrease the futures price? Explain your reasoning.

2.2. What are the most important aspects of the design of a new futures contract?

2.3. Explain how margins protect investors against the possibility of default.

2.4. A company enters into a short futures contract to sell 5,000 bushels of wheat for 250 cents per bushel. The initial margin is $3,000 and the maintenance margin is $2,000. What price change would lead to a margin call? Under what circumstances could $1,500 be withdrawn from the margin account?

2.5. An investor enters into two long futures contracts on frozen orange juice. Each contract is for the delivery of 15,000 pounds. The current futures price is 160 cents per pound, the initial margin is $6,000 per contract, and the maintenance margin is $4,500 per contract. What price change would lead to a margin call? Under what circumstances could $2,000 be withdrawn from the margin account?

2.6. Show that if the futures price of a commodity is greater than the spot price during the delivery period there is an arbitrage opportunity. Does an arbitrage opportunity exist if the futures price is less than the spot price? Explain your answer.

2.7. Explain the difference between a market-if-touched order and a stop order.

2.8. Explain what a stop-limit order to sell at 20.30 with a limit of 20.10 means.

2.9. At the end of one day, a clearinghouse member is long 100 contracts and the settlement price is $50,000 per contract. The original margin is $2,000 per contract. On the following day, the member becomes responsible for clearing an additional 20 long contracts. These were entered into at a price of $51,000 per contract. The settlement price at the end of this day is $50,200. How much does the member have to add to its margin account with the exchange clearinghouse?

2.10. On July 1, 1993, a company enters into a forward contract to buy 10 million Japanese yen on January 1, 1994. On September 1, 1993, it enters into a forward contract to sell 10 million Japanese yen on January 1, 1994. Describe the payoff from this strategy.

2.11. The forward price on the German mark for delivery in 45 days is quoted as 1.8204. The futures price for a contract that will be delivered in 45 days is 0.5479. Explain these two quotes. Which is more favorable for an investor wanting to sell marks?

2.12. Suppose you call your broker and issue instructions to sell one July hogs contract. Describe what happens.

2.13. "Speculation in futures markets is pure gambling. It is not in the public interest to allow speculators to buy seats on a futures exchange." Discuss this viewpoint.

2.14. Identify the most actively traded contracts in Table 2.3. Consider each of the following sections separately: grains and oilseeds, livestock and meat, food and fiber, and metals and petroleum.

2.15. What do you think would happen if an exchange started trading a contract where the quality of the underlying asset was incompletely specified?

2.16. "When a futures contract is traded on the floor of the exchange, it may be the case that the open interest increases by one, stays the same, or decreases by one." Explain this statement.

2.17. "A long forward contract is equivalent to a long position in a call option and a short position in a put option." Explain this statement.

2.18. Suppose that on October 24, 1993 you take a short position in an April 1994 live cattle futures contract. You close out your position on January 21, 1994. The futures price (per pound) is 61.20 cents when you enter into your contract, 58.30 cents when you close out your position, and 58.80 cents at the end of December 1993. One contract is for the delivery of 40,000 pounds of cattle. What is your total profit? How is it taxed if you are (a) a hedger and (b) a speculator?

3

THE DETERMINATION OF FORWARD AND FUTURES PRICES

In this chapter, we discuss how forward prices and futures prices are related to the price of the underlying asset. Forward contracts are generally easier to analyze than futures contracts because there is no daily settlement—only a single payment at maturity. Consequently, most of the analysis in the first part of the chapter is directed toward determining forward prices rather than futures prices. Key results are provided for forward contracts on

1. Securities providing no income
2. Securities providing a known cash income
3. Securities providing a known dividend yield

It can be shown that the forward price and futures price of an asset are generally very close to each other when the maturities of the two contracts are the same. This means that the key results obtained for forward prices can be assumed to be true for futures prices as well. The second part of the chapter uses the results to calculate futures prices for contracts on stock indices, foreign exchange, gold, and silver.

This chapter draws an important distinction between assets that are held solely for investment by a significant number of investors and those that are held almost exclusively for consumption. Arbitrage arguments enable the forward and futures prices for contracts on investment assets to be determined precisely in terms of spot prices and other observable variables. This is not possible for the forward and futures prices of contracts on consumption assets.

SOME PRELIMINARIES

Before we get into the calculation of forward prices, it will be useful to present some preliminary material.

Continuous Compounding

In this book, the interest rates used will be continuously compounded except where otherwise stated. Readers used to working with interest rates that are compounded annually, semiannually, or in some other way may find this a little strange at first. However, continuously compounded interest rates are used to such a great extent when options and other complex derivative securities are being priced that it makes sense to get used to working with them now.

Consider an amount A invested for n years at an interest rate of R per annum. If the rate is compounded once per annum, the terminal value of the investment is

$$A(1 + R)^n$$

If it is compounded m times per annum, the terminal value of the investment is

$$A\left(1 + \frac{R}{m}\right)^{mn} \tag{3.1}$$

Suppose $A = \$100$, $R = 10$ percent per annum, and $n = 1$ so that we are considering one year. When we compound once per annum ($m = 1$), this formula shows that the \$100 grows to

$$\$100 \times 1.1 = \$110$$

When we compound twice a year ($m = 2$), the formula shows that the \$100 grows to

$$\$100 \times 1.05 \times 1.05 = \$110.25$$

When we compound four times a year ($m = 4$), the formula shows that the \$100 grows to

$$\$100 \times 1.025^4 = \$110.38$$

Table 3.1 shows the effect of increasing the compounding frequency further (i.e., of increasing m). The limit as m tends to infinity is known as *continuous compound-*

Table 3.1 Effect of the Compounding Frequency on the Value of \$100 at the End of One Year When the Interest Rate Is 10 Percent per Annum

COMPOUNDING FREQUENCY	*VALUE OF \$100 AT END OF 1 YEAR (\$)*
Annually ($m = 1$)	110.00
Semiannually ($m = 2$)	110.25
Quarterly ($m = 4$)	110.38
Monthly ($m = 12$)	110.47
Weekly ($m = 52$)	110.51
Daily ($m = 365$)	110.52

ing. With continuous compounding, it can be shown that an amount A invested for n years at rate R grows to

$$Ae^{Rn} \tag{3.2}$$

where $e = 2.71828$. The function e^x is built into most calculators so the computation of the expression in (3.2) presents no problems. In the example in Table 3.1, $A = 100$, $n = 1$, and $R = 0.1$ so that the value to which A grows with continuous compounding is

$$100e^{0.1} = 110.52$$

This is (to two decimal places) the same as the value using daily compounding. For most practical purposes, continuous compounding can be thought of as being equivalent to daily compounding. Compounding a sum of money at a continuously compounded rate R for n years involves multiplying it by e^{Rn}. Discounting it at a continuously compounded rate R for n years involves multiplying by e^{-Rn}.

Suppose that R_1 is a rate of interest with continuous compounding and R_2 is the equivalent rate with compounding m times per annum. From the results in (3.1) and (3.2), we must have

$$Ae^{R_1 n} = A\left(1 + \frac{R_2}{m}\right)^{mn}$$

or

$$e^{R_1} = \left(1 + \frac{R_2}{m}\right)^{m}$$

This means that

$$R_1 = m \ln\left(1 + \frac{R_2}{m}\right) \tag{3.3}$$

and

$$R_2 = m(e^{R_1/m} - 1) \tag{3.4}$$

These equations can be used to convert a rate where the compounding frequency is m times per annum to a continuously compounded rate and vice versa. The function ln is the natural logarithm function and is built into most calculators. It is defined so that if $y = \ln x$, then $x = e^y$.

Examples

1. Consider an interest rate that is quoted as 10 percent per annum with semiannual compounding. From using Equation (3.3) with $m = 2$ and $R_2 = 0.1$, the equivalent rate with continuous compounding is

   $$2 \ln(1 + 0.05) = 0.09758$$

   or 9.758 percent per annum.
2. Suppose that a lender quotes the interest rate on loans as 8 percent per annum with continuous compounding and that interest is actually paid quarterly. From using Equation (3.4) with $m = 4$ and $R_1 = 0.08$, the equivalent rate with quarterly compounding is

   $$4(e^{0.02} - 1) = 0.0808$$

   or 8.08 percent per annum This means that on a $1,000 loan, interest payments of $20.20 would be required each quarter.

Short Selling

Some of the arbitrage strategies presented in this chapter involve short selling. It is appropriate at this stage to explain exactly what is meant by this trading strategy. *Short selling* involves selling securities that are not owned. An investor might contact his or her broker to short 500 IBM shares. The broker will then borrow the shares from another client and sell them in the open market in the usual way. The investor can maintain the short position for as long as he or she chooses provided there are always shares for the broker to borrow. At some stage, however, the investor will close out the position by purchasing 500 IBM shares. These are then replaced in the account of the client from which the shares were borrowed. The investor makes a profit if the stock price has declined and a loss if it has risen. If, at any time while the contract is open, the broker runs out of shares to borrow, the investor is *short-squeezed* and is forced to close out the position immediately even though he or she may not be ready to do so.

Regulators currently only allow shares to be sold short on an *uptick*, that is, when the most recent movement in the price of the security was an increase. A broker requires significant initial margins from clients with short positions, and as with futures contracts, if there are adverse movements (i.e., increases) in the price of the security, additional margin may be required. The proceeds of the initial sales of the security belong to the investor and normally form part of the margin account. Some brokers pay interest on margin accounts and marketable securities such as treasury bills can be deposited with a broker to meet initial margin requirements. As in the case of futures contracts, the margin does not, therefore, represent a real cost.

An investor with a short position must pay to his or her broker any income such as dividends or interest that would normally be received on the securities that have been shorted. The broker will transfer this to the account of the client from whom the securities have been borrowed. Consider the position of an investor who shorts 500 IBM shares in April when the price per share is \$50 and closes out his or her position by buying them back in July when the price per share is \$30. Suppose that a dividend of \$1 per share is paid in May. The investor receives $500 \times \$50 = \$25{,}000$ in April when the short position is initiated. The dividend leads to a payment of $500 \times \$1 = \$500$ in May. The investor also pays $500 \times \$30 = \$15{,}000$ when the position is closed out in July. The net gain is, therefore,

$$\$25{,}000 - \$500 - \$15{,}000 = \$9{,}500$$

This example is summarized in Table 3.2.

Table 3.2 Example of a Short Sale

From the Trader's Desk

An investor shorts 500 IBM shares in April when the price is \$50 and buys them back (to close out the position) in July when the price is \$30. A dividend of \$1 per share is paid in May.

The Profit

The investor receives $500 \times \$50$ in April. He or she must pay $500 \times \$1$ in May when the dividend is declared. The cost of closing out the position is $500 \times \$30$. The net gain is, therefore,

$$(500 \times \$50) - (500 \times \$1) - (500 \times \$30) = \$9{,}500$$

Assumptions

In this chapter, we will assume that the following are all true for some market participants:

1. There are no transactions costs.
2. All trading profits (net of trading losses) are subject to the same tax rate.
3. The market participants can borrow money at the same risk-free rate of interest as they can lend money.
4. The market participants take advantage of arbitrage opportunities as they occur.

Note that we do not require these assumptions to be true for all market participants. All that we require is that they be true for a subset of all market participants, for example, large investment houses. This is not unreasonable. As discussed in Chapter 1, the fact that these market participants are prepared to take advantage of arbitrage opportunities as they occur means that in practice arbitrage opportunities disappear almost as soon as they arise. It is reasonable, therefore, to assume for the purposes of our analyses that there are no arbitrage opportunities.

The Repo Rate

The relevant risk-free rate of interest for many arbitrageurs operating in the futures market is what is known as the *repo rate.* A *repo* or *repurchase agreement* is an agreement where the owner of securities agrees to sell them to a financial institution and buy them back later. The financial institution is providing a loan. The price at which the securities are bought back is slightly higher than the price at which they are sold. This provides the financial institution with its interest on the loan. The loan has virtually no risk since, if the borrowing company does not keep to its side of the agreement, the lender simply keeps the securities.

The repo rate is only slightly higher than the treasury bill rate. The most common type of repo is an *overnight repo* where the agreement is renegotiated each day. However, longer-term arrangements, known as *term repos,* are sometimes used.

Notation

The following notation will be used throughout this chapter:

- T: time until delivery date in forward contract (in years)
- S: price of asset underlying forward contract today
- K: delivery price in forward contract
- f: value of a long forward contract today
- F: forward price today
- r: risk-free rate of interest per annum today, with continuous compounding, for an investment maturing at the delivery date (i.e., in T years)

It is important to realize that the forward price, F, is quite different from the value of the forward contract, f. As explained in Chapter 2, the forward price at any given time is the delivery price that would make the contract have a zero value. When a contract is initiated, the delivery price is set equal to the forward price so that $F = K$ and $f = 0$. As time passes, both f and F change. The analysis and the examples in the next few sections should make clear the distinction between the two variables.

FORWARD PRICES FOR A SECURITY THAT PROVIDES NO INCOME

The easiest forward contract to value is one written on a security that provides the holder with no income. Nondividend-paying stocks and discount bonds are examples of such securities.[1]

An Example

Consider a long forward contract to purchase a nondividend-paying stock in three months. Assume the current stock price is $40 and the three-month risk-free interest rate is 5 percent per annum. We consider strategies open to an arbitrageur in two extreme situations.

Suppose first that the forward price is relatively high at $43. An arbitrageur can borrow $40 at the risk-free interest rate of 5 percent per annum, buy one share, and short a forward contract to sell one share in three months. At the end of the three months, the arbitrageur delivers the share and receives $43. The sum of money required to pay off the loan is

$$40e^{0.05\times 0.25} = \$40.50$$

The arbitrageur by following this strategy locks in a profit of $43.00 − $40.50 = $2.50 at the end of the three-month period. The strategy is summarized in Table 3.3.

Suppose next that the forward price is relatively low at $39. An arbitrageur can short one share, invest the proceeds of the short sale at 5 percent per annum for three months, and take a long position in a three-month forward contract. The proceeds of the short sale grow to

$$40e^{0.05\times 0.25}$$

or $40.50 in three months. At the end of the three months, the arbitrageur pays

[1] Some of the contracts that are used as examples in the first half of this chapter (e.g., forward contracts on individual stocks) do not normally arise in practice. However, they form useful examples for developing our ideas.

Table 3.3 Arbitrage Opportunity When Forward Price of a Nondividend-Paying Stock Is Too High

From the Trader's Desk

The forward price of a stock for a contract with delivery date in three months is \$43. The three-month risk-free interest rate is 5 percent per annum, and the current stock price is \$40. No dividends are expected.

Opportunity

The forward price is too high relative to the stock price. An arbitrageur can

1. Borrow \$40 to buy one share.
2. Enter into a forward contract to sell one share in three months.

At the end of three months, the arbitrageur delivers the share and receives \$43. The sum of money required to pay off the loan is $40e^{0.25 \times 0.05} = \$40.50$. The arbitrageur, therefore, makes a profit at the end of the three-month period of

$$\$43 - \$40.50 = \$2.50$$

\$39, takes delivery of the share under the terms of the forward contract, and uses it to close out the short position. A net gain of

$$\$40.50 - \$39.00 = \$1.50$$

is, therefore, made at the end of the three months. This trading strategy is summarized in Table 3.4.

Under what circumstances do arbitrage opportunitites such as those in Tables 3.3 and 3.4 not exist? The arbitrage in Table 3.3 works when the forward price is greater than \$40.50. The arbitrage in Table 3.4 works when the forward price is less than \$40.50. We deduce that for there to be no arbitrage the forward price must be exactly \$40.50.

Table 3.4 Arbitrage Opportunity When Forward Price of a Nondividend-Paying Stock Is Too Low

From the Trader's Desk

The forward price of a stock for a contract with a delivery date in three months is \$39. The three-month risk-free interest rate is 5 percent per annum and the current stock price is \$40. No dividends are expected.

Opportunity

The forward price is too low relative to the stock price. An arbitrageur can

1. Short one share investing the proceeds of the short sale at 5 percent per annum for three months.
2. Take a long position in a three-month forward contract on one share.

The proceeds of the short sale (i.e., \$40) grow to $40e^{0.25 \times 0.05} = \$40.50$. At the end of the three months, the arbitrageur pays \$39 and takes delivery of the share under the terms of the forward contract. The share is used to close out the short position. The arbitrageur, therefore, makes a net profit at the end of the three-month period of

$$\$40.50 - \$39.00 = \$1.50$$

A Generalization

To generalize this example, we consider a forward contract on a security with price S that provides no income. Using our notation, T is the time to maturity, r is the risk-free rate, and F is the forward price. We imagine an investor adopting the following strategy:

1. Buy one unit of the security.
2. Short one forward contract.

The forward contract has zero value at the time it is first entered into. The up-front cost of the strategy is, therefore, S. The forward contract requires the security to be exchanged for the forward price at time T. The security provides no income. By following the strategy, the investor is, therefore, simply exchanging a payment of S today for a riskless cash inflow equal to the forward price at time T. It follows that the forward price, F, must be the value to which S would grow if invested at the risk-free interest rate for a time T. This means that

$$F = Se^{rT} \tag{3.5}$$

In the example considered, $S = 40$, $r = 0.05$, and $T = 0.25$ so that

$$F = 40e^{0.05\times 0.25} = 40.50$$

which is in agreement with our earlier calculations.

Example

Consider a four-month forward contract to buy a discount bond that will mature one year from today. The current price of the bond is \$930. (Since the bond will have eight months to go when the forward contract matures, we can regard the contract as on an eight-month discount bond.) We assume that the four-month risk-free rate of interest (continuously compounded) is 6 percent per annum. Since discount bonds provide no income, we can use Equation (3.5) with $T = 0.333$, $r = 0.06$, and $S = 930$. The forward price, F, is given by

$$F = 930e^{0.06\times 0.3333} = 948.79$$

This would be the delivery price in a contract negotiated today.

FORWARD PRICES FOR A SECURITY THAT PROVIDES A KNOWN CASH INCOME

In this section, we consider a forward contract on a security that will provide a perfectly predictable cash income to the holder. Examples are stocks paying known dividends and coupon-bearing bonds. We adopt the same approach as in the previous section. We first present a numerical example and then provide the formal arguments.

An Example

Consider a long forward contract to purchase a coupon-bearing bond whose current price is \$900. We suppose that the forward contract matures in one year and the bond matures in five years so that the forward contract is a contract to purchase a four-year bond in one year. We also suppose coupon payments of \$40 are expected after six months and twelve months with the second coupon payment being immediately prior to the delivery date in the forward contract. We assume the six-month and one-year risk-free interest rates (continuously compounded) are 9 percent per annum, and 10 percent per annum, respectively.

Suppose, first, the forward price is relatively high at \$930. An arbitrageur can borrow \$900 to buy the bond and short a forward contract. The first coupon payment has a present value of $40e^{-0.09\times 0.5} = \$38.23$. Of the \$900, \$38.23 is therefore borrowed at 9 percent per annum for six months so that it can be repaid with the first coupon payment. The remaining \$861.77 is borrowed at 10 percent per annum for one year. The amount owing at the end of the year is $861.77e^{0.1} = \$952.40$. The second coupon provides \$40 toward this, and \$930 is received for the bond under the terms of the forward contract. The arbitrageur, therefore, makes a net profit of

$$40 + 930 - 952.40 = \$17.60$$

This strategy is summarized in Table 3.5.

Suppose next that the forward price is relatively low at \$905. An investor

Table 3.5 Arbitrage Opportunity When Forward Price on a Coupon-Bearing Bond Is Too High

From the Trader's Desk

The forward price of a bond for a contract with a delivery date in one year is \$930. The current spot price is \$900. Coupon payments of \$40 are expected in six months and one year. The six-month and one-year risk-free interest rates are 9 percent per annum and 10 percent per annum, respectively.

Opportunity

The forward price is too high. An arbitrageur can

1. Borrow \$900 to buy one bond.
2. Short a forward contract on one bond.

The \$900 loan is made up of \$38.23 borrowed at 9 percent per annum for six months and \$861.77 borrowed at 10 percent per annum for one year. The first coupon payment of \$40 is exactly sufficient to repay interest and principal on the \$38.23. At the end of one year, the second coupon of \$40 is received, \$930 is received for the bond under the terms of the forward contract, and \$952.40 is required to pay principal and interest on the \$861.77. The net profit is, therefore,

$$\$40.00 + \$930.00 - \$952.40 = \$17.60$$

Table 3.6 Opportunity When the Forward Price of a Coupon-Bearing Bond Is Too Low

From the Trader's Desk

The forward price of a bond for a contract with delivery date in one year is $905. The current spot price is $900. Coupon payments of $40 are expected in six months and one year. The six-month and one-year risk-free interest rates are 9 percent per annum and 10 percent per annum, respectively.

Opportunity

The futures price is too low. An investor who holds the bond can

1. Sell one bond.
2. Enter into a long forward contract to repurchase the bond in one year.

Of the $900 realized from selling the bond, $38.23 is invested for six months at 9 percent per annum and $861.77 is invested for one year at 10 percent per annum. This strategy produces a cash flow of $40 at the six-month point and a cash flow of $952.40 at the one-year point. The $40 replaces the coupon that would have been received on the bond at the six-month point. Of the $952.40, $40 replaces the coupon that would have been received on the bond at the one-year point. Under the terms of the forward contract, the bond is repurchased for $905.00. The strategy of selling the bond and buying it back is, therefore,

$$\$952.40 - \$40.00 - \$905.00 = \$7.40$$

more profitable than simply holding the bond for the year.

who holds the bond can sell it and enter into a long forward contract.[2] Of the $900 realized from selling the bond, $38.23 is invested for six months at 9 percent per annum so that it grows into an amount sufficient to equal the coupon that would have been paid on the bond. The remaining $861.77 is invested for twelve months at 10 percent per annum and grows to $952.40. Of this sum, $40.00 is used to replace the coupon that would have been received on the bond, and $905 is paid under the terms of the forward contract to replace the bond in the investor's portfolio. The investor, therefore, gains

$$\$952.40 - \$40.00 - \$905.00 = \$7.40$$

relative to the the situation the investor would have been in if he or she had kept the bond. This strategy is summarized in Table 3.6.

If F is the forward price, the strategy in Table 3.5 produces a profit when $F > 912.40$, while the strategy in Table 3.6 produces a profit when $F < 912.40$. It follows that if there are no arbitrage opportunities, the forward price must be $912.40.

[2] The argument here shows that, providing the asset underlying the forward contract is held by individuals solely for investment purposes, we do not need short selling for our no-arbitrage arguments to work. This point will be explored further later in this chapter.

A Generalization

To generalize from this example, we consider a forward contract on a security that provides income with a present value of I. Consider an investor adopting the following strategy.

1. Buy the security.
2. Enter into a short forward contract.

The forward contract has zero value at the time it is entered into so that the up-front cost of the strategy is the price of the security, S. The strategy provides the investor with income that has a present value of I and a cash flow at T equal to the forward price of the bond, F. Equating the initial outflow with the present value of the cash inflows,

$$S = I + Fe^{-rT}$$

or

$$F = (S - I)e^{rT} \tag{3.6}$$

In the example considered, $S = 900$, $I = 74.43$, $r = 0.1$ so that

$$F = (900 - 74.43)e^{0.1} = 912.40$$

Example

Consider a ten-month forward contract on a stock with a price of \$50. We assume that the risk-free rate of interest (continuously compounded) is 8 percent per annum and the term structure is flat. We also assume that dividends of \$0.75 per share are expected after three months, six months, and nine months. The present value of the dividends, I, is given by

$$I = 0.75e^{-0.02} + 0.75e^{-0.04} + 0.75e^{-0.06} = 2.162$$

The variable T is 0.8333 year so that the forward price, F, is from Equation (3.6) given by

$$F = (50 - 2.162)e^{0.08 \times 0.8333} = 51.14$$

If the forward price were less than this, an arbitrageur would short the stock and buy forward contracts. If the forward price were greater than this, an arbitrageur would short forward contracts and buy the stock.

FORWARD PRICES FOR A SECURITY THAT PROVIDES A KNOWN DIVIDEND YIELD

As will be explained in later sections, both currencies and stock indices can be regarded as securities that provide known dividend yields. In this section, we provide a general analysis of forward contracts on such securities.

A known dividend yield means that the income when expressed as a percentage of the security price is known. We will assume that the dividend yield is paid continuously at an annual rate q. To illustrate what this means, suppose that $q = 0.05$ so that the dividend yield is 5 percent per annum. When the security price is \$10, dividends in the next small interval of time are paid at the rate of 50 cents per annum; when the security price is \$100, dividends in the next small interval of time are paid at the rate of \$5 per annum; and so on. In practice, dividends are not paid continuously. But, in some situations, the continuous dividend yield assumption is a good approximation to reality.

Consider an investor adopting the following strategy:

1. Buy e^{-qT} of the security with income from the security being reinvested in the security.
2. Short a forward contract.

The holding of the security grows at rate q so that $e^{-qT} \times e^{qT}$ or exactly one unit of the security is held at time T.[3] Under the terms of the forward contract, the security is sold for F at time T. The strategy, therefore, leads to an initial outflow of Se^{-qT} and a final inflow of F. The present value of the inflow must equal the outflow. Hence

$$Se^{-qT} = Fe^{-rT}$$

or

$$F = Se^{(r-q)T} \quad \textbf{(3.7)}$$

If $F < Se^{(r-q)T}$, an arbitrageur can enter into a long forward contract and short the stock to lock in a riskless profit. If $F > Se^{(r-q)T}$, an arbitrageur can buy the stock and enter into a short forward contract to lock in a riskless profit.

If the dividend yield varies during the life of the forward contract but is a

[3] These arguments make the unrealistic assumption that one share is divisible. However, we can magnify the holdings in the two portfolios by 100, 10,000, or 1,000,000 and the basic argument is still the same. To illustrate the fact that the holding grows at rate q when dividends are reinvested, suppose that the stock price is \$100, the dividend yield, q, is 5 percent per annum and a short time interval of length 0.02 years is considered. If we hold 10,000 shares, the dividend received in the short time interval is $10{,}000 \times \$100 \times 0.05 \times 0.02 = \$1{,}000$. This enables ten new shares to be purchased so that the holding grows by 0.1 percent during the time period. This corresponds to the assumed growth rate of 5 percent per annum.

known function of time, it can be shown that Equation (3.7) is still correct with q equal to the average dividend yield rate during the life of the forward contract.

Example

Consider a six-month forward contract on a security that is expected to provide a continuous dividend yield of 4 percent per annum. The risk-free rate of interest (with continuous compounding) is 10 percent per annum. The stock price is \$25. In this case $S = 25$, $r = 0.10$, $T = 0.5$, $q = 0.04$. From Equation (3.7), the forward price F is given by

$$F = 25e^{0.06 \times 0.5} = 25.76$$

VALUING FORWARD CONTRACTS

The value of a forward contract at the time it is first entered into is zero. At a later stage it may prove to have a positive or negative value. There is a general result, applicable to all forward contracts, that gives the value of a long forward contract, f, in terms of the originally negotiated delivery price, K, and the current forward price, F. This is

$$f = (F - K)e^{-rT} \quad \textbf{(3.8)}$$

To see why Equation (3.8) is correct, we compare a long forward contract with delivery price F with an otherwise identical long forward contract that has a delivery price of K. The difference between the two is only in the amount that will be paid for the underlying asset at time T. Under the first contract this amount is F; under the second contract it is K. A cash outflow difference of $F - K$ at time T translates to a difference of $(F - K)e^{-rT}$ today. The contract with a delivery price F is, therefore, less valuable than the contract with delivery price K by an amount $(F - K)e^{-rT}$. The value of the contract that has a delivery price of F is by definition zero. It follows that the value of the contract with a delivery price of K is $(F - K)e^{-rT}$. This proves Equation (3.8).

Using Equation (3.8) in conjunction with (3.5) gives the following expression for the value of a forward contract on a security that provides no income

$$f = S - Ke^{-rT} \quad \textbf{(3.9)}$$

Similarly, using Equation (3.8) in conjunction with (3.6) gives the following expression for the value of a forward contract on a security that provides a known income with present value I

$$f = S - I - Ke^{-rT} \quad \textbf{(3.10)}$$

Finally, using Equation (3.8) in conjunction with (3.7) gives the following expression for the value of a forward contract on a security that provides a known dividend yield at rate q

$$f = Se^{-qT} - Ke^{-rT} \tag{3.11}$$

Note that in each case the forward price, F, is the value of K which makes f equal zero.

Example

Consider a six-month long forward contract on a nondividend-paying stock. The risk-free rate of interest (with continuous compounding) is 10 percent per annum, the stock price is \$25, and the delivery price is \$24. In this case $S = 25$, $r = 0.10$, $T = 0.5$, $K = 24$. From Equation (3.5), the forward price F is given by

$$F = 25e^{0.1 \times 0.5} = 26.28$$

From Equation (3.8), the value of the forward contract is

$$f = (26.28 - 24)e^{-0.1 \times 0.5} = 2.17$$

Alternatively, using Equation (3.9),

$$f = 25 - 24e^{-0.1 \times 0.5} = 2.17$$

ARE FORWARD PRICES AND FUTURES PRICES EQUAL?

Appendix 3A provides an arbitrage argument to show that when the risk-free interest rate is constant and the same for all maturities, the forward price for a contract with a certain delivery date is the same as the futures price for a contract with the same delivery date. The argument in Appendix 3A can be extended to cover situations where the interest rate is a known function of time.

When interest rates vary unpredictably (as they do in the real world), forward and futures prices are in theory no longer the same. The proof of the relationship between the two is beyond the scope of this book. However, we can get a sense of the nature of the relationship by considering the situation where the price of the underlying asset, S, is strongly positively correlated with interest rates. When S increases, an investor who holds a long futures position makes an immediate gain because of the daily settlement procedure. This gain will tend to be invested at a higher than average rate of interest. Similarly, when S decreases, the investor will make an immediate loss. This loss will tend to be financed at a lower than average rate of interest. An investor holding a forward contract rather than a futures contract is not affected in this way by interest-rate movements. It follows that a long futures contract will be more attractive than a long forward contract.

Hence, when S is strongly positively correlated with interest rates, futures prices will tend to be higher than forward prices. When S is strongly negatively correlated with interest rates, a similar argument shows that forward prices will tend to be higher than futures prices.

The theoretical differences between forward and futures prices are in most circumstances sufficiently small to be ignored. In practice, there are a number of factors not reflected in theoretical models that may cause forward and futures prices to be different. These include taxes, transaction costs, and the treatment of margins. The risk that the counterparty will default is generally less in the case of a futures contract because of the role of the exchange clearinghouse. Also, in some instances, futures contracts are more liquid and easier to trade than forward contracts. Despite all these points, it is reasonable for most purposes to assume forward and futures prices are the same. This is the assumption that will be made throughout this book. The symbol F will be used to represent both the futures price and the forward price of an asset.

Empirical Research

Some empirical research that has been carried out comparing forward and futures contracts is listed at the end of this chapter. Cornell and Reinganum studied forward and futures prices on the British pound, Canadian dollar, German mark, Japanese yen, and Swiss franc between 1974 and 1979. They found very few statistically significant differences between the two prices. Their results were confirmed by Park and Chen who as part of their study looked at the British pound, German mark, Japanese yen, and Swiss franc between 1977 and 1981.

French studied copper and silver during the period 1968 to 1980. The results for silver show that the futures price and the forward price are significantly different (at the 5 percent confidence level) with the futures price generally above the forward price. The results for copper are less clear-cut. Park and Chen looked at gold, silver, silver coin, platinum, copper, and plywood between 1977 and 1981. Their results are similar to those of French for silver. The forward and futures prices are significantly different with the futures price above the forward price. Rendleman and Carabini studied the treasury bill market between 1976 and 1978. They also found statistically significant differences between futures and forward prices. In all these studies it seems likely that the differences observed are due to the factors mentioned in the previous section (taxes, transaction costs, and so on).

STOCK INDEX FUTURES

A *stock index* tracks the changes in the value of a hypothetical portfolio of stocks. The weight of a stock in the portfolio equals the proportion of the portfolio invested in the stock. The stocks in the portfolio can have equal weights or weights that change in some way over time. The percentage increases in the value of a stock index over a small interval of time is usually defined so that it is equal to the percentage increase in the total value of the stocks comprising the portfolio at that time. A stock index is not usually adjusted for cash dividends. In other words, any cash dividends received on the portfolio are ignored when percentage changes in most indices are being calculated.

It is worth noting that if the hypothetical portfolio of stocks remains fixed, the weights assigned to individual stocks in the portfolio do not remain fixed. If the price of one particular stock in the portfolio rises more sharply than others, more weight is automatically given to that stock. A corollary to this is that, if the weights of the stocks in the portfolio are specified as constant over time, the hypothetical portfolio will change each day. If the price of one particular stock in the portfolio rises more sharply than others, fewer shares of the stock are included in the portfolio.

Stock Indices

Table 3.7 shows futures prices for contracts on five different stock indices as they were reported in *The Wall Street Journal* of August 12, 1993. The prices refer to the close of trading on August 11, 1993. The stock indices are as follows:

1. *The Standard & Poor's 500 (S&P 500) Index*. This is based on a portfolio of 500 different stocks: 400 industrials, 40 utilities, 20 transportation companies, and 40 financial institutions. The weights of the stocks in the portfolio at any given time reflect the stock's total market capitalization (= stock price × number of shares outstanding). The index accounts for about 80 percent of the market capitalization of all the stocks listed on the New York Stock Exchange.

Table 3.7 Stock Index Futures Quotes from *The Wall Street Journal* on August 12, 1993

INDEX

	Open	High	Low	Settle	Chg	High	Low	Open Interest
S&P 500 INDEX (CME) $500 times index								
Sept	450.40	451.90	450.10	450.60	− .20	458.55	391.00	175,005
Dec	451.30	452.65	451.00	451.50	− .10	459.30	429.70	8,545
Mr94		....	....	452.50	− .15	458.80	434.00	403
June	454.00	454.75	453.15	453.60	− .15	456.30	444.50	395
Est vol 30,101; vol Tues 31,300; open int 184,348, −1,559.								
Indx prelim High 451.00; Low 449.60; Close 450.46 +1.01								
S&P MIDCAP 400 (CME) $500 times index								
Sept	170.50	170.60	170.00	170.25	− .30	170.85	157.00	9,700
Est vol 195; vol Tues 351; open int 9,729, +222.								
The index: High 169.92; Low 169.36; Close 169.72 −.20								
NIKKEI 225 Stock Average (CME)−$5 times index								
Sept	20870.	21030.	20860.	21015.	+ 430.0	21380.	16340.	20,548
Est vol 2,678; vol Tues 589; open int 20,581, −73.								
The index: High 20756.08; Low 20489.05; Close 20732.57 +238.82								
NYSE COMPOSITE INDEX (NYFE) 500 times index								
Sept	250.05	250.70	249.65	249.95	− .15	251.85	222.50	3,636
Dec	250.25	250.95	250.25	250.35	− .15	252.00	241.10	483
Mr94		....	....	250.75	− .15	252.00	246.60	120
Est vol 1,427; vol Tues 1,936; open int 4,239, +81.								
The index: High 250.22; Low 249.63; Close 249.99 +.36								
MAJOR MKT INDEX (CBT) $500 times index								
Aug	362.00	362.40	361.00	361.55	− .55	364.90	351.40	1,730
Sept	362.20	362.20	361.20	361.65	− .65	364.50	340.00	168
Est vol 180; vol Tues 268; open int 1,898, +9.								
The index: High 362.56; Low 361.31; Close 362.04 + 45								

Reprinted by permission from *The Wall Street Journal*, August 12, 1993.

2. *The S&P MidCap 400 Index*. This is based on a portfolio of 400 stocks that have somewhat lower market capitalizations than the stocks used to compute the S&P 500 Index. When the MidCap was constructed, the market capitalizations of the stocks comprising it ranged from $300 million to $5 billion.
3. *The Nikkei 225 Stock Average*. This is based on a portfolio of 225 of the largest stocks trading on the Tokyo Stock Exchange. Stocks are weighted according to their prices.
4. *The New York Stock Exchange (NYSE) Composite Index*. This is based on a portfolio of all the stocks listed on the New York Stock Exchange. As with the S&P 500, weights reflect market capitalizations.
5. *The Major Market Index (MMI)*. This is based on a portfolio of 20 blue-chip stocks listed on the New York Stock Exchange. The stocks are weighted according to their prices. However, adjustments are made to reflect the effects of stock splits and stock dividends. The MMI is very closely correlated to the widely quoted Dow Jones Industrial Average, which is also based on relatively few stocks.

As mentioned in Chapter 2, futures contracts on stock indices are settled in cash, not by delivery of the underlying asset. All contracts are marked to market on the last trading day and the positions are deemed to be closed. For most contracts, the settlement price on the last trading day is set at the closing value of the index on that day. However, as discussed in Chapter 2, for the S&P 500 it is set as the value of the index based on opening prices the next day. For the futures on the NYSE Composite and MMI, the last trading day is the third Friday of the delivery month. For the S&P 500, it is the Thursday before the third Friday of the delivery month.

Futures Prices of Stock Indices

A stock index can be regarded as the price of a security that pays dividends. The security is the portfolio of stocks underlying the index and the dividends paid by the security are the dividends that would be received by the holder of this portfolio. To a reasonable approximation, the stocks underlying the index can be assumed to provide a continuous dividend yield. If q is the dividend yield rate, Equation (3.7) gives the futures price, F, as

$$F = Se^{(r-q)T} \tag{3.12}$$

Example

Consider a three-month futures contract on the S&P 500. Suppose that the stocks underlying the index provide a dividend yield of 3 percent per annum, that the current value of the index is 400, and that the continuously compounded risk-free interest rate is 8 percent per annum. In this case, $r = 0.08$, $S = 400$, $T = 0.25$, and $q = 0.03$. Hence, the futures price, F, is given by

$$F = 400e^{0.05 \times 0.25} = 405.03$$

In practice, the dividend yield on the portfolio underlying an index varies week by week throughout the year. For example, a large proportion of the dividends on NYSE stocks are paid in the first week of February, May, August, and November each year. The value of q that is used should represent the average annualized dividend yield during the life of the contract. The dividends used for estimating q should be those for which the ex-dividend date is during the life of the futures contract. Looking at Table 3.7, we see that the futures prices for the NYSE Composite appear to be increasing with maturity at about 0.6 percent per annum. This corresponds to the situation where the risk-free interest rate exceeds the dividend yield by about 0.6 percent per annum.

If an analyst is unhappy working in terms of dividend yields, he or she can estimate the dollar amount of dividends that will be paid by the portfolio underlying the index and the timing of those dividends. The index can then be considered to be a security providing known income, and the result in Equation (3.6) can be used to calculate the futures price.

Index Arbitrage

If $F > Se^{(r-q)T}$, profits can be made by buying the stocks underlying the index and shorting futures contracts. If $F < Se^{(r-q)T}$, profits can be made by doing the reverse, that is, shorting or selling the stocks underlying the index and taking a long position in futures contracts. These strategies are known as *index arbitrage.* When $F < Se^{(r-q)T}$, index arbitrage is often done by a pension fund that owns an indexed portfolio of stocks. When $F > Se^{(r-q)T}$, it is often done by a corporation holding short-term money market investments. For indices involving many stocks, index arbitrage is sometimes accomplished by trading a relatively small representative sample of stocks whose movements closely mirror those of the index. Often index arbitrage is implemented using *program trading*. This means that a computer system is used to generate the trades.

October 19, 1987

In normal market conditions, F is very close to $Se^{(r-q)T}$. However, it is interesting to note what happened on October 19, 1987, when the market fell by over 20 percent and the volume of shares traded on the New York Stock Exchange (604 million) easily exceeded all previous records. For most of the day futures prices were at a significant discount to the underlying index. For example, at the close of trading the S&P 500 Index was at 225.06 (down 57.88 on the day), while the futures price for December delivery on the S&P 500 was 201.50 (down 80.75 on the day). This was largely because the delays in processing orders made index arbitraging too risky. On the next day, October 20, 1987, the New York Stock Exchange placed temporary restrictions on the way in which program trading could be done. The result was that the breakdown of the traditional linkage between stock indices and stock index futures continued. At one point, the futures price for the December contract was 18 percent less than the S&P 500 Index.

The Nikkei Futures Contract

Equation (3.12) does not apply to the futures contract on the Nikkei 225. The reason for this is quite subtle. Define S_F as the value of the Nikkei 225 Index. This is the value of a portfolio measured in yen. The variable underlying the CME futures contract on the Nikkei 225 is a variable with a *dollar value* of $5S_F$. In other words, the futures contract takes a variable which is measured in yen and treats it as though it were dollars. We cannot invest in a portfolio whose value will always be $5S_F$ dollars. The best we can do is to invest in one that is always worth $5S_F$ yen or in one that is always worth $5QS_F$ dollars, where Q is the dollar value of 1 yen. The arbitrage arguments that have been used in this chapter require the spot price underlying the futures price to be the price of something that can be traded by investors. They do not, therefore, apply to the Nikkei Index contract.

FORWARD AND FUTURES CONTRACTS ON CURRENCIES

We now move on to consider forward and futures contracts on foreign currencies. The variable, S, is the current price in dollars of one unit of the foreign currency. A foreign currency has the property that the holder of the currency can earn interest at the risk-free interest rate prevailing in the foreign country. (For example, the holder can invest the currency in a foreign denominated bond.) We define r_f as the value of this foreign risk-free interest rate with continuous compounding.

Consider an investor adopting the following strategy:

1. Buy e^{-r_fT} of the foreign currency.
2. Short a forward contract on one unit of the foreign currency.

The holding in the foreign currency grows to one unit at time T because of the interest earned. Under the terms of the forward contract, this is exchanged for F at time T. The strategy, therefore, leads to an initial outflow of Se^{-r_fT} and a final inflow of F. The present value of the inflow must equal the outflow. Hence

$$Se^{-r_fT} = Fe^{-rT}$$

or

$$F = Se^{(r-r_f)T} \tag{3.13}$$

This is the well-known interest-rate parity relationship from the field of international finance. From the discussion earlier in this chapter, F is to a reasonable approximation also the futures price.

Note that Equation (3.13) is identical to Equation (3.7) with q replaced by r_f. This is because a foreign currency is analogous to a security paying a known dividend yield. The "dividend yield" is the risk-free rate of interest in the foreign

Table 3.8 Foreign Exchange Futures Quotes from *The Wall Street Journal* on August 12, 1993

CURRENCY

	Open	High	Low	Settle	Change	Lifetime High	Lifetime Low	Open Interest
JAPAN YEN (CME)–12.5 million yen; $ per yen (.00)								
Sept	.9554	.9664	.9552	.9661	+ .0114	.9620	.7945	72,427
Dec	.9640	.9670	.9620	.9667	+ .0115	.9615	.7970	4,554
Mr94	....	....	....	.9689	+ .0115	.9620	.8700	331
Est vol 21,843; vol Tues 17,547; open int 77,346, –380.								
DEUTSCHEMARK (CME)–125,000 marks; $ per mark								
Sept	.5806	.5824	.5780	.5788	– .0017	.6720	.5702	139,880
Dec	.5768	.5777	.5734	.5742	– .0016	.6650	.5657	7,780
Mr94	.5725	.5735	.5710	.5710	– .0016	.6200	.5646	99
Est vol 42,987; vol Tues 45,734; open int 147,771, +2,507.								
CANADIAN DOLLAR (CME)–100,000 dlrs.; $ per Can $								
Sept	.7725	.7725	.7650	.7658	– .0069	.8335	.7515	40,492
Dec	.7674	.7679	.7630	.7640	– .0069	.8310	.7470	1,749
Mr94	.7650	.7650	.7620	.7621	– .0070	.7860	.7550	665
June	.7628	.7628	.7600	.7600	– .0071	.7805	.7515	402
Sept	.7605	.7605	.7605	.7578	– .0072	.7740	.7555	150
Est vol 9,703; vol Tues 3,528; open int 43,458, +548.								
BRITISH POUND (CME)–62,500 pds.; $ per pound								
Sept	1.4660	1.4756	1.4630	1.4678	+ .0068	1.5800	1.3980	36,264
Dec	1.4580	1.4680	1.4534	1.4592	+ .0070	1.5670	1.3930	1,403
Est vol 14,472; vol Tues 29,499; open int 37,767, +10,296.								
SWISS FRANC (CME)–125,000 francs; $ per franc								
Sept	.6545	.6563	.6505	.6511	– .0024	.7100	.6380	39,301
Dec	.6525	.6545	.6485	.6490	– .0025	.7050	.6400	3,151
Est vol 19,355; vol Tues 25,682; open int 42,524, +1,873.								
AUSTRALIAN DOLLAR (CME)–100,000 dlrs.; $ per A.$								
Sept	.6848	.6852	.6815	.6818	– .0041	.7202	.6595	4,593
Est vol 514; vol Tues 832; open int 4,638, –349.								
U.S. DOLLAR INDEX (FINEX)–1,000 times USDX								
Sept	95.84	95.87	95.38	95.76	– .10	97.10	89.96	7,958
Dec	96.65	96.78	96.45	96.64	– .10	97.30	91.34	2,057
Est vol 2,500; vol Tues 1,583; open int 10,051, +313.								
The index: High 95.30; Low 94.91; Close 95.23 +.02								

currency. To see why this is so, note that interest earned on a foreign currency holding is denominated in the foreign currency. Its value when measured in the domestic currency is, therefore, proportional to the value of the foreign currency.

Table 3.8 shows futures prices on August 11, 1993 for contracts trading on the Japanese yen, German mark, Canadian dollar, British pound, Swiss franc, and Australian dollar in the International Monetary Market of the Chicago Mercantile Exchange. In the case of the Japanese yen, prices are expressed as the number of cents per unit of foreign currency. In the case of the other five currencies, prices are expressed as the number of U.S. dollars per unit of foreign currency. As mentioned in Chapter 2, this can be confusing because spot and forward rates on most currencies are quoted the other way around, that is, as the number of units of the foreign currency per U.S. dollar. A forward quote on the Canadian dollar of 1.2000 would become a futures quote of 0.8333. The table also shows the U.S dollar index contract traded on FINEX, which is a division of the New York Cotton Exchange. The U.S. dollar index is a weighted geometric average of the U.S. dollar's value in ten currencies: the Deutschemark, Japanese yen, French franc, British pound, Canadian dollar, Italian lire, Netherlands guilder, Belgian franc, Swedish krona, and Swiss franc.

Consider the contracts on a single currency in Table 3.8. When the foreign interest rate is greater than the domestic interest rate ($r_f > r$), Equation (3.13) shows that F is always less than S and that F decreases as the maturity of the contract, T, increases. Similarly, when the domestic interest rate is greater than the foreign interest rate ($r > r_f$), Equation (3.13) shows that F is always greater than S and that F increases as T increases. On August 11, 1993, interest rates in Germany, Canada, Britain, Switzerland, and Australia were higher than in the United States. This corresponds to the $r_f > r$ situation and explains why futures prices for these currencies decline with maturity. In Japan, interest rates were lower than in the United States. This corresponds to the $r > r_f$ situation and explains why the futures prices for this currency increase with maturity. The futures price of the U.S. dollar index contract is an increasing function of time because the underlying asset is the value of the U.S. dollar in other currencies, not the value of other currencies in the U.S. dollar.

Example

The futures price of the German mark in Table 3.8 appears to be decreasing at a rate of about 2.7 percent per annum with the maturity. This suggests that the risk-free interest rate was about 2.7 percent per annum lower in the United States than in Germany on August 11, 1993.

FUTURES ON COMMODITIES

We now move on to consider commodity futures contracts. Here it will prove to be important to distinguish between commodities that are held solely for investment by a significant number of investors (e.g., gold and silver) and those that are held primarily for consumption. Arbitrage arguments can be used to obtain exact futures prices in the case of investment commodities. However, it turns out that they can only be used to give an upper bound to the futures price in the case of consumption commodities.

Gold and Silver

Gold and silver are held by a significant number of investors solely for investment. If storage costs are zero, they can be considered as being analogous to securities paying no income. Using the notation introduced earlier, S is the current spot price of gold. As shown by Equation (3.5), the futures price, F, should be given by

$$F = Se^{rT} \tag{3.14}$$

Storage costs can be regarded as negative income. If U is the present value of all the storage costs that will be incurred during the life of a futures contract, it follows from Equation (3.6) that

$$F = (S + U)e^{rT} \tag{3.15}$$

If the storage costs incurred at any time are proportional to the price of the commodity, they can be regarded as providing a negative dividend yield. In this case, from Equation (3.7),

$$F = Se^{(r+u)T} \tag{3.16}$$

where u is the storage costs per annum as a proportion of the spot price.

If we return to Table 2.3, it can be seen that the futures price of gold increases at about 3 percent per annum with the maturity of the contract. This is close to the risk-free interest rate on August 11, 1993 and is consistent with the formulas just given.

Example

Consider a one-year futures contract on gold. Suppose that it costs \$2 per ounce per year to store gold, with the payment being made at the end of the year. Assume that the spot price is \$450 and the risk-free rate is 7 percent per annum for all maturities. This corresponds to $r = 0.07$, $S = 450$, $T = 1$, and

$$U = 2e^{-0.07} = 1.865$$

The futures price, F, is given by

$$F = (450 + 1.865)e^{0.07} = 484.6$$

If $F > 484.6$, an arbitrageur can buy gold and short one-year gold futures contracts to lock in a profit. If $F < 484.6$, an investor who already owns gold can improve his or her return by selling the gold and buying gold futures contracts. Tables 3.9 and 3.10 illustrate these strategies for the situations where $F = 500$ and $F = 470$.

Table 3.9 Arbitrage Opportunity in the Gold Market When Gold Futures Price Is Too High

From the Trader's Desk

The one-year futures price of gold is \$500 per ounce. The spot price is \$450 per ounce and the risk-free interest rate is 7 percent per annum. The storage costs for gold are \$2 per ounce per year payable in arrears.

Opportunity

The futures price of gold is too high. An arbitrageur can

1. Borrow \$45,000 at the risk-free interest rate to buy 100 ounces of gold.
2. Short one gold futures contract for delivery in one year.

At the end of the year \$50,000 is received for the gold under the terms of the futures contract, \$48,263 is used to pay interest and principal on the loan, and \$200 is used to pay storage. The net gain is

$$\$50,000 - \$48,263 - \$200 = \$1,537$$

Table 3.10 Arbitrage Opportunity in the Gold Market When Gold Futures Price Is Too Low

From the Trader's Desk

The one-year futures price of gold is \$470 per ounce. The spot price is \$450 per ounce and the risk-free interest rate is 7 percent per annum. The storage costs for gold are \$2 per ounce per year payable in arrears.

Opportunity

The futures price of gold is too low. Consider an investor who already holds 100 ounces of gold for investment purposes. He or she can

1. Sell the gold for \$45,000.
2. Enter into one long futures contract on gold for delivery in one year.

The \$45,000 is invested at the risk-free interest rate for one year and grows to \$48,263. At the end of the year, under the terms of the futures contract, 100 ounces of gold are purchased for \$47,000. The investor, therefore, ends up with 100 ounces of gold plus

$$\$48{,}263 - \$47{,}000 = \$1{,}263$$

in cash. If the investor had kept the gold throughout the year, he or she would have ended up with 100 ounces of gold less the \$200 paid for storage. The futures strategy, therefore, improves the investor's position by

$$\$1{,}263 + \$200 = \$1{,}463$$

Other Commodities

For commodities that are not held primarily for investment purposes, the arbitrage arguments leading to Equations (3.14), (3.15), and (3.16) need to be reviewed carefully.

Suppose that instead of Equation (3.15), we have

$$F > (S + U)e^{rT} \tag{3.17}$$

To take advantage of this, an arbitrageur should implement the following strategy:

1. Borrow an amount $S + U$ at the risk-free rate and use it to purchase one unit of the commodity and to pay storage costs.
2. Short a futures contract on one unit of the commodity.

If we regard the futures contract as a forward contract, this is certain to lead to a profit of $F - (S + U)e^{rT}$ at time T. The strategy is illustrated for gold in Table 3.9. There is no problem with implementing the strategy for any commodity. However, as arbitrageurs do so, there will be a tendency for S to increase and F to decrease until Equation (3.17) is no longer true. We conclude that Equation (3.17) cannot hold for any significant length of time.

Suppose next that

$$F < (S + U)e^{rT} \tag{3.18}$$

We might try to take advantage of this using a strategy analogous to that suggested in Table 3.6 for a forward contract on a bond when the forward price is too low. However, this would involve shorting the commodity in such a way that the storage costs are paid to the person with the short position. This is not usually possible.

For gold and silver, we can argue that there are many investors who hold the commodity solely for investment. When they observe the inequality in Equation (3.18), they will find it profitable to

1. Sell the commodity, save the storage costs, and invest the proceeds at the risk-free interest rate.
2. Buy the futures contract.

This is the strategy illustrated in Table 3.10. The result is a riskless profit at maturity of $(S + U)e^{rT} - F$ relative to the position the investors would have been in if they had held the gold or silver. It follows that Equation (3.18) cannot hold for long. Since neither Equation (3.17) nor (3.18) can hold for long, we must have $F = (S + U)e^{rT}$.

For commodities that are not to any significant extent held for investment, this argument cannot be used. Individuals and companies who keep the commodity in inventory do so because of its consumption value—not because of its value as an investment. They are reluctant to sell the commodity and buy futures contracts, since futures contracts cannot be consumed. There is, therefore, nothing to stop Equation (3.18) from holding. Since Equation (3.17) cannot hold, all we can assert for a consumption commodity is

$$F \leq (S + U)e^{rT} \tag{3.19}$$

If storage costs are expressed as a proportion u of the spot price, the equivalent result is

$$F \leq Se^{(r+u)T} \tag{3.20}$$

Convenience Yields

When Equation (3.19) or (3.20) holds, users of the commodity must feel that there are benefits from ownership of the physical commodity that are not obtained by the holder of a futures contract. These benefits may include the ability to profit from temporary local shortages or the ability to keep a production process running. The benefits are sometimes referred to as the *convenience yield* provided by the product. If the dollar amount of storage costs is known and has a present value, U, the convenience yield, y, is defined so that

$$Fe^{yT} = (S + U)e^{rT}$$

If the storage costs per unit are a constant proportion, u, of the spot price, y is defined so that

$$Fe^{yT} = Se^{(r+u)T}$$

or

$$F = Se^{(r+u-y)T} \quad \textbf{(3.21)}$$

The convenience yield simply measures the extent to which the left-hand side is less than the right-hand side in (3.19) or in (3.20). For investment assets, the convenience yield must be zero; otherwise, there are opportunities such as those in Table 3.10. Table 2.3 of Chapter 2 shows that the futures prices of commodities such as soybean meal, live cattle, and palladium decrease as the maturity of the contract increases on August 11, 1993. This suggests that the convenience yield, y, is greater than $r + u$.

The convenience yield reflects the market's expectations concerning the future availability of the commodity. The greater the possibility that shortages will occur during the life of the futures contract, the higher the convenience yield. If users of the commodity have high inventories, there is very little chance of shortages in the near future and the convenience yield tends to be low. On the other hand, low inventories tend to lead to high convenience yields.

THE COST OF CARRY

The relationship between futures prices and spot prices can be summarized in terms of what is known as the *cost of carry*. This measures the storage cost plus the interest that is paid to finance the asset less the income earned on the asset. For a nondividend-paying stock, the cost of carry is r since there are no storage costs and no income is earned; for a stock index, it is $r - q$ since income is earned at rate q on the asset; for a currency, it is $r - r_f$; for a commodity with storage costs that are a proportion u of the price, it is $r + u$; and so on.

Define the cost of carry as c. For an investment asset, the futures price is

$$F = Se^{cT} \quad \textbf{(3.22)}$$

For a consumption asset, it is

$$F = Se^{(c-y)T} \tag{3.23}$$

where y is the convenience yield.

DELIVERY OPTIONS

Whereas a forward contract normally specifies that delivery is to take place on a particular day, a futures contract often allows the party with the short position to choose to deliver at any time during a certain period. (Typically, the party has to give a few days notice of its intention to deliver.) This introduces a complication into the determination of futures prices. Should the maturity of the futures contract be assumed to be the beginning, middle, or end of the delivery period? Even though most futures contracts are closed out prior to maturity, it is important to know when delivery would have taken place in order to calculate the theoretical futures price.

If the futures price is an increasing function of the time to maturity, it can be seen from Equation (3.23) that the benefits from holding the asset (including convenience yield and net of storage costs) are less than the risk-free rate. It is then usually optimal for the party with the short position to deliver as early as possible. This is because the interest earned on the cash received outweighs the benefits of holding the asset. As a general rule, futures prices in these circumstances should, therefore, be calculated on the basis that delivery will take place at the beginning of the delivery period. If futures prices are decreasing as maturity increases, the reverse is true: It is usually optimal for the party with the short position to deliver as late as possible and futures prices should, as a general rule, be calculated on the assumption that this will happen.

FUTURES PRICES AND THE EXPECTED FUTURE SPOT PRICE

One question that is often raised is whether the futures price of an asset is equal to its expected future spot price. If you had to guess what the price of an asset will be in three months, is the futures price an unbiased estimate? In Chapter 2 we presented the arguments of Keynes and Hicks. These authors contend that speculators will not trade a futures contract unless their expected profit is positive. By contrast, hedgers are prepared to accept a negative profit because of the risk-reduction benefits they get from a futures contract. If more speculators are long than short, there will be a tendency for the futures price to be less than the expected future spot price. On average, speculators can then expect to make a gain, since the futures price converges to the spot price at maturity. Similarly, if more speculators are short than long, there will be a tendency for the futures price to be greater than the expected future spot price.

Risk and Return

Another explanation of the relationship between futures prices and expected future spot prices can be obtained by considering the relationship between risk and expected return in the economy. In general, the higher the risk of an investment, the higher the expected return demanded by an investor. Readers familiar with the capital asset pricing model will know that there are two types of risk in the economy: systematic and nonsystematic. Nonsystematic risk should not be important to an investor. This is because it can be almost completely eliminated by holding a well-diversified portfolio. An investor should not, therefore, require a higher expected return for bearing nonsystematic risk. Systematic risk, by contrast, cannot be diversified away. It arises from a correlation between returns from the investment and returns from the stock market as a whole. An investor in general requires a higher expected return than the risk-free interest rate for bearing positive amounts of systematic risk. Also, an investor is prepared to accept a lower expected return than the risk-free interest rate when the systematic risk in an investment is negative.

The Risk in a Futures Position

Consider a speculator who takes a long futures position in the hope that the price of the asset will be above the futures price at maturity. We suppose that the speculator puts the present value of the futures price into a risk-free investment while simultaneously taking a long futures position. We assume that the futures contract can be treated as a forward contract. The proceeds of the risk-free investment are used to buy the asset on the delivery date. The asset is then immediately sold for its market price. This means that the cash flows to the speculator are

Time 0: $-Fe^{-rT}$
Time T: $+S_T$

where S_T is the price of the asset at time T.

The present value of this investment is

$$-Fe^{-rT} + E(S_T)e^{-kT}$$

where k is the discount rate appropriate for the investment (that is, it is the expected return required by investors on the investment) and E denotes expected value. Assuming that all investment opportunities in securities markets have zero net present value,

$$-Fe^{-rT} + E(S_T)e^{-kT} = 0$$

or

$$F = E(S_T)e^{(r-k)T} \tag{3.24}$$

The value of k depends on the systematic risk of the investment. If S_T is uncorrelated with the level of the stock market, the investment has zero systematic risk. In this case $k = r$ and Equation (3.24) shows that $F = E(S_T)$. If S_T is positively correlated with the the stock market as a whole, the investment has positive systematic risk. In this case $k > r$ and Equation (3.24) shows that $F < E(S_T)$. Finally, if S_T is negatively correlated with the stock market, the investment has negative systematic risk. This means that $k < r$ and Equation (3.24) shows that $F > E(S_T)$.

Empirical Evidence

If $F = E(S_T)$, the futures price will drift up or down only if the market changes its views about the expected future spot price. Over a long period of time we can reasonably assume that the market revises its expectations about future spot prices upward as often as it does so downward. It follows that when $F = E(S_T)$, the average profit from holding futures contracts over a long period of time should be zero. The $F < E(S_T)$ situation corresponds to the positive systematic risk situation. Since the futures price and the spot price must be equal at maturity of the futures contract, it implies that a futures price should on average drift up and a trader should over a long period of time make positive profits from consistently holding long futures positions. Similarly, the $F > E(S_T)$ situation implies that a trader should over a long period of time make positive profits from consistently holding short futures positions.

How do futures prices behave in practice? Some of the empirical work that has been carried out is listed at the end of this chapter. The results are mixed. Houthakker's study looked at futures prices for wheat, cotton, and corn during the period from 1937 to 1957. It showed that it was possible to earn significant profits from taking long futures positions. This suggests that an investment in corn has positive systematic risk and $F < E(S_T)$. Telser's study contradicted the findings of Houthakker. His data covered the period from 1926 to 1950 for cotton and from 1927 to 1954 for wheat and gave rise to no significant profits for traders taking either long or short positions.[4] To quote from Telser "The futures data offer no evidence to contradict the simple . . . hypothesis that the futures price is an unbiased estimate of the expected future spot price." Gray's study looked at corn futures prices during the period from 1921 to 1959 and resulted in similar findings to those of Telser. Dusak's study used data on corn, wheat, and soybeans from 1952 to 1967 and took a different approach. It attempted to estimate the systematic risk of an investment in these commodities by calculating the correlation of movements in the commodity prices with movements in the S&P 500. The results suggest that there is no systematic risk and lend support to the $F = E(S_T)$ hypothesis. However, more recent work by Chang using the same commodities and more advanced statistical techniques supports the $F < E(S_T)$ hypothesis.

[4] See L. G. Telser "Futures trading and the storage of cotton and wheat." *Journal of Political Economy*, 66 (June 1958), 233–255.

SUMMARY

For most purposes, the futures price of a contract with a certain delivery date can be considered to be the same as the forward price for a contract with the same delivery date. It can be shown that in theory the two should be exactly the same when interest rates are perfectly predictable and should be very close to each other when interest rates vary unpredictably.

For the purposes of understanding futures (or forward) prices, it is convenient to divide futures contracts into two categories: those where the underlying asset is held for investment by a significant number of investors and those where the underlying investment is held primarily for consumption purposes.

In the case of investment assets, we have considered three different situations:

1. The asset provides no income.
2. The asset provides a known dollar income.
3. The asset provides a known dividend yield.

The results are summarized in Table 3.11. They enable futures prices to be obtained for contracts on stock indices, currencies, gold, and silver.

In the case of consumption assets, it is not possible to obtain the futures price as a function of the spot price and other observable variables. A parameter known as the asset's convenience yield becomes important. This measures the extent to which users of the commodity feel that there are benefits from ownership of the physical asset that are not obtained by the holders of the futures contract. These benefits may include the ability to profit from temporary local shortages or the ability to keep a production process running. It is possible to obtain only an upper bound for the futures price of consumption assets using arbitrage arguments.

The concept of a cost of carry is sometimes useful. The cost of carry is the storage cost of the underlying asset plus the cost of financing it minus the income received from it. In the case of investment assets, the futures price is greater than the spot price by an amount reflecting the cost of carry. In the case of consumption

Table 3.11 Summary of Results for a Contract with Maturity T on an Asset with Price S When the Risk-Free Interest Rate for a T-Year Period Is r

ASSET	*VALUE OF LONG FORWARD CONTRACT WITH DELIVERY PRICE* K	*FORWARD/ FUTURES PRICE*
Provides no income	$S - Ke^{-rT}$	Se^{rT}
Provides known income with present value, I	$S - I - Ke^{-rT}$	$(S - I)e^{rT}$
Provides known dividend yield, q	$Se^{-qT} - Ke^{-rT}$	$Se^{(r-q)T}$

assets, the futures price is greater than the spot price by an amount reflecting the cost of carry net of the convenience yield.

If we assume the capital asset pricing model is true, the relationship between the futures price and the expected future spot price depends on whether the spot price is positively or negatively correlated with the level of the stock market. Positive correlation will tend to lead to a futures price lower than the expected future spot price. Negative correlation will tend to lead to a futures price higher than the expected future spot price. Only when the correlation is zero will the theoretical futures price be equal to the expected future spot price.

Suggestions for Further Reading

On empirical research concerning forward and futures prices

CORNELL, B., and M. REINGANUM, "Forward and futures prices: Evidence from foreign exchange markets," *Journal of Finance*, 36 (December 1981), 1035–1045.

FRENCH, K., "A comparison of futures and forward prices," *Journal of Financial Economics*, 12 (November 1983), 311–342.

PARK, H. Y., and A. H. CHEN, "Differences between futures and forward prices: A further investigation of marking to market effects," *Journal of Futures Markets*, 5 (February 1985), 77–88.

RENDLEMAN, R., and C. CARABINI, "The efficiency of the Treasury bill futures markets," *Journal of Finance*, 34 (September 1979), 895–914.

On empirical research concerning the relationship between futures prices and expected future spot prices

CHANG, E. C., "Returns to speculators and the theory of normal backwardation," *Journal of Finance*, 40 (March 1985), 193–208.

DUSAK, K., "Futures trading and investor returns: an investigation of commodity risk premiums," *Journal of Political Economy*, 81 (December 1973), 1387–1406.

GRAY, R. W., "The search for a risk premium," *Journal of Political Economy*, 69 (June 1961), 250–260.

HOUTHAKKER, H. S., "Can speculators forecast prices?" *Review of Economics and Statistics*, 39 (1957), 143–151.

TELSER, L. G., "Futures trading and the storage of cotton and wheat," *Journal of Political Economy*, 66 (June 1958), 233–255.

On the theoretical relationship between forward and futures prices

COX, J. C., J. E. INGERSOLL, and S. A. ROSS, "The relation between forward prices and futures prices," *Journal of Financial Economics*, 9 (December 1981), 321–346.

JARROW, R. A., and G. S. OLDFIELD, "Forward contracts and futures contracts," *Journal of Financial Economics*, 9 (December 1981), 373–382.

KANE, E. J., "Market incompleteness and divergences between forward and futures interest rates," *Journal of Finance*, 35 (May 1980), 221–234.

MARGRABE, W., "A theory of forward and futures prices," Unpublished working paper, The Wharton School, University of Pennsylvania, 1976.

RICHARD, S., and M. SUNDARESAN, "A continuous time model of forward and futures prices in a multigood economy," *Journal of Financial Economics*, 9 (December 1981), 347–372.

Quiz

1. A bank quotes you an interest rate of 14 percent per annum with quarterly compounding. What is the equivalent rate with (a) continuous compounding and (b) annual compounding?

2. Explain what happens when an investor shorts a certain share.
3. Suppose that you enter into a six-month forward contract on a nondividend-paying stock when the stock price is \$30 and the risk-free interest rate (with continuous compounding) is 12 percent per annum. What is the forward price?
4. A stock index currently stands at 350. The risk-free interest rate is 8 percent per annum (with continuous compounding) and the dividend yield on the index is 4 percent per annum. What should the futures price for a four-month contract be?
5. Explain carefully why the futures price of gold can be calculated from its spot price and other observable variables while the futures price of copper cannot.
6. Explain carefully the meaning of the terms *convenience yield* and *cost of carry*. What is the relationship between the futures price, the spot price, the convenience yield, and the cost of carry?
7. Is the futures price of a stock index greater than or less than the expected future value of the index? Explain your answer.

Questions and Problems

3.1. An individual receives \$1100 in one year in return for an investment of \$1,000 now. Calculate the percentage return per annum with:
   a. Annual compounding
   b. Semiannual compounding
   c. Monthly compounding
   d. Continuous compounding

3.2. What rate of interest with continuous compounding is equivalent to 15 percent per annum with monthly compounding?

3.3. A deposit account pays 12 percent per annum with continuous compounding, but interest is actually paid quarterly. How much interest will be paid each quarter on a \$10,000 deposit?

3.4. A one-year long forward contract on a nondividend-paying stock is entered into when the stock price is \$40 and the risk-free rate of interest is 10 percent per annum with continuous compounding.
   a. What are the forward price and the initial value of the forward contract?
   b. Six months later, the price of the stock is \$45 and the risk-free interest rate is still 10 percent. What are the forward price and the value of the forward contract?

3.5. A stock is expected to pay a dividend of \$1 per share in two months and in five months. The stock price is \$50 and the risk-free rate of interest is 8 percent per annum with continuous compounding for all maturities. An investor has just taken a short position in a six-month forward contract on the stock.
   a. What are the forward price and the initial value of the forward contract?
   b. Three months later, the price of the stock is \$48 and the risk-free rate of interest is still 8 percent per annum. What are the forward price and the value of the short position in the forward contract?

3.6. The risk-free rate of interest is 7 percent per annum with continuous compounding and the dividend yield on a stock index is 3.2 percent per annum. The current value of an index is 150. What is the six-month futures price?

3.7. Assume that the risk-free interest rate is 9 percent per annum with continuous compounding and that the dividend yield on a stock index varies throughout the year. In February, May, August, and November, it is 5 percent per annum. In other months, it is 2 percent per annum. Suppose that the value of the index on July 31, 1994 is 300. What is the futures price for a contract deliverable on December 31, 1994?

3.8. Suppose that the risk-free interest rate is 10 percent per annum with continuous compounding and the dividend yield on a stock index is 4 percent per annum. The index is standing at 400 and the futures price for a contract deliverable in four months is 405. What arbitrage opportunities does this create?

3.9. Estimate the difference between risk-free rates of interest in Japan and the United States from the information in Table 3.8.

3.10. The two-month interest rates in Switzerland and the United States are 3 percent and 8 percent per annum, respectively, with continuous compounding. The spot price of the Swiss franc is \$0.6500. The futures price for a contract deliverable in two months is \$0.6600. What arbitrage opportunities does this create?

3.11. The current price of silver is \$9 per ounce. The storage costs are \$0.24 per ounce per year payable quarterly in advance. Assuming a flat term structure with a continuously compounded interest rate of 10 percent, calculate the futures price of silver for delivery in nine months.

3.12. A bank offers a corporate client a choice between borrowing cash at 11 percent per annum and borrowing gold at 2 percent per annum. (If gold is borrowed, interest must be repaid in gold. Thus, 100 ounces borrowed today would require 102 ounces to be repaid in one year.) The risk-free interest rate is 9.25 percent per annum and storage costs are 0.5 percent per annum. Discuss whether the rate of interest on the gold loan is too high or too low in relation to the rate of interest on the cash loan. The interest rates on the two loans are expressed with annual compounding. The risk-free interest rate and storage cost are expressed with continuous compounding.

3.13. Suppose that F_1 and F_2 are two futures contracts on the same commodity with maturity dates of t_1 and t_2 and $t_2 > t_1$. Prove that

$$F_2 \leq F_1 e^{r(t_2 - t_1)}$$

where r is the interest rate (assumed constant) and there are no storage costs. For the purposes of this problem, assume that a futures contract is the same as a forward contract.

3.14. When a known future cash outflow in a foreign currency is hedged by a company using a forward contract, there is no foreign exchange risk. When it is hedged using futures contracts, the marking-to-market process does leave the company exposed to some risk. Explain the nature of this risk. In particular, consider whether the company is better off using a futures contract or a forward contract when

a. The value of the foreign currency falls rapidly during the life of the contract.
b. The value of the foreign currency rises rapidly during the life of the contract.
c. The value of the foreign currency first rises and then falls back to its initial value.
d. The value of the foreign currency first falls and then rises back to its initial value.

Assume that the forward price equals the futures price.

3.15. It is sometimes argued that a forward exchange rate is an unbiased predictor of future exchange rates. Under what circumstances is this so?

3.16. A company that is uncertain about the exact date when it will pay or receive a foreign currency sometimes wishes to negotiate with its bank a forward contract where there is a period during which delivery can be made. The company wants to reserve the right to choose the exact delivery date to fit in with its own cash flows. Put yourself in the position of the bank. How would you structure the product that you would offer to the company?

Appendix 3A A Proof That Forward and Futures Prices Are Equal When Interest Rates Are Constant

In this appendix, we show that forward and futures prices are equal when interest rates are constant. Suppose that a futures contract lasts for n days and that F_i is the futures price at the end of day i ($0 < i < n$). Define δ as the risk-free rate per day (assumed constant). Consider the following strategy.[5]

1. Take a long futures position of e^{δ} at the end of day 0 (i.e., at the beginning of the contract).
2. Increase long position to $e^{2\delta}$ at the end of day 1.
3. Increase long position to $e^{3\delta}$ at the end of day 2.

And so on.

This strategy is summarized in Table 3.12. By the beginning of day i, the investor has a long position of $e^{\delta i}$. The profit (possibly negative) from the position on day i is

$$(F_i - F_{i-1})e^{\delta i}$$

Assume that this is compounded at the risk-free rate until the end of day n. Its value at the end of day n is

$$(F_i - F_{i-1})e^{\delta i}e^{(n-i)\delta} = (F_i - F_{i-1})e^{n\delta}$$

The value at the end of day n of the entire investment strategy is, therefore,

$$\sum_{i=1}^{n}(F_i - F_{i-1})e^{n\delta}$$

This is

$$[(F_n - F_{n-1}) + (F_{n-1} - F_{n-2}) + \cdots + (F_1 - F_0)]e^{n\delta} = (F_n - F_0)e^{n\delta}$$

Since F_n is the same as the terminal asset price, S_T, the terminal value of the investment strategy can be written

$$(S_T - F_0)e^{n\delta}$$

[5] This strategy was proposed by J. C. Cox, J. E. Ingersoll, and S. A. Ross, "The relationship between forward prices and futures prices," *Journal of Financial Economics*, 9 (December 1981), 321–346.

Table 3.12 The Investment Strategy to Show That Futures and Forward Prices Are Equal

Day	0	1	2	...	$n-1$	n
Futures price	F_0	F_1	F_2	...	F_{n-1}	F_n
Futures position	e^{δ}	$e^{2\delta}$	$e^{3\delta}$	...	$e^{n\delta}$	0
Gain/loss	0	$(F_1 - F_0)e^{\delta}$	$(F_2 - F_1)e^{2\delta}$	...	...	$(F_n - F_{n-1})e^{n\delta}$
Gain/loss compounded to day n	0	$(F_1 - F_0)e^{n\delta}$	$(F_2 - F_1)e^{n\delta}$	...	...	$(F_n - F_{n-1})e^{n\delta}$

An investment of F_0 in a risk-free bond combined with the strategy just given yields

$$F_0e^{n\delta} + (S_T - F_0)e^{n\delta} = S_Te^{n\delta}$$

at time T. No investment is required for all the long futures positions described. It follows that an amount F_0 can be invested to give an amount $S_Te^{n\delta}$ at time T.

Suppose next that the forward price at the end of day 0 is G_0. By investing G_0 in a riskless bond and taking a long forward position of $e^{n\delta}$ forward contracts, an amount $S_Te^{n\delta}$ is also guaranteed at time T. Thus, there are two investment strategies, one requiring an initial outlay of F_0, the other requiring an initial outlay of G_0, both of which yield $S_Te^{n\delta}$ at time T. It follows that in the absence of arbitrage opportunities

$$F_0 = G_0$$

In other words, the futures price and the forward price are identical. Note that in this proof there is nothing special about the time period of one day. The futures price based on a contract with weekly settlements is also the same as the forward price when corresponding assumptions are made.

4

HEDGING STRATEGIES USING FUTURES

Many of the participants in futures markets are hedgers. Their aim is to use futures markets to reduce a particular risk that they face. This risk might relate to the price of oil, a foreign exchange rate, the level of the stock market, or some other variable. A *perfect hedge* is one that completely eliminates the risk. In practice, perfect hedges are rare. To quote one trader: "The only perfect hedge is in a Japanese garden." A study of hedging using futures contracts is, therefore, for the most part a study of the ways in which hedges can be constructed so that they perform as close to perfectly as possible.

In this chapter, we consider a number of general issues associated with the way hedges are set up. When is a short futures position appropriate? When is a long futures position appropriate? Which futures contract should be used? What is the optimal size of the futures position for reducing risk? At this stage, we restrict our attention to what might be termed *hedge and forget* strategies. We assume that no attempt is made to adjust the hedge once it has been put in place. The hedger simply takes a futures position at the beginning of the life of the hedge and closes it out at the end of the life of the hedge. In Chapter 14, we will discuss dynamic hedging strategies where the hedge is monitored closely and frequent adjustments are made.

BASIC PRINCIPLES

When an individual or company chooses to use futures markets to hedge a risk, the objective is usually to take a position that neutralizes the risk as far as possible. Consider a company that knows it will gain $10,000 for each 1 cent increase in the price of a commodity over the next three months and lose $10,000 for each 1 cent decrease in its price during this period. To hedge, the company's treasurer should take a short futures position that is designed to offset this risk. The futures position should lead to a loss of $10,000 for each 1 cent increase in the price of the commodity over the three months and a gain of $10,000 for each 1 cent decrease in its price during the period. If the price of the commodity goes down, the gain on the futures position offsets the loss on the rest of the company's business. If the price of the commodity goes up, the loss on the futures position is offset by the gain on the rest of the company's business.

Short Hedges

A *short hedge* is a hedge, such as the one just described, that involves a short position in futures contracts. A short hedge is appropriate when the hedger already owns an asset and expects to sell it at some time in the future. For example, it could be used by a farmer who owns some hogs and knows that they will be ready for sale at the local market in two months. A short hedge can also be used when a hedger does not own an asset right now, but knows that the asset will be owned at some time in the future. Consider for example, a U.S. exporter who knows that he or she will receive German marks in three months. The exporter will realize a gain if the mark increases in value relative to the U.S. dollar and a loss if the mark decreases in value relative to the U.S. dollar. A short futures position leads to a loss if the mark increases in value and a gain if it decreases in value. It has the effect of offsetting the exporter's risk.

To provide a more detailed illustration of the operation of a short hedge in a specific situation, we assume that it is May 15 today and company X has just negotiated a contract to sell 1 million barrels of oil. It has been agreed that the price that will apply in the contract is the market price on August 15. Company X is, therefore, in the position where it will gain $10,000 for each 1 cent increase in the price of oil over the next three months and lose $10,000 for each 1 cent decrease in the price during this period. Suppose that the spot price on May 15 is $19 per barrel and the August oil futures price on the New York Mercantile Exchange (NYMEX) is $18.75 per barrel. Since each futures contract on NYMEX is for the delivery of 1,000 barrels, the company can hedge its exposure by shorting 1,000 August futures contracts. If company X closes out its position on August 15, the effect of the strategy should be to lock in a price close to $18.75 per barrel.

As an example of what might happen, suppose that the spot price on August 15 proves to be $17.50 per barrel. The company realizes $17.50 million for the oil under its sales contract. Since August is the delivery month for the futures contract, the futures price on August 15 should be very close to the spot price of $17.50 on that date. The company, therefore, gains approximately

$$\$18.75 - \$17.50 = \$1.25$$

per barrel or $1.25 million in total from the short futures position. The total amount realized from both the futures position and the sales contract is, therefore, approximately $18.75 per barrel or $18.75 million in total.

Tabe 4.1 A Short Hedge

From the Trader's Desk—May 15

Company X has negotiated a contract to sell 1 million barrels of oil. The price in the sales contract is the spot price on August 15. Quotes:
Spot price of crude oil: $19.00 barrel
August oil futures price: $18.75 per barrel

Hedging Strategy

May 15: Short 1,000 August futures contracts on crude oil
August 15: Close out futures position.

Result

The company ensures that it will receive a price close to $18.75 per barrel.
Example 1:
Price of oil on August 15 is $17.50 per barrel
Company receives $17.50 per barrel under the sales contract.
Company gains about $1.25 per barrel from the futures contract.
Example 2:
Price of oil on August 15 is $19.50 per barrel.
Company receives $19.50 per barrel from the sales contract.
Company loses about $0.75 per barrel from the futures contract.

For an alternative outcome, suppose that the price of oil on August 15 proves to be $19.50 per barrel. The company realizes $19.50 for the oil and loses approximately

$$\$19.50 - \$18.75 = \$0.75$$

per barrel on the short futures position. Again, the total amount realized is approximately $18.75 million. It is easy to see that in all cases the company ends up with approximately $18.75 million. This example is summarized in Table 4.1.

Long Hedges

Hedges where a long position is taken in a futures contract are known as *long hedges*. A long hedge is appropriate when a company knows it will have to purchase a certain asset in the future and wants to lock in a price now.

Suppose that it is now January 15. A copper fabricator knows it will require 100,000 pounds of copper on May 15 to meet a certain contract. The spot price of copper is 140 cents per pound and the May futures price is 120 cents per pound. The fabricator can hedge its position by taking a long position in four May futures contracts on COMEX and closing its position on May 15. Each contract is for the delivery of 25,000 pounds of copper. The strategy has the effect of locking in the price of the copper that is required at close to 120 cents per pound.

Table 4.2 A Long Hedge

From the Trader's Desk—January 15

A copper fabricator knows it will require 100,000 pounds of copper on May 15 to meet a certain contract. The spot price of copper is 140 cents per pound and the May futures price is 120 cents per pound.

Hedging Strategy

January 15: Take a long position in four May futures contracts on copper.
May 15: Close out the position.

Result

The company ensures that its cost will be close to 120 cents per pound.
Example 1:
Cost of copper on May 15 is 125 cents per pound.
The company gains 5 cents per pound from the futures contract.
Example 2:
Cost of copper on May 15 is 105 cents per pound.
The company loses 15 cents per pound from the futures contract.

This example is summarized in Table 4.2. Suppose that the price of copper on May 15 proves to be 125 cents per pound. Since May is the delivery month for the futures contract, this should be very close to the futures price. The fabricator, therefore, gains approximately

$$100{,}000 \times (\$1.25 - \$1.20) = \$5{,}000$$

on the futures contracts. It pays $100{,}000 \times \$1.25 = \$125{,}000$ for the copper. The total cost is, therefore, approximately $\$125{,}000 - \$5{,}000 = \$120{,}000$. For an alternative outcome, suppose that the futures price is 105 cents per pound on May 15. The fabricator then loses approximately

$$100{,}000 \times (\$1.20 - \$1.05) = \$15{,}000$$

on the futures contract and pays $100{,}000 \times \$1.05 = \$105{,}000$ for the copper. Again the total cost is approximately $120,000 or 120 cents per pound.

Note that it is better for the company to use futures contracts than to buy the copper on January 15 in the spot market. If it does the latter, it will pay 140 cents per pound instead of 120 cents per pound and will incur both interest costs and storage costs. For a company using copper on a regular basis, this disadvantage would be offset by the convenience yield associated with having the copper on hand. (See Chapter 3 for a discussion of convenience yields.) However, for a company that knows it will not require the copper until May 15, the convenience yield has no value.

Long hedges can also be used to partially offset an existing short position. Consider an investor who has shorted a certain stock. Part of the risk faced by the investor is related to the performance of the stock market as a whole. The investor can neutralize this risk by taking a long position in index futures contracts. This type of hedging strategy is discussed further later in this chapter.

In both the example in Table 4.2 and the example in Table 4.1, we assume that the futures position is closed out in the delivery month. The hedge has the same basic effect if delivery is allowed to happen. However, making or taking delivery can be a costly business. For this reason, delivery is not usually made even when the hedger keeps the futures contract until the delivery month. As will be discussed later, hedgers with long positions usually avoid any possibility of having to take delivery by closing out their positions before the delivery period.

We have also assumed in the two examples that a futures contract is the same as a forward contract. In practice, marking to market does have a small effect on the performance of a hedge. It means that the payoff from the futures contract is realized day by day throughout the life of the hedge rather than all at the end.

ARGUMENTS FOR AND AGAINST HEDGING

The arguments in favor of hedging are so obvious that they hardly need to be stated. Most companies are in the business of manufacturing or retailing or wholesaling or providing a service. They have no particular skills or expertise in predicting variables such as interest rates, exchange rates, commodity prices, and so on. It makes sense for them to hedge the risks associated with these variables as they arise. They can then focus on their main activities–where presumably they do have particular skills and expertise. By hedging, they avoid unpleasant surprises such as a sharp rise in the price of a commodity. In practice, many risks are left unhedged. In this section, we will explore some of the reasons for this.

Hedging and Shareholders

One argument sometimes put forward is that shareholders can, if they wish, do the hedging themselves. They do not need the company to do it for them. This argument is, however, open to question. It assumes that shareholders have as much information about the risks faced by a company as the company's management. In most instances, this is not the case. It also ignores commissions and other transactions costs. These are less expensive per dollar of hedging for large transactions than for small transactions. Hedging is, therefore, likely to be less expensive when carried out by the company than by individual shareholders. Indeed, the size of many futures contracts makes hedging by individual shareholders impossible in many situations.

However, this is not the whole story. One thing that shareholders can do far more easily than a corporation is diversify their risk. A shareholder with a well-diversified portfolio may be immune to many of the risks faced by a corporation. For example, in addition to holding shares in a company that uses copper, a well-diversified shareholder may also hold shares in a copper producer so that there is very little overall exposure to the price of copper. If companies are acting in the best interests of well-diversified shareholders, it can be argued that hedging is unnecessary in many situations.

Hedging and Competitors

If hedging is not the norm in a certain industry, it may not make sense for one particular company to choose to be different from everyone else. This is because competitive pressures within the industry may be such that the prices of the goods and services produced by the industry fluctuate up and down to reflect raw material costs, interest rates, exchange rates, and so on. A company that does not hedge can expect its profit margins to be roughly constant. However, a company that does hedge can expect its profit margins to fluctuate!

To illustrate this point, consider two manufacturers of gold jewelry, company A and company B. We assume that most companies in the industry do not hedge against movements in the price of gold and that company B is no exception. However, company A has decided to be different from its competitors and use futures contracts to hedge its purchase of gold over the next 18 months. If the price of gold goes up, economic pressures will tend to lead to a corresponding increase in the wholesale price of the jewelry so that company B's profit margin is unaffected. By contrast, company A's profit margin will increase after the effects of the hedge have been taken into account. If the price of gold goes down, economic pressures will tend to lead to a corresponding decrease in the wholesale price of the jewelry. Again, company B's profit margin is unaffected. However, company A's profit margin goes down. In extreme conditions, company A's profit margin could become negative as a result of the "hedging" carried out! This example is summarized in Table 4.3.

Other Considerations

It is important to realize that a hedge using futures contracts can result in a decrease or an increase in a company's profits relative to the position it would be in with no hedging. In the example in Table 4.1, if the price of oil goes down, the company loses money on its sale of 1 million barrels of oil and the futures position leads to an offsetting gain. The treasurer can be congratulated for having

Table 4.3 Danger in Hedging When Competitors Do Not

CHANGE IN GOLD PRICE	*EFFECT ON PRICE OF GOLD JEWELRY*	*EFFECT ON PROFITS OF NONHEDGER*	*EFFECT ON PROFITS OF HEDGER*
Increase	Increase	None	Increase
Decrease	Decrease	None	Decrease

had the foresight to put the hedge in place. Clearly the company is better off than it would be with no hedging. Other executives in the organization, it is hoped, will appreciate the contribution made by the treasurer. If the price of oil goes up, the company gains from its sale of the oil and the futures position leads to an offsetting loss. The company is in a worse position than it would be with no hedging. Although the hedging decision was perfectly logical, the treasurer may in practice have a difficult time justifying it. Suppose that the price of oil is $21.75 on August 15 in Table 4.1 so that the company loses $3 per barrel on the futures contract. It is easy to imagine a conversation such as the following between the treasurer and the president.

PRESIDENT: This is terrible. We've lost $3 million in the futures market in the space of three months. How could it happen? I want a full explanation.

TREASURER: The purpose of the futures contracts was to hedge our exposure to the price of oil—not to make a profit. Don't forget that we made about $3 million from the favorable effect of the oil price increases on our business.

PRESIDENT: What's that got to do with it? That's like saying that we do not need to worry when our sales are down in California because they are up in New York.

TREASURER: If the price of oil had gone down . . .

PRESIDENT: I don't care what would have happened if the price of oil had gone down. The fact is that it went up. I really do not know what you were doing playing the futures markets like this. Our shareholders will expect us to have done particularly well this quarter. I'm going to have to explain to them that your actions reduced profits by $3 million. I'm afraid this is going to mean no bonus for you this year.

TREASURER: That's unfair. I was only . . .

PRESIDENT: Unfair! You are lucky not to be fired. You lost $3 million.

TREASURER: It all depends how you look at it . . .

It is easy to see why many treasurers are reluctant to hedge! Hedging reduces risk for the company. However, it may increase risks for the treasurer if others do not fully understand what is being done. The only real solution to this problem involves ensuring that all senior executives within the organization fully understand the nature of hedging prior to a hedging program being put in place. Hedging strategies should ideally be set by a company's board of directors and be clearly communicated to both the company's management and shareholders.

BASIS RISK

The hedges in the examples considered so far have been almost too good to be true. The hedger was able to identify the precise date in the future when an asset would be bought or sold. He or she was then able to use futures contracts to remove almost all the risk arising from the price of the asset on that date. In practice, hedging is often not quite as straightforward as this. Some of the reasons are as follows:

1. The asset whose price is to be hedged may not be exactly the same as the asset underlying the futures contract.
2. The hedger may be uncertain as to the exact date when the asset will be bought or sold.
3. The hedge may require the futures contract to be closed out well before its expiration date.

These problems give rise to what is termed *basis risk*. This concept will now be explained.

The Basis

The *basis* in a hedging situation is as follows:[1]

$$\text{Basis} = \begin{array}{c}\text{Spot price of asset}\\ \text{to be hedged}\end{array} - \begin{array}{c}\text{Futures price of}\\ \text{contract used}\end{array}$$

If the asset to be hedged and the asset underlying the futures contract are the same, the basis should be zero at the expiration of the futures contract. Prior to expiration, the basis may be positive or negative. From the analysis in Chapter 3, when the underlying asset is a low-interest-rate currency or gold or silver, the futures price is greater than the spot price. This means that the basis is negative. For high-interest-rate currencies and many commodities, the reverse is true and the basis is positive.

When the spot price increases by more than the futures price, the basis increases. This is referred to as a *strengthening of the basis*. When the futures price increases by more than the spot price, the basis declines. This is referred to as a *weakening of the basis*. Figure 4.1 illustrates how a basis might change over time. In this example, the basis is positive prior to expiration of the futures contract.

To examine the nature of basis risk, we will use the following notation:

S_1: spot price at time t_1
S_2: spot price at time t_2
F_1: futures price at time t_1
F_2: futures price at time t_2
b_1: basis at time t_1
b_2: basis at time t_2

[1] This is the usual definition. However, the alternative definition

Basis = Futures price − Spot price

is sometimes used, particularly when the futures contract is on a financial asset.

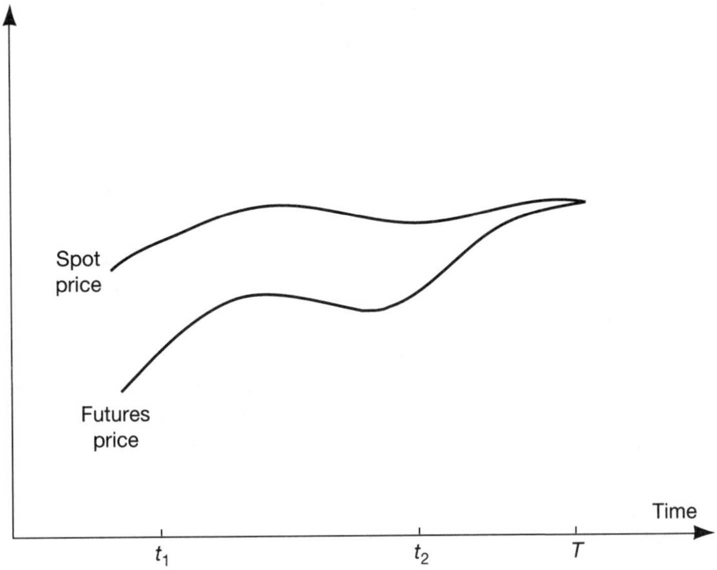

Figure 4.1 Variation of basis over time.

We will assume that a hedge is put in place at time t_1 and closed out at time t_2. As an example, we will consider the case where the spot and futures prices at the time the hedge is initiated are \$2.50 and \$2.20, respectively, and that at the time the hedge is closed out they are \$2.00 and \$1.90, respectively. This means that $S_1 = 2.50$, $F_1 = 2.20$, $S_2 = 2.00$, and $F_2 = 1.90$.

From the definition of the basis

$$b_1 = S_1 - F_1$$

$$b_2 = S_2 - F_2$$

and in our example, $b_1 = 0.30$ and $b_2 = 0.10$.

Consider first the situation of a hedger who knows that the asset will be sold at time t_2 and takes a short futures position at time t_1. The price realized for the asset is S_2 and the profit on the futures position is $F_1 - F_2$. The effective price that is obtained for the asset with hedging is, therefore,

$$S_2 + F_1 - F_2 = F_1 + b_2$$

In our example, this is \$2.30. The value of F_1 is known at time t_1. If b_2 were also known at this time, a perfect hedge would result. The hedging risk is the uncertainty associated with b_2. This is known as *basis risk*. Consider next a situation where a company knows it will buy the asset at time t_2 and initiates a long hedge at time t_1. The price paid for the asset is S_2 and the loss on the hedge is $F_1 - F_2$. The effective price that is paid with hedging is, therefore,

$$S_2 + F_1 - F_2 = F_1 + b_2$$

This is the same expression as before and is \$2.30 in the example. The value of F_1 is known at time t_1 and the term b_2 represents basis risk.

For investment assets such as currencies, stock indices, gold, and silver, the basis risk tends to be less than for consumption commodities. This is because, as shown in Chapter 3, arbitrage arguments lead to a well-defined relationship between the futures price and the spot price of an investment asset. The basis risk for an investment asset arises mainly from uncertainty as to the level of the risk-free interest rate in the future. In the case of a consumption commodity, imbalances between supply and demand and the difficulties sometimes associated with storing the commodity can lead to large variations in the convenience yield. This provides an additional source of basis risk.

The asset that gives rise to the hedger's exposure is sometimes different from the asset underlying the hedge.[2] The basis risk is then usually greater. Define S_2^* as the price of the asset underlying the futures contract at time t_2. As before, S_2 is the price of the asset being hedged at time t_2. By hedging, a company ensures that the price that will be paid (or received) for the asset is

$$S_2 + F_1 - F_2$$

This can be written

$$F_1 + (S_2^* - F_2) + (S_2 - S_2^*)$$

The terms $S_2^* - F_2$ and $S_2 - S_2^*$ represent the two components of the basis. The $S_2^* - F_2$ term is the basis that would exist if the asset being hedged were the same as the asset underlying the futures contract. The $S_2 - S_2^*$ term is the basis arising from the difference between the two assets.

Note that basis risk can lead to an improvement or a worsening of a hedger's position. Consider a short hedge. If the basis strengthens unexpectedly, the hedger's position improves, whereas if the basis weakens unexpectedly, the hedger's position worsens. For a long hedge, the reverse holds. If the basis strengthens unexpectedly, the hedger's position worsens whereas if the basis weakens unexpectedly, the hedger's position improves.

[2] For example, airlines sometimes use the NYMEX heating oil futures contract to hedge their exposure to the price of jet fuel. See the article by Nikkhah referenced at the end of this chapter for a description of this.

Choice of Contract

One key factor affecting basis risk is the choice of the futures contract to be used for hedging. This choice has two components:

1. The choice of the asset underlying the futures contract.
2. The choice of the delivery month.

If the asset being hedged exactly matches an asset underlying a futures contract, the first choice is generally fairly easy. In other circumstances, it is necessary to carry out a careful analysis to determine which of the available futures contracts has futures prices that are most closely correlated with the price of the asset being hedged.

The choice of the delivery month is likely to be influenced by several factors. In the examples earlier in this chapter, we assumed that when the expiration of the hedge corresponds to a delivery month, the contract with that delivery month is chosen. In fact, a contract with a later delivery month is usually chosen in these circumstances. This is because futures prices are in some instances quite erratic during the delivery month. Also, a long hedger runs the risk of having to take delivery of the physical asset if he or she holds the contract during the delivery month. This can be expensive and inconvenient.

In general, basis risk increases as the time difference between the hedge expiration and the delivery month increases. A good rule of thumb is, therefore, to choose a delivery month that is as close as possible to, but later than, the expiration of the hedge. Suppose delivery months are March, June, September, and December for a particular contract. For hedge expirations in December, January, and February, the March contract will be chosen; for hedge expirations in March, April, and May, the June contract will be chosen; and so on. This rule of thumb assumes that there is sufficient liquidity in all contracts to meet the hedger's requirements. In practice, liquidity tends to be greatest in short maturity futures contracts. The hedger may, therefore, in some situations be inclined to use short maturity contracts and roll them forward. This strategy is discussed at the end of this chapter.

Examples

We now illustrate some of the points made so far in this section. Suppose it is March 1. A U.S. company expects to receive 50 million Japanese yen at the end of July. Yen futures contracts on the IMM have delivery months of March, June, September, and December. One contract is for the delivery of 12.5 million yen. The criteria mentioned earlier for the choice of a contract suggest that the September contract be chosen for hedging purposes.

The company, therefore, shorts four September yen futures contracts on March 1. When the yen are received at the end of July, the company closes out its position. The basis risk arises from uncertainty about the difference between the futures price and the spot price at this time. We suppose that the futures price on March 1 in cents per yen is 0.7800 and that the spot and futures prices when the contract is closed out are 0.7200 and 0.7250, respectively. The basis is −0.0050 and the gain from the futures contracts is 0.0550. The effective price obtained in cents per yen is the spot price plus the gain on the futures:

$$0.7200 + 0.0550 = 0.7750$$

This can also be written as the initial futures price plus the basis:

$$0.7800 - 0.0050 = 0.7750$$

The company receives a total of 50×0.00775 million dollars or $387,500. This example is summarized in Table 4.4.

For our next example, we suppose it is June 8 and a company knows that it will need to purchase 20,000 barrels of crude oil at some time in October or November. Oil futures contracts are currently traded for delivery every month on NYMEX and the contract size is 1,000 barrels. Following the criteria indicated, the company decides to use the December contract for hedging. On June 8, it takes

Table 4.4 Basis Risk in a Short Hedge

From the Trader's Desk—March 1

It is March 1. A U.S. company expects to receive 50 million Japanese yen at the end of July. The September futures price for the yen is currently 0.7800.

Strategy

The company can

1. Short four September yen futures contracts on March 1.
2. Close out the contract when the yen arrive at the end of July.

Basis Risk

The basis risk arises from the hedger's uncertainty as to the difference between the spot price and September futures price of the Japanese yen at the end of July.

The Outcome

When the yen arrived at the end of July, it turned out that the spot price was 0.7200 and the futures price was 0.7250. It follows that

$$\text{Basis} = 0.7200 - 0.7250 = -0.0050$$
$$\text{Gain on futures} = 0.7800 - 0.7250 = +0.0550$$

The effective price in cents per yen received by the hedger is the end-of-July spot price plus the gain on the futures:

$$0.7200 + 0.0550 = 0.7750$$

This can also be written as the initial September futures price plus the basis:

$$0.7800 - 0.0050 = 0.7750$$

Table 4.5 Basis Risk in Long Hedge

From the Trader's Desk—June 8

It is June 8. A company knows that it will need to purchase 20,000 barrels of crude oil at some time in October or November. The current December oil futures price is \$18.00 per barrel.

Strategy

The company

1. Takes a long position in 20 NYM December oil futures contracts on June 8.
2. Closes out the contract when it finds it is ready to purchase the oil.

Basis Risk

The basis risk arises from the hedger's uncertainty as to the difference between the spot price and the December futures price of oil at the time when the oil is required.

The Outcome

The company was ready to purchase the oil on November 10 and closed out its futures contract on that date. The spot price was \$20.00 per barrel and the futures price was \$19.10 per barrel. It follows that

$$\text{Basis} = 20.00 - 19.10 = 0.90$$
$$\text{Gain on futures} = 19.10 - 18.00 = 1.10$$

The effective cost of the oil purchased is the November 10 price less the gain on the futures:

$$20.00 - 1.10 = 18.90 \text{ per barrel}$$

This can also be written as the initial December futures price plus the basis:

$$18.00 + 0.90 = 18.90 \text{ per barrel}$$

---

a long position in 20 December contracts. At that time, the futures price is \$18.00 per barrel. The company finds that it is ready to purchase the crude oil on November 10. It therefore closes out its futures contract on that date. The basis risk arises from uncertainty as to what the basis will be on the day the contract is closed out. We suppose that the spot price and futures price on November 10 are \$20.00 per barrel and \$19.10 per barrel, respectively. The basis is, therefore, \$0.90 and the effective price paid is \$18.90 per barrel or \$378,000 in total. This example is summarized in Table 4.5.

MINIMUM VARIANCE HEDGE RATIO

The *hedge ratio* is the ratio of the size of the position taken in futures contracts to the size of the exposure. Up to now, we have always used a hedge ratio of 1.0. In Table 4.5, for example, the hedger's exposure was on 20,000 barrels of oil and futures contracts were entered into for the delivery of exactly this amount of oil.

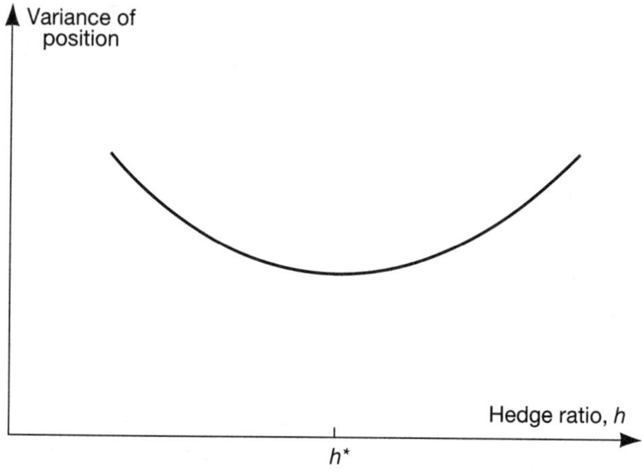

Figure 4.2 Dependence of variance of hedger's position on hedge ratio.

If the objective of the hedger is to minimize risk, setting the hedge ratio equal to 1.0 is not necessarily optimal.

We will use the following notation:

ΔS: Change in spot price, S, during a period of time equal to the life of the hedge
ΔF: Change in futures price, F, during a period of time equal to the life of the hedge
σ_S: Standard deviation of ΔS
σ_F: Standard deviation of ΔF
ρ: Coefficient of correlation between ΔS and ΔF
h^*: Hedge ratio that minimizes the variance of the hedger's position

In Appendix 4A we show that

$$h^* = \rho \frac{\sigma_S}{\sigma_F} \qquad \textbf{(4.1)}$$

The optimal hedge ratio is the product of the coefficient of correlation between ΔS and ΔF and the ratio of the standard deviation of ΔS to the standard deviation of ΔF. Figure 4.2 shows how the variance of the value of the hedger's position depends on the hedge ratio chosen.

If $\rho = 1$ and $\sigma_F = \sigma_S$, the hedge ratio, h^*, is 1.0. This is to be expected since in this case the futures price mirrors the spot price perfectly. If $\rho = 1$ and $\sigma_F = 2\sigma_S$, the hedge ratio h^* is 0.5. This result is also as expected since in this case the futures price always changes by twice as much as the spot price.

The optimal hedge ratio, h^*, is the slope of the best fit line when ΔS is regressed against ΔF, as indicated in Figure 4.3. This is intuitively reasonable since we require h^* to correspond to the ratio of changes in ΔS to changes in ΔF. The *hedge effectiveness* can be defined as the proportion of the variance that is eliminated by hedging. This is ρ^2 or

$$h^{*2} \frac{\sigma_F^2}{\sigma_S^2}$$

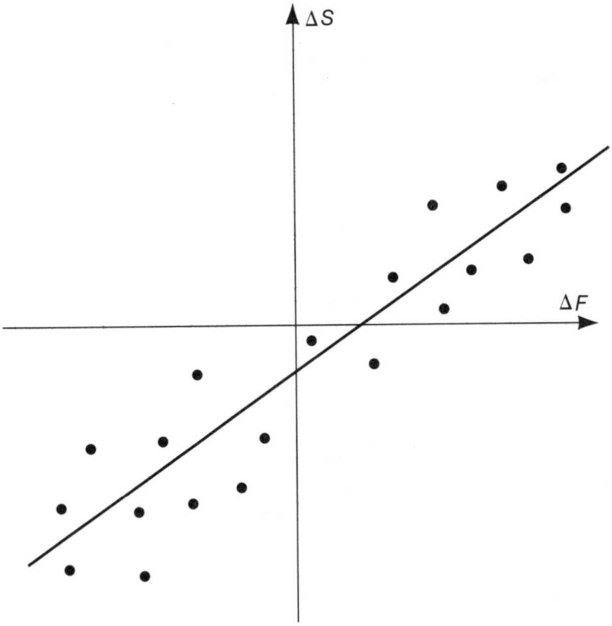

Figure 4.3 Regression of change in spot price against change in futures price.

Estimation

The parameters ρ, σ_F, and σ_S in Equation (4.1) are usually estimated from historical data on ΔS and ΔF. (This implicitly assumes that the future will in some sense be like the past.) A number of equal nonoverlapping time intervals are chosen and the values of ΔS and ΔF for each of the intervals are observed. Ideally, the length of each time interval should be the same as the length of the time interval for which the hedge is in effect. In practice, this sometimes severely limits the number of observations that are available and a shorter time interval is used.

To illustrate how the calculations are carried out, Table 4.6 gives sample data on ΔF and ΔS. We suppose that the duration of the hedge is one month, so that ΔF and ΔS measure the changes in F and S during successive one-month periods. The futures contract observed is the one that would actually be used for hedging an exposure during the month under consideration. We will denote the ith observations on ΔF and ΔS by x_i and y_i, respectively, and suppose that there n observations in total. It can be shown that

$$\sum x_i = -0.013; \qquad \sum x_i^2 = 0.0138$$

$$\sum y_i = 0.003; \qquad \sum y_i^2 = 0.0097$$

$$\sum x_i y_i = 0.0108$$

Table 4.6 Data to Calculate Minimum Variance Hedge Ratio

MONTH i	ΔF FOR MONTH = x_i	ΔS FOR MONTH = y_i
1	0.021	0.029
2	0.035	0.020
3	−0.046	−0.044
4	0.001	0.008
5	0.044	0.026
6	−0.029	−0.019
7	−0.026	−0.010
8	−0.029	−0.007
9	0.048	0.043
10	−0.006	0.011
11	−0.036	−0.036
12	−0.011	−0.018
13	0.019	0.009
14	−0.027	−0.032
15	0.029	0.023

Using standard formulas from statistics, the estimate of σ_F is

$$\sqrt{\frac{\Sigma x_i^2}{n-1} - \frac{(\Sigma x_i)^2}{n(n-1)}} = 0.00313$$

The estimate of σ_S is

$$\sqrt{\frac{\Sigma y_i^2}{n-1} - \frac{(\Sigma y_i)^2}{n(n-1)}} = 0.00262$$

The estimate of ρ is

$$\frac{n\Sigma x_i y_i - \Sigma x_i \Sigma y_i}{\sqrt{[n\Sigma x_i^2 - (\Sigma x_i)^2][n\Sigma y_i^2 - (\Sigma y_i)^2]}} = 0.928$$

The minimum variance hedge ratio, h^*, is therefore,

$$0.928 \times \frac{0.00262}{0.00313} = 0.786$$

This means that the futures contracts bought or sold should have 78.6 percent of the face value of the asset being hedged. In practice, of course, the number of futures contracts used must be an integer and the hedger can only achieve an approximation to the optimal hedge.

Optimal Number of Contracts

Define

N_A: size of position being hedged (units)
Q_F: size of one futures contract (units)
N^*: the optimal number of futures contracts for hedging

The futures contracts used should have a face value of h^*N_A. The number of futures contracts required is, therefore, given by

$$N^* = \frac{h^*N_A}{Q_F} \tag{4.2}$$

Suppose that for the example in Table 4.5, h^* is calculated as 0.7. Since $N_A = 20{,}000$ and $Q_F = 1{,}000$, the optimal number of contracts, N^*, is given by

$$N^* = \frac{0.7 \times 20{,}000}{1{,}000} = 14$$

A Change of Notation

For the rest of this chapter and the next chapter, it is convenient to redefine S, F, σ_S, and σ_F. From now onward, S will denote the value of the position being hedged ($= N_A$ times the old S) and F will denote the futures contract price ($= Q_F$ times the old F). The variables σ_S, σ_F, and ρ will denote the standard deviations of the new S, the standard deviation of the new F, and the coefficient between the new S and F, respectively. The new σ_S is N_A times the old σ_S, the new σ_F is Q_F times the old σ_F, and ρ is the same as before. From Equations (4.1) and (4.2), it can be seen that the equation for N^* is the same as our earlier equation for h^*:

$$N^* = \rho \frac{\sigma_S}{\sigma_F} \tag{4.3}$$

STOCK INDEX FUTURES

Stock index futures were introduced in Chapter 3. They are frequently used to hedge portfolios of stocks in the way described in the previous section. Readers familiar with the capital asset pricing model will know that the relationship between the return on a portfolio of stocks and the return on the market is described by a parameter β (= beta). This is the slope of the best fit line obtained when the excess return on the portfolio over the risk-free rate is regressed against the excess return on the market over the risk-free rate. When $\beta = 1.0$, the return on the portfolio tends to mirror the return on the market; when $\beta = 2.0$, the excess return on the portfolio tends to be twice as great as the excess return on the market; when $\beta = 0.5$, it tends to be half as great; and so on.

Consistent with our new notation, S is the value of the portfolio and F is the price of a futures contract (= futures price times size of contract). It can be shown that as an approximation, the optimal number of contracts, N^*, is given by: [3]

$$N^* = \beta \frac{S}{F} \tag{4.4}$$

We will illustrate that this gives reasonable results with an example. Suppose that

Value of S&P 500 index	= 200
Value of portfolio	= \$2,040,000
Risk-free interest rate	= 10 percent per annum
Dividend yield on S&P 500	= 4 percent per annum
Beta of portfolio	= 1.5

We assume that a futures contract on the S&P 500 with four months to maturity is used to hedge the value of the portfolio over the next three months. One futures contract is for delivery of \$500 times the index. From Equation (3.12), the current futures price should be

$$200e^{(0.10-0.04)\times 0.333} = 204.0$$

and the price of a futures contract, F, should be $500 \times 204.0 = \$102{,}000$. Using Equation (4.4), the number of futures contracts that should be shorted to hedge the portfolio is

$$1.5 \times \frac{2{,}040{,}000}{102{,}000} = 30$$

Suppose the index turns out to be 180 in three months. The futures price will be

$$180e^{(0.10-0.04)\times 0.0833} = 180.9$$

[3] To prove Equation (4.4), denote $\Delta S/S$ by R_S, and $\Delta F/F$ by R_F. Also, denote the standard deviations of R_S and R_F by σ_1 and σ_2, respectively, and the coefficient of correlation between R_S and R_F by ρ^*. R_S is the return on the portfolio and as an approximation we can assume that R_F is the return on the market. An approximate expression for β is, therefore, $\beta = \rho^*\sigma_1/\sigma_2$. Approximate expressions for σ_1, σ_2, and ρ^* are $\sigma_1 = \sigma_S/S$, $\sigma_2 = \sigma_F/F$, and $\rho^* = \rho$. It follows that β is approximately given by:

$$\beta = \rho \frac{\sigma_S F}{\sigma_F S}$$

When used in conjunction with Equation (4.3), this leads to Equation (4.4).

Table 4.7 Performance of Stock Index Hedge

Value of index in three months	180.0	190.0	200.0	210.0	220.0
Future prices of index in three months	180.9	191.0	201.0	211.1	221.1
Gain on futures position ($000s)	346.5	195.0	45.0	(106.5)	(256.5)
Value of portfolio (including dividends) in three months ($000s)	1739.1	1892.1	2045.1	2198.1	2351.1
Total value of position in three months ($000s)	2085.6	2087.1	2090.1	2091.6	2094.1

The gain from the short futures position is, therefore,

$$30 \times (204 - 180.9) \times 500 = \$346{,}500$$

The loss on the index is 10 percent. The index pays a dividend of 4 percent per annum or 1 percent per 3 months. When dividends are taken into account, an investor in the index would therefore earn −9 percent in the three-month period. The risk-free interest rate is approximately 2.5 percent per three months.[4] Since the portfolio has a β of 1.5,

$$\begin{aligned}&\text{Expected return on portfolio} - \text{Risk-free interest rate}\\&= 1.5 \times [\text{Return on index} - \text{Risk-free interest rate}]\end{aligned}$$

Using this, the expected return on the portfolio is

$$2.5 + [1.5 \times (-9.0 - 2.5)] = -14.75\%$$

The expected value of the portfolio (inclusive of dividends) at the end of the three months is, therefore,

$$\$2{,}040{,}000 \times (1 - 0.1475) = \$1{,}739{,}100$$

It follows that the expected value of the hedger's position including the gain on the hedge is

$$\$1{,}739{,}100 + \$346{,}500 = \$2{,}085{,}600$$

Table 4.7 summarizes these calculations together with similar calculations for other values of the index at maturity. It can be seen that the total value of the hedger's position in three months is almost independent of the value of the index.

Table 4.7 assumes that the dividend yield on the index is predictable, the risk-free interest rate remains constant, and the return on the index over the three-month period is perfectly correlated with the return on the portfolio. In practice,

[4] For ease of presentation, the fact that the interest rate and dividend yield are continuously compounded has been ignored. This makes very little difference.

these assumptions do not hold perfectly and the hedge works rather less well than is indicated by Table 4.7.

Reasons for Hedging a Portfolio

Table 4.7 shows that the hedging scheme results in a value for the hedger's position very close to \$2,090,000 at the end of three months. This is greater than the \$2,040,000 initial value of the position by about 2.5 percent. This should not be a surprise. The risk-free interest rate is 10 percent per annum or about 2.5 percent per quarter. The hedge results in the hedger's position growing at the risk-free interest rate.

It is natural to ask why the hedger should go to the trouble of using futures contracts. If the hedger's objective is to earn the risk-free interest rate, he or she can simply sell the portfolio and invest the proceeds in treasury bills.

One answer to this question is that hedging can be justified if the hedger feels that the stocks in the portfolio have been chosen well. In these circumstances, the hedger might be very uncertain about the performance of the market as a whole but confident that the stocks in the portfolio will outperform the market (after appropriate adjustments have been made for the β of the portfolio). A hedge using index futures removes the risk arising from market moves and leaves the hedger exposed only to the performance of the portfolio relative to the market. Another reason for hedging may be that the hedger is planning to hold a portfolio for a long period of time and requires short-term protection in an uncertain market situation. The alternative strategy of selling the portfolio and buying it back later might involve unacceptably high transaction costs.

Changing Beta

In the example in Table 4.7, the beta of the hedger's portfolio is reduced to zero. Sometimes futures contracts are used to change the beta of a portfolio to some value other than zero. In the example, to reduce the beta of the portfolio from 1.5 to 0.75, the number of contracts shorted should be 15 rather than 30; to increase the beta of the portfolio to 2.0 a long position in ten contracts should be taken; and so on. In general, to change the beta of the portfolio from β to β^* where $\beta > \beta^*$, a short position in

$$(\beta - \beta^*)\,\frac{S}{F}$$

contracts is required. When $\beta < \beta^*$, a long position in

$$(\beta^* - \beta)\,\frac{S}{F}$$

is required.

Exposure to the Price of an Individual Stock

Stock index futures can be used to hedge an exposure to the price of an individual stock. The number of contracts that the hedger should enter into is given by $\beta S/F$, where β is the beta of the stock, S is the total value of the shares being hedged, and F is the total price of one index futures contract. Note that although the number of contracts entered into is calculated in the same way as it is for the situation where a portfolio of stocks is being hedged, the performance of the hedge is considerably worse. This is because the hedge only provides protection against the risk arising from market movements and this risk is a relatively small proportion of the total risk in the price movements of individual stocks. The hedge is appropriate when an investor feels that the stock will outperform the market but is unsure about the performance of the market. It can also be used by an investment bank that has underwritten a new issue of the stock.

Consider an investor who in June holds 20,000 IBM shares each worth \$50. The investor feels that the market will be very volatile over the next month but feels that IBM has a good chance of outperforming the market. The investor decides to use the CBOT August futures contract on the Major Market Index (MMI) to hedge the position during the one-month period. The β of IBM is estimated at 1.1. The current futures price for the August contract on the MMI is 450, and each contract is for delivery of \$500 times the index. This means that the total futures price corresponding to one contract is $500 \times 450 = \$225{,}000$. The total value of the stocks being hedged is \$1 million. The number of contracts that should be shorted is, therefore,

$$1.1 \times \frac{1{,}000{,}000}{225{,}000} = 4.89$$

Rounding to the nearest integer, the hedger shorts five contracts closing out the position one month later. Suppose IBM rises to \$62.50 during the month and the Major Market Index rises to 540. The investor gains $20{,}000 \times (\$62.50 - \$50) = \$250{,}000$ on IBM while losing $5 \times 500 \times (540 - 450) = \$225{,}000$ on the futures contracts. The example is summarized in Table 4.8.

In this example, the hedge offsets a gain on the underlying asset with a loss on a futures contract. This might seem to be counterproductive. However, it cannot be emphasized often enough that the purpose of a hedge is to reduce risk. A hedge tends to make unfavorable outcomes less unfavorable and favorable outcomes less favorable.

ROLLING THE HEDGE FORWARD

Sometimes, the expiration date of the hedge is later than the delivery dates of all the futures contracts that can be used. The hedger must then roll the hedge forward. This involves closing out one futures contract and taking the same position

Table 4.8 Hedging a Position in an Individual Stock

From the Trader's Desk—June

An investor holds 20,000 IBM shares. The investor is concerned about the volatility in the market during the next month. The current market price of IBM is $50 and the August futures price of the Major Market Index is 450.

Strategy

The investor
1. Shorts five August contracts on the Major Market Index.
2. Closes out the position one month later.

Outcome

One month later the price of IBM is $62.50 and the futures price for the August Major Market Index contract is 540. The investor gains

$$20{,}000 \times (\$62.50 - \$50) = \$250{,}000$$

on the IBM shares and loses

$$5 \times 500 \times (540 - 450) = \$225{,}000$$

on the futures contract.

---

in a futures contract with a later delivery date. Hedges can be rolled forward many times. Consider a company that wishes to use a short hedge to reduce the risk associated with the price to be received for an asset at time T. If there are futures contracts 1, 2, 3, . . . , n (not all necessarily in existence at the present time) with progressively later delivery dates, the company can use the following strategy:

Time t_1: Short futures contract 1.
Time t_2: Close out futures contract 1.
Short futures contract 2.
Time t_3: Close out futures contract 2.
Short futures contract 3.
⋮ ⋮
Time t_n: Close out futures contract $n - 1$.
Short futures contract n.
Time T: Close out futures contract n.

An example of the use of this strategy is shown in Table 4.9. In April 1993, a company realizes that it will have 100,000 barrels of oil to sell in June 1994 and decides to hedge its risk with a hedge ratio of 1.0. The current spot price is $19. Although futures contracts are traded for every month of the year up to one year in the future, we suppose that only the first six delivery months have sufficient liquidity to meet the company's needs. The company, therefore, shorts 100 October 1993 contracts. In September 1993, it rolls the hedge forward into the March 1994 contract. In February 1994, it rolls the hedge forward again into the July 1994 contract.

As one possible outcome, we suppose that the price of oil drops \$3 to \$16 per barrel in June 1994. We suppose that the October 1993 futures contract was shorted at \$18.20 per barrel and closed out at \$17.40 per barrel for a profit of \$0.80 per barrel; the March 1994 contract was shorted at \$17.00 per barrel and closed out at \$16.50 per barrel for a profit of \$0.50 per barrel. The July 1994 contract was shorted at \$16.30 per barrel and closed out at \$15.90 per barrel for a profit of \$0.40 per barrel. In this case, the futures contracts provide a total of \$1.70 per barrel compensation for the \$3 per barrel oil price decline. This example is summarized in Table 4.9.

Only receiving \$1.70 per barrel compensation for a price decline of \$3.00 may appear unsatisfactory. However, we cannot expect total compensation for a price decline when futures prices are below spot prices. The best we can hope for is to lock in the futures price that would apply to a June 1994 contract if it were actively traded.

Table 4.9 Rolling the Hedge Forward

From the Trader's Desk—April 1993

The price of oil is \$19 per barrel. A company knows it will have 100,000 barrels of oil to sell in June 1994 and wishes to hedge its position. Contracts are traded on the NYMEX for every delivery month up to one year in the future. However, only the first six delivery months provide sufficient liquidity to meet the company's needs. The contract size is 1,000 barrels.

The Strategy

April 1993: The company shorts 100 October 1993 contracts.
September 1993: The company closes out the 100 October contracts. The company shorts 100 March 1994 contracts.
February 1994: The company closes out the 100 March contracts. The company shorts 100 July 1994 contracts.
June 1994: The company closes out the 100 July contracts. The company sells 100,000 barrels of oil.

The Outcome

October 1993 futures contract:
Shorted in April 1993 at \$18.20 and closed out in September 1993 at \$17.40.
March 1994 futures contracts:
Shorted in September 1993 at \$17.00 and closed out in February 1994 at \$16.50.
July 1994 futures contracts:
Shorted in February 1994 at \$16.30 and closed out in June 1994 at \$15.90.
Spot oil price in June 1994:
\$16 per barrel.

The gain from the futures contracts is (\$18.20 − \$17.40) + (\$17.00 − \$16.50) + (\$16.30 − \$15.90) = \$1.70 per barrel. This partly offsets the \$3 decline in oil prices between April 1993 and June 1994.

SUMMARY

This chapter has discussed various ways in which a company can take a position in futures contracts to offset an exposure to the price of an asset. If the exposure is such that the company gains when the price of the asset increases and loses when the price of the asset decreases, a short hedge is appropriate. If the exposure is the other way round (i.e., the company gains when the price of the asset decreases and loses when the price of the asset increases), a long hedge is appropriate.

Hedging is a way of reducing risk. As such, it should be welcomed by most executives. In reality, there are a number of theoretical and practical reasons why companies do not hedge. On a theoretical level, we can argue that shareholders, by holding well-diversified portfolios, can eliminate many of the risks that are faced by a company. They do not require the company to hedge these risks. On a practical level, a company may find that it is increasing rather than decreasing risk by hedging if none of its competitors does so. Also, a treasurer may feel that he or she will be criticized by other executives if the company makes a gain from movements in the price of the underlying asset and a loss on the hedge.

An important concept in hedging is basis risk. The basis is the difference between the spot price of an asset and its futures price. Basis risk is created by a hedger's uncertainty as to what the basis will be at maturity of the hedge. Basis risk is generally greater for consumption assets than for investment assets.

The hedge ratio is the ratio of the size of the position taken in futures contracts to the size of the exposure. It is not always optimal to use a hedge ratio of 1.0. If the hedger wishes to minimize the variance of his or her total position, a hedge ratio different from 1.0 may be appropriate. The optimal hedge ratio is the slope of the best fit line obtained when changes in the spot price are regressed against changes in the futures price. When a stock index futures contract is used to hedge a position in a portfolio of stocks or a position in an individual stock, the optimal number of futures contracts is equal to the beta of the position times the ratio of the value of the portfolio to the futures contract price.

When there is no liquid futures contract that matures later than the expiration of the hedge, a strategy known as rolling the hedge forward may be appropriate. This involves entering into a sequence of futures contracts. When the first futures contract is near expiration, it is closed out and the hedger enters into a second contract with a later delivery month. When the second contract is close to expiration, it is closed out and the hedger enters into a third contract with a later delivery month; and so on. Rolling the hedge works well if there is a close correlation between changes in the futures prices and changes in the spot prices.

Suggestions for Further Reading

CHICAGO BOARD OF TRADE, *Introduction to Hedging*. Chicago, 1984.

EDERINGTON, L. H., "The hedging performance of the new futures market," *Journal of Finance*, 34 (March 1979), 157–170.

FRANKCLE, C. T., "The hedging performance of the new futures market: Comment," *Journal of Finance*, 35 (December 1980), 1273–1279.

JOHNSON, L. L., "The theory of hedging and speculation in commodity futures markets," *Review of Economics Studies*, 27 (October 1960), 139–151.

McCabe, G. M., and C. T. Franckle, "The effectiveness of rolling the hedge forward in the treasury bill futures market," *Financial Management*, 12 (Summer 1983), 21–29.

Nikkhah, S., "How end users can hedge fuel costs in energy markets," *Futures* (October 1987), 66–67.

Stulz, R. M., "Optimal hedging policies," *Journal of Financial and Quantitative Analysis*, 19 (June 1984), 127–140.

Quiz

1. Under what circumstances are (a) a short hedge and (b) a long hedge appropriate.
2. Explain what is meant by *basis risk* when futures contracts are used for hedging.
3. Explain what is meant by a *perfect hedge*. Does a perfect hedge always lead to a better outcome than an imperfect hedge? Explain your answer.
4. Under what circumstances does a minimum variance hedge portfolio lead to no hedging at all?
5. Give three reasons why the treasurer of a company might not hedge the company's exposure to a particular risk.
6. Suppose that the standard deviation of quarterly changes in the prices of a commodity is \$0.65, the standard deviation of quarterly changes in a futures price on the commodity is \$0.81, and the coefficient of correlation between the two changes is 0.8. What is the optimal hedge ratio for a three-month contract? What does it mean?
7. A company has a \$10 million portfolio with a beta of 1.2. It would like to use futures contracts on the Major Market Index to hedge its risk. The index is currently standing at 270 and each contract is for delivery of \$500 times the index. What is the hedge that minimizes risk? What should the company do if it wants to reduce the beta of the portfolio to 0.6?

Questions and Problems

4.1. In the Chicago Board of Trade's corn futures contract, the following delivery months are available: March, May, July, September, and December. State the contract that should be used for hedging when the expiration of the hedge is in
   a. June.
   b. July.
   c. January.

4.2. Does a perfect hedge always succeed in locking in the current spot price of an asset for a future transaction? Explain your answer.

4.3. Explain why a short hedger's position improves when the basis strengthens unexpectedly and worsens when the basis weakens unexpectedly.

4.4. Imagine you are the treasurer of a Japanese company exporting electronic equipment to the United States. Discuss how you would design a foreign exchange hedging strategy and the arguments you would use to sell the strategy to your fellow executives.

4.5. Suppose that in Table 4.5, the company decides to use a hedge ratio of 0.8. How does this affect the way in which the hedge is implemented and the end result?

4.6. "If the minimum variance hedge ratio is calculated as 1.0, the hedge must be perfect." Is this statement true? Explain your answer.

4.7. "If there is no basis risk, the minimum variance hedge ratio is always 1.0." Is this statement true? Explain your answer.

4.8. "When the convenience yield is high, long hedges are likely to be particularly attractive." Explain this statement. Illustrate it with an example.

4.9. The standard deviation of monthly changes in the spot price of live cattle is (in cents per pound) 1.2. The standard deviation of monthly changes in the futures price of live cattle for the closest contract is 1.4. The correlation between the futures price changes and the spot price changes is 0.7. It is now October 15. A beef producer is committed to purchasing 200,000 pounds of live cattle on November 15. The producer wants to use the December live cattle futures contracts to hedge its risk. Each contract is for the delivery of 40,000 pounds of cattle. What strategy should the beef producer follow?

4.10. A U.S. company is interested in using the futures contracts traded on the CME to hedge its German mark exposure. Define r as the interest rate (all maturities) on the U.S. dollar and r_f as the interest rate (all maturities) on the mark. Assume that r and r_f are constant and suppose that the company uses a contract expiring at time T to hedge an exposure at time t ($T > t$). Using the results in Chapter 3, show that the optimal hedge ratio is

$$e^{(r_f - r)(T-t)}$$

4.11. On July 1, an investor holds 50,000 shares of a certain stock. The stock is \$30. The investor is interested in hedging against movements in the market over the next two months and decides to use the December NYSE Index futures contract. The futures price is currently 150 and one contract is for delivery of \$500 times the index. The beta of the stock is 1.3. What strategy should the investor follow?

4.12. It is July 16. A company has a portfolio of stocks worth \$10 million. The beta of the portfolio is 1.0. It would like to use the CME December futures contract on the S&P 500 to change the beta of the portfolio to 0.5 during the period July 16 to November 16. The contract's futures price is currently 400. What should the company do?

4.13. Suppose that in Problem 4.12 the company would like to change the beta of the portfolio to 1.5. What should it do?

4.14. The following table gives data on monthly changes in the spot price and the futures price for a certain commodity. Use the data to calculate a minimum variance hedge ratio.

Spot price change	+0.50	+0.61	−0.22	−0.35	+0.79
Futures price change	+0.56	+0.63	−0.12	−0.44	+0.60
Spot price change	+0.04	+0.15	+0.70	−0.51	−0.41
Futures price change	−0.06	+0.01	+0.80	−0.56	−0.46

4.15. Suppose that in Table 4.9 the company decides to use a hedge ratio of 1.5. How does this affect the way the hedge is implemented and the end result?

Appendix 4A A Proof of the Minimum Variance Hedge Ratio Formula

Suppose we expect to sell N_A units of an asset at time t_2 and choose to hedge at time t_1 by shorting futures contracts on N_F units of a similar asset. The hedge ratio, which we will denote by h, is

$$h = \frac{N_F}{N_A} \tag{4A.1}$$

We will denote the total amount realized for the asset when the profit or loss on the hedge is taken into account by Y so that

$$Y = S_2 N_A - (F_2 - F_1)N_F$$

or

$$Y = S_1 N_A + (S_2 - S_1)N_A - (F_2 - F_1)N_F \tag{4A.2}$$

where S_1 and S_2 are the asset prices at times t_1 and t_2, and F_1 and F_2 are the futures prices at times t_1 and t_2. Using Equation (4A.1), the expression for Y in (4A.2) can be written

$$Y = S_1 N_A + N_A(\Delta S - h\Delta F) \tag{4A.3}$$

where

$$\Delta S = S_2 - S_1$$

$$\Delta F = F_2 - F_1$$

Since S_1 and N_A are known at time t_1, the variance of Y in Equation (4A.3) is minimized when the variance of $\Delta S - h\Delta F$ is minimized. The variance of $\Delta S - h\Delta F$ equals

$$\sigma_S^2 + h^2\sigma_F^2 - 2h\rho\sigma_S\sigma_F$$

This can be written

$$(h\sigma_F - \rho\sigma_S)^2 + \sigma_S^2 - \rho^2\sigma_S^2$$

The second and third terms do not involve h. The variance is, therefore, minimized when

$$(h\sigma_F - \rho\sigma_S)^2$$

is zero, that is, when

$$h = \rho \frac{\sigma_S}{\sigma_F}$$

5

INTEREST-RATE FUTURES

An interest-rate futures contract is a futures contract on an asset whose price is dependent solely on the level of interest rates. In this chapter, we describe the mechanics of how interest rate futures contracts work and how prices are quoted. We also explain the way in which futures prices can be related to spot prices and consider a number of hedging strategies involving interest-rate futures.

Hedging a company's exposure to interest rates is more complicated than hedging its exposure to, say, the price of copper. This is because a whole term structure is necessary to provide a full description of the level of interest rates, whereas the price of copper can be described by a single number. A company, when wishing to hedge its interest rate exposure, must decide not only the maturity of the hedge it requires but also the maturity of the interest rate to which it is exposed. It must then find a way of using available interest rate futures contracts so that an appropriate hedge is obtained.

SOME PRELIMINARIES

Before we describe the nature of interest-rate futures contracts, it is appropriate to review a few topics concerned with the term structure of interest rates.

Spot and Forward Interest Rates

The n-year spot interest rate or n-year zero-coupon rate is the interest rate on an investment that is made for a period of time starting today and lasting for n years. Thus, the three-year spot rate is the rate of interest on an investment

Table 5.1 Calculation of Forward Rates

YEAR (n)	*SPOT RATE FOR AN* n*-YEAR INVESTMENT (% PER ANNUM)*	*FORWARD RATE FOR* n*TH YEAR (% PER ANNUM)*
1	10.0	
2	10.5	11.0
3	10.8	11.4
4	11.0	11.6
5	11.1	11.5

lasting three years, the five-year spot rate is the rate of interest on an investment lasting five years, and so on. The investment considered should be a "pure" n-year investment with no intermediate payments. This means that all the interest and the principal are repaid to the investor at the end of year n.

Forward interest rates are the rates of interest implied by current spot rates for periods of time in the future. To illustrate how they are calculated, we suppose that the spot rates are as shown in the second column of Table 5.1. The rates are assumed to be continuously compounded. Thus, the 10 percent per annum rate for one year means that, in return for an investment of $100 today, the investor receives $100e^{0.1} = \$110.52$ in one year; the 10.5 percent per annum rate for two years means that in return for an investment of $100 today, the investor receives $100e^{0.105\times 2} = \$123.37$ in two years, and so on.

The forward interest rate in Table 5.1 for year 2 is 11 percent per annum. This is the rate of interest that is implied by the spot rates for the period of time between the end of the first year and the end of the second year. It can be calculated from the one-year spot interest rate of 10 percent per annum and the two-year spot interest rate of 10.5 percent per annum. It is the rate of interest for year 2 that, when combined with 10 percent per annum for year 1, gives 10.5 percent overall for the two years. To show that the correct answer is 11 percent per annum, suppose that $100 is invested. A rate of 10 percent for the first year and 11 percent for the second year yields

$$100e^{0.1}e^{0.11} = \$123.37$$

at the end of the second year. A rate of 10.5 percent per annum for two years yields

$$100e^{0.105\times 2}$$

which is also $123.37. This example illustrates the general result that when interest rates are continuously compounded and rates in successive time periods are combined, the overall equivalent rate is simply the arithmetic average of the rates (10.5 percent is the average of 10 percent and 11 percent). The result is only approximately true when the rates are not continuously compounded.

The forward rate for the third year is the rate of interest that is implied by a 10.5 percent per annum two-year spot rate and a 10.8 percent per annum three-year spot rate. It is 11.4 percent per annum. This is because an investment for two years at 10.5 percent per annum averaged with an investment for one year at 11.4 percent per annum gives an overall return for the three years of 10.8 percent per annum. The other forward rates can be calculated similarly and are shown in the third column of the table. In general, if r is the spot rate of interest applying for T years and r^* is the spot rate of interest applying to T^* years where $T^* > T$, the forward interest rate for the period of time between T and T^*, $\hat{r}$, is given by

$$\hat{r} = \frac{r^*T^* - rT}{T^* - T} \tag{5.1}$$

To illustrate the use of this formula, consider the calculation of the year 4 forward rate from the data in Table 5.1: $T = 3$, $T^* = 4$, $r = 0.108$, and $r^* = 0.11$, and the formula gives $\hat{r} = 0.116$.

Assuming that an investor can borrow or invest at the spot rate, the investor can lock in the forward rate for borrowing or investing during a future time period. For example, with the interest rates in Table 5.1, if an investor borrows \$100 at 10 percent for one year and then invests the money at 10.5 percent for two years, the result is a cash outflow of $100e^{0.1} = \$110.52$ at the end of year 1 and an inflow of $100e^{0.105\times 2} = \$123.37$ at the end of year 2. Since $123.37 = 110.52e^{0.11}$, a return equal to the forward rate, 11.0 percent, is earned on \$110.52 during the second year. For another example, suppose that the investor borrows \$100 for four years at 11.0 percent and invests it for three years at 10.8 percent. The result is a cash inflow of $100e^{0.108\times 3} = 138.26$ at the end of the third year and a cash outflow of $100e^{0.11\times 4} = 155.27$ at the end of the fourth year. Since $155.27 = 138.26e^{0.116}$, money is being borrowed for the fourth year at the forward rate of 11.6 percent.

The Zero-Coupon Yield Curve

A *zero-coupon bond* is a bond that pays no coupons. The holder of the bond receives all interest and principal at the end of the bond's life. Zero-coupon bonds are not often issued in practice. However, they are sometimes created artificially by "stripping" coupons from regular coupon-bearing bonds and selling the coupons separately from the principal. By definition the yield on an n-year zero-coupon bond is the n-year spot rate.

The *zero-coupon yield curve* is a curve showing the relationship between the yields on zero-coupon bonds and maturity. (Equivalently, it is a curve showing the relationship between spot rates and maturity.) Figure 5.1 shows the zero-coupon yield curve for the data in Table 5.1. It is important to distinguish between the zero-coupon yield curve and a yield curve for coupon-bearing bonds. In a situation such as that shown in Figure 5.1 where the yield curve is upward sloping, the zero-coupon yield curve will always be above the yield curve for coupon-

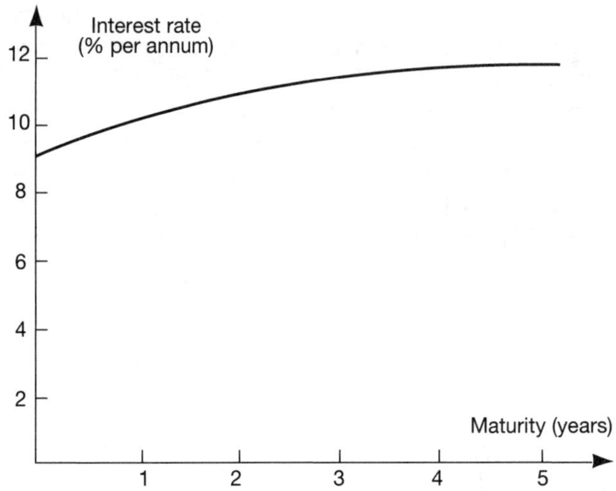

Figure 5.1 Zero-coupon yield curve for the data in Table 5.1.

bearing bonds. This is because the yield on a coupon-bearing bond is affected by the fact that the investor gets some payments before the maturity of the bond and the discount rates corresponding to these payment dates are lower than the discount rate corresponding to the final payment date. One particular coupon-bearing bond yield that is often considered is a *par bond yield*. This is the yield on a bond whose coupon is chosen so that it sells for exactly its face value of 100.

Analysts sometimes also look at the curve relating forward rates to the maturity of the forward contract. The forward rates can be defined so that they apply to future periods that have a length of three months or six months or any other convenient time period. In the situation where the zero-coupon yield curve is upward sloping, the forward rate curve is always above the zero-coupon yield curve. The reason for this should be clear from the nature of the calculations leading to the third column of Table 5.1.

Figure 5.2 shows the zero-coupon yield curve, coupon-bearing-bond yield

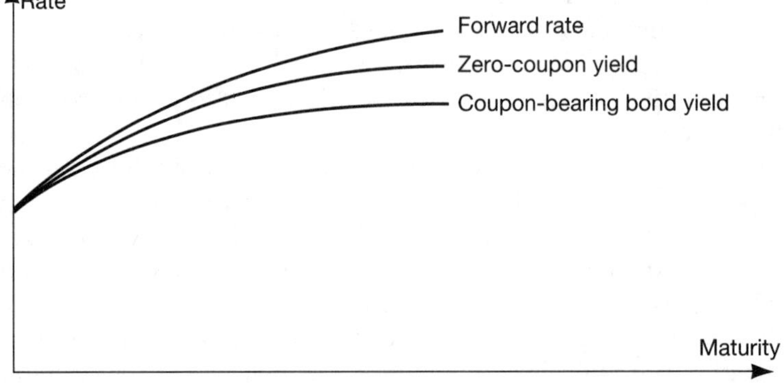

Figure 5.2 Situation when yield curve is upward sloping.

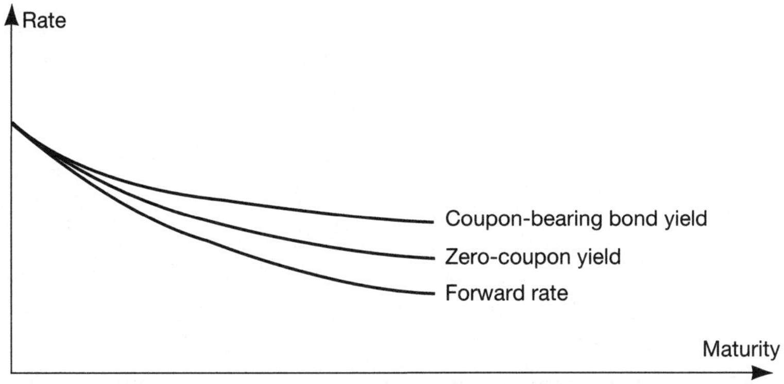

Figure 5.3 Situation when yield curve is downward sloping.

curve, and forward rate curve when the yield curve is upward sloping. As discussed, the forward rate curve is above the zero-coupon yield curve, which is in turn above the coupon-bearing-bond yield curve. Figure 5.3 shows the situation when the yield curve is downward sloping. Arguments similar to those just presented show that in this situation the coupon-bearing bond curve is above the zero-coupon yield curve, which is in turn above the forward rate curve.

Determination of Zero-Coupon Yield Curve

In practice, spot rates (or zero-coupon yields) cannot usually be observed directly. What can be observed are the prices of coupon-bearing bonds. An important issue, therefore, is how the zero-coupon yield curve can be extracted from the prices of coupon-bearing bonds.

One approach is known as the *bootstrap method*. To illustrate it, consider the data in Table 5.2 on the prices of five bonds. Since the first three bonds pay no coupons, the continuously compounded spot rates corresponding to the maturities of these bonds can easily be calculated using Equation (3.3). The three-month bond provides a return of 2.5 on an initial investment of 97.5 in three months. With quarterly compounding the rate is 2.5/97.5 = 2.56 percent per three months. With continuous compounding it becomes

$$4 \ln\left(1 + \frac{2.5}{97.5}\right) = 0.1012$$

or 10.12 percent per annum. Similarly, the six-month rate with continuous compounding is

$$2 \ln\left(1 + \frac{5.1}{94.9}\right) = 0.1047$$

Table 5.2 Data for Bootstrap Method

BOND PRINCIPAL ($)	*TIME TO MATURITY (YRS)*	*ANNUAL COUPON ($)**	*BOND PRICE ($)*
100	0.25	0	97.5
100	0.50	0	94.9
100	1.00	0	90.0
100	1.50	8	96.0
100	2.00	12	101.6

* Half of the stated coupon is assumed to be paid every six months.

or 10.47 percent per annum, and the one-year rate with continuous compounding is

$$\ln\left(1 + \frac{10}{90.0}\right) = 0.1054$$

or 10.54 percent per annum.

The fourth bond lasts 1.5 years. The payments are as follows:

6 months:	\$4
1 year:	\$4
1.5 years:	\$104

From our earlier calculations, we know that the discount rate for the payment at the end of six months is 10.47 percent and the discount rate for the payment at the end of 1 year is 10.54 percent. We also know that the bond's price, \$96, must equal the present value of all the payments received by the bondholder. Suppose the 1.5-year spot rate is denoted by R. It follows that

$$4e^{-0.1047\times 0.5} + 4e^{-0.1054} + 104e^{-1.5R} = 96$$

This reduces to

$$e^{-1.5R} = 0.85196$$

or

$$R = -\frac{\ln(0.85196)}{1.5} = 0.1068$$

The 1.5-year spot rate is, therefore, 10.68 percent. This is the only spot rate that is consistent with the six-month and one-year spot rate and consistent with the data in Table 5.2.

The two-year spot rate can be calculated similarly from the six-month, one-year, and 1.5-year spot rates and the information on the fifth bond in Table 5.2. If R is the two-year spot rate,

$$6e^{-0.1047\times 0.5} + 6e^{-0.1054\times 1.0} + 6e^{-0.1068\times 1.5} + 106e^{-2R} = 101.6$$

This gives $R = 0.1081$ or 10.81 percent.

By continuing in this way, a complete term structure can be obtained. Spot rates for intermediate maturities are calculated using linear interpolation. In the example just considered, the 1.25-year spot rate would be $0.5 \times 10.54 + 0.5 \times 10.68 = 10.61\%$.

Theories of the Term Structure

A number of different theories of the term structure have been proposed. The simplest is the *expectations theory*. This conjectures that long-term interest rates should reflect expected future short-term interest rates. More precisely, it argues that a forward interest rate corresponding to a certain period is equal to the expected future spot interest rate for that period. Another theory is known as the *market segmentation theory*. This conjectures that there need be no relationship between short-, medium-, and long-term interest rates. Under the theory, different institutions invest in bonds of different maturity and do not switch maturities. The short-term interest rate is determined by supply and demand in the short-term bond market, the medium-term interest rate is determined by supply and demand in the medium-term bond market, and so on.

The theory that is in some ways most appealing is known as *liquidity preference theory*. This argues that forward rates should always be higher than expected future spot interest rates. The basic assumption underlying the theory is that investors prefer to preserve their liquidity and invest funds for short periods of time. Borrowers, on the other hand, usually prefer to borrow at fixed rates for long periods of time. If the interest rates offered by banks and other financial intermediaries were such that the forward rate equaled the expected future spot rate, long-term interest rates would equal the average of expected future short-term interest rates. In the absence of any incentive to do otherwise, investors would tend to deposit their funds for short time periods and borrowers would tend to choose to borrow for long time periods. Financial intermediaries would then find themselves financing substantial amounts of long-term fixed-rate loans with short-term deposits. This would involve excessive interest-rate risk. In practice, in order to match depositors with borrowers and avoid interest-rate risk, financial intermediaries raise long-term interest rates relative to expected future short-term interest rates. This reduces the demand for long-term fixed-rate borrowing and encourages investors to deposit their funds for long terms.

Liquidity preference theory leads to a situation in which forward rates are greater than expected future spot rates. It is also consistent with the empirical result that yield curves tend to be upward sloping more often than they are downward sloping.

TREASURY BOND AND TREASURY NOTE FUTURES

The most popular long-term interest rate futures contracts are the treasury bond and treasury note futures contracts traded on the CBOT. In the treasury bond contract, any government bond with more than 15 years to maturity and not callable within 15 years can be delivered. As will be explained later, the exchange has developed a procedure for adjusting the price received by the party with the short position according to the particular bond delivered.

In the treasury note futures contract, any government bond (or note) with a maturity between 6.5 and 10 years can be delivered. Again, there is a way of adjusting the price received by the party with the short position according to the particular note delivered.

The rest of our discussion will focus on treasury bond futures. However, treasury note contracts work in an analogous way to treasury bond contracts and most of the points made are equally applicable to both contracts.

Quotes

Treasury bond prices are quoted in dollars and thirty-seconds of a dollar. The quoted price is for a bond with a face value of $100. Thus, a quote of 90-05 means that the indicated price for a bond with a face value of $100,000 is $90,156.25.

The quoted price is not the same as the cash price that is paid by the purchaser. In general,

$$\text{Cash price} = \text{Quoted price} + \text{Accrued interest since last coupon date}$$

To illustrate this formula, suppose that it is March 5, 1994 and the bond under consideration is an 11 percent coupon bond maturing on July 10, 2010 with a quoted price of 95-16 (or $95.50). Since coupons are paid semiannually on government bonds, the most recent coupon date is January 10, 1994 and the next coupon date is July 10, 1994. The number of days between January 10, 1994 and March 5, 1994 is 54 while the number of days between January 10, 1994 and July 10, 1994 is 181. On $100 face value of bonds, the coupon payment is $5.50 on January 10 and July 10. The accrued interest on March 5, 1994 is the share of the July 10 coupon accruing to the bondholder on March 5, 1994 and is calculated as

$$\frac{54}{181} \times \$5.5 = \$1.64$$

The cash price per $100 face value for the July 10, 2010 bond is, therefore,

$$\$95.5 + \$1.64 = \$97.14$$

The cash price of a $100,000 bond is, therefore, $97,140.

Table 5.3 shows quotes for interest-rate futures contracts as they appeared in *The Wall Street Journal* on August 12, 1993. Treasury bond futures prices are quoted in the same way as the treasury bond prices themselves. Table 5.3 shows

Table 5.3 Interest Rate Futures Quotes from *The Wall Street Journal* on August 12, 1993

INTEREST RATE

TREASURY BONDS (CBT) – $100,000; pts. 32nds of 100%

	Open	High	Low	Settle	Chg	Yield Settle	Yield Chg	Open Interest
Sept	116-04	116-15	115-28	116-08	+ 5	6.533	– .012	305,673
Dec	114-31	115-11	114-24	115-04	+ 5	6.624	.013	41,232
Mr94	113-24	114-08	113-24	114-02	+ 6	6.712	– .016	11,657
June	112-22	113-06	112-22	113-04	+ 8	6.791	– .021	2,351
Sept	111-27	112-11	111-27	112-11	+ 11	6.857	– .029	3,873
Dec	111-02	111-28	111-02	111-24	+ 18	6.907	– .049	3,302
Mr95	....	....	....	111-06	+ 23	6.957	– .062	45

Est vol 200,000; vol Tues 210,621; op int 368,190, +1,431.

TREASURY BONDS (MCE) – $50,000; pts. 32nds of 100%

	Open	High	Low	Settle	Chg	Yield Settle	Yield Chg	Open Interest
Sept	115-31	116-15	115-28	116-08	+ 5	6.533	– .012	10,084
Dec	114-25	115-10	114-25	115-04	+ 5	6.624	– .013	95

Est vol 3,100; vol Tues 2,557; open int 10,189, –108.

TREASURY NOTES (CBT) – $100,000; pts. 32nds of 100%

	Open	High	Low	Settle	Chg	Yield Settle	Yield Chg	Open Interest
Sept	113-10	113-19	113-06	113-16	+ 5	6.171	– .019	209,481
Dec	112-06	112-18	112-06	112-16	+ 5	6.296	– .020	30,025
Mr94	111-09	111-19	111-09	111-19	+ 5	6.412	– .020	890

Est vol 67,890; vol Tues 44,248; open int 240,424, +1,283.

5 YR TREAS NOTES (CBT) – $100,000; pts. 32nds of 100%

	Open	High	Low	Settle	Chg	Yield Settle	Yield Chg	Open Interest
Sept	11-155	111-19	11-125	11-165	+ 1½	5.345	– .010	143,324
Dec	110-21	10-255	110-20	10-235	+ 1	5.515	– .007	15,261

Est vol 25,600; vol Tues 23,168; open int 158,585, –1,709.

2 YR TREAS NOTES (CBT) – $200,000, pts. 32nds of 100%

	Open	High	Low	Settle	Chg	Yield Settle	Yield Chg	Open Interest
Sept	106-20	06-217	106-19	106-21	+ 5	4.483	– .008	17,132
Dec	06-052	106-06	06-052	06-057	+ 5	4.726	– .007	4,221

Est vol 1,800; vol Tues 1,770; open int 21,353, +694.

30-DAY FEDERAL FUNDS (CBT)-$5 million; pts. of 100%

	Open	High	Low	Settle	Chg	Yield Settle	Yield Chg	Open Interest
Aug	96.94	96.94	96.94	96.94	– .01	3.06	+ .01	2,791
Sept	96.91	96.92	96.91	96.91	....	3.09	....	2,797
Oct	96.88	96.90	96.88	96.90	+ .01	3.10	– .01	1,584
Nov	....	....	....	96.83	+ .01	3.17	– .01	1,524
Dec	....	....	....	96.64	+ .01	3.36	– .01	273

Est vol 444; vol Tues 176; open int 9,102, –118.

TREASURY BILLS (CME) – $1 mil.; pts. of 100%

	Open	High	Low	Settle	Chg	Discount Settle	Discount Chg	Open Interest
Sept	96.92	96.94	96.91	96.93	+ .01	3.07	– .01	22,205
Dec	96.70	96.73	96.69	96.72	+ .01	3.28	– .01	9,630
Mr94	96.56	96.57	96.54	96.56	+ .01	3.46	– .01	1,989

Est vol 1,860; vol Tues 1,329; open int 33,841, –319.

LIBOR-1 MO. (CME) – $3,000,000; points of 100%

	Open	High	Low	Settle	Chg	Discount Settle	Discount Chg	Open Interest
Aug	96.82	96.83	96.81	96.83	+ .01	3.17	– .01	17,841
Sep	96.78	96.80	96.77	96.79	+ .01	3.21	– .01	6,980
Oct	96.72	96.74	96.72	96.73	+ .01	3.27	– .01	2,513
Nov	96.66	96.67	96.66	96.66	....	3.34	....	2,113
Dec	96.04	96.04	96.03	96.94	....	3.06	....	2,080
Ja94	....	....	....	96.51	....	3.49	....	271
Mar	....	....	....	96.32	....	3.68	....	453

Est vol 3,666; vol Tues 2,057; open int 32,251, +29.

MUNI BOND INDEX (CBT)-$1,000; times Bond Buyer MBI

	Open	High	Low	Settle	Chg	High	Low	Open Interest
Sept	103-02	103-24	103-00	103-17	+ 14	102-28	96-00	22,772
Dec	102-04	102-28	102-04	102-21	+ 15	101-25	97-18	1,445

Est vol 4,500; vol Tues 3,602; open int 24,218, +559.
The index: Close 103-09; Yield 5.70.

EURODOLLAR (CME) – $1 million; pts of 100%

	Open	High	Low	Settle	Chg	Yield Settle	Yield Chg	Open Interest
Sept	96.68	96.69	96.66	96.67	....	3.33	....	293,630
Dec	96.27	96.30	96.26	96.28	....	3.72	....	334,333
Mr94	96.19	96.21	96.17	96.20	....	3.80	....	255,359
June	95.91	95.94	95.89	95.92	....	4.08	....	175,046
Sept	95.61	95.65	95.59	95.62	....	4.38	....	150,330
Dec	95.17	95.20	95.15	95.18	....	4.82	....	109,631
Mr95	95.07	95.10	95.05	95.08	....	4.92	....	110,460
June	94.86	94.89	94.84	94.87	....	5.13	....	74,993
Sept	94.67	94.72	94.66	94.70	+ .01	5.30	– .01	61,993
Dec	94.37	94.42	94.36	94.40	+ .01	5.60	– .01	60,610
Mr96	94.33	94.38	94.32	94.36	+ .01	5.64	– .01	53,912
June	94.15	94.20	94.14	94.19	+ .02	5.81	– .02	39,199
Sept	94.02	94.07	94.01	94.06	+ .02	5.94	– .02	33,914
Dec	93.78	93.83	93.77	93.82	+ .02	6.18	– .02	30,982
Mr97	93.78	93.83	93.77	93.82	+ .02	6.18	– .02	24,885
June	93.65	93.70	93.64	93.69	+ .02	6.31	– .02	21,329
Sept	93.55	93.60	93.55	93.59	+ .02	6.41	– .02	17,036
Dec	93.34	93.40	93.34	93.38	+ .02	6.62	– .02	13,833
Mr98	93.36	93.41	93.36	93.40	+ .02	6.60	– .02	12,826
June	93.28	93.33	93.28	93.32	+ .02	6.68	– .02	8,356

Est vol 138,739; vol Tues 154,110; open int 1,882,857, +1,277.

EURODOLLAR (LIFFE) – $1 million; pts of 100%

	Open	High	Low	Settle	Change	Lifetime High	Lifetime Low	Open Interest
Sept	96.67	96.68	96.67	96.67	....	96.76	92.50	5,808
Dec	96.29	96.29	96.26	96.28	....	96.70	92.24	4,871
Mr94	96.18	96.18	96.18	96.18	– .02	96.30	92.20	1,951
June	95.90	95.90	95.90	95.91	– .01	95.98	93.36	743
Sept	....	....	....	95.60	– .02	95.62	93.76	174

Est vol 803; vol Tues 502; open int 13,685, –112.

STERLING (LIFFE) – £500,000; pts of 100%

	Open	High	Low	Settle	Change	Lifetime High	Lifetime Low	Open Interest
Sept	94.21	94.27	94.19	94.27	+ .06	94.94	87.20	83,895
Dec	94.68	94.77	94.68	94.75	+ .08	94.85	88.95	104,000
Mr94	94.74	94.82	94.74	94.80	+ .08	94.82	89.87	60,546
June	94.64	94.70	94.64	94.70	+ .08	94.70	89.78	47,925
Sept	94.42	94.50	94.42	94.48	+ .08	94.50	90.10	23,825
Dec	94.20	94.23	94.19	94.23	+ .08	94.23	90.10	17,438
Mr95	93.94	93.97	93.92	93.97	+ .06	93.97	90.70	12,366
June	93.70	93.73	93.65	93.72	+ .08	93.73	91.73	6,664
Sept	93.47	93.48	93.45	93.47	+ .05	93.48	91.65	6,465
Dec	93.19	93.23	93.18	93.23	+ .09	93.23	92.25	6,533

Est vol 46,636; vol Tues 31,676; open int 369,657, +1,447.

LONG GILT (LIFFE) – £50,000; 32nds of 100%

	Open	High	Low	Settle	Change	Lifetime High	Lifetime Low	Open Interest
Sept	112-09	113-05	112-06	112-29	+ 0-28	113-05	102-06	89,754
Dec	111-16	112-07	111-16	112-05	+ 0-28	112-07	103-30	3,686

Est vol 67,383; vol Tues 59,980; open int 93,440, +1,982.

EUROMARK (LIFFE) – DM 1,000,000; pts of 100%

	Open	High	Low	Settle	Change	Lifetime High	Lifetime Low	Open Interest
Sept	93.49	93.55	93.48	93.53	+ .06	94.49	91.12	180,805
Dec	94.06	94.10	94.05	94.09	+ .05	94.62	91.31	168,485
Mr94	94.56	94.60	94.55	94.58	+ .03	94.77	91.53	104,514
June	94.76	94.80	94.76	94.79	+ .03	94.80	91.71	73,452
Sept	94.83	94.85	94.83	94.84	+ .02	94.85	91.81	55,853
Dec	94.72	94.78	94.72	94.73	+ .01	94.78	91.83	45,769
Mr95	94.65	94.70	94.64	94.70	+ .07	94.70	92.45	26,565
June	94.50	94.59	94.50	94.59	+ 11	94.59	93.15	15,011
Sept	94.40	94.46	94.40	94.46	+ .10	94.46	93.62	5,584
Dec	94.20	94.28	94.20	94.27	+ .10	94.28	93.72	3,756

Est vol 73,440; vol Tues 65,159; open int 679,804, +1,202.

EUROSWISS (LIFFE) – SFr 1,000,000; pts of 100%

	Open	High	Low	Settle	Change	Lifetime High	Lifetime Low	Open Interest
Sept	95.43	95.48	95.41	95.47	+ .04	96.11	93.35	29,179
Dec	95.73	95.78	95.73	95.78	+ .03	96.11	94.83	14,592
Mr94	95.92	95.97	95.92	95.97	+ .02	96.16	95.49	6,201
June	95.94	95.94	95.94	95.94	+ .03	96.02	95.79	3,020

Est vol 4,313; vol Tues 7,343; open int 52,992, –687.

GERMAN GOV'T. BOND (LIFFE)
250,000 marks; pts of 100%

	Open	High	Low	Settle	Change	Lifetime High	Lifetime Low	Open Interest
Sept	97.38	97.60	97.36	97.42	+ .07	104.15	91.65	165,157
Dec	97.57	97.69	97.52	97.56	+ .07	103.75	94.93	40,128

Est vol 82,735; vol Tues 63,295; open int 205,285, +1,982.

ITALIAN GOVT. BOND (LIFFE)
ITL 200,000,000; pts of 100%

	Open	High	Low	Settle	Change	Lifetime High	Lifetime Low	Open Interest
Sept	110.10	111.33	110.10	111.16	+ 1.27	111.33	95.45	54,798
Dec	109.95	110.90	109.95	110.68	+ 1.26	110.90	102.05	6,020

Est vol 28,308; vol Tues 18,380; open int 60,818, +1,130.

FT–SE 100 INDEX (LIFFE) – £25 per index point

	Open	High	Low	Settle	Change	Lifetime High	Lifetime Low	Open Interest
Sept	2981.	3023.	2976.	3019.	+ 36.0	3023.	2634.	49,162
Dec	3003.	3038.5	3003.	3039.	+ 36.0	3038.5	2804.	5,355
Mr94	....	....	....	3053.	+ 36.0	2980.	2873.	321

Est vol 11,285; vol Tues 6,860; open int 54,838, +783.

that the settlement price for the September 1993 contract on August 11, 1993 was 116-08 or $116\frac{1}{4}$. One contract involves the delivery of $100,000 face value of the bond. Thus, a $1 change in the quoted futures price would lead to a $1,000 change in the value of the futures contract. Delivery can take place at any time during the delivery month.

Conversion Factors

As mentioned, there is a provision in the treasury bond futures contract for the party with the short position to choose to deliver any bond with a maturity over 15 years and not callable within 15 years. When a particular bond is delivered, a parameter known as its *conversion factor* defines the price received by the party with the short position. The quoted price applicable to the delivery is the product of the conversion factor and the quoted futures price. Taking accrued interest into account, we have the following relationship for each $100 face value of the bond delivered:

$$\begin{array}{c}\text{Cash received by party}\\ \text{with short position}\end{array} = \begin{array}{c}\text{Quoted futures}\\ \text{price}\end{array} \times \begin{array}{c}\text{Conversion factor}\\ \text{for bond delivered}\end{array} + \begin{array}{c}\text{Accrued interest}\\ \text{on bond delivered}\end{array}$$

Each contract is for the delivery of $100,000 face value of bonds. Suppose the quoted futures price is 90-00, the conversion factor for the bond delivered is 1.3800, and the accrued interest on this bond at the time of delivery is $3.00 per $100 face value. The cash received by the party with the short position (and paid by the party with the long position) is then

$$(1.38 \times 90.00) + 3.00 = \$127.20$$

per $100 face value. A party with the short position in one contract would deliver bonds with face value of $100,000 and receive $127,200.

The conversion factor for a bond is equal to the value of the bond on the first day of the delivery month on the assumption that the interest rate for all maturities equals 8 percent per annum (with semiannual compounding). The bond maturity and the times to the coupon payment dates are rounded down to the nearest three months for the purposes of the calculation. This enables the CBOT to produce comprehensive tables. If after rounding, the bond lasts for an exact number of half years, the first coupon is assumed to be paid in six months. If after rounding, the bond does not last for an exact number of six months (i.e., there is an extra three months), the first coupon is assumed to be paid after three months and accrued interest is subtracted.

Examples

1. Consider a 14 percent coupon bond with 20 years and two months to maturity. For the purposes of calculating the conversion factor, the bond is assumed to have exactly 20 years to maturity. The first coupon payment

is assumed to be made after six months. Coupon payments are then assumed to be made at six-month intervals until the end of the 20 years when the principal payment is made. We will work in terms of a $100 face value bond. On the assumption that the discount rate is 8 percent per annum with semiannual compounding (or 4 percent per six months), the value of the bond is

$$\sum_{i=1}^{40} \frac{7}{1.04^i} + \frac{100}{1.04^{40}} = 159.38$$

Dividing by the face value, the credit conversion factor is 1.5938.

2. Consider a 14 percent coupon bond with 18 years and four months to maturity. For the purposes of calculating the conversion factor, the bond is assumed to have exactly 18 years and three months to maturity. Discounting all the payments back to a point in time three months from today gives a value of

$$\sum_{i=0}^{36} \frac{7}{1.04^i} + \frac{100}{1.04^{36}} = 163.73$$

The interest rate for a three-month period is $\sqrt{1.04} - 1$ or 1.9804 percent. Hence, discounting back to the present gives the bond's value as 163.73/1.019804 = 160.55. Subtracting the accrued interest of 3.5, this becomes 157.05. The conversion factor is, therefore, 1.5705.

Cheapest-to-Deliver Bond

At any given time, there are about 30 bonds that can be delivered in the CBOT treasury bond futures contract. These vary widely as far as coupon and maturity are concerned. The party with the short position can choose which of the available bonds is "cheapest" to deliver. Since the party with the short position receives

$$(\text{Quoted futures price} \times \text{Conversion factor}) + \text{Accrued interest}$$

and the cost of purchasing a bond is

$$\text{Quoted price} + \text{Accrued interest}$$

the cheapest-to-deliver bond is the one for which

$$\text{Quoted price} - \left(\text{Quoted futures price} \times \text{Conversion factor}\right)$$

is least. This can be found by examining each of the bonds in turn.

Table 5.4 Deliverable Bonds in Example

BOND	*QUOTED PRICE*	*CONVERSION FACTOR*
1	99.50	1.0382
2	143.50	1.5188
3	119.75	1.2615

Example

The party with the short position has decided to deliver and is trying to choose between the three bonds in Table 5.4. Assume the current quoted futures price is 93-08 or 93.25. The cost of delivering each of the bonds is as follows:

$$\text{Bond 1: } 99.50 - (93.25 \times 1.0382) = 2.69$$

$$\text{Bond 2: } 143.50 - (93.25 \times 1.5188) = 1.87$$

$$\text{Bond 3: } 119.75 - (93.25 \times 1.2615) = 2.12$$

The cheapest-to-deliver bond is bond 2.

A number of factors determine the cheapest-to-deliver bond. When yields are in excess of 8 percent, there is a tendency for the conversion factor system to favor the delivery of low coupon long-maturity bonds. When yields are less than 8 percent, there is a tendency for it to favor the delivery of high-coupon, short-maturity bonds. Also, when the yield curve is upward sloping, there is a tendency for bonds with a long time to maturity to be favored, whereas when it is downward sloping, there is a tendency for bonds with a short time to maturity to be delivered. Finally, some bonds tend to sell for more than their theoretical value. Examples are low-coupon bonds and bonds where the coupons can be stripped from the interest. These bonds are unlikely to prove to be cheapest to deliver in any circumstances.

The Wild Card Play

Trading in the CBOT treasury bond futures contract ceases at 2 p.m. (Chicago time). However, treasury bonds themselves continue trading until 4 p.m. Furthermore, the party with the short position has until 8 p.m. to issue to the clearinghouse a notice of intention to deliver. If the notice is issued, the invoice price is calculated on the basis of the settlement price that day. This is the price at which trading was being done just before the bell at 2 p.m.

This gives the party with the short position an option known as the *wild card play*. If bond prices decline after 2 p.m., he or she can issue a notice of intention to deliver and proceed to buy cheapest-to-deliver bonds in preparation for delivery. If the bond price does not decline, the party with the short position keeps the position open and waits until the next day when the same strategy can be used.

Like the other options open to the party with the short position, the wild card option is not free. Its value is reflected in the futures price, which is lower than it would be without the option.

Determining the Futures Price

An exact theoretical futures price for the treasury bond contract is difficult to determine because the short party's options concerned with the timing of delivery and choice of the bond that is delivered cannot easily be valued. However, if we assume that both the cheapest-to-deliver bond and the delivery date are known, the treasury bond futures contract is a futures contract on a security providing the holder with known income. Equation (3.6) from Chapter 3 then shows that futures price, F, is related to the spot price, S, by

$$F = (S - I)e^{rT} \tag{5.2}$$

where I is the present value of the coupons during the life of the futures contract, T is the time until the futures contract matures, and r is the risk-free interest rate applicable to a time period of length T.

In Equation (5.2), F is the cash futures price and S is the cash bond price. The correct procedure is, therefore, as follows:

1. Calculate cash price of the cheapest-to-deliver bond from quoted price.
2. Calculate cash futures price from cash bond price using Equation (5.2).
3. Calculate the quoted futures price from the cash futures price.
4. Divide the quoted futures price by the conversion factor to allow for difference between the cheapest-to-deliver bond and the standard 15-year 8 percent bond.

The procedure is best illustrated with an example.

Example

Suppose that in a treasury bond futures contract, it is known that the cheapest-to-deliver bond will be a 12 percent coupon bond with a conversion factor of 1.4000. Suppose also that it is known that delivery will take place in 270 days. Coupons are payable semiannually on the bond. As illustrated in Figure 5.4, the last coupon date was 60 days ago, the next coupon date is in 122 days, and the next-but-one coupon date is in 305 days. The term structure is flat and the rate of interest (with continuous compounding) is 10 percent per annum. We assume that the current quoted bond price is \$120. The cash price of the bond is obtained by adding to this quoted price

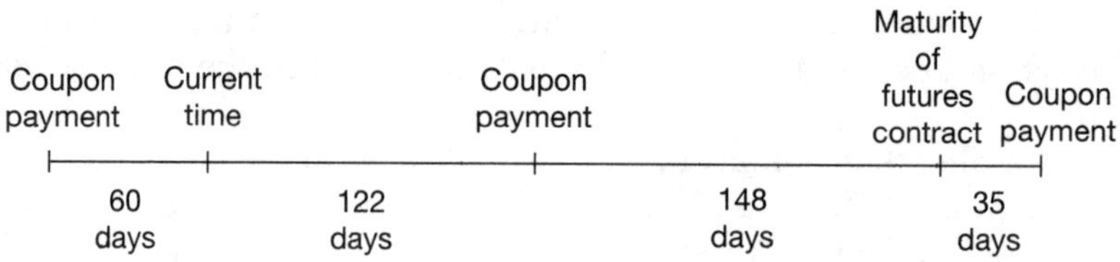

Figure 5.4 Time chart for Example.

the proportion of the next coupon payment that accrues to the holder. The cash price is, therefore,

$$120 + \frac{60}{182} \times 6 = 121.978$$

A coupon of 6 will be received after 122 days (= 0.3342 year). The present value of this is

$$6e^{-0.3342 \times 0.1} = 5.803$$

The futures contract lasts for 270 days (= 0.7397 year). The cash futures price if the contract were written on the 12 percent bond would, therefore, be

$$(121.978 - 5.803)e^{0.7397 \times 0.1} = 125.094$$

At delivery, there are 148 days of accrued interest. The quoted futures price if the contract were written on the 12 percent bond would, therefore, be

$$125.094 - 6 \times \frac{148}{183} = 120.242$$

The contract is in fact written on a standard 8 percent bond, and 1.4000 standard bonds are considered equivalent to each 12 percent bond. The quoted futures price should, therefore, be

$$\frac{120.242}{1.4000} = 85.887$$

TREASURY BILL AND EURODOLLAR FUTURES

Two of the most popular short-term interest rate contracts are the treasury bill and Eurodollar futures contracts traded on the CME.

Treasury Bill Futures

In the treasury bill futures contract, the underlying asset is a 90-day treasury bill. Under the terms of the contract, the party with the short position must deliver $1 million of treasury bills on any of three successive business days. The first delivery day is the first day of the delivery month on which a 13-week treasury bill is issued and a one-year treasury bill has 13 weeks remaining to maturity. In practice this means that the treasury bill may have 89 or 90 or 91 days to expiration when it is delivered.

A treasury bill is what is known as a *discount instrument*. It pays no coupons, and the investor receives the face value at maturity. Prior to maturity of the futures contract, the underlying asset is a treasury bill with a maturity longer than 90 days. For example, if the futures contract matures in 160 days, the underlying asset is a 250-day treasury bill.

To present a general analysis, we suppose that the futures contract matures in T years and the treasury bill underlying the futures contract matures in T^* years. (The difference between T^* and T is 90 days.) We suppose further that r and r^* are the continuously compounded interest rates for risk-free investments maturing at times T and T^*, respectively. Assuming the treasury bill underlying the futures contract has a face value of \$100, its current value, V^* is given by

$$V^* = 100e^{-r^*T^*}$$

Since no income is paid on the instrument, we know from Equation (3.5) that the futures price, F, is e^{rT} times this; that is,

$$F = 100e^{-r^*T^*}e^{rT} = 100e^{rT-r^*T^*} \tag{5.3}$$

From Equation (5.1), this reduces to

$$F = 100e^{-\hat{r}(T^*-T)}$$

where $\hat{r}$ is the forward rate for the time period between T and T^*. This expression shows that the futures price of a treasury bill is the price it will have if the 90-day interest rate on the delivery date proves to be equal to the current forward rate. Suppose that V is the price of a treasury bill maturing at time T so that

$$V = 100e^{-rT} \tag{5.4}$$

From Equation (5.3), another expression for F is

$$F = 100\frac{V^*}{V} \tag{5.5}$$

Implied Repo Rates

The repo rate was mentioned in Chapter 3. It is the rate of interest at which an investor can borrow by selling securities to a financial institution and agreeing to buy them back later. It is also the rate of interest at which financial institutions can lend without risk. The repo rate is generally close to the treasury bill rate. In testing for arbitrage opportunities in the treasury bill market, traders frequently calculate what is known as the *implied repo rate*. This is the rate of interest on a short-term treasury bill implied by

1. The treasury bill futures price for a contract maturing at the same time as the short-term treasury bill.
2. The price of a treasury bill maturing 90 days later than the short-term treasury bill.

Using the preceding notation, it is the T-year rate of interest implied by V^* and F. From Equation (5.5),

$$V = 100\frac{V^*}{F}$$

Substituting into Equation (5.4) and solving for r, the implied repo rate with continuous compounding is as follows

$$\text{Implied repo rate} = \frac{1}{T}\ln\left(\frac{F}{V^*}\right)$$

If the yield on a treasury bill lasting for time T is different from this, there are arbitrage opportunities.

Arbitrage Based on the Implied Repo Rate

We will illustrate these arbitrage opportunities by considering a situation where the cash price (per \$100 face value) of a treasury bill maturing in 146 days is \$95.21 and the cash futures price for a 90-day treasury bill futures contract maturing in 56 days is \$96.95. In this case $T = 56/365 = 0.1534$ and the implied repo rate is

$$\frac{1}{0.1534}\ln\left(\frac{96.95}{95.21}\right) = 0.1180$$

or 11.80 percent per annum with continuous compounding.

If the 56-day treasury bill rate is less than 11.80 percent per annum, a trader can

1. Borrow 56-day money at the treasury bill rate using a repo.
2. Short the futures.
3. Buy 146-day treasury bills.

At the end of the 56-day period, the trader delivers the treasury bills under the terms of the futures contract, repays the loan, and is left with a profit. Suppose, for example, that the 56-day treasury bill rate with continuous compounding is

11 percent per annum. A trader could borrow $952,100 for 56 days at 11 percent per annum, short one futures contract, and buy 146-day treasury bills with a face value of $1,000,000. At the end of 56 days, the treasury bills are delivered for $969,500. Of this $952{,}100e^{0.1534 \times 0.11} = \$968{,}302$ is used to repay the loan. The remaining $1,198 is profit.

If the actual 56-day treasury bill rate is greater than 11.80 percent per annum, a trader can

1. Borrow 146-day money at the treasury bill rate using a repo.
2. Buy 56-day treasury bills.
3. Go long futures.

At the end of the 56-day period, the trader takes delivery of the treasury bills. These are held to maturity, and the proceeds are used to repay the loan. Suppose, for example, that the 56-day treasury bill rate is 12.5 percent per annum with continuous compounding. The 146-day treasury bill rate is (365/146) ln (100/95.21) = 0.1227 or 12.27 percent per annum. A trader can borrow $969{,}500e^{-0.1534 \times 0.125} = \$951{,}087$ at this rate for 146 days, invest the money in 56-day treasury bills, and buy one futures contract. The proceeds of the investment are $969,500—just enough to take delivery of the treasury bill under the terms of the futures contract. The treasury bill is worth $1,000,000 in 146 days. An amount $951{,}087e^{0.1227 \times 146/365} = \$998{,}931$ of this $1,000,000 is required to repay the loan. The remaining $1,069 is profit.

This example assumes that a repo can be negotiated for as long as 146 days. In practice this is difficult. Nevertheless, implied repo rates are regularly calculated by traders and used as indicators of situations where an arbitrage opportunity might exist. In practice a trader may have to borrow using a short-term repo and take a chance that the repo can be rolled over at interest rates that are not too unfavorable.

Quoted Prices

Treasury bill price quotes are for a treasury bill with a face value of $100. There is a difference between the cash price and quoted price for a treasury bill. If Y is the cash price of a treasury bill that has a face value of $100 and n days to maturity, the quoted price is

$$\frac{360}{n}(100 - Y)$$

This is referred to as the *discount rate*. It is the annualized dollar return provided by the treasury bill expressed as a percentage of the face value. If for a 90-day treasury bill the cash price, Y, were 98, the quoted price would be 8.00.

The discount rate is not the same as the rate of return earned on the treasury bill. The latter is calculated as the dollar return divided by the cost. In the preceding example, where the quoted price is 8.00, the rate of return would be 2/98 or 2.04 percent per 90 days. This amounts to

$$\frac{2}{98} \times \frac{365}{90} = 0.0828$$

or 8.28 percent per annum with compounding every 90 days.[1] This rate of return is sometimes referred to as the *bond equivalent yield*.

A 90-day treasury bill futures contract is for delivery of \$1 million of treasury bills. Treasury bill futures prices are not quoted in the same way as the prices of treasury bills themselves. The following relationship is used:[2]

$$\begin{array}{c}\text{Treasury bill futures}\\ \text{price quote}\end{array} = 100 - \begin{array}{c}\text{Corresponding treasury bill}\\ \text{price quote}\end{array}$$

If Z is the quoted futures price and Y is the corresponding price that would be paid for delivery of \$100 of 90-day treasury bills, this means that

$$Z = 100 - 4(100 - Y)$$

or, equivalently,

$$Y = 100 - 0.25(100 - Z)$$

Thus, the closing quote of 96.93 for September 1993 treasury bills in Table 5.3 corresponds to a price of 100 − 0.25(100 − 96.93) = \$99.2325 per \$100 of 90-day treasury bills or a contract price of \$992,325.

If the treasury bills that are delivered have 89 days to maturity, the price received is calculated by replacing the 0.25 in the preceding formula for Y by 89/360 or 0.2472. If they have 91 days to maturity, the 0.25 in the formula becomes 91/360 or 0.2528.

Example

Suppose that the 140-day interest rate is 8 percent per annum and the 230-day rate is 8.25 percent per annum with continuous compounding being used for both rates. The forward rate for the time period between day 140 and day 230 is

$$\frac{0.0825 \times 230 - 0.08 \times 140}{90} = 0.0864$$

[1] It is interesting to note that the compounding frequency used when the yield on a money-market instrument such as a treasury bill is quoted is generally equal to the life of the instrument. This means that the quoted yields on money-market instruments of different maturities are not directly comparable.

[2] The reason for quoting treasury bill futures prices in this way is to ensure that the bid price is below the ask price.

or 8.64 percent. Since 90 days = 0.2466 year, the futures price for $100 of 90-day treasury bills deliverable in 140 days is

$$100e^{-0.0864 \times 0.2466} = 97.89$$

This would be quoted as 100 − 4(100 − 97.89) = 91.56.

Eurodollar Futures

The Eurodollar futures contract is the most successful of the short-term interest rate futures contracts. It is traded on the Chicago Mercantile Exchange (CME) and the London International Financial Futures Exchange (LIFFE). A Eurodollar is a dollar deposited in a U.S. or foreign bank outside the United States. The Eurodollar interest rate is the rate of interest earned on Eurodollars deposited by one bank with another bank and is also known as the 3-month London Interbank Offer Rate (LIBOR). Eurodollar interest rates are generally higher than the corresponding Treasury bill interest rates. This is because the Eurodollar interest rate is a commercial lending rate whereas the Treasury bill rate is the rate at which governments borrow.

On the surface, a Eurodollar futures contract appears to be structurally the same as the Treasury bill futures contract. The formula for calculating the value of one contract from the quoted futures price is the same as the formula used for Treasury bill futures. The quote of 96.67 for the September contract in Table 5.3 corresponds to a Eurodollar interest rate quote of 3.33 percent per annum and a contract price of

$$10{,}000[100 - 0.25(100 - 96.67)] = \$991{,}675$$

However, there are some important differences between the Treasury bill and Eurodollar futures contracts. For a Treasury bill futures, the contract price converges at maturity to the price of a 90-day $1 million face value Treasury bill and, if a contract is held until maturity, this is the instrument delivered. A Eurodollar futures contract is settled in cash on the second London business day before the third Wednesday of the month. The final marking to market sets the contract price equal to

$$10{,}000(100 - 0.25R)$$

where R is the quoted Eurodollar rate at that time. This quoted Eurodollar rate is the actual 90-day rate on Eurodollar deposits with quarterly compounding. It is not a discount rate. The Eurodollar futures contract is therefore a futures contract on an interest rate, whereas the Treasury bill futures contract is a futures contract on the price of a Treasury bill.

DURATION

Duration is an important concept in the use of interest-rate futures for hedging. The *duration* of a bond is a measure of how long on average the holder of the bond has to wait before receiving cash payments. A zero-coupon bond that matures in n years has a duration of n years. However, a coupon-bearing bond maturing in n years has a duration of less than n years. This is because some of the cash payments are received by the holder prior to year n.

Suppose that a bond provides the holder with payments c_i at time t_i $(1 \leq i \leq n)$. The price B and yield y (continuously compounded) are related by

$$B = \sum_{i=1}^{n} c_i e^{-yt_i} \tag{5.6}$$

The duration, D, of the bond is defined as

$$D = \frac{\sum_{i=1}^{n} t_i c_i e^{-yt_i}}{B} \tag{5.7}$$

This can be written

$$D = \sum_{i=1}^{n} t_i \left[\frac{c_i e^{-yt_i}}{B}\right]$$

The term in square brackets is the ratio of the present value of the payment at time t_i to the bond price. The bond price is the present value of all payments. The duration is, therefore, a weighted average of the times when payments are made with the weight applied to time t_i being equal to the proportion of the bond's total present value provided by the payment at time t_i. The sum of the weights is 1.0.

From Equation (5.6), it can be shown that

$$\Delta B = -\Delta y \sum_{i=1}^{n} c_i t_i e^{-yt_i} \tag{5.8}$$

where Δy is a small change in y and ΔB is the corresponding small change in B. (Note that there is a negative relationship between B and y. When bond yields increase, bond prices decrease. When bond yields decrease, bond prices increase.) From Equations (5.7) and (5.8),

$$\Delta B = -BD\Delta y \tag{5.9}$$

This is an important equation that underlies most duration-based hedging schemes. It can also be written

$$\frac{\Delta B}{B} = -D\Delta y \tag{5.10}$$

showing that the percentage change in a bond price for a particular small change in the yield is proportional to its duration.

Table 5.5 Calculation of Duration

TIME	*PAYMENT*	*PRESENT VALUE*	*WEIGHT*	*TIME × WEIGHT*
0.5	5	4.709	0.050	0.025
1.0	5	4.435	0.047	0.047
1.5	5	4.176	0.044	0.066
2.0	5	3.933	0.042	0.084
2.5	5	3.704	0.039	0.098
3.0	105	73.256	0.778	2.334
Total	130	94.213	1.000	2.654

Example

Consider a three-year 10 percent coupon bond with a face value of \$100. Suppose that the yield on the bond is 12 percent per annum with continuous compounding. This means that $y = 0.12$. Coupon payments of \$5 are made every six months. Table 5.5 shows the calculations necessary to determine the bond's duration. The present values of the payments using the yield as the discount rate are shown in column 3. (For example, the present value of the first payment is $5e^{-0.12\times 0.5} = 4.709$.) The sum of the numbers in column 3 gives the bond's price as \$94.213. The weights are calculated by dividing the numbers in column 3 by 94.213. The sum of the numbers in column 5 gives the duration as 2.654 years. From Equation (5.9),

$$\Delta B = -94.213 \times 2.654\Delta y$$

that is,

$$\Delta B = -250.04\Delta y$$

If $\Delta y = +0.001$ so that y increases to 0.121, this formula indicates that we expect ΔB to be -0.25. In other words, we expect the bond price to go down to $94.213 - 0.250 = 93.963$. By recomputing the bond price for a yield of 12.1 percent, the reader can verify that this is indeed what happens.

The duration of a bond portfolio can be defined as a weighted average of the durations of the individual bonds in the portfolio with the weights being proportional to the bond prices. Equation (5.9) then applies to a portfolio of bonds as well as to individual bonds providing the yields of all bonds in the portfolio are assumed to change by the same amount.

The preceding analysis is based on the assumption that y is expressed with continuous compounding. If y is expressed with annual compounding, it can be shown that Equation (5.9) becomes

$$\Delta B = -\frac{BD\Delta y}{1 + y}$$

More generally if y is expressed with a compounding frequency of m times per year,

$$\Delta B = -\frac{BD\Delta y}{1 + y/m}$$

The expression

$$\frac{D}{1 + y/m}$$

is sometimes referred to as the *modified duration.*

Duration Matching and Convexity

A portfolio of fixed-income securities can be described in terms of its average duration. Financial institutions frequently try to match the average duration of their assets with the average duration of their liabilities. (The liabilities can be regarded as short positions in bonds.) This is known as *duration matching* or *portfolio immunization*. It is based on the assumption that the yield curve always exhibits parallel shifts. When the durations of assets and liabilities are matched, a small parallel shift in interest rates should have little effect on the whole portfolio. Equation (5.9) shows that the gain (loss) on the assets should offset the loss (gain) on the liabilities.

When moderate or large changes in interest rates are considered, a factor known as *convexity* is sometimes important. Figure 5.5 shows the relationship

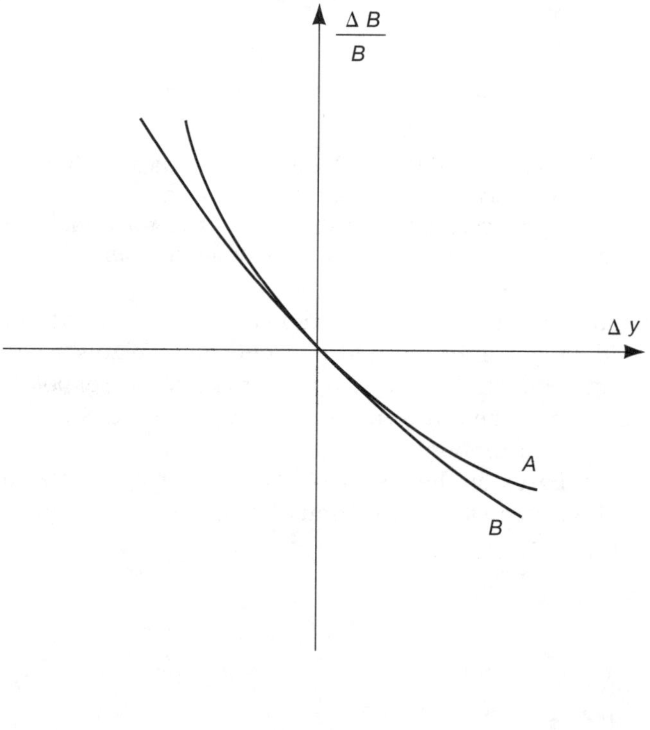

Figure 5.5 Bond portfolios with different convexity.

between the percentage change in value and change in yield for two portfolios having the same duration. The gradients of the two curves are the same for the current yield. This means that both portfolios change in value by the same percentage for small interest-rate changes and is consistent with Equation (5.10). For large interest-rate changes, the portfolios behave differently. Portfolio A has more convexity (or curvature) than portfolio B. Its value increases by a greater percentage amount than that of portfolio B when yields decline, and its value decreases by less than that of portfolio B when yields increase.

The convexity of a bond portfolio tends to be greatest when the portfolio provides payments evenly over a long period of time. It is least when the payments are concentrated around one particular point in time. For long positions in bond portfolios, it is clear from Figure 5.5 that a high-convexity portfolio with a certain duration is always more attractive than a low-convexity bond portfolio with the same duration. Not surprisingly, it is generally also more expensive.

DURATION-BASED HEDGING STRATEGIES

The general approach to hedging described in Chapter 4 required a historical analysis of the relationship between the change in the futures price and the change in the value of the asset being hedged. The optimal number of contracts, N^*, was given in Equation (4.3) by

$$N^* = \rho \frac{\sigma_S}{\sigma_F} \tag{5.11}$$

where σ_S and σ_F are the standard deviations of changes in the value of the asset position and changes in the futures contract price, respectively, and ρ is the coefficient of correlation between the two changes. This approach can be used when interest rate futures are used for hedging. However, the duration concept provides a useful alternative.

Consider the situation where a position in an interest-rate-dependent asset such as a bond portfolio or a money-market security is being hedged using an interest-rate futures contract. Define

F: contract price for the interest-rate futures contract
D_F: duration of asset underlying futures contract at expiration of the futures contract
S: value of asset being hedged
D_S: duration of asset being hedged at expiration of the hedge

We assume that the change in the yield, Δy, is the same for all maturities—which means that only parallel shifts in the yield curve can occur. From Equation (5.9)

$$\Delta S = -SD_S\Delta y \tag{5.12}$$

To a reasonable approximation, it is also true that

$$\Delta F = -FD_F\Delta y \tag{5.13}$$

Since the Δy's are assumed to be the same, $\rho = 1$ in Equation (5.11). From Equations (5.12) and (5.13), ΔS is always $(SD_S)/(FD_F)$ times ΔF. It follows that

$$\frac{\sigma_S}{\sigma_F} = \frac{SD_S}{FD_F}$$

and Equation (5.11) gives the optimal number of contracts to use for hedging as

$$N^* = \frac{SD_S}{FD_F} \tag{5.14}$$

This is the *duration-based hedge ratio*.[3] It is sometimes also called the *price sensitivity hedge ratio*. Using it has the effect of making the duration of the whole position zero.

Equation (5.14) is a useful result. However, the hedge to which it gives rise is by no means perfect. One reason for this is the assumption that Δy is the same for all yields. In practice, short-term yields are usually more volatile than, and are not closely correlated with, long-term yields. (Sometimes it even happens that short- and long-term yields move in opposite directions to each other.) As a result, hedge performance can be disappointing, particularly if there is a big difference between D_S and D_F. Another (less important) potential effect on the performance of the hedge is convexity. If the convexity of the asset underlying the futures contract is markedly different from the convexity of the asset being hedged, and there is a large change in interest rates, hedge performance may be worse than expected. Finally, it is worth noting that in order to calculate D_F, an assumption as what will be to the cheapest-to-deliver bond is necessary when treasury bond or treasury note futures contracts are used. If the duration of the cheapest-to-deliver bond changes, the optimal number of contracts also changes.

EXAMPLES

In this section, we give three examples of how the duration-based model can be used for interest-rate hedging. Generally, the hedger tries to choose the futures contract so that the duration of the underlying asset is as close as possible to the duration of the asset being hedged. Treasury bill and Eurodollar futures contracts

[3] If y is defined with annual compounding, Equation (5.14) becomes

$$h^* = [SD_S(1 + y_F)]/[FD_F(1 + y_S)]$$

where y_S and y_F are the yields on S and F. This is not the same as Equation (5.14) except when $y_S = y_F$. The reason for the difference is that the assumption that $\Delta y_S = \Delta y_F$ when yields are continuously compounded is not quite the same assumption as $\Delta y_S = \Delta y_F$ when yields are compounded once a year.

are, therefore, used for exposures to short-term interest rates while treasury bond and treasury note futures contracts are used for exposures to longer term rates.

When constructing hedges using interest-rate futures, it is important to bear in mind that interest rates and futures prices move in opposite directions. When interest rates go up, the price of the asset underlying the futures contract goes down. This, in turn, causes the futures price itself to go down. When interest rates go down, the reverse happens and the futures price goes up. This means that a company in the position where it will lose money if interest rates drop should hedge by taking a long futures position. Similarly, a company in the position where it will lose money if interest rates rise should hedge by taking a short futures position.

Hedging the Future Purchase of a Six-Month Treasury Bill

Suppose that on May 20, a corporate treasurer learns that $3.3 million will be received on August 5. The funds will be needed for a major capital investment the following February. The treasurer, therefore, plans to invest the funds in six-month treasury bills as soon as they are received. The current yield on six-month treasury bills, expressed with semiannual compounding, is 11.20 percent. The treasurer is concerned that this may decline between May 20 and August 5 and decides to hedge using treasury bill futures. The quoted price for the September treasury bill futures contract is 89.44.

In this case, the company will lose money if interest rates go down. A long hedge is therefore required. If interest rates do go down, the treasury bill price will go up and a gain will be made on the futures position.

To calculate the number of treasury bill futures contracts that should be purchased, we note that the asset underlying the futures contract lasts for three months. Since it is a discount instrument, its duration is also three months or 0.25 years. Similarly, the six-month treasury bill investment planned by the treasurer has a duration of six months or 0.50 years. Each treasury bill futures contract is for the delivery of $1 million of treasury bills. The contract price is

$$10{,}000[100 - 0.25(100 - 89.44)] = \$973{,}600$$

The number of contracts that should be purchased is, using Equation (5.14),

$$\frac{3{,}300{,}000}{973{,}600} \times \frac{0.5}{0.25} = 6.78$$

Rounding to the nearest whole number, the treasurer should purchase seven contracts.

Between May 20 and August 5, the treasurer's worst fears were realized and the yield on six-month treasury bills (with semiannual compounding) declined by 1.40 percent per annum from 11.20 percent per annum to 9.80 percent per annum. This cost the treasurer $\$3{,}300{,}000 \times 0.014 \times 0.5 = \$23{,}100$ in lost interest.

Table 5.6 Hedging the Future Purchase of a Six-Month Treasury Bill

From the Trader's Desk—May 20

A corporate treasurer has just learned that $3.3 million will be received on August 5. The treasurer plans to invest the money in six-month treasury bills and would like to hedge against a reduction in interest rates.

Quotes:

1. The six-month treasury bill yield, expressed with semiannual compounding, is 11.20 percent per annum.
2. The quoted price for the September treasury bill futures contract is 89.44. This corresponds to a contract price of $973,600.

The Strategy

1. Take a long position in seven September treasury bill futures contracts on May 20.
2. Close out the position on August 5.

The Result

The yield on six-month treasury bills, expressed with semiannual compounding, declined from 11.20 percent per annum to 9.80 percent per annum between May 20 and August 5. This cost the treasurer $3,300,000 × 0.014 × 0.5 = $23,100 in interest.

The price quoted for the September treasury bill futures contract was 90.56 on August 5. This corresponds to a contract price of $976,400. The gain on the futures contract was, therefore, 7 × ($976,400 − $973,600) = $19,600

When invested for six months at 9.80 percent, the gain grew to $20,560. The company was, therefore, only $23,100 − $20,560 = $2,540 worse off than it would have been if interest rates had remained unchanged between May 20 and August 5.

The price quote for the September treasury bill futures contract was 90.56 on August 5. This corresponds to a contract price of $976,400. The gain on the futures contract was, therefore, 7 × ($976,400 − $973,600) = $19,600. When invested for six months at 9.80 percent per annum, this gain grew to $20,560. The company, therefore, lost only $23,100 − $20,560 = $2,540 relative to the position it would have been in if the interest rate had remained unchanged between May 20 and August 5. The effective rate of interest earned on the six-month investment was

$$0.098 + \frac{20{,}560 \times 2}{3{,}330{,}000} = 0.1105$$

or 11.05 percent per annum. This example is summarized in Table 5.6.

Hedging a Bond Portfolio

For our next example, we suppose it is August 2. A fund manager has $10 million invested in government bonds and is concerned that interest rates are expected to be highly volatile over the next three months. The fund manager decides to use the December treasury bond futures contract to hedge the value of the portfolio. The current futures price is 93-02 or 93.0625. Since each contract is for the delivery of $100,000 face value of bonds, the futures contract price is $93,062.50.

The average duration of the bond portfolio in three months will be 6.80 years. The cheapest-to-deliver bond in the treasury bond contract is expected to be a 20-year, 12 percent per annum coupon bond. The yield on this bond is currently 8.80 percent per annum, and the duration will be 9.20 years at maturity of the futures contract.

The fund manager requires a short position in treasury bond futures to hedge the bond portfolio. If interest rates go up, a gain will be made on the short futures position and a loss will be made on the bond portfolio. If interest rates decrease, a loss will be made on the short position, but there will be a gain on the bond portfolio. The number of bond futures contracts that should be shorted can be calculated from Equation (5.14) as

$$\frac{10{,}000{,}000}{93{,}062.50} \times \frac{6.80}{9.20} = 79.42$$

Rounding to the nearest whole number, the portfolio manager should short 79 contracts.

During the period August 2 to November 2, interest rates declined rapidly. The value of the bond portfolio increased from $10 million to $10,450,000. On November 2, the T-bond futures price was 98-16. This corresponds to a contract price of $98,500. This means that the total loss on the treasury bond futures contracts was

$$79 \times (\$98{,}500.00 - \$93{,}062.50) = \$429{,}562.50$$

The net change in the value of the portfolio manager's position was, therefore, only

$$\$450{,}000.00 - \$429{,}562.50 = \$20{,}437.50$$

This example is summarized in Table 5.7. Since the fund manager makes a loss on the futures position, he or she may regret having implemented the hedge. On average, we can expect half our hedges to lead to these sorts of regrets. The problem is that we do not know in advance which half of the hedges it will be!

London Interbank Offer Rate

Before presenting the next example, it is appropriate to review the meaning of LIBOR, the London Interbank Offer Rate. LIBOR is widely used in specifying corporate borrowing rates in international markets. It is a floating reference rate of interest similar to prime. LIBOR is determined by the trading of deposits

Table 5.7 Hedging a Bond Portfolio

From the Trader's Desk—August 2

A fund manager responsible for a $10 million bond portfolio is concerned that interest rates are expected to be highly volatile over the next three months. The fund manager decides to use treasury bond futures to hedge the value of the bond portfolio. The quoted price for the December treasury bond futures contract is 93-02. This means that the contract price is $93,062.50.

The Strategy

1. Short 79 December treasury bond futures contracts on August 2.
2. Close out the position on November 2.

The Result

During the period August 2 to November 2, interest rates declined rapidly. The value of the bond portfolio increased from $10 million to $10,450,000.

On November 2, the treasury bond futures price was 98-16. This corresponds to a contract price of $98,500.00. A loss of 79 × ($98,500.00 − $93,062.50) = $429,562.50 was, therefore, made on the treasury bond futures contracts.

Overall, the value of the portfolio manager's position changed by only $450,000.00 − $429,562.50 = $20,437.50.

between banks on the Eurocurrency market. The one-month LIBOR at any given time is the rate of interest being offered by one bank to another on one-month deposits at that time. When the interest rate on a loan is equal to one-month LIBOR, it means that the interest rate on the loan is reset equal to one-month LIBOR at monthly intervals with interest being paid in arrears. Other LIBOR rates such as three-month LIBOR and six-month LIBOR are defined and used analogously.

Hedging a Floating-Rate Loan

Interest-rate futures can be used to hedge the rate of interest paid by a borrower on a floating-rate loan. Generally, Eurodollar futures are used in preference to treasury bill futures for this purpose. This is because the Eurodollar interest rate is more closely related to the rate of interest at which corporations borrow than is the treasury bill rate. We will consider the use of Eurodollar futures to hedge a three-month loan where the interest rate is reset every month. This will produce a simple example. The same principles can be used for loans that last far longer than three months. The liquid contracts traded on the CME have maturities up to about five years, and longer-maturity contracts can be created by rolling contracts forward in the way described in Chapter 4.

We suppose that it is April 29 and a company has just borrowed $15 million for three months at an interest rate equal to the one-month LIBOR rate plus 100 basis points. At the time the loan is negotiated, the one-month LIBOR rate is 8.00 percent per annum so that the company must pay 9.00 percent per annum for the first month. Since the one-month LIBOR rate is quoted with monthly compounding, this means that the interest for the first month is 0.75 percent of $15 million, or $112,500. This is known for certain at the time the loan is negotiated and does not have to be hedged.

The interest paid at the end of the second month is determined by the one-month LIBOR rate at the beginning of the second month. It can be hedged by taking a position in the June Eurodollar futures contract. Suppose that the quoted price for this contract is 91.88. Each contract is for a deposit with a face value of $1 million. The contract price is, therefore,

$$10{,}000[100 - 0.25(100 - 91.88)] = \$979{,}700$$

The company will lose money if interest rates rise and gain if interest rates fall. It therefore requires a short position in the futures contracts. The duration of the asset underlying the futures contract at maturity of the futures contract is three months or 0.25 years. The duration of the asset being hedged at maturity of the hedge is one month or 0.0833 years. Using Equation (5.14), the number of contracts that should be used to hedge the interest payment in the second month is

$$\frac{0.08333}{0.25} \times \frac{15{,}000{,}000}{979{,}700} = 5.10$$

Rounding to the nearest whole number, five contracts are required.

For the third month, the September Eurodollar futures contract can be used. The quoted price for this contract is 91.44, which corresponds to a futures price of $978,600. The number of futures contracts that should be shorted can be calculated as before:

$$\frac{0.08333}{0.25} \times \frac{15{,}000{,}000}{978{,}600} = 5.11$$

Again, we find that, to the nearest whole number, five contracts are required. Thus, five of the June contracts should be shorted to hedge the LIBOR rate applicable to the second month and five of the September contracts should be shorted to hedge the LIBOR rate applicable to the third month. The June contracts are closed out on May 29 and the September contracts are closed out on June 29.

On May 29, the one-month LIBOR rate was 8.8 percent and the June futures price was 91.12. The latter corresponds to a contract price of $977,800 so that the company made a profit of

$$5 \times (\$979{,}700 - \$977{,}800) = \$9{,}500$$

on the June contracts. This provided compensation for the extra interest equal to ($\frac{1}{12}$) of 0.8 percent of $15 million = $10,000 that had to be paid at the end of the second month as a result of the LIBOR increase from 8.0 percent to 8.8 percent.

On June 29, the one-month LIBOR rate was 9.4 percent and the September futures price was 90.16. A similar calculation to that just given shows that the company gained $16,000 on the short futures position but incurred extra interest

Table 5.8 Hedging a Floating-Rate Loan

From the Trader's Desk—April 29

A company has just borrowed $15 million for three months at an interest rate equal to one-month LIBOR plus 100 basis points and would like to hedge its risk.

Quotes:

1. The one-month LIBOR rate is 8.00 percent.
2. The June Eurodollar futures price is 91.88.
3. The September Eurodollar futures price is 91.44.

The Strategy

1. Short five June contracts and five September contracts.
2. Close out the June contracts on May 29.
3. Close out the September contracts on June 29.

The Result

On May 29, the one-month LIBOR rate was 8.8 percent and the June futures price was 91.12. The company gained 5($979,700 − $977,800) = $9,500 on the five June contracts. This provided compensation for the $10,000 extra interest payment necessary in the second month because of the increase in LIBOR from 8.0 percent to 8.8 percent.

On June 29, the one-month LIBOR rate was 9.4 percent and the September futures price was 90.16. The company gained $16,000 on the five September contracts. This provided compensation for extra interest costs of $17,500.

costs of $17,500 as a result of the increase in one-month LIBOR from 8 percent per annum to 9.4 percent per annum. This example is summarized in Table 5.8.

SUMMARY

In this chapter, we have discussed four of the most popular interest rate futures contracts: the treasury bond, treasury note, treasury bill, and Eurodollar contracts. We have also considered different ways in which these contracts can be used for hedging. Since bond prices are inversely related to interest rates, a long hedge provides protection against a reduction in interest rates; a short hedge provides protection against an increase in interest rates.

In the treasury bond and treasury note futures contracts, the party with the short position has a number of interesting delivery options:

1. Delivery can be made on any day during the delivery month.
2. There are a number of alternative bonds that can be delivered.
3. On any day during the delivery month, the notice of intention to deliver at the 2 p.m. settlement price can be made any time up to 8 p.m.

These options all tend to reduce the futures price.

The concept of duration is important in hedging interest-rate risk. Duration measures how long on average an investor has to wait before receiving payments. It is a weighted average of the times until payments are received, with the weight for a particular payment time being proportional to the present value of the payment.

A key result underlying the duration-based hedging scheme described in this chapter is

$$\Delta B = -BD\Delta y$$

where B is a bond price, D is its duration, Δy is a small change in its yield (continuously compounded), and ΔB is the resultant small change in B. The equation enables a hedger to assess the sensitivity of a bond to small changes in its yield. It also enables the hedger to assess the sensitivity of an interest-rate futures price to small changes in the yield of the underlying bond. If the hedger is prepared to assume that Δy is the same for all bonds, the result enables the hedger to calculate the number of futures contracts necessary to protect a bond or bond portfolio against small changes in interest rates.

The key assumption underlying the duration-based hedging scheme is that all interest rates change by the same amount. This means that only parallel shifts in the term structure are allowed for. In practice, short-term interest rates are generally more volatile than are long-term interest rates, and hedge performance is liable to be poor if the duration of the bond underlying the futures contract and the duration of the asset being hedged are markedly different.

We have looked at three situations in which the duration-based hedging model can be used. The reader should have no difficulty in applying the same basic principles to other situations. In all cases, the number of contracts used for hedging is chosen using Equation (5.14) so that the duration of the whole position is zero.

Suggestions for Further Reading

CHICAGO BOARD OF TRADE, *Interest Rate Futures for Institutional Investors*. Chicago, 1987.

FIGLEWSKI, S., *Hedging with Financial Futures for Institutional Investors*. Cambridge, MA: Ballinger, 1986.

GAY, G. D., R. W. KOLB, and R. CHIANG., "Interest rate hedging: An empirical test of alternative strategies," *Journal of Financial Research*, 6 (Fall 1983), 187–197.

KLEMKOSKY, R. C., and D. J. LASSER, "An efficiency analysis of the T-bond futures market," *Journal of Futures Markets*, 5 (1985), 607–620.

KOLB, R. W., *Interest Rate Futures: A Comprehensive Introduction*, Richmond, VA: R. F. Dame, 1982.

KOLB, R. W., and R. CHIANG, "Improving Hedging Performance using Interest Rate Futures," *Financial Management*, 10 (Autumn 1981), 72–79.

RESNICK, B. G., "The relationship between futures prices for U.S. Treasury bonds," *Review of Research in Futures Markets*, 3 (1984), 88–104.

RESNICK, B. G., and E. HENNIGAR, "The relationship between futures and cash prices for U.S. Treasury bonds," *Review of Research in Futures Markets*, 2 (1983), 282–299.

SENCHAK, A. J., and J. C. EASTERWOOD, "Cross hedging CDs with Treasury bill futures," *Journal of Futures Markets*, 3 (1983), 429–438.

VEIT, W. T., and W. W. REIFF, "Commercial banks and interest rate futures: a hedging survey," *Journal of Futures Markets*, 3 (1983), 283–293.

Quiz

1. Suppose that spot interest rates with continuous compounding are as follows:

MATURITY (YEARS)	RATE (% PER ANNUM)
1	8.0
2	7.5
3	7.2
4	7.0
5	6.9

Calculate forward interest rates for the second, third, fourth, and fifth years.

2. The term structure is upward sloping. Put the following in order of magnitude:
   a. The five-year spot rate.
   b. The yield on a five-year coupon-bearing bond.
   c. The forward rate corresponding to the period between 5 and 5.25 years in the future.

   What is the answer to this question when the term structure is downward sloping?
3. The six-month and the one-year spot rates are both 10 percent per annum. For a bond that lasts 18 months and pays a coupon of 8 percent per annum (with a coupon payment having just been made), the yield is 10.4 percent per annum. What is the bond's price? What is the 18-month spot rate? All rates are quoted with semiannual compounding.
4. It is January 9, 1994. The price of a treasury bond with a 12 percent coupon that matures on October 12, 1999 is quoted as 102-07. What is the cash price?
5. The price of a 90-day treasury bill is quoted as 10.00. What continuously compounded return does an investor earn on the treasury bill for the 90-day period?
6. What assumptions does a duration-based hedging scheme make about the way in which the term structure moves?
7. It is January 30. You are managing a bond portfolio worth \$6 million. The average duration of the portfolio is 8.2 years. The September treasury bond futures price is currently 108-15 and the cheapest-to-deliver bond has a duration of 7.6 years. How should you hedge against changes in interest rates over the next seven months?

Questions and Problems

5.1. Suppose that spot interest rates with continuous compounding are as follows:

MATURITY (YEARS)	RATE (% PER ANNUM)
1	12.0
2	13.0
3	13.7
4	14.2
5	14.5

Calculate forward interest rates for the second, third, fourth, and fifth years.

5.2. Suppose that spot interest rates with continuous compounding are as follows

MATURITY (MNTHS)	*RATE (% PER ANNUM)*
3	8.0
6	8.2
9	8.4
12	8.5
15	8.6
18	8.7

Calculate forward interest rates for the second, third, fourth, fifth, and sixth quarters.

5.3. The cash prices of six-month and one-year treasury bills are 94.0 and 89.0. A 1.5-year bond that will pay coupons of $4 every six months currently sells for $94.84. A two-year bond that will pay coupons of $5 every six months currently sells for $97.12. Calculate the six-month, one-year, 1.5-year, and two-year spot rates.

5.4. A ten-year, 8 percent coupon bond currently sells for $90. A ten-year, 4 percent coupon bond currently sells for $80. What is the ten-year spot rate? (Hint: Consider taking a long position in two of the 4 percent coupon bonds and a short position in one of the 8 percent coupon bonds.)

5.5. Explain carefully why liquidity preference theory is consistent with the observation that the term structure tends to be upward sloping more often than it is downward sloping.

5.6. It is May 5, 1994. The quoted price of a government bond with a 12 percent coupon that matures on July 27, 2001 is 110-17. What is the cash price?

5.7. Suppose that the treasury bond futures price is 101-12. Which of the following four bonds is cheapest to deliver?

BOND	*PRICE*	*CONVERSION FACTOR*
1	125-05	1.2131
2	142-15	1.3792
3	115-31	1.1149
4	144-02	1.4026

5.8. It is July 30, 1994. The cheapest-to-deliver bond in a September 1994 treasury bond futures contract is a 13 percent coupon bond, and delivery is expected to be made on September 30, 1994. Coupon payments on the bond are made on February 4 and August 4 each year. The term structure is flat and the rate of interest with semiannual compounding is 12 percent per annum The conversion factor for the bond is 1.5. The current quoted bond price is $110. Calculate the quoted futures price for the contract.

5.9. An investor is looking for arbitrage opportunities in the treasury bond futures market. What complications are created by the fact that the party with a short position can choose to deliver any bond with a maturity of over 15 years?

5.10. Suppose that the treasury bill futures price for a contract maturing in 33 days is quoted as 90.04 and the discount rate for a 123-day treasury bill is 10.03. What is the implied repo rate? How can it be used?

5.11. Suppose that the nine-month interest rate is 8 percent per annum and the six-month interest rate is 7.5 percent per annum (both with continuous compounding). Estimate the futures price of 90-day treasury bills with a face value of $1 million for delivery in six months. How would the price be quoted?

5.12. Assume that a bank can borrow or lend money at the same interest rate in Euromarkets. The 90-day rate is 10 percent per annum and the 180-day rate is 10.2 percent per annum, both expressed with continuous compounding. The Eurodollar futures price for a contract maturing in 90 days is quoted as 89.5. What arbitrage opportunities are open to the bank?

5.13. A Canadian company wishes to create a Canadian interest-rate futures contract from a U.S. treasury bill futures contract and forward contracts on foreign exchange. Using an example, explain how this can be done. For the purposes of this problem, assume that a futures contract is the same as a forward contract.

5.14. A five-year bond with a yield of 11 percent (continuously compounded) pays an 8 percent coupon at the end of each year.

a. What is the bond's price?
b. What is the bond's duration?
c. Use the duration to calculate the effect on the bond's price of a 0.2 percent decrease in its yield.
d. Recalculate the bond's price on the basis of a 10.8 percent per annum yield and verify that the result is in agreement with your answer to (c).

5.15. Portfolio A consists of a one-year discount bond with a face value of $2,000 and a ten-year discount bond with a face value of $6,000. Portfolio B consists of a 5.95-year discount bond with a face value of $5,000. The current yield on all bonds is 10 percent per annum

a. Show that both portfolios have the same duration.
b. Show that the percentage changes in the values of the two portfolios for a 10 basis point increase in yields is the same.
c. What are the percentage changes in the values of the two portfolios for a 5 percent per annum increase in yields?
d. Which portfolio has the higher convexity?

5.16. Suppose that a bond portfolio with a duration of 12 years is hedged using a futures contract where the underlying asset has a duration of four years. What is likely to be the impact on the hedge of the fact that the 12-year rate is less volatile than the four-year rate?

5.17. Suppose that it is February 20 and a treasurer realizes that on July 17, the company will have to issue $5 million of commercial paper with a maturity of 180 days. If the paper were issued today, it would realize $4,820,000. (In other words, the company would receive $4,820,000 for its paper and have to redeem it at $5,000,000 in 180 days time.) The September Eurodollar futures price is quoted as 92.00. How should the treasurer hedge the company's exposure?

5.18. On August 1, a portfolio manager has a bond portfolio worth \$10 million. The duration of the portfolio is 7.1 years. The December treasury bond futures price is currently 91-12 and the cheapest-to-deliver bond has a duration of 8.8 years. How should the portfolio manager immunize the portfolio against changes in interest rates over the next two months?

5.19. How can the portfolio manager change the duration of the portfolio to 3.0 years in Problem 5.18?

6

SWAPS

Swaps are private agreements between two companies to exchange cash flows in the future according to a prearranged formula. They can be regarded as portfolios of forward contracts. The study of swaps is, therefore, a natural extension of the study of forward and futures contracts.

The first swap contracts were negotiated in 1981. Since then, the market has grown very rapidly. Hundreds of billions of dollars of contracts are currently negotiated each year. In this chapter, we discuss how swaps are designed, how they are used, and how they can be valued. We also briefly consider the nature of the credit risk facing financial institutions when they trade swaps and other similar financial contracts.

MECHANICS OF INTEREST-RATE SWAPS

The most common type of swap is a "plain vanilla" interest-rate swap. In this, one party, B, agrees to pay to the other party, A, cash flows equal to interest at a predetermined fixed rate on a notional principal for a number of years. At the same time, party A agrees to pay party B cash flows equal to interest at a floating rate on the same notional principal for the same period of time. The currencies of the two sets of interest cash flows are the same. The life of the swap can range from two years to over 15 years.

Why should A and B enter into such an agreement? The reason most commonly put forward concerns comparative advantages.[1] Some companies appear to have a comparative advantage in fixed-rate markets while other companies appear to have a comparative advantage in floating-rate markets. When obtaining a new loan, it makes sense for a company to go to the market where it has a comparative advantage. However, this may lead to a company borrowing fixed when it wants floating or borrowing floating when it wants fixed. This is where a swap comes in. A swap has the effect of transforming a fixed rate loan into a floating-rate loan or vice versa.

London Interbank Offer Rate

The floating rate in many interest-rate swap agreements is the London Interbank Offer Rate (LIBOR). We have already encountered this in Chapter 5. It is appropriate at this stage to review how it works.

LIBOR is the rate of interest offered by banks on deposits from other banks in Eurocurrency markets. One-month LIBOR is the rate offered on one-month deposits, three-month LIBOR is the rate offered on three-month deposits, and so on. LIBOR rates are determined by trading between banks and change continuously as economic conditions change. Just as prime is often the reference rate of interest for floating-rate loans in the domestic financial market, LIBOR is frequently a reference rate of interest for loans in international financial markets. To understand how it is used, consider a loan where the rate of interest is specified as six-month LIBOR + 0.5 percent per annum. The life of the loan is divided into six-month time periods. For each period, the rate of interest is set 0.5 percent per annum above the six-month LIBOR rate at the beginning of the period. Interest is paid at the end of the period.

An Example of an Interest-Rate Swap

We now give an example of how an interest-rate swap might arise in practice. We suppose that two companies, A and B, both wish to borrow $10 million for five years and have been offered the following rates.

	FIXED	*FLOATING*
Company A	10.00%	6-month LIBOR + 0.30%
Company B	11.20%	6-month LIBOR + 1.00%

We assume that company B wants to borrow at a fixed rate of interest while company A wants to borrow floating funds at a rate linked to six-month LIBOR. Company B clearly has a lower credit rating than company A since it pays a higher rate of interest than company A in both fixed and floating markets.

[1] The comparative advantage argument is a useful way of introducing swaps but, as we will discuss later in this chapter, perceived comparative advantages may be largely illusory.

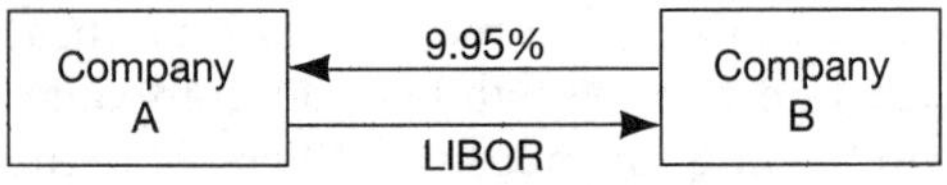

Figure 6.1 A direct swap agreement between A and B.

From the viewpoint of the swaps market, an interesting aspect of the rates offered to A and B is that the difference between the two fixed rates is greater than the difference between the two floating rates. Company B pays 1.20 percent more than company A in fixed rate markets and only 0.70 percent more than company A in floating-rate markets.

Company B has a comparative advantage in floating-rate markets, while company A has a comparative advantage in fixed-rate markets.[2] It is this apparent anomaly that allows a profitable swap to be negotiated. Company A borrows fixed-rate funds at 10 percent per annum. Company B borrows floating-rate funds at LIBOR + 1.00 percent per annum. They then enter into a swap agreement to ensure that A ends up with floating-rate funds and B ends up with fixed-rate funds.

As a first step in understanding how swaps work, we assume that A and B get in touch with each other directly. The sort of swap they might negotiate is shown in Figure 6.1. Company A agrees to pay company B interest at six-month LIBOR on $10 million. In return, company B agrees to pay company A interest at a fixed rate of 9.95 percent per annum on $10 million.

When the external borrowings of A and B are taken into account, we obtain Figure 6.2. Company A has three sets of interest-rate cash flows:

1. It pays 10.00 percent per annum to outside lenders.
2. It receives 9.95 percent per annum from B.
3. It pays LIBOR to B.

The first two cash flows taken together imply that A pays 0.05 percent per annum. It follows that the net effect of the three cash flows is that A pays LIBOR + 0.05 percent per annum. This is 0.25 percent per annum less than it would pay if it went directly to floating-rate markets. Company B also has three sets of interest-rate cash flows:

1. It pays LIBOR + 1.00 percent per annum to outside lenders.
2. It receives LIBOR from A.
3. It pays 9.95 percent per annum to A.

The first two cash flows taken together imply that B pays 1.00 percent per annum. It follows that the net effect of the three cash flows is that B pays 10.95 percent

[2] Note that B's comparative advantage in floating-rate markets does not imply that B pays less than A in this market. It means that the extra amount that B pays over the amount paid by A is less in this market. One of my students summarized the situation as follows: "A pays more less in fixed-rate markets; B pays less more in floating-rate markets."

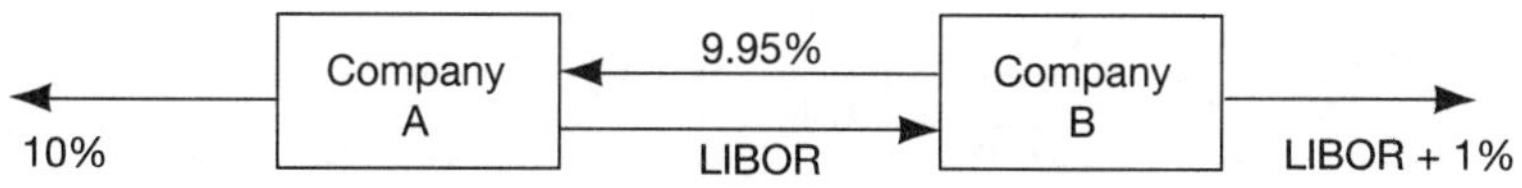

Figure 6.2 Direct swap agreement with outside borrowing.

per annum. This is 0.25 percent per annum less than it would pay if it went directly to fixed-rate markets.

The swap arrangement improves the position of both A and B by 0.25 percent per annum. The total gain is, therefore, 0.50 percent per annum. This could have been calculated in advance. The total potential gain from an interest-rate swap agreement is always $a - b$ where a is the difference between the interest rates facing the two companies in fixed-rate markets and b is the difference between the interest rates facing the two companies in floating-rate markets. In this case, $a = 1.20$ percent and $b = 0.70$ percent.

Role of Financial Intermediary

Usually, two companies do not get in touch with each other directly to arrange a swap. They each deal with a financial intermediary such as a bank. This means that the total potential gain (0.5 percent per annum in our example) has to be split three ways between A, B, and the financial intermediary. One possible arrangement is shown in Figure 6.3.

When the external borrowings of A and B are taken into account, we obtain Figure 6.4. Company A has three sets of interest-rate cash flows:

1. It pays 10.00 percent per annum to outside lenders.
2. It receives 9.9 percent per annum from the financial institution.
3. It pays LIBOR to the financial institution.

The net effect of these three cash flows is that company A pays LIBOR + 0.10 percent, which is a 0.20 percent per annum improvement over the rate it could get by going directly to floating rate markets. Company B also has three sets of interest-rate cash flows:

1. It pays LIBOR + 1.00 percent per annum to outside lenders.
2. It receives LIBOR from the financial institution.
3. It pays 10.0 percent per annum to the financial institution.

Figure 6.3 Interest-rate swap using financial intermediary.

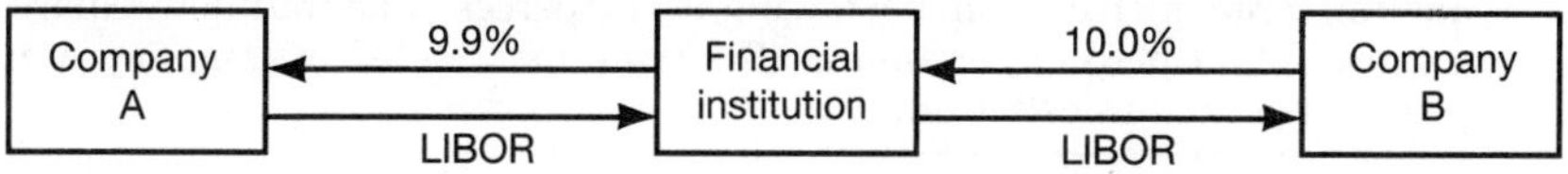

Figure 6.4 Interest-rate swap using financial intermediary and including outside borrowings.

The net effect of these three cash flows is that company B pays 11.0 percent per annum, which is a 0.20 percent per annum improvement over the rate it could get by going directly to fixed rate markets. The financial institution's net gain is 0.10 percent per annum. (The floating rate it receives is the same as the floating rate it pays, but the fixed rate it receives is 0.10 percent higher than the fixed rate it pays.) The total gain to all parties is as before 0.50 percent per annum.

The swap is summarized in Table 6.1. Note that the financial institution has two separate contracts, one with company A and the other with company B. If one of the companies defaults, the financial institution still has to honor its agreement with the other company. In most instances, company A will not even know

Table 6.1 An Interest-Rate Swap Arrangement

From the Trader's Desk

Company A and company B both wish to borrow $10 million for five years. Company A wants to arrange a floating-rate loan where the rate of interest is linked to six-month LIBOR. Company B wants to arrange a fixed-rate loan. They have been offered the following terms.

	FIXED	*FLOATING*
Company A	10.0%	6-month LIBOR + 0.3%
Company B	11.2%	6-month LIBOR + 1.0%

The Strategy

1. Company A borrows fixed-rate funds at 10 percent per annum.
2. Company B borrows floating-rate funds at LIBOR + 1.0 percent per annum.
3. They then enter into a swap agreement.

The Swap with No Intermediary

This is shown in Figure 6.2. Company A agrees to pay company B the six-month LIBOR rate of interest on $10 million. In return, company B agrees to pay company A 10.95 percent per annum on $10 million. The net result is that A ends up borrowing at LIBOR + 0.05 percent, while B ends up borrowing at 10.95 percent. The swap makes both sides 0.25 percent per annum better off.

The Swap with Intermediary

This is shown in Figure 6.4. Each side enters into a swap agreement with a financial intermediary. Company A ends up borrowing at LIBOR + 0.1 percent per annum, company B ends up borrowing at 11.0 percent, and the intermediary achieves a spread of 0.1 percent per annum. The swap makes each of company A and B 0.20 percent per annum better off.

that the financial institution has entered into an offsetting swap with company B and vice versa.

The Exchange of Payments

In the swap that has been described, interest payment dates would occur every six months, and all interest rates would be quoted with semiannual compounding. (This is because the swap is based on six-month LIBOR.) The terms of the swap agreement would specify that one party should send a check for the difference between the fixed and floating interest payments to the other party every six months. Suppose that in Figure 6.3 the six-month LIBOR rate applicable to a particular payment date is 12.0 percent. Company A pays the financial institution

$$0.5 \times (12.0 - 9.9)\% \text{ of } \$10 \text{ million}$$

or $105,000. The financial institution pays company B

$$0.5 \times (12.0 - 10.0)\% \text{ of } \$10 \text{ million}$$

or $100,000.

Principal payments are not exchanged in an interest-rate swap. This is because the dollar value of the principal remains the same throughout the contract for both the floating-rate loan and the fixed-rate loan. The exchange of principals in our example would involve $10 million being exchanged for $10 million—a transaction that would have no financial value to either party.

The six-month LIBOR rate that is actually used on a payment date is the rate prevailing six months earlier. This reflects the way in which interest is paid on LIBOR-based loans. The first payment date is six months after the start of the swap contract. The exchange of cash flows that will take place on that date is, therefore, based on six-month LIBOR at the start of the contract and is known with certainty when the contract is negotiated. The second payment is 12 months after the start of the swap. The exchange of payments that will take place on that date is based on the six-month LIBOR rate prevailing six months after the swap begins.

Table 6.2 considers a three-year swap where six-month LIBOR is exchanged for 5 percent. It shows the payments that would be exchanged for one particular set of future LIBOR rates.

Validity of the Comparative Advantage Argument

The comparative advantage argument, although a good way of introducing swaps, is open to question. Why in Table 6.1 should the spreads between the rates offered to A and B be different in fixed and floating markets? Now that the swap

Table 6.2 Cash Flows ($ Millions) Exchanged in a $100 Million Three-Year Interest-Rate Swap When a Fixed Rate of 5 Percent Is Paid and LIBOR Is Received

TIME (YRS)	*LIBOR RATE*	*FLOATING CASH FLOW*	*FIXED CASH FLOW*	*NET CASH FLOW*
0.0	4.20			
0.5	4.80	+2.10	−2.50	−0.40
1.0	5.30	+2.40	−2.50	−0.10
1.5	5.50	+2.65	−2.50	+0.15
2.0	5.60	+2.75	−2.50	+0.25
2.5	5.90	+2.80	−2.50	+0.30
3.0	6.40	+2.95	−2.50	+0.45

market has been in existence for some time, we might reasonably expect these types of differences to have been arbitraged away.

The reason why spread differentials appear to continue to exist may in part be due to the nature of the contracts available to companies in fixed and floating markets. The 10.0 percent and 11.2 percent rates available to A and B in fixed-rate markets are likely to be the rates at which the companies can issue five-year fixed-rate bonds. The LIBOR + 0.3 percent and LIBOR + 1.0 percent rates available to A and B in floating-rate markets are six-month rates. The lender usually has the opportunity to review the rates every six months. If the creditworthiness of A or B has declined, the lender has the option of increasing the spread over LIBOR that is charged. In extreme circumstances the lender can refuse to roll over the loan at all. The providers of fixed-rate finance do not have the option to change the terms of the loan in this way.

The spreads between the rates offered to A and B are a reflection of the extent to which B is more likely to default than A. During the next six months there is very little chance that either A or B will default. As we look further ahead, the probability of a default by B increases faster than the probability of a default by A. This is why the spread between the five-year rates is greater than the spread between the six-month rates.

After negotiating a floating-rate loan at LIBOR + 1.0 percent and entering into the swap shown in Figure 6.3, we argued that B obtained a fixed-rate loan at 11.0 percent. The arguments we are now presenting show that this is not really the case. In practice, the rate paid is 11.0 percent only if B can continue to borrow floating-rate funds at a spread of 1.0 percent over LIBOR. For example, if the credit rating of B declines so that the floating-rate loan is rolled over at LIBOR + 2.0 percent, the rate paid by B increases to 12.0 percent. The relatively high five-year borrowing rate offered to B in Table 6.1 suggests that the market considers that B's spread over six-month LIBOR for borrowed funds is expected to rise. Assuming this is so, B's expected total borrowing rate if it enters into the swap is greater than 11.0 percent and possibly greater than the 11.2 percent B could get by going to fixed-rate markets directly.

The swap in Figure 6.1 locks in LIBOR + 0.1 percent for company A for the

Table 6.3 Indication Pricing for Interest-Rate Swaps at 2:20 P.M. New York Time on July 22, 1993

MATURITY	*BANK PAYS FIXED RATE*	*BANK RECEIVES FIXED RATE*	*CURRENT TN RATE (%)*
2 years	2 yr TN + 20 bps	2 yr TN + 23 bps	4.19
3 years	3 yr TN + 31 bps	3 yr TN + 34 bps	4.52
4 years	4 yr TN + 30 bps	4 yr TN + 33 bps	4.87
5 years	5 yr TN + 22 bps	5 yr TN + 25 bps	5.22
7 years	7 yr TN + 24 bps	7 yr TN + 27 bps	5.56
10 years	10 yr TN + 32 bps	10 yr TN + 35 bps	5.88

whole of the next five years, not just for the next six months. Unless there is a strong reason for supposing that company A's credit rating will improve, it appears to be a good deal for company A. However, the company should consider the possibility of a default by the financial institution before making a final judgment on the attractiveness of the swap.

Pricing Schedules

The most common interest-rate swap involves an exchange of six-month LIBOR for a fixed rate of interest that is a certain number of basis points above the treasury note yield. Table 6.3 shows an *indication pricing schedule* that was used by swap traders working for financial institutions at 2:20 p.m. New York time on July 22, 1993. It indicates the prices quoted to prospective counterparties. For example, it indicates that for a five-year swap where the financial institution will pay fixed and receive six-month LIBOR, the fixed rate should be set 22 basis points above the current five-year treasury note rate of 5.22 percent. In other words, the financial institution should set the fixed rate at 5.44 percent. When it is negotiating a five-year swap where it will receive fixed and pay six-month LIBOR for five years, the schedule indicates that it should set the fixed rate at 25 basis points above the current five-year treasury note rate, or at 5.47 percent. The bank's profit or its bid-asked spread from negotiating two offsetting five-year swaps would be 3 basis points (= 0.03 percent) per annum.[3]

At any given time, swap spreads are determined by supply and demand. If more market participants want to receive fixed than receive floating, swap spreads tend to fall. If the reverse is true, swap spreads tend to rise. Table 6.3 would be updated regularly as market conditions changed. One point to note is that six-month LIBOR is quoted with semiannual compounding on the basis of a 360-day year, whereas the treasury note rate is quoted with semiannual compounding on the basis of a 365-day year. This can be confusing. To make a six-month LIBOR rate comparable with a treasury note rate, either the six-month LIBOR rate must

[3] In the early days of swaps, bid-asked spreads as high as 100 basis points were possible. As Table 6.3 indicates the market is now much more competitive.

be multiplied by 365/360 or the treasury note rate must be multiplied by 360/365.[4]

The CBOT trades futures contracts on the three- and five-year swap rates. The contracts are cash settled to a swap rate, which is the median of the average of the bid and offer quotes of seven dealers randomly selected from an approved list. The CBOT also trades options on swap futures.

Warehousing

In practice, it is unlikely that two companies will contact a financial institution at exactly the same time and want to take opposite positions in exactly the same swap. For this reason, most large financial institutions are prepared to warehouse interest-rate swaps. This involves entering into a swap with one counterparty and then hedging the interest-rate risk until a counterparty wanting to take an opposite position is found. The interest-rate futures contracts discussed in Chapter 5 are one way of carrying out the hedging.

VALUATION OF INTEREST-RATE SWAPS

If we assume no possibility of default, an interest-rate swap can be valued either as a long position in one bond combined with a short position in another bond or as a portfolio of forward contracts.

Relationship to Bond Prices

Consider the swap between company B and the financial institution in Figure 6.3. This is the same as an arrangement in which

1. Company B has lent the financial institution \$10 million at the six-month LIBOR rate.
2. The financial institution has lent company B \$10 million at a fixed rate of 10 percent per annum.

To put this another way, the financial institution has sold a \$10 million floating-rate (LIBOR) bond to company B and has purchased a \$10 million fixed-rate (10 percent per annum) bond from company B. The value of the swap is, therefore, the difference between the values of two bonds.

In general, suppose that under the terms of a swap, a financial institution

[4] Some of the numbers calculated earlier in this chapter are not perfectly accurate because they do not take into account these differences between the ways of quoting fixed and floating rates. For example, in calculating the LIBOR payment that is made in a semiannual swap, the LIBOR rate is adjusted to reflect the number of days to which it applies. If the 6-month LIBOR rate applicable to a payment date is 12% and the time since the last payment date is 182 days, the actual LIBOR payment on a principal of 100 is

$$100 \times 0.12 \times \frac{182}{360} = 6.067$$

receives fixed payments of k dollars at times t_i $(1 \leq i \leq n)$ and makes floating payments at the same times. Define

V: value of swap
B_1: value of fixed-rate bond underlying the swap
B_2: value of floating-rate bond underlying the swap
Q: notional principal in swap agreement

It follows that

$$V = B_1 - B_2 \tag{6.1}$$

The discount rates used in valuing the bonds should reflect the riskiness of the cash flows. We suppose that it is appropriate to use a discount rate with a risk level corresponding to the floating rate underlying the swap. In our example, the floating rate underlying the swap is LIBOR, and so our assumption means that the appropriate risk level is the risk associated with loans in the interbank market.

In practice the fixed-rate cash flow stream in a swap has roughly the same risk as the floating-rate cash flow stream since, if one of the cash flow streams stops because of a default, the other will stop as well. It is, therefore, correct to use the same discount rate for both B_1 and B_2. The overall value of the swap is not usually highly sensitive to the particular discount rate chosen providing the same discount rate is used for both bonds. Our assumption that the floating basis rate underlying the swap is the appropriate rate to use for discounting is a very common one and considerably simplifies the valuation.

It is reasonable to assume that a swap, if entered into at the average of the bid and offer quotes in Table 6.3, has a value of zero. Given our assumption about discount rates, $B_2 = Q$ for such a swap. It follows from Equation (6.1) that $B_1 = Q$ for the swap. An indication pricing schedule such as the one in Table 6.3, therefore, gives a number of fixed-rate bonds that are worth their par value. (These are known as *par yield bonds*.) The bootstrap procedure described in Chapter 5 can be used to determine a zero-coupon yield curve from these par yield bonds. This zero-coupon yield curve defines the appropriate discount rates for swap cash flows and can be used in conjunction with Equation (6.1) to determine the values of swaps that were negotiated some time ago.

Define r_i as the discount rate corresponding to a maturity t_i. Since B_1 is the present value of the fixed-rate bond's future cash flows,

$$B_1 = \sum_{i=1}^{n} ke^{-r_i t_i} + Qe^{-r_n t_n}$$

The floating rate of interest that is of equivalent risk to the r_i's must be the floating rate of interest underlying the swap. (This is because the r_i's were derived from the indication pricing schedule.) We can, therefore, use the floating rate underlying the swap to discount the cash flows of the floating-rate bond. This makes the calculation relatively easy. Immediately after a payment date the value of the floating-rate bond, B_2, is always its face value, Q. Between payment dates, we can use the fact that B_2 will equal Q immediately after the next payment date. In our notation, the time until the next payment date is t_1 so that

$$B_2 = Qe^{-r_1t_1} + k^*e^{-r_1t_1}$$

where k^* is the floating-rate payment (already known) that will be made at time t_1. As interest rates increase (decrease), the value, V, of the swap to the financial institution decreases (increases).

In the situation where the financial institution is paying fixed and receiving floating, B_1 and B_2 are calculated in the same way and

$$V = B_2 - B_1$$

It is interesting to note that the value of the swap is zero when it is first negotiated and zero at the end of its life.[5] During its life it may have a positive or negative value.

Example

Suppose that under the terms of a swap, a financial institution has agreed to pay six-month LIBOR and receive 8 percent per annum (with semiannual compounding) on a notional principal of \$100 million. The swap has a remaining life of 1.25 years. The relevant fixed rates of interest with continuous compounding for three-month, nine-month, and 15-month maturities are 10.0 percent, 10.5 percent, and 11.0 percent, respectively. The six-month LIBOR rate at the last payment date was 10.2 percent (with semiannual compounding). In this case, k = \$4 million and k^* = \$5.1 million so that

$$B_1 = 4e^{-0.25\times0.1} + 4e^{-0.75\times0.105} + 104e^{-1.25\times0.11}$$

$$= \$98.24 \text{ million}$$

$$B_2 = 5.1e^{-.25\times0.1} + 100e^{-0.25\times0.1}$$

$$= \$102.51 \text{ million}$$

Hence, the value of the swap is

$$98.24 - 102.51 = -\$4.27 \text{ million}$$

If the bank had been in the opposite position of paying fixed and receiving floating, the value of the swap would be + \$4.27 million.

Relationship to Forward Contracts

In the absence of default risk, an interest-rate swap can be decomposed into a series of forward contracts. This is best illustrated by returning to the example in Figure 6.3. Consider the swap agreement between the financial institution and

[5] Strictly speaking, the value of the swap to the financial institution is slightly positive when it is first negotiated because of the bid-ask spread effect.

company A. Since the principal amount is \$10 million and payments are exchanged every six months, the cash flow to the financial institution on a payment date is (in millions of dollars)

$$10 \times (0.5 \times \text{LIBOR} - 0.5 \times 0.099)$$

or

$$5 \times (\text{LIBOR} - 0.099)$$

This is the payoff from a forward contract on LIBOR with a "delivery price" of 9.9 percent and a principal of \$5 million. The only difference between this and a regular forward contract is that it is the value of LIBOR six months prior to maturity date that determines the payoff.

Suppose that $\hat{R}_i$ is the forward interest rate (expressed with semiannual compounding) for the six-month period prior to a payment date i ($i \geq 2$). The arguments in Chapter 3 show that the value of a long forward contract on an asset is the present value of the amount by which the current forward price exceeds the delivery price. Using the notation introduced earlier, the value of the forward contract corresponding to the payment number i ($i \geq 2$) for the party receiving fixed and paying floating can similarly be shown to be

$$(k - 0.5\,\hat{R}_i Q)e^{-r_i t_i}$$

The exchange that will take place on the first payment date (at time t_1) involves a payment k^* and receipt k. The value of this is

$$(k - k^*)e^{-r_1 t_1}$$

The total value of the swap is, therefore,

$$(k - k^*)e^{-r_1 t_1} + \sum_{i=2}^{n} (k - 0.5\,\hat{R}_i Q)e^{-r_i t_i}$$

For the party receiving floating and paying fixed, the value is

$$(k^* - k)e^{-r_1 t_1} + \sum_{i=2}^{n} (0.5\,\hat{R}_i Q - k)e^{-r_i t_i}$$

Example

Consider again the situation in the previous example. In millions of dollars, $k = 4.0$, $k^* = 5.1$, and $Q = 100$. Also, $r_1 = 0.10$, $r_2 = 0.105$, $r_3 = 0.11$, $t_1 = 0.25$, $t_2 = 0.75$, and $t_3 = 1.25$. Equation (5.1) gives the values of $\hat{R}_2$ and $\hat{R}_3$ with continuous compounding as

$$\hat{R}_2 = \frac{r_2 t_2 - r_1 t_1}{t_2 - t_1} = \frac{0.75 \times 0.105 - 0.25 \times 0.10}{0.5} = 0.1075$$

$$\hat{R}_3 = \frac{r_3 t_3 - r_2 t_2}{t_3 - t_2} = \frac{1.25 \times 0.11 - 0.75 \times 0.105}{0.5} = 0.1175$$

These can be converted to semiannual compounding using Equation (3.4): $\hat{R}_2 = 0.1104$, $\hat{R}_3 = 0.1210$. The value of the swap is, therefore,

$$(4.0 - 5.1)e^{-0.1\times 0.25} + (4.0 - 0.5 \times 0.1104 \times 100)e^{-0.105\times 0.75}$$
$$+ (4.0 - 0.5 \times 0.1210 \times 100)e^{-0.11\times 1.25} = -4.27$$

or $-\$4.27$ million. This is in agreement with the calculation based on bond prices in the previous example.

At the time the swap is entered into, it is worth zero. This means that the sum of the value of the forward contracts underlying the swap is zero at this time. However, it does not mean that the value of each individual forward contract is zero. In general, some will have positive values while others have negative values.

For the forward contracts underlying the swap between the financial institution and company A in Figure 6.3,

Value of forward contract > 0 when forward interest rate $> 9.9\%$

Value of forward contract $= 0$ when forward interest rate $= 9.9\%$

Value of forward contract < 0 when forward interest rate $< 9.9\%$

Suppose the term structure is upward sloping at the time the swap is negotiated. This means that the forward interest rates increase as the maturity of the forward contract increases. Since the sum of the values of the forward contracts is zero, this must mean that the forward interest rate is less than 9.9 percent for the early payment dates and greater than 9.9 percent for the later payment dates. The value to the financial institution of the forward contracts corresponding to early payment dates are therefore negative, while those corresponding to later payment dates are positive. If the term structure is downward sloping at the time the swap is negotiated, the reverse is true. This argument is illustrated in Figure 6.5.

A Simple Rule

Our analysis of the value of an interest-rate swap in terms of forward contracts shows that we can value a plain vanilla interest-rate swap on the basis that forward interest rates are certain to be realized. The procedure is:

1. Calculate forward rates for each of the LIBOR rates that will determine swap cash flows.
2. Calculate swap cash flows on the assumption that the LIBOR rates will equal the forward rates.
3. Set the swap value equal to the present value of these cash flows.

This procedure does not always work for non-plain-vanilla swaps.

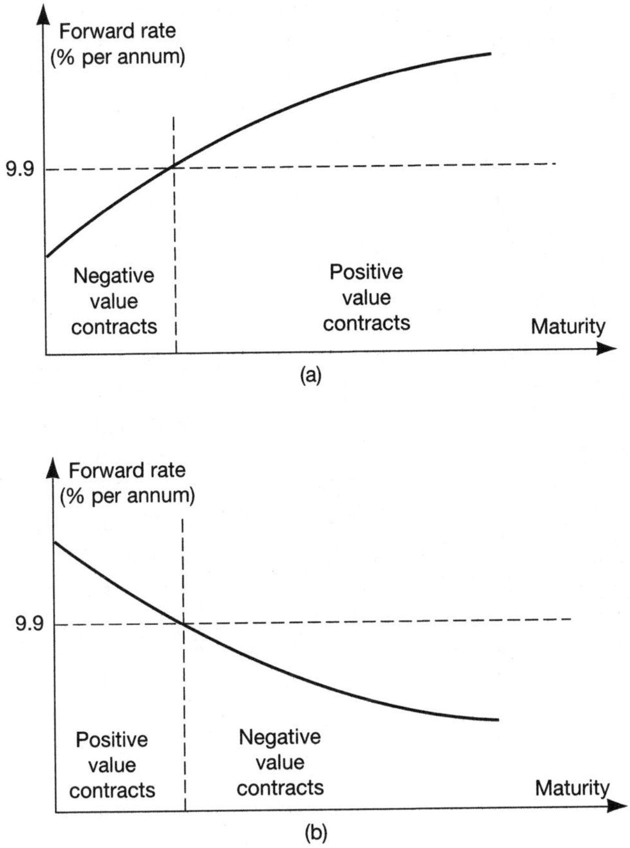

Figure 6.5 Value of forward contracts underlying financial institution's swap with company A in Figure 6.3 when term structure is (a) upward sloping and (b) downward sloping.

CURRENCY SWAPS

Another popular type of swap is known as a *currency swap*. In its simplest form, this involves exchanging principal and fixed-rate interest payments on a loan in one currency for principal and fixed-rate interest payments on an approximately equivalent loan in another currency.

An Example

Like interest-rate swaps, currency swaps can be motivated by comparative advantage. Suppose that company A and company B are offered the following fixed rates of interest in U.S. dollars and sterling.

	DOLLARS	*STERLING*
Company A	8.0%	11.6%
Company B	10.0%	12.0%

This table shows that sterling interest rates are generally higher than U.S. interest rates. Company A is clearly more creditworthy than company B, since it is offered a more favorable rate of interest in both currencies. However, the differences between the rates offered to A and B in the two markets are not the same. Company B pays 2.0 percent more than company A in the U.S. dollar market and only 0.4 percent more than company A in the sterling markets.

Company A has a comparative advantage in the U.S. dollar market, while company B has a comparative advantage in the sterling market. This might be because A is an American company that is better known to U.S. investors, while B is a U.K. company that is better known to British investors. Tax considerations may also play an important role in determining the rates. We suppose that A wants to borrow sterling while B wants to borrow dollars. This creates a perfect situation for a currency swap. Company A and B each borrow in the market where they have a comparative advantage; that is, company A borrows dollars while company B borrows sterling. They then use a currency swap to transform A's loan into a sterling loan and B's loan into a dollar loan.

As already mentioned, the difference between the dollar interest rates is 2.0 percent, while the difference between the sterling interest rates is 0.4 percent. By analogy with the interest-rate swap case, we expect the total gain to all parties to be 2.0 percent − 0.4 percent = 1.6 percent per annum.

There are many ways in which the swap can be organized. Figure 6.6 shows one possible arrangement. Company A borrows dollars while company B borrows sterling. The effect of the swap is to provide company A with a sterling interest rate of 11.0 percent per annum and company B with a 9.4 percent per annum dollar interest rate. This makes each company 0.6 percent better off than it would be if it went directly to the market it wants to borrow in. The financial intermediary gains 1.4 percent per annum on its dollar cash flows and loses 1.0 percent per annum on its sterling cash flows. Ignoring the difference between the two currencies, it makes a net gain of 0.4 percent per annum. As predicted, the total gain to all parties is 1.6 percent per annum.

A currency swap agreement requires the principal to be specified in each of the two currencies. The principal amounts are exchanged at the beginning and at the end of the life of the swap. They are chosen so that they are approximately equal at the exchange rate at the beginning of the swap's life. In the example in Figure 6.6, the principal amounts might be \$15 million and £10 million. Initially, the principal amounts flow in the opposite direction to the arrows in Figure 6.6. The interest payments during the life of the swap and the final principal payment flow in the same direction as the arrows. Thus, at the outset of the swap, company A pays \$15 million and receives £10 million. Each year during the life of the swap

Figure 6.6 A currency swap.

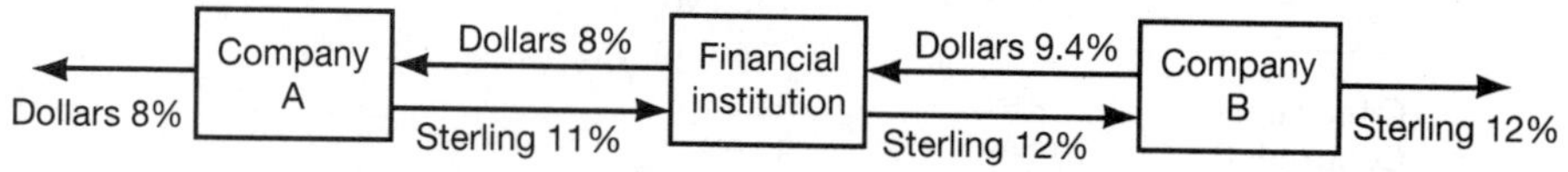

Table 6.4 A Currency Swap Arrangement

From the Trader's Desk

Company A wants to borrow £10 million at a fixed rate of interest for five years. Company B wants to borrow $15 million at a fixed rate of interest for five years. The companies have been offered the following rates

	DOLLARS	*STERLING*
Company A	8.0%	11.6%
Company B	10.0%	12.0%

The Strategy

1. Company A borrows dollars at 8.0 percent per annum.
2. Company B borrows sterling at 12.0 percent per annum.
3. They enter into a swap agreement.

The Swap

One possible arrangement is shown in Figure 6.6. Principal payments flow in the opposite direction to the arrows at the start of the swap and in the same direction as the arrows at the end of the life of the swap. Company A ends up borrowing sterling at 11.0 percent per annum. Company B ends up borrowing dollars at 9.4 percent per annum. The financial institution makes a gain of 1.4 percent per annum in dollars and loses 1.0 percent per annum in sterling. The financial institution can hedge its sterling outflows to lock in a profit in dollars.

contract, company A receives $1.20 million (= 8 percent of $15 million) and pays £1.10 million (= 11 percent of £10 million). At the end of the life of the swap, it pays a principal of £10 million and receives a principal of $15 million.

The swap is summarized in Table 6.4. The reader may feel that the swap is unsatisfactory because the financial institution is exposed to foreign exchange risk. Each year, it makes a gain of $210,000 (= 1.4 percent of $15 million) and a loss of £100,000 (= 1 percent of £10 million). However, the financial institution can avoid this risk by buying £100,000 per annum in the forward market for each year of the life of the swap. This will lock in a net gain in U.S. dollars. If we tried to redesign the swap so that the financial institution makes 0.4 percent spread in dollars and zero spread in sterling, we might come up with the arrangement in Figure 6.7 or Figure 6.8. In Figure 6.7, company B bears some foreign exchange risk because it pays 1.0 percent per annum in sterling and 8.4 percent in dollars. In Figure 6.8, company A bears some foreign exchange risk because it receives

Figure 6.7 Alternative arrangement for currency swap; company B bears some foreign exchange risk.

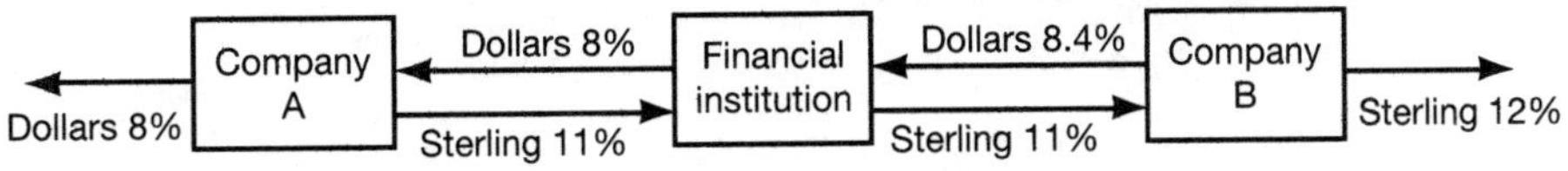

Figure 6.8 Alternative arrangement for currency swap; company A bears some foreign exchange risk.

1.0 percent per annum in dollars and pays 12.0 percent in sterling. In general, it makes sense for the financial institution to bear the foreign exchange risk as it is in the best position to hedge it.

Like interest-rate swaps, currency swaps are frequently warehoused by financial institutions. The financial institution then monitors its exposures to different currencies carefully so that it can hedge its risk.

VALUATION OF CURRENCY SWAPS

In the absence of default risk, a currency swap can be decomposed into a position in two bonds in a similar way to an interest-rate swap. Consider the position of company B in Figure 6.6. It is long a sterling bond that pays interest at 12.0 percent per annum and short a dollar bond that pays interest at 9.4 percent per annum. In general, if V is the value of a swap such as the one in Figure 6.6 to the party paying U.S. dollar interest rates,

$$V = SB_F - B_D$$

where B_F is the value, measured in the foreign currency, of the foreign-denominated bond underlying the swap, B_D is the value of the U.S. dollar bond underlying the swap, and S is the spot exchange rate (expressed as number of units of domestic currency per unit of foreign currency). The value of a swap can, therefore, be determined from the term structure of interest rates in the domestic currency, the term structure of interest rates in the foreign currency, and the spot exchange rate.

Example

Suppose that the term structure of interest rates is flat in both Japan and the United States. The Japanese rate is 4 percent per annum and the U.S. rate is 9 percent per annum (both with continuous compounding). A financial institution has entered into a currency swap where it receives 5 percent per annum in yen and pays 8 percent per annum in dollars once a year. The principals in the two currencies are \$10 million and 1,200 million yen. The swap will last for another three years and the current exchange rate is 110 yen = \$1. In this case

$$\begin{aligned} B_D &= 0.8e^{-0.09} + 0.8e^{-0.09\times 2} + 10.8e^{-0.09\times 3} \\ &= \$9.64 \text{ million} \\ B_F &= 60e^{-0.04} + 60e^{-0.04\times 2} + 1260e^{-0.04\times 3} \\ &= 1{,}230.55 \text{ million yen} \end{aligned}$$

The value of the swap is

$$\frac{1{,}230.55}{110} - 9.64 = \$1.55 \text{ million}$$

If the financial institution had been paying yen and receiving dollars, the value of the swap would have been −\$1.55 million.

Decomposition into Forward Contracts

An alternative decomposition of the currency swap is into a series of forward contracts. Suppose that in Figure 6.6 there is one payment date per year. On each payment date company B has agreed to exchange an inflow of £1.2 million (= 12 percent of £10 million) for an outflow of \$1.41 million (= 9.4 percent of \$15 million). In addition, at the final payment date it has agreed to exchange a £10 million inflow for a \$15 million outflow. Each of these exchanges represents a forward contract. Suppose t_i $(1 \le i \le n)$ is the time of the ith settlement date, r_i $(1 \le i \le n)$ is the continuously compounded U.S. dollar interest rate applicable to a time period of length t_i, and F_i $(1 \le i \le n)$ is the forward exchange rate applicable to time t_i. In Chapter 3, we showed that the value of a long forward contract is in all circumstances the present value of the amount by which the forward price exceeds the delivery price. The value to company B of the forward contract corresponding to the exchange of interest payments at time t_i is, therefore,

$$(1.2F_i - 1.41)e^{-r_i t_i}$$

for $1 \le i \le n$. The value to company B of the forward contract corresponding to the exchange of principal payments at time t_n is

$$(10F_n - 15)e^{-r_n t_n}$$

This shows that the value of a currency swap can always be calculated from the term structure of forward rates and the term structure of domestic interest rates.

Example

Consider again the situation in the previous example. The current spot rate is 110 yen per dollar or 0.009091 dollar per yen. Since the difference between the dollar and yen interest rates is 5 percent per annum, Equation (3.13) can be used to give the one-year, two-year, and three-year forward exchange rates as

$$0.009091e^{0.05\times 1} = 0.0096$$

$$0.009091e^{0.05\times 2} = 0.0100$$

$$0.009091e^{0.05\times 3} = 0.0106$$

respectively. The exchange of interest involves receiving 60 million yen and paying \$0.8 million. The riskfree interest rate in dollars is 9 percent per annum. The values of the forward contracts corresponding to the exchange of interest are, therefore, (in millions of dollars)

$$(60 \times 0.0096 - 0.8)e^{-0.09\times 1} = -0.21$$

$$(60 \times 0.0101 - 0.8)e^{-0.09\times 2} = -0.16$$

$$(60 \times 0.0106 - 0.8)e^{-0.09\times 3} = -0.13$$

The final exchange of principal involves receiving 1,200 million yen and paying \$10 million. The value of the forward contract corresponding to this is (in millions of dollars)

$$(1{,}200 \times 0.0106 - 10)e^{-0.09\times 3} = 2.04$$

The total value of the swap is $2.04 - 0.13 - 0.16 - 0.21 = \$1.54$ million which (allowing for rounding errors) is in agreement with the result of the calculations in the previous example.

Assume that the principal amounts in the two currencies are exactly equivalent at the start of a currency swap. At this time, the total value of the swap is zero. However, this does not mean that each of the individual forward contracts underlying the swap has zero value. It can be shown that when interest rates in two currencies are significantly different, the payer of the low-interest-rate currency is in the position where the forward contracts corresponding to the early exchanges of cash flows have positive values and the forward contract corresponding to the final exchange of principals has a negative expected value. The payer of the high-interest-rate currency is likely to be in the opposite position; that is, the early exchanges of cash flows have negative values and the final exchange has a positive expected value.

For the payer of the low-interest-rate currency, there will be a tendency for the swap to have a negative value during most of its life. This is because the forward contracts corresponding to the early exchanges of payments have positive values, and, once these exchanges have taken place, there is a tendency for the remaining forward contracts to have in total a negative value. For the payer of the high-interest-rate currency, the reverse is true. There is a tendency for the value of the swap to be positive during most of its life. These results are important when the credit risk in the swap is being evaluated.

OTHER SWAPS

A swap in its most general form is a security that involves the exchange of cash flows according to a formula that depends on the value of one or more underlying variables. There is, therefore, no limit to the number of different types of swaps that can be invented. In this section we discuss a few of the variants on the plain vanilla interest-rate swap and the plain deal currency swap that have been described so far.

In an interest-rate swap, a number of different floating reference rates can be used. Six-month LIBOR is the most common. Among the others used are: the three-month LIBOR, the one-month commercial paper rate, the treasury bill rate, and the tax-exempt rate. The particular reference rate chosen by a company will depend on the nature of its exposure. Swaps can be constructed to swap one floating rate (say, LIBOR) for another floating rate (say, prime). This allows a financial institution to hedge an exposure arising from assets and liabilities that are subject to different floating rates.

The principal in a swap agreement can be varied throughout the term of the swap to meet the needs of a counterparty. In an *amortizing swap*, the principal reduces in a way that corresponds to the amortization schedule on a loan. In a *step-up swap*, the principal increases in a way that corresponds to the drawdowns on a loan agreement. *Deferred swaps* or *forward swaps* in which parties do not begin to exchange interest payments until some future date can also be arranged.

One popular swap is an agreement to exchange a fixed interest rate in one currency for a floating interest rate in another currency. As such, it is a combination of a plain vanilla interest-rate swap and a plain deal currency swap. It can be valued using the procedures described earlier in this chapter.

Swaps can be extendable or puttable. In an *extendable swap*, one party has the option to extend the life of the swap beyond the specified period. In a *puttable swap*, one party has the option to terminate the swap early. Options on swaps or *swaptions* are also available. An option on an interest-rate swap is in essence an option to exchange a fixed-rate bond for a floating-rate bond. Since the floating-rate bond is worth close to its face value, swaptions can be considered as options on the value of the fixed-rate bond. Swaptions will be discussed further in Chapter 17.

A CMS swap is an agreement to exchange a LIBOR rate for a swap rate. (An example would be an agreement to exchange 6-month LIBOR for the ten-year swap rate every six months for the next five years.) A CMT swap is a similar agreement to exchange a LIBOR rate for a constant maturity treasury rate. An index amortizing rate swap (sometimes also called an *indexed principal swap*) is a swap where the principal reduces in a way dependent on the level of interest rates. (The lower the interest rates, the greater the reduction in the principal.) A *differential swap* or *diff swap* is a swap where a floating-interest rate in the domestic currency is exchanged for a floating interest rate in a foreign currency, with both interest rates being applied to the same domestic principal.

Swaps are now becoming increasingly available on commodities. A company that consumes 100,000 barrels of oil per year could agree to pay \$2 million each year for the next ten years and to receive in return $100{,}000S$, where S is the current market price of oil per barrel. This would in effect lock in its oil cost at \$20 per barrel. Similarly, an oil producer might agree to the opposite exchange. This would have the effect of locking in the price it realized for its oil at \$20 per barrel.

CREDIT RISK

Contracts such as swaps that are private arrangements between two companies entail credit risks. Consider a financial institution that has entered into offsetting contracts with two companies, A and B. (See Figure 6.3 or Figure 6.6.) If neither party defaults, the financial institution remains fully hedged. A decline in the value of one contract will always be offset by an increase in the value of the other contract. However, there is a chance that one party will get into financial difficulties and default. The financial institution would then still have to honor the contract it has with the other party.

Suppose that some time after the initiation of the contracts in Figure 6.3, the contract with company B has a positive value to the financial institution while the contract with company A has a negative value. If company B defaults, the financial institution would lose the positive value it has in this contract. To maintain a hedged position, it would have to find a third party willing to take company B's position. To induce the third party to do this, it would have to pay the third party an amount roughly equal to the value of the financial institution's contract with B prior to the default.

A financial institution has credit risk exposure from a swap only when the value of the swap to the financial institution is positive. What happens when this value is negative and the counterparty gets into financial difficulties? In theory, the financial institution could realize a windfall gain since a default would lead to it getting rid of a liability. In practice, it is likely that the counterparty would choose to sell the contract to a third party or rearrange its affairs in some way so that its positive value in the contract is not lost. The most realistic assumption for the financial institution is, therefore, as follows: If the counterparty goes bankrupt, there will be a loss if the value of the swap to the financial institution is positive and there will be no effect on the financial institution's position if the value of the swap to the financial institution is negative. The situation is illustrated in Figure 6.9.

Sometimes a financial institution can predict in advance which of two offsetting contracts is likely to have a positive value. Consider the currency swap in Figure 6.6. Sterling interest rates are higher than U.S. dollar interest rates. As mentioned earlier, this means that as time passes the financial institution is likely to find that its swap with A has a negative value, while its swap with B has a positive value. The creditworthiness of B is, therefore, far more important than the creditworthiness of A. In general, credit risk from a matched pair of currency swaps is greater than the credit risk from a matched pair of interest-rate swaps. This is because, in the case of a currency swap, principal amounts in different currencies are exchanged. In the case of both types of swaps, the expected loss from a default is much less than the expected loss from a default on a regular loan with approximately the same principal as the swap.

It is important to distinguish between the credit risk and market risk to a financial institution in any contract. As discussed earlier, the credit risk arises from the possibility of a default by the counterparty when the value of the contract to the financial institution is positive. The market risk arises from the possibility

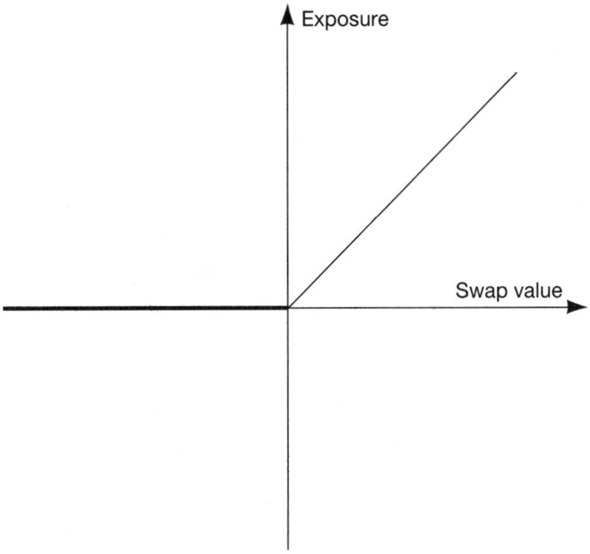

Figure 6.9 The credit exposure in a swap.

that market variables such as interest rates and exchange rates will move in such a way that the value of a contract to the financial institution becomes negative. Market risks can be hedged by entering into offsetting contracts; credit risks cannot be hedged.

SUMMARY

The two most common types of swaps are interest-rate swaps and currency swaps. In an interest-rate swap, one party agrees to pay the other party interest at a fixed rate on a notional principal for a number of years. In return, it receives interest at a floating rate on the same notional principal for the same period of time. In a currency swap, one party agrees to pay interest on a principal amount in one currency. In return, it receives interest on a principal amount in another currency.

Principal amounts are not exchanged in an interest-rate swap. In a currency swap, principal amounts are exchanged at both the beginning and the end of the life of the swap. For a party paying interest in the foreign currency the foreign principal is received and the domestic principal is paid at the beginning of the life of the swap. At the end of the life of the swap, the foreign principal is paid and the domestic principal is received.

An interest-rate swap can be used to transform a floating-rate loan into a fixed-rate loan or vice versa. A currency swap can be used to transform a loan in one currency into a loan in another currency. In essence, a swap is a long position in one bond combined with a short position in another bond. Alternatively, it can be considered as a portfolio of forward contracts.

Swaps are usually arranged by financial institutions. Ideally, in order to eliminate interest-rate or exchange-rate risk, a financial institution would like to enter into offsetting swap agreements with two parties at the same time. In practice, financial institutions frequently warehouse swaps. This means that they enter into a swap agreement with one party and then hedge their risk on a day-to-day basis while they attempt to find a party wanting to take the opposite position.

When a financial institution enters into a pair of offsetting swaps with different counterparties, it is exposed to credit risk. If one of the counterparties defaults when the financial institution has positive value in its swap with that counterparty, the financial institution loses money since it still has to honor its swap agreement with the other counterparty.

Suggestions for Further Reading

BICKSLER, J., and A. H. CHEN, "An economic analysis of interest rate swaps," *The Journal of Finance*, 41, No. 3 (1986), 645–655.

HULL, J., "Assessing credit risk in a financial institution's off-balance sheet commitments," *Journal of Financial and Quantitative Analysis*, 24 (December 1989), 489–502.

HULL, J., and A. WHITE, "The price of default," *RISK*, (September 1992), pp. 101–103.

HULL, J., and A. WHITE, "The impact of default risk on the prices of options and other derivative securities," forthcoming, *Journal of Banking and Finance*.

INTERNATIONAL SWAPS AND DERIVATIVES ASSOCIATION. "Code of Standard Working, Assumptions and Provisions for Swaps." New York.

LAYARD-LIESCHING, R., "Swap fever," *Euromoney*, supplement (January 1986), 108–113.

LITZENBERGER, R. H., "Swaps: plain and fanciful, " *Journal of Finance*, 47, no. 3 (1992), 831–50.

MARSHALL, J. F., and K. R. KAPNER, *Understanding Swap Finance*. Cincinnati, OH: South-Western, 1990.

SMITH, C. W., C. W. SMITHSON, and L. M. WAKEMAN, "The evolving market for swaps," *Midland Corporate Finance Journal*, 3(Winter 1986), 20–32.

TURNBULL, S. M., "Swaps: A zero sum game," *Financial Management*, 16, no. 1 (Spring 1987), 15–21.

Quiz

1. Companies A and B have been offered the following rates per annum on a \$20 million five-year loan:

	FIXED RATE	*FLOATING RATE*
Company A	12.0%	LIBOR + 0.1%
Company B	13.4%	LIBOR + 0.6%

Company A requires a floating-rate loan; company B requires a fixed-rate loan. Design a swap that will net a bank acting as intermediary 0.1 percent per annum and be equally attractive to both companies.

2. Company X wishes to borrow U.S. dollars at a fixed rate of interest. Company Y wishes to borrow Japanese yen at a fixed rate of interest. The amounts required by the two companies are roughly the same at the current exchange rate. The companies have been quoted the following interest rates:

	YEN	*DOLLARS*
Company X	5.0%	9.6%
Company Y	6.5%	10.0%

Design a swap that will net a bank, acting as intermediary, 50 basis points per annum. Make the swap equally attractive to the two companies and ensure that all foreign exchange risk is assumed by the bank.

3. A $100 million interest-rate swap has a remaining life of ten months. Under the terms of the swap, six-month LIBOR is exchanged for 12 percent per annum (compounded semiannually). The average of the bid and ask rate being exchanged for six-month LIBOR in swaps of all maturities is currently 10 percent per annum with continuous compounding. The six-month LIBOR rate was 9.6 percent per annum two months ago. What is the current value of the swap to the party paying floating? What is its value to the party paying fixed?
4. What is meant by warehousing swaps?
5. A currency swap has a remaining life of 15 months. It involves exchanging interest at 14 percent on £20 million for interest at 10 percent on $30 million once a year. The term structure of interest rates in both the United Kingdom and the United States is currently flat and if the swap were negotiated today the interest rates exchanged would be 8 percent in dollars and 11 percent in sterling. All interest rates are quoted with annual compounding. The current exchange rate is 1.6500. What is the value of the swap to the party paying sterling? What is the value of the swap to the party paying dollars?
6. Explain the difference between the credit risk and the market risk in a financial contract. Which of the risks can be hedged?
7. Explain why a bank is subject to credit risk when it enters into two offsetting swap contracts.

Questions and Problems

6.1. Companies X and Y have been offered the following rates per annum on a $5 million ten-year loan:

	FIXED RATE	*FLOATING RATE*
Company X	7.0%	LIBOR + 0.5%
Company Y	8.8%	LIBOR + 1.5%

Company X requires a floating-rate loan; company Y requires a fixed-rate loan. Design a swap that will net a bank acting as intermediary 0.2 percent per annum and which will be equally attractive to X and Y.

6.2. Company A, a British manufacturer, wishes to borrow U.S. dollars at a fixed rate of interest. Company B, a U.S. multinational, wishes to borrow sterling at a fixed rate of interest. They have been quoted the following rates per annum:

	STERLING	*U.S. DOLLARS*
Company A	11.0%	7.0%
Company B	10.6%	6.2%

Design a swap that will net a bank, acting as intermediary, 10 basis points per annum and which will produce a gain of 15 basis points per annum for each of the two companies.

6.3. Under the terms of an interest-rate swap, a financial institution has agreed to pay 10 percent per annum and to receive three-month LIBOR in return on a notional principal of $100 million with payments being exchanged every three months. The swap has a remaining life of 14 months. The average of the bid and ask fixed rate currently being swapped for three-month LIBOR is 12 percent per annum for all maturities. The three-month LIBOR rate one month ago was 11.8 percent per annum. All rates are compounded quarterly. What is the value of the swap?

6.4. Suppose that the term structure of interest rates is flat in the United States and Germany. The dollar interest rate is 11 percent per annum while the mark interest rate is 8 percent per annum. The current exchange rate is 2.1 marks = $1. Under the terms of a swap agreement, a financial institution pays 5 percent per annum in marks and receives 10 percent per annum in dollars. The principals in the two currencies are $10 million and 20 million marks. Payments are exchanged every year with one exchange having just taken place. The swap will last two more years. What is the value of the swap to the financial institution? Assume all interest rates are continuously compounded.

6.5. A financial institution has entered into an interest-rate swap with company X. Under the terms of the swap, it receives 10 percent per annum and pays six-month LIBOR on a principal of $10 million for five years. Payments are made every six months. Suppose that company X defaults on the sixth payment date (end of year 3) when the interest rate (with semiannual compounding) is 8 percent per annum for all maturities. What is the loss to the financial institution? Assume that six-month LIBOR was 9 percent per annum halfway through year 3.

6.6. A financial institution has entered into a ten-year currency swap with company Y. Under the terms of the swap, it receives interest at 3 percent per annum in Swiss francs and pays interest at 8 percent per annum in U.S. dollars. Interest payments are exchanged once a year. The principal amounts are $7 million and 10 million francs. Suppose that company Y defaults at the end of year 6 when the exchange rate is $0.80 per franc. What is the cost to the financial institution? Assume that at the end of year 6, the interest rate is 3 percent per annum in Swiss francs and 8 percent per annum in U.S. dollars for all maturities. All interest rates are quoted with annual compounding.

6.7. Companies A and B face the following interest rates:

	A	*B*
U.S. dollars (floating rate)	LIBOR + 0.5%	LIBOR + 1.0%
German marks (fixed rate)	5.0%	6.5%

Assume that A wants to borrow dollars at a floating rate of interest and B wants to borrow marks at a fixed rate of interest. A financial institution is planning to arrange a swap and requires a 50 basis point spread. If the swap is equally attractive to A and B, what rates of interest will A and B end up paying?

6.8. Company X is based in the United Kingdom and would like to borrow $U.S. 50 million at a fixed rate of interest for five years in U.S. funds. As the company is not well known in the United States, this has proved to be impossible. However, the company has been quoted 12 percent per annum on fixed-rate five-year sterling funds. Company Y is based in the United States and would like to borrow the equivalent of $U.S. 50 million in sterling funds for five years at a fixed rate of interest. It has been unable to get a quote, but has been offered U.S. dollar funds at 10.5 percent per annum. Five-year government bonds currently yield 9.5 percent per annum in the United States and 10.5 percent in the United Kingdom. Suggest an appropriate currency swap which will net the financial intermediary 0.5 percent per annum.

6.9. After it hedges its foreign exchange risk using forward contracts, is the financial institution's average spread in Figure 6.6 likely to be greater than or less than 40 basis points? Explain your answer.

6.10. How can a deferred swap be created from two other swaps?

6.11. "Companies with high credit risks are the ones that cannot access fixed-rate markets directly. They are the companies that are most likely to be paying fixed and receiving floating in an interest-rate swap." Assume that this is true. Do you think it increases or decreases the risk of a financial institution's swap portfolio? Assume that companies are most likely to default when interest rates are high.

6.12. How can a financial institution that warehouses interest-rate swaps monitor its exposure to interest-rate changes?

6.13. Why is the expected loss from a default on a swap less than the expected loss from the default on a loan with the same principal?

6.14. A bank finds that its assets are not matched with its liabilities. It is taking floating-rate deposits and making fixed-rate loans. How can swaps be used to offset the risk?

6.15. Explain how you would value a swap that is the exchange of a floating rate in one currency for a fixed rate in another currency.

7

MECHANICS OF OPTIONS MARKETS

The rest of this book is concerned with options. In this chapter, we explain how options markets are organized, what terminology is used, how the contracts are traded, how margin requirements are set, and so on. In later chapters, we will discuss such topics as trading strategies involving options, the determination of option prices, and the ways in which portfolios of options can be hedged. This chapter is concerned primarily with stock options. We will provide more details on the markets for currency options, index options, and futures options in Chapters 12 and 13.

Options are fundamentally different from forward and futures contracts. An option gives the holder of the option the right to do something. The holder does not have to exercise this right. By contrast, in a forward or futures contract, the two parties have committed themselves to doing something. Whereas it costs nothing (except for the margin requirements) to enter into a forward or futures contract, the purchase of an option requires an up-front payment.

TYPES OF OPTIONS

As mentioned in Chapter 1, there are two basic types of options. A call option gives the holder the right to buy an asset by a certain date for a certain price. A put option gives the holder the right to sell an asset by a certain date for a certain price. The date specified in the contract is known as the expiration date, the exercise date, the strike date, or the maturity. The price specified in the contract is known as the exercise price or strike price.

Options can be either American or European. This has nothing to do with geographical location. *American options* are options that can be exercised at any time up to the expiration date, whereas *European options* are options that can only be exercised on the expiration date itself. Most of the options that are traded on exchanges are American. However, European options are generally easier to analyze than American options, and some of the properties of an American option are frequently deduced from those of its European counterpart.

Example of a Call Option

Consider the situation of an investor who buys a European call option to purchase 100 IBM shares with a strike price of $40. Suppose that the current stock price is $38, the expiration date of the option is in four months, and the price of an option to purchase one share is $5. The initial investment is $500. Since the option is European, the investor can exercise only on the expiration date. If the share price on this date is less than $40, he or she will clearly choose not to exercise. (There is no point in buying for $40 a share that has a market value of less than $40.) In these circumstances, the investor loses the whole of the initial investment of $500. If the share price is above $40 on the expiration date, the option will be exercised. Suppose, for example, that the share price is $55. By exercising the option, the investor is able to buy 100 shares for $40 per share. If the shares are sold immediately, the investor makes a gain of $15 per share, or $1,500, ignoring transactions costs. When the initial cost of the option is taken into account, the net profit to the investor is $1,000.

Table 7.1 summarizes this example. Figure 7.1 shows the way in which the investor's net profit/loss on an option to purchase one share varies with the terminal share price in this example. It is important to realize that an investor sometimes exercises an option and makes a loss overall. Suppose that in the example the stock price of IBM is $42 at the expiration of the option. The investor would exercise the option for a gain of 100 × ($42 − $40) = $200 and realize a loss overall of $300 when the initial cost of the option is taken into account. It is tempting to argue that the investor should not exercise the option in these circumstances. However, not exercising would lead to an overall loss of $500—which is worse than the $300 loss when the investor exercises. In general, call options should always be exercised at the expiration date if the stock price is above the strike price.

Example of a Put Option

Whereas the purchaser of a call option is hoping that the stock price will increase, the purchaser of a put option is hoping that it will decrease. Consider an investor who buys a European put option to sell 100 Exxon shares with a strike price of $70. Suppose that the current share price is $65, the expiration date of the

Table 7.1 Profit from Call Option

From the Trader's Desk

An investor buys a call option to purchase 100 IBM shares.

Strike price = \$40
Current stock price = \$38
Price of an option to buy one share = \$5

The initial investment is 100 × \$5 = \$500.

The Outcome

At the expiration of the option, IBM's stock price is \$55. At this time, the option is exercised for a gain of

(\$55 − \$40) × 100 = \$1,500

When the initial cost of the option is taken into account, the net gain is

\$1,500 − \$500 = \$1,000

option is in three months, and the price of an option to sell one share is \$7. The initial investment is \$700. Since the option is European, it will be exercised only if the share price is below \$70 at the expiration date. Suppose that the share price is \$55 on this date. The investor can buy 100 shares for \$55 per share and, under the terms of the put option, sell the same shares for \$70 to realize a gain of \$15 per share, or \$1,500. (Again, transactions costs are ignored.) When the \$700 initial cost of the option is taken into account, the investor's net profit is \$800. Of course, there is no guarantee that the investor will make a gain. If the final stock price is above \$70, the put option expires worthless and the investor loses \$700. Table 7.2 summarizes this example. Figure 7.2 shows the way in which the investor's profit/

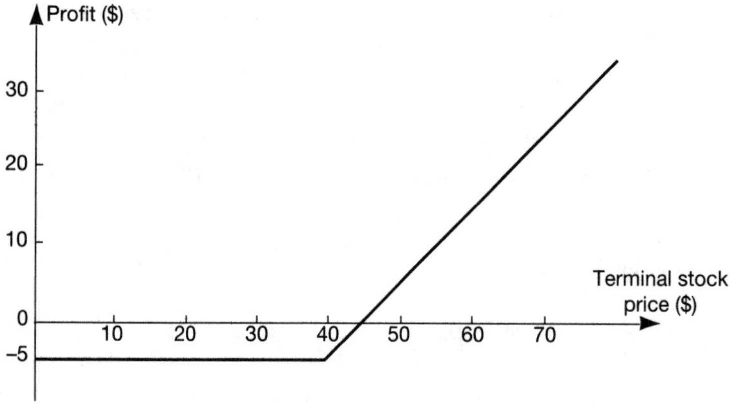

Figure 7.1 Profit from buying a European call option on one IBM share. Option price = \$5, strike price = \$40.

Table 7.2 Profit from Put Option

From the Trader's Desk

An investor buys a put option to sell 100 Exxon shares.

Strike price = \$70
Current share price = \$65
Price of put option to sell one share = \$7

The initial investment is 100 × \$7 = \$700.

The Outcome

At the expiration of the option Exxon's share price is \$55. At this time, the investor buys 100 Exxon shares and, under the terms of the put option, sells them for \$70 per share to realize a gain of \$15 per share or \$1,500 in total. When the initial cost of the option is taken into account, the net gain is

\$1,500 − \$700 = \$800

loss on an option to sell one share varies with the terminal stock price in this example.

Early Exercise

As already mentioned, stock options are generally American rather than European. This means that the investor in the foregoing examples does not have to wait until the expiration date before exercising the option. We will see later that there are some circumstances under which it is optimal to exercise American options prior to maturity.

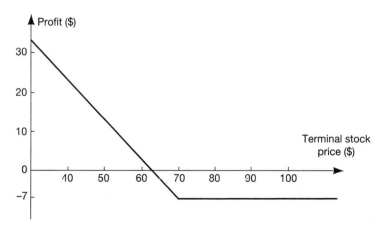

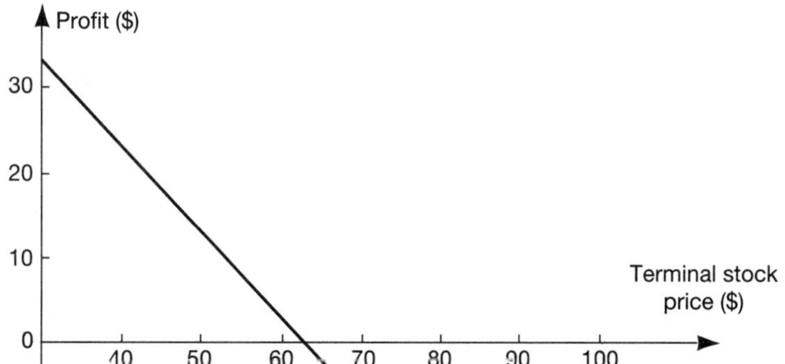

Figure 7.2 Profit from buying a European put option on one Exxon share. Option price = \$7, strike price = \$70.

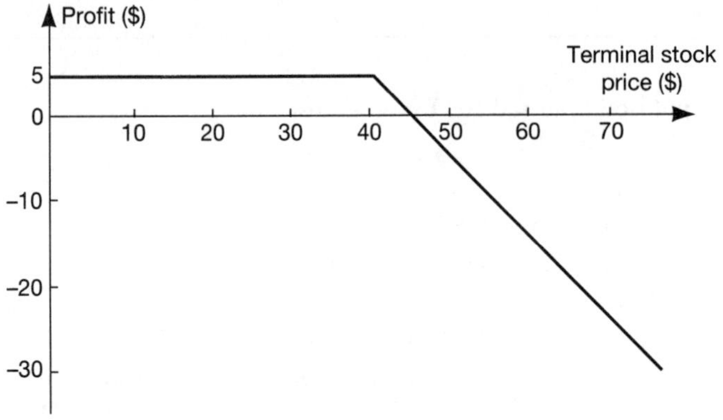

Figure 7.3 Profit from writing a European call option on one IBM share. Option price = $5, strike price = $40.

OPTION POSITIONS

There are two sides to every option contract. On one side is the investor who has taken the long position (i.e., has bought the option). On the other side is the investor who has taken a short position (i.e., has sold or *written* the option). The writer of an option receives cash up front but has potential liabilities later. His or her profit/loss is the reverse of that for the purchaser of the option. Figures 7.3 and 7.4 show the variation of the profit/loss with the final stock price for writers of the options considered in Figures 7.1 and 7.2.

There are four types of options positions:

1. A long position in a call option
2. A long position in a put option
3. A short position in a call option
4. A short position in a put option

Figure 7.4 Profit from writing a European put option on one Exxon share. Option price = $7, strike price = $70.

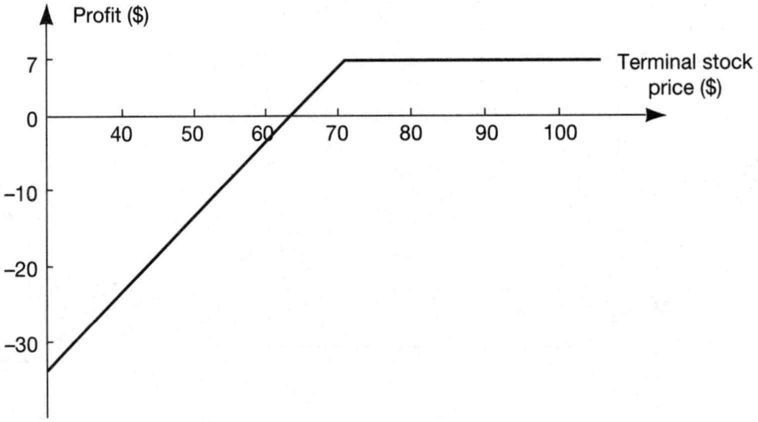

It is often useful to characterize European option positions in terms of the terminal value or payoff to the investor at maturity. The initial cost of the option is then not included in the calculation. If X is the strike price and S_T is the final price of the underlying asset, the payoff from a long position in a European call option is

$$\max(S_T - X, 0)$$

This reflects the fact that the option will be exercised if $S_T > X$ and will not be exercised if $S_T \leq X$. The payoff to the holder of a short position in the European call option is

$$-\max(S_T - X, 0) = \min(X - S_T, 0)$$

The payoff to the holder of a long position in a European put option is

$$\max(X - S_T, 0)$$

and the payoff from a short position in a European put option is

$$-\max(X - S_T, 0) = \min(S_T - X, 0)$$

Figure 7.5 illustrates these payoffs graphically.

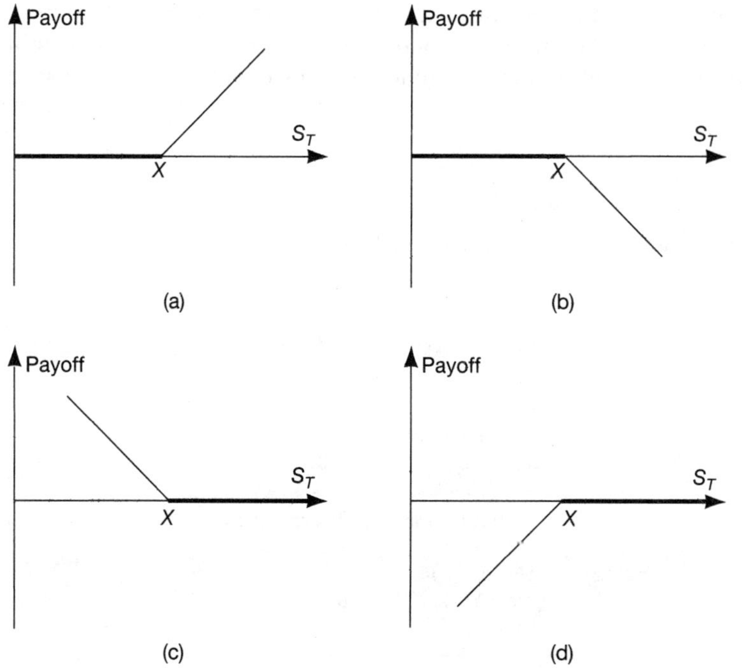

Figure 7.5 Payoffs from positions in European options: (a) long call, (b) short call, (c) long put, (d) short put. Strike price = X, price of asset at maturity = S_T.

THE UNDERLYING ASSETS

Exchange-traded options are currently actively traded on stocks, stock indices, foreign currencies, and futures contracts. Table 7.3 provides a list of U.S. exchanges that trade options. In addition, most of the exchanges in Table 2.1 trade options on futures contracts as well as the futures contracts themselves.

Stock Options

Options currently trade on over 500 stocks in the United States. One contract gives the holder the right to buy or sell 100 shares at the specified strike price. This is convenient since the shares themselves are normally traded in lots of 100. At one time, there was an arrangement whereby most stock options were traded on just one exchange (the CBOE, PHLX, AMEX, PSE, or NYSE). However, this is in the process of changing to a situation where all exchanges are allowed to trade all options.

Foreign Currency Options

The major exchange for trading foreign currency options is the Philadelphia Stock Exchange. It offers both European and American contracts on the Australian dollar, British pound, Canadian dollar, German mark, French franc, Japanese yen, and Swiss franc. The size of one contract depends on the currency. For example, in the case of the British pound, one contract gives the holder the right to buy or sell £31,250; in the case of the Japanese yen, one contract gives the holder the right to buy or sell 6.25 million yen. Foreign currency options contracts are discussed further in Chapter 12.

Table 7.3 U.S. Exchanges That Trade Options

Chicago Board Options Exchange (CBOE) LaSalle at Van Buren Chicago, IL 60604 312-786-5600	American Stock Exchange (AMEX) 86 Trinity Place New York, NY 10006 212-306-1000
Philadelphia Stock Exchange (PHLX) 1900 Market Street Philadelphia, PA 19103 215-496-5000	Pacific Stock Exchange (PSE) 301 Pine Street San Francisco, CA 94104 415-393-4000
New York Stock Exchange (NYSE) 11 Wall Street New York, NY 10005 212-263-8533	AMEX Commodities Corporation (ACC) 86 Trinity Place New York, NY 10006 212-306-1000

Index Options

Many different index options currently trade in the United States. The contracts with the greatest open interest are those on the S&P 500 Index (CBOE), the S&P 100 Index (CBOE), and the Major Market Index (AMEX). Some of the options which trade are European; others are American. For example, the contract on the S&P 500 is European while those on the S&P 100 and the Major Market Index are American. One contract is to buy or sell 100 times the index at the specified strike price. Settlement is always in cash rather than by delivering the portfolio underlying the index. Consider, for example, one call contract on the S&P 100 with a strike price of 280. If it is exercised when the value of the index is 292, the writer of the contract pays the holder $(292 - 280) \times 100 = \$1{,}200$. This cash payment is based on the index value at the end of the day on which exercise instructions are issued. Not surprisingly, investors usually wait until the end of a day before issuing these instructions.

Exchange-traded index options contracts typically have maturities no greater than four months, but longer-maturity contracts known as LEAPS are available on the S&P 500, the S&P 100, and the Major Market Index. These contracts always have December expiration dates. Recently the CBOE has introduced trading in flex options. These are options where the strike price and the maturity are determined by traders and do not have to conform to those specified by the exchange. Index option contracts are discussed further in Chapter 12.

Futures Options

In a futures option (or options on futures), the underlying asset is a futures contract. The futures contract normally matures shortly after the expiration of the option. Futures options are now available for most of the assets on which futures contracts are traded. When the holder of a call option exercises, he or she acquires from the writer a long position in the underlying futures contract plus a cash amount equal to the excess of the futures price over the strike price. When the holder of a put option exercises, he or she acquires a short position in the underlying futures contract plus a cash amount equal to the excess of the strike price over the futures price. In both cases, the futures contracts have zero value and can be closed out immediately. The payoff from a futures option is, therefore, the same as the payoff from a stock option with the stock price replaced by the futures price. The most actively traded futures option contracts are on the Eurodollar (CME) and the treasury bond (CBOT). The contracts on corn, soybeans, crude oil, gold, and some currencies are also popular. Futures options contracts are discussed further in Chapter 13.

SPECIFICATION OF STOCK OPTIONS

In the rest of this chapter, we will focus on stock options. The contract specifications and trading of index options, currency options, and futures options are discussed further in Chapters 12 and 13.

As already mentioned, a stock option contract is an American-style option contract to buy or sell 100 shares of the stock. Details of the contract such as the expiration date, the strike price, what happens when dividends are declared, how large a position investors can hold, and so on are specified by the exchange.

Expiration Dates

One of the items used to describe a stock option is the month in which the expiration date occurs. Thus, a January call on IBM is a call option on IBM with an expiration date in January. The precise expiration date is 10:59 p.m. Central Time on the Saturday immediately following the third Friday of the expiration month. The last day on which options trade is the third Friday of the expiration month. An investor with a long position in an option normally has until 4:30 p.m. Central Time on that Friday to instruct his or her broker to exercise the option. The broker then has until 10:59 p.m. the next day to complete the paperwork notifying the exchange that exercise is to take place.

Stock options are on a January, February, or March cycle. The January cycle consists of the months of January, April, July, and October. The February cycle consists of the months of February, May, August, and November. The March cycle consists of the months of March, June, September, and December. If the expiration date for the current month has not yet been reached, options trade with expiration dates in the current month, the following month, and the next two months in its cycle. If the expiration date of the current month has passed, options trade with expiration dates in the next month, the next-but-one month, and the next two months of the expiration cycle. For example, IBM is on a January cycle. At the beginning of January, options are traded with expiration dates in January, February, April, and July; at the end of January, they are traded with expiration dates in February, March, April, and July; at the beginning of May, they are traded with expiration dates in May, June, July, and October; and so on. When one option reaches expiration, trading in another is started. Longer-term options, known as LEAPS, also trade on some stocks. These have expiration dates up to three years into the future. The expiration dates for LEAPS on stocks are always in January.

Strike Prices

The exchange chooses the strike prices at which options can be written. For stock options, strike prices are normally spaced \$2½, \$5, or \$10 apart. (An exception occurs when there has been a stock split or a stock dividend as will be described shortly.) The usual rule followed by exchanges is to use a \$2½ spacing for strike prices when the stock price is less than \$25, a \$5 spacing when it is between \$25 and \$200, and a \$10 spacing when it is greater than \$200. For example, in mid-1993, Compaq had a stock price of 52⅝ and the options traded had strike prices of 40, 45, 50, 55, and 60. Bethlehem Steel had a stock price of 13⅞ and the options traded had strike prices of 12½, 15, and 17½.

When a new expiration date is introduced, the two strike prices closest to the current stock price are usually selected by the exchange. If one of these is very close to the existing stock price, the third strike price closest to the current stock price may also be selected. If the stock price moves outside the range defined by the highest and lowest strike price, trading is usually introduced in an option with a new strike price. To illustrate these rules, suppose that the stock price is $53 when trading in the October options start. Call and put options would first be offered with strike prices of 50 and 55. If the stock price rose above $55, a strike price of 60 would be offered; if it fell below $50, a strike price of 45 would be offered; and so on.

Terminology

For any given asset at any given time, there may be many different option contracts trading. Consider a stock where there are four expiration dates and five strike prices. If call and put options trade with every expiration date and every strike price, there are a total of 40 different contracts. All options of the same type (calls or puts) are referred to as an *option class*. For example, IBM calls are one class while IBM puts are another class. An *option series* consists of all the options of a given class with the same expiration date and strike price. In other words, an option series refers to a particular contract that is traded. The IBM 50 October calls are an option series.

Options are referred to as *in the money*, *at the money*, or *out of the money*. An in-the-money option is one that would lead to a positive cash flow to the holder if it were exercised immediately. Similarly, an at-the-money option would lead to zero cash flow if it were exercised immediately, and an out-of-the-money option would lead to a negative cash flow if it were exercised immediately. If S is the stock price and X is the strike price, a call option is in the money when $S > X$, at the money when $S = X$, and out of the money when $S < X$. A put option is in the money when $S < X$, at the money when $S = X$, and out of the money when $S > X$. Clearly, an option will only ever be exercised if it is in the money. In the absence of transaction costs, an in-the-money option will always be exercised on the expiration date if it has not been exercised previously.

The *intrinsic value* of an option is defined as the maximum of zero and the value it would have if it were exercised immediately. For a call option, the intrinsic value is therefore $\max(S - X, 0)$. For a put option, it is $\max(X - S, 0)$. An in-the-money American option must be worth at least as much as its intrinsic value, since the holder can realize the intrinsic value by exercising immediately. Often it is optimal for the holder of an in-the-money American option to wait rather than exercise immediately. The option is then said to have *time value*. The total value of an option can be thought of as the sum of its intrinsic value and its time value.

Dividends and Stock Splits

The early over-the-counter options were dividend protected. If a company declared a cash dividend, the strike price for options on the company's stock was reduced on the ex-dividend day by the amount of the dividend. Exchange-traded options are not generally adjusted for cash dividends. As we will see in Chapter 11, this has significant implications for the way in which options are valued.

Exchange-traded options are adjusted for stock splits. A stock split occurs when the existing shares are "split" into more shares. For example, in a 3-for-1 stock split, three new shares are issued to replace each existing share. Since a stock split does not change the assets or the earning ability of a company, we should not expect it to have any effect on the wealth of the company's shareholders. All else being equal, the 3-for-1 stock split just referred to should cause the stock price to go down to one third of its previous value. In general, an n-for-m stock split should cause the stock price to go down to m/n of its previous value. The terms of option contracts are adjusted to reflect expected changes in a stock price arising from a stock split. After an n-for-m stock split, the strike price is reduced to m/n of its previous value and the number of shares covered by one contract is increased to n/m of its previous value. If the stock price reduces in the way expected, the positions of both the writer and the purchaser of a contract remain unchanged.

Example

> Consider a call option to buy 100 shares of a company for $30 per share. Suppose that the company makes a 2-for-1 stock split. The terms of the option contract are then changed so that it gives the holder the right to purchase 200 shares for $15 per share.

Stock options are adjusted for stock dividends. A stock dividend involves a company issuing more shares to its existing shareholders. For example, a 20 percent stock dividend means that investors receive one new share for each five already owned. A stock dividend like a stock split has no effect on either the assets or the earning power of a company. The stock price can be expected to go down as a result of a stock dividend. The 20 percent stock dividend referred to is essentially the same as a 6-for-5 stock split. All else being equal, it should cause the stock price to decline to 5/6 of its previous value. The terms of an option are adjusted to reflect the expected price decline arising from a stock dividend in the same way as they are for that arising from a stock split.

Example

> Consider a put option to sell 100 shares of a company for $15 per share. Suppose that the company declares a 25 percent stock dividend. This is equivalent to a 5-for-4 stock split. The terms of the option contract are changed so that it gives the holder the right to sell 125 shares for $12.

Adjustments are also made for rights issues. The basic procedure is to calculate the theoretical price of the rights and then to reduce the strike price by this amount. As pointed out by Brown, this procedure leaves the option holder slightly worse off than he or she was before the issue.[1]

[1] See R. L. Brown, "Adjusting option contracts to reflect capitalization changes," *Journal of Business Finance and Accounting*, 16 (1989), pp 247–54.

Position Limits and Exercise Limits

The exchange specifies a *position limit* for each stock upon which options are traded. This defines the maximum number of option contracts that an investor can hold on one side of the market. For this purpose, long calls and short puts are considered to be on the same side of the market. Also, short calls and long puts are considered to be on the same side of the market. The *exercise limit* equals the position limit. It defines the maximum number of contracts that can be exercised by any individual (or group of individuals acting together) in any period of five consecutive business days. A position limit/exercise limit between 5,000 and 10,000 contracts is not uncommon.

Position limits and exercise limits are designed to prevent the market from being unduly influenced by the activities of an individual investor or group of investors. However, whether they are really necessary is a controversial issue.

NEWSPAPER QUOTES

Many newspapers carry option quotations. In *The Wall Street Journal*, stock option quotations can currently be found under the heading "Listed Options" in the Money and Investing section. Table 7.4 shows the quotations as they appeared in *The Wall Street Journal* of Thursday, August 12, 1993. These refer to trading that took place on the previous day (i.e., Wednesday, August 11, 1993).

The company on whose stock the option is written together with the closing stock price is listed in the first column. The strike price and maturity month appear in the second and third columns. If a call option traded with the strike price and maturity month traded, the next two columns show the volume of trading and price at last trade for the call option. The final two columns show the same for a put option.

The quoted price is the price of an option to buy or sell one share. As mentioned earlier, one contract is for the purchase or sale of 100 shares. A contract, therefore, costs 100 times the price shown. Since most options are priced at less than \$10 and some are priced at less than \$1, individuals do not have to be extremely wealthy to trade options.

The Wall Street Journal also shows the total call volume, put volume, call open interest, and put open interest for each exchange. The numbers for Wednesday, August 11, 1993 are shown in Table 7.5. The volume is the total number of contracts traded on the day. The open interest is the number of contracts outstanding.

From Table 7.4, it appears that there were arbitrage opportunities on August 11, 1993. For example, a September put on Abbt L with a strike price of 25 could be bought for $1\frac{7}{8}$. Since the stock price is 23, it appears that this put could be purchased and then exercised immediately for a profit of $\frac{1}{8}$. In fact, these arbitrage opportunities almost certainly did not exist. For both options and stocks, Table 7.4 gives the prices at which the last trade took place on August 11, 1993. The last

Table 7.4 Stock Option Quotations from *The Wall Street Journal* on August 12, 1993

LISTED OPTIONS QUOTATIONS

Option/Strike		Exp.	Call Vol.	Call Last	Put Vol.	Put Last
AEP	40	Feb	46	1/2	...	...
AMD	20	Oct	26	10	10	1/8
29 5/8	22 1/2	Aug	69	7 1/2	...	...
29 5/8	22 1/2	Oct	63	7 1/2	26	1/4
29 5/8	22 1/2	Jan	39	8 1/2	...	...
29 5/8	25	Aug	452	4 3/4	15	1/16
29 5/8	25	Sep	21	5	40	3/8
29 5/8	25	Oct	313	5 1/2	234	3/4
29 5/8	25	Jan	76	6 3/4	...	...
29 5/8	30	Aug	759	3/4	161	7/8
29 5/8	30	Sep	1027	1 3/4	155	2
29 5/8	30	Oct	465	2 5/16	107	2 1/2
29 5/8	30	Jan	242	3 3/4	299	3
29 5/8	35	Sep	50	3/8	...	...
29 5/8	35	Oct	224	3/4	2	5 1/4
29 5/8	35	Jan	97	1 3/4	20	6 5/8
AMP	65	Aug	75	1	...	...
AMR	55	Nov	...	...	50	5/8
65	60	Aug	70	5 1/8	204	3/16
65	60	Sep	22	6	20	5/8
65	60	Nov	60	7 1/4	...	...
65	65	Aug	390	1 1/16	169	1 1/8
65	65	Sep	363	2 1/4	29	2 1/8
65	65	Nov	465	4 1/4	1	3 3/4
65	70	Aug	50	1/16	10	4 1/4
65	70	Sep	71	5/8	...	...
65	70	Nov	78	2	...	...
65	75	Nov	35	1 1/8	...	...
ASA	40	Aug	...	...	40	1/16
45 1/2	40	Nov	2	6 5/8	50	1 1/4
45 1/2	45	Aug	259	1 3/16	60	7/8
45 1/2	45	Sep	250	2 7/16	9	2
45 1/2	45	Nov	61	3 5/8	39	3 3/8
45 1/2	50	Aug	4	1/8	23	4 7/8
45 1/2	50	Sep	100	3/4	...	...
45 1/2	50	Nov	34	1 3/4	23	6 3/8
ABrrck	17 1/2	Jan	550	8 1/4	...	...
25 1/8	20	Oct	19	5 3/8	39	5/16
25 1/8	20	Jan	66	6 3/8	...	...
25 1/8	22 1/2	Oct	76	3 1/2	85	3/4
25 1/8	25	Aug	250	1/2	50	5/8
25 1/8	25	Sep	93	1 7/16	10	1 1/4
25 1/8	25	Oct	224	2 1/8	3	1 3/4
25 1/8	25	Jan	373	3 1/4	4	2 5/8
25 1/8	30	Sep	30	3/8	10	5 1/8
25 1/8	30	Jan	101	1 3/8	...	...
ADT	10	Sep	40	7/16	40	3/4
9 3/4	10	Dec	510	7/8	...	...
AGreet	60	Dec	30	3 1/8	...	...
AInt o	80	Aug	180	16 1/2	...	...
...	93 3/8	Aug	...	...	100	7/16
...	93 3/8	Feb	360	8 1/4	...	...
AMedHI	12 1/2	Sep	50	1 1/4	...	...
13 3/8	15	Sep	4	1/4	30	1 7/8
APwrCv	40	Sep	100	7 1/4	16	1
45 7/8	45	Sep	150	3 3/8	10	2 3/4
45 7/8	50	Sep	43	1 1/2	34	5 3/4
45 7/8	50	Dec	35	4 1/8	...	...
AST Rs	15	Aug	40	1/4	5	1/2
AT&T	45	Jan	30	18 3/4	...	...
63 1/4	55	Oct	51	8 5/8	...	...
63 1/4	60	Sep	100	4 1/8	43	3/8
63 1/4	60	Oct	55	4 1/8	53	3/4
63 1/4	60	Jan	...	...	30	1 3/4
63 1/4	65	Aug	790	1/8	415	1 3/4
63 1/4	65	Sep	274	3/4	...	...
63 1/4	65	Oct	281	1 3/16	...	...
63 1/4	65	Jan	6	2 1/4	30	3 7/8
63 1/4	70	Jan	67	7/8	...	...
Abbt L	22 1/2	Sep	59	1 1/4	53	1/2
23	25	Aug	154	1/8	72	1 13/16
23	25	Sep	53	5/16	50	1 7/8
23	25	Nov	72	3/4	77	2 3/8
23	25	Feb	114	1 1/8	...	...
23	30	Nov	48	1/8	5	6 3/4
Aclaim	30	Aug	74	6	...	...
35 5/8	30	Sep	...	...	25	1
35 5/8	35	Aug	...	...	60	1 1/4
Adaptc	20	Oct	26	10	30	1/8
30 3/8	22 1/2	Aug	36	8 1/8	...	...
30 3/8	25	Oct	28	6	20	9/16
30 3/8	30	Aug	53	1 1/4	88	13/16
30 3/8	30	Sep	248	2 1/4	30	1 3/4
30 3/8	30	Oct	223	3	40	2 1/8
30 3/8	30	Jan	57	4 1/8	25	3 3/8
AdobeS	25	Aug	227	3 3/4	50	1/8
28 3/4	25	Sep	96	4	25	3/4
28 3/4	25	Oct	40	4 3/8	30	1
28 3/4	27 1/2	Aug	2195	1 1/2	568	3/8
28 3/4	27 1/2	Sep	120	2 3/8	6	1 5/8
28 3/4	27 1/2	Oct	25	2 11/16	31	2 1/8
47	45	Aug	350	2	136	3/16
47	45	Sep	25	2 1/4	4	3/4
47	45	Oct	69	3 1/8	8	1 5/16
47	45	Jan	24	4 1/4	...	...
47	50	Sep	44	7/16	10	4
47	50	Jan	339	2 1/8	...	...
BankNY	60	Sep	100	1/8	...	...
54 5/8	60	Oct	32	3/4	...	...
Bard	20	Sep	10	1 11/16	28	3/4
21 3/4	22 1/2	Aug	...	...	300	2 1/4
21 3/4	25	Aug	...	...	300	4 1/2
21 3/4	30	Oct	217	1/8	...	...
Barnet	45	Sep	...	...	25	13/16
BattlM	7 1/2	Aug	30	2	...	...
9 5/8	7 1/2	Oct	100	2 1/4	...	...
9 5/8	10	Aug	398	1/8	10	5/8
9 5/8	10	Sep	25	1/2	...	...
9 5/8	10	Oct	81	3/4	...	...
9 5/8	10	Jan	228	1 7/16	...	...
9 5/8	12 1/2	Sep	37	1/8	...	...
9 5/8	12 1/2	Jan	70	11/16	...	...
Baybks	50	Dec	30	3 7/8	...	...
Bear o	21 3/8	Oct	402	2 3/16	...	...
22 7/8	21 3/8	Jan	100	2 9/16	...	...
22 7/8	23 3/4	Aug	41	1/4	...	...
22 7/8	23 3/4	Jan	410	1 1/2	...	...
BellSo	55	Aug	300	1 5/8	...	...
56 3/8	55	Oct	200	2 1/2	...	...
BestBy	40	Aug	76	9 3/8	...	...
49 1/4	45	Sep	83	6	97	1 1/4
49 1/4	50	Sep	148	2 3/4	17	3 1/2
Beth S	12 1/2	Sep	...	...	40	1/4
13 7/8	15	Sep	20	1/2	350	1 1/4
13 7/8	15	Oct	...	...	394	1 5/8
13 7/8	17 1/2	Oct	49	1/4	...	...
13 7/8	17 1/2	Jan	31	5/8	...	...
BioTcG	5	Aug	42	1/16	...	...
Biogen	25	Sep	40	2 9/16	14	1
26 5/8	25	Oct	53	3	...	...
26 5/8	30	Oct	29	1	23	4 3/8
26 5/8	30	Jan	24	1 15/16	2	5
26 5/8	35	Oct	17	1/4	30	8 1/4
26 5/8	35	Jan	20	7/8	30	8 5/8
BirStl	25	Oct	39	1 3/4	...	...
BkBost	22 1/2	Aug	120	1 7/8	...	...
BkrsTr	80	Aug	95	7/8	3	1 7/16
Blk Dk	20	Aug	33	1	...	...
21	20	Sep	55	1 7/16	...	...
21	22 1/2	Nov	100	11/16	...	...
Blkbst	22 1/2	Aug	47	3 1/8	...	...
25 5/8	22 1/2	Dec	506	4	10	9/16
25 5/8	25	Aug	54	1	38	1/4
25 5/8	25	Sep	41	1 3/8	...	...
25 5/8	25	Dec	16	2 5/16	40	1 9/16
25 5/8	30	Sep	50	1/8	...	...
25 5/8	30	Dec	27	5/8	25	4 5/8
BncOne	60	Nov	150	5/8	...	...
BoatBn	55	Jan	100	5	...	...
59 1/2	60	Sep	22	15/16	...	...
Boeing	35	Aug	72	4 1/8	5	1/16
39	35	Sep	...	...	50	3/16
39	40	Aug	73	1/8	129	1 5/16
39	40	Sep	280	5/8	...	...
39	40	Nov	109	1 3/8	10	2 5/16
39	45	Sep	55	1/16	...	...
BordCh	10	Aug	39	3/8	...	...
...	10	Nov	50	15/16	...	...
Borden	15	Jan	60	1 3/4	10	1 1/16
15 1/8	17 1/2	Aug	...	...	50	2 3/8
15 1/8	17 1/2	Oct	...	...	41	2 1/2
Borlnd	15	Sep	44	2 5/8	...	...
17	15	Jan	...	...	90	1 9/16
17	17 1/2	Aug	80	1/2	479	1
17	17 1/2	Sep	21	1 1/8	25	1 7/16
17	17 1/2	Jan	27	2 3/4	8	3
17	20	Aug	59	1/8	22	3 1/8
17	20	Sep	79	5/8	...	...
17	20	Oct	658	7/8	...	...
17	25	Oct	612	1/4	...	...
BoxEnB	12 1/2	Sep	30	3/16	...	...
10 3/8	12 1/2	Oct	45	5/16	...	...
BrMSq	50	Aug	58	1 7/8	36	1/4
51 3/8	50	Sep	18	2 3/4	680	7/8
51 3/8	50	Dec	55	3 5/8	275	2 1/8
51 3/8	55	Aug	2	1/16	78	3 3/4
51 3/8	55	Sep	289	7/16	97	4
51 3/8	55	Dec	228	1 5/16	42	5
51 3/8	55	Mar	23	2	6	5 3/4
51 3/8	60	Sep	132	1/8	59	8 7/8
51 3/8	60	Dec	92	7/16	15	9 1/2
51 3/8	65	Sep	87	1/8	...	...
57 1/2	55	Aug	1130	3 5/8	1054	1 1/8
57 1/2	55	Sep	636	4 5/8	654	2 3/8
57 1/2	55	Oct	40	6 1/4	50	3 5/8
57 1/2	60	Aug	1315	1 1/8	363	3 5/8
57 1/2	60	Sep	483	2 3/16	17	5
57 1/2	60	Oct	223	3 3/4	...	...
Citicp	30	Aug	342	2 5/8	...	...
32 5/8	30	Oct	841	3 3/8	163	1/2
32 5/8	30	Jan	52	4 1/2	342	1 1/4
32 5/8	35	Aug	...	...	720	2 1/2
32 5/8	35	Sep	110	3/8	...	...
32 5/8	35	Oct	103	3/4	...	...
32 5/8	35	Jan	95	1 3/4	325	3 5/8
ClarkE	25	Aug	60	15 1/4	...	...
ClerCd	5	Nov	30	7/8	80	1/2
5 1/8	5	Feb	35	1 1/16	...	...
Cmdrln	5	Nov	29	1/4	...	...
CmpAsc	30	Aug	151	1/2	60	5/8
29 3/8	30	Sep	184	1 1/2	5	1 1/2
29 3/8	30	Oct	39	2	3	2 3/8
29 3/8	30	Jan	...	...	101	2 3/4
29 3/8	35	Sep	150	1/4	8	5
29 3/8	35	Oct	33	13/16	...	...
CmpUSA	20	Sep	60	3 5/8	...	...
23 1/8	30	Nov	40	1 1/16	350	8 1/2
23 1/8	35	Aug	...	...	50	12 1/4
23 1/8	35	Feb	...	...	50	12 7/8
23 1/8	40	Nov	...	...	350	17 1/4
CmprsL	15	Aug	40	7/16	2	7/8
14 1/8	15	Jan	50	1 15/16	...	...
Cnseco	50	Aug	411	9 3/4	...	...
59 3/4	55	Sep	...	...	36	1 1/4
59 3/4	55	Nov	400	8 1/2	...	...
59 3/4	60	Aug	74	1 3/8	25	1 1/2
59 3/4	60	Sep	25	3 1/4	...	...
59 3/4	60	Nov	23	5 5/8	1	5 1/2
59 3/4	65	Aug	207	1/8	3	5 1/2
59 3/4	65	Sep	332	1 1/8	...	...
CntCrd	35	Oct	50	1 1/4	...	...
Cntocr	7 1/2	Oct	50	3/4	5	3/4
7 1/4	10	Jan	57	5/8	...	...
7 1/4	30	Jan	40	1/16	...	...
CoeurM	20	Aug	47	1 1/2	...	...
Coke	40	Aug	428	3 5/8	280	1/16
43 3/4	40	Nov	263	4 1/2	60	3/4
43 3/4	45	Aug	211	1/8	45	1 9/16
43 3/4	45	Sep	212	1/2	...	...
ColHsp	22 1/2	Aug	175	6	...	...
28 1/2	25	Nov	50	3 1/2	...	...
ColgPl	45	Sep	50	4	...	...
48 1/8	50	Aug	6	1/8	29	1 3/4
48 1/8	50	Sep	27	3/4	31	2 1/2
48 1/8	50	Nov	52	1 5/8	...	...
48 1/8	55	Sep	166	1/8	...	...
48 1/8	55	Nov	153	1/2	2	7 3/8
Comcst	22 1/2	Sep	...	...	1000	1/4
Compaq	40	Sep	6	12 1/8	24	3/16
52 5/8	40	Oct	...	...	124	9/16
52 5/8	45	Aug	386	7 5/8	394	1/16
52 5/8	45	Sep	84	8 3/8	60	5/8
52 5/8	45	Oct	111	8 7/8	372	1 1/8
52 5/8	50	Aug	3659	3	3469	3/8
52 5/8	50	Sep	87	4 1/4	78	1 1/2
52 5/8	50	Oct	51	5 1/8	192	2 9/16
52 5/8	50	Jan	43	7 5/8	21	4 3/8
52 5/8	55	Aug	737	7/16	83	2 15/16
52 5/8	55	Sep	2894	1 13/16	79	4 1/4
52 5/8	55	Oct	113	2 7/8	...	...
52 5/8	60	Jan	31	3 3/8	...	...
Comsat	30	Oct	27	2 3/4	...	...
Comvrs	17 1/2	Oct	25	15/16	...	...
15 3/4	17 1/2	Jan	30	1 3/4	...	...
15 3/4	20	Jan	52	1 3/8	...	...
Con Ed	30	Nov	130	7 1/8	...	...
37 1/8	35	Aug	150	2 1/8	...	...
Conner	10	Jan	110	2 1/2	35	3/4
11 5/8	12 1/2	Jan	30	1 5/16	...	...
11 5/8	15	Jan	31	5/8	...	...
ContBk	25	Sep	55	5/8	...	...
Cooper	50	Jan	53	2 3/4	...	...
Copytl	12 1/2	Aug	20	7/8	50	1/4
13 1/2	12 1/2	Sep	...	...	40	5/8
13 1/2	12 1/2	Dec	30	2 3/4	50	1 3/8
13 1/2	17 1/2	Sep	90	1/4	...	...
13 1/2	17 1/2	Dec	25	7/8	...	...
13 1/2	20	Aug	24	1/16	...	...
13 1/2	20	Sep	100	1/8	...	...
Cordis	30	Jan	30	5 5/8	...	...
CoreFn	50	Oct	...	...	65	9/16
Corng	30	Aug	65	1 3/8	90	1/4
31 3/8	30	Sep	25	1 1/4	55	5/8

Reprinted by permission from *The Wall Street Journal*, August 12, 1993.

Table 7.5 Volume and Open Interest, August 11, 1993

EXCHANGE	CALL VOLUME	CALL OPEN INTEREST	PUT VOLUME	PUT OPEN INTEREST
Chicago Board	217,776	4,407,088	146,727	2,898,764
American	107,491	3,013,689	43,835	1,567,232
Philadephia	48,401	1,775,684	42,819	1,109,765
Pacific	46,092	977,253	22,771	449,075
New York	7,556	450,145	3,448	200,218
Total	427,316	10,623,859	259,600	6,225,054

trade for the September Abbt L put with a strike price of 25 probably occurred much earlier in the day than the last trade on the stock. If an option trade had been attempted at the time of the last trade on the stock, the put price would have been higher than $1\frac{7}{8}$.

TRADING

Options trading is in many respects similar to futures trading (see Chapter 2). An exchange has a number of members (individuals and firms) who are referred to as having seats on the exchange. Membership on an exchange entitles one to go on the floor of the exchange and trade with other members.

Market Makers

Most options exchanges (including the CBOE) use a market maker system to facilitate trading. A market maker for a certain option is an individual who will quote both a bid and an ask price on the option whenever he or she is asked to do so. The bid is the price at which the market maker is prepared to buy and the ask is the price at which the market maker is prepared to sell. At the time the bid and the ask are quoted, the market maker does not know whether the trader who asked for the quotes wants to buy or sell the option. The ask is of course higher than the bid and the amount by which the ask exceeds the bid is referred to as the bid-ask spread. The exchange sets upper limits for the bid-ask spread. For example, it might specify that this be no more than \$0.25 for options priced at less than \$0.50; \$0.50 for options priced between \$0.50 and \$10, \$0.75 for options priced between \$10 and \$20, and \$1 for options priced over \$20.

The existence of the market maker ensures that buy and sell orders can always be executed at some price without any delays. Market makers, therefore, add liquidity to the market. The market makers themselves make their profits from the bid-ask spread. They use some of the schemes that will be discussed later in this book to hedge their risks.

The Floor Broker

Floor brokers execute trades for the general public. When an investor contacts his or her broker to buy or sell an option, the broker relays the order to the firm's floor broker in the exchange on which the option trades. If the brokerage house does not have its own floor broker, it generally has an arrangement whereby it uses either an independent floor broker or the floor broker of another firm.

The types of orders that can be placed by the general public are similar to those that can be placed in the futures market (see Chapter 2). A market order is to be executed immediately; a discretionary or market-not-held order leaves the timing of the trade to the floor broker's discretion; a limit order specifies the least favorable price at which the order can be executed; and so on.

The floor broker trades either with another floor broker or with the market maker. A floor broker may be on commission or may be paid a salary by the brokerage house for which he or she executes trades.

The Order Book Official

Many orders that are relayed to floor brokers are limit orders. This means that they can only be executed at the specified price or a more favorable price. Often when a limit order reaches a floor broker, it cannot be executed immediately. (For example, a limit order to buy a call at \$5 cannot be executed immediately when the market maker is quoting a bid of \$4¾ and an ask of \$5¼.) In most exchanges, the floor broker will then pass the order to an individual known as the *order book official* (or *board broker*). This person enters the order into a computer along with other public limit orders. This ensures that as soon as the limit price is reached, the order is executed. The information on all outstanding limit orders is available to all traders.

The market maker/order book official system can be contrasted with the specialist system which is used in a few options exchanges (e.g., AMEX and PHLX) and is the most common system for trading stocks. Under the specialist system, an individual known as the *specialist* is responsible for being a market maker and keeping a record of limit orders. Unlike the order book official, the specialist does not make information on limit orders available to other traders.

Offsetting Orders

An investor who has purchased an option can close out his or her position by issuing an offsetting order to sell the same option. Similarly, an investor who has written an option can close out his or her position by issuing an offsetting order to buy the same option.

If, when an options contract is traded, neither investor is offsetting an existing position, the open interest increases by one contract. If one investor is offsetting an existing position and the other is not, the open interest stays the same. If both investors are offsetting existing positions, the open interest goes down by one contract.

COMMISSIONS

Commissions vary significantly from broker to broker. Discount brokers generally charge lower commissions than full-service brokers. The actual amount charged is usually calculated as a fixed cost plus a proportion of the dollar amount of the trade. Table 7.6 shows the sort of schedule that might be offered by a discount broker. Under this schedule, the purchase or sale of one contract always costs \$30 (since both the maximum and minimum commission is \$30 for the first contract). The purchase of eight contracts when the option price is \$3 would cost \$20 + (0.02 × 2,400) = \$68 in commissions.

If an option position is closed out by entering into an offsetting trade, the commission must be paid again. If the option is exercised, an investor pays the same commission as he or she would when placing an order to buy or sell the underlying stock. Typically, this is 1 percent to 2 percent of the stock's value.

Consider an investor who buys one call contract with an strike price of \$50 when the stock price is \$49. We suppose the option price is \$4.50 so that the cost of the contract is \$450. Using the schedule in Table 7.6, the commission paid when the option is bought is \$30. Suppose that the stock price rises and the option is exercised when it reaches \$60. Assuming that the investor pays 1.5 percent commission on stock trades, the commission payable when the option is exercised is

$$0.015 \times \$60 \times 100 = \$90$$

The total commission paid is, therefore, \$120 and the net profit to the investor is

$$\$1{,}000 - \$450 - \$120 = \$430$$

Note that if the investor could sell the option for \$10 instead of exercising it, he or she would save \$60 in commissions. (This is because the commission payable

Table 7.6 A Typical Commission Schedule for a Discount Broker

DOLLAR AMOUNT OF TRADE	*COMMISSION**
< \$2,500	\$20 + 0.02 of the dollar amount
\$2,500 to \$10,000	\$45 + 0.01 of the dollar amount
>\$10,000	\$120 + 0.0025 of the dollar amount

* Maximum commission is \$30 per contract for the first five contracts plus \$20 per contract for each additional contract. Minimum commission is \$30 per contract for the first contract plus \$2 per contract for each additional contract.

when an option is sold is only \$30 in our example.) In general, the commission system tends to push investors in the direction of selling options rather than exercising them.

A hidden cost in option trading (and in stock trading) is the market maker's bid-ask spread. Suppose that in the example just considered, the bid price was \$4.00 and the ask price was \$4.50 at the time the option was purchased. We can reasonably assume that a "fair" price for the option is halfway between the bid and the ask price, or \$4.25. The cost to the buyer and to the seller of the market maker system is the difference between the fair price and the price paid. This is \$0.25 per option, or \$25 per contract.

MARGINS

When shares are purchased, an investor can either pay cash or use a margin account. The initial margin is usually 50 percent of the value of the shares and the maintenance margin is usually 25 percent of the value of the shares. The margin account operates in the same way as it does for an investor entering into a futures contract (see Chapter 2). When call and put options are purchased, the option price must be paid in full. Investors are not allowed to buy options on margin. This is because options already contain substantial leverage. Buying on margin would raise this leverage to an unacceptable level.

When an investor writes options, he or she is required to maintain funds in a margin account. This is because the investor's broker and the exchange want to be satisfied that the investor will not default if the option is exercised. The size of the margin required depends on the circumstances.

Writing Naked Options

Consider first the situation where a stock option is naked. This means that the option position is not combined with an offsetting position in the underlying stock. The initial margin is the greater of the results of the following two calculations:

1. A total of 100 percent of the proceeds of the sale plus 20 percent of the underlying share price less the amount if any by which the option is out of the money.
2. A total of 100 percent of the option proceeds plus 10 percent of the underlying share price.

The maintenance margin is calculated in the same way with the option's current market price replacing the proceeds of the sale. For options on a broadly based index, the 20 percent in the preceding calculations is replaced by 15 percent.

Example

An investor writes four naked call option contracts on a stock. The option price is \$5, the strike price is \$40, and the stock price is \$38. Since the option is \$2 out of the money, the first calculation gives

$$400[5 + 0.2 \times 38 - 2] = 4{,}240$$

The second calculation gives

$$400[5 + 0.1 \times 38] = 3{,}520$$

The initial margin requirement is therefore \$4,240. Note that if the option had been a put, it would be \$2 in the money and the margin requirement would be

$$400[5 + 0.2 \times 38] = \$5{,}040$$

In both cases the proceeds of the sale, \$2,000, can be used to form part of the margin account.

A calculation similar to the initial margin calculation (but with the current market price replacing the proceeds of sale) is repeated every day. Funds can be withdrawn from the margin account when the calculation indicates that the margin required is less than the current balance in the margin account. When the calculation indicates that a significantly greater margin is required, a margin call will be made.

Writing Covered Calls

Writing covered calls involves writing call options when the shares that might have to be delivered are already owned. Covered calls are far less risky than naked calls since the worst that can happen is that the investor is required to sell shares already owned at below their market value. If covered call options are out of the money, no margin is required. The shares owned can be purchased using a margin account as described previously, and the price received for the option can be used to partially fulfill this margin requirement. If the options are in the money, no margin is required for the options. However, for the purposes of calculating the investor's equity position, the share price is reduced by the extent if any to which the option is in the money. This may limit the amount which the investor can withdraw from the margin account if the share price increases.

Example

An investor decides to buy 200 shares of a certain stock on margin and to write two call option contracts on the stock. The stock price is \$63, the strike price is \$60, and the price of the option is \$7. The margin account allows the investor to borrow 50 percent of the price of the stock, or \$6,300. The investor is also able to use the price received for the option, \$7 × 200 or \$1,400, to finance the purchase of the shares. The shares cost \$63 × 200 = \$12,600. The minimum cash initially required from the investor for his or her trades is, therefore,

$$\$12{,}600 - \$6{,}300 - \$1{,}400 = \$4{,}900$$

In Chapter 9, we will discuss more complicated option trading strategies such as spreads, combinations, straddles, strangles, and so on. There are special rules for determining the margin requirements when these trading strategies are used.

THE OPTIONS CLEARING CORPORATION

The Options Clearing Corporation (OCC) performs much the same sort of function for options markets as the clearinghouse does for futures markets (see Chapter 2). It guarantees that the option writer will fulfil his or her obligations under the terms of the option contract and keeps a record of all long and short positions. The OCC has a number of members, and all option trades must be cleared through a member. If a brokerage house is not itself a member of an exchange's OCC, it must arrange to clear its trades with a member. Members are required to have a certain minimum amount of capital and to contribute to a special fund that can be used if any member defaults on an option obligation.

When purchasing an option, the buyer must pay for it in full by the morning of the next business day. These funds are deposited with the OCC. The writer of the option maintains a margin account with his or her broker as described earlier. The broker maintains a margin account with the OCC member that clears its trades. The OCC member, in turn, maintains a margin account with the OCC. The margin requirements described in the previous section are the margin requirements imposed by the OCC on its members. A brokerage house may require higher margins from its clients. However, it cannot require lower margins.

Exercising an Option

When an investor wishes to exercise an option, the investor notifies his or her broker. The broker in turn notifies the OCC member that clears its trades. This member then places an exercise order with the OCC. The OCC randomly selects a member with an outstanding short position in the same option. The member using a procedure established in advance selects a particular investor who has written the option. If the option is a call, this investor is required to sell stock at the strike price. If it is a put, the investor is required to buy stock at the strike price. The investor is said to be *assigned*. When an option is exercised, the open interest goes down by one.

At the expiration of the option, all in-the-money options should be exercised unless the transactions costs are so high as to wipe out the payoff from the option. Some brokerage firms will automatically exercise options for their clients at expiration when it is in their clients' interest to do so. The OCC automatically exercises stock options owned by individuals that are in the money unless specifically instructed not to do so.

REGULATION

Options markets are regulated in a number of different ways. Both the exchanges and the Options Clearing Corporation have rules governing the behavior of traders. In addition, there are both federal and state regulatory authorities. In general, options markets have demonstrated a willingness to regulate themselves. There have been no major scandals or defaults by OCC members. Investors can have a high level of confidence in the way the market is run.

The Securities and Exchange Commission is responsible for regulating options markets in stocks, stock indices, currencies, and bonds at the federal level. The Commodity Futures Trading Commission is responsible for regulating markets for options on futures. The major options markets are in the states of Illinois and New York. These states actively enforce their own laws on unacceptable trading practices.

TAXATION

Determining the tax implications of options strategies can be tricky and an investor who is in doubt about his or her position should consult a tax specialist. In this section, we outline briefly the implications of U.S. tax rules for simple stock option trading strategies.

The general rule for all investors is that gains and losses from the trading of stock options are taxed as capital gains or losses. For a noncorporate taxpayer capital losses are deductible only to the extent of capital gains plus ordinary income up to $3,000. For a corporate investor capital losses are deductible only to the extent of capital gains. Having said this, the main issues concern exactly when gains and losses are realized.

The holder of an option recognizes a gain or loss when (a) the option is allowed to expire unexercised or (b) the option is closed out with an offsetting trade. If a call option is exercised, the writer is deemed to have sold stock at the strike price plus the original call price. The party with a long position is deemed to have purchased the stock at the strike price plus the call price. (This is then used as a basis for calculating this party's gain or loss when the stock is eventually sold.) If a put option is exercised, the party with a long position is deemed to have sold stock for the strike price less the original put price. The writer is deemed to have bought stock for the strike price less the original put price. (This is used as a basis for calculating the writer's gain or loss when the stock is eventually sold.) In all cases, brokerage commissions are deductible.

Wash Sale Rule

One tax consideration in option trading is the wash sale rule. To understand this rule, imagine an investor who buys a stock when the price is $60 and plans to keep it for the long term. If the stock price drops to $40, the investor might be tempted to sell the stock and then immediately repurchase it so that the $20 loss is realized for tax purposes. To prevent this sort of thing, the tax authorities have ruled that when the repurchase is within 30 days of the sale (that is, between 30 days before the sale and 30 days after the sale) any loss on the sale is not deductible. This rule is relevant to options' traders because, for the purposes of the wash sale rule, a call option on a stock is regarded as the same security as the stock itself. Thus, selling a stock at a loss and buying a call option within a 30-day period will lead to the loss being disallowed.

WARRANTS AND CONVERTIBLES

For the exchange-traded options that have been described so far, the writers and purchasers meet on the floor of the exchange and, as trading takes place, the number of contracts outstanding fluctuates. A warrant is an option that arises in a quite different way. *Warrants* are issued (i.e., written) by a company or a financial institution. In some cases they are subsequently traded on an exchange. The number of contracts outstanding is determined by the size of the original issue and changes only when options are exercised or expire. Warrants are bought and sold in much the same way as stocks and there is no need for an Options Clearing Corporation to become involved. When a warrant is exercised, the original issuer settles up with the current holder of the warrant.

Call warrants are frequently issued by companies on their own stock. For example, in a debt issue a company might offer investors a package consisting of bonds plus call warrants on its stock. If the warrants are exercised, the company issues new treasury stock to the warrant holders in return for the strike price specified in the contract. The strike price and exercise date of the warrants do not have to correspond to those of the regular exchange-traded call options. Typically warrants have longer maturities than regular exchange-traded call options.

Put and call warrants are also issued by financial institutions to satisfy a demand in the market. The underlying asset is typically an index, a currency, or a commodity. Once it has written the warrant, the financial institution must hedge its risk. The techniques for doing this will be described in Chapter 14.

Convertible bonds are debt instruments with embedded options issued by corporations. The holder has the right to exchange a convertible bond for equity in the issuing company at certain times in the future according to a certain exchange ratio. Very often the convertible is *callable*. This means that it can be repurchased by the issuer at a certain price at certain times in the future. Once the bonds have been called, the holder can always choose to convert prior to repurchase. Thus, the effect of a call provision is often to give the issuer the right to force conversion of the bonds into equity at an earlier time than the holders would otherwise choose. The company provides the holder with new treasury stock in exchange for the bonds when the convertible is converted. If, as a rough approximation, interest rates are assumed constant and call provisions are ignored, a convertible can be regarded as a regular debt instrument plus call warrants.

OVER-THE-COUNTER MARKETS

Not all options contracts are traded on exchanges. Foreign exchange options, interest rate options, and other types of options are frequently traded "over the counter" between two financial institutions or between a financial institution and one of its corporate clients.

Over-the-counter foreign exchange options are similar to the exchange-traded products. For a corporation wishing to hedge its foreign exchange exposure by buying a call or a put option as described in Chapter 1, the over-the-counter market has the advantage that the strike price and exercise date can be tailored to meet its precise needs. The disadvantage is that the option is usually more costly than it would be if it were exchange-traded. This is because the financial institution that is writing the option wishes to make a profit and requires compensation for the difficulties it may have in hedging its risks. Of course, competition between financial institutions prevents over-the-counter foreign exchange options from becoming too expensive. Foreign exchange options will be discussed in more detail in Chapter 12.

Examples of over-the-counter interest-rate option products are interest-rate caps, which were discussed in Chapter 1, and swaptions, which were mentioned in Chapter 6. Some traded securities have interest-rate options embedded in them. An extendible bond, for example, is a regular bond plus an option on a bond. Interest-rate options will be discussed in more detail in Chapter 17.

SUMMARY

There are two types of options: calls and puts. A call option gives the holder the right to buy the underlying asset for a certain price by a certain date. A put option gives the holder the right to sell the underlying asset by a certain date for a certain price. There are four possible positions in options markets: a long position in a call, a short position in a call, a long position in a put, and a short position in a put. Taking a short position in an option is known as writing it. Options are currently traded on stocks, stock indices, foreign currencies, futures contracts, and bonds.

An exchange must specify the terms of the option contracts it trades. In particular, it must specify the size of the contract, the precise expiration time, and the strike price. One stock option contract gives the holder the right to buy or sell 100 shares. The expiration of a stock option contract is 10.59 p.m. Central Time on the Saturday immediately following the third Friday of the expiration month. Options with four different expiration months trade at any given time. Strike prices are at $2\frac{1}{2}$, \$5, or \$10 intervals, depending on the stock price. The strike price is generally fairly close to the current stock price when trading in an option begins.

The terms of a stock option are not adjusted for cash dividends. However, they are adjusted for stock dividends, stock splits, and rights issues. The aim of the adjustment is to keep the positions of both the writer and the buyer of a contract unchanged.

Most options exchanges use a market maker system. A market maker is an individual who is prepared to quote both a bid (price at which he or she is prepared to buy) and an ask (price at which he or she is prepared to sell). Market makers improve the liquidity of the market and ensure that there is never any delay in executing market orders. They themselves make a profit from the difference between their bid and ask prices (known as their bid-ask spread). The exchange has rules specifying upper limits for the bid-ask spread.

Writers of options have potential liabilities and are required to maintain margins with their brokers. The broker if it is not a member of the Options Clearing Corporation will maintain a margin account with a firm that is a member. This firm will in turn maintain a margin account with the Options Clearing Corporation. The Options Clearing Corporation is responsible for keeping a record of all outstanding contracts, handling exercise orders, and so on.

Not all options are traded on exchanges. Interest-rate options, foreign exchange options, and other types of options are actively traded over the counter between two financial institutions or between a financial institution and one of its corporate clients. Over-the-counter options have the advantage that their expiration dates and strike prices do not have to correspond with the standards of an exchange.

Suggestions for Further Reading

BROWN, R. L., "Adjusting option contracts to reflect capitalization changes," *Journal of Business Finance and Accounting*, 16 (1989), 247–54.

CHANCE, D. M., *An Introduction to Options and Futures Markets*. Orlando, FL: Dryden Press, 1989.

CHICAGO BOARD OPTIONS EXCHANGE, *Margin Manual*. Chicago, 1991.

CHICAGO BOARD OPTIONS EXCHANGE, *Reference Manual*. Chicago, 1982.

CHICAGO BOARD OPTIONS EXCHANGE, *Understanding Options*. Chicago, 1985.

CLASING, H. K., *The Dow Jones–Irwin Guide to Put and Call Trading*. Homewood, IL: Dow Jones–Irwin, 1978.

COX, J. C., and M. RUBINSTEIN, *Options Markets*. Englewood Cliffs, NJ: Prentice Hall, 1985.

GASTINEAU, G., *The Stock Options Manual*. New York: McGraw-Hill, 1979.

MCMILLAN, L. G., *Options as a Strategic Investment*. New York: New York Institute of Finance, 1986.

PHILLIPS, S. M., and C. W. SMITH, "Trading costs for listed options; the implications for market efficiency," *Journal of Financial Economics*, 8 (1980), 179–201.

Quiz

1. An investor buys a European put on a share for $3. The stock price is $42 and the strike price is $40. Under what circumstances does the investor make a profit? Under what circumstances will the option be exercised? Draw a diagram showing the variation of the investor's profit with the stock price at the maturity of the option.
2. An investor sells a European call on a share for $4. The stock price is $47 and the strike price is $50. Under what circumstances does the investor make a profit? Under what circumstances will the option be exercised? Draw a diagram showing the variation of the investor's profit with the stock price at the maturity of the option.

3. An investor buys a call with strike price X and writes a put with the same strike price. Describe the investor's position.
4. Explain why brokers require margins from clients when they write options but not when they buy options.
5. A stock option is on a February, May, August, November cycle. What options trade on (a) April 1 and (b) May 30?
6. A company declares a 3-for-1 stock split. Explain how the terms of a call option with a strike price of $60 change.
7. Explain the difference between the specialist system and the market maker/order book official system for the organization of trading at an exchange.

Questions and Problems

7.1. Suppose that a European call option to buy a share for $50.00 costs $2.50 and is held until maturity. Under what circumstances will the holder of the option make a profit? Under what circumstances will the option be exercised? Draw a diagram illustrating how the profit from a long position in the option depends on the stock price at maturity of the option.

7.2. Suppose that a European put option to sell a share for $60.00 costs $4.00 and is held until maturity. Under what circumstances will the seller of the option (that is, the party with the short position) make a profit? Under what circumstances will the option be exercised? Draw a diagram illustrating how the profit from a short position in the option depends on the stock price at maturity of the option.

7.3. Describe the terminal value of the following portfolio: a newly-entered-into long forward contract on an asset and a long position in a European put option on the asset with the same maturity as the forward contract and a strike price that is equal to the forward price of the asset at the time the portfolio is set up. Show that the European put option has the same value as a European call option with the same strike price and maturity.

7.4. Draw a diagram showing the variation of an investor's profit/loss with the terminal stock price for a portfolio consisting of:
   a. One share and a short position in one call option.
   b. Two shares and a short position in one call option.
   c. One share and a short position in two call options.
   d. One share and a short position in four call options.

   In each case, assume that the call option has a strike price equal to the current stock price.

7.5. Explain why an American option is always worth at least as much as a European option on the same asset with the same strike price and exercise date.

7.6. Explain why an American option is always worth at least as much as its intrinsic value.

7.7. Explain carefully the difference between writing a call option and buying a put option.

7.8. The treasurer of a corporation is trying to choose between the use of options and forward contracts to hedge the corporation's foreign exchange risk. Discuss the advantages and disadvantages of each.

7.9. Suppose that sterling-U.S. dollar spot and forward exchange rates are as follows:

Spot	1.8470
90-day forward	1.8381
180-day forward	1.8291

What opportunities are open to an investor in the following situations?

a. A 180-day European call option to buy £1 for $1.80 costs $0.0250.
b. A 90-day European put option to sell £1 for $1.86 costs $0.0200.

7.10. Consider an exchange-traded call option contract to buy 500 shares with strike price $40 and maturity in four months. Explain how the terms of the option contract change when there is

a. A 10 percent stock dividend.
b. A 10 percent cash dividend.
c. A 4-for-1 stock split.

7.11. "If most of the call options on a stock are in the money, it is likely that the stock price has risen rapidly in the last few months." Discuss this statement.

7.12. What is the effect of an unexpected cash dividend on (a) a call option price and (b) a put option price?

7.13. Options on General Motors' stock are on a March, June, September, and December cycle. What options trade on (a) March 1, (b) June 30, and (c) August 5?

7.14. Explain why the market maker's bid-ask spread represents a real cost to options' investors.

7.15. An investor writes five naked call option contracts. The option price is $3.50, the strike price is $60.00 and the stock price is $57.00. What is the initial margin requirement?

7.16. An investor buys 500 shares of a stock and sells five call option contracts on the stock. The strike price is $30. The price of the option is $3. What is the investor's minimum cash investment if the stock price is $28?

8

BASIC PROPERTIES OF STOCK OPTIONS

In this chapter, we discuss the factors affecting stock option prices. We use a number of different arbitrage arguments to explore the relationships between European option prices, American option prices, and the underlying stock price. We show that it is never optimal to exercise an American call option on a nondividend-paying stock prior to expiration, but that there are some circumstances under which the early exercise of an American put option on such a stock is optimal.

FACTORS AFFECTING OPTION PRICES

There are six factors affecting the price of a stock option:

1. The current stock price
2. The strike price
3. The time to expiration
4. The volatility of the stock price
5. The risk-free interest rate
6. The dividends expected during the life of the option

In this section, we consider what happens to option prices when one of these factors changes with all the others remaining fixed.

Stock Price and Strike Price

If it is exercised at some time in the future, the payoff from a call option will be the amount by which the stock price exceeds the strike price. Call options, therefore, become more valuable as the stock price increases and less valuable as the strike price increases. For a put option, the payoff on exercise is the amount by which the strike price exceeds the stock price. Put options, therefore, behave in the opposite way to call options. They become less valuable as the stock price increases and more valuable as the strike price increases. Figures 8.1a, b, c, and d show the general way in which put and call prices depend on the stock price and strike price.

Time to Expiration

Consider next the effect of the expiration date. Both put and call American options become more valuable as the time to expiration increases. To see this, consider two options that differ only as far as the expiration date is concerned. The owner of the long-life option has all the exercise opportunities open to the owner of the short-life option—and more. The long-life option must, therefore, always be worth at least as much as the short-life option. Figures 8.1e and f show the general way in which American calls and puts depend on the time to expiration. The figures have been drawn on the assumption that the stock price is less than the exercise price. This explains why the call is worth zero when the time to expiration is zero, while the put has a positive value at this time.

European put and call options do not necessarily become more valuable as the time to expiration increases. This is because it is not true that the owner of a long-life European option has all the exercise opportunities open to the owner of a short-life European option. The owner of the long-life European option can only exercise at the maturity of that option. Consider two European call options on a stock, one with an expiration date in one month, the other with an expiration date in two months. Suppose that a very large dividend is expected in six weeks. The dividend will cause the stock price to decline. It is possible that this will lead to the short-life option being worth more than the long-life option.

Volatility

The precise way in which the volatility is defined will be discussed in Chapter 11. Roughly speaking, the *volatility* of a stock price is a measure of how uncertain we are about future stock price movements. As volatility increases, the chance that the stock will do very well or very poorly increases. For the owner of a stock, these two outcomes tend to offset each other. However, this is not so for the owner of a call or put. The owner of a call benefits from price increases but has limited downside risk in the event of price decreases, since the most that he or she can lose is the price of the option. Similarly, the owner of a put benefits from price

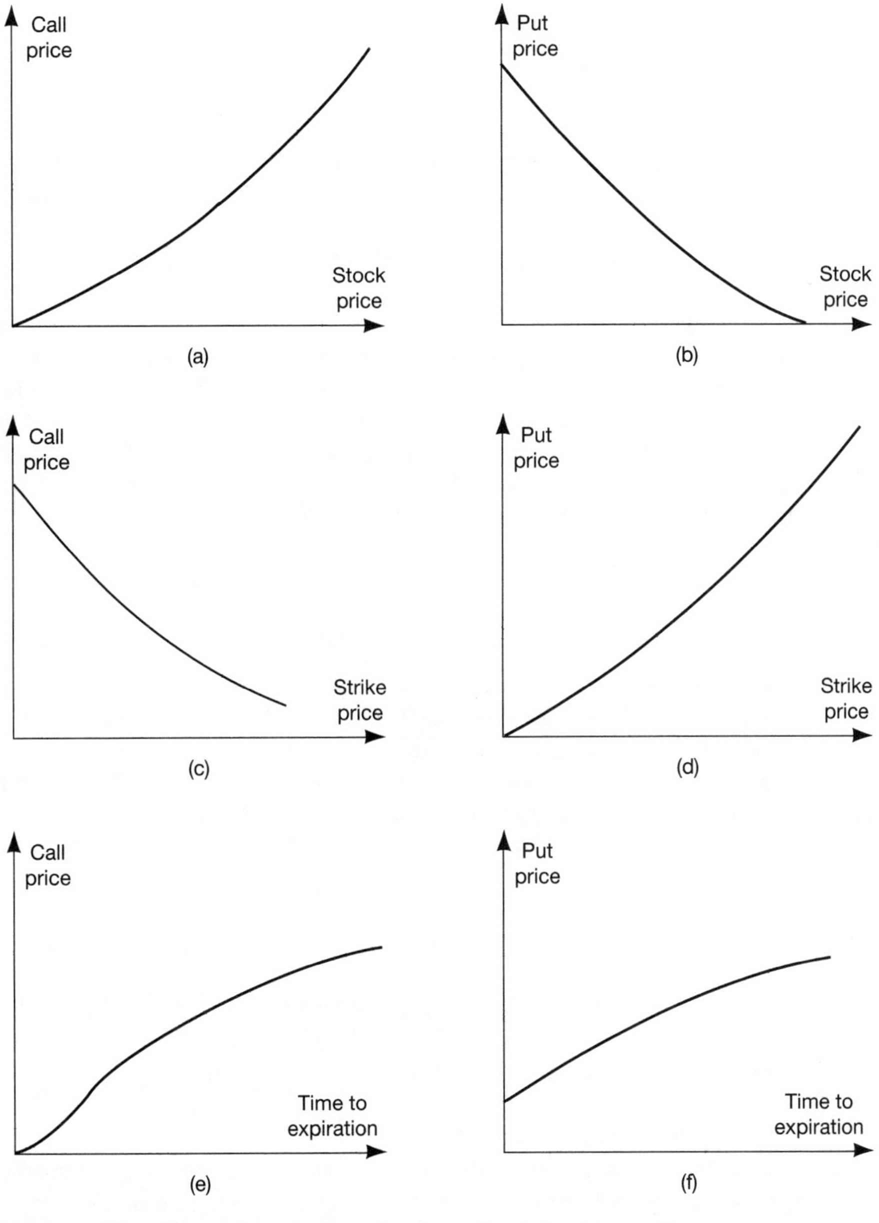

Figure 8.1 Effect of changes in stock price, strike price, and expiration date on options prices.

decreases but has limited downside risk in the event of price increases. The values of both calls and puts, therefore, increase as volatility increases. (See Figures 8.2a and b.)

Risk-Free Interest Rate

The risk-free interest rate affects the price of an option in a less clear-cut way. As interest rates in the economy increase, the expected growth rate of the stock price tends to increase. However, the present value of any future cash flows received by the holder of the option decreases. These two effects both tend to decrease the value of a put option. Hence, put option prices decline as the risk-free interest rate increases (see Figure 8.2d). In the case of calls, the first effect tends to increase the price while the second effect tends to decrease it. It can be shown that the first effect always dominates the second effect; that is, the prices of calls always increase as the risk-free interest rate increases (see Figure 8.2c).

It should be emphasized that these results assume all other variables remain fixed. In practice when interest rates rise (fall), stock prices tend to fall (rise). The net effect of an interest-rate change and the accompanying stock price change may, therefore, be the opposite of that just given.

Dividends

Dividends have the effect of reducing the stock price on the ex-dividend date. This is bad news for the value of call options and good news for the value of put options. The values of call options are, therefore, negatively related to the sizes of any anticipated dividends and the values of put options are positively related to the sizes of any anticipated dividends. Figures 8.2e and f show the relationship between the present value of anticipated dividends and option prices.

ASSUMPTIONS

In this chapter, we will make assumptions similar to those we made when deriving forward and futures prices in Chapter 3. We assume that there are some market participants, such as large investment banks, for which

1. There are no transaction costs.
2. All trading profits (net of trading losses) are subject to the same tax rate.
3. Borrowing and lending at the risk-free interest rate are possible.

We assume that these market participants are prepared to take advantage of arbitrage opportunities as they arise. As discussed in Chapters 1 and 3, this means that any available arbitrage opportunities disappear very quickly. For the purposes

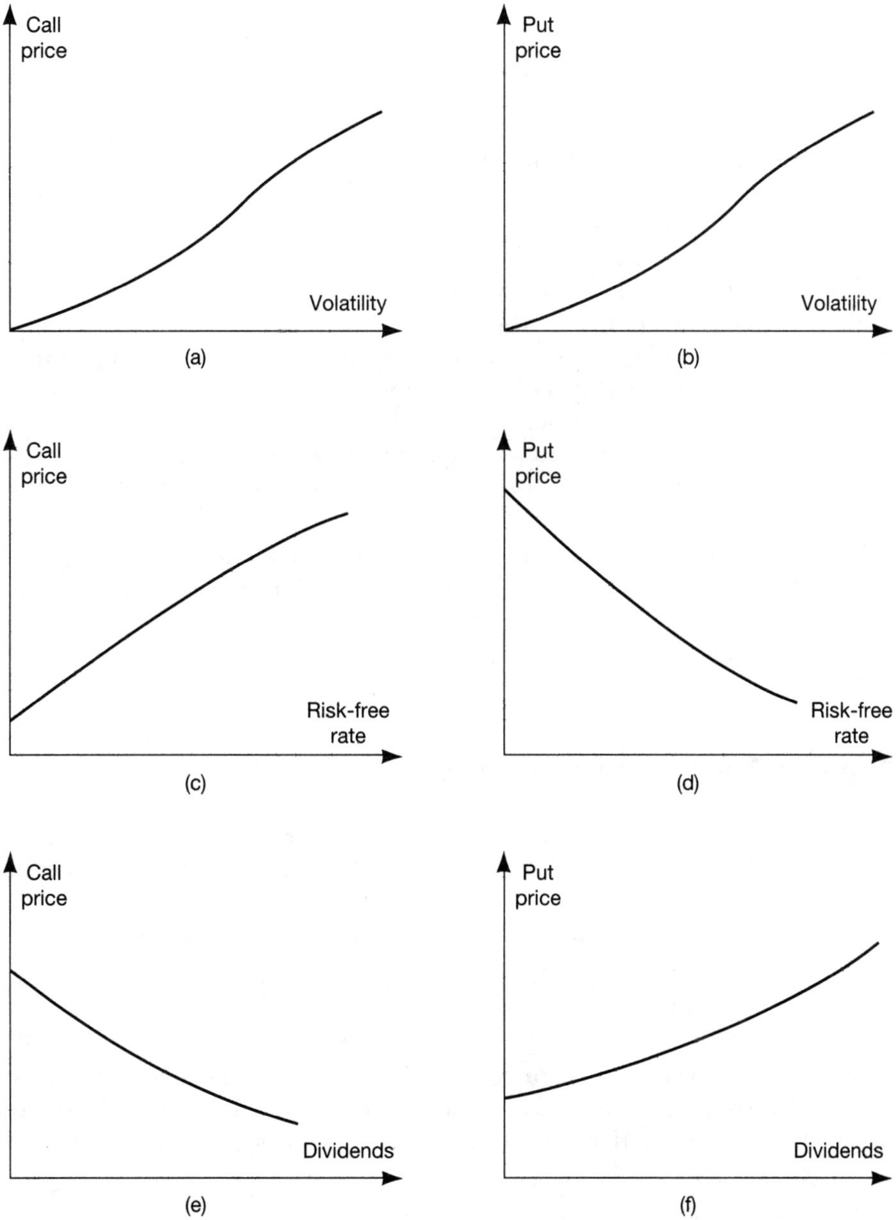

Figure 8.2 Effect of changes in volatility, risk-free interest rate, and dividends on option prices.

of our analyses, it is therefore reasonable to assume that there are no arbitrage opportunities.

NOTATION

We will use the following notation:

S: current stock price
X: exercise price of option
T: time to expiration of option
S_T: stock price at time T
r: risk-free rate of interest for an investment maturing at time T
C: value of American call option to buy one share
P: value of American put option to sell one share
c: value of European call option to buy one share
p: value of European put option to sell one share

It should be noted that r is the nominal rate of interest, not the real rate of interest. We can assume that $r > 0$. Otherwise, a risk-free investment would provide no advantages over cash. (Indeed, if $r < 0$, cash would be preferable to a risk-free investment.)

UPPER AND LOWER BOUNDS FOR OPTION PRICES

In this section, we derive upper and lower bounds for option prices. These do not depend on any particular assumptions about the factors mentioned in the previous section (except $r > 0$). If the option price is above the upper bound or below the lower bound, there are profitable opportunities for arbitrageurs.

Upper Bounds

An American or European call option gives the holder the right to buy one share of a stock for a certain price. No matter what happens, the option can never be worth more than the stock. Hence, the stock price is an upper bound to the option price:

$$c \leq S \quad \text{and} \quad C \leq S$$

If these relationships are not true, an arbitrageur can easily make a riskless profit by buying the stock and selling the call option.

An American or European put option gives the holder the right to sell one share of a stock for X. No matter how low the stock price becomes, the option can never be worth more than X. Hence,

$$p \leq X \quad \text{and} \quad P \leq X$$

For European options, we know that at time T, the option will be worth less than X. It follows that it must now be worth less than the present value of X:

$$p \leq Xe^{-rT}$$

If this were not true, an arbitrageur could make a riskless profit by writing the option and investing the proceeds of the sale at the risk-free interest rate.

Lower Bound for Calls on Nondividend-Paying Stocks

A lower bound for the price of a European call option on a nondividend-paying stock is

$$S - Xe^{-rT}$$

We first illustrate this with a numerical example and then present a more formal argument.

Suppose that $S = \$20$, $X = \$18$, $r = 10$ percent per annum, and $T =$ one year. In this case,

$$S - Xe^{-rT} = 20 - 18e^{-0.1} = 3.71$$

or \$3.71. Consider the situation where the European call price is \$3.00, which is less than the theoretical minimum of \$3.71. An arbitrageur can buy the call and short the stock. This provides a cash inflow of \$20.00 − \$3.00 = \$17.00. If invested for one year at 10 percent per annum, the \$17.00 grows to $17e^{0.1} = \$18.79$. At the end of the year, the option expires. If the stock price is greater than \$18, the arbitrageur exercises the option for \$18, closes out the short position and makes a profit of

$$\$18.79 - \$18.00 = \$0.79$$

If the stock price is less than \$18, the stock is bought in market and the short position is closed out. The arbitrageur then makes an even greater profit. For example, if the stock price is \$17, the arbitrageur's profit is

$$\$18.79 - \$17.00 = \$1.79$$

This example is illustrated in Table 8.1.

Table 8.1 Arbitrage Opportunity When European Call Price Is Less Than the Lower Bound

From the Trader's Desk

An investor has just obtained the following quotes for a European call option on a nondividend-paying stock with a strike price of \$18 and an expiration date in one year:

Stock price:	\$20
Option price:	\$3

The risk-free interest rate for a one-year investment is 10 percent per annum.

Opportunity

1. Buy the option.
2. Short the stock.
3. Invest surplus cash at 10 percent per annum.

The Result

This strategy provides an immediate positive cash flow of \$20.00 − \$3.00 = \$17.00. The \$17.00 is invested at 10 percent per annum and grows to $17e^{0.1}$ = \$18.79 at the end of one year. At this time, the option expires. If the price of the stock is greater than \$18.00, the investor exercises the option and closes out the short position for a profit of

$$\$18.79 - \$18.00 = \$0.79$$

If the price of the stock is less than \$18.00 at the end of one year, the stock is bought in the market and the short position is closed out. The investors then makes a profit equal to

$$18.79 - S_T$$

where S_T is the stock price. Since $S_T < 18$, this is at least as great as \$0.79.

For a more formal argument, we consider the following two portfolios:

Portfolio A: One European call option plus an amount of cash equal to Xe^{-rT}

Portfolio B: One share

In portfolio A, the cash, if it is invested at the risk-free interest rate, will grow to X at time T. If $S_T > X$, the call option is exercised at time T and portfolio A is worth S_T. If $S_T < X$, the call option expires worthless and the portfolio is worth X. Hence, at time T, portfolio A is worth

$$\max(S_T, X)$$

Portfolio B is worth S_T at time T. Hence, portfolio A is always worth as much as, and is sometimes worth more than, portfolio B at time T. It follows that in the absence of arbitrage opportunities this must also be true today. Hence,

$$c + Xe^{-rT} > S$$

or

$$c > S - Xe^{-rT}$$

Since the worst that can happen to a call option is that it expires worthless, its value must be positive. This means that $c > 0$ and, therefore,

$$c > \max(S - Xe^{-rT}, 0) \quad \textbf{(8.1)}$$

Example

Consider an American call option on a nondividend-paying stock when the stock price is \$51, the exercise price is \$50, the time to maturity is six months, and the risk-free rate of interest is 12 percent per annum. In this case, $S = 51$, $X = 50$, $T = 0.5$, and $r = 0.12$. From Equation (8.1), a lower bound for the option price is $S - Xe^{-rT}$ or

$$51 - 50e^{-0.12\times 0.5} = \$3.91$$

Lower Bound for European Puts on Nondividend-Paying Stocks

For a European put option on a nondividend-paying stock, a lower bound for the price is

$$Xe^{-rT} - S$$

Again, we first illustrate this with a numerical example and then present a more formal argument.

Suppose that $S = \$37$, $X = \$40$, $r = 5$ percent per annum, and $T = 0.5$ years. In this case,

$$Xe^{-rT} - S = 40e^{-0.05\times 0.5} - 37 = 2.01$$

or \$2.01. Consider the situation where the European put price is \$1.00, which is less than the theoretical minimum of \$2.01. An arbitrageur can borrow \$38.00 for six months to buy both the put and the stock. At the end of the six months, the arbitrageur will be required to repay $38e^{0.05\times 0.5} = \$38.96$. If the stock price is below \$40.00, the arbitrageur exercises the option to sell the stock for \$40.00, repays the loan, and makes a profit of

$$\$40.00 - \$38.96 = \$1.04$$

If the stock price is greater than \$40.00, the arbitrageur discards the option, sells

Table 8.2 Arbitrage Opportunities When European Put Price Is Less Than the Lower Bound

From the Trader's Desk

An investor has just obtained the following quotes for a European put option on a nondividend-paying stock with a strike price of \$40 and an expiration date in six months.

Stock price:	\$37
Option price:	\$1

The risk-free interest rate for a six-month investment is 10 percent per annum.

Opportunity

1. Borrow \$38 for six months.
2. Buy one option.
3. Buy one share of the stock.

The Result

At the end of the six months, $38e^{0.05\times 0.5} = \$38.96$ is required to pay off the loan. If the stock price at this time is below \$40.00, the investor exercises the option to sell the stock for \$40.00 and makes a profit of

$$\$40.00 - \$38.96 = \$1.04$$

If the price of the stock is greater than \$40.00, the investor sells the stock and repays the loan for a profit of

$$S_T - 38.96$$

where S_T is the stock price. This is at least as great as \$1.04.

the stock, and repays the loan for an even greater profit. For example, if the stock price is \$42.00, the arbitrageur's profit is

$$\$42.00 - \$38.96 = \$3.04$$

This example is illustrated in Table 8.2.

For a more formal argument, we consider the following two portfolios:

Portfolio C: One European put option plus one share
Portfolio D: An amount of cash equal to Xe^{-rT}

If $S_T < X$, the option in portfolio C is exercised at time T and the portfolio becomes worth X. If $S_T > X$, the put option expires worthless and the portfolio is worth S_T at time T. Hence, portfolio C is worth

$$\max(S_T, X)$$

at time T. Assuming the cash is invested at the risk-free interest rate, portfolio D is worth X at time T. Hence, portfolio C is always worth as much as, and is sometimes worth more than, portfolio D at time T. It follows that in the absence of arbitrage opportunities portfolio C must be worth more than portfolio D today. Hence,

$$p + S > Xe^{-rT}$$

or

$$p > Xe^{-rT} - S$$

Since the worst that can happen to a put option is that it expires worthless, its value must be positive. This means that

$$p > \max(Xe^{-rT} - S, 0) \qquad \textbf{(8.2)}$$

Example

Consider a European put option on a nondividend-paying stock when the stock price is \$38, the exercise price is \$40, the time to maturity is three months, and the risk-free rate of interest is 10 percent per annum. In this case, $S = 38$, $X = 40$, $T = 0.25$, and $r = 0.10$. From Equation (8.2), a lower bound for the option price is $Xe^{-rT} - S$ or

$$40e^{-0.1\times 0.25} - 38 = \$1.01$$

EARLY EXERCISE: CALLS ON A NONDIVIDEND-PAYING STOCK

In this section, we show that it is never optimal to exercise an American call option on a nondividend-paying stock early.

To illustrate the general nature of the argument, consider an American call option on a nondividend-paying stock with one month to expiration when the stock price is \$50 and the strike price is \$40. The option is deep in the money and the investor who owns the option might well be tempted to exercise it immediately. However, if the investor plans to hold the stock for more than one month, this is not the best strategy. A better course of action is to keep the option and exercise it at the end of the month. The \$40 strike price is then paid out one month later than it would be if the option were exercised immediately. This means that interest is earned on the \$40 for one month. Since the stock pays no dividend, no income from the stock is sacrificed. A further advantage of waiting rather than exercising immediately is that there is some chance (however remote) that the stock price will be below \$40 in one month. In this case, the investor will not exercise and will be glad that the decision to exercise early was not taken!

This argument shows that there are no advantages to exercising early if the investor plans to keep the stock for the rest of the life of the option (one month, in this case). What if the investor thinks the stock is currently overpriced and is wondering whether to exercise the option and sell the stock? In this case, the investor is better off selling the option than exercising it.[1] The option will be bought by another investor who does want to hold the stock. Such investors must exist. Otherwise the current stock price would not be \$50. The price obtained for the option will be greater than its intrinsic value of \$10 for the reasons mentioned earlier. In fact, Equation (8.1) shows that the market price of the option must always be greater than

$$50 - 40e^{-0.1\times 0.08333} = \$10.33$$

Otherwise there are arbitrage opportunities.

To present a more formal argument, consider again the following two portfolios:

Portfolio E: One American call option plus an amount of cash equal to Xe^{-rT}

Portfolio F: One share

The value of the cash in portfolio E at expiration of the option is X. At some earlier time t, it is $Xe^{-r(T-t)}$. If the call option is exercised at time t, the value of portfolio E is

$$S - X + Xe^{-r(T-t)}$$

This is always less than S when $t < T$ since $r > 0$. Portfolio E is, therefore, always worth less than portfolio F if the call option is exercised prior to maturity. If the call option is held to expiration, the value of portfolio E at time T is

$$\max(S_T, X)$$

The value of portfolio F is S_T. There is always some chance that $S_T < X$. This means that portfolio E is always worth as much as, and is sometimes worth more than, portfolio F.

We have shown that portfolio E is worth less than portfolio F if the option is exercised immediately but is worth at least as much as portfolio F if the holder of the option delays exercise until the expiration date. It follows that a call option on a nondividend-paying stock should never be exercised prior to the expiration date. An American call option on a nondividend-paying stock is, therefore, worth the same as the corresponding European option on the same stock:

$$C = c$$

For a quicker proof, we can use Equation (8.1):

$$c > S - Xe^{-rT}$$

[1] As an alternative strategy the investor can keep the option and short the stock. This locks in a better profit than \$10.

Since the owner of an American call has all the exercise opportunities open to the owner of the corresponding European call, we must have

$$C \geq c$$

Hence,

$$C > S - Xe^{-rT}$$

Since $r > 0$, it follows from this that $C > S - X$. If it were optimal to exercise early, C would equal $S - X$. We deduce that it can never be optimal to exercise early.

Figure 8.3 shows the general way in which the call price varies with S and X. It indicates that the call price is always above its intrinsic value of $\max(S - X, 0)$. As r, σ, or T increase, the call price moves in the direction indicated by the arrows (i.e., farther away from the intrinsic value).

One reason why a call option should not be exercised early can be considered as being due to the insurance that it provides. A call option, when held instead of the stock itself, in effect insures the holder against the stock price falling below the exercise price. Once the option has been exercised and the exercise price has been exchanged for the stock price, this insurance vanishes. Another reason is

Figure 8.3 Variation of price of an American or European call option on a nondividend-paying stock with the stock price, S.

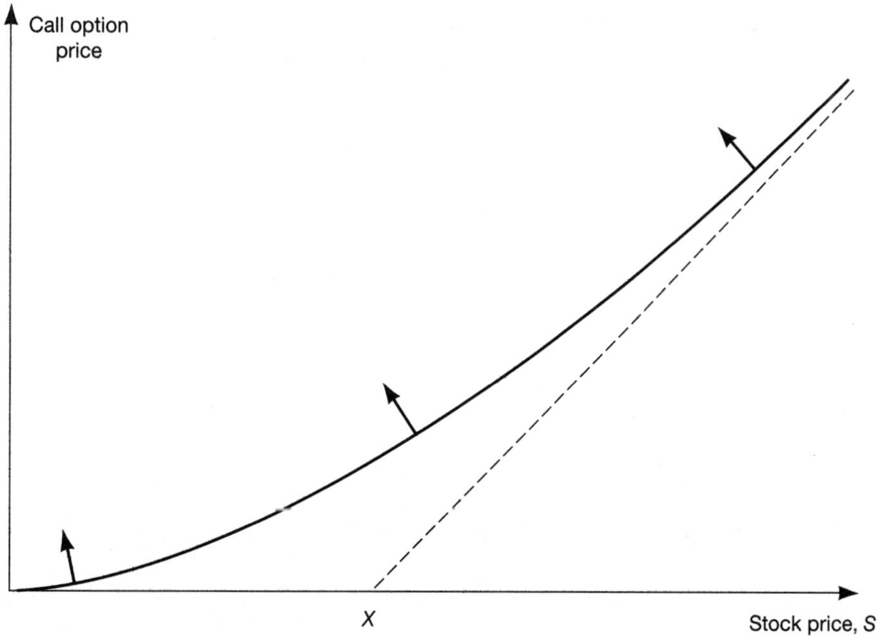

concerned with the time value of money. The later the strike price is paid out the better.

EARLY EXERCISE: PUTS ON A NONDIVIDEND-PAYING STOCK

It can be optimal to exercise an American put option on a nondividend-paying stock early. Indeed, at any given time during its life, a put option should always be exercised early if it is sufficiently deeply in the money.

To illustrate this, consider an extreme situation. Suppose that the strike price is \$10 and the stock price is virtually zero. By exercising immediately, an investor makes an immediate gain of \$10. If the investor waits, the gain from exercise might be less than \$10 but it cannot be more than \$10, since negative stock prices are impossible. Furthermore, receiving \$10 now is preferable to receiving \$10 in the future. It follows that the option should be exercised immediately.

It is instructive to consider the following two portfolios:

Portfolio G: One American put option plus one share
Portfolio H: An amount of cash equal to Xe^{-rT}

If the option is exercised at time $t < T$, portfolio G becomes worth X while portfolio H is worth $Xe^{-r(T-t)}$. Portfolio G is, therefore, worth more than portfolio H. If the option is held to expiration, portfolio G becomes worth

$$\max(X, S_T)$$

while portfolio H is worth X. Portfolio G is, therefore, worth at least as much as, and possibly more than, portfolio H. Note the difference between this situation and the one in the previous section. Here, we cannot argue that early exercise is undesirable since portfolio G looks more attractive than portfolio H regardless of the decision on early exercise.

Like a call option, a put option can be viewed as providing insurance. A put option, when held in conjunction with the stock, insures the holder against the stock price falling below a certain level. However, a put option is different from a call option in that it may be optimal for an investor to forgo this insurance and exercise early in order to realize the strike price immediately. In general, the early exercise of a put option becomes more attractive as S decreases, as r increases, and as σ decreases.

It will be recalled from Equation (8.2) that

$$p > Xe^{-rT} - S$$

For an American put with price P, the stronger condition

$$P \geq X - S$$

must always hold, since immediate exercise is always possible.

Figure 8.4 shows the general way in which the price of an American put

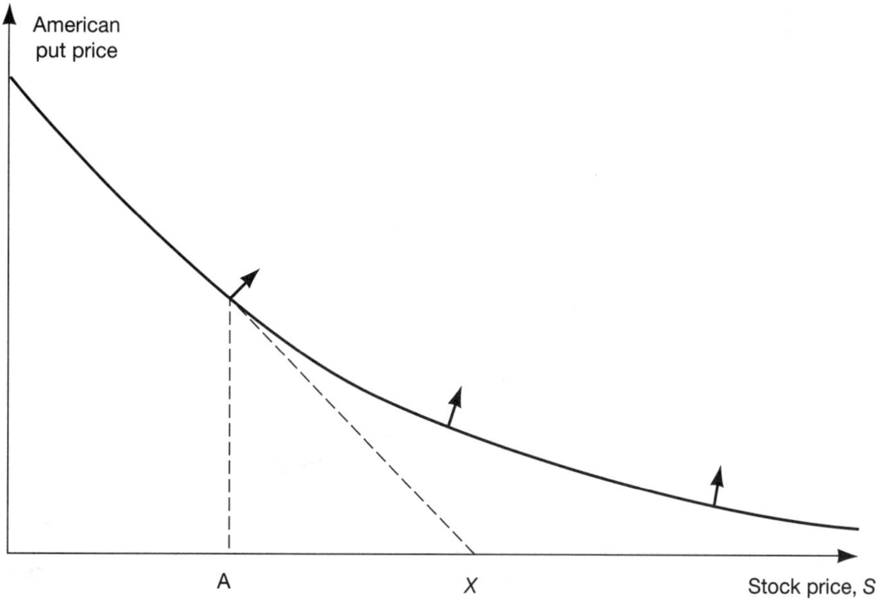

Figure 8.4 Variation of price of an American put option with the stock price, S.

varies with S. Provided that $r > 0$, it is always optimal to exercise an American put immediately when the stock price is sufficiently low. When early exercise is optimal, the value of the option is $X - S$. The curve representing the value of the put, therefore, merges into the put's intrinsic value, $X - S$, for a sufficiently small value of S. In Figure 8.4, this value of S is shown as point A. The value of the put moves in the direction indicated by the arrows when r decreases, when σ increases, and when T increases.

Since there are some circumstances when it is desirable to exercise an American put option early, it follows that an American put option is always worth more than the corresponding European put option. Since an American put is sometimes worth its intrinsic value (see Figure 8.4), it follows that a European put option must sometimes be worth less than its intrinsic value. Figure 8.5 shows the variation of the European put price with the stock price. Note that point B in Figure 8.5, at which the price of the option is equal to its intrinsic value, must represent a higher value of the stock price than point A in Figure 8.4. Point E in Figure 8.5 is where $S = 0$ and the European put price is Xe^{-rT}.

PUT-CALL PARITY

It will be recalled that P and C are the prices of American put and call options, while p and c are the prices of European put and call options. The variables, P,

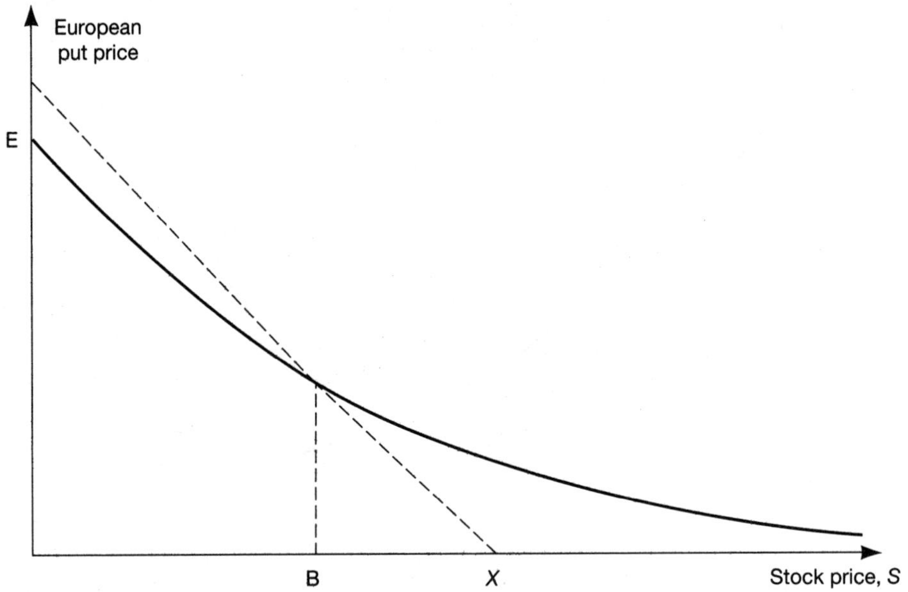

Figure 8.5 Variation of price of a European put option with the stock price, S.

p, C, and c are all functions of S, X, r, T, and σ. We have shown that for a nondividend-paying stock,

$$C = c$$

$$P > p \quad \text{when} \quad r > 0$$

We now derive an important relationship between p and c. Consider the following two portfolios:

Portfolio A: One European call option plus an amount of cash equal to Xe^{-rT}

Portfolio C: One European put option plus one share

Both are worth

$$\max(S_T, X)$$

at expiration of the options. Since the options are European, they cannot be exercised prior to the expiration date. The portfolios must, therefore, have identical values today. This means that

$$c + Xe^{-rT} = p + S \tag{8.3}$$

This relationship is known as *put-call parity*. It shows that the value of a European call with a certain exercise price and exercise date can be deduced from the value of a European put with the same exercise price date, and vice versa.

If Equation (8.3) does not hold, there are arbitrage opportunities. Suppose that the stock price is \$31, the exercise price is \$30, the risk-free interest rate is 10 percent per annum, the price of a three-month European call option is \$3, and the price of a three-month European put option is \$2.25. In this case,

$$c + Xe^{-rT} = 3 + 30e^{-0.1 \times 0.25} = 32.26$$

$$p + S = 2.25 + 31 = 33.25$$

Portfolio C is overpriced relative to portfolio A. The correct arbitrage strategy is to buy the securities in portfolio A and short the securities in portfolio C. This involves buying the call and shorting both the put and the stock. The strategy generates a positive cash flow of

$$-3 + 2.25 + 31 = \$30.25$$

up front. When invested at the risk-free interest rate, this grows to $30.25e^{0.1 \times 0.25} = 31.02$ in three months. If the stock price at expiration of the option is greater than \$30, the call will be exercised. If it is less than \$30, the put will be exercised. In either case, the investor ends up buying one share for \$30. This share can be used to close out the short position. The net profit is, therefore,

$$\$31.02 - \$30.00 = \$1.02$$

This example is illustrated in Table 8.3.

For an alternative situation, suppose that the call price is \$3 and the put price is \$1. In this case

$$c + Xe^{-rT} = 3 + 30e^{-0.1 \times 0.25} = 32.26$$

$$p + S = 1 + 31 = 32.00$$

Portfolio A is overpriced relative to portfolio C. An arbitrageur can short the securities in portfolio A and buy the securities in portfolio C to lock in a profit. This involves shorting the call and buying both the put and the stock. The strategy involves an initial investment of

$$\$31 + \$1 - \$3 = \$29$$

at time zero. When financed at the risk-free interest rate, a repayment of $29e^{0.1 \times 0.25} = \$29.73$ is required at the end of the three months. As in the previous case, either the call or the put will be exercised. The short call and long put option position, therefore, leads to the stock being sold for \$30.00. The net profit is, therefore,

$$\$30.00 - \$29.73 = \$0.27$$

This example is illustrated in Table 8.4.

Table 8.3 Arbitrage Opportunity When Put-Call Parity Does Not Hold: Call Price Too Low Relative to Put Price

From the Trader's Desk

An investor has just obtained the following quotes for options on a stock worth \$31 when the three-month risk-free interest rate is 10 percent per annum. Both options have a strike price of \$30 and an expiration date in three months.

European call: \$3
European put: \$2¼

Strategy

1. Buy the call.
2. Short the put.
3. Short the stock.

The Result

This strategy leads to an initial cash flow of \$31.00 − \$3.00 + \$2.25 = \$30.25. When invested for three months at the risk-free interest rate, this grows to $30.25e^{0.1 \times 025}$ = \$31.02. At the end of the three months, the possible situations are as follows:

1. Stock price is greater than \$30.00. The investor exercises the call. This involves buying one share for \$30.00. The short position is closed out and the net profit is \$31.02 − \$30.00 = \$1.02.
2. Stock price is less than \$30.00. The counterparty exercises the put. This also involves the investor in buying one share for \$30.00. The short position is closed out and the net profit is again \$31.02 − \$30.00 = \$1.02.

Relationship Between American Call and Put Prices

Put-call parity holds only for European options. However, it is possible to derive some relationships between American option prices. Since $P > p$, it follows from Equation (8.3) that

$$P > c + Xe^{-rT} - S$$

and since $c = C$,

$$P > C + Xe^{-rT} - S$$

or

$$C - P < S - Xe^{-rT} \tag{8.4}$$

Table 8.4 Arbitrage Opportunity When Put-Call Parity Does Not Hold: Put Price Too Low Relative to Call Price

From the Trader's Desk

An investor has just obtained the following quotes for options on a stock worth \$31 when the three-month risk-free interest rate is 10 percent per annum. Both options have a stock price of \$30 and an expiration date in three months.

European call:	\$3
European put:	\$1

Strategy

The investor
1. Sells the call.
2. Buys the put.
3. Buys the stock.

The Outcome

This involves an investment of \$31 + \$1 − \$3 = \$29 at time zero. When financed at the risk-free interest rate, a repayment of $29e^{0.1\times0.25}$ = \$29.73 is required at the end of three months. The possible situations are as follows:
1. Stock price is greater than \$30.00. The counterparty exercises the call. This means that the investor has to sell the share owned for \$30.00. The net profit is \$30.00 − \$29.73 = \$0.27.
2. Stock price is less than \$30.00. The investor exercises the put. This also means that the share is sold for \$30.00. The net profit is again \$30.00 − \$29.73 = \$0.27.

For a further relationship between C and P, consider:

Portfolio I: European call option plus an amount of cash equal to X
Portfolio J: American put option plus one share

Both options have the same exercise price and expiration date. Assume that the cash in portfolio I is invested at the risk-free interest rate. If the put option is not exercised early, portfolio J is worth

$$\max(S_T, X)$$

at time T. Portfolio I is worth

$$\max(S_T, X) + Xe^{rT} - X$$

at this time. Portfolio I is, therefore, worth more than portfolio J. Suppose next that the put option in portfolio J is exercised early, say, at time t. This means that portfolio J is worth X at time t. However, even if the call option were worthless, portfolio I would be worth Xe^{rt} at time t. It follows that portfolio I is worth more than portfolio J in all circumstances. Hence,

$$c + X > P + S$$

Since $c = C$,

$$C + X > P + S$$

or

$$C - P > S - X$$

Combining this with (8.4), we obtain

$$S - X < C - P < S - Xe^{-rT} \tag{8.5}$$

Example

Consider the situation where an American call option on a nondividend-paying stock with exercise price \$20.00 and maturity in five months is worth \$1.50. This must also be the value of a European call option on the same stock with the same exercise price and maturity. Suppose that the current stock price is \$19.00 and the risk-free interest rate is 10 percent per annum. From a rearrangement of Equation (8.3), the price of a European put with exercise price \$20 and maturity in five months is

$$1.50 + 20e^{-0.1\times 0.4167} - 19 = \$1.68$$

From Equation (8.5)

$$19 - 20 < C - P < 19 - 20e^{-0.1\times 0.4167}$$

or

$$1 > P - C > 0.18$$

showing that $P - C$ lies between \$1.00 and \$0.18. Since C is \$1.50, P must lie between \$1.68 and \$2.50. In other words, upper and lower bounds for the price of an American put with the same strike price and expiration date as the American call are \$2.50 and \$1.68.

EFFECT OF DIVIDENDS

The results produced so far in this chapter have assumed that we are dealing with options on a nondividend-paying stock. In this section, we discuss the impact of dividends. In the United States, exchange-traded stock options generally have less than eight months to maturity. The dividends payable during the life of the option can usually be predicted with reasonable accuracy. We will use D to denote the present value of the dividends during the life of the option. In the calculation of D, a dividend is assumed to occur at the time of its ex-dividend date.

Lower Bound for Calls and Puts

We can redefine portfolios A and B as follows:

Portfolio A: One European call option plus an amount of cash equal to $D + Xe^{-rT}$

Portfolio B: One share

A similar argument to the one used to derive (8.1) shows that

$$c > S - D - Xe^{-rT} \tag{8.6}$$

We can also redefine portfolios C and D as follows:

Portfolio C: One European put option plus one share

Portfolio D: An amount of cash equal to $D + Xe^{-rT}$

A similar argument to the one used to derive (8.2) shows that

$$p > D + Xe^{-rT} - S \tag{8.7}$$

Early Exercise

When dividends are expected, we can no longer assert than an American call option will not be exercised early. Sometimes it is optimal to exercise an American call immediately prior to an ex-dividend date. This is because the dividend will cause the stock price to jump down making the option less attractive. It is never optimal to exercise a call at other times. This point will be discussed further in Chapter 11.

Put-Call Parity

Comparing the value at time T of the redefined portfolios A and C shows that when there are dividends put-call parity becomes

$$c + D + Xe^{-rT} = p + S \tag{8.8}$$

Dividends cause Equation (8.5) to be modified to

$$S - D - X < C - P < S - Xe^{-rT} \tag{8.9}$$

To prove this inequality consider

Portfolio I: European call option plus an amount of cash equal to $D + X$
Portfolio J: American put option plus a share

Regardless of what happens, it can be shown that portfolio I is worth more than portfolio J. Hence,

$$P + S < c + D + X$$

Since a European call is never worth more than its American counterpart, or $c < C$, it follows that

$$P + S < C + D + X$$

or

$$S - D - X < C - P$$

This proves the first half of the inequality in (8.9). For a nondividend-paying stock, we showed in (8.5) that

$$C - P < S - Xe^{-rT}$$

Since dividends decrease the value of a call and increase the value of a put, this inequality must also be true for options on a dividend-paying stock. This proves the second half of the inequality in (8.9).

EMPIRICAL RESEARCH

Empirical research to test the results in this chapter might seem to be relatively simple to carry out once the appropriate data have been assembled. In fact there are a number of complications:

1. It is important to be sure that option prices and stock prices are being observed at exactly the same time. For example, testing for arbitrage opportunities by looking at the price at which the last trade is done each day is inappropriate. This point was made in Chapter 7 in connection with the numbers in Table 7.5.
2. It is important to consider carefully whether a trader could have taken advantage of any observed arbitrage opportunity. If the opportunity exists only momentarily, there might in practice be no way of exploiting it.

3. Transactions costs must be taken into account when determining whether arbitrage opportunities were possible.
4. Put-call parity only holds for European options. Exchange-traded stock options are American.
5. Dividends to be paid during the life of the option must be estimated.

Some of the empirical research that has been carried out is described in the papers by Bhattacharya, Galai, Gould and Galai, Klemkosky and Resnick, and Stoll that are referenced at the end of this chapter. Galai and Bhattacharya test whether option prices are ever less than their theoretical lower bounds; Stoll, Gould and Galai, and the two papers by Klemkosky and Resnick test whether put-call parity holds. We will consider the results of Bhattacharya and Klemkosky and Resnick.

Bhattacharya's study examined whether the theoretical lower bounds for call options applied in practice. He used data consisting of the transaction prices for options on 58 stocks over a 196-day period between August 1976 and June 1977. The first test examined whether the options satisfied the condition that price be greater than intrinsic value, that is, whether $C > \max(S - X, 0)$. Over 86,000 option prices were examined and about 1.3 percent were found to violate this condition. In 29 percent of the cases the violation disappeared by the next trade, indicating that in practice traders would not have been able to take advantage of it. When transaction costs were taken into account, the profitable opportunities created by the violation disappeared. Bhattacharya's second test examined whether options sold for more than the lower bound $S - D - Xe^{-rT}$. (See Equation (8.6).) He found that 7.6 percent of his observations did in fact sell for less than this lower bound. However, when transaction costs were taken into account these did not give rise to profitable opportunities.

Klemkosky and Resnick's tests of put-call parity used data on option prices taken from trades between July 1977 and June 1978. They subjected their data to several tests to determine the likelihood of options being exercised early and discarded data where early exercise was considered probable. By doing this they felt they were justified in treating Amerian options as European. They identified 540 situations where an arbitrage opportunity similar to that in Table 8.3 existed and 540 situations where an arbitrage opportunity similar to that in Table 8.4 existed. After allowing for transaction costs, 38 of the Table 8.3 opportunities (call price too low relative to put price) and 147 of the Table 8.4 opportunities (call price too high relative to the put price) were still profitable. The opportunities persisted when either a 5- or a 15-minute delay between the opportunity being noted and trades being executed was assumed. Klemkosky and Resnick's conclusion is that arbitrage opportunities were available to some traders, particularly market makers, during the period they studied.

SUMMARY

There are six factors affecting the value of a stock option: the current stock price, the strike price, the expiration date, the stock price volatility, the risk-free interest rate, and the dividends expected during the life of the option. The value of a call generally increases as the current stock price, the time to expiration, the volatility, and the risk-free interest rate increase. The value of a call decreases as the strike price and expected dividends increase. The value of a put generally increases as the strike price, the time to expiration, the volatility, and the expected dividends increase. The value of a put decreases as the current stock price and the risk-free interest rate increase.

It is possible to reach some conclusions about the values of stock options without making any assumptions about the behavior of stock prices. For example, the price of a call option on a stock must always be worth less than the price of the stock itself. Similarly, the price of a put option on a stock must always be worth less than the option's strike price.

A call option on a nondividend-paying stock must be worth more than

$$\max(S - Xe^{-rT}, 0)$$

where S is the stock price, X is the exercise price, r is the risk-free interest rate, and T is the time to expiration. A put option on a nondividend-paying stock must be worth more than

$$\max(Xe^{-rT} - S, 0)$$

When dividends with present value D will be paid, the lower bound for a call option becomes

$$\max(S - D - Xe^{-rT}, 0)$$

and the lower bound for a put option becomes

$$\max(Xe^{-rT} + D - S, 0)$$

Put-call parity is a relationship between the price, c, of a European call option on a stock and the price, p, of a European put option on a stock. For a nondividend-paying stock, it is

$$c + Xe^{-rT} = p + S$$

For a dividend-paying stock, the put-call parity relationship is

$$c + D + Xe^{-rT} = p + S$$

Put-call parity does not hold for American options. However, it is possible to use arbitrage arguments to obtain upper and lower bounds for the difference between the price of an American call and the price of an American put.

In Chapter 11, we will carry the analyses in this chapter further by making specific assumptions about the probabilistic behavior of stock prices. This will enable us to derive exact pricing formulas for European stock options. In Chapter 15, we will show how numerical procedures can be used to price American options.

Suggestions for Further Reading

BHATTACHARYA, M., "Transaction data tests of efficiency of the Chicago Board Options Exchange," *Journal of Financial Economics*, 12 (1983), 161–185.

GALAI, D., "Empirical tests of boundary conditions for CBOE options," *Journal of Financial Economics*, 6 (1978), 187–211.

GOULD, J. P., and D. GALAI, "Transactions costs and the relationship between put and call prices," *Journal of Financial Economics*, 1 (1974), 105–129.

KLEMKOSKY, R. C., and B. G. RESNICK, "An ex-ante analysis of put-call parity," *Journal of Financial Economics*, 8 (1980), 363–378.

KLEMKOSKY, R. C., and B. G. RESNICK, "Put-call parity and market efficiency," *Journal of Finance*, 34 (December 1979), 1141–1155.

MERTON, R. C., "The relationship between put and call prices: Comment," *Journal of Finance*, 28 (March 1973), 183–184.

MERTON, R. C., "Theory of rational option pricing," *Bell Journal of Economics and Management Science*, 4 (Spring 1973), 141–183.

STOLL, H. R., "The relationship between put and call option prices," *Journal of Finance*, 31 (May 1969), 319–332.

Quiz

1. List the six factors affecting stock option prices.
2. What is a lower bound for the price of a four-month call option on a nondividend-paying stock when the stock price is \$28, the strike price is \$25, and the risk-free interest rate is 8 percent per annum?
3. What is a lower bound for the price of a one-month European put option on a nondividend-paying stock when the stock price is \$12, the strike price is \$15, and the risk-free interest rate is 6 percent per annum?
4. Give two reasons why the early exercise of an American call option on a nondividend-paying stock is not optimal. The first reason should involve the time value of money. The second reason should apply even if interest rates are zero.
5. "The early exercise of an American put is a trade-off between the time value of money and the insurance value of a put." Explain this statement.
6. A European call and put option on a stock both have a strike price of \$20 and an expiration date in three months. Both sell for \$3. The risk-free interest rate is 10 percent per annum, the current stock price is \$19, and a \$1 dividend is expected in one month. Identify the arbitrage opportunity open to a trader.
7. Explain why the arguments leading to put-call parity for European options cannot be used to give a similar result for American options.

Questions and Problems

8.1. What is a lower bound for the price of a six-month call option on a nondividend-paying stock when the stock price is \$80, the strike price is \$75, and the risk-free interest rate is 10 percent per annum?

8.2. What is a lower bound for the price of a two-month European put option on a nondividend-paying stock when the stock price is \$58, the strike price is \$65, and the risk-free interest rate is 5 percent per annum?

8.3. A four-month European call option on a dividend-paying stock is currently selling for \$5. The stock price is \$64, the strike price is \$60, and a dividend of \$0.80 is expected in one month. The risk-free interest rate is 12 percent per annum for all maturities. What opportunities are there for an arbitrageur?

8.4. A one-month European put option on a nondividend-paying stock is currently selling for \$2½. The stock price is \$47, the strike price is \$50, and the risk-free interest rate is 6 percent per annum. What opportunities are there for an arbitrageur?

8.5. Give an intuitive explanation of why the early exercise of an American put becomes more attractive as the risk-free rate increases and volatility decreases.

8.6. The price of a European call which expires in six months and has a strike price of \$30 is \$2. The underlying stock price is \$29, and a dividend of \$0.50 is expected in two months and in five months. The term structure is flat with all risk-free interest rates being 10 percent. What is the price of a European put option that expires in six months and has a strike price of \$30?

8.7. Explain carefully the arbitrage opportunities in Problem 8.6 if the European put price is \$3.

8.8. The price of an American call on a nondividend-paying stock is \$4. The stock price is \$31, the strike price is \$30, and the expiration date is in three months. The risk-free interest rate is 8 percent. Derive upper and lower bounds for the price of an American put on the same stock with the same strike price and expiration date.

8.9. Explain carefully the arbitrage opportunities in Problem 8.8 if the American put price is greater than the calculated upper bound.

8.10. Suppose that c_1, c_2, and c_3 are the prices of European call options with strike prices X_1, X_2, and X_3, respectively, where $X_3 > X_2 > X_1$ and $X_3 - X_2 = X_2 - X_1$. All options have the same maturity. Show that

$$c_2 \leq 0.5(c_1 + c_3)$$

(Hint: Consider a portfolio that is long one option with strike price X_1, long one option with strike price X_3, and short two options with strike price X_2.)

8.11. What is the result corresponding to that in Problem 8.10 for American put options?

8.12. Suppose that you are the manager and sole owner of a highly leveraged company. All the debt will mature in one year. If at that time the value of the company is greater than the face value of the debt, you will pay off the debt. If the value of the company is less than the face value of the debt, you will declare bankruptcy and the debtholders will own the company.

a. Express your position as an option on the value of the company.

b. Express the position of the debtholders in terms of options on the value of the company.

c. What can you do to increase the value of your position?

9

TRADING STRATEGIES INVOLVING OPTIONS

The profit pattern from an investment in a single stock option was discussed in Chapter 7. In this chapter we cover more fully the range of profit patterns obtainable using options. In the first section we consider what happens when a position in a stock option is combined with a position in the stock itself. We then move on to discuss the profit patterns obtained when an investment is made in two or more different options on the same stock. One of the attractions of options is that they can be used to create a wide range of different payoff functions. Toward the end of this chapter, we will argue that if European options were available with every single possible strike price, any payoff function could in theory be created.

STRATEGIES INVOLVING A SINGLE OPTION AND A STOCK

There are a number of different trading strategies involving a single option on a stock and the stock itself. The profits from these are illustrated in Figure 9.1. In this figure, and in other figures throughout this chapter, the dashed line shows the relationship between profit and stock price for the individual securities constituting the portfolio, while the solid line shows the relationship between profit and stock price for the whole portfolio.

In Figure 9.1a the portfolio consists of a long position in a stock plus a short position in a call option. The investment strategy represented by this portfolio is known as *writing a covered call*. This is because the long stock position "covers"

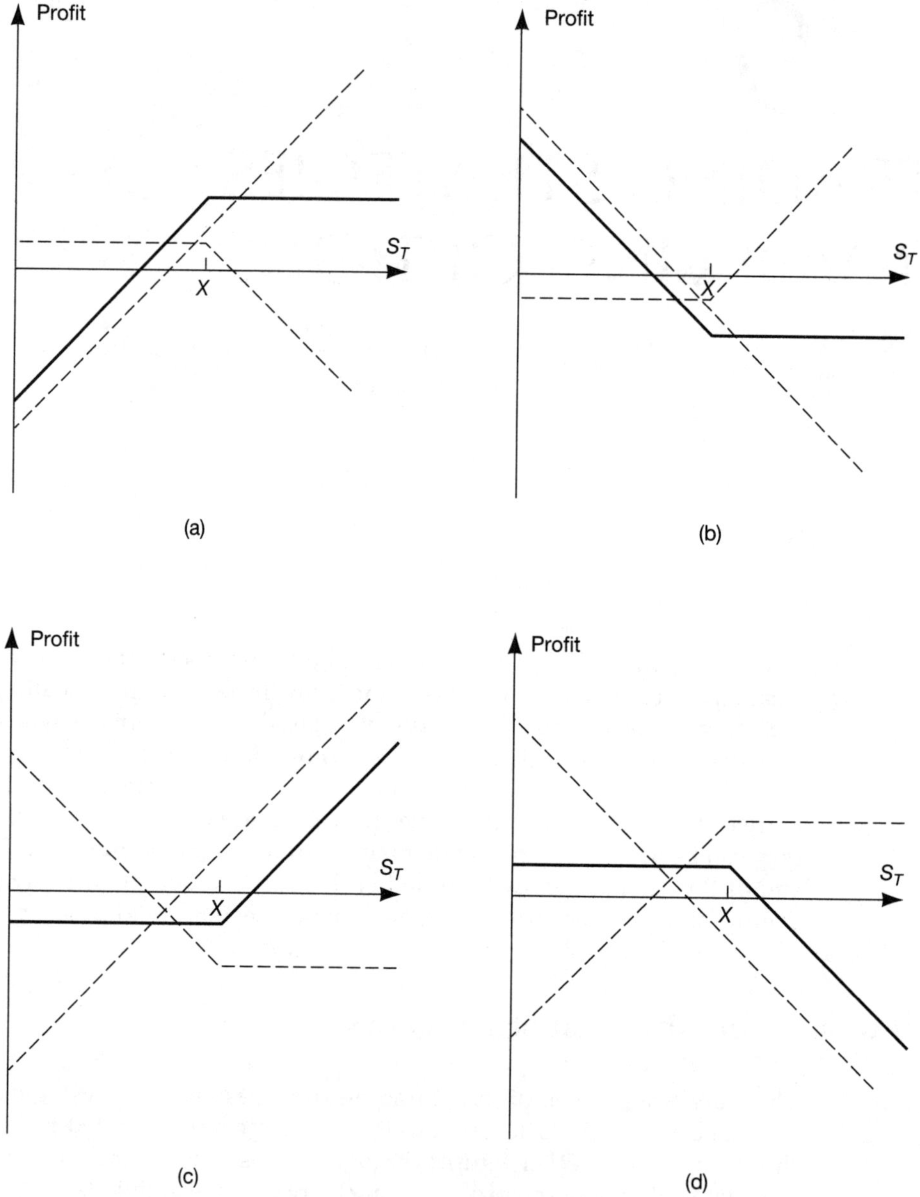

Figure 9.1 Profit from (a) a long position in a stock combined with a short position in a call, (b) a short position in a stock combined with a long position in a call, (c) a long position in a put combined with a long position in a stock, (d) a short position in a put combined with a short position in a stock.

or protects the investor from the possibility of a sharp rise in the stock price. In Figure 9.1b a short position in a stock is combined with a long position in a call option. This is the reverse of writing a covered call. In Figure 9.1c the investment strategy involves buying a put option on a stock and the stock itself. This is sometimes referred to as a *protective put* strategy. In Figure 9.1d a short position in a put option is combined with a short position in the stock. This is the reverse of a protective put.

The profit patterns in Figures 9.1a, b, c, and d have the same general shape as the profit patterns discussed in Chapter 7 for short put, long put, long call, and short call, respectively. Put-call parity provides a way of understanding why this is so. It will be recalled from Chapter 8 that the put-call parity relationship is

$$p + S = c + Xe^{-rT} + D \tag{9.1}$$

where p is the price of a European put, S is the stock price, c is the price of a European call, X is the strike price of both call and put, r is the risk-free interest rate, T is the time to maturity of both call and put, and D is the present value of the dividends anticipated during the life of the option.

Equation (9.1) shows that a long position in a put combined with a long position in the stock is equivalent to a long call position plus a certain amount $(= Xe^{-rT} + D)$ of cash. This explains why the profit pattern in Figure 9.1c is similar to the profit pattern from a long call position. The position in Figure 9.1d is the reverse of that in Figure 9.1c and, therefore, leads to a profit pattern similar to that from a short call position.

Equation (9.1) can be rearranged to become

$$S - c = Xe^{-rT} + D - p$$

This shows that a long position in a stock combined with a short position in a call is equivalent to a short put position plus a certain amount $(= Xe^{-rT} + D)$ of cash. This explains why the profit pattern in Figure 9.1a is similar to the profit pattern from a short put position. The position in Figure 9.1b is the reverse of that in Figure 9.1a and, therefore, leads to a profit pattern similar to that from a long put position.

SPREADS

A spread trading strategy involves taking a position in two or more options of the same type (that is, two or more calls or two or more puts).

Bull Spreads

One of the most popular types of spreads is a *bull spread*. This can be created by buying a call option on a stock with a certain strike price and selling a call

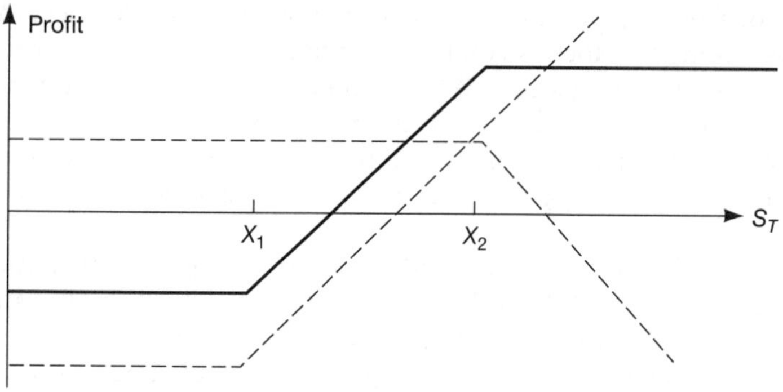

Figure 9.2 Bull spread created using call options.

option on the same stock with a higher strike price. Both options have the same expiration date. The strategy is illustrated in Figure 9.2. The profits from the two option positions taken separately are shown by the dashed lines. The profit from the whole strategy is the sum of the profits given by the dashed lines and is indicated by the solid line. Since a call price always decreases as the strike price increases, the value of the option sold is always less than the value of the option bought. A bull spread, when created from calls, therefore requires an initial investment.

Suppose that X_1 is the strike price of the call option bought, X_2 is the strike price of the call option sold, and S_T is the stock price on the expiration date of the options. Table 9.1 shows the total payoff that will be realized from a bull spread in different circumstances. If the stock price does well and is greater than the higher strike price, the payoff is the difference between the two strike prices, $X_2 - X_1$. If the stock price on the expiration date lies between the two strike prices, the payoff is $S_T - X_1$. If the stock price on the expiration date is below the lower strike price, the payoff is zero. The profit in Figure 9.2 is calculated by subtracting the initial investment from the payoff.

A bull spread strategy limits both the investor's upside potential and his or her downside risk. We can describe the strategy by saying that the investor has a call option with a strike price equal to X_1 and has chosen to give up some upside potential by selling a call option with strike price X_2 ($X_2 > X_1$). In return for giving

Table 9.1 Payoff from a Bull Spread

STOCK PRICE RANGE	*PAYOFF FROM LONG CALL OPTION*	*PAYOFF FROM SHORT CALL OPTION*	*TOTAL PAYOFF*
$S_T \geq X_2$	$S_T - X_1$	$X_2 - S_T$	$X_2 - X_1$
$X_1 < S_T < X_2$	$S_T - X_1$	0	$S_T - X_1$
$S_T \leq X_1$	0	0	0

up the upside potential, the investor gets the price of the option with strike price X_2. Three types of bull spreads can be distinguished:

1. Both calls initially out of the money
2. One call initially in the money, the other call initially out of the money
3. Both calls initially in the money

The most aggressive bull spreads are those of type 1. They cost very little to set up and have a small probability of giving a relatively high payoff ($= X_2 - X_1$). As we move from type 1 to type 2 and from type 2 to type 3, the spreads become more conservative.

Example

An investor buys for \$3 a call with a strike price of \$30 and sells for \$1 a call with a strike price of \$35. The payoff from this bull spread strategy is \$5 if the stock price is above \$35 and zero when it is below \$30. If the stock price is between \$30 and \$35, the payoff is the amount by which the stock price exceeds \$30. The cost of the strategy is \$3 − \$1 = \$2. The profit is, therefore, as follows:

STOCK PRICE RANGE	*PROFIT*
$S_T \leq 30$	-2
$30 < S_T < 35$	$S_T - 32$
$S_T \geq 35$	3

Bull spreads can also be created by buying a put with a low strike price and selling a put with a high strike price. This is illustrated in Figure 9.3. Unlike the bull spread created using calls, bull spreads created from puts involve a positive cash flow to the investor up front. (This ignores margin requirements.) Needless

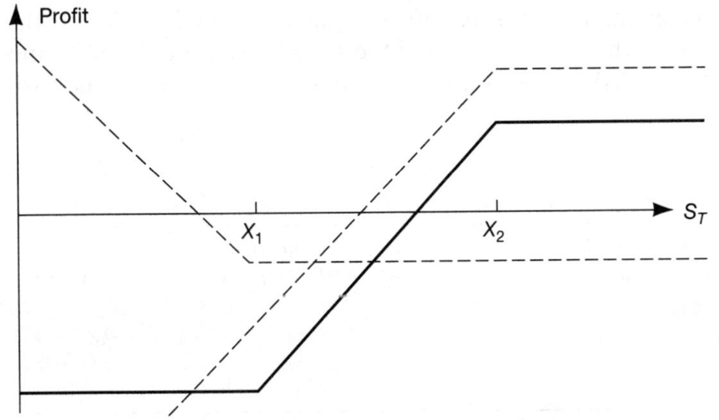

Figure 9.3 Bull spread created using put options.

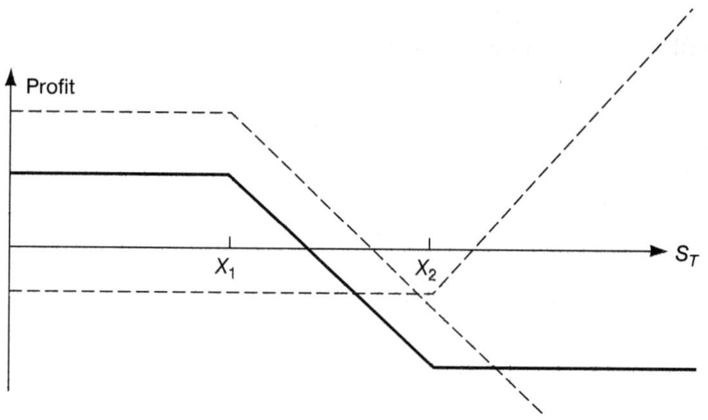

Figure 9.4 Bear spread created using call options.

to say, the final payoffs from bull spreads created using puts are lower than from those created using calls.

Bear Spreads

An investor entering into a bull spread is hoping that the stock price will increase. By contrast an investor who enters into a *bear spread* is hoping that the stock price will decline. Like a bull spread, a bear spread can be created by buying a call with one strike price and selling a call with another strike price. However, in the case of a bear spread, the strike price of the option purchased is greater than the strike price of the option sold. This is illustrated in Figure 9.4 where the profit from the spread is shown by the solid line. A bear spread created from calls involves an initial cash inflow (when margin requirements are ignored), since the price of the call sold is greater than the price of the call purchased.

Assuming that the strike prices are X_1 and X_2 with $X_1 < X_2$, Table 9.2 shows the payoff that will be realized from a bear spread in different circumstances. If the stock price is greater than X_2, the payoff is negative at $-(X_2 - X_1)$. If the stock price is less than X_1, the payoff is zero. If the stock price is between X_1 and X_2, the payoff is $-(S_T - X_1)$. The profit is calculated by adding the initial cash inflow to the payoff.

Table 9.2 Payoff from a Bear Spread

STOCK PRICE RANGE	*PAYOFF FROM LONG CALL OPTION*	*PAYOFF FROM SHORT CALL OPTION*	*TOTAL PAYOFF*
$S_T \geq X_2$	$S_T - X_2$	$X_1 - S_T$	$-(X_2 - X_1)$
$X_1 < S_T < X_2$	0	$X_1 - S_T$	$-(S_T - X_1)$
$S_T \leq X_1$	0	0	0

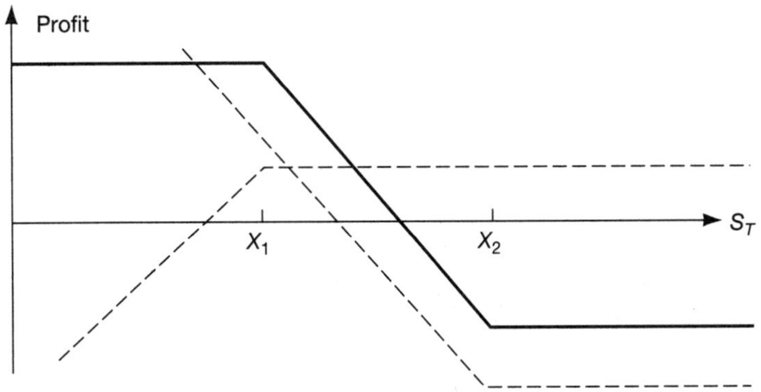

Figure 9.5 Bear spread created using put options.

Example

An investor buys for $1 a call with a strike price of $35 and sells for $3 a call with a strike price of $30. The payoff from this bear spread strategy is –$5 if the stock price is above $35 and zero if it is below $30. If the stock price is between $30 and $35, the payoff is $-(S_T - 30)$. The investment generates $3 − $1 = $2 up front. The profit is, therefore, as follows:

STOCK PRICE RANGE	*PROFIT*
$S_T \leq 30$	$+2$
$30 < S_T < 35$	$32 - S_T$
$S_T \geq 35$	-3

Like bull spreads, bear spreads limit both the upside profit potential and the downside risk. Bear spreads can be created using puts instead of calls. The investor buys a put with a high strike price and sells a put with a low strike price. This is illustrated in Figure 9.5. Bear spreads created with puts require an initial investment. In essence the investor has bought a put with a certain strike price and chosen to give up some of the profit potential by selling a put with a lower strike price. In return for the profit given up, the investor gets the price of the option sold.

Butterfly Spread

A *butterfly spread* involves positions in options with three different strike prices. It can be created by buying a call option with a relatively low strike price, X_1, buying a call option with a relatively high strike price, X_3, and selling two call options with a strike price, X_2, halfway between X_1 and X_3. Generally X_2 is close to the current stock price. The pattern of profits from the strategy is shown

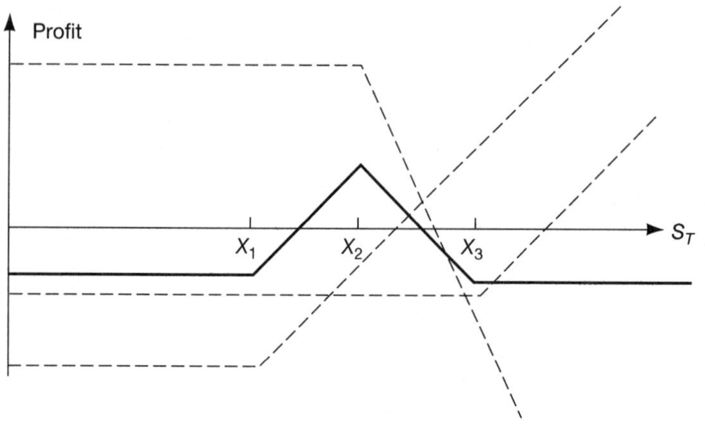

Figure 9.6 Butterfly spread using call options.

in Figure 9.6. A butterfly spread leads to a profit if the stock price stays close to X_2 but gives rise to a small loss if there is a significant stock price move in either direction. It is, therefore, an appropriate strategy for an investor who feels that large stock price moves are unlikely. The strategy requires a small investment initially. The payoff from a butterfly spread is shown in Table 9.3.

Suppose that a certain stock is currently worth \$61. Consider an investor who feels that it is unlikely that there will be a significant price move in the next six months. Suppose that the market prices of six-month calls are as follows:

STRIKE PRICE (\$)	*CALL PRICE* (\$)
55	10
60	7
65	5

The investor could create a butterfly spread by buying one call with a \$55 strike price, buying one call with a \$65 strike price, and selling two calls with a \$60 strike price. It costs \$10 + \$5 − (2 × \$7) = \$1 to create the spread. If the stock price in six months is greater than \$65 or less than \$55, there is no payoff and the investor makes a net loss of \$1. If the stock price is between \$56 and \$64,

Table 9.3 Payoff from a Butterfly Spread

STOCK PRICE RANGE	*PAYOFF FROM FIRST LONG CALL*	*PAYOFF FROM SECOND LONG CALL*	*PAYOFF FROM SHORT CALLS*	*TOTAL PAYOFF**
$S_T < X_1$	0	0	0	0
$X_1 < S_T < X_2$	$S_T - X_1$	0	0	$S_T - X_1$
$X_2 < S_T < X_3$	$S_T - X_1$	0	$-2(S_T - X_2)$	$X_3 - S_T$
$S_T > X_3$	$S_T - X_1$	$S_T - X_3$	$-2(S_T - X_2)$	0

* These payoffs are calculated using the relationship $X_2 = 0.5(X_1 + X_3)$.

Table 9.4 Use of Butterfly Spread

From the Trader's Desk

A stock is currently selling for $61. The prices of call options expiring in six months are quoted as follows:

Strike price = $55, call price = $10
Strike price = $60, call price = $7
Strike price = $65, call price = $5

An investor feels it is unlikely that the stock price will move significantly in the next six months.

Strategy

The investor sets up a butterfly spread by
1. Buying one call with a $55 strike.
2. Buying one call with a $65 strike.
3. Selling two calls with a $60 strike.

This costs $10 + $5 − (2 × $7) = $1. The strategy leads to a net loss (maximum $1) if the stock price moves outside the $56 to $64 range but leads to a profit if it stays within this range. The maximum profit of $4 is realized if the stock price is $60 on the expiration date.

a profit is made. The maximum profit, $4, occurs when the stock price in six months is $60. This example is summarized in Table 9.4.

Butterfly spreads can be created using put options. The investor buys a put with a low strike price, buys a put with a high strike price, and sells two puts with an intermediate strike price. This is illustrated in Figure 9.7. The butterfly spread in the example just considered would be created by buying a put with a strike price of $55, buying a put with a strike price of $65, and selling two puts with a strike price of $60. If all options are European, the use of put options results in exactly the same spread as the use of call options. Put-call parity can be used to show that the initial investment is the same in both cases.

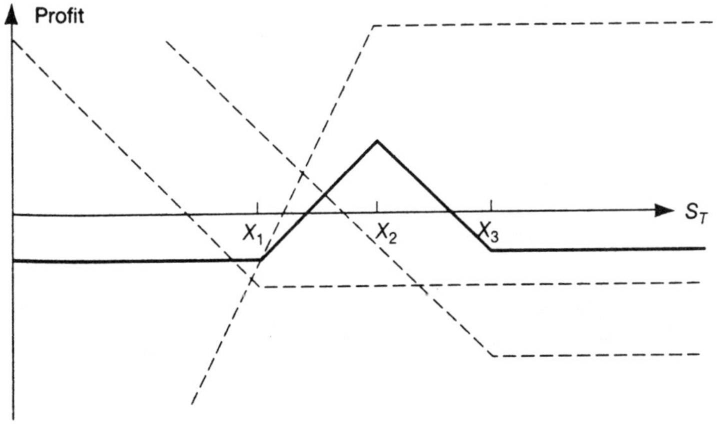

Figure 9.7 Butterfly spread using put options.

A butterfly spread can be sold or shorted by following the reverse strategy to that described earlier. Options are sold with strike prices of X_1 and X_3, and two options with the middle strike price X_2 are purchased. This strategy produces a modest profit if there is a significant movement in the stock price.

Calendar Spreads

Up to now we have assumed that the options used to create a spread all expire at the same time. We now move on to discuss *calendar spreads* where the options used have the same strike price and different expiration dates.

A calendar spread can be created by selling a call option with a certain strike price and buying a longer-maturity call option with the same strike price. The longer the maturity of an option, the more expensive it is. A calendar spread, therefore, requires an initial investment. Assuming that the long-maturity option is sold when the short-maturity option expires, the profit pattern given by a calendar spread is as shown in Figure 9.8. This is similar to the profit pattern from the butterfly spread in Figure 9.6. The investor makes a profit if the stock price at the expiration of the short-maturity option is close to the strike price of the short-maturity option. However, a loss is incurred when the stock price is significantly above or significantly below this strike price.

To understand the profit pattern from a calendar spread, first consider what happens if the stock price is very low when the short-maturity option expires. The short-maturity option is worthless and the value of the long-maturity option is close to zero. The investor, therefore, incurs a loss that is only a little less than the cost of setting up the spread initially. Consider next what happens if the stock price, S_T, is very high when the short-maturity option expires. The short-maturity option costs the investor $S_T - X$ and the long-maturity option (assuming early

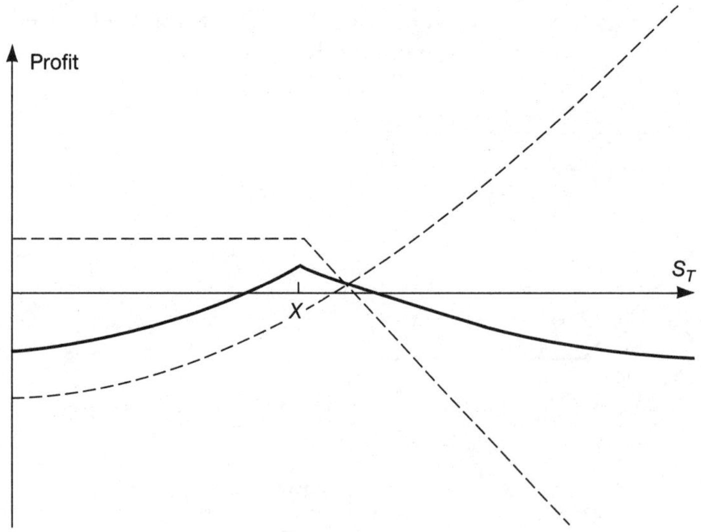

Figure 9.8 Calendar spread created using two calls.

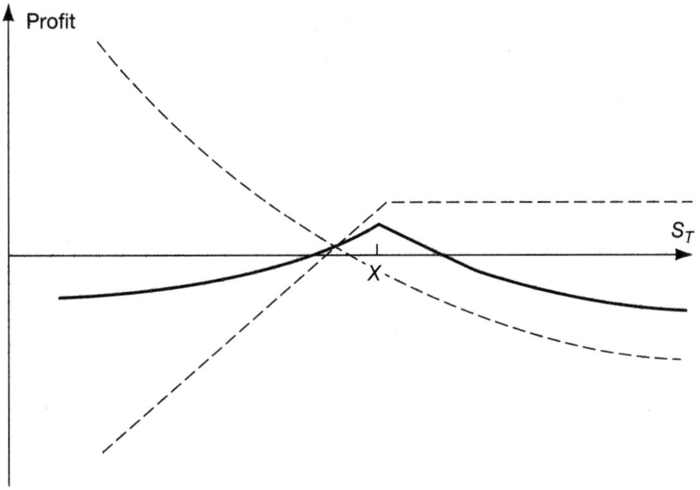

Figure 9.9 Calendar spread created using two puts.

exercise is not optimal) is worth a little more than $S_T - X$, where X is the strike price of the options. Again the investor makes a net loss that is a little less than the cost of setting up the spread initially. If S_T is close to X, the short-maturity option costs the investor either a small amount or nothing at all. However, the long-maturity option is still quite valuable. In this case a significant net profit is made.

In a *neutral calendar spread* a strike price close to the current stock price is chosen. A *bullish calendar spread* would involve a higher strike price, while a *bearish calendar spread* would involve a lower strike price.

Calendar spreads can be created with put options as well as call options. The investor buys a long-maturity put option and sells a short-maturity put option. As shown in Figure 9.9, the profit pattern is similar to that obtained from using calls.

A *reverse calendar spread* is the opposite to that in Figures 9.8 or 9.9. The investor buys a short-maturity option and sells a long-maturity option. This creates a small profit if the stock price at the expiration of the short-maturity option is well above or well below the strike price of the short-maturity option. However, it leads to a significant loss if it is close to the strike price.

Diagonal Spreads

Bull, bear, and calendar spreads can all be created from a long position in one call and a short position in another call. In the case of bull and bear spreads, the calls have different strike prices and the same expiration date. In the case of calendar spreads, the calls have the same strike price and different expiration dates. A *diagonal spread* is a spread which is such that both the expiration date and the strike price of the calls are different. There are several different types of

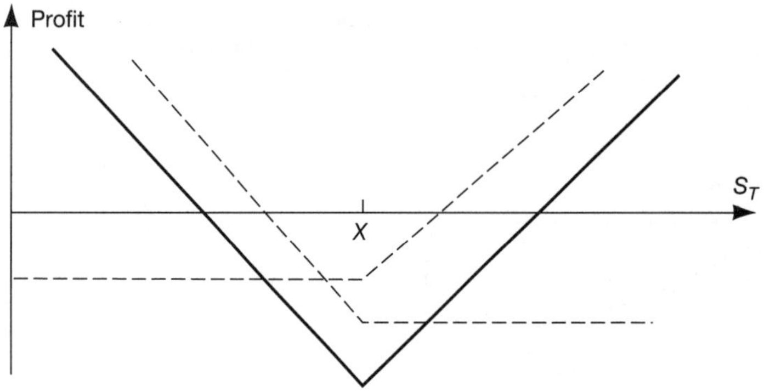

Figure 9.10 A straddle.

diagonal spreads. Their profit patterns are generally variations on the profit patterns from the corresponding bull or bear spreads.

COMBINATIONS

A *combination* is an option trading strategy that involves taking a position in both calls and puts on the same stock. We will consider what are known as straddles, strips, straps, and strangles.

Straddle

One popular combination is a *straddle*. This involves buying a call and put with the same strike price and expiration date. The profit pattern is shown in Figure 9.10. The strike price is denoted by X. If the stock price is close to this strike price at expiration of the options, the straddle leads to a loss. However, if there is a sufficiently large move in either direction, a significant profit will result. The payoff from a straddle is calculated in Table 9.5.

A straddle is appropriate when an investor is expecting a large move in a stock price but does not know in which direction the move will be. Consider an investor who feels that the price of a certain stock, currently valued at \$69 by the market, will move significantly in the next three months. The investor could create a straddle by buying both a put and a call with a strike price of \$70 and an expiration date in three months. Suppose that the call costs \$4 and the put costs

Table 9.5 Payoff from a Straddle

RANGE OF STOCK PRICE	*PAYOFF FROM CALL*	*PAYOFF FROM PUT*	*TOTAL PAYOFF*
$S_T \leq X$	0	$X - S_T$	$X - S_T$
$S_T > X$	$S_T - X$	0	$S_T - X$

Table 9.6 Use of a Straddle

From the Trader's Desk

A stock is currently trading at \$69. A three-month call with a strike price of \$70 costs \$4 while a three-month put with the same strike price costs \$3. An investor feels that the stock price is likely to experience a significant jump (either up or down) in the next three months.

The Strategy

The trader buys both the put and the call. The worst that can happen is that the stock price is \$70 in three months. In this case the strategy costs \$7. The farther away from \$70 the stock price is, the more profitable the strategy is. For example, if the stock price is \$90, the strategy leads to a profit of \$13. If the stock price is \$55, the strategy leads to a profit of \$8.

\$3. If the stock price stays at \$69, it is easy to see that the strategy costs the investor \$6. (An up-front investment of \$7 is required, the call expires worthless, and the put expires worth \$1.) If the stock price moves to \$70, a loss of \$7 is experienced. (This is the worst that can happen.) However, if the stock price jumps up to \$90, a profit of \$13 is made; if the stock move down to \$55, a profit of \$8 is made; and so on. This example is summarized in Table 9.6.

For a straddle to be an effective strategy, the investor's beliefs about the stock must be different from those of most other market participants. If the general view of the market is that there will be a large jump in the stock price, this will be reflected in the prices of options. When the investor attempts to buy options on the stock, he or she will find them significantly more expensive than for a similar stock where no jump is expected. (This point is explored further in Chapter 16.)

The straddle in Figure 9.10 is sometimes referred to as a *bottom straddle* or *straddle purchase*. A *top straddle* or *straddle write* is the reverse position. It is created by selling a call and a put with the same exercise price and expiration date. It is a highly risky strategy. If the stock price on the expiration date is close to the strike price, it leads to a significant profit. However, the loss arising from a large move in either direction is unlimited.

Strips and Straps

A *strip* consists of a long position in one call and two puts with the same strike price and expiration date. A *strap* consists of a long position in two calls and one put with the same strike price and expiration date. The profit patterns from strips and straps are shown in Figure 9.11. In a strip the investor is betting that there will be a big stock price move and considers a decrease in the stock price to be more likely than an increase. In a strap the investor is also betting that there will be a big stock price move. However, in this case, an increase in the stock price is considered to be more likely than a decrease.

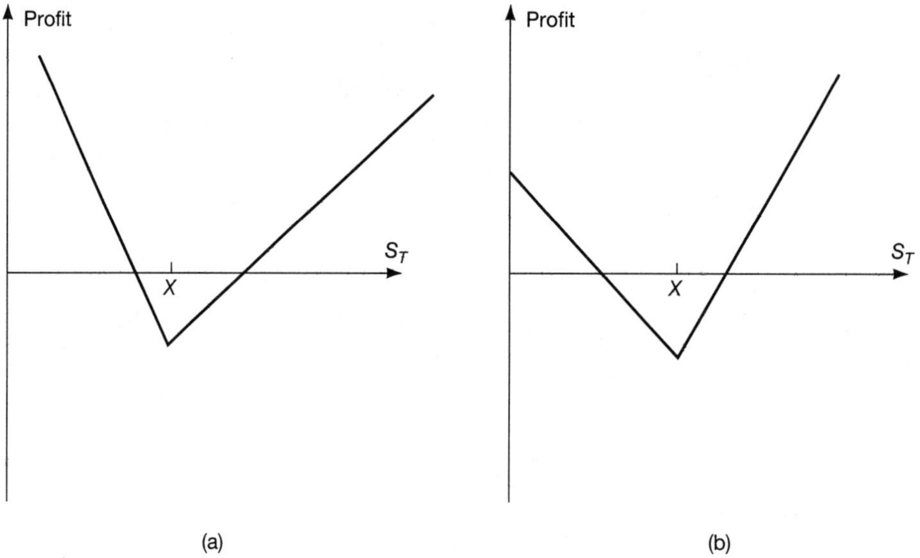

Figure 9.11 Profit patterns from (a) a strip and (b) a strap.

Strangles

In a *strangle,* sometimes called a *bottom vertical combination,* an investor buys a put and a call with the same expiration date and different strike prices. The profit pattern that is obtained is shown in Figure 9.12. The call strike price, X_2, is higher than the put strike price, X_1. The payoff function for a strangle is calculated in Table 9.7.

A strangle is a similar strategy to a straddle. The investor is betting that there will be a large price move but is uncertain whether it will be an increase or a decrease. Comparing Figures 9.12 and 9.10, we see that the stock price has to move farther in a strangle than in a straddle for the investor to make a profit.

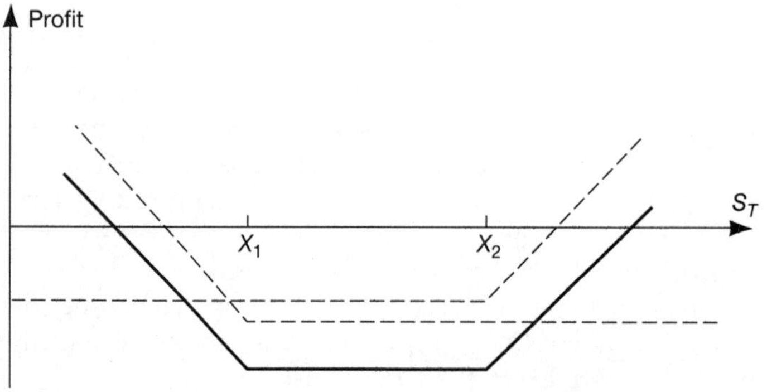

Figure 9.12 A strangle.

Table 9.7 Payoff from a Strangle

RANGE OF STOCK PRICE	*PAYOFF FROM CALL*	*PAYOFF FROM PUT*	*TOTAL PAYOFF*
$S_T \leq X$	0	$X_1 - S_T$	$X_1 - S_T$
$X_1 < S_T < X_2$	0	0	0
$S_T \geq X_2$	$S_T - X_2$	0	$S_T - X_2$

However, the downside risk if the stock price ends up at a central value is less with a strangle.

The profit pattern obtained with a strangle depends on how close the strike prices are together. The farther they are apart the less the downside risk and the farther the stock price has to move for a profit to be realized.

The sale of a strangle is sometimes referred to as a *top vertical combination.* It can be appropriate for an investor who feels that large stock price moves are unlikely. However, like the sale of a straddle, it is a risky strategy since the investor's potential loss is unlimited.

OTHER PAYOFFS

This chapter has demonstrated just a few of the ways in which options can be used to produce an interesting relationship between profit and stock price. If European options expiring at time T were available with every single possible strike price, any payoff function at time T could in theory be obtained. The easiest way to see this is in terms of butterfly spreads. It will be recalled that a butterfly spread is created by buying options with strike prices X_1 and X_3 and selling two options with strike price X_2 where $X_1 < X_2 < X_3$ and $X_3 - X_2 = X_2 - X_1$. Figure 9.13 shows the payoff from a butterfly spread. This could be described as a "spike." As X_1 and X_3 become closer together, the spike becomes smaller. By judiciously combining together a large number of very small spikes, any payoff function can be approximated.

SUMMARY

A number of common trading strategies involve a single option and the underlying stock. For example, writing a covered call involves buying the stock and selling a call option on the stock; a protective put involves buying a put option and

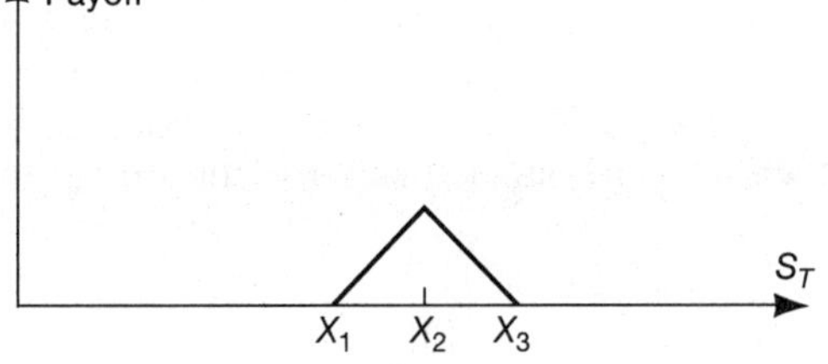

Figure 9.13 Payoff from a butterfly spread.

buying the stock. The former is similar to selling a put option; the latter is similar to buying a call option.

Spreads involve either taking a position in two or more calls or taking a position in two or more puts. A bull spread can be created by buying a call (put) with a low strike price and selling a call (put) with a high strike price. A bear spread can be created by buying a call (put) with a high strike price and selling a call (put) with a low strike price. A butterfly spread involves buying calls (puts) with a low and high strike price and selling two calls (puts) with some intermediate strike price. A calendar spread involves selling a call (put) with a short time to expiration and buying a call (put) with a longer time to expiration. A diagonal spread involves a long position in one option and a short position in another option where both the strike price and expiration date are different.

Combinations involve taking a position in both calls and puts on the same stock. A straddle combination involves taking a long position in a call and a long position in a put with the same strike price and expiration date. A strip consists of a long position in one call and two puts with the same strike price and expiration date. A strap consists of a long position in two calls and one put with the same strike price and expiration date. A strangle consists of a long position in a call and a put with different strike prices and the same expiration date. There are many other ways in which options can be used to produce interesting payoffs. It is not surprising that option trading has steadily increased in popularity and continues to fascinate investors.

Suggestions for Further Reading

BOOKSTABER, R. M., *Option Pricing and Strategies in Investing*. Reading, MA: Addison-Wesley, 1981.
CHANCE, D. M., *An Introduction to Options and Futures*. Orlando, FL.: Dryden Press, 1989.
DEGLER, W. H. and H. P. BECKER, "19 option strategies and when to use them," *Futures*, June 1984.
GASTINEAU, G., *The Stock Options Manual*, 2nd ed. New York: McGraw-Hill, 1979.
MCMILLAN, L. G., *Options as a strategic investment*, 2nd ed. New York: New York Institute of Finance, 1986.
SLIVKA, R, "Call option spreading,," *Journal of Portfolio Management*, 7 (Spring 1981), 71–76.
WELCH, W. W., *Strategies for Put and Call Option Trading*. Cambridge, MA: Winthrop, 1982.
YATES, J. W., and R. W. KOPPRASCH, "Writing covered call options: Profits and risks," *Journal of Portfolio Management*, 6 (Fall 1980), 74–80.

Quiz

1. What is meant by a protective put? What position in call options is equivalent to a protective put?
2. Explain two ways in which a bear spread can be created.
3. When is it appropriate for an investor to purchase a butterfly spread?
4. Call options on a stock are available with strike prices of \$15, \$17½, and \$20 and expiration dates in three months. Their prices are \$4, \$2, and \$½, respectively. Explain how the options can be used to create a butterfly spread. Construct a table showing how profit varies with stock price for the butterfly spread.
5. What trading strategy creates a reverse calendar spread?
6. What is the difference between a strangle and a straddle?

7. A call option with a strike price of \$50 costs \$2. A put option with a strike price of \$45 costs \$3. Explain how a strangle can be created from these two options. What is the pattern of profits from the strangle?

Questions and Problems

9.1. Analyze carefully the difference between a bull spread created from puts and a bull spread created from calls.

9.2. Explain how an aggressive bear spread can be created using put options.

9.3. Suppose that put options on a stock with strike prices \$30 and \$35 cost \$4 and \$7, respectively. How can the options be used to create (a) a bull spread and (b) a bear spread? Construct a table that shows the profit and payoff for both spreads.

9.4. Three put options on a stock have the same expiration date and strike prices of \$55, \$60, and \$65. The market prices are \$3, \$5, and \$8, respectively. Explain how a butterfly spread can be created. Construct a table showing the profit from the strategy. For what range of stock prices would the butterfly spread lead to a loss?

9.5. Use put-call parity to show that the cost of a butterfly spread created from European puts is identical to the cost of a butterfly spread created from European calls.

9.6. A diagonal spread is created by buying a call with strike price X_2 and exercise date T_2, and selling a call with strike price X_1 and exercise date T_1 ($T_2 > T_1$). Draw a diagram showing the profit when (a) $X_2 > X_1$ and (b) $X_2 < X_1$.

9.7. A call with a strike price of \$50 costs \$6. A put with the same strike price and expiration date costs \$4. Construct a table that shows the profits from a straddle. For what range of stock prices would the straddle lead to a loss?

9.8. Construct a table showing the payoff from a bull spread when puts with strike prices X_1 and X_2 are used ($X_2 > X_1$).

9.9. An investor believes that there will be a big jump in a stock price but is uncertain as to the direction. Identify six different strategies the investor can follow and explain the differences between them.

9.10. How can a forward contract on a stock with a certain delivery price and delivery date be created from options?

9.11. A box spread is a combination of a bull call spread with strike prices X_1 and X_2 and a bear put spread with the same strike prices. The expiration dates of all options are the same. What are the characteristics of a box spread?

9.12. What is the result if the strike price of the put is higher than the strike price of the call in a strangle?

10

AN INTRODUCTION TO BINOMIAL TREES

A useful and very popular technique for pricing a stock option involves constructing what is known as a *binomial tree*. This is a tree which represents different possible paths that might be followed by the stock price over the life of the option. In this chapter we will take a first look at binomial trees and explain their relationship to an important principle known as *risk-neutral valuation*. The general approach we will take is similar to that in an important paper published by Cox, Ross, and Rubinstein in 1976.

The material in this chapter is intended to be introductory. More details on how numerical procedures involving binomial trees can be implemented in practice are in Chapter 15.

A ONE-STEP BINOMIAL MODEL

We start by considering a very simple situation where a stock price is currently \$20 and it is known that at the end of three months the stock price will be either \$22 or \$18. We suppose that we are interested in valuing a European call option to buy the stock for \$21 in three months. This option will have one of two values at the end of the three months. If the stock price turns out to be \$22, the value of the option will be \$1; if the stock price turns out to be \$18, the value of the option will be zero. The situation is illustrated in Figure 10.1.

It turns out that a relatively simple argument can be used to price the option in this example. The only assumption we need is that there are no arbitrage opportunities for an investor. We set up a portfolio of the stock and the option

Figure 10.1 Stock price movements in numerical example.

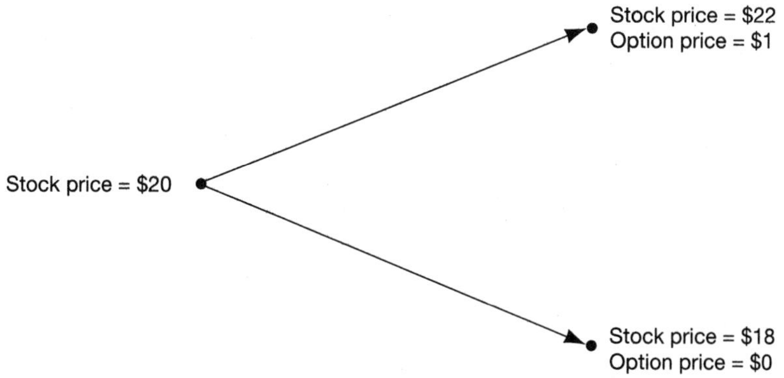

in such a way that there is no uncertainty about the value of the portfolio at the end of the three months. We then argue that, since the portfolio has no risk, the return earned on it must equal the risk-free interest rate. This enables us to work out the cost of setting up the portfolio and therefore the option's price. Since there are two securities (the stock and the stock option) and only two possible outcomes, it is always possible to set up the riskless portfolio.

Consider a portfolio consisting of a long position in Δ shares of the stock and a short position in one call option. We will calculate the value of Δ that makes the portfolio riskless. If the stock price moves up from 20 to 22, the value of the shares is 22Δ and the value of the option is 1 so that the total value of the portfolio is $22\Delta - 1$. If the stock price moves down from 20 to 18, the value of the shares is 18Δ and the value of the option is zero so that the total value of the portfolio is 18Δ. The portfolio is riskless if the value of Δ is chosen so that the final value of the portfolio is the same for both of the alternative stock prices. This means

$$22\Delta - 1 = 18\Delta$$

or

$$\Delta = 0.25$$

A riskless portfolio is, therefore:

Long: 0.25 shares
Short: 1 option

If the stock price moves up to 22, the value of the portfolio is

$$22 \times 0.25 - 1 = 4.5$$

If the stock price moves down to 18, the value of the portfolio is

$$18 \times 0.25 = 4.5$$

Regardless of whether the stock price moves up or down, the value of the portfolio is always 4.5 at the end of the life of the option.

Riskless portfolios must, in the absence of arbitrage opportunities, earn the risk-free rate of interest. Suppose that in this case the risk-free rate is 12 percent per annum. It follows that the value of the portfolio today must be the present value of 4.5 or

$$4.5e^{-0.12\times 0.25} = 4.367$$

The value of the stock price today is known to be 20. Suppose the option price is denoted by f. The value of the portfolio today is, therefore,

$$20 \times 0.25 - f = 5 - f$$

It follows that

$$5 - f = 4.367$$

or

$$f = 0.633$$

This shows that in the absence of arbitrage opportunities the current value of the option must be \$0.633. If the value of the option were more than 0.633, the portfolio would cost less than 4.367 to set up and would earn more than the risk-free rate. If the value of the option were less than 0.633, shorting the portfolio would provide a way of borrowing money at less than the risk-free rate.

A Generalization

We can generalize the argument that has just been presented by considering a stock whose price is S and an option on the stock whose current price is f. We suppose that the option lasts for time T and that during the life of the option the stock price can either move up from S to a new level Su or down from S to a new level Sd ($u > 1$; $d < 1$). The proportional increase in the stock price when there is an up movement is $u - 1$; the proportional decrease when there is a down movement is $1 - d$. If the stock price moves up to Su, we suppose that the payoff from the option is f_u; if the stock price moves down to Sd, we suppose the payoff from the option is f_d. The situation is illustrated in Figure 10.2.

As before we imagine a portfolio consisting of a long position in Δ shares and a short position in one option. We calculate the value of Δ that makes the portfolio riskless. If there is an up movement in the stock price, the value of the portfolio at the end of the life of the option is

$$Su\Delta - f_u$$

If there is a down movement in the stock price, this becomes

$$Sd\Delta - f_d$$

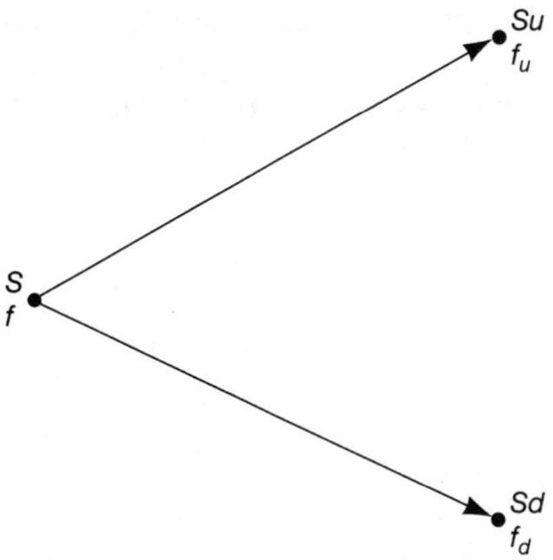

Figure 10.2 Stock and option prices in general one-step tree.

The two are equal when

$$Su\Delta - f_u = Sd\Delta - f_d$$

or

$$\Delta = \frac{f_u - f_d}{Su - Sd} \tag{10.1}$$

In this case the portfolio is riskless and must earn the risk-free interest rate. Equation (10.1) shows that Δ is the ratio of the change in the option price to the change in the stock price as we move between the nodes.

Denoting the risk-free interest rate by r, the present value of the portfolio must be

$$[Su\Delta - f_u]e^{-rT}$$

The cost of setting up the portfolio is:

$$S\Delta - f$$

It follows that

$$S\Delta - f = [Su\Delta - f_u]e^{-rT}$$

Substituting from Equation (10.1) for Δ and simplifying, this equation reduces to

$$f = e^{-rT}[pf_u + (1 - p)f_d] \tag{10.2}$$

where

$$p = \frac{e^{rT} - d}{u - d} \tag{10.3}$$

Equations (10.2) and (10.3) enable an option to be priced using a one-step binomial model.

In the numerical example considered previously (see Figure 10.1), $u = 1.1$, $d = 0.9$, $r = 0.12$, $T = 0.25$, $f_u = 1$, and $f_d = 0$. From Equation (10.3),

$$p = \frac{e^{0.03} - 0.9}{1.1 - 0.9} = 0.6523$$

and from Equation (10.2),

$$f = e^{-0.03}[0.6523 \times 1 + 0.3477 \times 0] = 0.633$$

This agrees with the answer obtained earlier in this section.

The Irrelevance of the Stock's Expected Return

The option pricing formula in Equation (10.2) does not involve the probabilities of the stock price moving up or down. For example, we get the same option price when the probability of an upward movement is 0.5 as we do when it is 0.9. This is surprising and seems counterintuitive. It is natural to assume that, as the probability of an upward movement in the stock price increases, the value of a call option on the stock increases and the value of a put option on the stock decreases. This is not the case.

The key reason for this is that we are not valuing the option in absolute terms. We are calculating its value in terms of the price of the underlying stock. The probabilities of future up or down movements are already incorporated into the price of the stock. It turns out that we do not need to take them into account again when valuing the option in terms of the stock price.

RISK-NEUTRAL VALUATION

Although we do not need to make any assumptions about the probabilities of up and down movements in order to derive Equation (10.2), it is natural to interpret the variable p in Equation (10.2) as the probability of an up movement in the stock price. The variable $1 - p$ is then the probability of a down movement and the expression

$$pf_u + (1 - p)f_d$$

is the expected payoff from the option. With this interpretation of p, Equation (10.2) then states that the value of the option today is its expected future value discounted at the risk-free rate.

We now investigate the expected return from the stock when the probability of an up movement is assumed to be p. The expected stock price at time T, $E(S_T)$, is given by

$$E(S_T) = pSu + (1 - p)Sd$$

or

$$E(S_T) = pS(u - d) + Sd$$

Substituting from Equation (10.3) for p, this reduces to

$$E(S_T) = Se^{rT} \tag{10.4}$$

showing that the stock price grows on average at the risk-free rate. Setting the probability of the up movement equal to p is, therefore, equivalent to assuming that the return on the stock equals the risk-free rate.

We will refer to a world where all individuals are risk neutral as a *risk-neutral world*. In such a world investors require no compensation for risk and the expected return on all securities is the risk-free interest rate. An important general principle in option pricing is known as *risk-neutral valuation*. This states that we can with complete impunity assume the world is risk neutral when pricing options. The prices we get are correct not just in a risk-neutral world, but in other worlds as well. A risk-neutral world is a particularly easy world to work with. The expected return on all stocks in a risk-neutral world is the risk-free rate. Also, an option can be valued in a risk-neutral world by discounting its expected payoff at the risk-free rate.

The analysis in this chapter shows that the principle of risk-neutral valuation applies to options when they are valued using binomial trees. Equation (10.4) shows that we are assuming a risk-neutral world when we set the probability of an up movement to p. Equation (10.2) shows that the value of the option is its expected payoff in a risk-neutral world discounted at the risk-free rate.

The One-Step Binomial Example Revisited

To illustrate the principle of risk-neutral valuation further, consider again the example in Figure 10.1. The stock price is currently \$20 and will move either up to \$22 or down to \$18 at the end of three months. The option considered is a European call option with a strike price of \$21 and an expiration date in three months. The risk-free interest rate is 12 percent per annum.

We denote the probability of an upward movement in the stock price in a risk-neutral world by p. In such a world the expected return on the stock must be the risk-free rate of 12 percent. This means that p must satisfy

$$22p + 18(1 - p) = 20e^{0.12\times 0.25}$$

or

$$4p = 20e^{0.12\times 0.25} - 18$$

That is, p must be 0.6523.

At the end of the three months the call option has a 0.6523 probability of being worth 1 and a 0.3477 probability of being worth zero. Its expected value is, therefore,

$$0.6523 \times 1 + 0.3477 \times 0 = \$0.6523$$

Discounting at the risk-free rate, the value of the option today is

$$0.6523e^{-0.12 \times 0.25}$$

or $0.633. This is the same as the value obtained earlier, demonstrating that no-arbitrage arguments and risk-neutral valuation give the same answer.

TWO-STEP BINOMIAL TREES

We can extend the analysis that has been given to a two-step binomial tree such as that shown in Figure 10.3. Here the stock price starts at $20 and in each of two time steps may go up by 10 percent or down by 10 percent. We suppose that each time step is three months in length and the risk-free interest rate is 12 percent per annum. As before we consider an option with a strike price of $21.

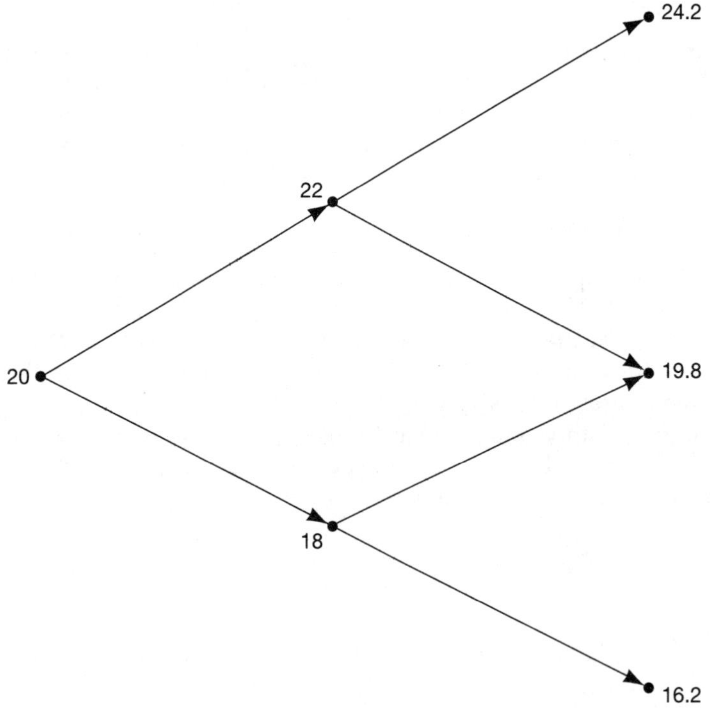

Figure 10.3 Stock prices in a two-step tree.

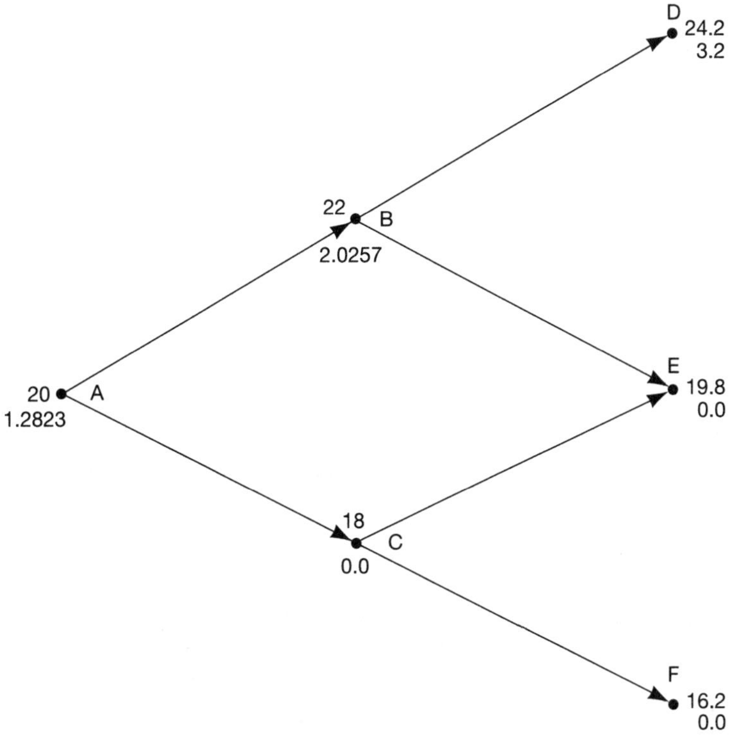

Figure 10.4 Stock and option prices in a two-step tree. The upper number at each node is the stock price; the lower number is the option price.

The objective of our analysis is to calculate the option price at the initial node of the tree. This can be done by repeatedly applying the principles established earlier in this chapter. Figure 10.4 shows the same tree as Figure 10.3, but with both the stock price and the option price at each node. (The stock price is the upper number and the option price is the lower number.) The option prices at the final nodes of the tree are easily calculated. They are the payoffs from the option. At node D the stock price is 24.2 and the option's price is $24.2 - 21 = 3.2$; at nodes E and F the option is out of the money and its value is zero.

At node C the option price is zero, since node C leads to either node E or node F and at both of these nodes the option price is zero. We calculate the option price at node B by focusing our attention on the part of the tree shown in Figure 10.5. Using the notation introduced earlier in the chapter, $u = 1.1$, $d = 0.9$, $r = 0.12$, $T = 0.25$ so that $p = 0.6523$ and Equation (10.2) gives the value of the option at node B as

$$e^{-0.12 \times 0.25}[0.6523 \times 3.2 + 0.3477 \times 0] = 2.0257$$

It remains to calculate the option price at the initial node A. We do this by focusing on the first step of the tree. We know that the value of the option at node

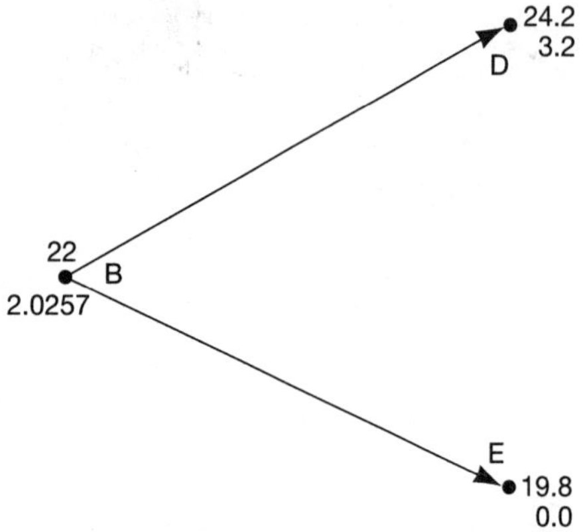

Figure 10.5 Evaluation of option price at node B.

B is 2.0257 and that at node C it is zero. Equation (10.2), therefore, gives the value at node A as

$$e^{-0.12\times0.25}[0.6523 \times 2.0257 + 0.3477 \times 0] = 1.2823$$

The price of the option is \$1.2823.

Note that this example was constructed so that u and d (the proportional up and down movements) were the same at each node of the tree and so that the time steps were of the same length. This led to the risk-neutral probability, p, as calculated by Equation (10.3), being the same at each node.

A Generalization

We can generalize the case of two time steps by considering the situation shown in Figure 10.6. The stock price is initially S. During each time step, it either moves up to u times its initial value or down to d times its initial value. The notation for the value of the option is shown on the tree. (For example, after two up movements the value of the option is f_{uu}.) We suppose that the risk-free interest rate is r and the length of the time step is ΔT years.

Repeated application of Equation (10.2) gives

$$f_u = e^{-r\Delta T}[pf_{uu} + (1 - p)f_{ud}] \tag{10.5}$$

$$f_d = e^{-r\Delta T}[pf_{ud} + (1 - p)f_{dd}] \tag{10.6}$$

$$f = e^{-r\Delta T}[pf_u + (1 - p)f_d] \tag{10.7}$$

Substituting from Equations (10.5) and (10.6) in (10.7), we get

$$f = e^{-2r\Delta T}[p^2 f_{uu} + 2p(1 - p)f_{ud} + (1 - p)^2 f_{dd}] \tag{10.8}$$

This is consistent with the principle of risk-neutral valuation mentioned earlier. The variables p^2, $2p(1 - p)$, and $(1 - p)^2$ are the probabilities of the upper, middle,

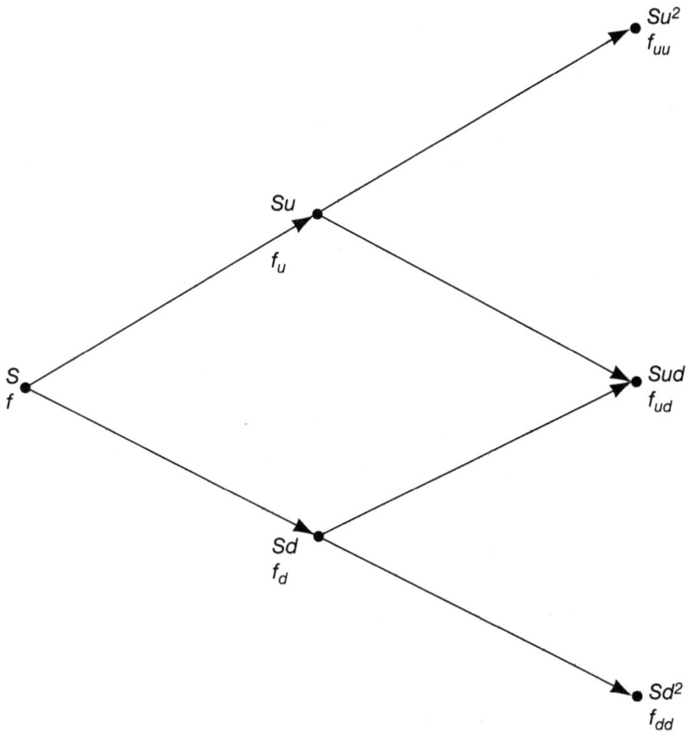

Figure 10.6 Stock and option prices in general two-step tree.

and lower final nodes being reached. The option price is equal to its expected payoff in a risk-neutral world discounted at the risk-free interest rate.

If we generalize the use of binomial trees still further by adding more steps to the tree, we find that the risk-neutral valuation principle continues to hold. The option price is always equal to its expected payoff in a risk-neutral world, discounted at the risk-free interest rate.

A PUT EXAMPLE

The procedures described in this chapter can be used to price any derivative dependent on a stock whose price changes are binomial. Consider for example a two-year European put with a strike price of 52 on a stock whose current price is 50. We suppose that there are two time steps of one year and in each time step the stock price either moves up by a proportional amount of 20 percent or down by a proportional amount of 20 percent. We also suppose that the risk-free interest rate is 5 percent.

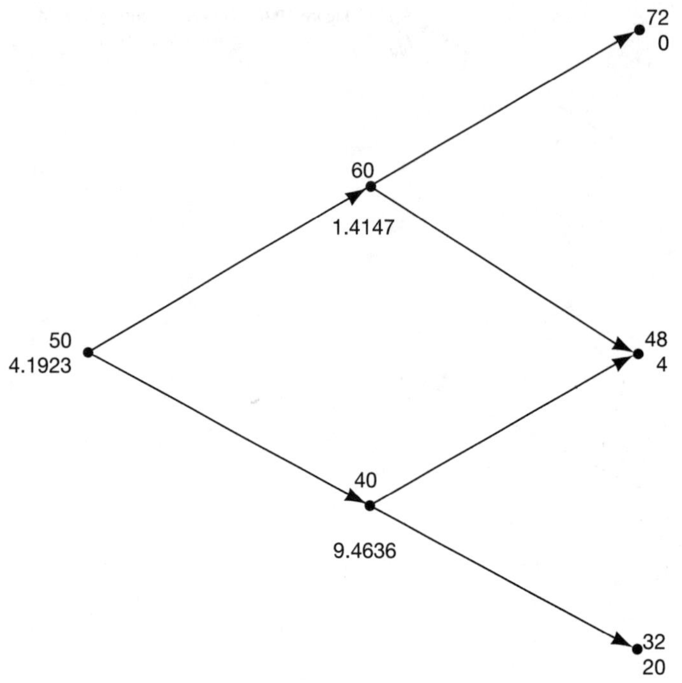

Figure 10.7 Use of two time-step tree to value European put option. At each node the upper number is the stock price; the lower number is the option price.

The tree is shown in Figure 10.7. The value of the risk-neutral probability, p, is given by

$$p = \frac{e^{0.05\times 1} - 0.8}{1.2 - 0.8} = 0.6282$$

The possible final stock prices are: 72, 48, and 32. In this case $f_{uu} = 0$, $f_{ud} = 4$, and $f_{dd} = 20$. Using Equation (10.8),

$$\begin{aligned} f &= e^{-2\times 0.05\times 1}[0.6282^2 \times 0 + 2 \times 0.6282 \times 0.3718 \times 4 + 0.3718^2 \times 20] \\ &= 4.1923 \end{aligned}$$

The value of the put is \$4.1923. This result can also be obtained using Equation (10.2) and working back through the tree one step at a time. Figure 10.7 shows the intermediate option prices that are calculated.

AMERICAN OPTIONS

Up to now all the options we have considered have been European. We now move on to consider how American options can be valued using a binomial tree such as that in Figures 10.4 or 10.7. The procedure is to work back through the tree from the end to the beginning, testing at each node to see whether early exercise is optimal. The value of the option at the final nodes is the same as for the European option. At earlier nodes the value of the option is the greater of

1. The value given by Equation (10.2); and
2. The payoff from early exercise.

As an illustration, we consider how Figure 10.7 is affected if the option under consideration is American rather than European. The stock prices and their probabilities are of course unchanged. The values for the option at the final nodes are also unchanged. At node B, Equation (10.2) gives the value of the option as 1.4147, while the payoff from early exercise is negative ($= -8$). Clearly early exercise is not optimal at node B and the value of the option at this node is 1.4147. At node C, Equation (10.2) gives the value of the option as 9.4636, while the payoff from early exercise is 12.0. In this case early exercise is optimal and the value of the option is 12.0. At the initial node A the value given by Equation (10.2) is

$$e^{-0.05\times 1}[0.6282 \times 1.4147 + 0.3718 \times 12.0] = 5.0894$$

while the payoff from early exercise is 2.0. In this case early exercise is not optimal. The value of the option is, therefore, \$5.0894. Figure 10.8 shows the new tree values.

More details on the use of binomial trees to value American options are in Chapter 15.

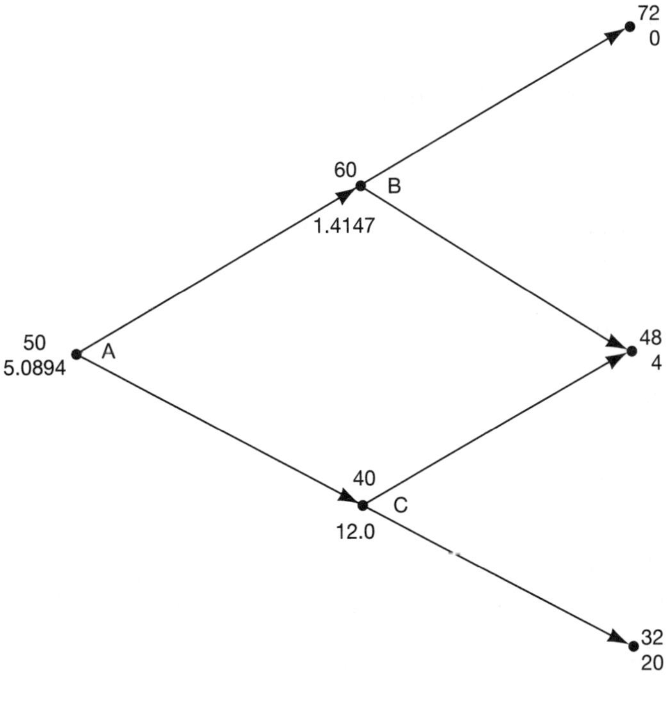

Figure 10.8 Use of two time-step tree to value American put option. At each node the upper number is the stock price; the lower number is the option price.

DELTA

At this stage it is appropriate to discuss *delta*, an important parameter in the pricing and hedging of options.

The delta of a stock option is the ratio of the change in the price of a stock option to the change in the price of the underlying stock. It is the number of units of the stock we should hold for each option shorted in order to create a riskless hedge. It is the same as the Δ introduced earlier in this chapter. The construction of a riskless hedge is sometimes referred to as *delta hedging*. The delta of a call option is positive, whereas the delta of a put option is negative.

From Figure 10.1 we can calculate the value of the delta of the call option being considered as

$$\frac{1 - 0}{22 - 18} = 0.25$$

This is because when the stock price changes from 18 to 22, the option price changes from 0 to 1.

In Figure 10.4 the delta corresponding to stock price movements over the first time step is

$$\frac{2.0257 - 0}{22 - 18} = 0.5064$$

The delta for stock price movements over the second time step is

$$\frac{3.2 - 0}{24.2 - 19.8} = 0.7273$$

if there is an upward movement over the first time step and

$$\frac{0 - 0}{19.8 - 16} = 0$$

if there is a downward movement over the first time step.

From Figure 10.7, delta is

$$\frac{1.4147 - 9.4636}{60 - 40} = -0.4024$$

for the first time step and either

$$\frac{0 - 4}{72 - 48} = -0.1667$$

or

$$\frac{4 - 20}{48 - 32} = -1.0000$$

over the second time step.

The two-step examples show that delta changes over time. (In Figure 10.4 delta changes from 0.5064 to either 0.7273 or 0; in Figure 10.7 it changes from -0.4024 to either -0.1667 or -1.0000.) This means that in order to maintain a riskless hedge using an option and the underlying stock, we need to adjust our holdings in the stock periodically. This is a feature of options that we will return to later in Chapters 11 and 14.

USING BINOMIAL TREES IN PRACTICE

The binomial models presented so far have been unrealistically simple. Clearly an analyst can expect to obtain only a very rough approximation to an option price by assuming that stock price movements during the life of the option consist of one or two binomial steps.

When binomial trees are used in practice the life of the option is typically divided into 30 or more time steps. In each time step there is a binomial stock price movement. With 30 time steps this means that 31 terminal stock prices and 2^{30}, or about one billion, possible stock price paths are considered.

The values of u and d are determined from the stock price volatility, σ. There are a number of different ways this can be done. If we define Δt as the length of one time step, one possibility is to set

$$u = e^{\sigma\sqrt{\Delta t}}$$

and

$$d = \frac{1}{u}$$

The complete set of equations defining the tree is then

$$u = e^{\sigma\sqrt{\Delta t}}; \qquad d = e^{-\sigma\sqrt{\Delta t}}$$

$$p = \frac{e^{r\Delta t} - d}{u - d}$$

Chapter 15 provides a further discussion of these formulas and practical issues involved in the construction and use of binomial trees.

SUMMARY

This chapter has provided a first look at the valuation of stock options. If stock price movements during the life of an option are governed by a one-step binomial tree, it is possible to set up a portfolio consisting of a stock option and the stock that is riskless. In a world where there are no arbitrage opportunities, riskless portfolios must earn the risk-free interest. This enables the stock option to be priced in terms of the stock. It is interesting to note that no assumptions are required about the probabilities of up and down movements in the stock price at each node.

When stock price movements are governed by a multistep binomial tree, we can treat each binomial step separately and work back from the end of the life of the option to the beginning to obtain the current value of the option. Again only no-arbitrage arguments are used and no assumptions are required about the probabilities of up and down movements in the stock price at each node.

Another approach to valuing stock options involves the use of what is known as risk-neutral valuation. This is a very important principle that states that it is permissible to assume that the world is risk neutral when valuing an option in terms of the underlying stock. In this chapter we have shown using both numerical examples and algebra that no-arbitrage arguments and risk-neutral valuation always lead to the same option prices.

The delta of a stock option, Δ, considers the effect of a small change in the underlying stock price on the change in the option price. It is the ratio of the change in the option price to the change in the stock price. For a riskless position an investor should buy Δ shares for each option sold. An inspection of a typical binomial tree shows that delta is liable to change during the life of an option. This means that riskless positions do not automatically remain riskless. They must be adjusted periodically.

In the next chapter we discuss the Black–Scholes analytic approach to pricing stock options. In Chapters 12 and 13 we discuss other types of options. In Chapter 14 we move on to consider hedge statistics such as delta. We then in Chapter 15 return to binomial trees and provide a more complete discussion of how they are used in practice.

Suggestions for Further Reading

COX, J., S. ROSS, and M. RUBINSTEIN, "Option pricing: a simplified approach," *Journal of Financial Economics*, 7 (October 1979), 229–264.

Quiz

1. A stock price is currently $40. It is known that at the end of one month it will be either $42 or $38. The risk-free interest rate is 8 percent per annum with continuous compounding. What is the value of a one-month European call option with a strike price of $39?
2. Explain the no-arbitrage and risk-neutral valuation approaches to valuing a European option using a one-step binomial tree.
3. What is meant by the delta of a stock option?
4. A stock price is currently $50. It is known that at the end of six months it will be either $45 or $55. The risk-free interest rate is 10 percent per annum with continuous compounding. What is the the value of a six-month European put option with a strike price of $50?

5. A stock price is currently \$100. Over each of the next two six-month periods it is expected to go up by 10 percent or down by 10 percent. The risk-free interest rate is 8 percent per annum with continuous compounding. What is the value of a one-year European call option with a strike price of \$100?
6. For the situation considered in the previous question, what is the value of a one-year European put option with a strike price of \$100? Verify that the European call and European put prices satisfy put–call parity.
7. Consider the situation where stock price movements during the life of a European option are governed by a two-step binomial tree. Explain why it is not possible to set up a position in the stock and the option that remains riskless for the whole of the life of the option.

Questions and Problems

10.1. A stock price is currently \$50. It is known that at the end of two months it will be either \$53 or \$48. The risk-free interest rate is 10 percent per annum with continuous compounding. What is the value of a two-month European call option with a strike price of \$49? Use no-arbitrage arguments.

10.2. A stock price is currently \$80. It is known that at the end of four months it will be either \$75 or \$85. The risk-free interest rate is 5 percent per annum with continuous compounding. What is the value of a four-month European put option with a strike price of \$80? Use no-arbitrage arguments.

10.3. A stock price is currently \$50. It is known that at the end of six months it will be either \$60 or \$42. The risk-free rate of interest with continuous compounding is 12 percent per annum. Calculate the value of a six-month European call option on the stock with exercise price of \$48. Verify that no-arbitrage arguments and risk-neutral valuation arguments give the same answers.

10.4. A stock price is currently \$40. It is known that at the end of three months it will be either \$45 or \$35. The risk-free rate of interest with quarterly compounding is 8 percent per annum. Calculate the value of a three-month European put option on the stock with an exercise price of \$40. Verify that no-arbitrage arguments and risk-neutral valuation arguments give the same answers.

10.5. A stock price is currently \$50. Over each of the next two three-month periods it is expected to go up by 6 percent or down by 5 percent. The risk-free interest rate is 5 percent per annum with continuous compounding. What is the value of a six-month European call option with a strike price of \$51?

10.6. For the situation considered in Problem 10.5, what is the value of a six-month European put option with a strike price of \$51? Verify that the European call and European put prices satisfy put–call parity. If the put option were American, would it ever be optimal to exercise it early at any of the nodes of the tree?

10.7. A stock price is currently \$40. Over each of the next two three-month periods it is expected to go up by 10 percent or down by 10 percent. The risk-free interest rate is 12 percent per annum with continuous compounding.

   a. What is the value of a 6-month European put option with a strike price of \$42?

b. What is the value of a 6-month American put option with a strike price of $42?

10.8. Using "trial and error," estimate how high the strike price has to be in Problem 10.7 for it to be optimal to exercise the option immediately.

10.9. A stock price is currently $25. It is known that at the end of two months it will be either $23 or $27. The risk-free interest rate is 10 percent per annum with continuous compounding. Suppose S_T is the stock price at the end of two months. What is the value of a derivative that pays off S_T^2 at this time?

11

THE PRICING OF STOCK OPTIONS USING BLACK–SCHOLES

In the early 1970s, Fischer Black and Myron Scholes made a major breakthrough in the pricing of stock options. This has had a huge influence on the way in which market participants price and hedge options. In this chapter, we explain the Black–Scholes results and the assumptions upon which they are based. We also discuss more fully than in previous chapters the meaning of volatility. We explain how volatility can be either estimated from historical data or implied from option prices. Towards the end of the chapter we show how the Black–Scholes results can be extended to deal with European call options on dividend-paying stocks.

THE LOGNORMAL ASSUMPTION

A stock option pricing model must make some assumptions about how stock prices evolve over time. If a stock price is $100 today, what is the probability distribution for the price in one day or in one week or in one year?

The assumption underlying the Black–Scholes model is that stock prices follow what is termed a *random walk*. This means that proportional changes in the stock price in a short period of time are normally distributed. This in turn implies that the stock price at any future time has what is known as a *lognormal* distribution. The general shape of a lognormal distribution is shown in Figure 11.1. It can be contrasted with the more familiar normal distribution in Figure 11.2. Whereas a variable with a normal distribution can take any positive or negative value, a

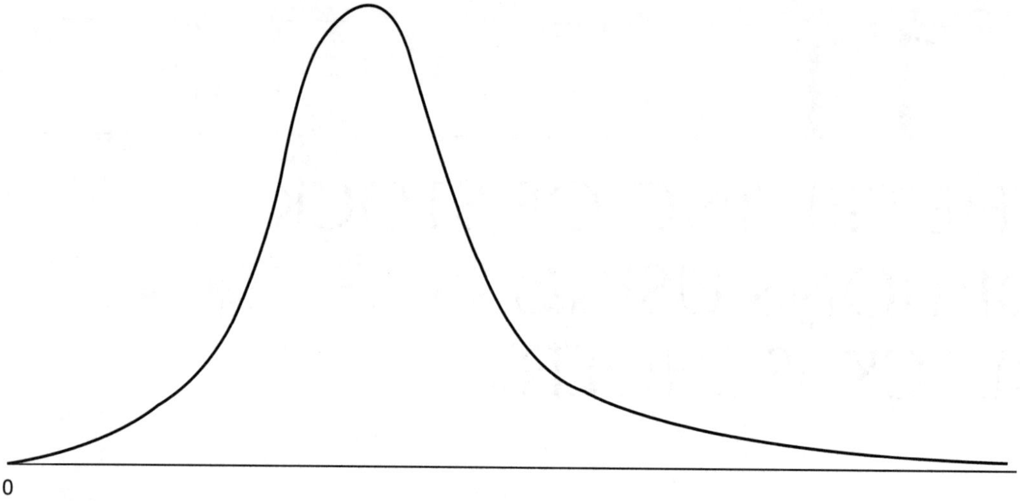

Figure 11.1 A lognormal distribution.

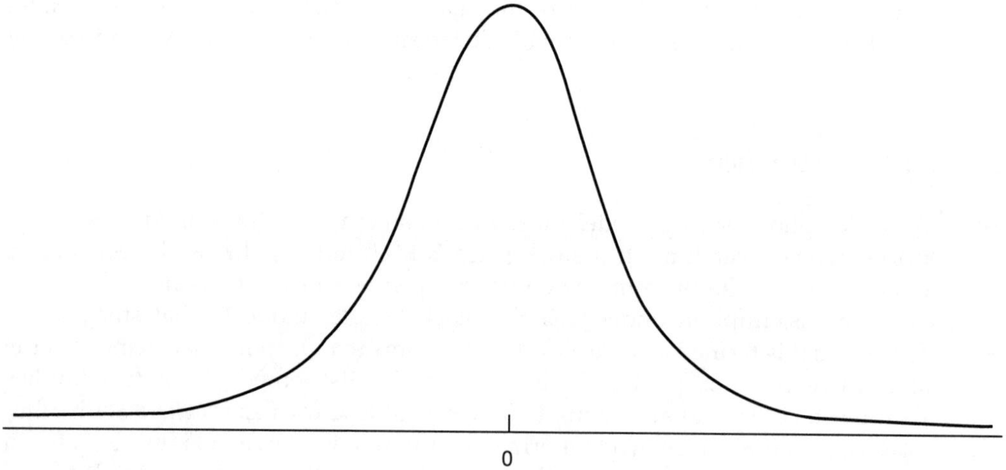

Figure 11.2 A normal distribution.

lognormally distributed variable is restricted to being positive. A normal distribution is symmetrical; a lognormal distribution is skewed with the mean, median, and mode all different.

The Parameters

The two key parameters describing the behavior of a stock price when the lognormal assumption is made are

1. The expected return from the stock
2. The volatility of the stock price

The expected return is the annualized average return earned by investors in a short period of time. We will denote the expected return parameter by μ. The volatility is a measure of our uncertainty about future stock price movements. More precisely, it is a measure of our uncertainty about proportional stock price changes. We will denote the volatility parameter by σ.

A variable with a lognormal distribution has the property that its natural logarithm is normally distributed. The lognormal assumption for stock prices, therefore, implies that $\ln S_T$ is normal where S_T is the stock price at a future time T. The mean and standard deviation of $\ln S_T$ can be shown to be

$$\ln S + (\mu - \frac{\sigma^2}{2})T$$

and

$$\sigma\sqrt{T}$$

where S is the current stock price, μ is the expected return per annum from an investment in the stock, and σ is the volatility per annum of the stock price. We can write this result as

$$\ln S_T \sim \phi\left[\ln S + \left(\mu - \frac{\sigma^2}{2}\right)T,\ \sigma\sqrt{T}\right] \quad \textbf{(11.1)}$$

where $\phi(m,s)$ denotes a normal distribution with mean m and standard deviation s. The expected value or mean value of S_T, $E(S_T)$, is given by

$$E(S_T) = Se^{\mu T} \quad \textbf{(11.2)}$$

This fits in with the definition of μ as the expected rate of return. The variance of S_T, var (S_T), can be shown to be given by

$$\text{var}\,(S_T) = S^2e^{2\mu T}(e^{\sigma^2 T} - 1) \quad \textbf{(11.3)}$$

Example

Consider a stock with an initial price of \$40, an expected return of 16 percent per annum, and a volatility of 20 percent per annum. From Equation (11.1), the probability distribution of the stock price, S_T, in six months' time is given by

$$\ln S_T \sim \phi\left[\ln 40 + \left(0.16 - \frac{0.04}{2}\right)0.5,\ 0.2\sqrt{0.5}\right]$$

or

$$\ln S_T \sim \phi(3.759,\ 0.141)$$

There is a 95 percent probability that a normally distributed variable has a value within two standard deviations of its mean. Hence, with 95 percent confidence,

$$3.477 < \ln S_T < 4.041$$

This can be written as

$$e^{3.477} < S_T < e^{4.041}$$

or

$$32.36 < S_T < 56.88$$

Thus, there is a 95 percent probability that the stock price in six months will lie between 32.36 and 56.88. The mean and variance of S_T are

$$40e^{0.16\times 0.5} = 43.33$$

and

$$40^2 e^{2\times 0.16\times 0.5}(e^{0.2\times 0.2\times 0.5} - 1) = 37.93$$

From Equation (11.1), it can be shown that

$$\ln\frac{S_T}{S} \sim \phi\left[\left(\mu - \frac{\sigma^2}{2}\right)T,\ \sigma\sqrt{T}\right] \qquad \textbf{(11.4)}$$

The expression $\ln(S_T/S)$ is the continuously compounded return provided by the stock in time T.[1] Equation (11.4) shows that this is normally distributed. Putting $T = 1$, we see that the mean and standard deviation of the continuously compounded return in one year are $\mu - \sigma^2/2$ and σ, respectively.

[1] As discussed in Chapter 3, it is important to distinguish between the continuously compounded return and the return with no compounding. The latter is $(S_T - S)/S$.

Example

Consider a stock with an expected return of 17 percent per annum and a volatility of 20 percent per annum. The probability distribution for the actual rate of return (continuously compounded) realized over one year is normal with mean

$$0.17 - \frac{0.04}{2} = 0.15$$

or 15 percent and standard deviation 20 percent. Since there is a 95 percent chance that a normally distributed variable will lie within two standard deviations of its mean, we can be 95 percent confident that the actual return realized over one year will be between -25 percent and $+55$ percent.

We now consider in more detail the nature of the expected return and volatility parameter in the lognormal stock price model.

THE EXPECTED RETURN

The expected return, μ, required by investors from a stock depends on the riskiness of the stock. The higher the risk, the higher the return. It also depends on the level of interest rates in the economy. The higher the risk-free interest rate, the higher the expected return required on any given stock. Fortunately, we do not have to concern ourselves with the determinants of μ in any detail. This is because it turns out that the value of a stock option, when expressed in terms of the value of the underlying stock, does not depend on μ at all. However, there is one aspect of the expected return from a stock that frequently causes confusion and is worth explaining.

Equation (11.4) states that the expected (continuously compounded) return in one year is $\mu - \sigma^2/2$. This appears to be inconsistent with the definition of μ, the expected return per annum. To understand what is going on, it is useful to consider a simple example. Suppose that the following is a sequence of returns per annum on a stock, measured using annual compounding:

$$15\%, \quad 20\%, \quad 30\%, \quad -20\%, \quad 25\%$$

The arithmetic mean of the returns, calculated by taking the sum of the returns and dividing by 5, is 14 percent. However, an investor would actually earn less than 14 percent per annum if he or she left money invested in the stock for five years. The dollar value of \$100 at the end of the five years would be

$$100 \times 1.15 \times 1.20 \times 1.30 \times 0.80 \times 1.25 = 179.40$$

By contrast a 14 percent return with annual compounding would give

$$100 \times 1.14^5 = 192.54$$

The actual average return earned by the investor, with annual compounding, is

$$(1.7940)^{1/5} - 1 = 0.124$$

or 12.4 percent per annum.

This example illustrates the general result that the mean of the returns earned in different years is not necessarily the same as the mean return per annum over several years with annual compounding. It can be shown that unless the returns happen to be the same in each year, the former is always greater than the latter.[2]

There is, of course, nothing magical about the time period of one year in this result. Suppose that the time period over which returns are measured is made progressively shorter and the number of observations is increased. In the limit, we obtain the following two estimates:

1. The expected rate of return in a very short period of time
2. The expected continuously compounded rate of return over a longer period of time

Analogously to the foregoing, we would expect estimate 1 to be greater than estimate 2. This is in fact the case. The expected rate of return in a very short period of time is μ. The expected continuously compounded rate of return over a longer period of time is $\mu - \sigma^2/2$.

The arguments in this section show that the term *expected return* is ambiguous. It can refer to either μ or to $\mu - \sigma^2/2$. Unless otherwise stated, we will use it to refer to μ throughout this book.

VOLATILITY

The volatility of a stock, σ, is a measure of our uncertainty about the returns provided by the stock. Typical values of the volatility of a stock are in the range 0.2 to 0.4 per annum. Often volatilities are expressed as percentages. Thus, we might refer to the volatility of IBM as being 25 percent per annum. Assuming time is measured in years, this means that $\sigma = 0.25$.

Equation (11.4) suggests the following as a precise definition of volatility:

> The volatility of a stock price is the standard deviation of the return provided by the stock in one year when the return is expressed using continuous compounding.

As a rough approximation, $\sigma\sqrt{T}$ is the standard deviation of the proportional change in the stock price in time T. Consider the situation where $\sigma = 0.3$, or 30 percent per annum. The standard deviation of the proportional change in one year is approximately 30 percent, the standard deviation of the proportional change in six months is approximately $30\sqrt{0.5} = 21.2$ percent, the standard deviation of the proportional change in three months is approximately $30\sqrt{0.25} = 15$ percent, and so on.

The square root effect is important in the assessment of risks. In general our uncertainty about a stock price (or a stock index or an exchange rate or a futures

[2] Some readers may recognize this as equivalent to the statement that the arithmetic mean of a set of numbers is always greater than the geometric mean if the numbers are not all equal to each other.

price) increases as the square root of how far ahead we are looking. It does not increase linearly with time.

ESTIMATING VOLATILITY FROM HISTORICAL DATA

A record of stock price movements can be used to estimate volatility. The stock price is usually observed at fixed intervals of time (e.g., every day, every week, or every month). Define

$n + 1$: number of observations
S_i: stock price at end of ith interval ($i = 0, 1, \ldots, n$)
τ: length of time interval in years

and let

$$u_i = \ln\left(\frac{S_i}{S_{i-1}}\right)$$

An estimate, s, of the standard deviation of the u_i's is given by

$$s = \sqrt{\frac{1}{n-1}\sum_{i=1}^{n}(u_i - \bar{u})^2}$$

or

$$s = \sqrt{\frac{1}{n-1}\sum_{i=1}^{n}u_i^2 - \frac{1}{n(n-1)}\left(\sum_{i=1}^{n}u_i\right)^2}$$

where $\bar{u}$ is the mean of the u_i's.

From Equation (11.4), the standard deviation of the u_i's is $\sigma\sqrt{\tau}$. The variable, s, is therefore an estimate of $\sigma\sqrt{\tau}$. It follows that σ itself can be estimated as s^*, where

$$s^* = \frac{s}{\sqrt{\tau}}$$

The standard error of this estimate can be shown to be approximately $s^*/\sqrt{2n}$.

Choosing an appropriate value for n is not easy. More data generally lead to more accuracy. However, σ does change over time and data that are too old may not be relevant for predicting the future. A compromise which seems to work reasonably well is to use closing prices from daily data over the most recent 90 to 180 days. There is an important issue concerned with whether time should be measured in calendar days or trading days when volatility parameters are being estimated and used. This will be discussed more fully later.

Table 11.1 Computation of Volatility

DAY	*CLOSING STOCK PRICE (DOLLARS)*	*PRICE RELATIVE* S_i/S_{i-1}	*DAILY RETURN* $u_i = \ln(S_i/S_{i-1})$
0	20		
1	$20\frac{1}{8}$	1.00625	0.00623
2	$19\frac{7}{8}$	0.98758	−0.01250
3	20	1.00629	0.00627
4	$20\frac{1}{2}$	1.02500	0.02469
5	$20\frac{1}{4}$	0.98781	−0.01227
6	$20\frac{7}{8}$	1.03086	0.03040
7	$20\frac{7}{8}$	1.00000	0.00000
8	$20\frac{7}{8}$	1.00000	0.00000
9	$20\frac{3}{4}$	0.99401	−0.00601
10	$20\frac{3}{4}$	1.00000	0.00000
11	21	1.01205	0.01198
12	$21\frac{1}{8}$	1.00595	0.00593
13	$20\frac{7}{8}$	0.98817	−0.01190
14	$20\frac{7}{8}$	1.00000	0.00000
15	$21\frac{1}{4}$	1.01796	0.01780
16	$21\frac{3}{8}$	1.00588	0.00587
17	$21\frac{3}{8}$	1.00000	0.00000
18	$21\frac{1}{4}$	0.99415	−0.00587
19	$21\frac{3}{4}$	1.02353	0.02326
20	22	1.01149	0.01143

Example

Table 11.1 shows a possible sequence of stock prices during 21 consecutive trading days. Since

$$\sum u_i = 0.09531 \quad \text{and} \quad \sum u_i^2 = 0.00333$$

an estimate of the standard deviation of the daily return is

$$\sqrt{\frac{0.00333}{19} - \frac{0.09531^2}{380}} = 0.0123$$

Assuming that there are 250 trading days per year, $\tau = 1/250$ and the data give an estimate for the volatility per annum of $0.0123\sqrt{250} = 0.194$. The estimated volatility is 19.4 percent per annum. The standard error of this estimate is

$$\frac{0.194}{\sqrt{2 \times 20}} = 0.031$$

or 3.1 percent per annum.

The foregoing analysis assumes that the stock pays no dividends. It can be adapted to accommodate dividend-paying stocks. The return, u_i, during a time interval that includes an ex-dividend day is given by

$$u_i = \ln \frac{S_i + D}{S_{i-1}}$$

where D is the amount of the dividend. The return in other time intervals is still

$$u_i = \ln \frac{S_i}{S_{i-1}}$$

However, as tax factors play a part in determining returns around an ex-dividend date, it is probably best to discard altogether data for intervals that include an ex-dividend date.

ASSUMPTIONS UNDERLYING BLACK–SCHOLES

The assumptions made by Black and Scholes when they derived their option pricing formula were as follows:

1. Stock price behavior corresponds to the lognormal model developed earlier in this chapter with μ and σ constant.
2. There are no transactions costs or taxes. All securities are perfectly divisible.
3. There are no dividends on the stock during the life of the option.
4. There are no riskless arbitrage opportunities.
5. Security trading is continuous.
6. Investors can borrow or lend at the same risk-free rate of interest.
7. The short-term risk-free rate of interest, r, is constant.

Some of these assumptions have been relaxed by other researchers. For example, variations on the Black–Scholes formula can be used when r and σ are functions of time and the formula can be adjusted to take dividends into account.

THE BLACK–SCHOLES ANALYSIS

The Black–Scholes analysis is analogous to the no-arbitrage analysis we used in Chapter 10 to value options when stock price changes are binomial. A riskless portfolio consisting of a position in the option and a position in the underlying stock is set up. In the absence of arbitrage opportunities, the return from the portfolio must be the risk-free interest rate, r.

The reason why a riskless portfolio can be set up is because the stock price and the option price are both affected by the same underlying source of uncertainty: stock price movements. In any short period of time, the price of a call

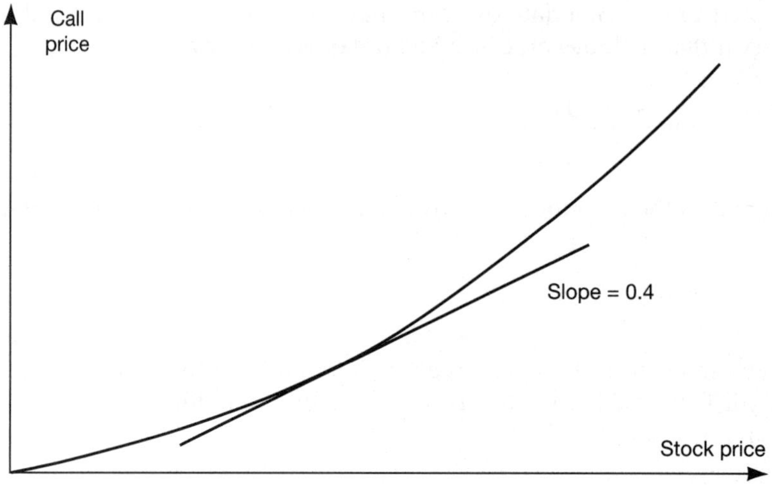

Figure 11.3 Relationship between c and S.

option is perfectly positively correlated with the price of the underlying stock; the price of a put option is perfectly negatively correlated with the price of the underlying stock. In both cases, when an appropriate portfolio of the stock and the option is set up, the gain or loss from the stock position always offsets the gain or loss from the option position so that the overall value of the portfolio at the end of the short period of time is known with certainty.

Suppose, for example, that at a particular point in time the relationship between a small change in the stock price, ΔS, and the resultant small change in the price of a European call option, Δc, is given by

$$\Delta c = 0.4\,\Delta S$$

This means that the slope of the line representing the relationship between c and S is 0.4 as indicated in Figure 11.3. The riskless portfolio would consist of

1. A long position in 0.4 share
2. A short position in 1 call option

There is one important difference between the Black–Scholes analysis and our analysis using a binomial model in Chapter 10. In Black–Scholes the position that is set up is riskless for only a very short period of time. (Theoretically, it remains riskless only for an instantaneously short period of time.) To remain riskless it must be frequently adjusted or *rebalanced*.[3] For example, the relationship between Δc and ΔS might change from $\Delta c = 0.4\Delta S$ today to $\Delta c = 0.5\Delta S$ in two

[3] We will discuss the rebalancing of portfolios in more detail in Chapter 14.

weeks. This would mean that 0.5 rather than 0.4 shares must then be owned for each call option sold. It is nevertheless true that the return from the riskless portfolio in any short period of time must be the risk-free interest rate. This is the key element in the Black–Scholes arguments and leads to their pricing formulas.

The Pricing Formulas

The Black–Scholes formulas for the prices of European calls and puts on nondividend-paying stocks are

$$c = SN(d_1) - Xe^{-rT}N(d_2) \tag{11.5}$$

$$p = Xe^{-rT}N(-d_2) - SN(-d_1) \tag{11.6}$$

where

$$d_1 = \frac{\ln(S/X) + (r + \sigma^2/2)T}{\sigma\sqrt{T}}$$

$$d_2 = \frac{\ln(S/X) + (r - \sigma^2/2)T}{\sigma\sqrt{T}} = d_1 - \sigma\sqrt{T}$$

The function $N(x)$ is the cumulative probability function for a standardized normal variable. In other words, it is the probability that a variable with a standard normal distribution, $\phi(0,1)$, will be less than x. It is illustrated in Figure 11.4. By now, the reader should be familiar with the other notation used in Equations (11.5) and (11.6). The variables c and p are the European call and put prices, S is the stock price, X is the strike price, r is the risk-free interest rate, T is the time to expiration, and σ is the volatility of the stock price. Since the American call price, C, equals the European call price, c, for a nondividend-paying stock, Equation (11.5) also gives the price of an American call. Unfortunately no exact analytic formula for the value of an American put on a nondividend-paying stock has been produced. We will discuss numerical procedures in Chapter 15.

Figure 11.4 Shaded area represents $N(x)$.

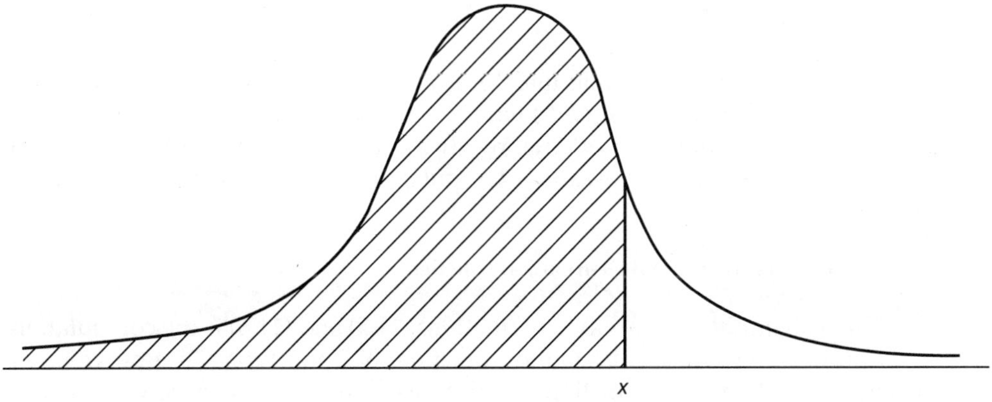

In theory, the Black–Scholes formula is only correct if the short-term interest rate, r, is constant. In practice, it is usually used with the interest rate, r, being set equal to the risk-free interest rate on an investment that lasts for time T.

Properties of the Black–Scholes Formulas

A full proof of the Black–Scholes formulas is beyond the scope of this book. At this stage we show that the formulas have the right general properties by considering what happens when some of the parameters take extreme values.

When the stock price, S, becomes very large, a call option is almost certain to be exercised. It then becomes very similar to a forward contract with delivery price X. From Equation (3.9) we, therefore, expect the call price to be

$$S - Xe^{-rT}$$

This is in fact the call price given by Equation (11.5) since, when S becomes very large, both d_1 and d_2 become very large and $N(d_1)$ and $N(d_2)$ are both close to 1.0.

When the stock price becomes very large, the price of a European put option, p, approaches zero. This is consistent with Equation (11.6), since $N(-d_1)$ and $N(-d_2)$ are both close to zero.

Consider next what happens when the volatility σ approaches zero. Since the stock is virtually riskless, its price will grow at rate r to Se^{rT} at time T and the payoff from a call option is

$$\max(Se^{rT} - X, 0)$$

Discounting at rate r, the value of the call today is

$$e^{-rT}\max(Se^{rT} - X, 0) = \max(S - Xe^{-rT}, 0)$$

To show that this is consistent with Equation (11.5), consider first the case where $S > Xe^{-rT}$. This implies $\ln(S/X) + rT > 0$. As σ tends to zero, d_1 and d_2 tend to $+\infty$ so that $N(d_1)$ and $N(d_2)$ tend to 1.0, and Equation (11.5) becomes

$$c = S - Xe^{-rT}$$

When $S < Xe^{-rT}$, it follows that $\ln(S/X) + rT < 0$. As σ tends to zero, d_1 and d_2 tend to $-\infty$ so that $N(d_1)$ and $N(d_2)$ tend to zero, and Equation (11.5) gives a call price of zero. The call price is, therefore, always $\max(S - Xe^{-rT}, 0)$ as σ tends to zero. Similarly, it can be shown that the put price is always $\max(Xe^{-rT} - S, 0)$ as σ tends to zero.

The Cumulative Normal Distribution Function

The only problem in applying Equations (11.5) and (11.6) is the computation of the cumulative normal distribution function, N. Tables for N are provided at the end of this book. The function can also be evaluated using a polynomial approximation. One such approximation that can easily be obtained using a hand calculator is given by the equations

$$N(x) = 1 - (a_1k + a_2k^2 + a_3k^3)N'(x) \quad \text{when } x \geq 0$$

$$N(x) = 1 - N(-x) \quad \text{when } x < 0$$

where

$$k = \frac{1}{1 + \alpha x}$$

$$\alpha = 0.33267$$

$$a_1 = 0.4361836$$

$$a_2 = -\ 0.1201676$$

$$a_3 = 0.9372980$$

and

$$N'(x) = \frac{1}{\sqrt{2\pi}} e^{-x^2/2}$$

This provides values for $N(x)$ that are always accurate to 0.0002.

Example

Consider the situation where the stock price six months from the expiration of an option is \$42, the exercise price of the option is \$40, the risk-free interest rate is 10 percent per annum, and the volatility is 20 percent per annum. This means that $S = 42$, $X = 40$, $r = 0.1$, $\sigma = 0.2$, $T = 0.5$,

$$d_1 = \frac{\ln 1.05 + 0.12 \times 0.5}{0.2\sqrt{0.5}} = 0.7693$$

$$d_2 = \frac{\ln 1.05 + 0.08 \times 0.5}{0.2\sqrt{0.5}} = 0.6278$$

and

$$Xe^{-rT} = 40e^{-0.05} = 38.049$$

Hence, if the option is a European call, its value, c, is given by

$$c = 42N(0.7693) - 38.049N(0.6278)$$

If the option is a European put, its value, p, is given by

$$p = 38.049N(-0.6278) - 42N(-0.7693)$$

Using the polynomial approximation just given or the tables at the end of the book,

$$N(0.7693) = 0.7791, \qquad N(-0.7693) = 0.2209$$

$$N(0.6278) = 0.7349, \qquad N(-0.6278) = 0.2651$$

so that

$$c = 4.76, \qquad p = 0.81$$

The stock price has to rise by \$2.76 for the purchaser of the call to break even. Similarly, the stock price has to fall by \$2.81 for the purchaser of the put to break even.

RISK-NEUTRAL VALUATION

A general result in the pricing of derivative securities is known as risk-neutral valuation. This was introduced in Chapter 10 and can be stated as follows:

> Any security dependent on other traded securities can be valued on the assumption that investors are risk neutral.

Note that risk-neutral valuation does not state that investors are risk neutral. What it does state is that derivative securities such as options can be valued on the assumption that investors are risk neutral. It means that investors' risk preferences have no effect on the value of a stock option when it is expressed as a function of the price of the underlying stock. It explains why Equations (11.5) and (11.6) do not involve μ.

Risk-neutral valuation is a very powerful tool. This is because in a risk-neutral world two particularly simple results hold:

1. The expected return from all securities is the risk-free interest rate.
2. The risk-free interest rate is the appropriate discount rate to apply to any expected future cash flow.

Using Risk-Neutral Valuation

The Black–Scholes stock option formulas can be derived using risk-neutral valuation. The procedure is:

1. Assume that the expected return from the stock is the risk-free interest rate r (i.e., assume $\mu = r$).
2. Calculate the expected payoff from the option at its maturity.
3. Discount the expected payoff at the risk-free interest rate.

The mathematics is fairly complicated. We will illustrate how these steps work by using them to value a forward contract on a nondividend-paying stock. (This has already been valued in Chapter 3 using a different approach.) We will make the assumption that interest rates are constant and equal to r.

Consider a long forward contract that matures at time T with delivery price, K. The value of the contract at maturity is

$$S_T - K$$

The expected value of S_T was shown earlier in this chapter to be $Se^{\mu T}$. In a risk-neutral world this becomes Se^{rT}. The expected payoff from the contract at maturity in a risk-neutral world is, therefore,

$$Se^{rT} - K$$

Discounting this at the risk-free rate r for time T gives the value, f, of the forward contract today as

$$f = e^{-rT}(Se^{rT} - K) = S - Ke^{-rT}$$

This is in agreement with the result in Equation (3.9).

IMPLIED VOLATILITIES

The one parameter in the Black–Scholes pricing formulas that cannot be observed directly is the volatility of the stock price. Earlier in this chapter, we discussed how this can be estimated from a history of the stock price. At this stage it is appropriate to mention an alternative approach that uses what is termed an *implied volatility*. This is the volatility implied by an option price observed in the market.

To illustrate the basic idea, suppose that the value of a call on a nondividend-paying stock is $1\frac{7}{8}$ (= 1.875) when $S = 21$, $X = 20$, $r = 0.1$, and $T = 0.25$. The implied volatility is the value of σ, which when substituted into Equation (11.5), gives $c = 1.875$. Unfortunately, it is not possible to invert Equation (11.5) so that σ is expressed as a function of S, X, r, T, and c. However, an iterative search procedure can be used to find the implied σ. We could start by trying $\sigma = 0.20$. This gives a value of c equal to 1.76, which is too low. Since c is an increasing function of σ, a higher value of σ is required. We could next try a value of 0.30 for σ. This gives a value of c equal to 2.10, which is too high and means that σ must lie between 0.20 and 0.30. Next, a value of 0.25 can be tried for σ. This also proves to be too high, showing that σ lies between 0.20 and 0.25. Proceeding in this way, the range for σ can be halved at each iteration and the correct value of σ can be calculated to any required accuracy.[4] In this example, the implied volatility is 0.235 or 23.5 percent per annum.

Implied volatilities can be used to monitor the market's opinion about the volatility of a particular stock. This does change over time. They can also be used

[4] This method is presented for illustration. Other more powerful procedures are usually used in practice.

to estimate the price of one option from the price of another option. Very often, several implied volatilities are obtained simultaneously from different options on the same stock, and a composite implied volatility for the stock is then calculated by taking a suitable weighted average of the individual implied volatilities. The amount of weight given to each implied volatility in this calculation should reflect the sensitivity of the option price to the volatility. To illustrate this point, suppose that two implied volatility estimates are available. The first is 21 percent per annum and is based on an at-the-money option; the second is 26 percent per annum and is based on a deep-out-of-the-money option with the same maturity. The price of the at-the-money option is far more sensitive to volatility than the price of the deep-out-of-the-money option. It is, therefore, providing more information about the "true" implied volatility. We might then choose a weight of 0.9 for the at-the-money implied volatility and a weight of 0.1 for the deep-out-of-the-money option. The weighted-average implied volatility would then be

$$0.9 \times 0.21 + 0.1 \times 0.26 = 0.215$$

or 21.5 percent per annum. Different weighting schemes are discussed by Beckers, Chiras and Manaster, Latane and Rendleman, and Whaley (see end-of-chapter references). The sensitivity of an option price to volatility is the rate of change of the price with respect to volatility.[5] Beckers, after examining various weighting schemes, concluded that best results are obtained by using only the option whose price is most sensitive to σ. Thus, the Beckers approach would estimate 21 percent for the volatility in our example.

THE CAUSES OF VOLATILITY

Proponents of the efficient markets hypothesis have traditionally claimed that the volatility of a stock price is caused solely by the random arrival of new information about the future returns from the stock. Others have claimed that volatility is caused largely by trading. An interesting question, therefore, is whether volatility is the same when the exchange is open as when it is closed.

Fama and French have tested this question empirically. (See end-of-chapter references.) They collected data on the stock price at the close of each trading day over a long period of time and then calculated

1. The variance of stock price returns between the close of trading on one day and the close of trading on the next trading day when there are no intervening nontrading days.
2. The variance of the stock price returns between the close of trading on Friday and the close of trading on Monday.

If trading and nontrading days are equivalent, the variance in situation 2 should be three times as great as the variance in situation 1. Fama found that it was only

[5] The calculation of the rate of change of the price with respect to volatility is discussed in Chapters 14 and 15.

22 percent higher. French's results were similar. He found that it was 19 percent higher.

These results suggest that the volatility is far larger when the exchange is open than when it is closed. Proponents of the traditional view that volatility is caused only by new information might be tempted to argue that most new information on stocks arrives during trading hours.[6] However, studies of futures prices of agricultural commodities, which depend largely on the weather, have shown that they exhibit much the same behavior as stock prices; that is, they are much more volatile during trading hours. Presumably, news about the weather is equally likely to arise on any day. The only reasonable conclusion seems to be that volatility is to some extent caused by trading itself.[7]

What are the implications of all this for the measurement of volatility and the Black–Scholes model? If daily data are used to measure volatility, the results suggest that days when the exchange is closed can be ignored. The volatility per annum should be calculated from the volatility per trading day using the formula

$$\text{Volatility per annum} = \begin{matrix}\text{Volatility per}\\ \text{trading day}\end{matrix} \times \sqrt{\begin{matrix}\text{Number of trading}\\ \text{days per annum}\end{matrix}}$$

This is the approach that was used earlier in this chapter in connection with the data in Table 11.1. The number of trading days in a year is usually assumed to be either 250 or 252.

DIVIDENDS

Up to now we have assumed that the stock upon which the option is written pays no dividends. In practice, this is not always the case. We now extend our results by assuming that the dividends paid on the stock during the life of an option can be predicted with certainty. As traded options usually last for less than eight months, this is not an unreasonable assumption.

The model of stock price behavior developed earlier is reasonable for a dividend-paying stock except when it goes ex-dividend. At this point, the stock's price goes down by an amount reflecting the dividend paid per share. The effect of this is to reduce the value of calls and to increase the value of puts. For tax reasons the stock price may go down by somewhat less than the cash amount of the dividend. To take account of this, the word dividend should be interpreted in the context of option pricing as the reduction in the stock price on the ex-dividend date caused by the dividend. Thus, if a dividend of $1 per share is anticipated and the share price normally goes down by 80 percent of the dividend on the ex-

[6] In fact, this is questionable. Often important announcements (e.g., those concerned with sales and earnings) are made when exchanges are closed.

[7] For a discussion of this, see the article by French and Roll referred to at the end of the chapter. We will consider one way in which trading can generate volatility when we discuss portfolio insurance schemes in Chapter 14.

dividend date, the dividend should be assumed to be \$0.80 for the purposes of the analysis.

European Options

European options can be analyzed by assuming that the stock price is the sum of two components: a riskless component that will be used to pay the known dividends during the life of the option and a risky component. The riskless component at any given time is the present value of all the dividends during the life of the option discounted from the ex-dividend dates to the present at the risk-free rate. The Black–Scholes formula is then correct if S is put equal to the risky component. Operationally, this means that the Black–Scholes formula can be used provided that the stock price is reduced by the present value of all the dividends during the life of the option, the discounting being done from the ex-dividend dates at the risk-free rate. A dividend is included in calculations only if its ex-dividend date occurs during the life of the option.

Example

Consider a European call option on a stock when there are ex-dividend dates in two months and five months. The dividend on each ex-dividend date is expected to be \$0.50. The current share price is \$40, the exercise price is \$40, the stock price volatility is 30 percent per annum, the risk-free rate of interest is 9 percent per annum, and the time to maturity is six months. The present value of the dividends is

$$0.5e^{-0.1667\times 0.09} + 0.5e^{-0.4167\times 0.09} = 0.9741$$

The option price can, therefore, be calculated from the Black–Scholes formula with $S = 39.0259$, $X = 40$, $r = 0.09$, $\sigma = 0.3$, and $T = 0.5$.

$$d_1 = \frac{\ln 0.9756 + 0.135 \times 0.5}{0.3\sqrt{0.5}} = 0.2017$$

$$d_2 = \frac{\ln 0.9756 + 0.045 \times 0.5}{0.3\sqrt{0.5}} = -0.0104$$

Using the polynomial approximation gives

$$N(d_1) = 0.5800, \qquad N(d_2) = 0.4959$$

and from Equation (11.5), the call price is

$$39.0259 \times 0.5800 - 40e^{-0.09\times 0.5} \times 0.4959 = 3.67$$

or \$3.67.

When using this procedure, σ in the Black–Scholes formula should be the volatility of the risky component of the stock price—not the volatility of the stock price itself. In practice, the two are often assumed to be the same. In theory, the volatility of the risky component is approximately $S/(S - D)$ times the volatility of the stock price where D is the present value of the dividends and S is the stock price.

American Call Options

In Chapter 8 we showed that American call options should never be exercised early when the underlying stock pays no dividends. When dividends are paid, it is sometimes optimal to exercise at a time immediately before the stock goes ex-dividend. The reason for this is easy to understand. The dividend will make both the stock and the call option less valuable. If the dividend is sufficiently large and the call option is sufficiently in the money, it may be worth forgoing the remaining time value of the option in order to avoid the adverse effects of the dividend on the stock price.

In practice, call options are most likely to be exercised early immediately before the final ex-dividend date. Appendix 11A provides an analysis that indicates why this is so and derives the conditions under which early exercise is liable to be optimal. Here we will describe an approximate procedure suggested by Fischer Black for valuing American calls on dividend-paying stocks.

Black's Approximation

Black's approximation involves calculating the prices of two European options:

1. An option that matures at the same time as the American option.
2. An option maturing just before the final ex-dividend date occurring during the life of the option.

The strike price, initial stock price, risk-free interest rate, and volatility are the same as for the option under consideration. The American option price is set equal to the higher of these two European option prices.

Example

Consider the situation in our previous example but suppose that the option is American rather than European. The present value of the first dividend is given by

$$0.5e^{-0.1667 \times 0.09} = 0.4926$$

The value of the option on the assumption that it expires just before the final ex-dividend date can be calculated using the Black–Scholes formula with $S = 39.5074$, $X = 40$, $r = 0.09$, $\sigma = 0.30$, and $T = 0.4167$. It is \$3.52. Black's approximation involves taking the greater of this and the value of the option when it can only be exercised at the end of six months. From the previous example, we know that the latter is \$3.67. Black's approximation, therefore, gives the value of the American call as \$3.67.

SUMMARY

The usual assumption made in stock option pricing is that the price of a stock at some future time given its price today is lognormal. This in turn implies that the continuously compounded return from the stock in a period of time is normally distributed. Our uncertainty about future stock prices increases as we look further ahead. As a rough approximation, we can say that the standard deviation of the stock price is proportional to the square root of how far ahead we are looking.

To estimate the volatility, σ, of a stock price empirically, the stock price is observed at fixed intervals of time (for example, every day, every week, or every month). For each time period the natural logarithm of the ratio of the stock price at the end of the time period to the stock price at the beginning of the time period is calculated. The volatility is estimated as the standard deviation of these numbers divided by the square root of the length of the time period in years. Usually days when the exchanges are closed are ignored in measuring time for the purposes of volatility calculations.

Stock option valuation involves setting up a position in the option and the stock that is riskless. Since the stock price and the option price both depend on the same underlying source of uncertainty, this can always be done. The position that is set up remains riskless for only a very short period of time. However, the return on a riskless position must always be the risk-free interest rate if there are to be no arbitrage opportunities. It is this fact that enables the option price to be valued in terms of the stock price. The original Black–Scholes equation gives the value of a European call or put option on a nondividend-paying stock in terms of five variables: the stock price, the strike price, the risk-free interest rate, the volatility, and the time to expiration.

The expected return on the stock does not enter into the Black–Scholes equations. This is surprising but follows from a general principle known as risk-neutral valuation. This states that any security dependent on other traded securities can be valued on the assumption that the world is risk neutral. This result proves to be very useful in practice. In a risk-neutral world the expected return from all securities is the risk-free interest rate and the correct discount rate for expected cash flows is also the risk-free interest rate.

An implied volatility is the volatility which, when substituted into the Black–Scholes equation or its extensions, gives the market price of the option. Traders monitor implied volatilities and sometimes use the implied volatility from one stock option price to calculate the price of another option on the same stock. Empirical results show that the volatility of a stock is much higher when the exchange is open than when it is closed. This suggests that to some extent trading itself causes stock price volatility.

The Black–Scholes results can easily be extended to cover European call and put options on dividend-paying stocks. One procedure is to use the Black–Scholes formula with the stock price reduced by the present value of the dividends anticipated during the life of the option, and the volatility equal to the volatility of the stock price net of the present value of these dividends. Fischer Black has suggested an approximate way of valuing American call options on a dividend-paying stock. This involves setting the price equal to the greater of two European option prices. The first European option expires at the same time as the American option; the second expires immediately prior to the final ex-dividend date.

Suggestions for Further Reading

On the Black–Scholes formula and its extensions

BLACK, F., "Fact and fantasy in the use of options and corporate liabilities," *Financial Analysts Journal*, 31 (July–August 1975), 36–41, 61–72.

BLACK, F., and M. SCHOLES, "The pricing of options and corporate liabilities," *Journal of Political Economy*, 81 (May–June 1973), 637–659.

HULL, J., *Options, Futures, and Other Derivative Securities*, Englewood Cliffs, NJ: Prentice Hall, 1989.

MERTON, R. C., "Theory of rational option pricing," *Bell Journal of Economics and Management Science*, 4 (Spring 1973), 141–183.

SMITH, C. W., "Option pricing: A review," *Journal of Financial Economics*, 3 (March 1976), 3–51.

On weighting schemes for implied volatilities

BECKERS, S, "Standard deviations in option prices as predictors of future stock price variability," *Journal of Banking and Finance*, 5 (September 1981), 363–382.

CHIRAS, D. P., and S. MANASTER, "The information content of option prices and a test of market efficiency," *Journal of Financial Economics*, 6 (1978), 213–234.

LATANE, H., and R. J. RENDLEMAN, "Standard deviation of stock price ratios implied by option premia," *Journal of Finance*, 31 (May 1976), 369–382.

WHALEY, R. E., "Valuation of American call options on dividend-paying stocks: Empirical tests," *Journal of Financial Economics*, 10 (March 1982), 29–58.

On the causes of volatility

FAMA, E. E., "The behavior of stock market prices," *Journal of Business*, 38 (January 1965), 34–105.

FRENCH, K. R., "Stock returns and the weekend effect," *Journal of Financial Economics*, 8 (March 1980), 55–69.

FRENCH, K., and R. ROLL, "Stock return variances: The arrival of information and the reaction of traders," *Journal of Financial Economics*, 17 (September 1986), 5–26.

On analytic solutions to the pricing of American calls

GESKE, R., "Comments on Whaley's Note," *Journal of Financial Economics*, 9 (June 1981), 213–215.

GESKE, R., "A note on an analytic valuation formula for unprotected American call options on stocks with known dividends," *Journal of Financial Economics*, 7 (1979), 375–380.

ROLL, R., "An analytical formula for unprotected American call options on stocks with known dividends," *Journal of Financial Economics*, 5 (1977), 251–258.

WHALEY, R., "On the valuation of American call options on stocks with known dividends," *Journal of Financial Economics*, 9 (1981), 207–211.

Quiz

1. What does the Black–Scholes stock option pricing model assume about the probability distribution of the stock price in one year? What does it assume

about the continuously compounded rate of return on the stock during the year?

2. The volatility of a stock price is 30 percent per annum. What is the standard deviation of the proportional price change in one trading day?
3. Explain how risk-neutral valuation could be used to derive the Black–Scholes formulas.
4. Calculate the price of a three-month European put option on a nondividend-paying stock with a strike price of $50 when the current stock price is $50, the risk-free interest rate is 10 percent per annum, and the volatility is 30 percent per annum.
5. What difference does it make to your calculations in the previous question if a dividend of $1.50 is expected in two months?
6. What is meant by implied volatility? How would you calculate the volatility implied by a European put option price?
7. What is Black's approximation for valuing an American call option on a dividend-paying stock?

Questions and Problems

11.1. A stock price is currently $50. Assume that the expected return from the stock is 18 percent per annum and its volatility is 30 percent per annum. What is the probability distribution for the stock price in two years? Calculate the mean and standard deviation of the distribution. Determine 95 percent confidence intervals.

11.2. A stock price is currently $40. Assume that the expected return from the stock is 15 percent and that its volatility is 25 percent. What is the probability distribution for the rate of return (with continuous compounding) earned over a one-year period?

11.3. A stock price has an expected return of 16 percent and a volatility of 35 percent. The current price is $38.

a. What is the probability that a European call option on the stock with an exercise price of $40 and a maturity date in six months will be exercised?

b. What is the probability that a European put option on the stock with the same exercise price and maturity will be exercised?

11.4. Prove that with the notation in the chapter, a 95 percent confidence interval for S_T is between

$$Se^{(\mu-\sigma^2/2)T-2\sigma\sqrt{T}} \quad \text{and} \quad Se^{(\mu-\sigma^2/2)T+2\sigma\sqrt{T}}$$

11.5. A portfolio manager announces that the average of the returns realized in each year of the last ten years is 20 percent per annum. In what respect is this statement misleading?

11.6. Suppose that observations on a stock price (in dollars) at the end of each of 15 consecutive weeks are as follows:

$30\frac{1}{4}$, 32, $31\frac{1}{8}$, $30\frac{1}{8}$, $30\frac{1}{4}$, $30\frac{3}{8}$, $30\frac{5}{8}$, 33,
$32\frac{7}{8}$, 33, $33\frac{1}{2}$, $33\frac{1}{2}$, $33\frac{3}{4}$, $33\frac{1}{2}$, $33\frac{1}{4}$

Estimate the stock price volatility. What is the standard error of your estimate?

11.7. Assume that an nondividend-paying stock has an expected return of μ and a volatility of σ. An innovative financial institution has just announced that it will trade a security which pays off a dollar amount equal to

$$\frac{1}{T}\ln\left(\frac{S_T}{S_0}\right)$$

at time T. The variables S_0 and S_T denote the values of the stock price at time zero and time T.

a. Describe the payoff from this security.

b. Use risk-neutral valuation to calculate the price of the security at time t when $0 \le t \le T$.

11.8. If the security in Problem 11.7 is a success, the financial institution plans to offer another security which pays off a dollar amount equal to

$$(S_T - S_0)^2$$

at time T.

a. Describe the payoff from this security.

b. Use risk-neutral valuation to calculate the price of the security at time t in terms of the stock price S when $0 \le t \le T$. (Hint: The expected value of S_T^2 can be calculated from the mean and variance of S_T given in this chapter.)

11.9. What is the price of a European call option on a nondividend-paying stock when the stock price is \$52, the strike price is \$50, the risk-free interest rate is 12 percent per annum, the volatility is 30 percent per annum, and the time to maturity is three months?

11.10. What is the price of a European put option on a nondividend-paying stock when the stock price is \$69, the strike price is \$70, the risk-free interest rate is 5 percent per annum, the volatility is 35 percent per annum, and the time to maturity is six months?

11.11. Consider an option on a nondividend-paying stock when the stock price is \$30, the exercise price is \$29, the risk-free interest rate is 5 percent per annum, the volatility is 25 percent per annum, and the time to maturity is four months.

a. What is the price of the option if it is a European call?

b. What is the price of the option if it is an American call?

c. What is the price of the option if it is a European put?

d. Verify that put-call parity holds.

11.12. Assume that the stock in Problem 11.11 is due to go ex-dividend in 1.5 months. The expected dividend is 50 cents.

a. What is the price of the option if it is a European call?

b. What is the price of the option if it is a European put?

11.13. A call option on a nondividend-paying stock has a market price of \$2½. The stock price is \$15, the exercise price is \$13, the time to maturity is three months, and the risk-free interest rate is 5 percent per annum. What is the implied volatility?

11.14. Show that the Black–Scholes formula for a call option gives a price which tends to max $(S - X, 0)$ as $T \to 0$.

11.15. Consider an American call option when the stock price is \$18, the exercise price is \$20, the time to maturity is six months, the volatility is 30 percent per annum, and the risk-free interest rate is 10 percent per annum. Two equal dividends of 40 cents are expected during the life of the option with ex-dividend dates at the end of two months and five months. Use Black's approximation to value the option.

11.16. Explain carefully why Black's approach to evaluating an American call option on a dividend-paying stock may give an approximate answer even when only one dividend is anticipated. Does the answer given by Black's approach understate or overstate the true option value? Explain your answer.

11.17. Consider an American call option on a stock. The stock price is \$70, the time to maturity is eight months, the risk-free rate of interest is 10 percent per annum, the exercise price is \$65, and the volatility is 32 percent. Dividends of \$1 are expected after three months and six months. Use the results in the appendix to show that it can never be optimal to exercise the option on either of the two dividend dates. Calculate the price of the option.

Appendix 11A The Early Exercise of American Call Options on Dividend-Paying Stocks

In Chapter 8 we showed that it is never optimal to exercise an American call option on a nondividend-paying stock early. A similar argument shows that a call option on a dividend-paying stock is only ever likely to be exercised early immediately before an ex-dividend date. We assume that n ex-dividend dates are anticipated and that $t_1, t_2, \ldots, t_n$ are the moments in time immediately prior to the stock going ex-dividend with $t_1 < t_2 < t_3 < \ldots < t_n$. The dividends at these times will be denoted by $D_1, D_2, \ldots, D_n$, respectively.

We start by considering the possibility of early exercise immediately prior to the final ex-dividend date (i.e., at time t_n). If the option is exercised at time t_n, the investor receives

$$S(t_n) - X$$

If the option is not exercised, the stock price drops to $S(t_n) - D_n$. As shown in Chapter 8, a lower bound for the price of the option is then

$$S(t_n) - D_n - Xe^{-r(T-t_n)}$$

It follows that if

$$S(t_n) - D_n - Xe^{-r(T-t_n)} \geq S(t_n) - X$$

that is,

$$D_n \leq X(1 - e^{-r(T-t_n)}) \quad \textbf{(11A.1)}$$

it cannot be optimal to exercise at time t_n. On the other hand, if

$$D_n > X(1 - e^{-r(T-t_n)}) \quad \textbf{(11A.2)}$$

it can be shown that it is always optimal to exercise at time t_n for a sufficiently high value of $S(t_n)$. The inequality in (11A.2) is most likely to be satisfied when the final ex-dividend date is fairly close to the maturity of the option (i.e., $T - t_n$ is small) and the dividend is large.

Consider next, time t_{n-1}, the penultimate ex-dividend date. If the option is exercised at time t_{n-1}, the investor receives

$$S(t_{n-1}) - X$$

If the option is not exercised at time t_{n-1}, the stock price drops to $S(t_{n-1}) - D_{n-1}$ and the earliest subsequent time at which exercise could take place is t_n. A lower bound to the option price if it is not exercised at time t_{n-1} is

$$S(t_{n-1}) - D_{n-1} - Xe^{-r(t_n - t_{n-1})}$$

It follows that if

$$S(t_{n-1}) - D_{n-1} - Xe^{-r(t_n - t_{n-1})} \geq S(t_{n-1}) - X$$

or

$$D_{n-1} \leq X(1 - e^{-r(t_n - t_{n-1})})$$

it is not optimal to exercise at time t_{n-1}. Similarly, for any $i < n$, if

$$D_i \leq X(1 - e^{-r(t_{i+1} - t_i)}) \quad \textbf{(11A.3)}$$

it is not optimal to exercise at time t_i.

The inequality in (11A.3) is approximately equivalent to

$$D_i \leq Xr(t_{i+1} - t_i)$$

Assuming that X is fairly close to the current stock price, the dividend yield on the stock would have to be either close to or above the risk-free rate of interest for this inequality not to be satisfied. This is not usually the case.

We can conclude from this analysis that, in most circumstances, the only time that needs to be considered for the early exercise of an American call is the final ex-dividend date, t_n. Furthermore, if inequality (11A.3) holds for $i = 1, 2, \ldots n - 1$ and inequality (11A.1) holds, we can be certain that early exercise is never optimal.

Example

Consider the example that was used in this chapter to value European options on dividend-paying stocks: $S = 40$, $X = 40$, $r = 0.09$, $\sigma = 0.30$, $t_1 = 0.1667$, $t_2 = 0.4167$, $T = 0.5$, $D_1 = D_2 = 0.5$. We suppose that the option is American rather than European. In this case,

$$X(1 - e^{-r(T_2 - t_1)}) = 40(1 - e^{-0.09 \times 0.25}) = 0.89$$

Since this is greater than 0.5, it follows from Equation (11A.3) that the option should never be exercised on the first ex-dividend date. Also

$$X(1 - e^{-r(T-t_2)}) = 40(1 - e^{-0.09 \times 0.08333}) = 0.30$$

Since this is less than 0.5, it follows from Equation (11A.1) that when it is sufficiently in the money, the option should be exercised on the second ex-dividend date.

12

OPTIONS ON STOCK INDICES AND CURRENCIES

In this chapter, we tackle the problem of valuing options on stock indices and currencies. As a first step, some of the results in Chapters 8, 10, and 11 are extended to cover European options on a stock paying a continuous dividend yield. It is then argued that stock indices and currencies are both analogous to stocks paying continuous dividend yields. The basic results for options on a stock paying a continuous dividend yield can, therefore, be used for these types of options as well.

A SIMPLE RULE

In this section we present a simple rule that enables results produced for European options on a nondividend-paying stock to be extended so that they apply to European options on stocks paying a known dividend yield.

Consider the difference between a stock that pays a continuous dividend yield at a rate q per annum and a similar stock that pays no dividends. As explained in Chapter 11, the payment of a dividend causes a stock price to drop by an amount equal to the dividend. The payment of a continuous dividend yield at rate q, therefore, causes the growth rate in the stock price to be less than it would otherwise be by an amount q. If, with a continuous dividend yield of q, the stock price grows from S today to S_T at time T, then in the absence of dividends, it would grow from S today to $S_T e^{qT}$ at time T. Alternatively, in the absence of dividends it would grow from Se^{-qT} today to S_T at time T.

This argument shows that we get the same probability distribution for the stock price at time T in each of the following two cases:

1. The stock starts at price S and pays a continuous dividend yield at rate q; and
2. The stock starts at price Se^{-qT} and pays no dividend yield.

This leads to a simple rule:

When valuing a European option lasting for time T on a stock paying a known dividend yield at rate q, we reduce the current stock price from S to Se^{-qT} and then value the option as though the stock pays no dividends.

Bounds for Option Prices

As a first application of this rule, consider the problem of determining bounds for the price of a European option on a stock paying a dividend yield at rate q. Substituting Se^{-qT} for S into Equation (8.1), we see that a lower bound for the European price, c, is given by

$$c > Se^{-qT} - Xe^{-rT} \tag{12.1}$$

We can also prove this directly by considering the following two portfolios:

Portfolio A: One European call option plus an amount of cash equal to Xe^{-rT}

Portfolio B: e^{-qT} shares with dividends being reinvested in additional shares

In portfolio A, the cash, if it is invested at the risk-free interest rate, will grow to X at time T. If $S_T > X$, the call option is exercised at time T and portfolio A is worth S_T. If $S_T < X$, the call option expires worthless and the portfolio is worth X. Hence, at time T, portfolio A is worth

$$\max(S_T, X)$$

Because of the reinvestment of dividends, portfolio B becomes one share at time T. It is, therefore, worth S_T at this time. It follows that portfolio A is always worth as much as, and is sometimes worth more than, portfolio B at time T. In the absence of arbitrage opportunities, this must also be true today. Hence,

$$c + Xe^{-rT} > Se^{-qT}$$

or

$$c > Se^{-qT} - Xe^{-rT}$$

To obtain a lower bound for a European put option, we can similarly replace S by Se^{-qT} in Equation (8.2) to get

$$p > Xe^{-rT} - Se^{-qT} \tag{12.2}$$

This result can also be proved directly by considering:

Portfolio C: One European put option plus e^{-qT} shares with dividends on the shares being reinvested in additional shares

Portfolio D: An amount of cash equal to Xe^{-rT}

Put–Call Parity

Replacing S by Se^{-qT} in Equation (8.3) we obtain put–call parity for an option on a stock paying a continuous dividend yield at rate q:

$$c + Xe^{-rT} = p + Se^{-qT} \tag{12.3}$$

This result can also be proved directly by considering the following two portfolios:

Portfolio A: One European call option plus an amount of cash equal to Xe^{-rT}

Portfolio C: One European put option plus e^{-qT} shares with dividends on the shares being reinvested in additional shares

Both portfolios are both worth $\max(S_T, X)$ at time T. They must, therefore, be worth the same today and the put–call parity result in Equation (12.3) follows.

PRICING FORMULAS

By replacing S by Se^{-qT} in the Black–Scholes formulas, Equations (11.5) and (11.6), we obtain the price, c, of a European call and the price, p, of a European put on a stock paying a continuous dividend yield at rate q as:

$$c = Se^{-qT}N(d_1) - Xe^{-rT}N(d_2) \tag{12.4}$$

$$p = Xe^{-rT}N(-d_2) - Se^{-qT}N(-d_1) \tag{12.5}$$

Since

$$\ln \frac{Se^{-qT}}{X} = \ln \frac{S}{X} - qT$$

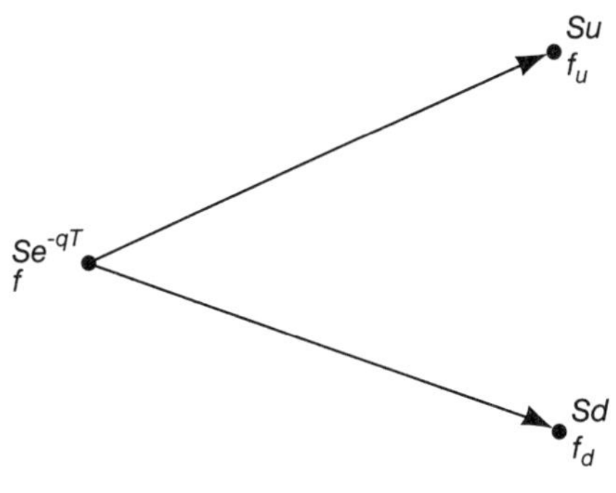

Figure 12.1 Stock price and option price in one-step binomial tree when stock pays a dividend at rate q.

d_1 and d_2 are given by

$$d_1 = \frac{\ln(S/X) + (r - q + \sigma^2/2)T}{\sigma\sqrt{T}}$$

and

$$d_2 = \frac{\ln(S/X) + (r - q - \sigma^2/2)T}{\sigma\sqrt{T}} = d_1 - \sigma\sqrt{T}$$

These results were first derived by Merton. As discussed in Chapter 11, the word *dividend* should, for the purposes of option valuation, be defined as the reduction in the stock price on the ex-dividend date arising from any dividends declared. If the dividend yield rate is not constant during the life of the option, Equations (12.4) and (12.5) are still true, with q equal to the average annualized dividend yield.

BINOMIAL TREES

We now move on to examining the effect of a dividend yield equal to q on the results for the binomial model in Chapter 10.

Consider the situation in Figure 10.2 where a stock price starts at S and moves either up to Su or down to Sd. If we follow our rule of changing the initial stock price from S to Se^{-qT}, we obtain the situation shown in Figure 12.1. As in Chapter 10 we imagine a portfolio consisting of a long position in Δ shares and a short position in one option. We calculate the value of Δ that makes the portfolio riskless.

$$\Delta = \frac{f_u - f_d}{Su - Sd}$$

The present value of the portfolio must be

$$(Su\Delta - f_u)e^{-rT}$$

The current value of the portfolio is

$$Se^{-qT}\Delta - f$$

It follows that

$$Se^{-qT}\Delta - f = (Su\Delta - f_u)e^{-rT}$$

Substituting for Δ and simplifying this equation reduces to

$$f = e^{-rT}[pf_u + (1 - p)f_d] \tag{12.6}$$

where

$$p = \frac{e^{(r-q)T} - d}{u - d} \tag{12.7}$$

These are the equations for pricing an option on a stock paying a continuous dividend yield at rate q under a one-step binomial model.

We now show that this is consistent with risk-neutral valuation. Define p^* as the probability of an up movement in a risk-neutral world. The value of the option is then

$$f = e^{-rT}[p^*f_u + (1 - p^*)f_d] \tag{12.8}$$

In a risk-neutral world the stock provides a return in the form of dividends equal to q. The return in the form of capital gains must be $r - q$. This means that p^* must satisfy

$$p^*Su + (1 - p^*)Sd = Se^{(r-q)T}$$

or

$$p^* = \frac{e^{(r-q)T} - d}{u - d}$$

From Equation (12.7), $p = p^*$. The risk-neutral valuation in Equation (12.8) is, therefore, identical to the no-arbitrage valuation in Equation (12.6).

OPTIONS ON STOCK INDICES

As discussed in Chapter 7, several exchanges trade options on stock indices. Some of the indices used track the movement of the market as a whole. Others are based on the performance of a particular sector (e.g., computer technology, oil and gas, transportation, or telephone).

Quotes

Table 12.1 shows quotes on the three most popular index options as they appeared in the Money and Investing section of *The Wall Street Journal* of Thursday, August 12, 1993. These quotes refer to the price at which the last trade was done on Wednesday, August 11, 1993.

The option on the S&P 500 Index is European while those on the S&P 100 and Major Market Index are American. All are settled in cash rather than by delivering the securities underlying the index. This means that upon exercise of the option, the holder of a call option receives $S - X$ in cash and the writer of the option pays this amount in cash, where S is the value of the index and X is the strike price. Similarly, the holder of a put option receives $X - S$ in cash and the writer of the option pays this amount in cash. The cash payment is based on the index value at the end of the day on which the exercise instructions are issued. Each contract is for $100 times the value of the index.

Example

In Table 12.1, one September call option contract on the S&P 100 with strike price of 400 cost $18\frac{1}{2} \times 100 = \$1{,}850$ on August 11, 1993. The value of the index at the close of trading on that day was 417.29, so that the option was in the money. If the option contract was exercised on August 11, 1993, the holder would receive $(417.29 - 400.00) \times 100 = \$1{,}729$ in cash.

Table 12.1 shows that in addition to relatively short-dated options, the exchanges trade longer-maturity contracts known as LEAPS. The acronym *LEAPS* stands for Long-term Equity AnticiPation Securities and was originated by the CBOE. LEAPS are long-term exchange-traded options. They last up to three years. The index is divided by ten for the purposes of quoting the strike price and the option price. One contract is an option on 100 times one-tenth of the index (or ten times the index). LEAPS on indices have expiration dates in December. LEAPS on the S&P 100 and Major Market Index are American while those on the S&P 500 are European. The CBOE and several other exchanges also trade LEAPS on many individual stocks. These have expirations in January.

Another innovation of the CBOE is *caps*. These trade on the S&P 100 and S&P 500. These are options where the payout is capped so that it cannot exceed $30. The options are European except for the following: a call cap is automatically exercised on a day when the index closes more than $30 above the strike price; a put cap is automatically exercised on a day when the index closes more than $30 below the cap level.

A more recent innovation of the CBOE is *flex options*. These are options where the traders can choose the expiration date, the strike price, whether the option is American or European, and the settlement basis.

Portfolio Insurance

Index options can be used by portfolio managers to limit their downside risk. Suppose that the value of an index is S. Consider a manager in charge of a well-diversified portfolio whose beta is 1.0. A beta of 1.0 implies that the returns

INDEX OPTIONS TRADING

S & P 100 INDEX(OEX)

Sep	370p	99	5/16	...	3,181
Aug	375p	325	1/16	...	4,485
Sep	375p	125	7/16	...	1,881
Oct	375p	57	7/8	− 1/16	1,752
Aug	380p	1,378	1/16	− 1/16	12,445
Sep	380p	53	1/2	...	5,860
Oct	380p	12	1 3/16	+ 1/16	3,081
Nov	380p	21	2	− 1/8	4,344
Aug	385p	188	1/16	− 1/16	12,227
Sep	385p	111	11/16	− 1/16	4,892
Oct	385p	4	1 7/16	− 1/16	1,774
Aug	390p	419	1/8	− 1/16	16,730
Sep	390p	1,040	7/8	− 1/16	16,594
Oct	390p	91	1 3/4	− 1/16	4,693
Nov	390p	1,035	3 1/4	...	1,821
Aug	395p	1,873	3/16	− 1/8	32,738
Sep	395p	1,291	1 1/4	− 1/16	4,835
Oct	395p	38	2 7/16	...	1,716
Aug	400c	127	17 1/4	+ 1/4	3,691
Aug	400p	3,341	5/16	− 1/8	34,558
Sep	400c	2	18 1/2	− 1/2	598
Sep	400p	1,900	1 11/16	− 1/16	12,509
Oct	400p	72	3 1/4	...	4,234
Nov	400p	58	5	...	1,858
Aug	405c	310	12 1/2	+ 1/4	3,675
Aug	405p	4,883	9/16	− 1/8	44,585
Sep	405c	429	14 5/8	+ 1/8	2,376
Sep	405p	1,180	2 7/16	...	10,176
Oct	405c	102	16 1/4	+ 1	367
Oct	405p	95	3 7/8	− 3/8	2,364
Aug	410c	13,483	7 7/8	...	28,958
Aug	410p	13,133	1 1/16	− 1/16	56,014
Sep	410c	937	10 1/2	...	9,782
Sep	410p	1,910	3 3/8	− 1/8	13,934
Oct	410p	61	5 1/2	...	4,619
Nov	410c	701	14 5/8	+ 1/8	1,650
Nov	410p	764	7 5/8	− 1/8	3,467
Aug	415c	18,836	3 7/8	− 1/8	51,053
Aug	415p	19,331	2 3/16	− 1/8	40,324
Sep	415c	2,467	7	+ 1/8	10,796
Sep	415p	2,294	4 7/8	− 1/4	12,132
Oct	415c	209	9 1/8	+ 1/8	2,498
Oct	415p	259	7 1/4	− 1/8	2,323
Aug	420c	13,226	1 7/16	− 1/16	46,123
Aug	420p	9,668	4 3/4	− 1/8	13,490
Sep	420c	1,911	4 1/8	...	13,717
Sep	420p	898	7 1/4	− 1/4	2,893
Oct	420c	291	6 1/4	...	4,158
Oct	420p	87	9	− 3/4	1,281
Nov	420c	99	8 1/4	...	10,624
Nov	420p	97	11 5/8	+ 1/4	1,013
Aug	425c	6,659	3/8	− 1/16	37,413
Aug	425p	184	8 3/4	− 1/4	1,353
Sep	425c	2,819	2 3/16	− 1/16	11,303
Sep	425p	31	10 5/8	− 1/8	347
Oct	425c	154	4	...	2,124
Oct	425p	7	12	− 1/2	11
Aug	430c	1,909	1/8	...	29,543
Sep	430c	1,418	1 1/16	...	26,558
Oct	430c	338	2 1/4	− 1/8	6,046
Nov	430c	208	3 7/8	...	3,515
Aug	435c	949	1/16	...	22,908
Sep	435c	742	1/2	+ 1/16	19,819
Oct	435c	968	1 1/4	− 1/16	3,466
Sep	440c	250	1/4	...	8,140
Oct	440c	540	5/8	− 1/16	4,969
Nov	440c	295	1 3/8	− 1/8	5,491
Sep	445c	1,004	9 1/2	...	15,135
Sep	445p	768	4	− 1/8	22,829
Oct	445p	706	6 1/8	− 1/8	978
Aug	450c	496	3	...	22,765
Aug	450p	1,033	2 1/2	− 3/8	22,981
Sep	450c	1,285	6 1/4	...	26,330
Sep	450p	829	5 1/2	− 1/2	21,259
Oct	450c	226	9	+ 1/2	1,186
Aug	455c	722	15/16	− 1/16	12,009
Aug	455p	36	5 1/8	− 1/2	2,322
Sep	455c	955	3 3/4	− 1/8	22,837
Sep	455p	73	7 1/2	− 1	389
Oct	455c	508	6 1/4	...	7,050
Aug	460c	2,001	1/4	− 1/16	12,256
Aug	460p	9	9 5/8	− 7/8	668
Sep	460c	2,806	2	− 1/16	14,670
Sep	460p	63	11 3/4	− 1/8	9,006
Oct	460c	853	4 1/8	...	294
Oct	460p	20	12 1/4	− 1 3/4	63
Aug	465c	140	1/16	− 1/16	20,731
Sep	465c	912	7/8	− 1/16	11,022
Sep	470c	434	7/16	− 1/16	20,129
Oct	470c	408	1 1/4	− 3/8	9,335
Oct	470p	1	19 7/8	− 2 3/8	10
Sep	475c	1,000	1/4	...	19,200
Oct	475c	105	3/4	− 1/8	5,716
Sep	480c	160	1/16	− 1/16	4,071

Call vol...... 70,379 Open Int.......395,838
Put vol....... 68,413 Open Int.......404,443

Call vol...... 16,981 Open Int.......437,708
Put vol.........9,680 Open Int.......570,785

S & P 500 INDEX-AM(SPX)

Sep	410p	463	7/16	− 1/16	9,961
Aug	415p	205	1/16	− 1/8	1,831
Sep	415p	100	9/16	+ 1/16	11,894
Sep	425c	20	26 3/8	− 1 7/8	11,149
Sep	425p	145	1 1/8	+ 1/8	27,245
Oct	425p	5	2 1/8	...	446
Aug	430p	289	3/16	− 1/16	12,817
Sep	430p	162	1 3/8	...	10,320
Oct	430p	5	2 3/4	...	328
Aug	435c	10	16 1/8	− 1/8	1,119
Aug	435p	111	1/4	− 1/8	8,718
Sep	435p	17	1 3/4	− 3/8	5,687
Oct	435p	3	3 5/8	− 1/8	860
Aug	440c	14	11 1/4	+ 3/4	4,065
Aug	440p	616	9/16	− 1/8	15,601
Sep	440c	200	13 1/2	− 1/8	6,797
Sep	440p	855	2 7/8	...	38,575
Oct	440c	104	15 5/8	− 3/4	4,954
Oct	440p	100	4 5/8	− 1/8	4,191
Aug	445c	43	6 7/8	+ 3/8	13,753
Aug	445p	490	1 1/8	− 1/4	18,431

MAJOR MARKET(XMI)

Aug	330p	80	1/16	...	116
Aug	340p	90	1/8	− 1/16	522
Aug	345p	40	3/16	− 1/8	564
Sep	345p	10	1 1/4	− 1/16	180
Aug	350c	30	12	− 1/8	343
Aug	350p	8	5/16	− 1/16	1,140
Aug	355c	95	7 1/4	− 3/4	322
Aug	355p	65	7/8	...	1,270
Aug	360c	366	3 3/8	− 1/4	2,318
Aug	360p	701	1 3/4	− 1/8	1,632
Sep	360c	162	6	− 3/8	305
Sep	360p	55	4 3/8	− 1/4	237
Aug	365c	263	1 1/16	− 1/4	1,452
Aug	365p	56	4 3/4	+ 1/4	651
Sep	365c	13	3 1/2	− 1/2	283
Aug	370c	14	1/4	− 1/16	1,408
Aug	370p	25	8 3/4	+ 3/8	690
Sep	370c	30	1 5/8	− 1/16	294
Sep	370p	1	9 1/2	+ 1/2	13
Oct	370c	33	3 1/4	...	46
Oct	370p	1	11 1/2	− 1/4	1
Aug	375c	800	1/16	− 1/16	2,239
Oct	375c	2	1 5/8	− 1/4	75

Call vol.........1,808 Open Int.........31,762
Put vol..........1,132 Open Int.........47,689

LEAPS—LONG TERM OPTIONS

MAJOR MARKET – AM

Dec 94	25p	60	1/8	− 1/16	2507

Call vol..............0 Open Int.........49,918
Put vol..............60 Open Int.........98,386

S & P 100 INDEX – CB

Dec 94	32 1/2p	90	7/16	...	4188
Dec 93	35p	35	1/8	...	22416
Dec 94	37 1/2p	20	1 1/4	...	5366
Dec 93	40p	985	3/4	+ 1/8	18847
Dec 94	40p	89	1 7/8	− 1/16	12565

Call vol..............0 Open Int...........8,015
Put vol..........1,219 Open Int.......127,751

S & P 500 INDEX – CB

Dec 93	45p	2	1 1/4	+ 1/16	6283
Dec 94	47 1/2p	20	3 5/8	...	2322

Call vol..............0 Open Int.........20,653
Put vol..............62 Open Int.......169,807

Table 12.1 Quotes for Stock Index Options from *The Wall Street Journal,* August 12, 1993

Table 12.2 Using Options to Protect the Value of a Portfolio That Mirrors the S&P 100

From the Trader's Desk

A manager in charge of a portfolio worth $500,000 is concerned that the market might decline rapidly during the next three months and would like to use index options as a hedge. The portfolio is expected to mirror closely the S&P 100, which is currently standing at 250. A three-month put option on the S&P 100 with a strike price of 240 is available.

The Strategy

The manager buys 20 put option contracts with a strike price of 240. This is designed to ensure that the value of the manager's position does not decline below $480,000.

The Outcome

The index dropped to 225 in the three months. The portfolio was worth $450,000. The payoff from the options was 20 × ($240 − $225) × 100 = $30,000 bringing the total value of the position up to $450,000 + $30,000 = $480,000.

from the portfolio mirror those from the index. If the dividend yield from the portfolio is the same as the dividend yield from the index, the percentage changes in the value of the portfolio can be expected to be approximately the same as the percentage changes in the value of the index. Each contract on the S&P 500 is for 100 times the index. It follows that the value of the portfolio is protected against the possibility of the index falling below X if, for each $100S$ dollars in the portfolio, the manager buys one put option contract with strike price X. For instance, suppose that the manager's portfolio is worth $500,000 and the value of the index is 250. The portfolio is worth 2,000 times the index. The manager can obtain insurance against the value of the portfolio dropping below $480,000 in the next three months by buying 20 put option contracts with a strike price of 240. To illustrate how this would work, consider the situation where the index drops to 225 in three months. The portfolio will be worth about $450,000. However, the payoff from the options will be 20 × ($240 − $225) × 100 = $30,000, bringing the total value of the portfolio up to the insured value of $480,000. This example is summarized in Table 12.2.

When the Portfolio's Beta Is Not 1.0

If the portfolio's returns are not expected to equal those of an index, the capital asset pricing model can be used. This model asserts that the expected excess return of a portfolio over the risk-free interest rate equals β times the excess return of a market index over the risk-free interest rate. Consider a portfolio with a β of 2.0. Suppose that it is currently worth $1 million. Suppose further that the current risk-free interest rate is 12 percent per annum, the dividend yield on both the portfolio and the index is expected to be 4 percent per annum, and the current value of the index is 250. Table 12.3 shows the expected relationship between the level of the index and the value of the portfolio in three months. To illustrate the

Table 12.3 Relation between Value of Index and Value of Portfolio for a Situation Where $\beta = 2$

VALUE OF INDEX IN THREE MONTHS	*VALUE OF PORTFOLIO IN THREE MONTHS ($ MILLIONS)*
270	1.14
260	1.06
250	0.98
240	0.90
230	0.82

sequence of calculations necessary to derive Table 12.3, consider what happens when the value of the index in three months proves to be 260:

Value of index in three months	260
Return from change in index	10/250 or 4 percent per three months
Dividends from index	$0.25 \times 4 = 1$ percent per three months
Total return from index	$4 + 1 = 5$ percent per three months
Risk-free interest rate	$0.25 \times 12 = 3$ percent per three months
Excess return from index over risk-free interest rate	$5 - 3 = 2$ percent per three months
Excess return from portfolio over risk-free interest rate	$2 \times 2 = 4$ percent per three months
Return from portfolio	$3 + 4 = 7$ percent per three months
Dividends from portfolio	$0.25 \times 4 = 1$ percent per three months
Increase in value of portfolio	$7 - 1 = 6$ percent per three months
Value of portfolio	$1 \times 1.06 = \$1.06$ million

Suppose that S is the value of the index. It can be shown that for each $100S$ dollars in the portfolio, a total of β put contracts should be purchased. The strike price should be the value the index is expected to have when the value of the portfolio reaches the insured value. Suppose that the insured value is $0.90 million in our example. Table 12.3 shows that the appropriate strike price for the put options purchased is 240. In this case $100S = \$25{,}000$ and the value of the portfolio is $1 million. Since $1{,}000{,}000/25{,}000 = 40$ and $\beta = 2$, the correct strategy is to buy 80 put contracts with a strike price of 240.

To illustrate that this gives the required result, consider what happens if the value of the index falls to 230. As shown in Table 12.3, the value of the portfolio is $0.82 million. The put options pay off $(240 - 230) \times 80 \times 100 = \$80{,}000$ and this is exactly what is necessary to move the total value of the portfolio manager's position up from $0.82 million to the required level of $0.90 million. This example is summarized in Table 12.4.

Table 12.4 Using Options to Protect the Value of a Portfolio That Has a Beta of 2.0

From the Trader's Desk

A manager in charge of a portfolio worth $1,000,000 is concerned that the market might decline rapidly during the next three months and would like to use index options as a hedge. The portfolio has a β of 2.0, the S&P 100 is standing at 250, and a three-month put option on the S&P 500 with a strike price of 240 is available. The dividend yield on both the index and the portfolio is expected to be 4 percent per annum and the risk-free interest rate is 12 percent per annum.

The Strategy

The manager buys 80 put option contracts with a strike price of 240. This is designed to ensure that the value of the manager's position does not decline below $0.90 million.

The Outcome

The portfolio's value declined to $0.82 million during the three-month period. The value of the index declined to 230. The options provided a payoff of 80 $\times$ (240 $-$ 230) $\times$ 100 = $80,000. This was equal to the amount needed to bring the value of the portfolio up to $0.90 million.

Valuation

It will be recalled that when we were valuing index futures in Chapter 3, we assumed that the index could be treated as a security paying a known dividend yield. When valuing index options, we make similar assumptions. This means that Equations (12.1) and (12.2) provide a lower bound for European index options; Equation (12.3) is the put–call parity result for European index options; Equations (12.4) and (12.5) can be used to value European options on an index. In all cases S is equal to the value of the index, σ is equal to the volatility of the index, and q is equal to the average annualized yield on the index during the life of the option. In calculating q only dividends where the ex-dividend date is during the life of the option should be included.

In the United States there is a tendency for ex-dividend dates to be during the first week of February, May, August, and November. At any given time the correct value of q is, therefore, likely to depend on the life of the option. This is even more the case for some foreign indices. For example, in Japan all companies tend to use the same ex-dividend dates.

Example

Consider a European call option on the S&P 500 which is two months from maturity. The current value of the index is 310, the exercise price is 300, the risk-free interest rate is 8 percent per annum, and the volatility of the index is 20 percent per annum. Dividend yields of 0.2 percent and 0.3 percent are expected in the first month and the second month, respectively. In this case,

$S = 310, X = 300, r = 0.08, \sigma = 0.2$, and $T = 0.1667$. The average dividend yield is 0.5 percent per two months or 3 percent per annum. Hence, $q = 0.03$,

$$d_1 = \frac{\ln 1.03333 + 0.07 \times 0.1667}{0.2\sqrt{0.1667}} = 0.5444$$

$$d_2 = \frac{\ln 1.0333 + 0.03 \times 0.1667}{0.2\sqrt{0.1667}} = 0.4628$$

$$N(d_1) = 0.7069, \qquad N(d_2) = 0.6782$$

so that the call price, c, from Equation (12.4) is given by

$$c = 310 \times 0.7069e^{-0.03 \times 0.1667} - 300 \times 0.6782e^{-0.08 \times 0.1667} = 17.28$$

One contract would cost \$1,728.

If the absolute amount of the dividend that will be paid rather than the dividend yield is assumed to be known, the basic Black–Scholes formula can be used with the initial stock price being reduced by the present value of the dividends. This is the approach recommended in Chapter 11 for a stock paying known dividends. It is liable to be difficult to implement for a broadly based stock index, since it requires a knowledge of the dividends expected on every stock underlying the index.

In some circumstances, it is optimal to exercise American put options on an index prior to the exercise date. To a lesser extent, this is also true of American call options on an index. American stock index option prices are, therefore, always worth slightly more than the corresponding European stock index option prices. We will discuss numerical procedures for valuing American index options in Chapter 15.

CURRENCY OPTIONS

The Philadelphia Stock Exchange commenced trading in currency options in 1982. Since then the size of the market has grown very rapidly. By 1993 the currencies traded were the Australian dollar, British pound, Canadian dollar, German mark, Japanese yen, French franc, and Swiss franc. For most of these currencies the Philadelphia Stock Exchange trades European as well as American options.

A significant amount of trading in foreign currency options is also done outside the organized exchanges. Many banks and other financial institutions are prepared to sell or buy foreign currency options that have strike prices and exercise dates tailored to meet the needs of their corporate clients. For a corporate client wishing to hedge a foreign exchange exposure, foreign currency options are an interesting alternative to forward contracts. A company due to receive sterling at a known time in the future can hedge its risk by buying put options on sterling which mature at that time. This guarantees that the value of the sterling will not be less than the exercise price, while allowing the company to benefit from any favorable exchange rate movements. Similarly, a company due to pay sterling at a known time in the future can hedge by buying calls on sterling which mature at that time. This guarantees that the cost of the sterling will not be greater than a certain amount while allowing the company to benefit from favorable exchange rate movements. Whereas a forward contract locks in the exchange rate for a future transaction, an option provides a type of insurance. Of course, insurance is not free. It costs nothing to enter into a forward transaction, while options require a premium to be paid up front.

Quotes

Table 12.5 shows the closing prices of some of the currency options traded on the Philadelphia Stock Exchange on Wednesday, August 11, 1993, as reported in *The Wall Street Journal* of Thursday, August 12, 1993. Options are traded with maturity dates in March, June, September, and December for up to nine months in the future. They are also traded with maturity dates in each of the next two months. The precise expiration date is the Saturday preceding the third Wednesday of the month. The sizes of contracts are indicated at the beginning of each section of the table. The option prices are for the purchase or sale of one unit of a foreign currency with U.S. dollars. For the Japanese yen the prices are in hundredths of a cent. For the other currencies, they are in cents. Thus, one put option contract on the British pound with exercise price 142½ cents and exercise month Sept. would give the holder the right to sell £31,250 for U.S. \$44,531.25 (= 1.425 × 31,250). The indicated price of the contract is 31,250 × 0.0062 = \$193.75. The spot exchange rate on sterling is shown as 146.66 cents per pound sterling.

Valuation

To value currency options, we define S as the spot exchange rate. To be precise, S is the value of one unit of the foreign currency in U.S. dollars. As noted in Chapter 3, a foreign currency is analogous to a stock paying a known dividend yield. The owner of foreign currency receives a "dividend yield" equal to the risk-free interest rate, r_f, in the foreign currency. Equations (12.1) and (12.2), with q replaced by r_f, provide bounds for the European call price, c, and the European put price, p,

$$c > Se^{-r_f T} - Xe^{-rT}$$

$$p > Xe^{-rT} - Se^{-r_f T}$$

Table 12.5 Currency Option Prices on the Philadelphia Exchange, August 11, 1993

PHILADELPHIA OPTIONS

Wednesday, August 11, 1993

		Calls Vol.	Calls Last	Puts Vol.	Puts Last
DMark					**58.05**
62,500 German Mark EOM-European style.					
54	Sep	...	...	10	0.05
55	Sep	...	...	10	0.11
62	Sep	10	0.07	...	...
62,500 German Marks EOM-European style.					
53½	Sep	...	...	10	0.03
54½	Sep	...	...	10	0.07
55½	Aug	...	...	25	0.02
61½	Sep	10	0.10	...	...
62½	Sep	10	0.05	...	...
Australian Dollar					**68.28**
50,000 Australian Dollars-cents per unit.					
69	Aug	200	0.06	...	...
69	Sep	2	0.59	3	1.10
70	Dec	10	0.84	...	...
72	Dec	2	0.38	...	...
British Pound					**146.66**
31,250 British Pound EOM-cents per unit.					
145	Aug	...	...	4	0.73
31,250 British Pounds-European Style.					
150	Aug	...	...	5	2.77
150	Sep	...	...	10	4.05
152½	Aug	...	...	1	5.15
155	Aug	...	...	1	7.65
160	Dec	32	0.60	...	...
31,250 British Pounds-European units.					
145	Aug	1	2.45	...	...
147½	Aug	1	0.65	...	...
31,250 British Pounds-cents per unit.					
142½	Sep	...	...	16	0.62
145	Aug	3	2.12	...	...
145	Sep	5	3.30	...	...
145	Dec	1	4.74	50	3.65
147½	Aug	14	0.76	21	0.87
147½	Sep	70	1.83	145	2.53
150	Aug	...	...	23	2.90
150	Sep	160	0.90	10	4.00
150	Dec	...	...	7	6.80
152½	Dec	...	...	50	8.18
155	Dec	31	1.37	...	...
160	Sep	...	...	4	13.20
British Pound-GMark					**253.20**
31,250 British Pound-German Mark cross.					
246	Sep	6	6.80	...	...
250	Sep	...	...	100	1.20
254	Sep	2	1.94	...	...
31,250 British Pound-German mark EOM.					
256	Aug	16	0.56	...	...
Canadian Dollar					**76.62**
50,000 Canadian Dollars-cents per unit.					
76½	Aug	...	...	200	0.06
76½	Sep	...	...	40	0.37
77	Aug	...	...	15	0.30
77	Sep	1150	0.40	54	0.65
77	Dec	...	...	6	1.19
77½	Sep	150	0.20	30	0.96
77½	Dec	...	...	6	1.53
78	Sep	...	...	20	1.32
78½	Dec	6	0.39	...	...
79½	Dec	10	0.22	...	...
80	Sep	10	0.01	...	...
87½	Sep	...	...	40	0.19
French Franc					**165.84**
250,000 French Francs-10ths of a cent per unit.					
15½	Dec	...	...	100	1.46
15¾	Dec	...	...	21	2.18
16	Dec	...	...	27	2.88
16¾	Sep	...	...	25	3.60
250,000 French Francs-European Style.					
15¼	Dec	...	...	5	0.90
16¼	Sep	...	...	8615	1.10
16½	Sep	...	...	4242	2.10
16¾	Dec	5	2.92	...	...
17¾	Dec	5	0.70	...	...
German Mark					**58.05**
62,500 German Marks EOM-cents per unit.					
57½	Aug	40	0.89	...	...
58	Aug	12	0.67	...	...
58½	Aug	65	0.41	20	0.78
58½	Sep	130	0.60	...	...
59	Sep	130	0.45	...	...
62,500 German Marks-European Style.					
55	Sep	...	...	25	0.05
55½	Sep	...	...	25	0.08
57	Sep	...	...	5	0.37
58	Aug	...	...	10	0.25
59	Aug	...	...	400	0.77
59	Sep	1000	0.35	...	...
60	Aug	...	...	200	1.68
61	Sep	50	0.07	...	...
61½	Sep	25	0.04	...	...
62,500 German Marks-cents per unit.					
56	Sep	...	...	250	0.14
56½	Sep	6	1.70	28	0.22
57	Aug	8	0.99	...	...
57	Sep	...	...	282	0.41
57	Dec	200	1.93	31	1.33
57½	Sep	3	1.10	33	0.49
58	Aug	1275	0.23	3572	0.22
58	Sep	70	0.68	115	0.80
58	Dec	...	...	3	1.74
58½	Aug	4310	0.08	1154	0.58
58½	Sep	4	0.60	5	0.97
59	Aug	11	0.04	2720	0.82
59	Sep	115	0.43	5	1.30
59½	Sep	10	0.27	...	...
60	Sep	...	...	124	2.15
61	Sep	500	0.08	...	...
62	Dec	3	0.30	...	...
63	Dec	200	0.19	...	...
Japanese Yen					**96.52**
6,250,000 Japanese Yen EOM-100ths of a cent per unit.					
95	Aug	...	...	550	0.52
6,250,000 Japanese Yen-100ths of a cent per unit.					
85	Dec	...	...	10	0.14
90	Dec	...	...	3	0.51
91	Aug	1	5.42	...	...
91	Sep	...	...	1	0.09
91	Dec	...	...	103	0.70
92	Aug	...	...	100	0.01
92	Sep	...	...	50	0.19
92	Dec	10	5.40	...	...
92½	Sep	...	...	34	0.27
93	Sep	5	3.01	...	...
93	Dec	...	...	200	1.18
93½	Sep	1	3.28	80	0.45
94	Sep	4	2.24	15	0.55
94	Dec	...	...	8	1.58
94½	Aug	...	...	30	0.05
95	Aug	144	1.57	100	0.12
95	Sep	16	2.29	51	0.86
95	Dec	...	...	36	1.99
95½	Aug	...	...	162	0.16
95½	Sep	34	1.63	10	1.05
96	Aug	37	0.79	10	0.29
96	Sep	2	1.15	23	1.30
96	Dec	...	...	74	2.37
97	Aug	275	0.33	...	...
97	Sep	24	1.17	...	...
100	Sep	35	0.42	...	...
6,250,000 Japanese Yen-European Style.					
97	Aug	170	0.33	...	...
Swiss Franc					**65.18**
62,500 Swiss Francs-European Style.					
64	Aug	...	...	23	0.02
66	Aug	...	...	23	0.53
62,500 Swiss Francs-cents per unit.					
62	Dec	...	...	15	0.74
65	Sep	4	1.04	133	0.80
66	Dec	...	...	4	2.30
66½	Aug	...	...	46	0.99
67½	Sep	10	0.18	...	...
68	Sep	...	...	4	2.71
68½	Sep	50	0.14	...	...
69	Sep	...	...	2	3.60

Call Vol ...... 12,129 Open Int ... 744,573
Put Vol .... 28,941 Open Int ... 660,297

Equation (12.3), with q replaced by r_f, provides the put–call parity result for currency options:

$$c + Xe^{-rT} = p + Se^{-r_f T}$$

Finally, Equations (12.4) and (12.5) provide pricing the formulas for currency options when q is replaced by r_f

$$c = Se^{-r_f T}N(d_1) - Xe^{-rT}N(d_2) \tag{12.9}$$

$$p = Xe^{-rT}N(-d_2) - Se^{-r_f T}N(-d_1) \tag{12.10}$$

where

$$d_1 = \frac{\ln(S/X) + (r - r_f + \sigma^2/2)T}{\sigma\sqrt{T}}$$

and

$$d_2 = \frac{\ln(S/X) + (r - r_f - \sigma^2/2)T}{\sigma\sqrt{T}} = d_1 - \sigma\sqrt{T}$$

Both the domestic interest rate, r, and the foreign interest rate, r_f, are assumed to be constant and the same for all maturities. Put and call options on a currency are symmetrical in that a put option to sell currency A for currency B at an exercise price X is the same as a call option to buy B with A at $1/X$.

Example

Consider a four-month European call option on the British pound. Suppose that the current exchange rate is 1.6000, the exercise price is 1.6000, the risk-free interest rate in the United States is 8 percent per annum, the risk-free interest rate in Britain is 11 percent per annum, and the option price is 4.3 cents. In this case $S = 1.6$, $X = 1.6$, $r = 0.08$, $r_f = 0.11$, $T = 0.3333$, and $c = 0.043$. The implied volatility can be calculated by trial and error. A volatility of 20 percent gives an option price of 0.0639; a volatility of 10 percent gives an option price of 0.0285; and so on. The implied volatility is 14.1 percent.

From Equation (3.13), the forward rate, F, for a maturity T is given by

$$F = Se^{(r-r_f)T}$$

This enables Equations (12.9) and (12.10) to be simplified to

$$c = e^{-rT}[FN(d_1) - XN(d_2)] \tag{12.11}$$

$$p = e^{-rT}[XN(-d_2) - FN(-d_1)] \tag{12.12}$$

where

$$d_1 = \frac{\ln(F/X) + (\sigma^2/2)T}{\sigma\sqrt{T}}$$

$$d_2 = \frac{\ln(F/X) - (\sigma^2/2)T}{\sigma\sqrt{T}} = d_1 - \sigma\sqrt{T}$$

Note that the maturities of the forward contract and the option must be the same for Equations (12.11) and (12.12) to apply.

In some circumstances it is optimal to exercise American currency options prior to maturity. Thus, American currency options are worth more than their

European counterparts. In general, call options on high-interest currencies and put options on low-interest currencies are the most likely to be exercised prior to maturity. This is because a high-interest currency (e.g., sterling in 1993) is expected to depreciate relative to the U.S. dollar and a low-interest currency (e.g., the Japanese yen in 1993) is expected to appreciate relative to the U.S. dollar. Unfortunately, analytic formulas do not exist for the evaluation of American currency options. We will discuss numerical procedures in Chapter 15.

SUMMARY

The Black–Scholes formula for valuing European options on a nondividend-paying stock can be extended to cover European options on a stock paying a continuous known dividend yield. In practice stocks do not pay continuous dividend yields. However, a number of other assets upon which options are written can be considered to be analogous to a stock paying a continous dividend yield. In particular,

1. A stock index is analogous to a stock paying a continuous dividend yield. The dividend yield is the dividend yield on the stocks comprising the index.
2. A foreign currency is analogous to a stock paying a continuous dividend yield where the dividend yield is the foreign risk-free interest rate.

The extension to Black–Scholes can, therefore, be used to value European options on stock indices and foreign currencies. As we will see in Chapter 15, these analogies are also useful in valuing numerically American options on these assets.

Index options are settled in cash. Upon exercise of an index call option, the holder receives the amount by which the index exceeds the strike price at the close of trading. Similarly, upon exercise of an index put option, the holder receives the amount by which the strike price exceeds the index at the close of trading. Index options can be used for portfolio insurance. If the value of the portfolio mirrors the index, it is appropriate to buy one put option for each $100S$ dollars in the portfolio where S is the value of the index. If the portfolio does not mirror the index, β put options should be purchased for each $100S$ dollars in the portfolio where β is the beta of the portfolio calculated using the capital asset pricing model. The strike price of the put options purchased should reflect the level of insurance required.

Currency options are traded both on organized exchanges and over the counter. They can be used by corporate treasurers to hedge foreign exchange exposure. For example, a U.S. corporate treasurer who knows sterling will be received by his or her company at a certain time in the future can hedge by buying put options that mature at that time. Similarly, a U.S. corporate treasurer who knows sterling will be paid at a certain time in the future can hedge by buying call options that mature at that time.

Suggestions for Further Reading

General

MERTON, R. C., "Theory of rational option pricing," *Bell Journal of Economics and Management Science*, 4 (Spring 1973), 141–183.

STOLL, H. R., and R. E. WHALEY, "New option instruments; arbitrageable linkages and valuation," *Advances in Futures and Options Research*, 1, pt. A (1986), 25–62.

On options on stock indices

CHANCE, D. M., "Empirical tests of the pricing of index call options," *Advances in Futures and Options Research*, 1, Pt. A (1986), 141–166.

On options on currencies

BIGER, N., and J. HULL, "The valuation of currency options," *Financial Management*, 12 (Spring 1983), 24–28.

BODURTHA, J. N., and G. R. COURTADON, "Tests of an American option pricing model on the foreign currency options market," *Journal of Financial and Quantitative Analysis*, 22 (June 1987), 153–167.

GARMAN, M. B., and S. W. KOHLHAGEN, "Foreign currency option values," *Journal of International Money and Finance*, 2 (December 1983), 231–253.

GRABBE, J. O., "The pricing of call and put options on foreign exchange," *Journal of International Money and Finance*, 2 (December 1983), 239–253.

Quiz

1. A portfolio is currently worth $10 million and has a beta of 1.0. The S&P 100 is currently standing at 250. Explain how a put option on the S&P 100 with a strike of 240 can be used to provide portfolio insurance.
2. "Once we know how to value options on a stock paying a continuous dividend yield, we know how to value options on stock indices and currencies." Explain this statement.
3. A stock index is currently 300, the dividend yield on the index is 3 percent per annum, and the risk-free interest rate is 8 percent per annum. What is a lower bound for the price of a six-month European call option on the index when the strike price is 290?
4. A currency is currently worth $0.80. Over each of the next two months it is expected to increase or decrease in value by 2 percent. The domestic and foreign risk-free interest rates are 6 percent and 8 percent. What is the value of a two-month European call option with a strike price of 0.80?
5. Explain how currency options can be used by corporations to hedge their foreign exchange risk.
6. Calculate the value of a three-month at-the-money European call option on a stock index when the index is at 250, the risk-free interest rate is 10 percent per annum, the volatility of the index is 18 percent per annum, and the dividend yield on the index is 3 percent per annum.
7. Calculate the value of an eight-month European put option on a currency with a strike price of 0.50. The current exchange rate is 0.52, volatility of the exchange rate is 12 percent, the domestic risk-free interest rate is 4 percent and the foreign risk-free interest rate is 8 percent per annum.

Questions and Problems

12.1. Suppose that an exchange constructs a stock index which tracks the return, including dividends, on a certain portfolio. Explain how you would value (a) futures contracts and (b) European options on the index.

12.2. A foreign currency is currently worth \$1.50. The domestic and foreign risk-free interest rates are 5 percent and 9 percent. Calculate a lower bound for the value of a six-month call option on the currency with a strike price of 1.40 if it is (a) European and (b) American.

12.3. Consider a stock index currently standing at 250. The dividend yield on the index is 4 percent per annum and the risk-free rate is 6 percent per annum. A three-month call option on the index with a strike price of 245 is currently worth 10. What is the value of a three-month put option on the index with a strike price of 245?

12.4. The S&P index currently stands at 348 and has a volatility of 30 percent per annum. The risk-free rate of interest is 7 percent per annum and the index provides a dividend yield of 4 percent per annum. Calculate the value of a three-month European put with an exercise price of 350.

12.5. Suppose that the spot price of the Canadian dollar is U.S. \$0.75 and that the Canadian dollar/U.S. dollar exchange rate has a volatility of 4 percent per annum. The risk-free rates of interest in Canada and the United States are 9 percent and 7 percent per annum, respectively. Calculate the value of a European call option with an exercise price of 0.75 and an exercise date in 9 months.

12.6. Show that if C is the price of an American call with exercise price X and maturity T on a stock paying a dividend yield of q, and P is the price of an American put on the same stock with the same strike price and exercise date,

$$Se^{-qT} - X < C - P < S - Xe^{-rT}$$

where S is the stock price, r is the risk-free rate, and $r > 0$. (Hint: To obtain the first half of the inequality, consider possible values of:

Portfolio A: A European call option plus an amount X invested at the risk-free rate

Portfolio B: An American put option plus e^{-qT} of stock with dividends being reinvested in the stock

To obtain the second half of the inequality, consider possible values of:

Portfolio C: An American call option plus an amount Xe^{-rT} invested at the risk-free rate

Portfolio D: A European put option plus one stock with dividends being reinvested in the stock)

12.7. Show that a call option on a currency has the same price as the corresponding put option on the currency when the forward price equals the strike price.

12.8. A stock index currently stands at 300. It is expected to increase or decrease by 10 percent over each of the next two time periods of three months. The risk-free interest rate is 8 percent and the dividend yield on the index is 3 percent. What is the value of a six-month put option on the index with a strike price of 300 if it is (a) European and (b) American?

12.9. Would you expect the volatility of a stock index to be greater or less than the volatility of a typical stock? Explain your answer.

12.10. A mutual fund announces that the salaries of its fund managers will depend on the performance of the fund. If the fund loses money, the salaries will be zero. If the fund makes a profit, the salaries will be proportional to the profit. Describe the salary of a fund manager as an option. How is a fund manager motivated to behave with this type of remuneration package?

12.11. Does the cost of portfolio insurance increase or decrease as the beta of a portfolio increases? Explain your answer.

12.12. Suppose that a portfolio is worth $60 million and the S&P 500 is at 300. If the value of the portfolio mirrors the value of the index, what options should be purchased to provide protection against the value of the portfolio falling below $54 million in one year's time?

12.13. Consider again the situation in Problem 12.12. Suppose that the portfolio has a beta of 2.0, that the risk-free interest rate is 5 percent per annum, and that the dividend yield on both the portfolio and the index is 3 percent per annum. What options should be purchased to provide protection against the value of the portfolio falling below $54 million?

13

OPTIONS ON FUTURES

The options we have considered so far have provided the holder with the right to buy or sell a certain asset by a certain date. These can be termed *options on spot* or *spot options*. This is because, when the option is exercised, the sale or purchase of the asset at the agreed price takes place immediately. In this chapter we move on to consider *options on futures*, also known as *futures options*. In these contracts, an exercise of the option gives the holder the right to buy or sell the asset at the agreed price at a future date.

The Commodity Futures Trading Commission authorized the trading of options on futures on an experimental basis in 1982. Permanent trading was approved in 1987 and since then the popularity of the contract with investors has grown very fast.

In this chapter we describe how futures options work and discuss the differences between futures options and spot options. We explain how European futures options can be priced using either binomial trees or formulas similar to the ones produced by Black and Scholes for stock options. We also discuss the relative pricing of futures options and spot options.

NATURE OF FUTURES OPTIONS

An option on a futures is the right, but not the obligation, to trade a futures contract at a certain futures price by a certain date. Specifically, a call option on a futures is the right to enter into a long futures contract at a certain price; a put option on a futures is the right to enter into a short futures position at a certain price. Most options on futures are American; that is, they can be exercised any time during the life of the contract. The expiration date of an option on a futures contract is generally on or a few days before the earliest delivery date of the underlying futures contract.

To illustrate the operation of futures options contracts further, consider the position of an investor who has bought a call futures option with a strike price of X. As with other exchange-traded option contracts, the investor is required to pay for the option when he or she first enters into the contract. If the call futures option is exercised, the investor obtains a long futures contract and there is a cash settlement to reflect the investor entering into the contract at a price of X. As explained in Chapter 2, futures contracts are marked to market daily. This means that an amount $F^* - X$ is added to the investor's margin account where F^* is the most recent settlement price.

Once the investor has exercised, he or she can choose to either close out the futures position or keep it. If the investor closes out the position immediately after exercise, there is a cash settlement of $F - F^*$ where F is the futures contract at the time of exercise. The total payoff is therefore

$$(F^* - X) + (F - F^*) = F - X$$

If the investor decides to keep the futures position, he or she may be required to provide some margin in addition to the cash settlement mentioned previously.

The payoff from a European call futures option contract is

$$\max(F_T - X, 0)$$

where F_T is the futures price of the asset on the expiration date of the option. If $F_T > X$, the holder of the option will choose to exercise and can realize the payoff by closing out the long futures position that is acquired immediately. If $F_T \leq X$, the holder of the option will choose not to exercise. In the $F_T > X$ case, the payoff can be realized in cash by immediately closing out the long futures position that is obtained on exercise.

The investor who sells (or writes) a call futures option receives the option premium but takes the risk that the contract will be exercised. When the contract is exercised, this investor assumes a short futures position. An amount $F^* - X$ is deducted from the investor's margin account where F^* is the most recent settlement price. The exchange clearinghouse arranges for this sum to be transferred to the investor on the other side of the transaction who chose to exercise the option.

Put futures options work similarly. When an investor with a long position in a put futures option chooses to exercise the option, he or she obtains a short futures position plus a cash amount equal to the amount by which the strike price exceeds the most recent settlement price. The investor on the other side of the transaction (that is, the investor who sold the put futures option) obtains a long futures position and has the excess of the strike price over the most recent settlement price deducted from his or her margin account. The payoff from a European put futures contract is

$$\max(X - F_T, 0)$$

This payoff is realized in cash by the purchaser of the option if the short futures position acquired by the purchaser of the option is closed out immediately. Similarly, it is paid in cash immediately by the seller of the option if the long futures position acquired by the seller is closed out immediately.

Examples

1. Consider an investor who has a September futures call option on 25,000 pounds of copper with an exercise price of 70 cents per pound. Suppose that the current futures price of copper for delivery in September is 80 cents and the most recent settlement price for the futures contract is also 80 cents. If the option is exercised, the investor receives \$2,500 (= 25,000 × 10 cents) plus a long position in a futures contract to buy 25,000 pounds of copper in September. If desired, the position in the futures contract can be immediately closed out. This would leave the investor with the \$2,500 cash payoff.
2. Consider an investor who has a December futures put option on 5,000 bushels of corn with an exercise price of 200 cents per bushel. Suppose that the current futures price of corn for delivery in December is 180 cents and the most recent settlement price is 181 cents. If the option is exercised, the investor receives \$950 (= 5,000 × (200 − 181) cents) plus a short position in a futures contract to sell 5000 bushels of corn in December. The short position in the futures contract is worth \$50 (= 5,000 × (181 − 180) cents). If this is closed out immediately the total payoff to the investor would be \$1,000. (Both this example and the previous example ignore transactions costs.)

QUOTES

As mentioned earlier, most futures options are American and are referred to by the month in which the underlying futures contract matures — not by the expiration month of the option. The maturity date of the options contract is generally on, or a few days before, the earliest delivery date of the underlying futures contract. For example, the NYSE index futures option and the S&P index futures options both expire on the same day as the underlying futures contract; the CME currency futures options expire two business days prior to the expiration of the futures contract; the CBOT treasury bond futures option expires on the first Friday preceding by at least five business days the end of the month, just prior to the futures contract expiration month.

Table 13.1 shows quotes for futures options as they appeared in *The Wall Street Journal* on August 12, 1993. The most popular contracts are on treasury bonds (CBOT) and Eurodollars (CME). The total of the put and call open interest for treasury bonds is over 600,000, while that for Eurodollars is over 1,500,000. Other popular contracts with an open interest greater than 50,000 are on corn (CBOT), soybeans (CBOT), wheat (CBOT), sugar (CSCE), crude oil (NYMEX), heating oil (NYMEX), gold (COMEX), silver (COMEX), yen (CME), deutschemark (CME), treasury notes (CBOT), five-year treasury notes (CBOT), long gilts (LIFFE), and S&P 500 (CME).

REASONS FOR THE POPULARITY OF FUTURES OPTIONS

It is natural to ask why people choose to trade options on futures rather than options on the underlying asset. The main reason appears to be that a futures contract is, in many circumstances, more liquid and easier to trade than the underlying asset. Furthermore, a futures price is known immediately from trading on the futures exchange, whereas the spot price of the underlying asset may not be so readily available.

Consider for example treasury bonds. The market for treasury bond futures is much more active than the market for any particular treasury bond. Also the price of treasury bond futures contracts is known immediately from trading on the CBOT. By contrast, the current market price of a bond can be obtained only by contacting one or more dealers. It is not surprising that investors would rather take delivery of a treasury bond futures contract than treasury bonds.

Other examples of assets where the futures is easier to trade than the underlying asset are commodities. For example, it is much easier and more convenient to make or take delivery of a live hogs futures contract than it is to make or take delivery of the hogs themselves.

An important point about a futures option is that the exercise of the option does not usually lead to delivery of the underlying asset, since in most circumstances the underlying futures contract is closed out prior to delivery. Futures options are, therefore, normally settled in cash. This is appealing to many investors, particularly those with limited capital who may find it difficult to come up with the funds to buy the underlying asset when an option is exercised.

Another advantage sometimes cited for futures options is that the trading of futures and futures options are arranged in pits side by side in the same exchange. This facilitates hedging, arbitrage, and speculation. It also tends to make the markets more efficient.

A final point is that futures options tend to entail lower transactions costs than spot options in many situations.

Table 13.1 Closing Prices of Commodity Futures Options on August 11, 1993

FUTURES OPTIONS PRICES

Wednesday, August 11, 1993.

AGRICULTURAL

CORN (CBT)
5,000 bu.; cents per bu.

Strike	Calls–Settle			Puts–Settle		
Price	Sep	Dec	Mar	Sep	Dec	Mar
220	20½	29¼	36¼	⅛	2	2¼
230	11¾	21¼	28	1	4⅝	4
240	5⅝	15⅝	21½	4¾	8¾	7¾
250	2⅜	11⅜	16½	11½	14¼	13½
260	¾	8	13	20½	20¾	19
270	⅛	5¾	9	....	28½	....

Est vol 15,000 Tues 9,271 calls 2,442 puts
Op int Tues 137,790 calls 67,550 puts

SOYBEANS (CBT)
5,000 bu.; cents per bu.

Strike	Calls–Settle			Puts–Settle		
Price	Sep	Nov	Jan	Sep	Nov	Jan
625	58	65	70¾	1	6¾	10
650	36	48½	55½	4½	15½	20
675	20	36	44	12½	29	34
700	10½	28¾	38	30	44⅜	47
725	5½	22	29	50	62½	67
750	2⅜	16¾	23	72½	83	....

Est vol 23,000 Tues 14,942 calls 6,-
130 puts
Op int Tues 141,412 calls 67,418 puts

SOYBEAN MEAL (CBT)
100 tons; $ per ton

Strike	Calls–Settle			Puts–Settle		
Price	Sep	Oct	Dec	Sep	Oct	Dec
200	17.10	17.70	17.25	.40	1.00	1.75
210	8.00	10.00	11.00	1.60	3.25	5.75
220	3.25	5.70	7.50	6.00	8.50	11.60
230	1.25	3.40	5.25	14.50	16.15	19.40
240	.50	1.90	4.00	23.60	24.90	27.75
250	.25	1.25	2.75	33.30	....	....

Est vol 1,500 Tues 1,669 calls 774 puts
Op int Tues 20,444 calls 15,476 puts

SOYBEAN OIL (CBT)
60,000 lbs.; cents per lb.

Strike	Calls–Settle			Puts–Settle		
Price	Sep	Oct	Dec	Sep	Oct	Dec
2300	1.020	1.310	1.750	.130	.300	.500
2350	.670	....	1.500	.280	.460	.730
2400	.450	.790	1.300	.540	.730	1.000
2450	.270	.650	1.100	.880	1.050	1.300
2500	.200	.480	1.000	1.260	1.400	1.650
2550	....	....	....	....	....	....

Est vol 1,100 Tues 480 calls 102 puts
Op int Tues 10,784 calls 9,036 puts

WHEAT (CBT)
5,000 bu.; cents per bu.

Strike	Calls–Settle			Puts–Settle		
Price	Sep	Dec	Mar	Sep	Dec	Mar
290	24	34½	38½	⅝	3¾	6⅝
300	15	26¾	31¾	1½	6½	9½
310	8	20¼	26	4¾	9½	12¾
320	3½	15	21	10	14¼	17½
330	1½	11½	17⅛	18	20½	24
340	¾	8¾	13¼	....	27½	....

Est vol 7,500 Tues 1,724 calls 799 puts
Op int Tues 32,726 calls 19,146 puts

WHEAT (KC)
5,000 bu.; cents per bu.

Strike	Calls–Settle			Puts–Settle		
Price	Sep	Dec	Mar	Sep	Dec	Mar
290	19¾	30⅝	37⅜	⅛	4	....
300	11¼	23⅜	33	1¾	8	13
310	5¼	18½	26⅜	6¼	10¼	....
320	1⅝	13⅞	22¾	12½	17⅜	....
330	¼	9½	18	20½	24	....
340	⅛	6½	13⅝	30½	....	....

Est vol 265 Tues 149 calls 83 puts
Op int Tues 4,311 calls 3,151 puts

COTTON (CTN)
50,000 lbs.; cents per lb.

Strike	Calls–Settle			Puts–Settle		
Price	Oct	Dec	Mar	Oct	Dec	Mar
54	2.40	4.05	....	.75	1.35	1.55
55	1.78	3.40	....	1.15	1.65	1.90
56	1.28	2.85	....	1.65	2.05	2.29
57	.92	2.40	4.05	2.24	2.61	2.68
58	.67	2.00	3.55	2.94	3.08	3.15
59	.43	1.65	3.10	3.74	3.75	3.70

Est vol 1,700 Tues 131 calls 514 puts
Op int Tues 17,968 calls 17,875 puts

ORANGE JUICE (CTN)
15,000 lbs.; cents per lb.

Strike	Calls–Settle			Puts–Settle		
Price	Oct	Nov	Jan	Oct	Nov	Jan
105	....	15.75	20.10	....	1.85	5.00
110	....	11.60	16.75	....	2.75	....
115	....	8.15	14.25	....	4.25	9.25
120	3.50	5.50	11.50	4.75	6.60	....
125	....	3.50	9.00	....	9.60	....
130	....	2.40	7.25	....	13.40	....

Est vol 60 Tues 89 calls 40 puts
Op int Tues 1,055 calls 1,113 puts

Strike	Calls–Settle			Puts–Settle		
Price	Sep	Oct	Nov	Sep	Oct	Nov

LIVESTOCK

CATTLE-FEEDER (CME)
44,000 lbs.; cents per lb.

Strike	Calls–Settle			Puts–Settle		
Price	Aug	Sep	Oct	Aug	Sep	Oct
84	4.90	3.70	3.30	0.02	0.30	0.62
86	2.92	2.07	1.87	0.05	0.67	1.20
88	1.10	0.90	0.85	0.22	1.50	....
90	0.17	0.25	0.30	1.30	....	....
92	0.02	0.05	0.07	....	....	....
94	....	....	....	....	....	....

Est vol 194 Tues 91 calls 196 puts
Op int Tues 3,181 calls 9,852 puts

CATTLE-LIVE (CME)
40,000 lbs.; cents per lb.

Strike	Calls–Settle			Puts–Settle		
Price	Sep	Oct	Dec	Sep	Oct	Dec
72	3.45	3.67	4.10	0.07	0.32	0.67
74	1.70	2.22	2.70	....	0.85	1.25
76	0.57	1.07	1.55	....	1.70	2.07
78	0.15	0.40	0.82	....	3.00	3.32
80	....	0.12	0.35	....	....	....
82	....	....	0.15	....	....	....

Est vol 699 Tues 561 calls 678 puts
Op int Tues 12,256 calls 19,881 puts

HOGS–LIVE (CME)
40,000 lbs.; cents per lb.

Strike	Calls–Settle			Puts–Settle		
Price	Oct	Dec	Feb	Oct	Dec	Feb
44	1.77	2.17	2.22	0.85	1.50	1.80
46	0.82	1.27	1.40	1.90	2.57	....
48	0.30	0.70	0.85	....	....	4.30
50	0.15	0.35	0.50	....	....	5.95
52	0.05	0.20	....	....	....	7.75
54	....	0.10	....	....	....	....

Est vol 118 Tues 141 calls 262 puts
Op int Tues 1,415 calls 1,416 puts

METALS

COPPER (CMX)
25,000 lbs.; cents per lb.

Strike	Calls–Settle			Puts–Settle		
Price	Sep	Dec	Mar	Sep	Dec	Mar
80	3.85	5.95	7.50	.15	1.95	2.80
82	2.10	4.70	6.30	.40	2.70	3.60
84	.90	3.50	5.20	1.20	3.50	4.55
86	.25	2.90	4.30	2.55	4.90	5.60
88	.10	2.25	3.55	4.40	6.25	6.85
90	.05	1.70	2.90	6.35	7.70	8.20

Est vol 500 Tues 253 calls 339 puts
Op int Tues 10,207 calls 6,144 puts

GOLD (CMX)
100 troy ounces; $ per troy ounce

Strike	Calls–Settle			Puts–Settle		
Price	Sep	Oct	Dec	Sep	Oct	Dec
360	16.90	18.60	23.70	.20	1.80	5.20
3.70	7.30	11.50	18.00	.50	4.70	9.40
3.80	1.30	6.50	13.10	4.50	9.70	14.40
390	.30	3.30	9.20	13.50	16.40	21.10
400	.10	1.80	6.50	23.20	24.90	27.80
410	.10	.90	4.80	33.20	33.90	36.00

Est vol 8,500 Tues 5,519 calls 2,412 puts
Op int Tues 126,891 calls 50,954 puts

SILVER (CMX)
5,000 troy ounces; cts per troy ounce

Strike	Calls–Settle			Puts–Settle		
Price	Sep	Oct	Dec	Sep	Oct	Dec
425	43.2	50.5	59.5	0.4	3.2	12.0
450	19.8	32.0	44.0	2.0	9.5	21.5
475	4.0	19.0	32.5	11.2	21.7	35.0
500	0.5	11.0	23.5	32.7	38.3	51.0
525	0.1	5.8	18.5	57.2	58.5	70.0
550	0.1	3.3	14.2	82.2	80.5	90.5

Est vol 6,500 Tues 3,259 calls 2,604 puts
Op int Tues 74,938 calls 35,632 puts

OTHER OPTIONS

Final or settlement prices of selected contracts. Volume and open interest are totals in all contract months.

CORN (MCE)
1,000 bu.; cents per bu.

Strike	Calls–Settle			Puts–Settle		
Price	Sep	Dec	Mar	Sep	Dec	Mar
240	5⅝	15⅝	21½	4¾	8¾	7¾

Est vol 15 Tues 23 calls 28 puts
Op int Tues 800 calls 239 puts

EUROMARK (CME)
DM 1,000,000; pts. of 100%

Strike	Calls–Settle			Puts–Settle		
Price	Aug	Sep	Oct	Aug	Sep	Oct
9350	0.07	0.13	....	0.02	0.08	....

Est vol 0 Tues 58 calls 0 puts
Op int Tues 2,362 calls 598 puts

Strike	Calls–Settle			Puts–Settle		
Price	Sep	Oct	Nov	Sep	Oct	Nov
9700	1.14	1.78	2.13	1.53	....	....
9750	0.94	1.57	....	....	....	....
9800	0.76	....	....	....	....	....

Est vol 14,800 Tues 3,541 calls 3,158 puts
Op int Tues 40,176 calls 49,101 puts

DEUTSCHEMARK (CME)
125,000 marks; cents per mark

Strike	Calls–Settle			Puts–Settle		
Price	Sep	Oct	Nov	Sep	Oct	Nov
5700	1.20	1.28	....	0.32	0.86	....
5750	0.86	1.02	....	0.48	1.10	....
5800	0.60	0.80	1.04	0.72	1.38	....
5850	0.41	0.61	....	1.03	....	1.92
5900	0.25	0.46	....	1.37	....	....
5950	0.17	0.35	0.56	1.78	....	....

Est vol 7,521 Tues 3,022 calls 15,225 puts
Op int Tues 125,729 calls 108,834 puts

CANADIAN DOLLAR (CME)
100,000 Can.$, cents per Can.$

Strike	Calls–Settle			Puts–Settle		
Price	Sep	Oct	Nov	Sep	Oct	Nov
7550	....	....	....	0.11	....	....
7600	....	....	....	0.20	0.54	....
7650	0.46	0.64	....	0.38	0.77	....
7700	0.25	0.47	....	0.67	1.06	....
7750	0.12	0.31	....	1.04	1.40	....
7800	0.05	0.20	....	1.48	1.79	....

Est vol 1,195 Tues 230 calls 229 puts
Op int Tues 3,345 calls 4,258 puts

BRITISH POUND (CME)
62,500 pounds; cents per pound

Strike	Calls–Settle			Puts–Settle		
Price	Sep	Oct	Nov	Sep	Oct	Nov
1425	4.70	....	....	0.44	1.44	....
1450	2.84	3.32	....	1.06	2.40	....
1475	1.46	2.16	....	2.18	3.72	....
1500	0.66	1.32	....	3.88	5.38	....
1525	0.26	0.76	....	5.96	....	....
1550	0.12	0.44	0.80	8.32	....	....

Est vol 1,808 Tues 3,757 calls 3,432 puts
Op int Tues 11,869 calls 10,137 puts

SWISS FRANC (CME)
125,000 francs; cents per franc

Strike	Calls–Settle			Puts–Settle		
Price	Sep	Oct	Nov	Sep	Oct	Nov
6400	1.46	....	....	0.35	0.86	....
6450	1.13	....	....	0.52	1.06	....
6500	0.84	....	....	0.73	1.31	....
6550	0.61	0.98	....	1.00	....	....
6600	0.43	0.79	....	1.32	1.88	....
6650	0.29	0.64	....	1.68	....	....

Est vol 1,361 Tues 1,086 calls 700 puts
Op int Tues 17,729 calls 9,152 puts

U.S. DOLLAR INDEX (FINEX)
1,000 times index

Strike	Calls–Settle			Puts–Settle		
Price	Sep	Oct	Nov	Sep	Oct	Nov
93	2.89	....	....	0.14	....	....
94	2.07	....	....	0.31	....	....
95	1.37	....	....	0.62	....	....
96	0.82	....	....	1.07	....	....
97	0.46	....	....	....	....	....
98	0.23	....	....	....	....	....

Est vol 119 Tues 105 calls 7 puts
Op int Tues 2,376 calls 1,243 puts

INTEREST RATE

T-BONDS (CBT)
$100,000; points and 64ths of 100%

Strike	Calls–Settle			Puts–Settle		
Price	Sep	Dec	Mar	Sep	Dec	Mar
112	4-17	3-54	3-52	0-01	0-47	1-46
114	2-20	2-34	2-46	0-04	1-25	2-40
116	0-44	1-32	1-52	0-26	2-25	....
118	0-06	0-51	1-12	1-54	3-43	....
120	0-01	0-24	0-46	3-49	5-16	6-35
122	0-01	0-10	0-26	....	....	....

Est. vol. 75,000;
Tues vol. 31,723 calls; 27,340 puts
Op. int. Tues 316,153 calls; 301,700 puts

T-NOTES (CBT)
$100,000; points and 64ths of 100%

Strike	Calls–Settle			Puts–Settle		
Price	Sep	Dec	Mar	Sep	Dec	Mar
111	2-33	2-62	....	0-01	0-46	1–40
112	1-35	2-14	1-45	0-03	1-05	....
113	0-45	1-37	....	0-13	1-37	....
114	0-12	1-05	....	0-44	....	....
115	0-02	0-44	....	1-34	....	....
116	0-01	0-16	0-29	....	....	....

Est vol 24,734 Tues 4,434 calls 12,-
258 puts
Op int Tues 83,574 calls 135,191 puts

MUNICIPAL BOND INDEX (CBT)
$100,000; pts. & 64ths of 100%

Strike	Calls–Settle			Puts–Settle		
Price	Sep	Dec	Mar	Sep	Dec	Mar
101	2-38	2-14	....	0-05	0-38	....
102	1-43	1-36	....	0-11	0-58	....
103	0-60	1-02	....	0-26	1-23	....
104	0-27	0-41	....	....	....	....
105	....	....	....	....	....	....
106	....	....	....	....	....	....

Est vol 202 Tues 550 calls 416 puts
Op int Tues 5,512 calls 5,757 puts

col. continues on next page *col. continues on next page* *col. continues on next page*

Table 13.1 *(continued)*

COFFEE (CSCE)
37,500 lbs.; cents per lb.

Strike Price	Calls–Settle Dec	Mar	May	Puts–Settle Dec	Mar	May
67.50	8.45	11.00	12.80	2.95	3.60	4.10
70.00	6.75	9.53	10.70	4.00	4.63	4.50
72.50	5.80	8.13	8.85	5.20	5.73	5.15
75.00	4.70	7.50	8.00	6.70	7.60	6.80
77.50	4.00	6.15	7.00	8.50	8.75	8.30
80.00	3.16	5.40	6.30	10.16	10.50	10.10

Est vol 6,231 Tues 1,424 calls 1,536 puts
Op int Tues 25,707 calls 11,875 puts

SUGAR–WORLD (CSCE)
112,000 lbs.; cents per lb.

Strike Price	Calls–Settle Sep	Oct	Nov	Puts–Settle Sep	Oct	Nov
8.50	1.20	1.24	1.44	0.01	0.05	0.14
9.00	0.70	0.81	1.00	0.01	0.12	0.20
9.50	0.28	0.48	0.78	0.05	0.29	0.48
10.00	0.04	0.28	0.35	0.35	0.59	0.55
10.50	0.02	0.16	0.27	0.83	0.95	0.97
11.00	0.01	0.11	0.20	1.32	1.39	1.40

Est vol 1,128 Tues 1,253 calls 646 puts
Op int Tues 59,071 calls 24,983 puts

COCOA (CSCE)
10 metric tons; $ per ton

Strike Price	Calls–Settle Dec	Mar	May	Puts–Settle Dec	Mar	May
850	129	167	205	14	20	40
900	94	135	157	29	38	42
950	69	109	141	54	62	76
1000	51	92	117	86	95	102
1050	36	73	100	121	126	135
1100	24	58	78	159	161	163

Est vol 367 Tues 636 calls 524 puts
Op int Tues 11,553 calls 9,646 puts

OIL

CRUDE OIL (NYM)
1,000 bbls.; $ per bbl.

Strike Price	Calls–Settle Sep	Oct	Nov	Puts–Settle Sep	Oct	Nov
1700	.89	1.39	1.72	.01	.06	.18
1750	.41	.97	....	.01	.08	.24
1800	.12	.63	.94	.01	.14	.32
1850	.02	.35	.65	.03	.22	.45
1900	.01	.19	.46	.24	.38	.66
1950	.01	.09	.30	.64	.60	.97

Est vol 33,001 Tues 12,388 calls 22,-722 puts
Op int Tues 237,460 calls 221,658 puts

HEATING OIL No.2 (NYM)
42,000 gal.; $ per gal.

Strike Price	Calls–Settle Sep	Oct	Nov	Puts–Settle Sep	Oct	Nov
48	....	.0498	....	.0010	.0038	.0040
50	.0185	.0331	....	.0028	.0070	.0070
52	.0058	.0142	.0311	.0101	.0130	.0135
54	.0012	.0098	.0186	.0255	.0235	.0209
56	.0004	.0043	.0107	.0447	.0379	.0329
58	.0002	.0023	.0057	.0645	.0559	.0477

Est vol 5,472 Tues 1,785 calls 1,277 puts
Op int Tues 41,669 calls 31,342 puts

GASOLINE – Unlead (NYM)
42,000 gal.; $ per gal.

Strike Price	Calls–Settle Sep	Oct	Nov	Puts–Settle Sep	Oct	Nov
52	.0384	.0220	.0165	.0006	.0108	.0176
54	.0204	.0112	.0090	.0030	.0200	.0300
56	.0080	.0060	.0045	.0102	.0347	.0453
58	.0022	.0025	.0025	.0244	.0511	.0632
60	.0005	.0012	.0015	.0427	....	....
62	.0002	....	.0010	.0624	....	....

Est vol 3,929 Tues 807 calls 506 puts
Op int Tues 15,762 calls 18,088 puts

NATURAL GAS (NYM)
10,000 MMBtu.; $ per MMBtu.

Strike Price	Calls–Settle Sep	Oct	Nov	Puts–Settle Sep	Oct	Nov
215	.105	.170	.289	.002	.027	.027
220	.057	.132	.248	.008	.038	.035
225	.025	.102	.207	.022	.058	.044
230	.008	.075	.170	.055	.087	.057
235	.002	.054	.141	.099	.110	.077
240	.001	.08	.116	.148	.144	.102

Est vol 575 Tues 209 calls 620 puts
Op int Tues 22,686 calls 21,364 puts

BRENT CRUDE (IPE)
1,000 net bbls.; $ per bbl.

Strike Price	Calls–Settle Sep	Oct	Nov	Puts–Settle Sep	Oct	Nov

NOT AVAILABLE

GAS OIL (IPE)
100 metric tons; $ per ton

Strike Price	Calls–Settle Sep	Oct	Nov	Puts–Settle Sep	Oct	Nov
150	9.35	12.40	14.55	0.35	0.65	0.80
155	5.40	8.35	10.50	1.40	1.60	1.75
160	2.50	5.20	7.10	3.50	3.45	3.35
165	0.05	2.70	4.35	6.83	3.93	5.60
170	0.30	1.40	2.50	11.30	9.65	8.75
175	0.10	0.70	1.30	16.10	13.95	12.55

Est vol 190 Tues 450 calls 150 puts
Op int Tues 9,240 calls 10,569 puts

cont. 2nd col. fr. p. 306

LUMBER (CME)
160,000 bd .ft., $ per 1,000 bd.ft.

Strike Price	Calls–Settle Sep	Nov	Jan	Puts–Settle Sep	Nov	Jan
275	8.90	....	....	10.40	....	....

Est vol 118 Tues 38 calls 31 puts
Op int Tues 546 calls 398 puts

NYSE COMPOSITE INDEX (NYFE)
$500 times premium

Strike Price	Calls–Settle Aug	Sep	Dec	Puts–Settle Aug	Sep	Dec
250	1.75	3.25	4.75	1.85	3.40	4.60

Est vol 51 Tues 9 calls 32 puts
Op int Tues 694 calls 704 puts

NIKKEI 225 STOCK AVG. (CME)
$5 times Prem.

Strike Price	Calls–Settle Aug	Sep	Oct	Puts–Settle Aug	Sep	Oct
21000	260	470	....	....	455	....

Est vol 59 Tues 0 calls 1 puts
Op int Tues 544 calls 274 puts

OATS (CBT)
5,000 bu.; cents per bu.

Strike Price	Calls–Settle Sep	Dec	Mar	Puts–Settle Sep	Dec	Mar
140	6	14¾	....	3½	6½	....

Est vol 100 Tues 28 calls 1 puts
Op int Tues 1,860 calls 689 puts

PLATINUM (NYM)
50 troy oz.; $ per troy oz.

Strike Price	Calls–Settle Sep	Oct	Nov	Puts–Settle Sep	Oct	Nov
390	3.90	10.10	....	....	8.80	....

Est vol 101 Tues 170 calls 22 puts
Op int Tues 3,171 calls 868 puts

PORK BELLIES (CME)
40,000 lbs.; cents per lb.

Strike Price	Calls–Settle Nov	Feb	Mar	Puts–Settle Nov	Feb	Mar
42	6.90	7.52	....	1.05	....	1.72

Est vol 97 Tues 44 calls 10 puts
Op int Tues 576 calls 392 puts

RICE-ROUGH (MCE)
2,000 cwt.; $ per cwt.

Strike Price	Calls–Settle Sep	Nov	Jan	Puts–Settle Sep	Nov	Jan
5800	.100	.450	....	.060	.145	....

Est vol 5 Tues 4 calls 0 puts
Op int Tues 276 calls 270 puts

SILVER (CBT)
1,000 troy oz.; cents per troy oz.

Strike Price	Calls–Settle Oct	Dec	....	Puts–Settle Oct	Dec	....
475	10.0	30.0	....	....	85.0	....

Est vol 10 Tues 4 calls 0 puts
Op int Tues 373 calls 5 puts

S&P MIDCAP 400 (CME)
$500 times index

Strike Price	Calls–Settle Aug	Sep	Oct	Puts–Settle Aug	Sep	Oct
1700	1.30	....	....	....	....	....

Est vol 0 Tues 30 calls 0 puts
Op int Tues 80 calls 51 puts

SOYBEANS (MCE)
1,000 bu.; cents per bu.

Strike Price	Calls–Settle Sep	Nov	Jan	Puts–Settle Sep	Nov	Jan
675	20	36	44	12½	29	40

Est vol 100 Tues 76 calls 7 puts
Op int Tues 1,738 calls 917 puts

2 YR TREAS NOTE (CBT)
$200,000; pts. 32nds of 100%

Strike Price	Calls–Settle Sep	Dec	Mar	Puts–Settle Sep	Dec	Mar
10625	....	....	....	....	....	....

Est vol 0 Tues 0 calls 0 puts
Op int Tues 130 calls 170 puts

WHEAT (MCE)
1,000 bu.; cents per bu.

Strike Price	Calls–Settle Sep	Dec	Mar	Puts–Settle Sep	Dec	Mar
310	8	20¼	26	4¾	9½	12¾

Est vol 10 Tues 15 calls 0 puts
Op int Tues 517 calls 98 puts

WHEAT (MPLS)
5,000 bu.; cents per bu.

Strike Price	Calls–Settle Sep	Dec	Mar	Puts–Settle Sep	Dec	Mar
320	4	15	23½	7	15½	19

Est vol 109 Tues 30 calls 0 puts
Op int Tues 798 calls 356 puts

CURRENCY

JAPANESE YEN (CME)
12,500,000 yen; cents per 100 yen

Strike Price	Calls–Settle Sep	Oct	Nov	Puts–Settle Sep	Oct	Nov
9550	1.95	2.56	....	0.84	1.40	....
9600	1.65	2.28	2.62	1.04	1.61	1.95
9650	1.38	2.02	....	1.27	1.85	....

cont. 3rd col. fr. p. 306

5 YR TREAS NOTES (CBT)
$100,000; points and 64ths of 100%

Strike Price	Calls–Settle Sep	Dec	Mar	Puts–Settle Sep	Dec	Mar
11000	1-34	1-18	....	0-01	0-36	....
11050	1-03	0-63	....	0-02	0-48	....
11100	0-39	0-47	....	0-06	1-00	....
11150	0-18	0-34	....	0-17	1-18	....
11200	0-05	0-24	....	0-36	1-40	....
11250	0-01	0-16	....	....	....	....

Est vol 5,555 Tues 1,551 calls 1,112 puts
Op int Tues 47,185 calls 74,087 puts

EURODOLLAR (CME)
$ million; pts. of 100%

Strike Price	Calls–Settle Sep	Dec	Mar	Puts–Settle Sep	Dec	Mar
9625	0.42	0.18	0.21	.0004	0.15	0.26
9650	0.19	0.07	0.10	0.02	0.29	0.40
9675	0.01	0.02	0.04	0.09	0.49	0.58
9700	.0004	0.01	0.01	0.33	0.72	0.80
9725	.0004	.0004	.0004	0.58	0.97	....
9750	.0004	....	....	....	....	....

Est. vol. 58,954;
Tues vol. 19,031 calls; 16,087 puts
Op. int. Tues 632,706 calls; 869,589 puts

LIBOR – 1 Mo. (CME)
$3 million; pts. of 100%

Strike Price	Calls–Settle Aug	Sep	Oct	Puts–Settle Aug	Sep	Oct
9625	0.58	0.54	....	.0004	.0004	....
9650	0.33	0.30	0.25	.0004	0.01	0.02
9675	0.08	0.07	0.08	0.01	0.03	0.10
9700	.0004	0.01	0.02	0.17	0.22	0.29
9725	....	.0004	.0004	....	....	0.52
9750	....	....	....	....	....	....

Est vol 1,159 Tues 25 calls 88 puts
Op int Tues 2,322 calls 2,183 puts

TREASURY BILLS (CME)
$1 million; pts. of 100%

Strike Price	Calls–Settle Sep	Dec	Mar	Puts–Settle Sep	Dec	Mar
9650	0.43	0.29	....	.0004	0.07	0.20
9675	0.19	0.13	....	0.01	0.16	....
9700	0.02	0.05	....	0.09	....	....
9725	.0004	....	....	0.32	....	....
9750	....	....	....	....	....	....
9775	....	....	....	....	....	....

Est vol 65 Tues 1 calls 48 puts
Op int Tues 190 calls 1,462 puts

EURODOLLAR (LIFFE)
$1 million; pts. of 100%

Strike Price	Calls–Settle Sep	Dec	Mar	Puts–Settle Sep	Dec	Mar
9625	0.43	0.19	0.21	0.01	0.16	0.28
9650	0.18	0.07	0.10	0.01	0.29	0.42
9675	0.02	0.03	0.05	0.10	0.50	0.62
9700	0.01	0.02	0.02	0.34	0.74	0.84
9725	0.00	0.01	0.01	0.58	0.98	1.08
9750	0.00	0.00	....	0.83	1.22	....

Est vol Wed 0 calls 0 puts
Op int Tues 4,140 calls 1,660 puts

LONG GILT (LIFFE)
£50,000; 64ths of 100%

Strike Price	Calls–Settle Sep	Dec	....	Puts–Settle Sep	Dec	....
110	2-61	3-15	....	0-03	1-05	....
111	2-01	2-38	....	0-07	1-28	....
112	1-13	2-02	....	0-19	1-56	....
113	0-39	1-36	....	0-45	2-26	....
114	0-16	1-15	....	1-22	3-05	....
115	0-06	0-57	....	2-12	3-47	....

Est vol Wed 16,311 calls 3,508 puts
Op int Tues 70,827 calls 62,660 puts

INDEX

S&P 500 STOCK INDEX (CME)
$500 times premium

Strike Price	Calls–Settle Aug	Sep	Oct	Puts–Settle Aug	Sep	Oct
440	11.15	13.20	15.90	0.55	2.65	4.50
445	6.70	9.45	12.30	1.10	3.85	5.85
450	3.20	6.20	9.10	2.60	5.60	7.60
455	1.05	3.70	6.35	5.45	8.10	9.85
460	0.25	1.95	4.15	9.65	11.30	....
465	0.05	0.90	2.55	14.45	....	....

Est vol 7,253 Tues 1,576 calls 2,284 puts
Op int Tues 40,609 calls 108,224 puts

GSCI (CME)
$250 times GSCI nearby index

Strike Price	Calls–Settle Oct	Dec	Mar	Puts–Settle Oct	Dec	Mar
174	4.50	....	....	2.50	....	....
175	....	....	....	....	....	....
176	3.80	....	....	3.80	....	....
177	....	....	....	....	....	....
178	2.90	5.60	....	4.90	5.60	....
179	....	....	....	....	....	....

Est vol 0 Tues 50 calls 50 puts
Op int Tues 2,113 calls 2,116 puts

PUT–CALL PARITY

In Chapter 8 we derived a put–call parity relationship for European stock options. We now use a similar argument to derive a put–call parity relationship for European futures options.

Consider European call and put futures options, both with strike price X and time to expiration T. We can form two portfolios:

Portfolio A: A European call futures option plus an amount of cash equal to Xe^{-rT}
Portfolio B: A European put option plus a long futures contract plus an amount of cash equal to Fe^{-rT}

In portfolio A the cash can be invested at the risk-free rate, r, and grows to X at time T. Let F_T be the futures price at maturity of the option. If $F_T > X$, the call option in portfolio A is exercised and portfolio A is worth F_T. If $F_T \leq X$, the call is not exercised and portfolio A is worth X. The value of portfolio A at time T is, therefore,

$$\max(F_T, X)$$

In portfolio B the cash can be invested at the risk-free rate to grow to F at time T. The put option provides a payoff of $\max(X - F_T, 0)$. The futures contract provides a payoff of $F_T - F$.[1] The value of portfolio B at time T is, therefore,

$$F + (F_T - F) + \max(X - F_T, 0) = \max(F_T, X)$$

Since the two portfolios have the same value at time T and there are no early exercise opportunities, it follows that they are worth the same today. The value of portfolio A today is

$$c + Xe^{-rT}$$

The marking-to-market process ensures that the futures contract in portfolio B is worth zero today. Portfolio B is, therefore, worth

$$p + Fe^{-rT}$$

Hence

$$c + Xe^{-rT} = p + Fe^{-rT} \quad \textbf{(13.1)}$$

Example

Suppose that the price of a European call option on silver futures for delivery in six months is 56 cents per ounce when the exercise price is \$8.50. Assume that the silver futures price for delivery in six months is currently \$8.00 and

[1] This assumes no difference between the payoffs from futures contracts and forward contracts when they are both entered into at the same time.

the risk-free interest rate for an investment which matures in six months is 10 percent per annum. From a rearrangement of Equation (13.1), the price of a European put option on silver futures with the same maturity and exercise date as the call option is

$$0.56 + 8.50e^{-0.5\times0.1} - 8.00e^{-0.5\times0.1} = 1.04$$

Consider next an American call futures option with price C and an American put with price P. Both have the same strike price, X, and time to maturity, T. The no-arbitrage relationship between C and P is

$$Fe^{-rT} - X < C - P < F - Xe^{-rT} \tag{13.2}$$

To prove this we can consider:

Portfolio C: One European call futures option plus an amount of cash equal to X

Portfolio D: An American put option plus a long futures contract plus an amount of cash equal to Fe^{-rT}

Portfolio E: An American call plus an amount Xe^{-rT} invested at the risk-free rate

Portfolio F: A European put plus an amount of cash F plus a long position in a futures contract

Regardless of the decision made on the early exercise of the American option in portfolio D, portfolio D is always worth less than portfolio C at the time of the exercise of the American option. Hence, portfolio D is worth less than portfolio C today and

$$P + Fe^{-rT} < c + X$$

Since a European call is always worth less than its American counterpart,

$$c \leq C$$

so that

$$P + Fe^{-rT} < C + X$$

or

$$Fe^{-rT} - X < C - P$$

This proves half the relationship in Equation (13.2).

Regardless of the decision on early exercise of the American option in portfolio E, portfolio F is always worth more than portfolio E at the time of the exercise of the American option. Portfolio F must, therefore, be worth more than portfolio E today. Hence:

$$C + Xe^{-rT} < p + F$$

Since $p \leq P$,

$$C + Xe^{-rT} < P + F$$

or

$$C - P < F - Xe^{-rT}$$

This proves the second half of the relationship in Equation (13.2).

BOUNDS FOR FUTURES OPTIONS

The put–call parity relationship in Equation (13.1) provides bounds for European call and put options. Since the price of a put, p, must always be greater than zero it follows from Equation (13.1) that

$$c + Xe^{-rT} > Fe^{-rT}$$

or

$$c > (F - X)e^{-rT} \quad \textbf{(13.3)}$$

Similarly, since the price of a call option must be greater than zero, it follows from Equation (13.1) that

$$Xe^{-rT} < Fe^{-rT} + p$$

or

$$p > (X - F)e^{-rT} \quad \textbf{(13.4)}$$

These are similar to the bounds derived for European stock options in Chapter 8. The prices of European call and put options are very close to their lower bounds when the options are deep in the money. To see why this is so we return to the put–call parity relationship in Equation (13.1). Consider a call option. When this is deep in the money, the corresponding put option is deep out of the money. This means that p is very close to zero. Since the difference between c and its lower bound equals p, the price of the call option must be very close to its lower bound. A similar argument applies to put options.

Since American futures options can be exercised at any time, we must have

$$C > F - X$$

and

$$P > X - F$$

This shows that if interest rates are positive, the lower bound for an American option price is always higher than the lower bound for a European option. This is consistent with the fact that there is always some chance that an American futures option will be exercised early.

VALUATION OF FUTURES OPTIONS USING BINOMIAL TREES

In this section we use a binomial tree approach, similar to that developed in Chapter 10 to price futures options. We will find that the key difference between the argument presented here and the argument in Chapter 10 is that there are no up-front costs when a futures contract is entered into.

Suppose the current futures price is 30 and that it is considered that it will either move up to 33 or down to 28 over the next month. Consider a one-month call option on the futures with a strike price of 29. The situation is as indicated in Figure 13.1. If the futures price proves to be 33, the payoff from the option is 4 and the value of the futures contract is 3. If the futures price proves to be 28, the payoff from the option is 0 and the value of the futures contract is -2.

To set up a riskless hedge, we consider a portfolio consisting of a short position in one options contract and a long position in Δ futures contracts. If the futures price moves up to 33, the value of the portfolio is $3\Delta - 4$; if it moves down to 28, the value of the portfolio is -2Δ. The portfolio is riskless when these are the same; that is, when

$$3\Delta - 4 = -2\Delta$$

or $\Delta = 0.8$.

For this value of Δ, we know that the portfolio will be worth

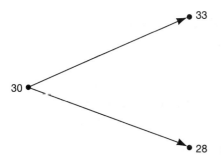

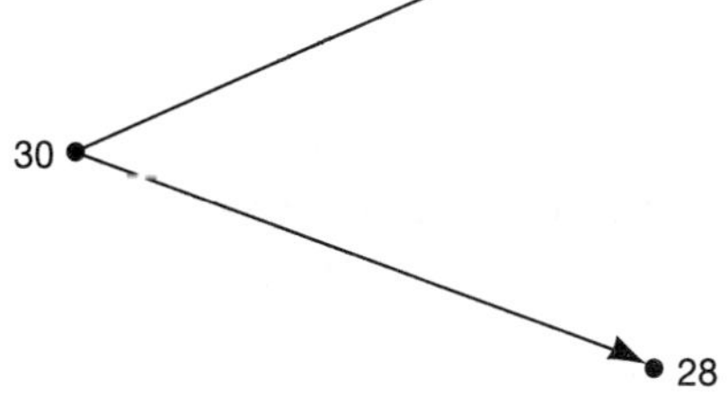

Figure 13.1 Futures price movements in numerical example.

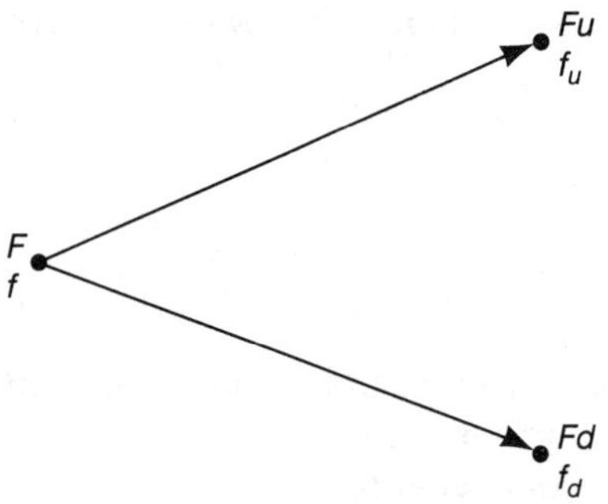

Figure 13.2 Futures price and option price in general situation.

$3 \times 0.8 - 4 = -1.6$ in one month. Assume a risk-free interest rate of 6 percent. The value of the portfolio today must be

$$-1.6e^{-0.06\times 0.08333} = -1.592$$

The portfolio consists of one short option and Δ futures contracts. Since the value of the futures contract today is zero, the value of the option today must be 1.592.

A Generalization

We can generalize this analysis by considering a futures price that starts at F and is anticipated to rise to Fu or move down to Fd over the time period T. We consider an option maturing at time T and suppose that its payoff is f_u if the futures price moves up and f_d if it moves down. The situation is summarized in Figure 13.2.

The riskless portfolio in this case consists of a short position in one option combined with a long position in Δ futures contracts where

$$\Delta = \frac{f_u - f_d}{Fu - Fd}$$

The value of the portfolio at time T is then always

$$(Fu - F)\Delta - f_u$$

Denoting the risk-free interest rate by r, the value of the portfolio today must be

$$[(Fu - F)\Delta - f_u]e^{-rT}$$

Another expression for the present value of the portfolio is $-f$ where f is the value of the option today. It follows that

$$-f = [(Fu - F)\Delta - f_u]e^{-rT}$$

Substituting for Δ and simplifying this equation reduces to

$$f = e^{-rT}[pf_u + (1 - p)f_d] \tag{13.5}$$

where

$$p = \frac{1 - d}{u - d} \tag{13.6}$$

In the numerical example considered previously (see Figure 13.1), $u = 1.1$, $d = 0.9333$, $r = 0.06$, $T = 0.08333$, $f_u = 4$, and $f_d = 0$. From Equation (13.6),

$$p = \frac{1 - 0.9333}{1.1 - 0.93333} = 0.4$$

and from Equation (13.5),

$$f = e^{-0.06 \times 0.08333}[0.4 \times 4 + 0.6 \times 0] = 1.592$$

This agrees with the answer obtained for this example earlier in this section.

A FUTURES PRICE AS A STOCK PAYING A CONTINUOUS DIVIDEND YIELD

There is a general result that makes the analysis of futures options analogous to the analysis of options on a stock paying a continuous dividend yield. This result is that futures prices behave in the same way as a stock paying a continuous dividend yield at the domestic risk-free rate r.

One clue that this might be so is given by comparing Equations (13.5) and (13.6) with (12.6) and (12.7). The two sets of equations are identical when we set $q = r$. Another clue is that the lower bounds for futures options prices and the put–call parity relationship for futures options prices are the same as those for options on a stock paying a continuous dividend yield at rate q when we replace the stock price by the futures price and set $q = r$.

We can understand the result by noting that a futures contract requires zero investment. In a risk-neutral world the expected profit from holding a position in an investment that costs zero to set up must be zero. The expected payoff from a futures contract in a risk-neutral world must, therefore, be zero. Another way of putting this is to say that the expected growth rate of the futures price in a risk-neutral world must be zero. As pointed out in Chapter 12, a stock paying a dividend at rate q grows at an expected rate $r - q$ in a risk-neutral world. If we put $q = r$, the expected growth rate of the stock price is zero, making it analogous to a futures price.

BLACK'S MODEL FOR VALUING FUTURES OPTIONS

In a paper published in 1976 Fischer Black extended the Black–Scholes model to cover European options on futures contracts. He assumed that the futures price has the same lognormal property that we assumed for stock prices in Chapter 11. He showed that the European call price, c, and the European put price, p, for a futures option are given by Equations (12.4) and (12.5) with S replaced by F and $q = r$:

$$c = e^{-rT}[FN(d_1) - XN(d_2)] \qquad \textbf{(13.7)}$$

$$p = e^{-rT}[XN(-d_2) - FN(-d_1)] \qquad \textbf{(13.8)}$$

where

$$d_1 = \frac{\ln(F/X) + \sigma^2 T/2}{\sigma\sqrt{T}}$$

$$d_2 = \frac{\ln(F/X) - \sigma^2 T/2}{\sigma\sqrt{T}} = d_1 - \sigma\sqrt{T}$$

and σ is the volatility of the futures price. In situations where the cost of carry and the convenience yield are functions only of time, it can be shown that the volatility of the futures price is the same as the volatility of the underlying asset. Note that Black's formula does not require the options contract and the futures contract to mature at the same time.

Example

Consider a European put futures option on crude oil. Suppose that the time to maturity is four months, the current futures price is \$20, the exercise price is \$20, the risk-free interest rate is 9 percent per annum, and the volatility of the futures price is 25 percent per annum. In this case, $F = 20$, $X = 20$, $r = 0.09$, $T = 0.333$, and $\sigma = 0.25$, $\ln(F/X) = 0$, so that

$$d_1 = \frac{\sigma\sqrt{T}}{2} = 0.07216$$

$$d_2 = -\frac{\sigma\sqrt{T}}{2} = -0.07216$$

$$N(-d_1) = 0.4712, \qquad N(-d_2) = 0.5288$$

and the put price p is given by

$$p = e^{-0.09\times 0.3333}(20 \times 0.5288 - 20 \times 0.4712) = 1.12$$

or \$1.12.

COMPARISON OF FUTURES OPTION AND SPOT OPTION PRICES

The payoffs from a European spot call option with strike price X is

$$\max(S_T - X, 0)$$

where S_T is the spot price at the option's maturity. The payoff from a European futures call option with the same strike price is

$$\max(F_T - X, 0)$$

where F_T is the futures price at the option's maturity. If the European futures option matures at the same time as the futures contract, $F_T = S_T$ and the two options are in theory equivalent. If the European call futures option matures before the futures contract, it is worth more than the corresponding spot option in a normal market (where futures prices are higher than the spot prices) and less than the corresponding spot option in an inverted market (where futures prices are lower than spot prices).[2]

Similarly, a European futures put option is worth the same as its spot option counterpart when the futures option matures at the same time as the futures contract. If the European put futures option matures before the futures contract, it is worth less than the corresponding spot option in a normal market and more than the corresponding spot option in an inverted market.

Results for American Options

Traded futures options are in practice usually American. Assuming that the risk-free rate of interest, r, is positive, there is always some chance that it will be optimal to exercise an American futures option early. American futures options are, therefore, worth more than their European counterparts. We will discuss numerical procedures for valuing American futures options in Chapter 15.

It is not generally true that an American futures option is worth the same as the corresponding American option on the underlying asset when the futures and options contracts have the same maturity. Suppose, for example, that there is a normal market with futures prices consistently higher than spot prices prior to maturity. This is the case with most indices, gold, silver, low-interest currencies, and some commodities. An American call futures option must be worth more than the corresponding American call option on the underlying asset. This is because there are some situations when it will be exercised early, and in these situations, it will provide a greater profit to the holder. Similarly, an American put futures option must be worth less than the corresponding American put option on the underlying asset. If there is an inverted market with futures prices consis-

[2] The spot option "corresponding" to a futures option is defined here as one with the same strike price and the same expiration date.

tently lower than spot prices, as is the case with high-interest currencies and some commodities, the reverse must be true. American call futures options are worth less than the corresponding American call option on the underlying asset, while American put futures options are worth more than the corresponding American put option on the underlying asset.

The differences between American futures options and American asset options that have just been outlined are true when the futures contract expires later than the options contract as well as when the two expire at the same time. In fact, the differences tend to be greater, the later the futures contract expires.

SUMMARY

Futures options require the delivery of the underlying futures contract upon exercise. When a call is exercised, the holder acquires a long futures position plus a cash amount equal to the excess of the futures price over the strike price. Similarly, when a put is exercised the holder acquires a short position plus a cash amount equal to the excess of the strike price over the futures price. The futures contract that is delivered typically expires slightly later than the option.

A futures price behaves in the same way as a stock that provides a continuous dividend yield equal to the risk-free rate r. This means the results produced in Chapter 12 for options on stock paying a continuous dividend yield provide results for futures options when the stock price is replaced by the futures price and the dividend yield is set equal to the risk-free interest rate.

Pricing formulas for European futures options were first produced by Fischer Black in 1976. They assume that the futures price has a constant volatility so that futures prices are lognormally distributed at the expiration of the option.

If we assume that the two expiration dates are the same, a European futures option is worth exactly the same as the corresponding European option on the underlying asset. However, this is not true of American options. If the futures market is normal, an American call futures is worth more than the American call on the underlying asset, while an American put futures is worth less than the American put on the underlying asset. If the futures market is inverted, the reverse is true.

Suggestions for Further Reading

Black, F., "The pricing of commodity contracts," *Journal of Financial Economics*, 3 (1976), 167–179.

Brenner, M., G. Courtadon, and M. Subrahmanyam, "Options on spot and options on futures," *Journal of Finance*, 40 (December 1985), 1303–1317.

Ramaswamy, K., and S. M. Sundaresan, "The valuation of options on futures contracts," *Journal of Finance*, 40 (December 1985), 1319–1340.

Wolf, A., "Fundamentals of commodity options on futures," *Journal of Futures Markets*, 2 (1982), 391–408.

Quiz

1. Explain the difference between a call option on yen and a call option on yen futures.

2. Why are options on bond futures more actively traded than options on bonds?
3. "A futures price is like a stock paying a continuous dividend yield." What is the continuous dividend yield?
4. A futures price is currently 50. At the end of six months it will be either 56 or 46. The risk-free interest rate is 6 percent per annum. What is the value of a six-month European call option with a strike price of 50?
5. How does the put–call parity formula for a futures option differ from put–call parity for an option on a nondividend-paying stock?
6. Consider an American futures call option where the futures contract and the option contract expire at the same time. Under what circumstances is the futures option worth more than the corresponding American option on the underlying asset?
7. Calculate the value of a five-month European put futures option when the futures price is \$19, the strike price is \$20, the risk-free interest rate is 12 percent per annum, and the volatility of the futures price is 20 percent per annum.

Questions and Problems

13.1. Suppose you buy a put option contract on October gold futures with a strike price of \$400 per ounce. Each contract is for the delivery of 100 ounces. What happens if you exercise when the October futures price is \$380?

13.2. Suppose you sell a call option contract on April live cattle futures with a strike price of 70 cents per pound. Each contract is for the delivery of 40,000 pounds. What happens if the contract is exercised when the futures price is 75 cents?

13.3. Consider a two-month call futures option with a strike price of 40 when the risk-free interest rate is 10 percent per annum. The current futures price is 47. What is a lower bound for the value of the futures option if it is (a) European and (b) American?

13.4. Consider a four-month put futures option with a strike price of 50 when the risk-free interest rate is 10 percent per annum. The current futures price is 47. What is a lower bound for the value of the futures option if it is (a) European and (b) American?

13.5. A futures price is currently 40. It is known that at the end of three months the price will be either 35 or 45. What is the value of a three-month European call option on the futures with a strike price of 42 if the risk-free interest rate is 7 percent per annum?

13.6. A futures price is currently 60. It is known that over each of the next two three-month periods it will either rise by 10 percent or fall by 10 percent. The risk-free interest rate is 8 percent per annum. What is the value of a six-month European call option on the futures with a strike price of 60? If the call were American, would it ever be worth exercising it early?

13.7. In Problem 13.6 what is the value of a six-month European put option on futures with a strike price of 60? If the put were American, would it ever be worth exercising it early? Verify that the call prices calculated in Problem 13.6 and the put prices calculated here satisfy put–call parity relationships.

13.8. A futures price is currently 25, its volatility is 30 percent per annum, and the risk-free interest rate is 10 percent per annum. What is the value of a nine-month European call on the futures with a strike price of 26?

13.9. A futures price is currently 70, its volatility is 20 percent per annum, and the risk-free interest rate is 6 percent per annum. What is the value of a five-month European put on the futures with a strike price of 65?

13.10. Calculate the implied volatility of soybean futures prices from the following information concerning a European put on soybean futures:

Current futures price	525
Exercise price	525
Risk-free rate	6 percent per annum
Time to maturity	5 months
Put price	20

13.11. Suppose that a futures price is currently 35. A European call option and a European put option on the futures with a strike price of 34 are both priced at 2 in the market. The risk-free interest rate is 10 percent per annum. Identify an arbitrage opportunity.

13.12. "The price of an at-the-money European call futures option always equals the price of a similar at-the-money European put futures option." Explain why this statement is true.

13.13. Suppose that a futures price is currently 30. The risk-free interest rate is 5 percent per annum. A three-month American call futures option with a strike price of 28 is worth 4. Calculate bounds for the price of a three-month American put futures option with a strike price of 28.

14

HEDGING POSITIONS IN OPTIONS AND THE CREATION OF OPTIONS SYNTHETICALLY

A financial institution frequently offers products that involve options to its clients. If the options happen to be the same as securities that are traded on an exchange, the financial institution can buy on the exchange the same options as it has sold to its clients. This neutralizes its exposure. However, when the options have been tailored to the needs of clients and do not correspond to the standardized securities traded by exchanges, the financial institution may find the problem of hedging its exposure far more difficult. In this chapter we discuss some of the alternative approaches to this problem. The analysis presented is applicable to market makers in options on an exchange as well as to financial institutions.

An option is tricky to hedge. One reason for this is that the sensitivity of an option to the price of the underlying asset changes as time passes and market conditions change. This means that the appropriate position for a hedger to take in the underlying asset also changes. Another reason is that the value of an option is also sensitive to volatility changes. This second dimension of the option's risk cannot be hedged using the underlying asset at all.

A problem closely related to that of hedging option positions is that of creating options synthetically. Portfolio managers are sometimes interested in creating a put option on a portfolio synthetically in order to ensure that the value of the portfolio does not fall below a certain level. The last part of this chapter discusses how this can be done—and the reasons why it does not always work well!

OPTIONS OFFERED BY FINANCIAL INSTITUTIONS

We start by briefly reviewing some of the products involving options that are offered by financial institutions. These can be categorized as:

1. Currency options
2. Interest-rate options
3. Equity options

Currency Options

Many financial institutions are prepared to offer their corporate clients foreign currency options as an alternative to forward contracts for hedging foreign exchange risk. Whereas a forward contract guarantees the exchange rate that will apply to a particular transaction in the future, a currency option insures that the exchange rate will not be worse than some level (the strike price).

When a forward contract is sold, the position can be hedged relatively simply. For example, if a financial institution agrees to sell £150,000 at the forward rate in 63 days, it can hedge by buying in the spot market an amount of sterling which, when invested at the sterling risk-free rate of interest, will grow to £150,000 in 63 days. Options, as we shall see, are more difficult to hedge than forward contracts. This is because when a financial institution buys or sells an option, it is uncertain whether the option will be exercised.

Interest-Rate Options

Examples of situations where a financial institution is explicitly or implicitly offering a product involving an interest-rate option are as follows:

1. A financial institution guarantees the interest rate on a five-year mortgage at 10 percent per annum for three months.
2. A financial institution agrees to cap a floating rate loan at 10 percent per annum for five years.
3. A financial institution offers prepayment privileges on a fixed-rate loan.
4. A financial institution offers early redemption privileges on a fixed-rate deposit.

In situation 1 the financial institution has provided its client with an option on the five-year mortgage interest rate in three months. The client will choose to exercise the option only if the actual five-year mortgage rate in three months is greater than 10 percent per annum. Otherwise, the client will insist on the actual rate being used. In situation 2, the financial institution has provided its client with a portfolio of European options on interest rate. When the floating rate on an interest payment date is above 10 percent, one of the options will be exercised. In situation 3, we can consider the loan as a bond purchased by the financial institution. The prepayment privilege gives the borrower the right to buy back the bond for its face value at any time in the future. The financial institution has, therefore, sold an American call option on the bond to the borrower. In situation 4, we can consider the deposit as a bond sold by the financial institution to the depositor. The early redemption privilege gives the depositor the right to sell the bond back to the financial institution at any time in the future for its face value. The financial institution has, therefore, sold an American put option to the depositor.

Equity Options

One example of a product involving an equity option is an underwriting contract. In an underwriting contract a financial institution guarantees the price at which a new issue of stock will be sold at some time in the future. If, before the financial institution has had a chance to sell the new shares, the stock price declines to below the guaranteed level, the financial institution has to make up the difference. This arrangement is equivalent to the financial institution selling a put option on the company's stock to the company's current owners.

Equity-linked investments also sometimes involve options. For example, some financial institutions offer products that provide investors with:

1. A guarantee that they will not lose any of their principal.
2. A return that is some proportion of the return provided by the market.

These products have options on the market index embedded in them.

AN EXAMPLE

In the next few sections we use as an example the position of a financial institution that has sold for \$300,000 a European call option on 100,000 shares of a nondividend-paying stock. We assume that the stock price is \$49, the strike price is \$50, the risk-free interest rate is 5 percent per annum, the stock price volatility is 20% per annum, the time to maturity is 20 weeks, and the expected return from the stock is 13 percent per annum.[1] With our usual notation, this means that

$$S = 49,\ X = 50,\ r = 0.05,\ \sigma = 0.20,\ T = 0.3846,\ \mu = 0.13$$

Financial institutions do not normally write call options on individual stocks. However, a call option on a stock is a convenient example with which to develop our ideas. The points that will be made apply to other types of options and to other derivative securities.

The Black–Scholes price of the option is about \$240,000. The financial institu-

[1] It was shown in Chapters 10 and 11 that the expected return is irrelevant to the pricing of an option. However, it can have some bearing on the effectiveness of a particular hedging scheme.

tion has, therefore, sold the option for $60,000 more than its theoretical value. However, it is faced with the problem of hedging its exposure.

NAKED AND COVERED POSITIONS

One strategy open to the financial institution is to do nothing. This involves what is known as a *naked position*. If the call is exercised, the financial institution will have to buy 100,000 shares at the current market price to cover the call. The cost to the financial institution will be 100,000 times the amount by which the stock price exceeds the strike price. Thus, if after 20 weeks the stock price is $60, the option costs the financial institution $1,000,000, which is considerably greater than the $300,000 charged. However, if the stock price is below $50 at the end of the 20 weeks, the option costs the financial institution nothing and it makes a profit of $300,000 on the whole deal.

As an alternative to a naked position, the financial institution can adopt a *covered position*. This involves buying 100,000 shares as soon as the option has been sold. If the option is exercised, this strategy works well. However, if the option is not exercised, the covered position could prove to be expensive. For example, if the stock price drops to $40, the financial institution loses $900,000 on its stock position. Again, this is considerably greater than the $300,000 charged for the option.

Neither a naked position nor a covered position provides a satisfactory hedge. If the assumptions underlying the Black–Scholes formula hold, the cost to the financial institution of writing the option should always be $240,000 on average for both approaches.[2] However, on any one occasion the cost is liable to range from zero to over $1,000,000. A perfect hedge would ensure that the cost is always $240,000; that is, the standard deviation of the cost of writing the option and hedging it is zero.

A STOP-LOSS STRATEGY

One interesting hedging scheme that is sometimes proposed involves a *stop-loss strategy*. To illustrate the basic idea, consider an institution that has written a call option with strike price X to buy one unit of a stock. The hedging scheme involves buying the stock as soon as its price rises above X and selling as soon as its price falls below X. The objective is to hold a naked position whenever the stock price is less than X and a covered position whenever the stock price is greater than X. The scheme is designed to ensure that the institution owns the stock at time T if the option closes in the money and does not own it if the option closes out

[2] More precisely, the present value of the expected cost is $240,000 for both approaches assuming that appropriate risk-adjusted discount rates are used. This is because the value of any security must in equilibrium equal the present value of the expected cash flows that the security provides for the holder.

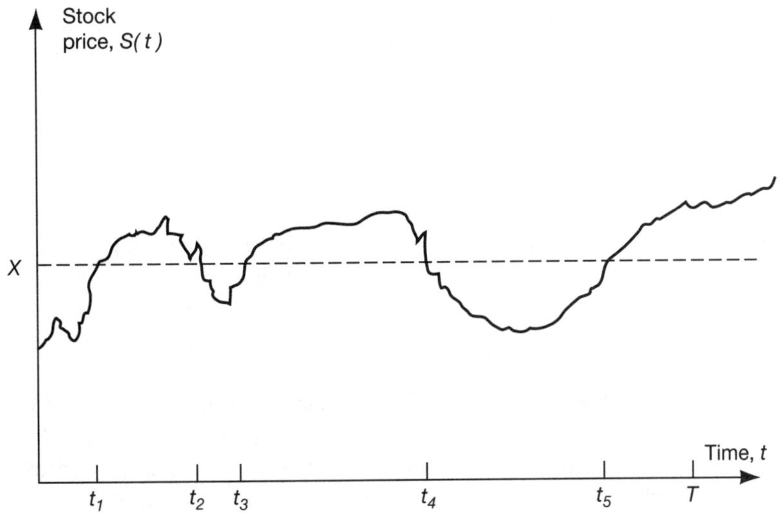

Figure 14.1 A stop-loss strategy.

of the money. It appears to produce payoffs that are the same as the payoffs on the option. In the situation illustrated in Figure 14.1, it involves buying the stock at time t_1, selling it at time t_2, buying it at time t_3, selling it at time t_4, buying it at time t_5, and delivering it at time T.

As usual, we denote the initial stock price by S. The cost of setting up the hedge initially is S if $S > X$ and zero otherwise. At first blush, the total cost, Q, of writing and hedging the option would appear to be given by

$$Q = \max(S - X, 0) \tag{14.1}$$

since all purchases and sales subsequent to time zero are made at price X. If this were in fact correct, the hedging scheme would work perfectly in the absence of transactions costs. Furthermore, the cost of hedging the option would always be less than its Black–Scholes price. Thus, one could earn riskless profits by writing options and hedging them.

There are two basic reasons why Equation (14.1) is incorrect. The first is that the cash flows to the hedger occur at different times and must be discounted. The second is that purchases and sales cannot be made at exactly the same price X. This second point is critical. If we assume a risk-neutral world with zero interest rates, we can justify ignoring the time value of money. However, we cannot legitimately assume that both purchases and sales are made at the same price. If markets are efficient, the hedger cannot know whether, when the stock price equals X, it will continue above or below X.

As a practical matter, purchases will be made at a price $X + \delta$ and sales will be made at a price $X - \delta$, for some small positive number, δ. Thus, every purchase and subsequent sale involves a cost (apart from transactions costs) of

Table 14.1 Performance of Stop-Loss Strategy

Δt (WEEKS)	*5*	*4*	*2*	*1*	*0.5*	*0.25*
Hedge performance	1.02	0.93	0.82	0.77	0.76	0.76

2δ. A natural response to this on the part of the hedger is to monitor price movements more closely so that δ is reduced. Assuming that stock prices change continuously, δ can be made arbitrarily small by monitoring the stock prices closely. However, as δ is made smaller, trades tend to occur more frequently. Thus, while the cost per trade is reduced, this is offset by the increasing frequency of trading. As $\delta \to 0$, the expected number of trades tend to infinity.

A stop-loss strategy, although superficially attractive, does not work particularly well as a hedging scheme. If the stock price never reaches the strike price X, the hedging scheme costs nothing for an out-of-the-money option. However, if the path of the stock price is such that the stock price equals X many times, the scheme is liable to be quite expensive. Monte Carlo simulation can be used to assess the overall performance of the scheme. Table 14.1 shows the results for the option considered earlier. It assumes that the stock price is observed at the end of time intervals of length Δt.[3] The hedge performance measure is the ratio of the standard deviation of the cost of hedging the option to the Black-Scholes price of the option. Each result is based on 1,000 sample paths for the stock price and has a standard error of about 2 percent. It appears to be impossible to produce a value for the hedge performance measure below 0.70 regardless of how small Δt is made.

MORE SOPHISTICATED HEDGING SCHEMES

Most option traders use more sophisticated hedging schemes than those that have been described so far. As a first step they attempt to make their portfolio immune to small changes in the price of the underlying asset in the next small interval of time. This is known as *delta hedging*. They then look at what are known as *gamma* and *vega*. Gamma is the rate of change of the value of the portfolio with respect to delta; vega is the rate of change of the portfolio with respect to the asset's volatility. By zeroing gamma, a portfolio can be made relatively insensitive to fairly large changes in the price of the asset; by zeroing vega, it can be made insensitive to changes in its volatility. Option traders may also look at *theta* and *rho*. Theta is the rate of change of the option portfolio with the passage of time and rho is its rate of change with respect to the risk-free interest rate.

In the next few sections we will discuss these hedge parameters in more detail.

[3] The precise hedging rule used was as follows. If the stock price moves from below X to above X in a time interval of length Δt, it is bought at the end of the interval. If it moves from above X to below X in the time interval, it is sold at the end of the interval. Otherwise, no action is taken.

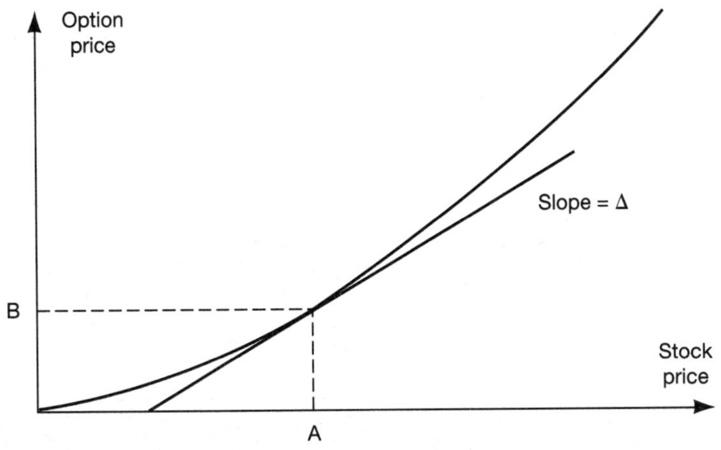

Figure 14.2 Calculation of delta.

DELTA HEDGING

The *delta* of an option, Δ, was first introduced in Chapter 10. It is defined as the rate of change of its price with respect to the price of the underlying asset. It is the slope of the curve that relates the option price to the underlying asset price. Suppose that the delta of a call option on a stock is 0.6. This means that when the stock price changes by a small amount, the option price changes by about 60 percent of that amount. Figure 14.2 shows the relationship between a call price and the underlying stock price. When the stock price corresponds to point A, the option price corresponds to point B, and Δ is the gradient indicated. As an approximation,

$$\Delta = \frac{\Delta c}{\Delta S} \qquad \textbf{(14.2)}$$

where ΔS is a small change in the stock price and Δc is the corresponding change in the call price.

Consider a call option whose delta is 0.6. Suppose that the option price is \$10 and the stock price is \$100. Imagine an investor who has sold 20 option contracts, that is, options to buy 2,000 shares. The investor's position could be hedged by buying $0.6 \times 2{,}000 = 1{,}200$ shares. The gain (loss) on the option position would tend to be offset by the loss (gain) on the stock position. For example, if the stock price goes up by \$1 (producing a gain of \$1,200 on the shares purchased), the option price will tend to go up by $0.6 \times \$1 = \$0.60$ (producing a loss of \$1,200 on the options written); if the stock price goes down by \$1 (producing a loss of \$1,200 on the shares purchased), the option price will tend to go down by \$0.60 (producing a gain of \$1,200 on the options written).

In this example the delta of the investor's option position is $0.6 \times (-2{,}000) = -1{,}200$. In other words the investor loses $1{,}200\Delta S$ when the stock

Table 14.2 Use of Delta Hedging

From the Trader's Desk

An investor has sold 20 option contracts (2,000 options) on a certain stock. The option price is \$10, the stock price is \$100, and the option's delta is 0.6. The investor wishes to hedge the position.

Strategy

The investor immediately buys $0.6 \times 2{,}000 = 1{,}200$ shares. Over the next short period of time, the call price will tend to change by 60 percent of the stock price and the gain (loss) on the call will be offset by the loss (gain) on the stock. As time passes, delta will change and the position in the stock will have to be adjusted. For example, if after three days the delta increases to 0.65, a further $0.05 \times 2{,}000 = 100$ shares will have to be bought.

price increases by ΔS. The delta of the stock is by definition 1.0 and the long position in 1,200 shares has a delta of $+1{,}200$. The delta of the investor's overall position is, therefore, zero. The delta of the asset position offsets the delta of the option position. A position with a delta of zero is referred to as being *delta neutral.*

It is important to realize that the investor's position only remains delta hedged (or delta neutral) for a relatively short period of time. This is because delta changes. (We showed that this is so in the case of a two-step binomial model in Chapter 10.) In practice when delta hedging is implemented, the hedge has to be adjusted periodically. This is known as *rebalancing*. In our example, at the end of three days the stock price might increase to \$110. As indicated by Figure 14.2, an increase in the stock price leads to an increase in delta. Suppose that delta rises from 0.60 to 0.65. This would mean that an extra $0.05 \times 2{,}000 = 100$ shares would have to be purchased to maintain the hedge. This example is summarized in Table 14.2. Hedging schemes such as this that involve frequent adjustments are known as *dynamic hedging schemes.*

Delta is closely related to the Black–Scholes analysis. As we explained in Chapter 11, Black and Scholes showed that it is possible to set up a riskless portfolio consisting of a position in an option on a stock and a position in the stock. Expressed in terms of Δ, the Black and Scholes portfolio is

-1: option
$+\Delta$: shares of the stock

Using our new terminology, we can say that Black and Scholes valued options by setting up a delta-neutral position and arguing that the return on the position should be the risk-free interest rate.

Forward Contracts

The concept of delta can be applied to other derivative securities besides options. It is instructive to consider forward contracts on nondividend-paying stocks.

Equation (3.9) shows that when the price of a nondividend-paying stock changes by ΔS, with all else remaining the same, the value of a forward contract on the stock also changes by ΔS. The delta of a forward contract on one share of a nondividend-paying stock is, therefore, always 1.0. This means that a short forward contract on one share can be hedged by purchasing one share, while a long forward contract on one share can be hedged by shorting one share. Unlike hedging schemes involving options, these are "hedge and forget" schemes in the sense that no changes need to be made to the position in the stock during the life of the contract. This is because delta remains constant. Rebalancing of the hedge is unnecessary.

Delta of European Calls and Puts

For a European call option on a nondividend-paying stock, it can be shown that

$$\Delta = N(d_1)$$

where d_1 is defined in Equation (11.5). Using delta hedging for a short position in a European call option, therefore, involves keeping a long position of $N(d_1)$ shares at any given time. Similarly, using delta hedging for a long position in a European call option involves maintaining a short position of $N(d_1)$ shares at any given time.

For a European put option on a nondividend-paying stock, delta is given by

$$\Delta = N(d_1) - 1$$

where d_1 is defined as in Equation (11.5). This is negative, which means that a long position in a put option should be hedged with a long position in the underlying stock, and a short position in a put option should be hedged with a short position in the underlying stock. The variation of the delta of a call option and a put option with the stock price is shown in Figure 14.3. Figure 14.4 shows the variation of delta with the time to maturity for an at-the-money, in-the-money, and out-of-the-money call option.

Simulations

Tables 14.3 and 14.4 provide two simulations of the operation of delta hedging for the example considered earlier where a financial institution sells an option worth $240,000. The hedge is assumed to be adjusted or rebalanced weekly. In Table 14.3 delta is initially calculated as 0.522. This means that as soon as the option is written, $2,557,800 must be borrowed to buy 52,200 shares at a price of $49. An interest cost of $2,500 is incurred in the first week. The stock price falls

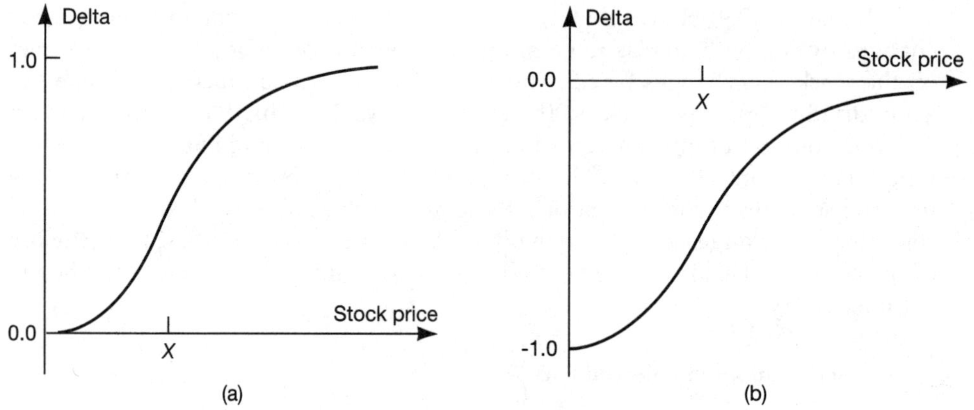

Figure 14.3 Variation of delta with the stock price for (a) a call option and (b) a put option on a nondividend-paying stock.

by the end of the first week to \$48⅛. This reduces the delta to 0.458, and 6,400 of shares are sold to maintain the hedge. This realizes \$308,000 in cash and the cumulative borrowings at the end of week 1 are reduced to \$2,252,300. On the second week the stock price reduces to \$47⅜ and delta declines again, and so on. Toward the end of the life of the option, it becomes apparent that the option will be exercised and delta approaches 1.0. By week 20, therefore, the hedger has a fully covered position. The hedger receives \$5,000,000 for the stock held, so that the total cost of writing the option and hedging it is \$263,400.

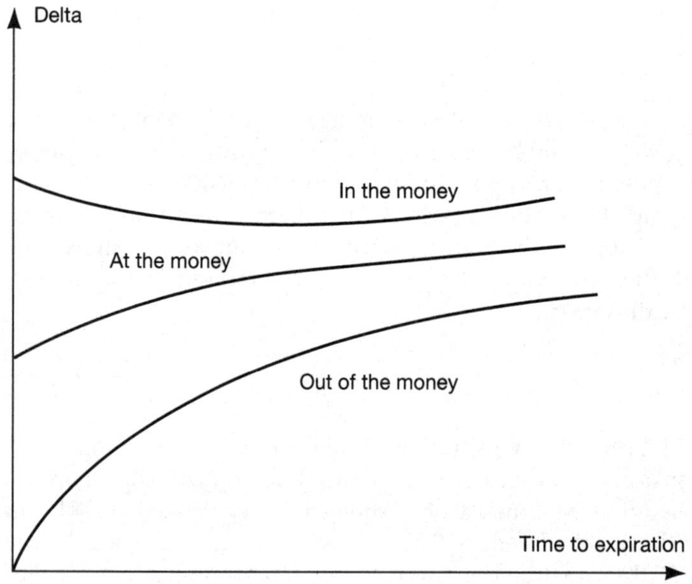

Figure 14.4 Variation of delta with time to maturity for a call option.

Table 14.3 Simulation of Delta Hedging. Option Closes in the Money. Cost of Hedging = $263,400.

WEEK	*STOCK PRICE*	*DELTA*	*SHARES PURCHASED*	*COST OF SHARES PURCHASED (THOUSANDS OF DOLLARS)*	*CUMULATIVE COST (INCLUDING INTEREST IN THOUSANDS OF DOLLARS)*	*INTEREST COST (THOUSANDS OF DOLLARS)*
0	49	0.522	52,200	2,557.8	2,557.8	2.5
1	48⅛	0.458	(6,400)	(308.0)	2,252.3	2.2
2	47⅜	0.400	(5,800)	(274.8)	1,979.7	1.9
3	50¼	0.595	19,600	984.9	2,996.5	2.9
4	51¾	0.693	9,700	502.0	3,471.3	3.3
5	53⅛	0.774	8,100	430.3	3,904.9	3.8
6	53	0.771	(300)	(15.9)	3,892.8	3.7
7	51⅞	0.706	(6,500)	(337.2)	3,559.3	3.4
8	51⅜	0.674	(3,200)	(164.4)	3,398.4	3.3
9	53	0.787	11,300	598.9	4,000.5	3.8
10	49⅞	0.550	(23,700)	(1,182.0)	2,822.3	2.7
11	48½	0.413	(13,700)	(664.4)	2,160.6	2.1
12	49⅞	0.542	12,900	643.4	2,806.1	2.7
13	50⅜	0.591	4,900	246.8	3,055.6	2.9
14	52⅛	0.768	17,700	922.6	3,981.2	3.8
15	51⅞	0.759	(900)	(46.7)	3,938.3	3.8
16	52⅞	0.865	10,600	560.5	4,502.6	4.3
17	54⅞	0.978	11,300	620.1	5,127.0	4.9
18	54⅝	0.990	1,200	65.6	5,197.5	5.0
19	55⅞	1.000	1,000	55.9	5,258.3	5.1
20	57¼	1.000	0	0.0	5,263.4	

Table 14.4 illustrates an alternative sequence of events which are such that the option closes out of the money. As it becomes progressively clearer that the option will not be exercised, delta approaches zero. By week 20 the hedger has a naked position and has incurred costs totaling $256,600.

In Tables 14.3 and 14.4 the costs of hedging the option, when discounted to the beginning of the period, are close to but not exactly the same as the Black–Scholes price of $240,000. If the hedging scheme worked perfectly, the cost of hedging would, after discounting, be exactly $240,000 on every simulation. The reason that there is a variation in the cost of delta hedging is that the hedge is rebalanced only once a week. As rebalancing takes place more frequently, the variation in the cost of hedging is reduced.

Table 14.5 shows statistics on the performance of delta hedging from 1,000 simulations of stock price movements for our example. As in Table 14.1, the performance measure is the ratio of the standard deviation of the cost of hedging the option to the Black–Scholes price of the option. It is clear that delta hedging is a great improvement over a stop-loss strategy. Unlike a stop-loss strategy, a delta

Table 14.4 Simulation of Delta Hedging. Option Closes Out of the Money. Cost of Hedging = $256,600.

WEEK	STOCK PRICE	DELTA	SHARES PURCHASED	COST OF SHARES PURCHASED (THOUSANDS OF DOLLARS)	CUMULATIVE COST (INCLUDING INTEREST IN THOUSANDS OF DOLLARS)	INTEREST COST (THOUSANDS OF DOLLARS)
0	49	0.522	52,200	2,557.8	2,557.8	2.5
1	$49\frac{3}{4}$	0.568	4,600	228.9	2,789.1	2.7
2	52	0.705	13,700	712.4	3,504.2	3.4
3	50	0.579	(12,600)	(630.0)	2,877.6	2.8
4	$48\frac{3}{8}$	0.459	(12,000)	(580.5)	2,299.8	2.2
5	$48\frac{1}{2}$	0.443	(1,600)	(77.2)	2,224.8	2.1
6	$48\frac{3}{4}$	0.475	3,200	156.0	2,383.0	2.3
7	$49\frac{5}{8}$	0.540	6,500	322.6	2,707.8	2.6
8	$48\frac{1}{4}$	0.420	(12,000)	(579.0)	2,131.4	2.0
9	$48\frac{1}{4}$	0.410	(1,000)	(48.2)	2,085.2	2.0
10	$51\frac{1}{8}$	0.658	24,800	1,267.9	3,355.1	3.2
11	$51\frac{1}{2}$	0.692	3,400	175.1	3,533.5	3.4
12	$49\frac{7}{8}$	0.542	(15,000)	(748.1)	2,788.7	2.7
13	$49\frac{7}{8}$	0.538	(400)	(20.0)	2,771.5	2.7
14	$48\frac{3}{4}$	0.400	(13,800)	(672.7)	2,101.4	2.0
15	$47\frac{1}{2}$	0.236	(16,400)	(779.0)	1,324.4	1.3
16	48	0.261	2,500	120.0	1,445.7	1.4
17	$46\frac{1}{4}$	0.062	(19,900)	(920.4)	526.7	0.5
18	$48\frac{1}{8}$	0.183	12,100	582.3	1,109.5	1.1
19	$46\frac{5}{8}$	0.007	(17,600)	(820.6)	290.0	0.3
20	$48\frac{1}{8}$	0.000	(700)	(33.7)	256.6	

hedging strategy has a performance that gets steadily better as the hedge is monitored more frequently.

Delta hedging aims to keep the total wealth of the financial institution as close to unchanged as possible. Initially, the value of the written option is $240,000. In the situation depicted in Table 14.3, the value of the option can be calculated as $414,500 on week 9. Thus, the financial institution has lost $174,500 on its option position. Its cash position, as measured by the cumulative cost, is $1,442,700 worse in week 9 than in week 0. However, the value of the shares held has increased from $2,557,800 to $4,171,100. The net effect of all this is that the overall wealth of the financial institution has changed by only $3,900.

Table 14.5 Performance of Delta Hedging

TIME BETWEEN HEDGE REBALANCING (WEEKS)	5	4	2	1	0.5	0.25
Performance Measure	0.43	0.39	0.26	0.19	0.14	0.09

Where the Cost Comes From

The delta hedging scheme in Tables 14.3 and 14.4 in effect creates a long position in the option synthetically. This neutralizes the short position arising from the option that has been written. The scheme generally involves selling stock just after the price has gone down and buying stock just after the price has gone up. It might be termed a buy high, sell low scheme! The cost of $240,000 comes from the average difference between the price paid for the stock and the price realized for it. Of course, the simulations in Tables 14.3 and 14.4 are idealized in that they assume that the volatility is constant, and that there are no transactions costs.

Delta of Other European Options

For European call options on a stock index paying a dividend yield, q,

$$\Delta = e^{-qT}N(d_1)$$

where d_1 is defined in Equation (12.4). For European put options on the stock index,

$$\Delta = e^{-qT}[N(d_1) - 1]$$

For European call options on a currency,

$$\Delta = e^{-r_fT}N(d_1)$$

where r_f is the foreign risk-free interest rate and d_1 is defined as in Equation (12.9). For European put options on a currency,

$$\Delta = e^{-r_fT}[N(d_1) - 1]$$

For European call futures options,

$$\Delta = e^{-rT}N(d_1)$$

where d_1 is defined as in Equation (13.7) and for European put futures options,

$$\Delta = e^{-rT}[N(d_1) - 1]$$

Example

A bank has written a six-month European option to sell £1,000,000 at an exchange rate of 1.6000. Suppose that the current exchange rate is 1.6200, the risk-free interest rate in the United Kingdom is 13 percent per annum, the risk-free interest rate in the United States is 10 percent per annum, and the volatility of sterling is 15 percent. In this case $S = 1.6200$, $X = 1.6000$, $r = 0.10$, $r_f = 0.13$, $\sigma = 0.15$, and $T = 0.5$. The delta of a put option on a currency is

$$[N(d_1) - 1]e^{-r_f T}$$

where d_1 is given by Equation (12.9). It can be shown that

$$d_1 = 0.0287$$

$$N(d_1) = 0.5115$$

so that the delta of the put option is -0.458. This is the delta of a long position in one put option. (It means that the price of the put goes down by 45.8 percent of the increase in the value of the currency.) The delta of the bank's total short position is $+458{,}000$. Delta hedging, therefore, requires that a short sterling position of £458,000 be set up initially. This short sterling position has a delta of $-458{,}000$ and neutralizes the delta of the option position. As time passes, the short position must be changed.

Using Futures

The delta of the underlying asset is by definition 1.0. In practice, delta hedging is often carried out using a position in a futures contract rather than a position in the underlying asset. The contract that is used does not have to mature at the same time as the option. Define

T^*: maturity of futures contract
H_A: required position in asset at time t for delta hedging
H_F: alternative required position in futures contracts at time t for delta hedging

If the underlying asset is a nondividend-paying stock, the futures price, F, is from Equation (3.5) given by

$$F = Se^{rT^*}$$

When the stock price increases by ΔS, the gain from the futures contract is $e^{rT^*}\Delta S$. Thus, $e^{rT^*}\Delta S$ futures contracts have the same sensitivity to stock price movements as one stock. Hence,

$$H_F = e^{-rT^*}H_A$$

When the underlying asset is a stock or index paying a dividend yield q, a similar argument shows that

$$H_F = e^{-(r-q)T^*}H_A \qquad \textbf{(14.3)}$$

When it is a currency,

$$H_F = e^{-(r-r_f)T^*}H_A$$

Example

Consider again the option in the previous example. Suppose that the bank decides to hedge using nine-month currency futures contracts. In this case $T^* = 0.75$ and

$$e^{-(r-r_f)T^*} = 1.0228$$

so that the short position in currency futures required for delta hedging is $1.0228 \times 458{,}000 = £468{,}442$. Since each futures contract is for the purchase or sale of £62,500, this means that (to the nearest whole number) seven contracts should be shorted.

It is interesting to note that the delta of a futures contract is different from the delta of the corresponding forward. This is true even when interest rates are constant and the forward price equals the futures price. Consider the situation where the underlying asset is a nondividend-paying stock. The delta of a futures contract on one unit of the asset is e^{rT^*}, whereas the delta of a forward contract on one unit of the asset is as discussed earlier, 1.0.

Delta of a Portfolio

When a portfolio of options on an asset are held, the delta of the portfolio is simply the sum of the deltas of the individual options in the portfolio. If a portfolio consists of an amount w_i of option i ($1 \le i \le n$), the delta of the portfolio is given by

$$\Delta = \sum_{i=1}^{n} w_i\Delta_i$$

where Δ_i is the delta of ith option. This can be used to calculate the position in the underlying asset, or in a futures contract on the underlying asset, necessary to carry out delta hedging. When this position has been taken, the delta of the portfolio is zero and the portfolio is referred to as being delta neutral.

Consider a financial institution that has the following three positions in options to buy or sell German marks:

1. A long position in 100,000 call options with strike price 0.55 and expiration date in three months. The delta of each option is 0.533.
2. A short position in 200,000 call options with strike price 0.56 and expiration date in five months. The delta of each option is 0.468.
3. A short position in 50,000 put options with strike price 0.56 and expiration date in two months. The delta of each option is -0.508.

Table 14.6 Making a Portfolio Delta Neutral

From the Trader's Desk

A financial institution has the following three positions in the German mark:

1. A long position in 100,000 call options with strike price 0.55 and expiration date in three months. The option's delta is 0.553.
2. A short position in 200,000 call options with strike price 0.56 and expiration date in five months. The option's delta is 0.468.
3. A short position in 50,000 put options with strike price 0.56 and expiration date in two months. The option's delta is -0.508.

The financial institution would like to make the portfolio delta neutral. The risk-free interest rates in the United States and Germany are 8 percent per annum and 4 percent per annum, respectively.

Calculation of Delta

The delta of the portfolio is

$$0.533 \times 100{,}000 - 0.468 \times 200{,}000 + 0.508 \times 50{,}000 = -14{,}900$$

Strategy 1

Take a long position in 14,900 marks.

Strategy 2

Take a long position in six-month futures contracts on

$$14{,}900e^{-(0.08-0.04)\times 0.5} = 14{,}605 \text{ marks}$$

The delta of the whole portfolio is

$$0.533 \times 100{,}000 - 200{,}000 \times 0.468 - 50{,}000 \times (-0.508) = -14{,}900$$

This means that the portfolio can be made delta neutral with a long position of 14,900 marks.

A six-month futures contract could also be used to achieve delta neutrality in this example. Suppose that the risk-free rate of interest is 8 percent per annum in the United States and 4 percent per annum in Germany. The long position in mark futures for delta neutrality is

$$14{,}900e^{-(0.08-0.04)\times 0.5} = 14{,}605$$

This example is summarized is Table 14.6.

THETA

The *theta* of a portfolio of options, Θ, is the rate of change of the value of the portfolio as time passes (i.e., as T decreases) with all else remaining the same. It is sometimes referred to as the *time decay* of the portfolio. For a European call option on a nondividend-paying stock,

$$\Theta = -\frac{SN'(d_1)\sigma}{2\sqrt{T}} - rXe^{-rT}N(d_2)$$

where d_1 and d_2 are defined as in Equation (11.5) and

$$N'(x) = \frac{1}{\sqrt{2\pi}}e^{-x^2/2} \tag{14.4}$$

For a European put option on the stock,

$$\Theta = -\frac{SN'(d_1)\sigma}{2\sqrt{T}} + rXe^{-rT}N(-d_2)$$

For a European call option on a stock index paying a dividend at rate q,

$$\Theta = -\frac{SN'(d_1)\sigma e^{-qT}}{2\sqrt{T}} + qSN(d_1)e^{-qT} - rXe^{-rT}N(d_2)$$

where d_1 and d_2 are defined as in Equation (12.4). For a European put option on the stock index,

$$\Theta = -\frac{SN'(d_1)\sigma e^{-qT}}{2\sqrt{T}} - qSN(-d_1)e^{-qT} + rXe^{-rT}N(-d_2)$$

With q equal to r_f, these last two equations give thetas for European call and put options on currencies. With q equal to r and S equal to F, they give thetas for European futures options.

Example

Consider a four-month put option on a stock index. The current value of the index is 305, the strike price is 300, the dividend yield is 3 percent per annum, the risk-free interest rate is 8 percent per annum, and the volatility of the index is 25 percent per annum. In this case $S = 305$, $X = 300$, $q = 0.03$, $r = 0.08$, $\sigma = 0.25$, and $T = 0.3333$. The option's theta is

$$-\frac{SN'(d_1)\sigma e^{-qT}}{2\sqrt{T}} - qSN(-d_1)e^{-qT} + rXe^{-rT}N(-d_2) = -18.15$$

This means that, if 0.01 year (or 2.5 trading days) passes with no changes to the value of the index or its volatility, the value of the option declines by 0.1815.

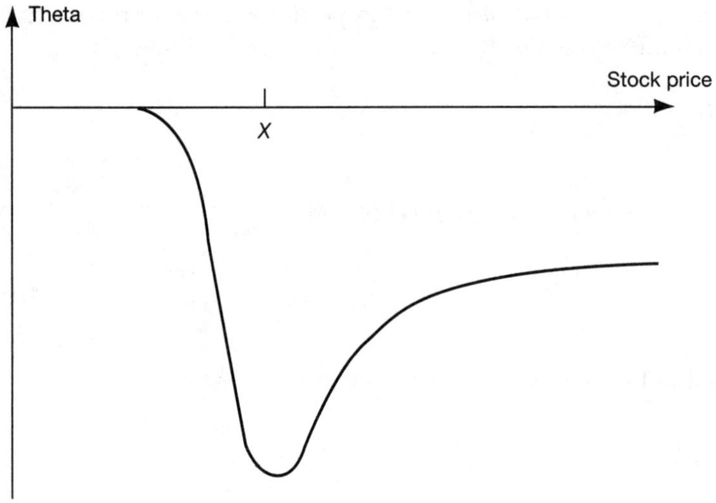

Figure 14.5 Variation of theta of a European call option with stock price.

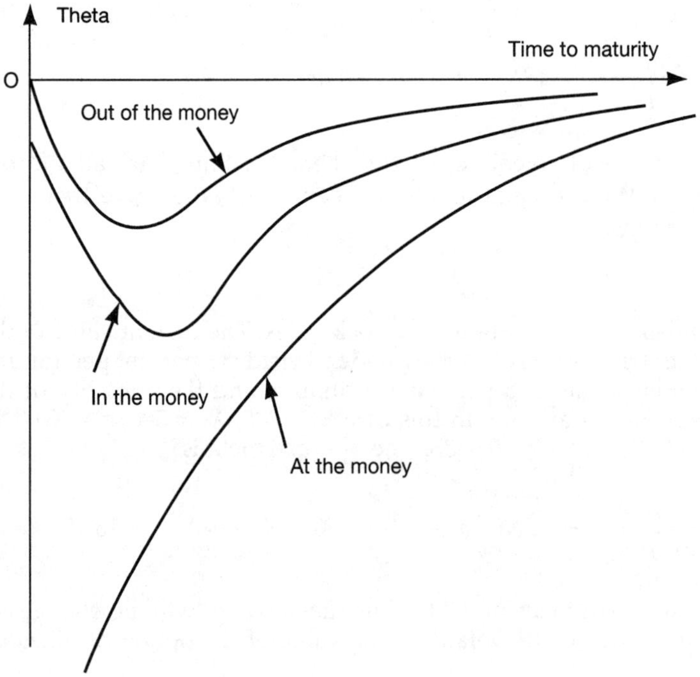

Figure 14.6 Variation of the theta of a European call option with time to maturity.

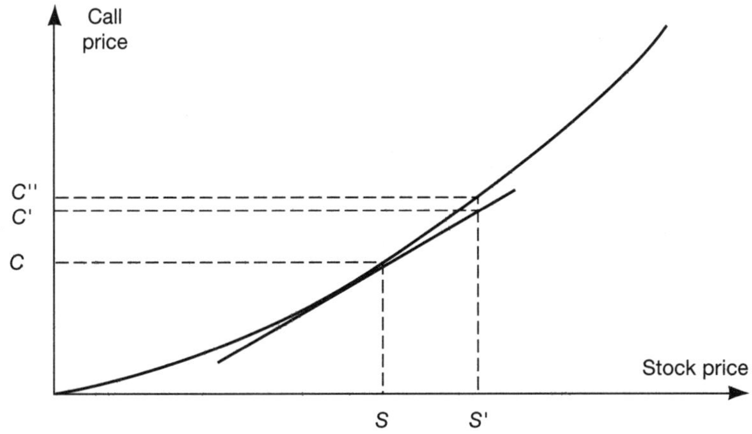

Figure 14.7 Illustration of hedging error introduced by curvature or gamma.

Theta is almost always negative for an option.[4] This is because as the time to maturity decreases, the option tends to become less valuable. The variation of Θ with the stock price for a call option on a stock is shown in Figure 14.5. When the stock price is very low, theta is close to zero. For an at-the-money option, theta is relatively large and negative. As the stock price becomes larger, theta tends to $-Xe^{-rT}$. Figure 14.6 shows the variation of Θ with the time to maturity for an in-the-money, at-the-money, and out-of-the-money option.

GAMMA

The gamma, Γ, of a portfolio of options on an underlying asset is the rate of change of the portfolio's delta with respect to the price of the underlying asset. If gamma is small, delta changes only very slowly, and adjustments to keep a portfolio delta neutral need only be made relatively infrequently. However, if gamma is large in absolute terms, delta is highly sensitive to the price of the underlying asset. It is then quite risky to leave a delta-neutral portfolio unchanged for any length of time. Figure 14.7 illustrates this point. When the stock price moves from S to S', delta hedging assumes that the option price moves from C to C' when in fact it moves from C to C''. The difference between C' and C'' leads to a hedging error. This error depends on the curvature of the relationship between the option price and the stock price. Gamma measures this curvature.[5]

Suppose that ΔS is the change in the price of an underlying asset in a small interval of time, Δt, and $\Delta\Pi$ is the corresponding change in the price of the portfo-

[4] An exception to this could be an in-the-money European put option on a nondividend-paying stock or an in-the-money European call option on a currency with a very high interest rate.

[5] Indeed, the gamma of an option is sometimes referred to as its *curvature* by practitioners.

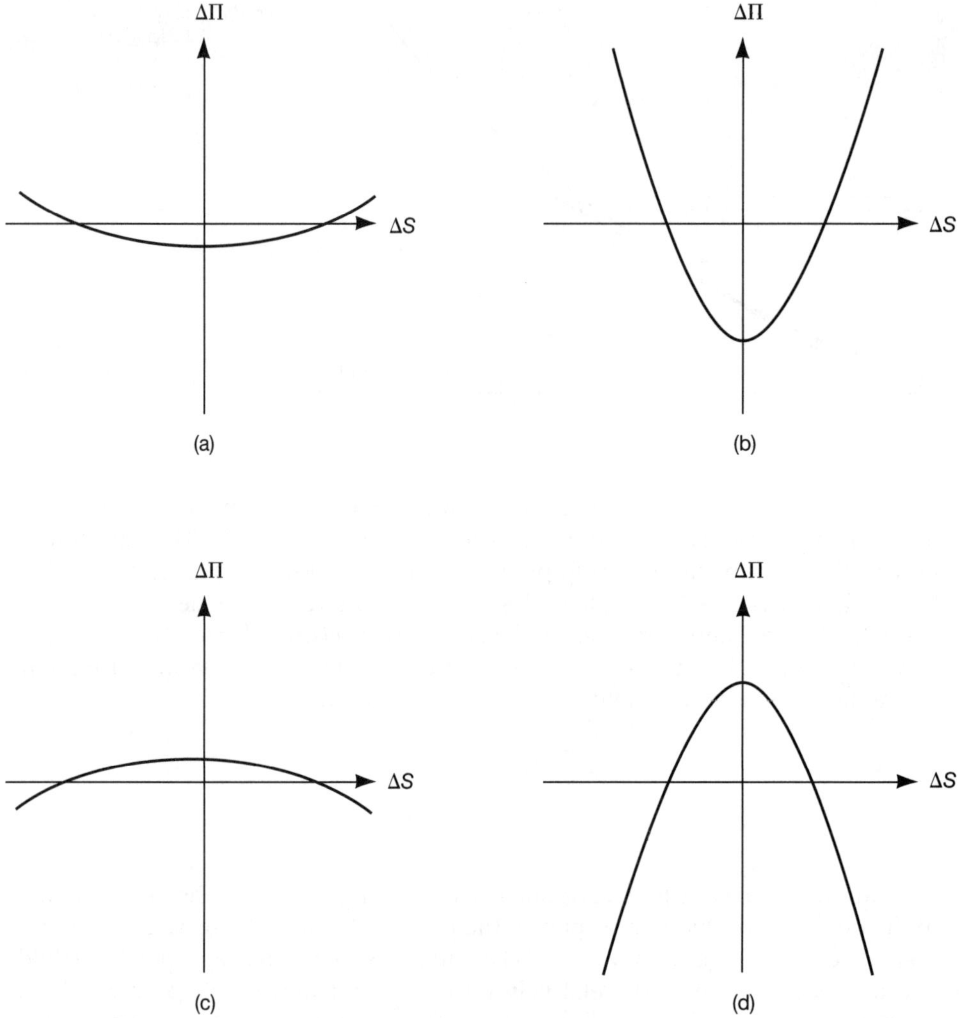

Figure 14.8 Alternative relationships between $\Delta\Pi$ and ΔS for a delta-neutral portfolio: (a) slightly positive gamma, (b) large positive gamma, (c) slightly negative gamma, (d) large negative gamma.

lio. If terms such as Δt^2 are ignored, it can be shown that for a delta-neutral portfolio,

$$\Delta\Pi = \Theta\Delta t + \frac{\Gamma\Delta S^2}{2}$$

where Θ is the theta of the portfolio. Figure 14.8 shows the nature of this relationship between $\Delta\Pi$ and ΔS. It can be seen that when gamma is positive, the portfolio declines in value if there is no change in S, but increases in value if there is a large positive or negative change in S. When gamma is negative the reverse is true; the portfolio increases in value if there is no change in S, but decreases in value if there is a large positive or negative change in S. As the absolute value of gamma increases, the sensitivity of the value of the portfolio to S increases.

Making a Portfolio Gamma Neutral

A position in the underlying asset or in a futures contract on the underlying asset has zero gamma. The only way a financial institution can change the gamma of its portfolio is by taking a position in a traded option. Suppose that a delta-neutral portfolio has gamma equal to Γ and a traded option has a gamma equal to Γ_T. If the number of traded options added to the portfolio is w_T, the gamma of the portfolio is

$$w_T \Gamma_T + \Gamma$$

Hence, the position in the traded option necessary to make the portfolio gamma neutral is $-\Gamma/\Gamma_T$. Of course, including the traded option is liable to change the delta of the portfolio, so the position in the underlying asset (or futures contract on the underlying asset) then has to be changed to maintain delta neutrality. Note that the portfolio is only gamma neutral instantaneously. As time passes, gamma neutrality can be maintained only if the position in the traded option is adjusted so that it is always equal to $-\Gamma/\Gamma_T$.

Making a delta-neutral portfolio gamma neutral can be regarded as a first correction for the fact that the position in the underlying asset (or futures contracts on the underlying asset) cannot be changed continuously when delta hedging is used. Delta neutrality provides protection against relatively small stock price moves between rebalancing. Gamma neutrality provides protection against larger movements in this stock price between hedge rebalancing. Suppose that a portfolio is delta neutral and has a gamma of $-3{,}000$. The delta and gamma of a particular traded call option are 0.62 and 1.50, respectively. The portfolio can be made gamma neutral by including a long position of

$$\frac{3{,}000}{1.5} = 2{,}000$$

traded call options in the portfolio. However, the delta of the portfolio will then change from zero to $2{,}000 \times 0.62 = 1{,}240$. A quantity, 1,240, of the underlying asset must, therefore, be sold from the portfolio to keep it delta neutral. This example is summarized in Table 14.7.

Calculation of Gamma

For a European call or put option on a nondividend-paying stock, the gamma is given by

$$\Gamma = \frac{N'(d_1)}{S\sigma\sqrt{T}}$$

Table 14.7 Making a Portfolio Gamma and Delta Neutral

From the Trader's Desk

An investor's portfolio is delta neutral and has a gamma of −3,000. The delta and gamma of a particular traded call option are 0.62 and 1.50, respectively. The investor would like to make the portfolio gamma neutral as well as delta neutral.

Strategy

The portfolio can be made gamma neutral by buying 2,000 options (20 contracts). However, this creates a delta of 1,240. A quantity, 1,240, of the underlying asset must, therefore, be sold at the same time as the traded options are purchased.

where d_1 is defined as in Equation (11.5) and $N'(x)$ is as given by (14.4). This is always positive and varies with S in the way indicated in Figure 14.9. The variation of gamma with time to maturity for out-of-the-money, at-the-money, and in-the-money options is shown in Figure 14.10. For an at-the-money option, gamma increases as the time to maturity decreases. Short-life at-the-money options have very high gammas—which means that the value of the option holder's position is highly sensitive to jumps in the stock price.

For a European call or put option on a stock index paying a continuous dividend at rate q,

$$\Gamma = \frac{N'(d_1)e^{-qT}}{S\sigma\sqrt{T}}$$

where d_1 is defined as in Equation (12.4). This formula gives the gamma for a European option on a currency when q is put equal to the foreign risk-free rate and gives the gamma for a European futures option with $q = r$ and $S = F$.

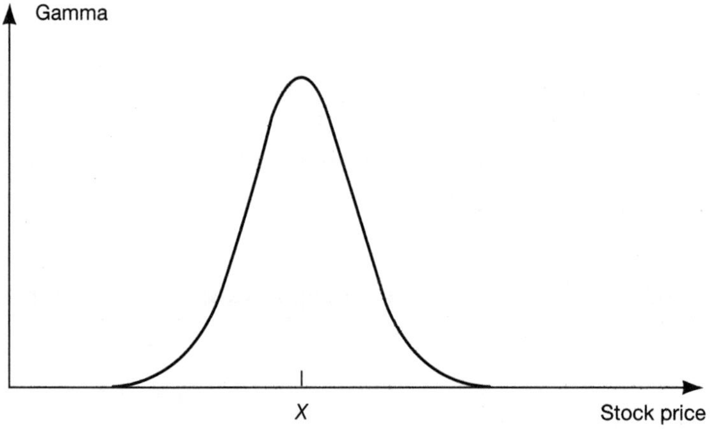

Figure 14.9 Variation of gamma with stock price for an option.

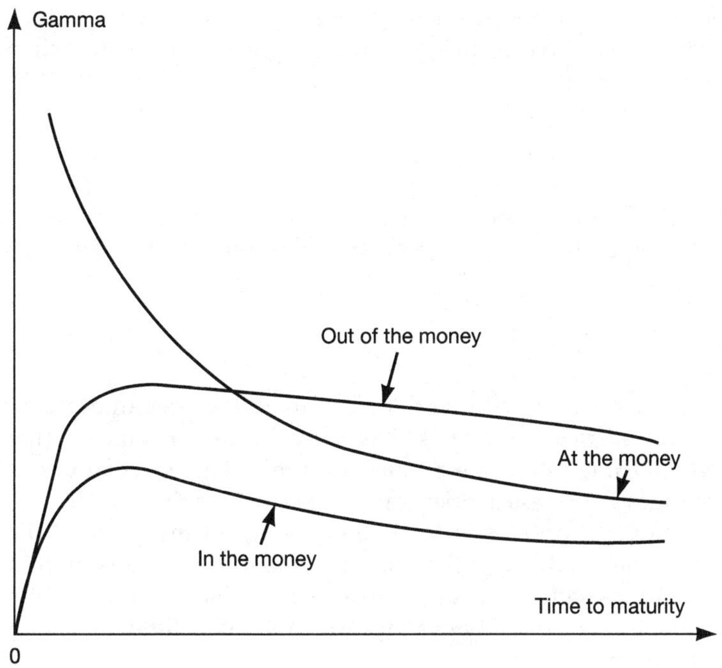

Figure 14.10 Variation of gamma with time to maturity for a stock option.

Example

Consider a four-month put option on a stock index. Suppose that the current value of the index is 305, the strike price is 300, the dividend yield is 3 percent per annum, the risk-free interest rate is 8 percent per annum, and volatility of the index is 25 percent per annum. In this case $S = 305$, $X = 300$, $q = 0.03$, $r = 0.08$, $\sigma = 0.25$, and $T = 0.3333$. The gamma of the index option is given by

$$\frac{N'(d_1)e^{-qT}}{S\sigma\sqrt{T}} = 0.00857$$

Thus, an increase of 1 in the index (from 305 to 306) increases the delta of the option by approximately 0.00857.

THE RELATIONSHIP BETWEEN DELTA, THETA, AND GAMMA

Suppose that f is the value of a call option or a put option or any other derivative security where the underlying asset is the price of a stock paying a continuous dividend at rate q. It can be shown that

$$\Theta + (r - q)S\Delta + \tfrac{1}{2}\sigma^2 S^2 \Gamma = rf \qquad (14.5)$$

This is true when f is the value of a portfolio of derivative securities on the stock as well as for individual derivative securities. An analogous result holds when the underlying asset is a currency ($q = r_f$) and when it is a futures price ($q = r$).

For a delta-neutral portfolio, $\Delta = 0$ and

$$\Theta + \tfrac{1}{2}\sigma^2 S^2 \Gamma = rf$$

This shows that when Θ is large and positive, gamma tends to be large and negative, and vice versa. The equation is consistent with the way in which Figure 14.8 has been drawn.

VEGA

Up to now we have implicitly assumed that the volatility of the asset underlying an option is constant. In practice, volatilities change over time. This means that the value of an option is liable to change because of movements in volatility as well as because of changes in the asset price and the passage of time.

The *vega* of a portfolio of options is the rate of change of the value of the portfolio with respect to the volatility of the underlying asset.[6] If vega is high in absolute terms, the portfolio's value is very sensitive to small changes in volatility. If vega is low in absolute terms, volatility changes have relatively little impact on the value of the portfolio.

A position in the underlying asset or in a futures contract has zero vega. However, the vega of a portfolio can be changed by adding a position in a traded option. If Λ is the vega of the portfolio and Λ_T is the vega of a traded option, a position of $-\Lambda/\Lambda_T$ in the traded option makes the portfolio instantaneously vega neutral. Unfortunately, a portfolio that is gamma neutral will not in general be vega neutral, and vice versa. If a hedger requires a portfolio to be both gamma and vega neutral, at least two traded options dependent on the underlying asset must be used.

Example

Consider a portfolio that is delta neutral, has a gamma of $-5{,}000$, and a vega of $-8{,}000$. Suppose that a traded option has a gamma of 0.5, a vega of 2.0, and a delta of 0.6. The portfolio can be made vega neutral by including a long position in 4,000 traded options. This would increase delta to 2,400 and require that 2,400 units of the asset be sold to maintain delta neutrality. The gamma of the portfolio would change from $-5{,}000$ to $-3{,}000$.

To make the portfolio gamma and vega neutral, we suppose that there is a second traded option with a gamma of 0.8, a vega of 1.2, and a delta of 0.5. If w_1 and w_2 are the amounts of the two traded options included in the portfolio, we require that

$$-5{,}000 + 0.5w_1 + 0.8w_2 = 0$$
$$-8{,}000 + 2.0w_1 + 1.2w_2 = 0$$

[6] Vega is also sometimes referred to as kappa or as sigma or as lambda.

The solution to these equations is $w_1 = 400$, $w_2 = 6{,}000$. The portfolio can, therefore, be made gamma and vega neutral by including 400 of the first traded option and 6,000 of the second traded option. The delta of the portfolio after the addition of the positions in the two traded options is $400 \times 0.6 + 6{,}000 \times 0.5 = 3{,}240$. Hence, 3,240 units of the asset would have to be sold to maintain delta neutrality.

For a European call or put option on a nondividend-paying stock, vega is given by

$$\Lambda = S\sqrt{T}N'(d_1)$$

where d_1 is defined as in Equation (11.5) and $N'(x)$ is defined in (14.4). For a European call or put option on a stock or stock index paying a continuous dividend yield at rate q,

$$\Lambda = S\sqrt{T}N'(d_1)e^{-qT}$$

where d_1 is defined as in Equation (12.4). This equation gives the vega for a European currency option with q replaced by r_f. It also gives the vega for a European futures option with q replaced by r and S replaced by F. The vega of an option is always positive. Figure 14.11 shows the general way in which vega varies with S. The general variation of vega with time to maturity is the same for in-the-money, at-the-money, and out-of-the-money options. This is shown in Figure 14.12.

Figure 14.11 Variation of vega with stock price for an option.

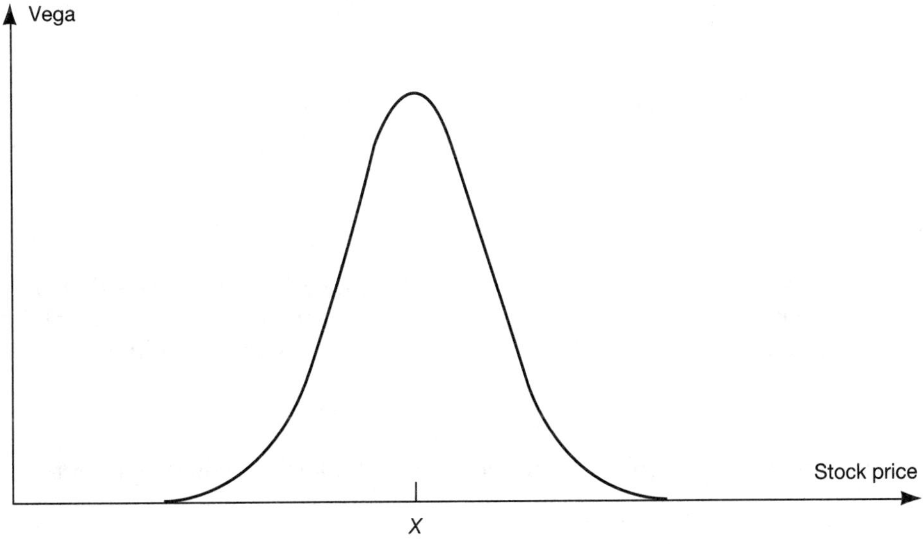

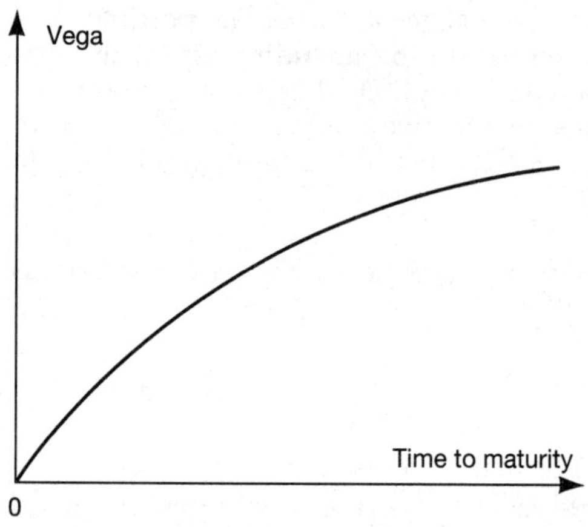

Figure 14.12 Variation of vega with time to maturity for an option.

Gamma neutrality protects against the fact that time elapses between hedge rebalancing. Vega neutrality protects against a variable volatility. As might be expected, whether it is best to use an available traded option for vega or gamma hedging depends on the time between hedge rebalancing and the volatility of the volatility.

Example

Consider again the four-month put option on a stock index. The current value of the index is 305, the strike price is 300, the dividend yield is 3 percent per annum, the risk-free interest rate is 8 percent per annum, and the volatility of the index is 25 percent per annum. In this case $S = 305$, $X = 300$, $q = 0.03$, $r = 0.08$, $\sigma = 0.25$, and $T = 0.3333$. The option's vega is

$$S\sqrt{T}N'(d_1)e^{-qT} = 66.44$$

Thus, a one-percentage-point or 0.01 increase in volatility (from 25 percent to 26 percent) increases the value of the option by approximately 0.6644.

RHO

The rho of a portfolio of options is the rate of change of the value of the portfolio with respect to the interest rate. It measures the sensitivity of the value of a portfolio to interest rates. For a European call option on a nondividend-paying stock,

$$\text{rho} = XTe^{-rT}N(d_2)$$

where d_2 is defined as in Equation (11.5). For a European put option,

$$\text{rho} = -XTe^{-rT}N(-d_2)$$

These same formulas apply to European call and put options on stocks and stock indices paying a dividend yield at rate q when appropriate changes are made to the definition of d_2.

Example

Consider again the four-month put option on a stock index. The current value of the index is 305, the strike price is 300, the dividend yield is 3 percent per annum, the risk-free interest rate is 8 percent per annum, and the volatility of the index is 25 percent per annum. In this case $S = 305$, $X = 300$, $q = 0.03$, $r = 0.08$, $\sigma = 0.25$, and $T = 0.333$. The option's rho is

$$-XTe^{-rT}N(-d_2) = -42.57$$

This means that for a one-percentage-point or 0.01 change in the risk-free interest rate (from 8 percent to 9 percent) the value of the option decreases by 0.4257.

In the case of currency options there are two rhos corresponding to the two interest rates. The rho corresponding to the domestic interest rate is given by the formulas already presented. The rho corresponding to the foreign interest rate for a European call on a currency is given by

$$\text{rho} = -Te^{-r_f T}SN(d_1)$$

while for a European put it is

$$\text{rho} = Te^{-r_f T}SN(-d_1)$$

HEDGING OPTION PORTFOLIOS IN PRACTICE

Up to now we may have given the impression that option traders are continually rebalancing their portfolios to maintain delta neutrality, gamma neutrality, vega neutrality, and so on. In practice transaction costs make frequent rebalancing very expensive. Rather than trying to eliminate all risks, an option trader usually concentrates on assessing risks and deciding whether they are acceptable.

Option traders tend to use the delta, gamma, and vega measures to quantify the different aspects of the risk inherent in their option portfolios. They then consider different possible future scenarios for movements in the stock price and the stock price volatility. If the downside risk is acceptable, no adjustment is made to the portfolio. If it is unacceptable, they take an appropriate position in either the underlying security or a traded option.

PORTFOLIO INSURANCE

Portfolio managers holding a well-diversified stock portfolio are sometimes interested in insuring themselves against the value of the portfolio dropping below a certain level. One way of doing this is by holding, in conjunction with the stock portfolio, put options on a stock index. This strategy was discussed in Chapter 12.

Consider, for example, a fund manager with a \$30 million portfolio whose value mirrors the value of the S&P 500. Suppose that the S&P 500 is standing at 300 and the manager wishes to insure against the value of the portfolio dropping below \$29 million in the next six months. The manager can buy 1,000 six-month put option contracts on the S&P 500 with an exercise price of 290 and a maturity in six months. If the index drops below 290, the put options will become in the money and provide the manager with compensation for the decline in the value of the portfolio. Suppose, for example, that the index drops to 270 at the end of six months. The value of the manager's stock portfolio is likely to be about \$27 million. Since each option contract is on 100 times the index, the total value of the put options is \$2 million. This brings the value of the entire holding back up to \$29 million. Of course, insurance is not free. In this example the put options could cost the portfolio manager as much as \$1 million.

Creating Options Synthetically

An alternative approach open to the portfolio manager involves creating the put options synthetically. This involves taking a position in the underlying asset (or futures on the underlying asset) so that the delta of the position is maintained equal to the delta of the required option. If more accuracy is required, the next step is to use traded options to match the gamma and vega of the required option. The alert reader will recognize that the position necessary to create an option synthetically is the reverse of that necessary to hedge it. This is simply a reflection of the fact that a procedure for hedging an option involves the creation of an equal and opposite option synthetically.

There are two reasons why it may be more attractive for the portfolio manager to create the required put option synthetically than to buy it in the market. The first is that options markets do not always have the liquidity to absorb the trades that managers of large funds would like to carry out. The second is that fund managers often require strike prices and exercise dates that are different from those available in traded options markets.

The synthetic option can be created from trades in stocks themselves or from trades in index futures contracts. We will first examine the creation of a put option by trades in the stocks themselves. Consider again the fund manager with a well-diversified portfolio worth \$30 million who wishes to buy a European put on the portfolio with a strike price of \$29 million and an exercise date in six months. Recall that the delta of a European put on an index is given by

$$\Delta = e^{-qT}[N(d_1) - 1] \tag{14.6}$$

where, with the usual notation,

$$d_1 = \frac{\ln(S/X) + (r - q + \sigma^2/2)T}{\sigma\sqrt{T}}$$

Since, in this case, the fund manager's portfolio mirrors the index, this is also the delta of a put on the portfolio when it is regarded as a single security. The delta is negative. Accordingly, in order to create the put option synthetically, the fund manager should ensure that at any given time a proportion

$$e^{-qT}[1 - N(d_1)]$$

of the stocks in the original \$30 million portfolio have been sold and the proceeds invested in riskless assets. As the value of the original portfolio declines, the delta of the put becomes more negative and the proportion of the portfolio sold must be increased. As the value of the original portfolio increases, the delta of the put becomes less negative and the proportion of the portfolio sold must be decreased (i.e., some of the original portfolio must be repurchased).

Using this strategy to create portfolio insurance means that at any given time funds are divided between the stock portfolio on which insurance is required and riskless assets. As the value of the stock portfolio increases, riskless assets are sold and the position in the stock portfolio is increased. As the value of the stock portfolio declines, the position in the stock portfolio is decreased and riskless assets are purchased. The cost of the insurance arises from the fact that the portfolio manager is always selling in a declining market and buying after a rise.

Use of Index Futures

Using index futures to create portfolio insurance can be preferable to using the underlying stocks, as the transactions costs associated with trades in index futures are generally less than those associated with the corresponding trades in the underlying stocks. The portfolio manager considered earlier would keep the \$30 million stock portfolio intact and short index futures contracts. The dollar amount of futures contracts shorted as a proportion of the value of the portfolio should from Equations (14.3) and (14.6) be

$$e^{-qT}e^{-(r-q)T^*}[1 - N(d_1)] = e^{q(T^*-T)}e^{-rT^*}[1 - N(d_1)]$$

where T^* is the maturity time of the futures contract. If the portfolio is worth K_1 times the index and each index futures contract is on K_2 times the index, this means that the number of futures contracts shorted at any given time should be

$$e^{q(T^*-T)}e^{-rT^*}[1 - N(d_1)]\frac{K_1}{K_2}$$

Example

In the example given at the beginning of this section, suppose that the volatility of the market is 25 percent per annum, the risk-free interest rate is 9 percent per annum, and the dividend yield on the market is 3 percent per annum. In this case $S = 300$, $X = 290$, $r = 0.09$, $q = 0.03$, $\sigma = 0.25$, and $T = 0.5$. The delta of the option that is required is

$$e^{-qT}[N(d_1) - 1] = -0.322$$

Hence, if trades in the portfolio are used to create the option, 32.2 percent of the portfolio should be sold initially. If nine-month futures contracts on the S&P 500 are used, $T^* - T = 0.25$, $T^* = 0.75$, $K_1 = 100{,}000$, $K_2 = 500$, so that the number of futures contracts shorted should be

$$e^{q(T^*-T)}e^{-rT^*}[1 - N(d_1)]\frac{K_1}{K_2} = 61.6$$

Up to now we have assumed that the portfolio mirrors the index. As discussed in Chapter 12, the hedging scheme can be adjusted to deal with other situations. The strike price for the options used should be the expected level of the market index when the portfolio's value reaches its insured value. The number of index options used should be β times the number of options that would be required if the portfolio had a beta of 1.0.

Frequency of Rebalancing and October 19, 1987

An important issue when put options are created synthetically for portfolio insurance is the frequency with which the portfolio manager's position should be adjusted or rebalanced. With no transaction costs, continuous rebalancing is optimal. However, as transactions costs increase, the optimal frequency of rebalancing declines.

Creating put options on the index synthetically does not work well if the volatility of the index changes rapidly or if the index exhibits large jumps. On Monday, October 19, 1987, the Dow Jones Industrial Average dropped by over 500 points. Portfolio managers who had insured themselves by buying traded put options survived this crash well. Those who had chosen to create put options synthetically found that they were unable to sell either stocks or index futures fast enough to protect their position.

STOCK MARKET VOLATILITY

We have already raised the issue of whether volatility is caused solely by the arrival of new information or whether trading itself generates volatility. Portfolio insurance schemes such as those just described have the potential to increase volatility. When the market declines, they cause portfolio managers either to sell stock or to sell index futures contracts. This may accentuate the decline. The sale of stock is liable to drive down the market index further in a direct way. The sale of index futures contracts is liable to drive down futures prices. This creates selling pressure on stocks via the mechanism of index arbitrage (see Chapter 3) so that the market index is liable to be driven down in this case as well. Similarly, when the market rises, the portfolio insurance schemes cause portfolio managers either to buy stock or to buy futures contracts. This may accentuate the rise.

In addition to formal portfolio insurance schemes, we can speculate that many investors consciously or subconsciously follow portfolio insurance schemes of their own. For example, an investor may be inclined to enter the market when it is rising but will sell when it is falling to limit his or her downside risk.

Whether portfolio insurance schemes (formal or informal) affect volatility depends on how easily the market can absorb the trades that are generated by portfolio insurance. If portfolio insurance trades are a very small fraction of all trades, there is likely to be no effect. However, as portfolio insurance becomes more widespread, it is liable to have a destabilizing effect on the market.

Brady Commission Report

The report of the Brady commission on the October 19, 1987 crash provides interesting insights into the effect of portfolio insurance on the market at that time.[7] The Brady commission estimates that $60 billion to $90 billion of equity assets were under portfolio insurance administration in October 1987. During the period Wednesday, October 14, 1987, to Friday, October 16, 1987, the market declined by about 10 percent with much of this decline taking place on the Friday afternoon. This should have generated at least $12 billion of equity or index futures sales as a result of portfolio insurance schemes.[8] In fact, less than $4 billion were sold, which means that portfolio insurers approached the following week with huge amounts of selling already dictated by their models. The Brady commission estimated that on Monday, October 19, sell programs by three portfolio insurers accounted for almost 10 percent of the sales on the New York Stock Exchange, and that portfolio insurance sales amount to 21.3 percent of all sales in index futures markets. It seems likely that portfolio insurance caused some downward pressure on the market. It is significant that in aggregate, portfolio insurers executed only a relatively small proportion of the total trades generated by their models. Needless to say, the popularity of portfolio insurance schemes based on dynamic trading in stocks and futures has declined considerably since October 1987.

SUMMARY

Financial institutions offer a variety of option products to their clients. Often the options do not correspond to the standardized products traded by exchanges. This presents the financial institutions with the problem of hedging their exposure.

[7] See "Report of the Presidential Task Force on Market Mechanisms," January 1988.

[8] To put this in perspective, on Monday, October 19, all previous records were broken when 604 million shares worth $21 billion were traded on the New York Stock Exchange. Approximately $20 billion of S&P 500 futures contracts were traded on that day.

Naked and covered positions leave them subject to an unacceptable level of risk. One strategy that is sometimes proposed is a stop-loss strategy. This involves holding a naked position when an option is out of the money and converting it to a covered position as soon as the option moves in the money. Surprisingly, the strategy does not work at all well.

The delta, Δ, of an option is the rate of change of its price with respect to the price of the underlying asset. Delta hedging involves creating a position with zero delta (sometimes referred to as a delta-neutral position). Since the delta of the underlying asset is 1.0, one way of doing this is to take a position of $-\Delta$ in the underlying asset for each long option being hedged. The delta of an option changes over time. This means that the position in the underlying asset has to be frequently adjusted.

Once an option position has been made delta neutral, the next stage is often to look at its gamma. The gamma of an option is the rate of change of its delta with respect to the price of the underlying asset. It is a measure of the curvature of the relationship between the option price and the asset price. The impact of this curvature on the performance of delta hedging can be reduced by making an option position gamma neutral. If Γ is the gamma of the position being hedged, this is usually achieved by taking a position in a traded option that has a gamma of $-\Gamma$.

Delta and gamma hedging are both based on the assumption that the volatility of the underlying asset is constant. In practice volatilities do change over time. The vega of an option or an option portfolio measures the rate of change of its value with respect to volatility. If a trader wishes to hedge an option position against volatility changes, he or she can make the position vega neutral. Like the procedure for creating gamma neutrality, this usually involves taking an offsetting position in a traded option. If the trader wishes to achieve both gamma and vega neutrality, two traded options are usually required.

Two other measures of the risk of an option position are theta and rho. Theta measures the rate of change of the value of the position with respect to the passage of time with all else remaining constant. Rho measures the rate of change of the value of the position with respect to the short-term interest rate with all else remaining constant.

Portfolio managers are sometimes interested in creating put options synthetically for the purposes of insuring an equity portfolio. They can do this either by trading the portfolio or by trading index futures on the portfolio. Trading the portfolio involves splitting the portfolio between equities and risk-free securities. As the market declines, more is invested in risk-free securities. As the market increases, more is invested in equities. Trading index futures involves keeping the equity portfolio intact and selling index futures. As the market declines, more index futures are sold; as it rises fewer are sold. This works well in normal market conditions. However, on Monday, October 19, 1987, when the Dow Jones Industrial Average dropped by over 500 points, it worked badly. Portfolio insurers were unable to sell either stocks or index futures fast enough to protect their positions.

Suggestions for Further Reading

On hedging option positions

BOYLE, P. P., and D. EMANUEL, "Discretely adjusted option hedges," *Journal of Financial Economics*, 8 (1980), 259–282.

DILLMAN, S., and J. HARDING, "Life after delta: The gamma factor," *Euromoney*, Supplement (February 1985), pp. 14–17.

FIGLEWSKI, S., "Options arbitrage in imperfect markets," *Journal of Finance*, 44 (December 1989), 1289–1311.

GALAI, D., "The components of the return from hedging options against stocks," *Journal of Business*, 56 (January 1983), 45–54.

HULL, J., and A. WHITE, "Hedging the risks from writing foreign currency options," *Journal of International Money and Finance*, 6 (June 1987), 131–152.

On portfolio insurance

ASAY, M., and C. EDELBERG, "Can a dynamic strategy replicate the returns on an option?" *Journal of Futures Markets*, 6 (Spring 1986), 63–70.

BOOKSTABER, R., and J. A. LANGSAM, "Portfolio insurance trading rules," *Journal of Futures Markets*, 8 (February 1988), 15–31.

ETZIONI, E. S., "Rebalance disciplines for portfolio insurance," *Journal of Portfolio Insurance*, 13 (Fall 1986), 59–62.

LELAND, H. E., Option pricing and replication with transactions costs," *Journal of Finance*, 40 (December 1985), 1283–1301.

LELAND, H. E., "Who should buy portfolio insurance?" *Journal of Finance*, 35 (May 1980), 581–594.

RUBINSTEIN, M., "Alternative paths for portfolio insurance," *Financial Analysts Journal*, 41 (July-August 1985), 42–52.

RUBINSTEIN, M., AND H. E. Leland, "Replicating options with positions in stock and cash," *Financial Analysts Journal*, 37 (July-August 1981), 63–72.

TILLEY, J. A., and G. O. LATAINER, "A synthetic option framework for asset allocation," *Financial Analysts Journal*, 41 (May–June 1985), 32–41.

Quiz

1. Explain how a stop-loss hedging scheme can be implemented for the writer of an out-of-the-money call option. Why does it provide a relatively poor hedge?
2. What does it mean to assert that the delta of a call option is 0.7? How can a short position in 1,000 options be made delta neutral when the delta of each option is 0.7?
3. Calculate the delta of an at-the-money six-month European call option on a nondividend-paying stock when the risk-free interest rate is 10 percent per annum and the stock price volatility is 25 percent per annum.
4. What does it mean to assert that the theta of an option position is -0.1 when time is measured in years? If a trader feels that neither a stock price nor its implied volatility will change, what type of option position is appropriate?
5. What is meant by the gamma of an option position? Consider the situation of an option writer when the gamma of his or her position is large and negative and the delta is zero. What are the risks?
6. "The procedure for creating an option position synthetically is the reverse of the procedure for hedging the option position." Explain this statement.
7. Why did portfolio insurance not work well on October 19, 1987?

Questions and Problems

14.1. A deposit instrument offered by a bank guarantees that investors will receive a return during a six-month period that is the greater of (a) zero and (b) 40 percent of the return provided by a market index. An individual is planning to invest $100,000 in the instrument. Describe the payoff as an option on the index. Assuming that the risk-free rate of interest is 8 percent per annum, the dividend yield on the index is 3 percent per annum, and the volatility of the index is 25 percent per annum, is the product a good deal for the individual?

14.2. The Black–Scholes price of an out-of-the-money call option with an exercise price of $40 is $4. A trader who has written the option plans to use a stop-loss strategy. The trader's plan is to buy at $40⅛ and to sell at $39⅞. Estimate the expected number of times the stock will be bought or sold.

14.3. Suppose that a stock price is currently $20 and that a call option with an exercise price of $25 is created synthetically using a continually changing position in the stock. Consider the following two scenarios:

a. Stock price increases steadily from $20 to $35 during the life of the option.

b. Stock price oscillates wildly ending up at $35.

Which scenario would make the synthetically created option more expensive? Explain your answer.

14.4. What is the delta of a short position in 1,000 European call options on silver futures? The options mature in eight months and the futures contract underlying the option matures in nine months. The current nine-month futures price is $8 per ounce, the exercise price of the options is $8, the risk-free interest rate is 12 percent per annum, and the volatility of silver is 18 percent per annum.

14.5. In Problem 14.4, what initial position in nine-month silver futures is necessary for delta hedging? If silver itself is used, what is the initial position? If one-year silver futures are used, what is the initial position? Assume no storage costs for silver.

14.6. A company uses delta hedging to hedge a portfolio of long positions in put and call options on a currency. Which of the following would give the most favorable result?

a. A virtually constant spot rate.

b. Wild movements in the spot rate.

Explain your answer.

14.7. Repeat Problem 14.6 for a financial institution with a portfolio of short positions in put and call options for a currency.

14.8. A financial institution has just sold 1,000 seven-month European call options on the Japanese yen. Suppose that the spot exchange rate is 0.80 cent per yen, the exercise price is 0.81 cent per yen, the risk-free interest rate in the United States is 8 percent per annum, the risk-free interest rate in Japan is 5 percent per annum, and the volatility of the yen is 15 percent per annum. Calculate the delta, gamma, vega, theta, and rho of the financial institution's position. Interpret each number.

14.9. A financial institution has the following portfolio of over-the-counter options on sterling:

TYPE	*POSITION*	*DELTA OF OPTION*	*GAMMA OF OPTION*	*VEGA OF OPTION*
Call	−1,000	0.50	2.2	1.8
Call	−500	0.80	0.6	0.2
Put	−2,000	−0.40	1.3	0.7
Call	−500	0.70	1.8	1.4

A traded option is available which has a delta of 0.6, a gamma of 1.5, and a vega of 0.8.

a. What position in the traded option and in sterling would make the portfolio both gamma neutral and delta neutral?

b. What position in the traded option and in sterling would make the portfolio both vega neutral and delta neutral?

14.10. Consider again the situation in Problem 14.9. Suppose that a second traded option with a delta of 0.1, a gamma of 0.5, and a vega of 0.6 is available. How could the portfolio be made delta, gamma, and vega neutral?

14.11. Under what circumstances is it possible to make a position in an over-the-counter European option on a stock index both gamma neutral and vega neutral by introducing a single traded European option into the portfolio?

14.12. A fund manager has a well-diversified portfolio that mirrors the performance of the S&P 500 and is worth $90 million. The value of the S&P 500 is 300 and the portfolio manager would like to buy insurance against a reduction of more than 5 percent in the value of the portfolio over the next six months. The risk-free interest rate is 6 percent per annum. The dividend yield on both the portfolio and the S&P 500 is 3 percent, and the volatility of the index is 30 percent per annum.

a. If the fund manager buys traded European put options, how much would the insurance cost?

b. Explain carefully alternative strategies open to the fund manager involving traded European call options, and show that they lead to the same result.

c. If the fund manager decides to provide insurance by keeping part of the portfolio in risk-free securities, what should the initial position be?

d. If the fund manager decides to provide insurance by using nine-month index futures, what should the initial position be?

14.13. Repeat Problem 14.12 on the assumption that the portfolio has a beta of 1.5. Assume that the dividend yield on the portfolio is 4 percent per annum.

14.14. Show by substituting for the various terms in Equation (14.5) that the equation is true for:

a. A single European call option on a nondividend-paying stock.

b. A single European put option on a nondividend-paying stock.

c. Any portfolio of European put and call options on a nondividend-paying stock.

14.15. Suppose that $70 billion of equity assets are the subject of portfolio insurance schemes. Assume that the schemes were designed to insure that the value of the assets do not decline by more than 5 percent within one year. Making whatever estimates you find necessary, calculate the value of the stock or futures contracts that the administrators of the portfolio insurance schemes will attempt to sell if the market falls by 23 percent in a single day.

14.16. Does a forward contract have the same delta as the corresponding futures contract? Explain your answer.

15

VALUING OPTIONS NUMERICALLY USING BINOMIAL TREES

The Black–Scholes model and its extensions can be used to value European call and put options on stocks, stock indices, currencies, and futures contracts. It can also be used for valuing American call options on nondividend-paying stocks and for some American call options on dividend-paying stocks. However, it cannot be used for valuing most other American options. In this chapter we extend the binomial tree analysis of Chapter 10 to develop a procedure for valuing these other options numerically.

THE BINOMIAL MODEL FOR A NONDIVIDEND-PAYING STOCK

In Chapter 10 we introduced one- and two-step binomial trees for nondividend-paying stocks and showed how they lead to valuations for European and American options. These models are clearly unrealistic and were used only for illustrative purpose. A more realistic model is one that assumes stock price movements are composed of a large number of small binomial movements. This is the assumption that underlies a widely used numerical procedure that was first proposed by Cox, Ross, and Rubinstein.

Consider the evaluation of an option on a nondividend-paying stock. We start by dividing the life of the option into a large number of small time intervals of length Δt. We assume that in each time interval the stock price moves from its initial value of S to one of two new values, Su or Sd. This model is illustrated in

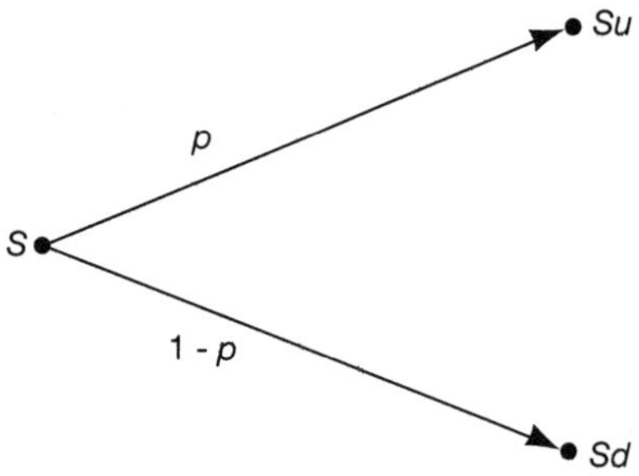

Figure 15.1 Stock price movements in time Δt under the binomial model.

Figure 15.1. In general, $u > 1$ and $d < 1$. The movement from S to Su is, therefore, an "up" movement and the movement from S to Sd is a "down" movement. The probability of an up movement is assumed to be p and the probability of a down movement is assumed to be $1 - p$.

Risk-Neutral Valuation

In Chapters 10 and 11 we introduced what is known as the risk-neutral valuation principle. This states that any security dependent on a stock price can be valued on the assumption that the world is risk neutral. It means that for the purposes of valuing an option (or any other derivative security), we can assume that:

1. The expected return from all traded securities is the risk-free interest rate.
2. Future cash flows can be valued by discounting their expected values at the risk-free interest rate.

When using the binomial model, we will make use of the risk-neutral valuation principle and assume that the world is risk neutral. This simplifies the determination of p, u, and d in Figure 15.1.

Determination of *p*, *u*, and *d*

The parameters p, u, and d must give correct values for the mean and variance of the stock price during a time interval Δt. Since we are working in a risk-neutral world, the expected return from a stock is the risk-free interest rate, r. Hence, the expected value of the stock price at the end of a time interval Δt is $Se^{r\Delta t}$, where S is the stock price at the beginning of the time interval. It follows that

$$Se^{r\Delta t} = pSu + (1 - p)Sd \tag{15.1}$$

or

$$e^{r\Delta t} = pu + (1 - p)d \tag{15.2}$$

It will be recalled from the stock price model assumed in Chapter 11 that the standard deviation of the proportional change in the stock price in a small time interval Δt is $\sigma\sqrt{\Delta t}$. This means that the variance of the actual change in Δt is $S^2\sigma^2\Delta t$. Since the variance of a variable Q is defined as $E(Q^2) - E(Q)^2$, where E denotes expected value, it follows that

$$S^2\sigma^2\Delta t = pS^2u^2 + (1 - p)S^2d^2 - S^2[pu + (1 - p)d]^2$$

or

$$\sigma^2\Delta t = pu^2 + (1 - p)d^2 - [pu + (1 - p)d]^2 \tag{15.3}$$

Equations (15.2) and (15.3) impose two conditions on p, u, and d. A third condition that is usually used is

$$u = \frac{1}{d}$$

It can be shown that provided Δt is small, the three conditions imply

$$p = \frac{a - d}{u - d} \tag{15.4}$$

$$u = e^{\sigma\sqrt{\Delta t}} \tag{15.5}$$

$$d = e^{-\sigma\sqrt{\Delta t}} \tag{15.6}$$

where

$$a = e^{r\Delta t} \tag{15.7}$$

Equations (15.4) and (15.7) correspond to Equation (10.3), which was shown to be correct using no-arbitrage arguments as well as risk-neutral valuation arguments.

The Tree of Stock Prices

The complete tree of stock prices that is considered when the binomial model is used is illustrated in Figure 15.2. At time zero the stock price S is known. At time Δt, there are two possible stock prices, Su and Sd; at time $2\Delta t$, there are three possible stock prices, Su^2, S, and Sd^2; and so on. In general at time $i\Delta t$, $i + 1$ stock prices are considered. These are

$$Su^jd^{i-j} \qquad j = 0, 1 \ldots, i$$

Note that the relationship $u = 1/d$ is used in computing the stock price at each node of the tree in Figure 15.2. For example $Su^2d = Su$. Note also that the tree recombines in the sense that an up movement followed by a down movement

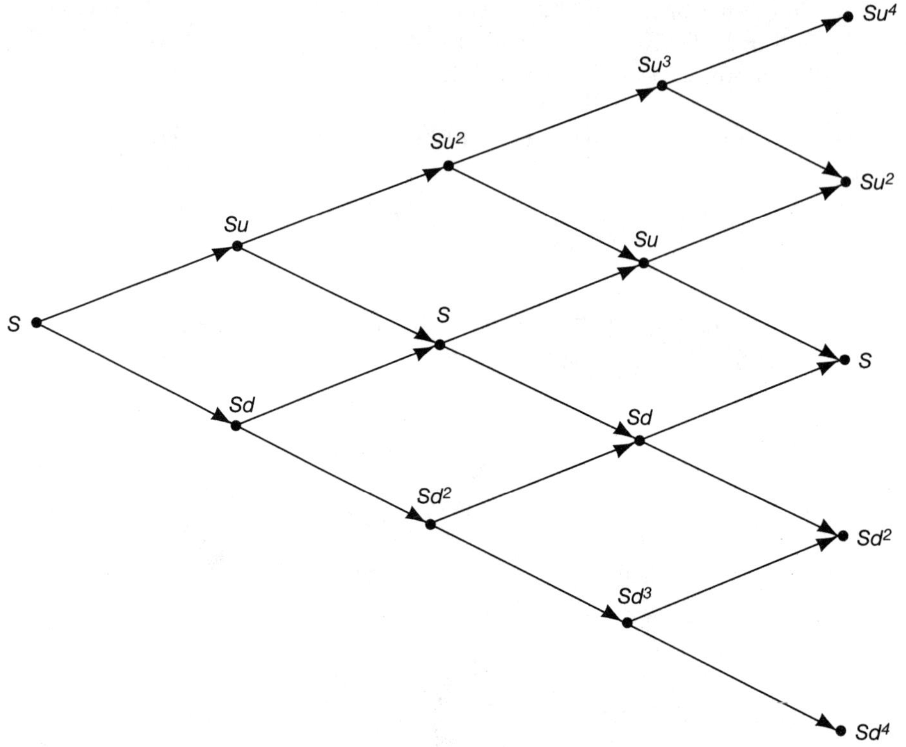

Figure 15.2 Tree used to value a stock option.

leads to the same stock price as a down movement followed by an up movement. This considerably reduces the number of nodes on the tree.

Working Backward Through the Tree

Options are evaluated by starting at the end of the tree (time T) and working backward. The value of the option is known at time T. For example, a put option is worth $\max(X - S_T, 0)$ and a call option is worth $\max(S_T - X, 0)$, where S_T is the stock price at time T and X is the strike price. Since a risk-neutral world is being assumed, the value at each node at time $T - \Delta t$ can be calculated as the expected value at time T discounted at rate r for a time period Δt. Similarly, the value at each node at time $T - 2\Delta t$ can be calculated as the expected value at time $T - \Delta t$ discounted for a time period Δt at rate r, and so on. If the option is American, it is necessary to check at each node to see whether early exercise is preferable to holding the option for a further time period Δt. Eventually, by working back through all the nodes, the value of the option at time zero is obtained.

An Example

The basic idea is best illustrated with an example. Consider a five-month American put option on a nondividend-paying stock when the stock price is \$50, the strike price is \$50, the risk-free interest rate is 10 percent per annum, and the volatility is 40 percent per annum. With our usual notation, this means that $S = 50, X = 50, r = 0.10, \sigma = 0.40$, and $T = 0.4167$. Suppose that we divide the life of the option into five intervals of length 1 month (= 0.0833 year) for the purposes of constructing a binomial tree. Then $\Delta t = 0.0833$ and using Equations (15.4) to (15.7)

$$u = e^{\sigma\sqrt{\Delta t}} = 1.1224, \qquad d = e^{-\sigma\sqrt{\Delta t}} = 0.8909$$

$$a = e^{r\Delta t} = 1.0084, \qquad p = \frac{a - d}{u - d} = 0.5076$$

$$1 - p = 0.4924$$

Figure 15.3 shows the binomial tree. At each node there are two numbers. The top one shows the stock price at the node; the lower one shows the value of the option at the node. The probability of an up movement is always 0.5076; the probability of a down movement is always 0.4924.

The stock price at the jth node ($j = 0, 1 \ldots, i$) at time $i\Delta t$ is calculated as $Su^j d^{i-j}$. For example, the stock price at the node labeled A ($i = 4, j = 1$) is $50 \times 1.1224 \times 0.8909^3 = \$39.69$. The option prices at the final nodes are calculated as $\max(X - S_T, 0)$. For example, the option price at node G is $50 - 35.36 = 14.64$.

The option prices at the penultimate nodes are calculated from the option prices at the final nodes. First, we assume no exercise of the option at the nodes. This means that the option price is calculated as the present value of the expected option price in time Δt. For example, at node E the option price is calculated as

$$(0.5076 \times 0 + 0.4924 \times 5.45)e^{-0.10 \times 0.0833} = 2.66$$

while at node A it is calculated as

$$(0.5076 \times 5.45 + 0.4924 \times 14.64)e^{-0.10 \times 0.0833} = 9.90$$

We then check to see if early exercise is preferable to waiting. At node E early exercise would give a value for the option of zero, since both the stock price and strike price are \$50. Clearly it is best to wait. The correct value for the option at node E is, therefore, \$2.66. At node A it is a different story. If the option is exercised, it is worth \$50.00 − \$39.69 or \$10.31. This is more than \$9.90. If node A is reached,

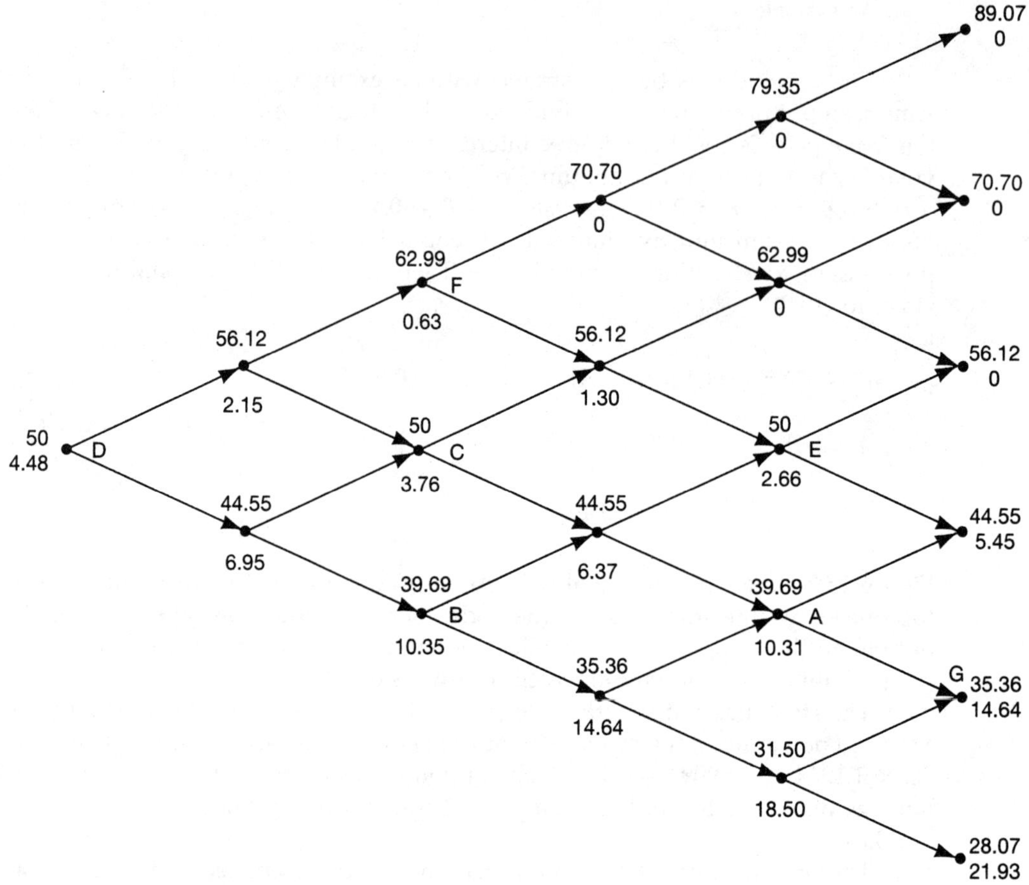

Figure 15.3 Binomial tree for American put on nondividend-paying stock.

the option should, therefore, be exercised and the correct value to put for the option at node A is \$10.31.

Option prices at earlier nodes are calculated in a similar way. Note that it is not always best to exercise an option early when it is in the money. Consider node B. If the option is exercised, it is worth \$50.00 − \$39.69 or \$10.31. However, if it is held, it is worth

$$(0.5076 \times 6.37 + 0.4924 \times 14.64)e^{-0.10 \times 0.0833} = 10.35$$

The option should, therefore, not be exercised at this node, and the correct option value at the node is \$10.35.

Working back through the tree, we find the value of the option at the initial node to be \$4.48. This is our numerical estimate for the option's current value. In practice a smaller value of Δt and many more nodes would be used. The true value of the option obtained using a very small value of Δt is \$4.29.

Expressing the Approach Algebraically

Suppose that the life of an American put option on a nondividend-paying stock is divided into N subintervals of length Δt. Define f_{ij} as the value of the option at time $i\Delta t$ when the stock price is $Su^j d^{i-j}$ for $0 \le i \le N, 0 \le j \le i$. We will refer to this as the value of the option at the (i,j) node. Since the value of an American put at its expiration date is $\max(X - S_T, 0)$, we know that

$$f_{Nj} = \max[X - Su^j d^{N-j}, 0] \qquad j = 0, 1 \ldots, N$$

There is a probability p of moving from the (i,j) node at time $i\Delta t$ to the $(i + 1, j + 1)$ node at time $(i + 1)\Delta t$ and a probability $1 - p$ of moving from the (i,j) node at time $i\Delta t$ to the $(i + 1,j)$ node at time $(i + 1)\Delta t$. Assuming no early exercise, risk-neutral valuation gives

$$f_{ij} = e^{-r\Delta t}\,[pf_{i+1,j+1} + (1 - p)f_{i+1,j}]$$

for $0 \le i \le N - 1$ and $0 \le j \le i$. When early exercise is taken into account, this value for f_{ij} must be compared with the option's intrinsic value, and we obtain

$$f_{ij} = \max\{X - Su^j d^{i-j}, e^{-r\Delta t}[pf_{i+1,j+1} + (1 - p)f_{i+1,j}]\}$$

Note that because the calculations start at time T and work backward, the value at time $i\Delta t$ captures not only the effect of early exercise possibilities at time $i\Delta t$, but also the effect of early exercise at subsequent times. In the limit, as Δt tends to zero an exact value for the American put is obtained. In practice $N = 30$ usually gives reasonable results.

Estimating Delta and Other Hedge Parameters

It will be recalled that the delta, Δ, of an option is the rate of change of its price with respect to the underlying stock price. In other words,

$$\Delta = \frac{\Delta f}{\Delta S}$$

where ΔS is a small change in the stock price and Δf is the corresponding small change in the option price. At time Δt we have an estimate f_{11} for the option price when the stock price is Su and an estimate f_{10} for the option price when the stock price is Sd. In other words, when $\Delta S = Su - Sd$, $\Delta f = f_{11} - f_{10}$. An estimate of Δ at time Δt is, therefore,

$$\Delta = \frac{f_{11} - f_{10}}{Su - Sd}$$

To determine gamma, Γ, we note that we have two estimates of Δ at time $2\Delta t$. When $S = (Su^2 + S)/2$ (half way between the second and third node), delta is $(f_{22} - f_{21})/(Su^2 - S)$; when $S = (S + Sd^2)/2$ (half way between the first and second node) delta is $(f_{21} - f_{20})/(S - Sd^2)$. The difference between the two values of S is h where

$$h = 0.5(Su^2 - Sd^2)$$

Gamma is the change in delta divided by the change in S or

$$\Gamma = \frac{[(f_{22} - f_{21})/(Su^2 - S)] - [(f_{21} - f_{20})/(S - Sd^2)]}{h} \tag{15.8}$$

These procedures provide estimates of delta at time Δt and of gamma at time $2\Delta t$. In practice, these are often used as estimates of delta and gamma at time zero as well. If slightly more accuracy is required, it makes sense to start the binomial tree at time $-2\Delta t$ and assume that the stock price is S at this time. The required estimate of the price of the option is then f_{21} (rather than f_{00}). More nodes have to be evaluated, but three different values of S are considered at time zero: Sd^2, S, and Su^2. An estimate of delta is

$$\Delta = \frac{f_{22} - f_{20}}{Su^2 - Sd^2} \tag{15.9}$$

and Equation (15.8) provides the estimate of gamma.

A further hedge parameter that can be obtained directly from the tree is theta, Θ. This is the rate of change of the option price with time when all else is kept constant. If the tree starts at time zero, an estimate of theta is

$$\Theta = \frac{f_{21} - f_{00}}{2\Delta t}$$

If the tree starts at time $-2\Delta t$, an estimate of theta is

$$\Theta = \frac{f_{42} - f_{00}}{4\Delta t} \tag{15.10}$$

Vega can be calculated by making a small change, $\Delta\sigma$, in the volatility and constructing a new tree to obtain a new value of the option (Δt should be kept the same). The estimate of vega is

$$\text{vega} = \frac{f^* - f}{\Delta\sigma}$$

where f and f^* are the estimates of the option price from the original and the new tree, respectively. Rho can be calculated similarly.

To illustrate the use of Equations (15.8), (15.9), and (15.10) consider a three-month American put option on a nondividend-paying stock when the stock price is \$50, the strike price is \$50, the risk-free interest rate is 10 percent per annum, and the volatility is 40 percent per annum. In this case $S = 50$, $X = 50$, $r = 0.10$, $\sigma = 0.4$, and $T = 0.25$. The option is exactly the same as the option considered in our earlier example (see Figure 15.3) except that it lasts for three months instead of five months. Choosing Δt equal to one month (= 0.0833 year), an estimate of the value of the option is the value of being at point C in Figure 15.3, that is, \$3.76.

In the context of our new example, Figure 15.3 starts at time $-2\Delta t$. From Equation (15.9), an estimate of delta can be obtained from the values at nodes B and F as

$$\frac{0.63 - 10.35}{62.99 - 39.69} = 0.42$$

From Equation (15.8), an estimate of the gamma of the option can be obtained from the values at nodes B, C, and F as

$$\frac{[(0.63 - 3.76)/(62.99 - 50.00)] - [(3.76 - 10.35)/(50.00 - 39.69)]}{11.65}$$

From Equation (15.10), an estimate of the theta of the option can be obtained from the values at nodes D and E as

$$\frac{2.66 - 4.48}{0.333} = -5.5$$

These are of course only rough estimates. They would be improved if a tree with a smaller Δt were constructed.

USING THE BINOMIAL TREE FOR OPTIONS ON INDICES, CURRENCIES, AND FUTURES CONTRACTS

As shown in Chapter 12, the binomial tree approach to valuing options on nondividend-paying stocks can easily be adapted to valuing American calls and puts on a stock paying a continuous dividend yield at rate q.

Since the dividends provide a return of q, the stock price itself must on average in a risk-neutral world provide a return of $r - q$. Hence, Equation (15.1) becomes:

$$Se^{(r-q)\Delta t} = pSu + (1 - p)Sd$$

so that Equation (15.2) becomes

$$e^{(r-q)\Delta t} = pu + (1 - p)d$$

It turns out that Equations (15.4), (15.5), and (15.6) are still correct but with

$$a = e^{(r-q)\Delta t} \qquad \textbf{(15.11)}$$

The binomial tree numerical procedure can, therefore, be used exactly as before with this new value of a.

It will be recalled from Chapters 12 and 13 that stock indices, currencies, and futures contracts can for the purposes of option evaluation be considered as stocks paying continuous dividend yields. In the case of a stock index, the relevant dividend yield is the dividend yield on the stock portfolio underlying the index; in the case of a currency it is the foreign risk-free interest rate; in the case of a futures contract, it is the domestic risk-free interest rate. The binomial tree approach can, therefore, be used to value options on stock indices, currencies, and futures contracts.

Example 1

Consider a four-month American call option on index futures where the current futures price is 300, the exercise price is 300, the risk-free interest rate is 8 percent per annum, and the volatility of the index is 40 percent per annum. We divide the life of the option into four one-month periods for the purposes of constructing the tree. In this case, $F = 300$, $X = 300$, $r = 0.08$, $\sigma = 0.4$, $T = 0.3333$, and $\Delta t = 0.0833$. Since a futures contract is analogous to a stock paying dividends at a continuous rate r, q should be set equal to r in Equation (15.11). This gives $a = 1$. The other parameters necessary to construct the tree are

$$u = e^{\sigma\sqrt{\Delta t}} = 1.1224, \qquad d = \frac{1}{u} = 0.8909$$

$$p = \frac{a - d}{u - d} = 0.4713, \qquad 1 - p = 0.5287$$

The tree is shown in Figure 15.4. (The upper number is the futures price; the lower number is the option price.) The estimated value of the option is 25.54.

Example 2

Consider a one-year American put option on the British pound. The current exchange rate is 1.6100, the strike price is 1.6000, the U.S. risk-free interest rate is 8 percent per annum, the sterling risk-free interest rate is 10 percent per annum, and the volatility of the sterling exchange rate is 12 percent per annum. In this case, $S = 1.61$, $X = 1.60$, $r = 0.08$, $r_f = 0.10$, $\sigma = 0.12$, and $T = 1.0$. We divide the life of the option into four three-month periods for the purposes of constructing the tree so that $\Delta t = 0.25$. In the case $q = r_f$ and Equation (15.11) gives

$$a = e^{(0.08 - 0.10)\times 0.25} = 0.9950$$

The other parameters necessary to construct the tree are

$$u = e^{\sigma\sqrt{\Delta t}} = 1.0618, \qquad d = \frac{1}{u} = 0.9418$$

$$p = \frac{a - d}{u - d} = 0.4433, \qquad 1 - p = 0.5567$$

The tree is shown in Figure 15.5. (The upper number is the exchange rate; the lower number is the option price.) The estimated value of the option is \$0.0782.

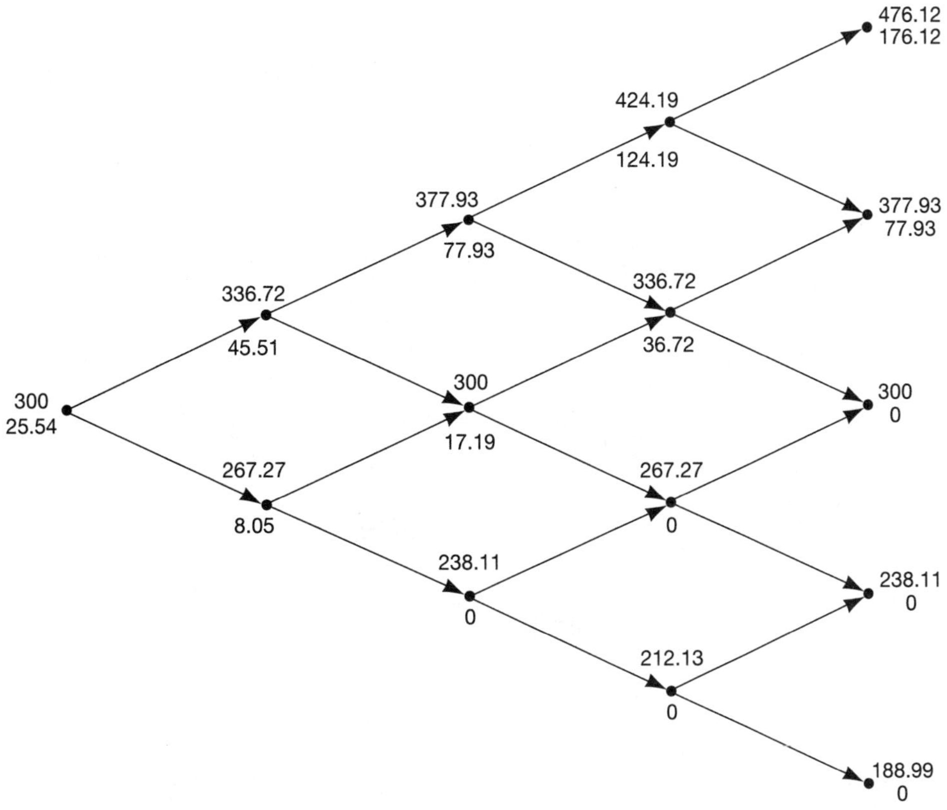

Figure 15.4 Binomial tree for American call option on an index futures contract.

THE BINOMIAL MODEL FOR A DIVIDEND-PAYING STOCK

We now move on to the more tricky issue of how the binomial model can be used for a dividend-paying stock. As in Chapter 11, the word "dividend" will for the purposes of our discussion be used to refer to the reduction in the stock price on the ex-dividend date as a result of the dividend.

If it is assumed that a known dividend yield, δ, is to be paid at a certain time in the future, the tree takes the form shown in Figure 15.6 and can be analyzed in a way that is analogous to that just described. If the time $i\Delta t$ is prior to the stock going ex-dividend, the nodes on the tree correspond to stock prices

$$Su^j d^{i-j} \qquad j = 0, 1, \ldots, i$$

where u and d are defined as in Equations (15.5) and (15.6). If the time $i\Delta t$ is after the stock goes ex-dividend, the nodes correspond to stock prices

$$S(1 - \delta)u^j d^{i-j} \qquad j = 0, 1, \ldots, i$$

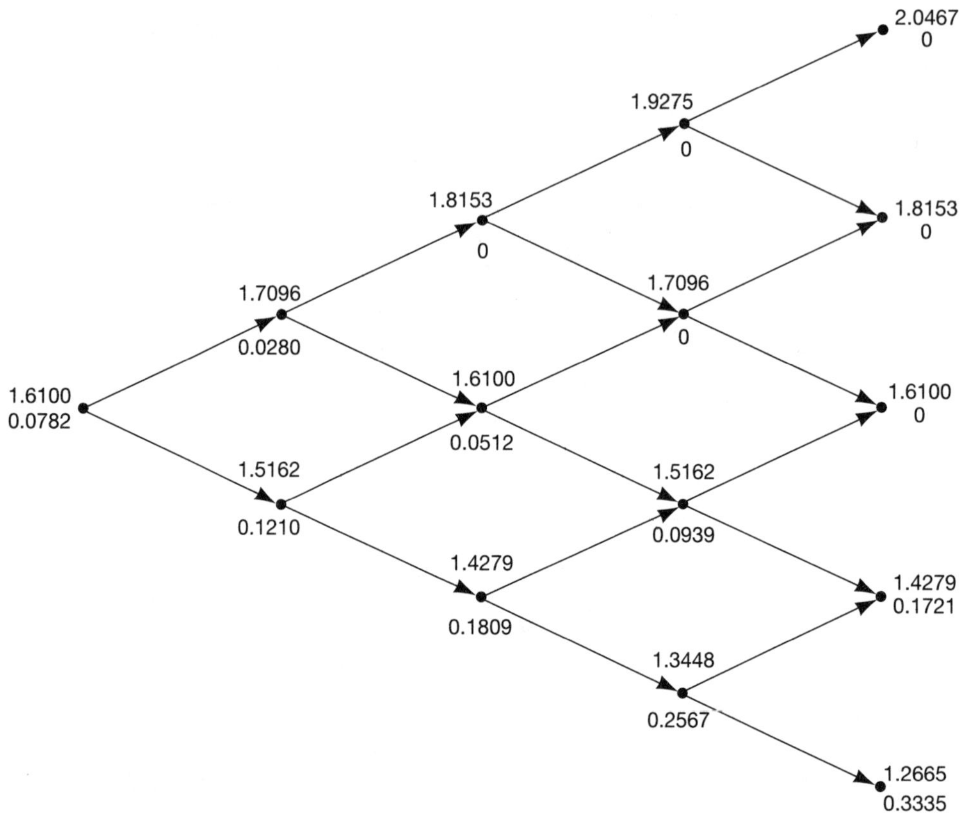

Figure 15.5 Binomial model for American put option on a currency.

Several known dividend yields during the life of an option can be dealt with similarly. If δ_i is the total dividend yield associated with all ex-dividend dates between time zero and time $i\Delta t$, the nodes at time $i\Delta t$ correspond to stock prices

$$S(1 - \delta_i)u^j d^{i-j}$$

A rather more realistic assumption is that the dollar amount of the dividend rather than the dividend yield is known in advance. If the volatility of the stock, σ, is assumed constant, the tree then takes the form shown in Figure 15.7. It does not recombine, which means that the number of nodes that have to be evaluated, particularly if there are several dividends, is liable to become very large. Suppose that there is only one dividend, that the ex-dividend date, τ, is between $k\Delta t$ and $(k + 1)\Delta t$, and that the dollar amount of the dividend is D. When $i \leq k$, the nodes on the tree at time $i\Delta t$ correspond to stock prices

$$Su^j d^{i-j} \qquad j = 0, 1, 2, \ldots, i$$

as before. When $i = k + 1$, the nodes on the tree correspond to stock prices

$$Su^j d^{i-j} - D \qquad j = 0, 1, 2, \ldots, i$$

When $i = k + 2$, the nodes on the tree correspond to stock prices

$$(Su^j d^{i-1-j} - D)u \qquad \text{and} \qquad (Su^j d^{i-1-j} - D)d$$

for $j = 0, 1, 2 \ldots, i - 1$, so that there are $2i$ rather than $i + 1$ nodes. At time $(k + m)\Delta t$, there are $m(k + 1)$ rather than $k + m + 1$ nodes.

The problem can be simplified by assuming, as in the analysis of European options in Chapter 11, that the stock price has two components: a part that is uncertain and a part that is the present value of all future dividends during the

Figure 15.6 Tree when stock pays a known dividend yield at one particular time.

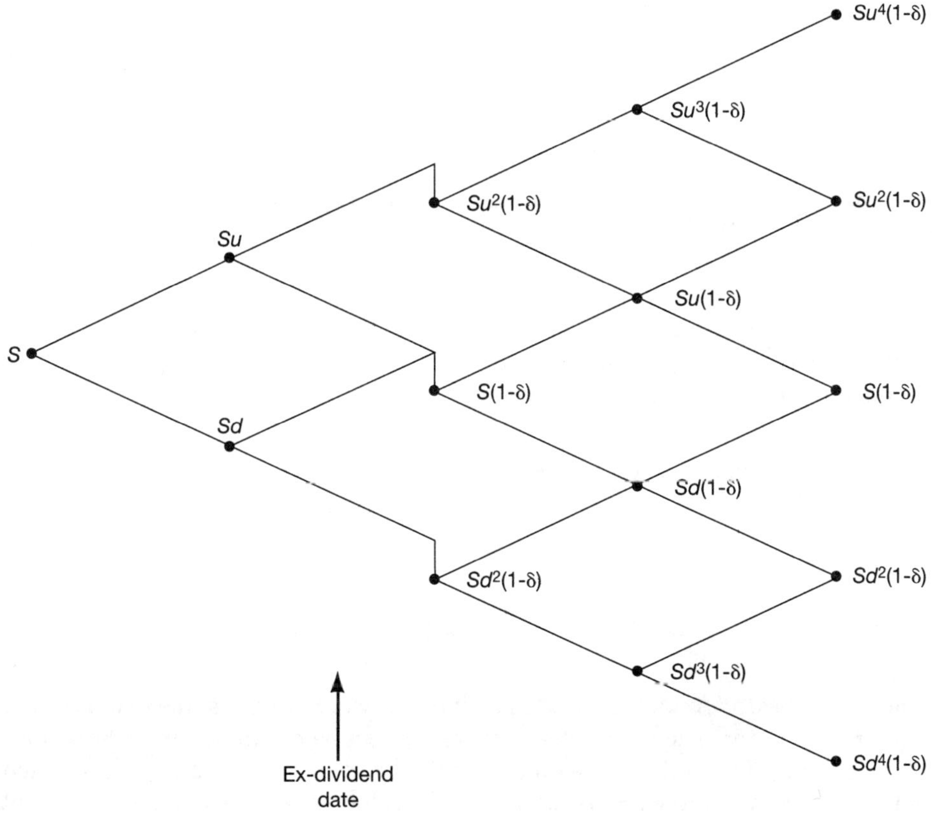

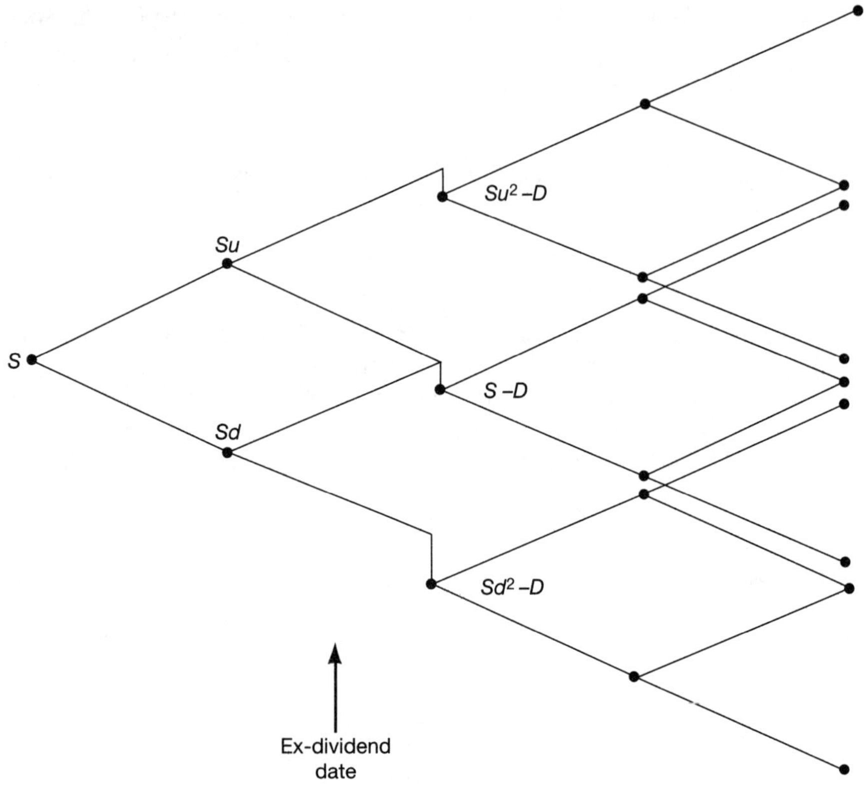

Figure 15.7 Tree when dollar amount of dividend is assumed known and volatility is assumed constant.

life of the option. Suppose as before that there is only one ex-dividend date, τ, during the life of the option and that $k\Delta t \leq \tau \leq (k + 1)\Delta t$. The value of the uncertain component, S^*, at time x is given by

$$S^*(x) = S(x) \qquad \text{when } x > \tau$$

and

$$S^*(x) = S(x) - De^{-r(\tau - x)} \qquad \text{when } x \leq \tau$$

where D is the dividend. Define σ^* as the volatility of S^* and assume that σ^* rather than σ is constant. The parameters p, u, and d can be calculated from Equations (15.4), (15.5), (15.6), and (15.7) with σ replaced by σ^* and a tree can be constructed in the usual way to model S^*. By adding to the stock price at each node the present value of future dividends (if any), the tree can be converted into another tree that models S. At time $i\Delta t$, the nodes on this tree correspond to the stock prices

$$S^*(t)u^j d^{i-j} + De^{-r(\tau - i\Delta t)} \qquad j = 0, 1, \ldots, i$$

when $i\Delta t < \tau$ and

$$S^*(t)u^j d^{i-j} \qquad j = 0, 1, \ldots, i$$

when $i\Delta t > \tau$. This approach, which involves a perfectly reasonable assumption about the stock price volatility, succeeds in achieving a situation where the tree recombines so that there are $i + 1$ nodes at time $i\Delta t$. It can be generalized in a straightforward way to deal with the situation where there are several dividends.

An Example

To illustrate the approach, consider a five-month put option on a stock that is expected to pay a single dividend of $2.06 during the life of the option. The initial stock price is $52, the strike price is $50, the risk-free interest rate is 10 percent per annum, the volatility is 40 percent per annum, and the ex-dividend date is in 3.5 months.

We first construct a tree to model S^*, the stock price less the present value of future dividends during the life of the option. Initially, the present value of the dividend is

$$2.06e^{-0.2917 \times 0.1} = 2.00$$

The initial value of S^* is, therefore, 50.0. Assuming that the 40 percent per annum volatility refers to S^*, Figure 15.3 provides a binomial tree for S^*. (S^* has the same initial value and volatility as the stock price upon which Figure 15.3 was based.) Adding the present value of the dividend at each node leads to Figure 15.8, which is a binomial model for S. The probabilities at each node are, as in Figure 15.3, 0.5076 for an up movement and 0.4924 for a down movement. Working back through the tree in the usual way gives the option price as $4.43.

THE CONTROL VARIATE TECHNIQUE

In most circumstances the binomial tree approach for valuing American options can be improved by using what is known as the *control variate technique*. This technique involves using the same tree to value both the American option that is of interest and the corresponding European option. This may seem wasteful since

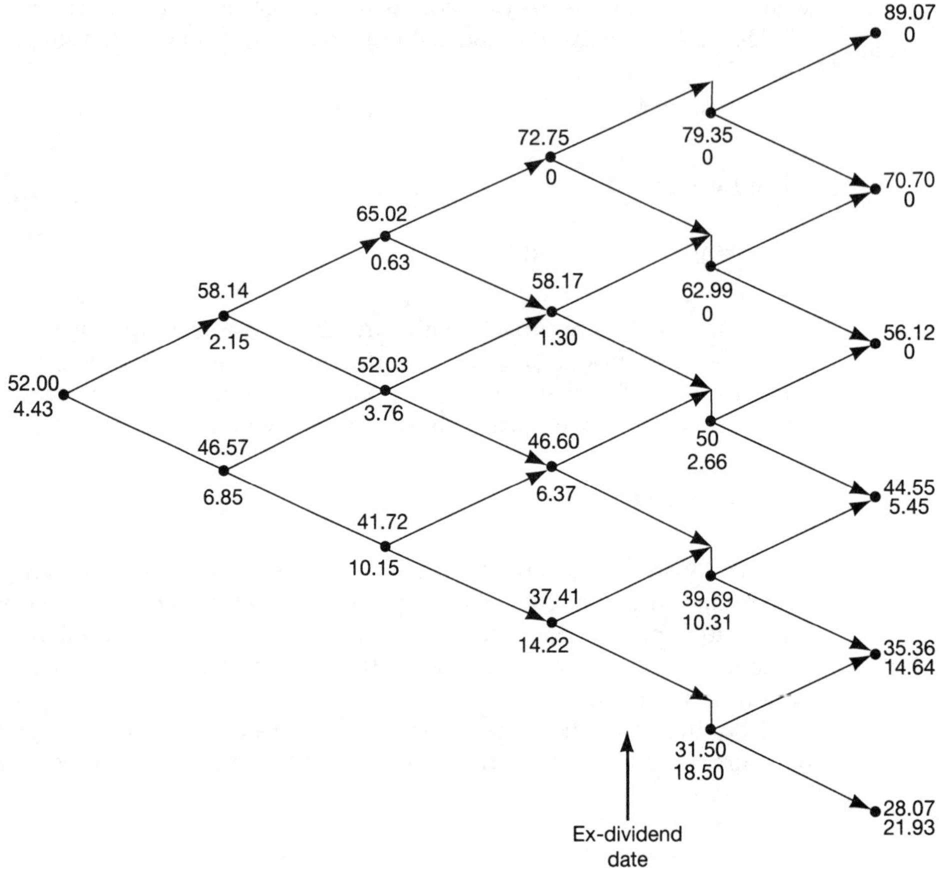

Figure 15.8 Tree for stock paying a known stock dividend at a certain time.

the European option price is known from the Black–Scholes formulas and its extensions. However, since errors in the calculated price of the American option are generally closely correlated with errors in the calculated price of the European option, it leads to a way of improving the estimate of the price of the American option.

Define

f_A: price of American option calculated from tree
f_E: price of European option calculated from tree
f_{BS}: Black–Scholes price of European option

An improved estimate of the price of the American option is

$$f_A + f_{BS} - f_E$$

Example

Consider again the American put option being valued in Figure 15.3 ($S = 50$, $X = 50$, $r = 0.10$, $\sigma = 0.40$, $T = 0.4167$). Figure 15.9 uses the same tree as Figure 15.3 to value the corresponding European option. The resulting price is \$4.31 (compared with \$4.48 for the American option in Figure 15.3). From the Black–Scholes formula, the true European price is \$4.08. The control variate estimate of the American price is, therefore,

$$4.48 + 4.08 - 4.31 = 4.25$$

The true American price is \$4.29. The control variate approach does, there-

Figure 15.9 Tree for European version of option in Figure 15.3. At each node upper number is stock price, lower number is option price.

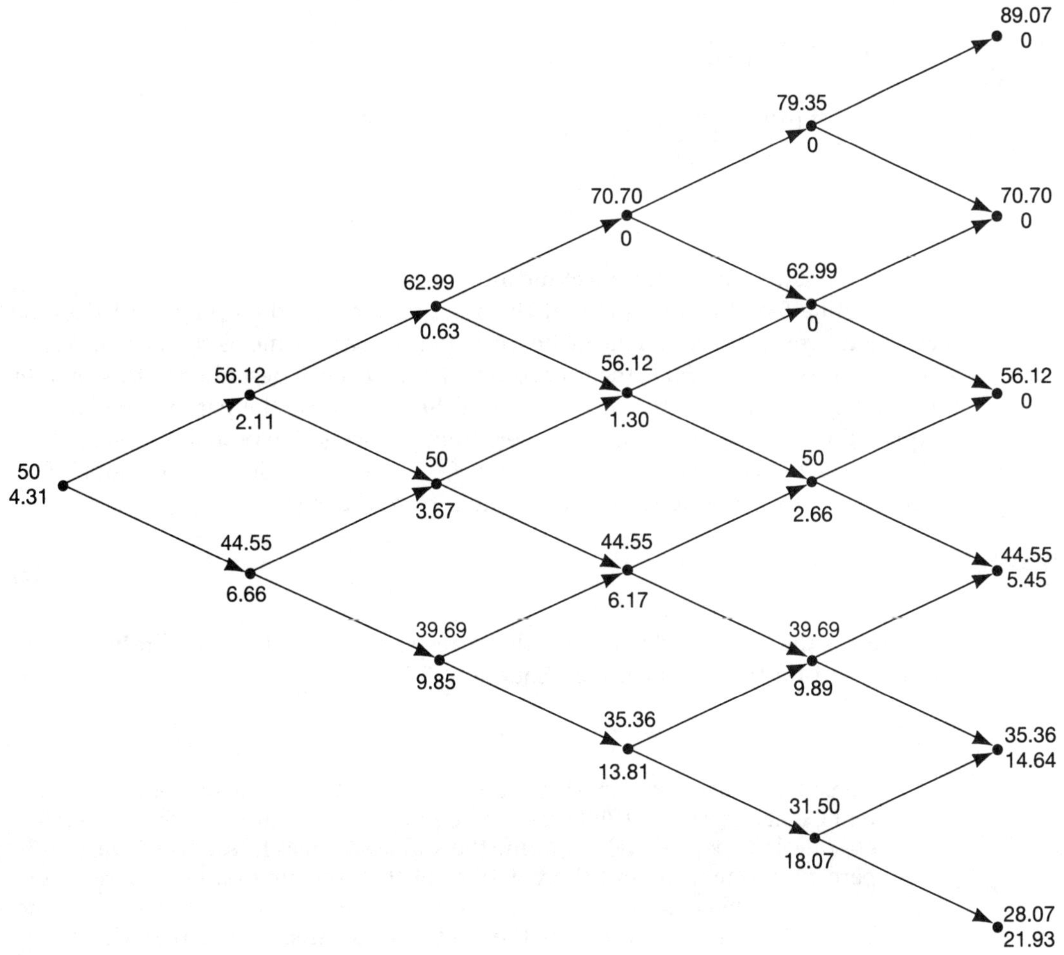

fore, produce a considerable improvement over the original estimate in this particular case.

AVOIDING NEGATIVE PROBABILITIES

The procedures that have been described so far produce a satisfactory tree in most circumstances. However, when σ is very small, they sometimes lead to one of the two probabilities being either very small or negative. For example, if r is 12 percent per annum, σ is 1 percent per annum, and $\Delta t = 0.1$, Equations (15.4) to (15.7) give:

$$a = e^{0.1 \times 0.12} = 1.0121$$

$$u = e^{0.01 \times \sqrt{0.1}} = 1.0032$$

$$d = \frac{1}{u} = 0.9968$$

$$p = \frac{1.0121 - 0.9968}{1.0032 - 0.9968} = 2.39$$

$$1 - p = -1.39$$

The probabilities are in this case meaningless!

Define S as the spot price of the asset underlying the option and F as the asset's futures price for a contract expiring at the same time as the option. When the tree is used to model F, the procedures that have been described in this chapter never give rise to negative probabilities. (This is because the parameter a always equals 1.0.) This suggests a way of overcoming the negative probabilities problem. Regardless of whether the option is on F, we construct the tree to model F. If necessary, at each node we can calculate S from F using

$$S = Fe^{-(r-q)(T-\tau)} \tag{15.12}$$

where τ is the time to which the node corresponds and T is the expiration of the option and futures contract. (See Equation (3.7).)

Example

Consider a one-year American call option on the Canadian dollar. The current exchange rate is 0.7900, the strike price is 0.8000, the U.S. risk-free interest rate is 6 percent per annum, the Canadian risk-free interest rate is 10 percent per annum, and the volatility of the exchange rate is 4 percent per annum. In this case $S = 0.79$, $X = 0.80$, $r = 0.06$, $r_f = 0.10$, $\sigma = 0.04$, and $T = 1$. We divide the life of the option into three-month periods for the purpose of constructing the tree so that $\Delta t = 0.25$. When using the tree to model the futures price for a contract maturing in one year,

$$a = 1$$

$$u = e^{0.04 \times \sqrt{0.25}} = 1.0202$$

$$d = \frac{1}{u} = 0.9802$$

$$p = \frac{a - d}{u - d} = 0.4950$$

$$1 - p = 0.5050$$

The initial futures price is, from Equation (3.7),

$$0.79e^{(0.06 - 0.10) \times 1} = 0.7590$$

The tree for the futures price is shown in Figure 15.10. At each node the

Figure 15.10 Binomial tree for American call option on a low-volatility currency. At each node, the uppermost number is the spot exchange rate, the middle number is the futures exchange rate, and the lower number is the option price.

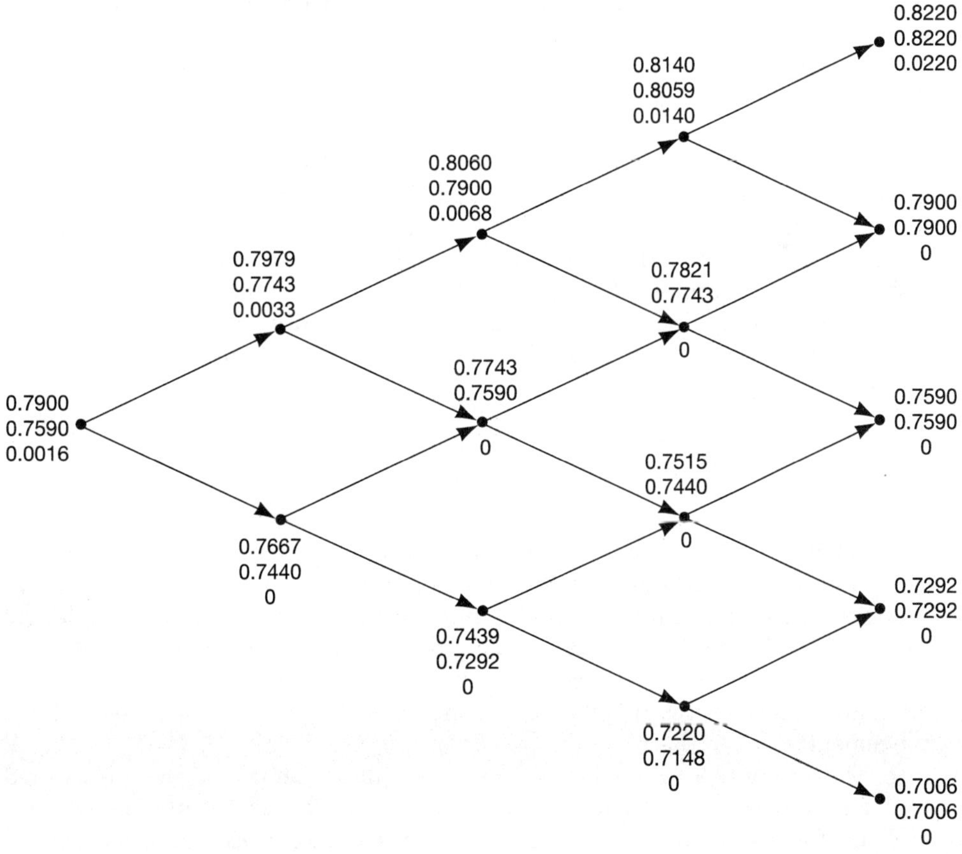

middle number shows the futures exchange rate, the upper number shows the spot exchange rate [calculated using Equation (15.12)], and the lower number shows the option price. The tree gives the value of the option as \$0.0016.

MONTE CARLO SIMULATION

Binomial trees can be used in conjunction with a technique known as *Monte Carlo simulation*. This involves randomly sampling paths through the tree. Instead of working backwards from the end of the tree to the beginning, we work forward through the tree. The basic procedure is as follows. At the first node we sample a random number between 0 and 1. If the number lies between 0 and p, we take the upper branch; if it lies between p and 1, we take the lower branch. We repeat this procedure at the node that is then reached and at all subsequent nodes that are reached until we get to the end of the tree. We then calculate the payoff on the option for the particular path sampled. This completes the first trial. We then carry out many trials by repeating the whole procedure. Our estimate of the value of the option is the arithmetic average of the payoffs from all the trials discounted at the risk-free interest rate.

Monte Carlo simulation, as just described, cannot be used for American options since we have no way of knowing whether early exercise is optimal when a certain node is reached. It can be used to value European options so that a check is provided on the pricing formulas for these options. It can also sometimes be used to price what are known as *exotic options*. These are options with more complicated payoffs than the standard call and put. Examples of exotic options that can be priced using Monte Carlo simulation are Asian options and lookback options. Asian options are options that provide a payoff based on the average asset price during the life of the option. Lookback options are options that provide a payoff based on the maximum or minimum stock price achieved during the life of the option.

SUMMARY

In this chapter we have been concerned with describing how options can be valued using the binomial tree approach. This approach, when used for stock options, involves dividing the life of the option into a number of small intervals of length Δt and assuming that a stock price at the beginning of an interval can only lead to one of two alternative stock prices at the end of the interval. One of these alternative stock prices involves an up movement; the other involves a down movement.

The size of the up movements and down movements, and their associated probabilities, are chosen so that the change in the stock price has the correct mean and standard deviation for a risk-neutral world. Option prices are calculated by starting at the end of the tree and working backward. At the end of the tree, the price of the option is its intrinsic value. At earlier nodes on the tree, the value of an option, if it is American, must be calculated as the greater of

1. The value it has if exercised immediately
2. The value it has if held for a further period of time of length Δt

If it is exercised immediately the value of the option is its intrinsic value. If it is held for a further period of length Δt, its value is the discounted value of its expected worth at the end of the time period Δt.

Delta, gamma, and theta can be estimated directly from the values of the option at the various nodes of the tree. Vega can be estimated by making a small change to the volatility and recomputing the value of the option using a similar tree. Rho can be estimated by making a small change to the interest rate and recomputing the tree.

The binomial tree approach can easily be extended to accommodate options on stocks paying continuous dividend yields. Since stock indices, currencies, and most futures contracts can be regarded as analogous to stocks paying continuous yields, they can be used to value options on these assets as well.

When the binomial tree approach is used to value options on a stock paying known dollar dividends, it is convenient to use the tree to model the stock price less the present value of all future dividends during the life of the option. This avoids the number of nodes on the tree becoming unmanageable. When one of the probabilities becomes low or negative, the binomial tree approach does not work well. It is then appropriate to use the tree to model the futures price of the asset rather than the asset price itself.

The computational efficiency of the binomial tree approach can be improved by using the control variate technique. This involves valuing both the American option that is of interest and the corresponding European option using the same tree. The error in the price of the European option is used as an estimate of the error in the price of the American option.

Binomial trees can be used in conjunction with a technique known as Monte Carlo simulation. This technique is particularly useful for European options that provide nonstandard payoffs.

Suggestions for Further Reading

On binomial trees

BOYLE, P. P., "A lattice framework for option pricing with two state variables," *Journal of Financial and Quantitative Analysis*, 23 (March 1988), 1–12.

COX, J., S. ROSS, and M. RUBINSTEIN, "Option pricing: a simplified approach," *Journal of Financial Economics*, 7 (October 1979), 229–264.

HULL, J., and A. WHITE, "The use of the control variate technique in option pricing," *Journal of Financial and Quantitative Analysis*, 23 (September, 1988), 237–251.

On other approaches

BARONE-ADESI, G., and R. E. WHALEY, "Efficient analytic approximation of American option values," *Journal of Finance*, 42 (June 1987), 301–320.

BOYLE, P. P., "Options: a Monte Carlo approach," *Journal of Financial Economics*, 4 (1977), 323–338.

BRENNAN, M. J., and E.S. SCHWARTZ, "Finite difference methods and jump processes arising in the pricing of contingent claims: A synthesis," *Journal of Financial and Quantitative Analysis*, 13 (September 1978), 462–474.

BRENNAN, M., and E. S. SCHWARTZ, "The valuation of American put options," *Journal of Finance*, 32 (May 1977), 449–462.

COURTADON, G, "A more accurate finite difference approximation for the valuation of options," *Journal of Financial and Quantitative Analysis*, 17 (December 1982), 697–705.

GESKE, R., and H.E. JOHNSON, "The American put valued analytically," *Journal of Finance*, 39 (December 1984), 1511–1524.

HULL, J., *Options, Futures, and Other Derivative Securities*. Englewood Cliffs, NJ: Prentice Hall, 1989.

HULL, J., and A. WHITE, "Valuing derivative securities using the explicit finite difference method," *Journal of Financial and Quantitative Analysis*, 25 (March 1990), 87–100.

JOHNSON, H. E., "An analytic approximation to the American put price," *Journal of Financial and Quantitative Analysis*, 18 (March 1983), 141–148.

MACMILLAN, L. W., "Analytic approximation for the American put option," *Advances in Futures and Options Research*, 1 (1986), 119–139.

SCHWARTZ, E. S., "The valuation of warrants: implementing a new approach," *Journal of Financial Economics*, 4 (1977), 79–94.

Quiz

1. Which of the following can be estimated for an American option by constructing a single binomial tree: delta, gamma, vega, theta, rho?
2. Calculate the price of a three-month American put option on a nondividend-paying stock when the stock price is \$60, the strike price is \$60, the risk-free interest rate is 10 percent per annum, and the volatility is 45 percent per annum. Use a binomial tree with a time interval of one month.
3. Explain how the control variate technique is implemented.
4. Calculate the price of a nine-month American call option on corn futures when the current futures price is 198 cents, the strike price is 200 cents, the risk-free interest rate is 8 percent per annum, and the volatility is 30 percent per annum. Use a binomial tree with a time interval of three months.
5. Consider an option that pays off the amount by which the final stock price exceeds the average stock price achieved during the life of the option. Can this be valued by the binomial tree approach?
6. "For a dividend-paying stock the tree for the stock price does not recombine, but the tree for the stock price less the present value of future dividends does recombine." Explain this statement.
7. Under what circumstances are the probabilities in a binomial tree negative? How can this problem be overcome?

Questions and Problems

15.1. A one-year American put option on a nondividend-paying stock has an exercise price of \$18. The current stock price is \$20, the risk-free interest rate is 15 percent per annum and the volatility of the stock is 40 percent per annum. Divide the year into four three-month time intervals and use the binomial tree approach to estimate the value of the option. Use the control variate technique to improve this estimate.

15.2. A one-year American call option on silver futures has an exercise price of \$9. The current futures price is \$8.50, the risk-free rate of interest is 12 percent per annum, and the volatility of the futures price is 25 percent per annum.

Divide the year into four three-month intervals and use the binomial tree approach to estimate the value of the option. Use the control variate technique to improve this estimate. Extend the tree to estimate the delta of the option.

15.3. A two-month American put option on the Major Market Index has an exercise price of 480. The current level of the index is 484, the risk-free interest rate is 10 percent per annum, the dividend yield on the index is 3 percent per annum, and the volatility of the index is 25 percent per annum. Divide the life of the option into four half-month periods and use the binomial tree approach to estimate the value of the option.

15.4. A six-month American call option on a stock is expected to pay dividends of \$1 per share at the end of the second month and the fifth month. The current stock price is \$30, the exercise price is \$34, the risk-free interest rate is 10 percent per annum and the volatility of the part of the stock price that will not be used to pay the dividends is 30 percent per annum. Divide the life of the option into six one-month periods and use the binomial tree approach to estimate the value of the option. Compare your answer to that given by Black's method (see Chapter 11). Estimate the delta of the option from your tree.

15.5. How would you use the control variate approach to improve the estimate of the delta of an American option when the binomial tree approach is used?

15.6. How would you use the binomial tree approach to value an American option on a stock index when the dividend yield on the index is a function of time?

16

BIASES IN THE BLACK–SCHOLES MODEL

Since Black and Scholes published their pathbreaking paper in 1973, there has been a great deal of interest in refining their model and identifying differences between the prices calculated from the model and the prices observed in the market. Several alternatives to Black–Scholes have been suggested and a great deal of empirical research has been carried out. In this chapter we review these developments. Most of the analysis is presented in the context of valuing European options on nondividend-paying stocks. However, the analysis can in most instances be extended to cover American stock options, situations where there are dividends, and the options considered in Chapters 12 and 13.

DEPARTURES FROM LOGNORMALITY

As explained in Chapter 11, the model of stock price behavior underlying Black–Scholes assumes that the distribution of the stock price at some future time, conditional on its value today, is lognormal. Equivalently, it assumes that the continuously compounded rate of return on the stock in any given time interval is normally distributed. Tests of option pricing frequently show that in-the-money and/or out-of-the-money options appear to be mispriced relative to at-the-money options. That is, the volatility for which the Black–Scholes equation correctly prices at-the-money options causes it to misprice in-the-money and out-of-the-money options. These pricing biases can be explained by differences between the lognormal distribution assumed by Black–Scholes and the true distribution.

Figure 16.1 shows four ways in which the true terminal distribution can be

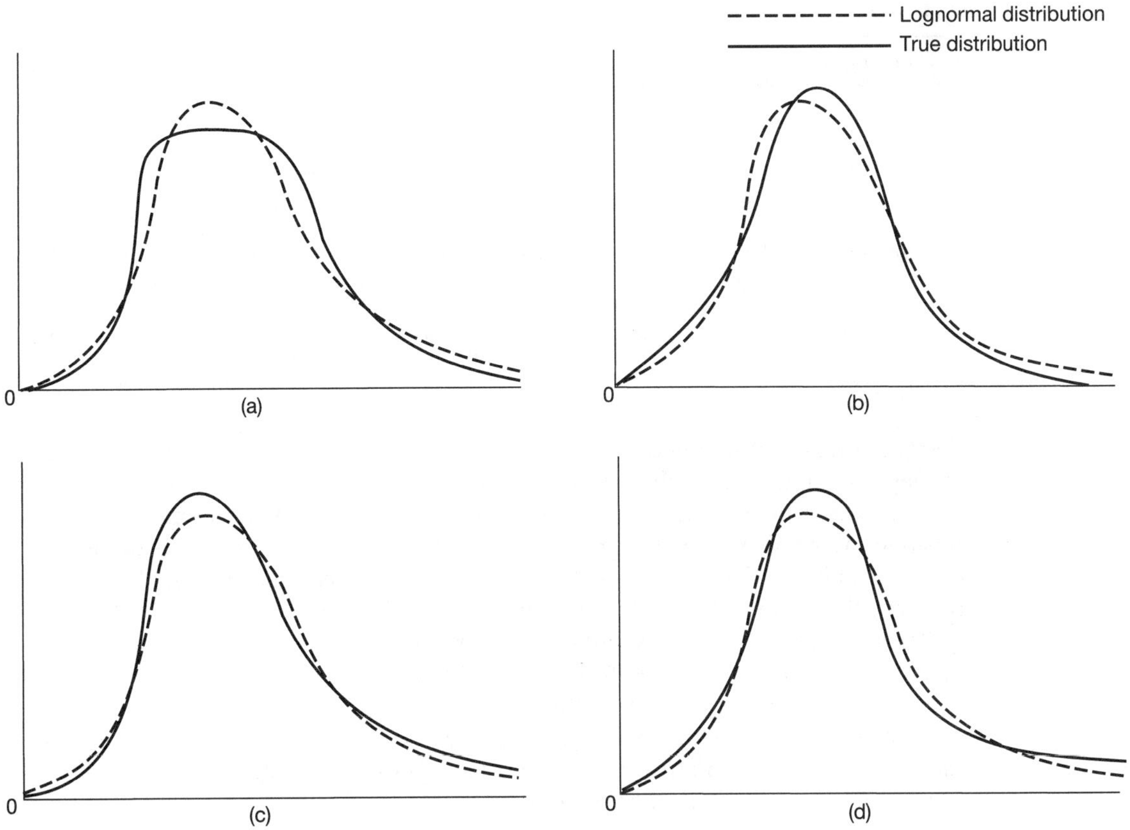

Figure 16.1 Alternative stock price distributions. Dashed line, lognormal distribution; solid line, true distribution. All distributions have same mean and standard deviation.

different from a lognormal distribution, while still giving the same mean and standard deviation for the stock price return. In Figure 16.1a, both tails are thinner than the lognormal distribution; in Figure 16.1d, both tails are fatter; in Figures 16.1b and 16.1c, one tail is thinner and the other is fatter.

Effect on Option Prices

We now consider the difference between the correct option price and the Black–Scholes price that would be observed in the four situations. We refer to this difference as a *bias*. Consider, first, a call option that is significantly out of the money. It has a positive value only if there is a large increase in the stock price. Its value, therefore, depends only on the right tail of the terminal stock price distribution. The fatter this tail, the more valuable the option is. Consequently, Black–Scholes will tend to underprice out-of-the-money calls when the stock price

Table 16.1 Biases Corresponding to Alternative Stock Price Distributions in Figure 16.1

DISTRIBUTION	*CHARACTERISTICS*	*BIASES*
Figure 16.1a	Both tails thinner	Black-Scholes overprices both out-of-the-money and in-the-money calls and puts.
Figure 16.1b	Left tail fatter, right tail thinner	Black-Scholes overprices out-of-the-money calls and in-the-money puts. It underprices out-of-the-money puts and in-the-money calls.
Figure 16.1c	Left tail thinner, right tail fatter	Black-Scholes overprices out-of-the-money puts and in-the-money calls. It underprices in-the-money puts and out-of-the-money calls.
Figure 16.1d	Both tails fatter	Black-Scholes underprices both out-of-the-money and in-the-money calls and puts.

distribution is as illustrated in Figures 16.1c and 16.1d and overprice out-of-the-money calls in the cases shown in Figures 16.1a and 16.1b.

Consider next a put option that is significantly out of the money. It has a positive value only if there is a large decrease in the stock price. Its value, therefore, depends only on the left tail of the terminal stock price distribution. The fatter this tail, the more valuable the option is. Black–Scholes will, therefore, tend to underprice out-of-the-money puts in Figures 16.1b and 16.1d and overprice out-of-the-money puts in Figures 16.1a and 16.1c.

To obtain the biases for in-the-money European options, we can use put-call parity. If S is the stock price, X is the exercise price, r is the risk-free interest rate, T is the time to maturity, c is the price of European call, p is the price of a European put, and no dividends are paid,

$$p + S = c + Xe^{-rT}$$

This relationship is independent of the terminal stock price distribution. If the European call with price c is out of the money, the corresponding European put with price p is in the money, and vice versa. Consequently, an in-the-money European put must exhibit the same pricing biases as the corresponding out-of-the-money European call. Similarly, an in-the-money European call must exhibit the same pricing biases as the corresponding out-of-the-money European put. The biases are, therefore, as indicated in Table 16.1.

ALTERNATIVES TO BLACK–SCHOLES

In this section we consider a number of alternatives to the basic Black–Scholes model and show how they can be categorized in the way indicated previously.

Uncertain Volatility

The Black–Scholes model assumes that volatility is constant. In practice the future volatility of the stock price is uncertain. Consider first the case where the volatility is positively correlated with the stock price. When the stock price increases, volatility tends to increase. This means that very high stock prices are more likely than when the volatility is constant. When the stock price decreases, volatility tends to decrease. This means that very low stock prices are less likely than when the volatility is constant. The situation where volatility and stock price are positively correlated, therefore, corresponds to Figure 16.1c.

Consider next the case where the volatility is negatively correlated with the stock price. When the stock price increases, volatility tends to decrease, making it less likely that very high stock prices will be achieved. When the stock price decreases, volatility tends to increase, making it more likely that very low stock prices will be achieved. The situation in which the volatility and stock price are negatively correlated, therefore, corresponds to the situation in Figure 16.1b.

It can be shown that when there is no significant correlation between stock price and volatility, the situation corresponds to Figure 16.1d; Black–Scholes tends to underprice both significantly in-the-money and significantly out-of-the-money options.

Compound Option Model

Geske has proposed a model that recognizes that the equity in a levered firm can be viewed as a call option on the assets of the firm. Suppose that the value of the firm is V and that the face value of outstanding debt is D. Suppose further that all debt matures at a single time T. If $V < D$ at time T, the value of the equity at this time is zero, since all the company's assets go to the bondholders. If $V > D$ at time T, the value of the equity at this time is $V - D$. The value of the equity at time T can, therefore, be written as

$$\max(V - D, 0)$$

Thus, the equity can be regarded as a European call option on V with maturity T and strike price D.

An option on the equity of the firm that expires earlier than T can be regarded as an option on an option on V. This is known as a *compound option*. Geske assumes that the volatility of V is constant and that the amount of debt, D, is also constant. The volatility of the stock price is then negatively correlated with S. This is because the volatility of S increases with leverage. When V increases, S increases and the leverage decreases so that the volatility of S decreases. When V decreases, S decreases and the leverage increases so that the volatility of S increases. From our discussion of the uncertain volatility situation, we know that this means that the biases are the same as those implied by the distribution in Figure 16.1b. If the compound option model accurately describes the world, we can expect Black–Scholes to overprice out-of-the-money calls and in-the-money puts and to underprice out-of-the-money puts and in-the-money calls.

Jumps

A number of researchers have suggested models where the stock price moves with jumps rather than by changing continuously. The general effect of jumps is that extreme outcomes become more likely. The probability distribution of a future stock price, therefore, exhibits the pattern shown in Figure 16.1d. This means that Black–Scholes tends to underprice call and put options that are both out of the money and in the money.

THE TIME-TO-MATURITY EFFECT

In addition to being categorized according to the terminal stock price distribution, the alternatives to Black–Scholes can be categorized according to whether the bias increases or decreases as the time to maturity of the option increases.

Consider first the biases caused by an uncertain volatility. An uncertain volatility has relatively little effect when the time to maturity is small. However, its effect increases as the maturity of the option increases. The reason for this is easy to understand. Just as the effect of volatility on the standard deviation of the stock price distribution increases as we look farther ahead, so the distortions to that distribution caused by uncertainties in the volatility become greater as we look farther ahead. For a similar reason, the biases in the compound option model become more pronounced as the time to maturity increases.

Jumps are different in that they produce proportionately greater effects when the time to maturity of the option is small. When we look sufficiently far into the future, jumps tend to get "averaged out" so that the stock price distribution arising from jumps is almost indistinguishable from that arising from continuous changes.

WHEN A SINGLE LARGE JUMP IS ANTICIPATED

Up to now, when talking about models involving jumps, we have been referring to situations where a stock price regularly exhibits modest jumps. We now move on to consider cases where a single large jump in the stock price is anticipated. This may be because some important announcement concerning the fortunes of the company (for example, the outcome of a takeover attempt) is anticipated. The Black–Scholes model is then inappropriate.

Suppose that a stock price is currently \$50 and an important announcement in one month is expected to either increase the stock price by \$8 or reduce it by \$8. The probability distribution of the stock price in, say, two months might then consist of two lognormal distributions superimposed upon each other, the first corresponding to favorable news in one month, the second to unfavorable news in one month. This situation is illustrated in Figure 16.2. The solid line shows the true stock price distribution in two months; the broken line shows a lognormal distribution with the same standard deviation as the true distribution.

The true probability distribution in Figure 16.2 is bimodal. One easy way to investigate the general effect of a bimodal stock price distribution is to consider the extreme case where the distribution is binomial. This is the approach we will now take.

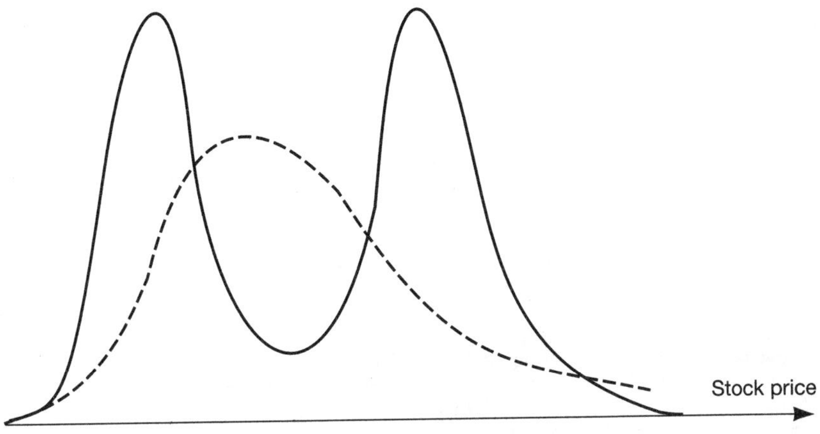

Figure 16.2 Effect of a single large jump. Solid line, true distribution; broken line, lognormal distribution.

Suppose that a stock price is currently \$50 and that it is known that in one month it will either be \$42 or \$58. Suppose further that the risk-free interest rate is 12 percent per annum. This situation is illustrated in Figure 16.3. We can use an approach similar to that developed in Chapter 10. The stock price must on average grow from \$50 to $50e^{0.12\times0.0833} = \$50.50$ in a risk-neutral world. The probability p of an up movement in a risk-neutral world must, therefore, satisfy

$$58p + 42(1 - p) = 50.50$$

which means that p is 0.53. This value of p implies that the standard deviation of the change in the stock price in one month is 8.0. Its volatility per month is, therefore, 8/50 or 16 percent, and its volatility per year is $16\sqrt{12} = 55$ percent per annum.

Table 16.2 shows the call and put price calculated on the basis of the binomial model using the approach explained in Chapter 10. Table 16.3 shows the volatilities implied by the prices in Table 16.2 when the Black–Scholes model is used. (From put-call parity, the volatilities implied by the call prices must be the same as the volatilities implied by the put prices.) If the same volatility were used for the whole range of strike prices, it is clear that Black–Scholes would significantly overprice very deep-in-the-money and very deep-out-of-the-money options. However, it would underprice options that are relatively close to the money.

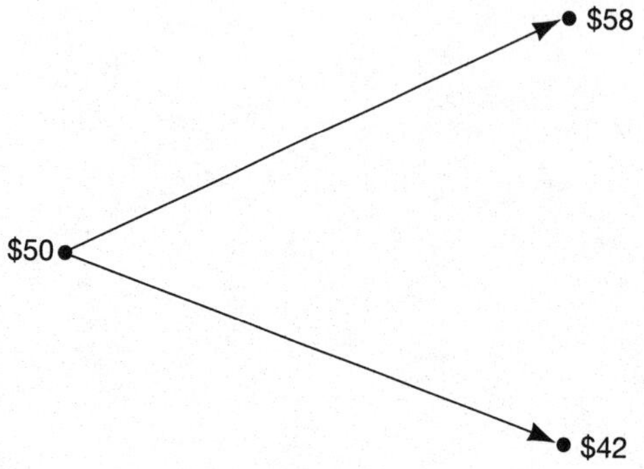

Figure 16.3 Change in stock price in one month.

Table 16.2 Option Prices Using the Binomial Model

STRIKE PRICE ($)	*CALL PRICE ($)*	*PUT PRICE ($)*
42	8.42	0.00
44	7.37	0.93
46	6.31	1.86
48	5.26	2.78
50	4.21	3.71
52	3.16	4.64
54	2.10	5.57
56	1.05	6.50
58	0.00	7.42

Table 16.3 Implied Volatilities When Black-Scholes Is Used and True Distribution of Stock Prices Is Binomial

STRIKE PRICE ($)	*IMPLIED VOLATILITY (% PER ANNUM)*
42	0.0
44	58.8
46	66.6
48	69.5
50	69.2
52	66.1
54	60.0
56	49.0
58	0.0

EMPIRICAL RESEARCH

There are a number of problems in carrying out empirical research to test the Black–Scholes and other option pricing models. The first problem is that any statistical hypothesis about how options are priced has to be a joint hypothesis to the effect that (1) the option pricing formula is correct and (2) markets are efficient. If the hypothesis is rejected, it may be the case that (1) is untrue, (2) is untrue, or both (1) and (2) are untrue. A second problem is that the stock price volatility is an unobservable variable. One approach is to estimate the volatility from historical stock price data. Alternatively, implied volatilities can be used in some way. A third problem for the researcher is to make sure that data on the stock price and option price are synchronous. For example, if the option is thinly traded, it is not likely to be acceptable to compare closing option prices with closing stock prices. This is because the closing option price might correspond to a trade at 1:00 p.m., while the closing stock price corresponds to a trade at 4:00 p.m.

Black and Scholes and Galai have tested whether it is possible to make excess returns above the risk-free rate of interest by buying options that are undervalued by the market (relative to the theoretical price) and selling options that are overvalued by the market (relative to the theoretical price). A riskless delta-neutral portfolio is assumed to be maintained at all times by trading the underlying stocks on a regular basis as described in Chapter 14. Black and Scholes used data from the over-the-counter options market where options are dividend protected. Galai used data from the Chicago Board Options Exchange (CBOE) where options are not protected against the effects of cash dividends. Galai used Black's procedure as described in Chapter 11 to incorporate the effect of anticipated dividends into the option price. Both studies showed that in the absence of transactions costs significant excess returns over the risk-free rate can be obtained by buying undervalued options and selling overvalued options. However, it is possible that these excess returns are available only to market makers and that when transaction costs are considered, they vanish.

A number of researchers have chosen to make no assumptions about the behavior of stock prices and have tested whether arbitrage strategies can be used to make a riskless profit in options markets. Garman provides a very efficient computational procedure for finding any arbitrage possibilities that exist in a given situation.[1] One study by Klemkosky and Resnick which is frequently cited tests whether the relationship in Equation (8.9), is ever violated. It concludes that some small arbitrage profits were possible from using the relationship. These were due mainly to the overpricing of American calls.

Chiras and Manaster have carried out a study using CBOE data comparing the weighted implied standard deviation from options on a stock at a point in

[1] See M. B. Garman, "An algebra for evaluating hedge portfolios," *Journal of Financial Economics*, 3 (October 1976), 403–427.

time with the standard deviation calculated from historical data. They found that the former provide a much better forecast of the volatility of the stock price during the life of the option. The study has been repeated by other authors using other data and has always given similar results. We can conclude that option traders are using more than just historical data when determining future volatilities. Chiras and Manaster also tested to see whether it was possible to make above-average returns by buying options with low implied standard deviations and selling options with high implied standard deviations. This strategy showed a profit of 10 percent per month. The Chiras and Manaster study can be interpreted as providing good support for the Black–Scholes model, while showing that the CBOE was inefficient in some respects.

MacBeth and Merville have tested the Black–Scholes model using a different approach. They looked at different call options on the same stock at the same time and compared the volatilities implied by the option prices. The stocks chosen were AT&T, Avon, Kodak, Exxon, IBM, and Xerox, and the time period considered was the year 1976. They found that implied volatilities tended to be relatively high for in-the-money options and relatively low for out-of-the-money options. A relatively high implied volatility is indicative of a relatively high option price, and a relatively low implied volatility is indicative of a relatively low option price. Therefore, if it is assumed that Black–Scholes prices at-the-money options correctly, it can be concluded that out-of-the-money call options are overpriced by Black–Scholes and in-the-money call options are underpriced by Black–Scholes. These effects become more pronounced as the time to maturity increases and the degree to which the option is in or out of the money increases. MacBeth and Merville's results are consistent with the compound option model. They are also consistent with other models where stock price and volatility are negatively correlated.

Rubinstein has carried out a similar type of study to MacBeth and Merville, but using a far larger data set and a different time period. He looked at all reported trades on the 30 most active Chicago Board Option Exchange options classes between August 23, 1976 and August 31, 1978. Special care was taken to incorporate the effects of dividends and early exercise. Rubinstein compared implied volatilities of matched pairs of call options, which differed either only as far as exercise price was concerned or only as far as maturity was concerned. He found that his time period could be conveniently divided into two subperiods: August 23, 1976 to October 21, 1977 and October 22, 1977 to August 31, 1978. For the first period, his results were consistent with those of MacBeth and Merville. However, for the second period, the opposite result from MacBeth and Merville was obtained; that is, implied volatilities were relatively high for out-of-the-money options and relatively low for in-the-money options. Throughout the entire period Rubinstein, found that for out-of-the-money options, short-maturity options had significantly higher implied volatilities than long-maturity options. The results for at-the-money and in-the-money options were less clear cut.

No single alternative to the Black–Scholes model for stock options seems superior for both of Rubinstein's time periods. Indeed, it is difficult to imagine a model that leads to the changes in the biases that were observed between the first time period and the second time period. Possibly macroeconomic variables affect option prices in a way that is as yet not fully understood. At present, there does not seem to be any really compelling arguments for using any of the models introduced earlier in this chapter in preference to Black–Scholes.

A number of authors have researched the pricing of options on assets other than stocks. For example, Shastri and Tandon, and Bodurtha and Courtadon have examined the market prices of currency options; Shastri and Tandon in another paper have examined the market prices of futures options; Chance has examined the market prices of index options. The authors find that the Black–Scholes model and its extensions misprice some options. There appears to be some evidence that currencies follow jump processes. However, the mispricing was not sufficient in most cases to present profitable opportunities to investors when transactions costs and bid-ask spreads were taken into account. When considering profitable opportunities, it is important to bear in mind that, even for a market maker, some time must elapse between a profitable opportunity being identified and action being taken. This delay, even if it is only to the next trade, can be sufficient to eliminate the profitable opportunity.

SUMMARY

The Black–Scholes model and its extensions assume that the probability distribution of the stock price at any given future time is lognormal. If this assumption is incorrect, there are liable to be biases in the prices produced by the model. If the right tail of the true distribution is fatter than the right tail of the lognormal distribution, there will be a tendency for the Black–Scholes model to underprice out-of-the-money calls and in-the-money puts. If the left tail of the true distribution is fatter than the left tail of the lognormal distribution, there will be a tendency for the Black–Scholes model to underprice out-of-the-money puts and in-the-money calls. When either tail is too thin relative to the lognormal distribution, the opposite biases are observed.

A number of alternatives to the Black–Scholes model have been suggested. These include models where the future volatility of a stock price is uncertain, models where the company's equity is assumed to be an option on its assets, and models where the stock price experiences occasional jumps rather than continuous changes. The models can be categorized according to the biases they give rise to. It is interesting to note that biases arising from jumps become less pronounced as an option's life increases, while biases arising in other ways become more pronounced as the option's life increases.

When a stock is expected to experience a single large jump in the near future, the Black–Scholes model is liable to be misleading. This is because the future stock consists of two lognormal distributions superimposed upon each other.

Generally, the empirical research that has been done has been very supportive of the Black–Scholes model. It is a model that has stood the test of time.

Differences between market prices and the Black–Scholes prices have been observed. However, these differences have usually been small when compared to transactions costs.

Suggestions for Further Reading

On alternative models

BLACK, F., "How to use the holes in Black–Scholes," *RISK*, 1 No. 4 (March 1988).

COX, J. C., and S. A. ROSS, "The valuation of options for alternative stochastic processes," *Journal of Financial Economics*, 3 (March 1976), 145–160.

COX, J. C., S. A. ROSS, and M. RUBINSTEIN, "Option pricing: A simplified approach," *Journal of Financial Economics*, 7 (September 1979), 229–263.

GESKE, R., "The valuation of compound options," *Journal of Financial Economics*, 7 (1979), 63–81.

HULL, J., *Options, Futures, and Other Derivative Securities*. Englewood Cliffs, NJ: Prentice Hall, 1989.

HULL, J., and A. WHITE, "The pricing of options on assets with stochastic volatilities," *Journal of Finance*, 42 (June 1987), 281–300.

MERTON, R. C., "Option pricing when underlying stock returns are discontinuous," *Journal of Financial Economics*, 3 (March 1976), 125–144.

MERTON, R. C., "Theory of rational option pricing," *Bell Journal of Economics and Management Science*, 4 (Spring 1973), 141–183.

RUBINSTEIN, M., "Displaced diffusion option pricing," *Journal of Finance*, 38 (March 1983), 213–217.

On empirical research

BLACK, F., and M. SCHOLES, "The valuation of option contracts and a test of market efficiency," *Journal of Finance*, 27 (May 1972), 399–418.

BODURTHA, J. N. and G. R. COURTADON, "Tests of an American option pricing model on the foreign currency options market," *Journal of Financial and Quantitative Analysis*, 22 (June 1987), 153–168.

CHANCE, D. M., "Empirical tests of the pricing of index call options," *Advances in Futures and Options Research*, 1, pt. A (1986), 141–166.

CHIRAS D., and S. MANASTER, "The information content of option prices and a test of market efficiency," *Journal of Financial Economics*, 6 (September 1978), 213–234.

GALAI, D., "Tests of market efficiency and the Chicago Board Options Exchange," *Journal of Business*, 50 (April 1977), 167–197.

KLEMKOSKY, R. C., and B. G. RESNICK, "Put-call parity and market efficiency," *Journal of Finance*, 34 (December 1979), 1141–1155.

MACBETH, J. D. and L. J. MERVILLE, "An empirical examination of the Black-Scholes call option pricing model," *Journal of Finance*, 34 (December 1979), 1172–1186.

RUBINSTEIN, M., "Non-parametric tests of alternative option pricing models using all reported trades and quotes on the 30 most active CBOE option classes from August 23, 1976 through August 31, 1978," *Journal of Finance*, 40 (June 1985), 455–480.

SHASTRI, K., and K. TANDON, "Valuation of foreign currency options: some empirical tests," *Journal of Financial and Quantitative Analysis*, 21 (June 1986), 145–160.

SHASTRI, K., and K. TANDON, "An empirical test of a valuation model for American options on futures contracts," *Journal of Financial and Quantitative Analysis*, 21 (December 1986), 377–392.

Quiz

1. Determine the option pricing biases likely to be observed when
   a. Both tails of the stock price distribution are thinner than those of the lognormal distribution.
   b. The right tail is thinner and the left tail is fatter than that of a lognormal distribution.
2. What biases are caused by an uncertain volatility when the stock price is positively correlated with volatility?

3. What biases are caused by jumps in the movements of a stock price? Are these biases likely to be more pronounced for a six-month option than for a three-month option?
4. Assume that a stock price follows the compound option model. The Black–Scholes model is used to calculate implied volatilities for call and put options with different exercise prices and different times to maturity. What patterns would you expect to observe in the implied volatilities?
5. Why are the biases (relative to Black–Scholes) for the market prices of in-the-money call options usually the same as the biases for the market prices of out-of-the-money put options?
6. A stock price is currently \$20. Tomorrow news is expected to be announced that will either increase the price by \$5 or decrease the price by \$5. What are the problems in using Black–Scholes to value options on the stock?
7. What are the major problems in testing a stock option pricing model empirically?

Questions and Problems

16.1. Suppose that a stock price exhibits jumps. Explain carefully why Black–Scholes will give misleading prices for short-life options, but will give reasonable answers for longer-life options.

16.2. Suppose that a foreign currency exchange rate follows a jump process and has an uncertain volatility that is uncorrelated with the exchange rate. What sort of biases would you expect in the option prices observed in the market relative to those given by the Black–Scholes formulas? Assume that implied volatilities are calculated on the basis of at-the-money options.

16.3. Option traders sometimes refer to deep out-of-the-money options as being options on volatility. Why do you think they do this?

16.4. Explain carefully why the implied volatilities are the same for both put and call options in Table 16.3.

16.5. Explain why the implied volatility of options with strike prices of 42 and 58 are zero in Table 16.3.

16.6. The risk-free interest rate is 15 percent per annum and the current price of a stock is \$30. It is known that the price will be either \$20 or \$35 in three months. Calculate prices of call options with strike prices of \$21, \$25, and \$34. What are the volatilities implied by the Black–Scholes model in each of these cases?

17

INTEREST-RATE OPTIONS

Interest-rate options are options whose payoffs are dependent in some way on the level of interest rates. In recent years they have become increasingly popular. A variety of different types of interest-rate options are now actively traded both over the counter and on exchanges. In this chapter we first describe how interest-rate options work and how they are used. We then explain some of the relatively simple approaches that are used to value them. Finally, we review some of the more complicated models that have been suggested and discuss current research directions.

EXCHANGE–TRADED BOND OPTIONS

The most popular exchange-traded interest-rate options are those on treasury bond futures, treasury note futures, and Eurodollar futures. Table 13.1 shows prices for these securities on August 11, 1993. The prices are quoted as a percentage of the principal amount of the underlying debt security. In the case of Eurodollars, the price is quoted to two decimal places and one contract is for the delivery of futures contracts with a face value of $1 million. In the case of treasury bonds and treasury notes, the price is quoted to the nearest $\frac{1}{64}$ of 1 percent and one contract is for the delivery of futures contracts with a face value of $100,000. Table 13.1 gives the price of the September call futures option on Eurodollars as 0.42 percent of the debt principal when the strike price is 96.25 (implying that one

Table 17.1 Speculation Using a Treasury Bond Futures Option Contract

From the Trader's Desk—August

The yield on long-term government bonds is currently about 8.4 percent per annum. An investor feels that long-term yields are likely to decline. The December treasury bond futures contract on the CBT is priced at 96-09. Options on the contract with a strike price of 98 are priced at 1-04.

Strategy

The investor buys one call option contract on the December treasury bond futures. This costs $1\frac{1}{16}$ percent of \$100,000 or \$1,062.50.

Outcome

By the time the option contract matured, long-term yields had fallen to 8.0 percent per annum and the December treasury bond futures contract was priced at 100-00. The contract, therefore, provided a payoff of \$2,000 and the investor made a profit of \$2,000 − \$1,062.50 = \$937.50.

contract would cost \$4,200). It also gives the price of the September call futures option on treasury bonds as $4\frac{17}{64}$ percent of the debt principal when the strike price is 112 (implying that one contract would cost \$4,265.62).

When interest rates rise, bond prices fall; when interest rates fall, bond prices rise. An investor who thinks that short-term interest rates will rise can speculate by buying put options on Eurodollar futures, while an investor who thinks that they will fall can speculate by buying call options on Eurodollar futures. An investor who thinks that long-term interest rates will rise can speculate by buying put options on treasury notes or treasury bonds, while an investor who thinks they will fall can speculate by buying call options on these instruments.

Suppose that it is August and the futures price for the December treasury bond contract traded on the CBOT is 96-09 (or $\frac{9}{32}$ = 96.28125). The yield on long-term government bonds is about 8.4 percent per annum. An investor who feels that this yield will fall by December might choose to buy December calls with a strike price of 98. Assume that the price of these calls is 1-04 (or $1\frac{4}{64} = 1.0625$ percent of the principal). If long-term rates fall to 8 percent per annum, the treasury bond futures price will rise to 100-00 and the investor will make a net profit per \$100 of bond futures of

$$100.00 - 98.00 - 1.0625 = 0.9375$$

Since one option contract is for the purchase or sale of instruments with a face value of \$100,000, the investor would make a profit of \$937.50 per option contract bought. This example is summarized in Table 17.1.

EMBEDDED BOND OPTIONS

Some bonds contain embedded call and put options. For example, a callable bond contains provisions that allow the issuing firm to buy back the bond at a predetermined price at certain times in the future. The holder of such a bond has sold a call option to the issuer. The value of the call option is reflected in the yields on bonds so that bonds with call features provide an investor with a higher yield than bonds with no call features. A puttable bond contains provisions that allow the holder to demand early redemption at a predetermined price at certain times in the future. The holder of such a bond has purchased a put option on the bond as well as the bond itself. This is also reflected in the yield on bonds, so that bonds with put features provide lower yields to the holder than bonds with no put features.

A number of other instruments with embedded bond options have already been mentioned in this book. Early redemption privileges on fixed rate deposits are analogous to the put features of a bond. Prepayment privileges on fixed rate loans are analogous to the call features of a bond. Also, mortgage commitments made by a bank or other financial institution are put options. Consider, for example, the situation where a bank quotes a five-year mortgage rate of interest of 12 percent per annum to a client and states that the rate is good for the next two months. The client has in effect obtained the right to sell a bond with a 12 percent coupon to the financial institution for its face value any time within the next two months.

MORTGAGE-BACKED SECURITIES

A type of interest-rate option is embedded in what are known as *mortgage-backed securities* (MBS). These securities have become very popular in recent years. They are created when a financial institution decides to sell part of its residential mortgage portfolio to investors. The mortgages sold are put into a pool and investors acquire a stake in the pool by buying units. A secondary market is usually created for the units so that investors can sell them to other investors as desired. An investor who owns units representing X percent of a certain pool is entitled to X percent of the principal and interest cash flows received from the mortgages in the pool.

The mortgages in a pool are generally insured so that investors are protected against defaults. This makes an MBS sound like a regular fixed-income security. However, there is one important complicating feature. The mortgages in an MBS pool have certain prepayment privileges. This means that the holder of an MBS has granted a series of interest-rate options to the borrowers of the mortgage funds.[1] In general, investors require a higher rate of interest on an MBS than on other fixed-income securities to compensate for these prepayment options.

[1] These options are not pure interest-rate options in the sense that the decision to exercise may depend on more than just the level of interest rates. For example, a family might prepay a mortgage when rates are relatively high simply because it is selling the house—not because it can refinance more cheaply.

SWAPTIONS

Swaptions are options on interest-rate swaps and are another increasingly popular type of interest-rate option. They give the holder the right to enter into a certain interest-rate swap at a certain time in the future. (The holder does not of course have to exercise this right.) Many large financial institutions that offer interest-rate swap contracts to their corporate clients are also prepared to sell them swaptions or buy swaptions from them.

To give an example of how a swaption might be used, consider a company that knows it will enter into a five-year floating-rate loan agreement in six months and knows that it will wish to swap the floating-interest payments for fixed-interest payments in order to convert the loan into a fixed-rate loan. (See Chapter 6 for how swaps can be used in this way.) At a cost the company could enter into a swaption and obtain the right to swap the floating-interest payments for a certain fixed-interest payment, say, 12 percent per annum, for a five-year period starting in six months. If the fixed rate on a regular five-year swap in six months turns out to be less than 12 percent per annum, the company will choose not to exercise the swaption and will enter into a swap agreement in the usual way. However, if it turns out to be greater than 12 percent per annum, the company will choose to exercise the swaption and will obtain a swap at more favorable terms than those available in the market. This example is summarized in Table 17.2.

Swaptions provide companies such as the one just considered with an alternative to forward swaps (sometimes called *deferred swaps*). The latter involve no up-front cost but have the disadvantage that they obligate the company to enter into a certain swap agreement. With a swaption the company is able to benefit from favorable interest-rate movements while acquiring protection from unfavorable movements. The difference between a swaption and a forward swap is analogous to the difference between an option on foreign exchange and a forward contract on foreign exchange.

Table 17.2 Use of a Swaption

From the Trader's Desk

A company knows it will be entering into a five-year floating-rate loan agreement in six months and plans to swap the floating-interest payments for fixed-interest payments. It would like to ensure that the fixed-interest payments are no more than 12 percent per annum.

The Strategy

The company buys a swaption. The swaption gives it the right (but not the obligation) to exchange the floating-interest payments for fixed-interest payments of 12 percent per annum for a five-year period starting in six months. If the fixed rate on a regular five-year swap in six months time turns out to be greater than 12 percent the company will exercise the swaption; under other circumstances, it will choose to negotiate a swap reflecting the market rates of interest.

Relation to Bond Options

It will be recalled from Chapter 6 that an interest-rate swap can be regarded as an agreement to exchange a fixed-rate bond for a floating-rate bond. At the start of a swap the value of the floating-rate bond always equals the principal amount of the swap. A swaption can, therefore, be regarded as an option to exchange a fixed-rate bond for the principal amount of the swap. If a swaption gives the holder the right to pay fixed and receive floating, it is a put option on the fixed-rate bond with a strike price equal to the principal. If a swaption gives the holder the right to pay floating and receive fixed, it is a call option on the fixed-rate bond with a strike price equal to the principal.

INTEREST-RATE CAPS

Another type of over-the-counter interest-rate option offered by financial institutions is an *interest-rate cap*. Caps are designed to provide insurance against the rate of interest on a floating-rate loan going above a certain level. This level is known as the *cap rate*.

Interest-Rate Caps

The operation of an interest-rate cap is illustrated in Figure 17.1. The instrument is designed so that it guarantees that the rate charged on a loan at any given time will be the lesser of the prevailing rate and the cap rate. Suppose that the rate on a loan, where the principal amount is $10 million, is reset every three months equal to three-month LIBOR, and that a financial institution has provided an interest-rate cap of 10 percent per annum. To fulfill its obligations under the cap agreement, the financial institution must pay to the borrower at the end of each quarter (in millions of dollars)

$$0.25 \times 10 \times \max(R - 0.1, 0)$$

where R is the three-month LIBOR rate at the beginning of the quarter. For example, when the three-month LIBOR rate at the beginning of the quarter is 11 percent per annum, the financial institution must pay $0.25 \times 10{,}000{,}000 \times 0.01 = \$25{,}000$ at the end of the quarter. When it is 9 percent per annum, the financial institution is not required to pay anything. This example is summarized in Table 17.3. The expression $\max(R - 0.1, 0)$ is the payoff from a call option on R. The cap can be viewed as a portfolio of call options on R with the payoffs from the options occurring three months in arrears.

In general if the cap rate is R_X, the principal is L, and interest payments are made at times $\tau, 2\tau, \ldots, n\tau$, the writer of the cap is required to make a payment of

$$\tau L \times \max(R_{k-1} - R_X, 0) \tag{17.1}$$

at time $k\tau$, where R_{k-1} is the LIBOR rate at time $(k - 1)\tau$. Suppose that F is the forward interest rate for the time period between $(k - 1)\tau$ and $k\tau$. We can use

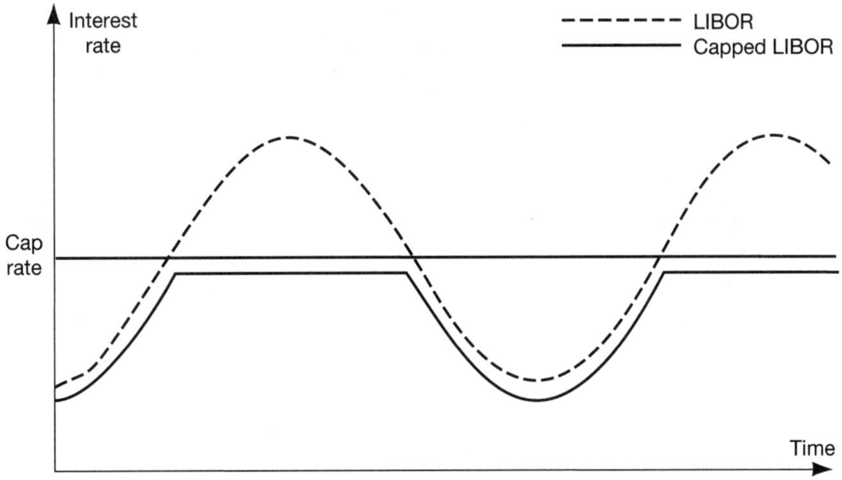

Figure 17.1 Borrower's effective interest rate with an interest-rate cap. Dashed line, LIBOR; solid line, capped LIBOR.

F as the discount rate for the payment in (17.1) so that it becomes equivalent to a payment of

$$\frac{\tau L}{1 + \tau F} \max(R_{k-1} - R_X, 0) \qquad \textbf{(17.2)}$$

at time $(k - 1)\tau$. The advantage of doing this is that we can view the cap as a portfolio of European call options on the 90-day interest rate with payoffs occurring at the maturity of the option rather than 90 days later. The principal amount for each option is $\tau L/(1 + F\tau)$.

Table 17.3 Use of an Interest-Rate Cap

From the Trader's Desk

A company entering into a five-year floating-rate loan agreement is concerned about possible increases in interest rates. The rate on the loan is three-month LIBOR and is currently set at 8 percent per annum. The company would like to buy protection against the rate rising above 10 percent per annum.

The Strategy

The company buys from a financial institution a five-year interest-rate cap with a cap rate of 10 percent per annum. The financial institution guarantees that whenever the floating rate proves to be greater than 10 percent per annum, it will pay the difference between the floating rate and 10 percent per annum. The cap can be viewed as a portfolio of call options on the three-month rate.

When an interest-rate cap and the corresponding loan are both provided by the same financial institution, the cost of the options underlying the cap is often incorporated into the interest rate charged. When they are provided by different financial institutions, an up-front payment for the cap is likely to be required.

A Simple Model for Valuing Caps

Equation (17.2) leads to a commonly used valuation model. At time $k\tau$, $F = R_k$. We can, therefore, regard the caplet corresponding to the period between $k\tau$ and $(k + 1)\tau$ as a European call option on F rather than R_k. If we assume that the forward interest rate, F, has a constant volatility, σ_F, Black's model for futures options (see Chapter 13) gives the price of the option as

$$\frac{\tau L}{1 + \tau F} e^{-rk\tau}[FN(d_1) - R_X N(d_2)] \tag{17.3}$$

where

$$d_1 = \frac{\ln(F/R_X) + \sigma_F^2 k\tau/2}{\sigma_F\sqrt{k\tau}}$$

$$d_2 = \frac{\ln(F/R_X) - \sigma_F^2 k\tau/2}{\sigma_F\sqrt{k\tau}} = d_1 - \sigma\sqrt{k\tau}$$

and r is the risk-free interest rate for an instrument that matures at time $k\tau$. If r is defined as the risk-free rate for an instrument maturing at $(k + 1)\tau$, an expression equivalent to (17.3) for the value of a caplet is

$$\tau L e^{-r(k+1)\tau}[FN(d_1) - R_X N(d_2)]$$

Example

Consider a contract that caps the interest on a \$10,000 loan at 8 percent per annum (with quarterly compounding) for three months starting in one year. This could be one element of a cap. Suppose that the forward interest rate for a three-month period starting in one year is 7 percent per annum (with quarterly compounding), the current one-year interest rate is 6.5 percent per annum (with continuous compounding), and the volatility of the 90-day forward rate is 20 percent per annum. It follows that $F = 0.07$, $\tau = 0.25$, $L = 10{,}000$, $R_X = 0.08$, $r = 0.065$, $\sigma = 0.20$, and $T = 1.0$.

$$\frac{\tau L}{1 + \tau F} = \frac{0.25 \times 10{,}000}{1 + 0.07 \times 0.25} = 2{,}457$$

Since

$$d_1 = \frac{\ln 0.875 + 0.02}{0.20} = -0.5677$$

$$d_2 = d_1 - 0.20 = -0.7677$$

Equation (17.3) gives the cap price as

$$2457e^{-0.065}[0.07N(-0.5677) - 0.08N(-0.7677)] = 5.19$$

or \$5.19.

Black's model involves the assumption that σ_F is constant. This assumption is at best only a rough approximation to the truth. When the time to the maturity of the forward contract is long, F is relatively insensitive to current interest-rate movements and has a low volatility. However, as the time to maturity becomes smaller, F is more affected by changes in the current level of interest rates, and its volatility increases. When using Black's model, the appropriate σ_F can be thought of as the average volatility of the forward rate during the life of the option. Figure 17.2 shows the way in which the appropriate σ_F varies with the maturity of the option being considered.

In practice, the following procedure is sometimes adopted to overcome the weaknesses in Black's model. First, the model is used to calculate implied volatilities for forward interest rates from traded Eurodollar futures options. These implied volatilities are then used to value the options underlying interest-rate caps. A three-month option is valued on the basis of the volatility implied by the price of a Eurodollar futures option with approximately three months to maturity; a six-month option is valued on the basis of the volatility implied by the price of a Eurodollar futures option with approximately six months to maturity; and so on. This twofold use of the model (to calculate implied volatilities for exchange-traded options and to calculate prices of over-the-counter options from the implied volatilities of exchange-traded options) tends to reduce errors caused by the use of an imperfect model and to ensure that calculated option prices are reasonably consistent with exchange-traded option prices. The interest-rate volatilities implied by the market prices of Eurodollar futures options of different maturities are regularly quoted by traders and published by investment houses. Since most caps last beyond the longest maturity of traded Eurodollar options, the relation-

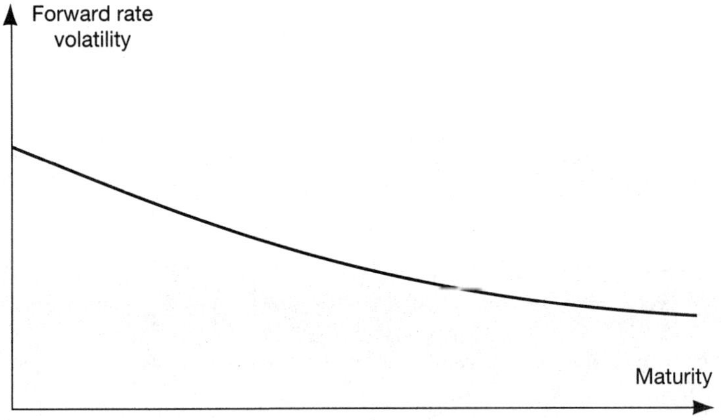

Figure 17.2 Variation of forward-rate volatility with maturity of forward contract.

ship between volatility and maturity which is observed for traded Eurodollar options must be extrapolated in some way.

Traders applying Black's model using the approach just discussed would change the volatility, σ_F, according to the caplet considered. The volatilities are then referred to as *forward forward volatilities*. An alternative approach is to use the same volatility for all the caplets comprising any particular cap, but to vary this volatility according to the life of the cap. The volatilities used are then referred to as a *forward volatilities* or *flat volatilities*.

Floors and Collars

Interest-rate floors and interest-rate collars (which are sometimes called floor-ceiling agreements) can be defined analogously to caps. A *floor* places a lower limit on the interest rate that will be charged. *Collars* specify both the upper and lower limits for the rate that will be charged. An interest-rate floor is a portfolio of put options on interest rates. It is written by the borrower of floating-rate funds. A collar is a combination of a cap and a floor. It is usually constructed so that the price of the cap equals the price of the floor. The net cost of the collar is then zero.

VALUING BOND OPTIONS USING BLACK–SCHOLES

The simplest model for valuing bond options is the Black–Scholes model described in Chapter 11. Define:

B: current bond price
T: maturity date of option
σ: volatility of bond price
X: strike price of option
R: current interest rate applicable to a risk-free investment maturing at time T[2]

When the underlying asset is a zero-coupon bond, the Black–Scholes model gives the European call and put prices, c and p, as

$$c = BN(d_1) - e^{-RT}XN(d_2) \tag{17.4}$$

and

$$p = e^{-RT}XN(-d_2) - BN(-d_1) \tag{17.5}$$

where

$$d_1 = \frac{\ln(B/X) + (R + \sigma^2/2)T}{\sigma\sqrt{T}}$$

$$d_2 = \frac{\ln(B/X) + (R - \sigma^2/2)T}{\sigma\sqrt{T}} = d_1 - \sigma\sqrt{T}$$

[2] As mentioned in Chapter 11, when Black–Scholes and similar models are implemented, the risk-free interest rate is usually chosen to correspond to an investment maturing at the end of the life of the option.

An argument similar to that in Chapter 8 shows that an American call on a bond that pays no coupons should never be exercised early and can be treated as a European option.

If coupon payments are due to be received during the life of the option, the present value of the coupons should be subtracted from B before Equations (17.4) and (17.5) are used. The volatility parameter, σ, should be the volatility of the bond price net of the present value of these coupons. This procedure is similar to the procedure we outlined in Chapter 11 for dealing with European options on dividend-paying stocks.

The precise terms of the option are important when the bond pays coupons. If the strike price is the cash amount that is exchanged for the bond when the option is exercised, X should be put equal to this strike price in Equations (17.4) and (17.5). If the strike price is the quoted price applicable when the option is exercised (as it is in exchange-traded bond options), X should be set equal to the strike price plus accrued interest at the expiration date of the option in Equations (17.4) and (17.5).

Example

Consider a ten-month European call option on a 9.75-year bond with a face value of \$1,000. (When the option matures the bond will have eight years and 11 months remaining.) Suppose that the current cash bond price is \$960, the strike price is \$1,000, the ten-month risk-free interest rate is 10 percent per annum, and the volatility of the bond price is 9 percent per annum. The bond pays a semiannual coupon of 10 percent and coupon payments of \$50 are expected in three months and nine months. (This means that the quoted bond price is \$935.) The 3-month and 9-month risk-free interest rates are 9.0 percent and 9.5 percent per annum, respectively. The present value of the coupon payments is

$$50e^{-0.25\times 0.09} + 50e^{-0.75\times 0.095} = 95.45$$

or \$95.45.

a. If the strike price is the cash price that would be paid for the bond on exercise, the parameters for Equation (17.4) are $B = 960 - 95.45 = 864.55$, $X = 1{,}000$, $R = 0.1$, $\sigma = 0.09$, and $T = 0.8333$. The price of the call option is \$9.49.

b. If the strike price is the quoted price that would be paid for the bond on exercise, one month's accrued interest must be added to X since the maturity of the option is one month after a coupon date. This produces a value for X of

$$1{,}000 + 50 \times 0.16667 = 1{,}008.33$$

The values for the other parameters in Equation (17.4) are unchanged (i.e., $B = 864.55$, $R = 0.1$, $\sigma = 0.09$, and $T = 0.8333$). The price of the option is \$7.97.

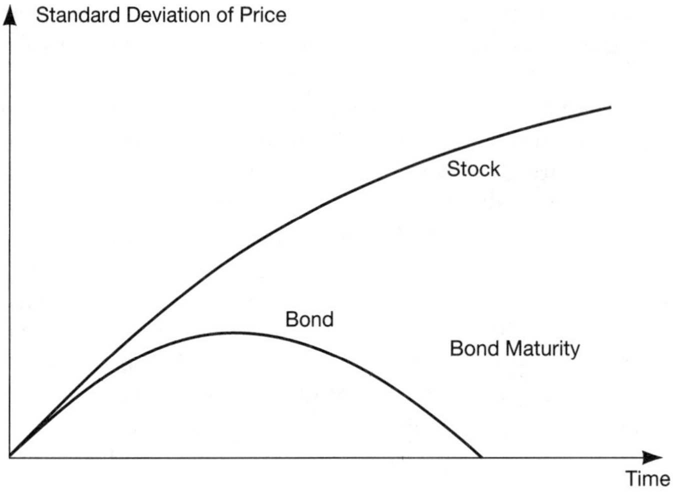

Figure 17.3 Standard deviation of a future bond price and a future stock price.

Problems in Applying the Black–Scholes Model to Bond Prices

The Black–Scholes model that has just been described assumes that the volatility of a bond's price is constant. In practice, a bond's price volatility is dependent on its time to maturity. The longer the time to maturity, the greater a bond's price volatility. Schaefer and Schwartz argue that a bond's price volatility is roughly proportional to its duration.[3] This means that the volatility of a bond with a duration of ten years is twice the volatility of a bond with a duration of five years, and so on. This idea seems to be reasonably well supported by empirical studies.

When the life of the option is short in relation to the life of the underlying bond (as it is in the case of most exchange-traded bond options), it can be assumed that the volatility of the bond is constant during the life of the option. The duration argument can then be used. For example, suppose we wish to value a three-month option on a bond with a duration of four years and a one-month option on a bond with a duration of eight years. The volatility used in Black–Scholes when the first option is valued should be half that used when the second option is valued.

For longer-term options, the assumption that the volatility of a bond is constant during the life of the option is no longer reasonable. A natural suggestion is to make the bond's price volatility proportional to the average duration of the bond during the life of the option. However, this approach overstates the values of long-dated options because it does not capture one key aspect of the behavior of bond prices. This is that the price of a bond must equal its face value at its maturity. This is sometimes referred to as the *pull-to-par phenomenon*. Figure 17.3 illustrates the phenomenon by showing how the standard deviation of the future

[3] See S. M. Schaefer and E. S. Schwartz, "Time-Dependent Variance and the Pricing of Bond Options," *Journal of Finance*, 42 (December 1987), 1113–1128.

price of a bond and a stock change as we look further ahead. The stock's price becomes progressively more uncertain, but our uncertainty about the bond's price first increases and then decreases.

Using Forward Bond Prices

One approach to valuing European options when the life of the option is significant in relation to the life of the underlying bond is to regard the option as being written on the forward price of the bond that will be delivered if the option is exercised. This is the forward price of a bond lasting between the end of the life of the option and the end of the life of the bond. When the option matures, the forward bond price equals the price of the underlying bond—which means that the forward bond option being considered is the same as the spot bond option whose value is required. This approach enables Black's model for options on futures (see Chapter 13) to be used. The correct volatility to use for the forward bond price will depend on the time between the end of the life of the option and the end of the life of the bond. It also tends to depend on the life of the option itself. The longer the option lasts, the lower the volatility. The valuation formulas are

$$c = e^{-RT}[FN(d_1) - XN(d_2)] \tag{17.6}$$

and

$$p = e^{-RT}[XN(-d_2) - FN(-d_1)] \tag{17.7}$$

where

$$d_1 = \frac{\ln(F/X) + \sigma^2 T/2}{\sigma\sqrt{T}}$$

$$d_2 = \frac{\ln(F/X) - \sigma^2 T/2}{\sigma\sqrt{T}} = d_1 - \sigma\sqrt{T}$$

F is the forward bond price, σ is its volatility, and other variables are defined as before.

This approach turns out to be identical to the earlier Black–Scholes valuation using bond prices. The forward bond price can be calculated using Equation (3.6)

$$F = (B - I)e^{RT}$$

where I is equal to the present value of the coupons during the life of the option. Substituting for F in Equations (17.6) and (17.7) shows that there is in essence no difference between this approach and the Black–Scholes approach just mentioned. Both approaches give option prices that satisfy the put–call parity condition for bond prices:

$$c + Xe^{-RT} = p + Fe^{-RT} \tag{17.8}$$

Example

Consider a three-year European call option on a five-year bond with a face value of \$100 and a coupon of 10 percent per annum. We suppose that the forward price of the bond that would be delivered if the option were exercised is \$95. We also suppose that the strike price is \$98, the three-year risk-free interest rate is 11 percent per annum, and the volatility of the forward bond price is 2.5 percent per annum. This means that $F = 95$, $X = 98$, $R = 0.11$, $\sigma = 0.025$, and $T = 3.0$. Equation (17.6) gives the call price as \$0.42.

Modeling Forward Bond Yields

One attempt to overcome the pull-to-par problem in modeling bond prices is to regard a bond option as a yield option. Consider the three-year option on a five-year bond in the preceding example. We define the forward yield, Y_F, on the bond as equal to the continuously compounded yield on the bond in three years' time if the bond's price equals its forward price. We define the strike yield, Y_X, as equal to the continuously compounded yield on the bond in three years' time if the bond's price equals the strike price. From Equation (5.10) in Chapter 5, an approximate relationship between the change in a forward bond price, ΔB, and the change in its forward yield, Δy, is

$$\frac{\Delta B}{B} = -D\Delta y$$

where D is the bond's duration at the maturity of the option. Using this formula

$$B - X = DX(Y_X - Y_F)$$

The payoff on a call option can be written as

$$\max[DX(Y_X - Y_F), 0]$$

and the payoff from a put option on the bond can be written as

$$\max[DX(Y_F - Y_X), 0]$$

These equations convert a call option on a bond price into a put option on a forward bond yield and a put option on a bond price into a call option on a forward bond yield. If forward bond yield volatilities are assumed constant, Black's model can be used to value the option.

This approach, although simple, has a weakness. As explained in Chapter 5, the duration of a bond measures the sensitivity of the bond's price to bond yields for only very small changes in the yield. The expressions, just given, for the payoffs in terms of yields are, therefore, approximations. A problem related to this weakness is that the option prices produced using this approach do not satisfy put-call parity.

The assumption that the forward bond yield volatilities are constant is attractive to many practitioners. To overcome the weakness just mentioned, some practitioners use numerical procedures to convert the lognormal yield distribution into a price distribution. The center of the distribution is chosen so that it represents a possible behavior for bond prices in a risk-neutral world. Option prices are then obtained numerically.

YIELD CURVE MODELS

Most traders would like to value both caps and bond options on a consistent basis. They can then assess the extent to which the risks in a cap portfolio can be offset by bond options or swaptions. It is, therefore, natural to ask what the relationship is between the volatilities used in cap pricing models and the volatilities used in bond option/swaption pricing models. Unfortunately, there is no easy answer to this question. The cap valuation approach that has been presented assumes that forward interest rates are lognormal, while the bond option valuation approach assumes that either bond prices or forward bond prices are lognormal. It can be shown that the models are inconsistent with each other. When forward interest rates are lognormal, bond prices are not lognormal and vice versa.

Another problem with the cap and bond option valuation models presented so far is that it is difficult to extend them so that they can be used to value other securities. For example, Black's model for valuing a European bond option cannot be extended to value American bond options. The problem is that, in the case of an American bond option, the uncertain exercise date means that there is not a single forward bond underlying the option.

A more sophisticated approach to valuing interest-rate derivative securities involves constructing what is known as a *yield curve model*. This is a model that describes the probabilistic behavior of the yield curve over time. Yield curve models are more complicated than the models used to describe the movements of a stock price or currency exchange rate. This is because it is concerned with movements in a whole curve—not with changes to a single variable. As time passes, the individual interest rates in the term structure change. In addition, the shape of the curve itself is liable to change. Figure 17.4 shows four different term structure patterns that have been observed at different times. In Figure 17.4a the term structure is upward sloping, with long-term rates higher than short-term rates. In Figure 17.4b it is downward sloping, with long-term rates lower than short-term rates. In Figure 17.4c the term structure is flat with all rates equal. In Figure 17.4d it is humped with rates being first an increasing and then a decreasing function of the time to maturity.

It is beyond the scope of this book to provide a complete description of how yield curve models are constructed. In the rest of this section we will discuss in a general way some of the key issues in this important area.

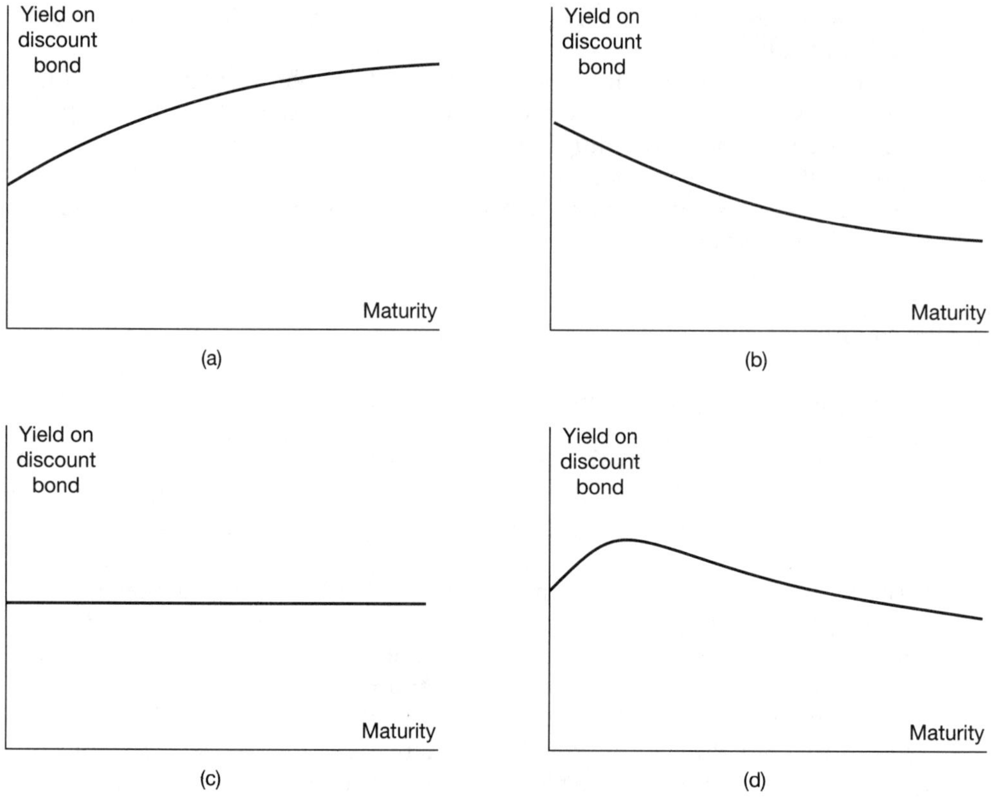

Figure 17.4 Alternative term structures for interest rates.

The Short-Term Rate

The short-term interest rate, r, is of central importance in the construction of yield curve models. It can be shown that if we specify a model describing the probabilistic behavior of the short-term interest rate and some information on individual risk preferences, then we have completely specified both the current term structure of interest rates and the yield curve model. (In other words, we have completely specified a probabilistic model for how the term structure changes over time.)

Mean Reversion

What sort of model is appropriate for r? We can think of r as having an average *drift* or expected change, with volatility superimposed upon the drift. In practice the drift in r seems to incorporate what is known as *mean reversion*. This means that the drift tends to pull interest rates back to some long-run average level. When the short-term interest rate is very high, r tends to have a negative

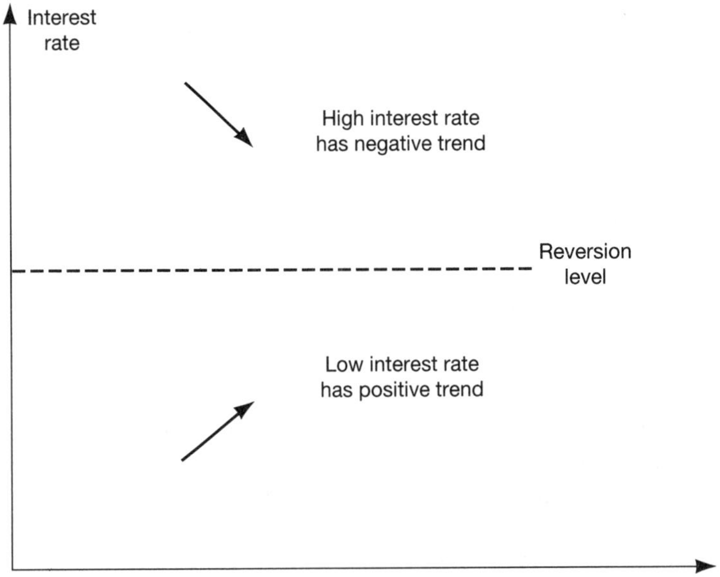

Figure 17.5 Mean reversion.

drift; when the short-term interest rate is very low, r tends to have a positive drift. This is illustrated in Figure 17.5.

The effect of mean reversion is to make us more certain about long-term interest rates than short-term interest rates. The volatility of a spot interest rate, therefore, tends to be a decreasing function of its maturity. The ten-year spot interest rate tends to have a lower volatility than the five-year spot interest rate; the five-year spot interest rate tends to have a lower volatility than the one-year spot interest rate; and so on. This effect is illustrated in Figure 17.6.

Mean reversion can be shown to be responsible for the fact that a forward-rate volatility declines as the maturity of the forward contract increases. This effect was illustrated in Figure 17.2. The volatility of the three-month forward interest

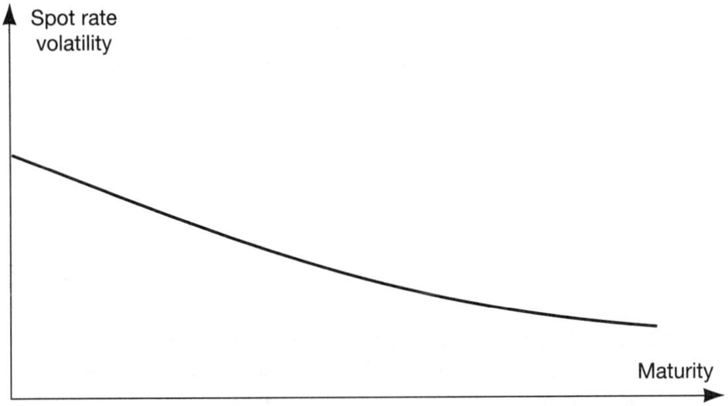

Figure 17.6 Variation of spot interest-rate volatility with maturity.

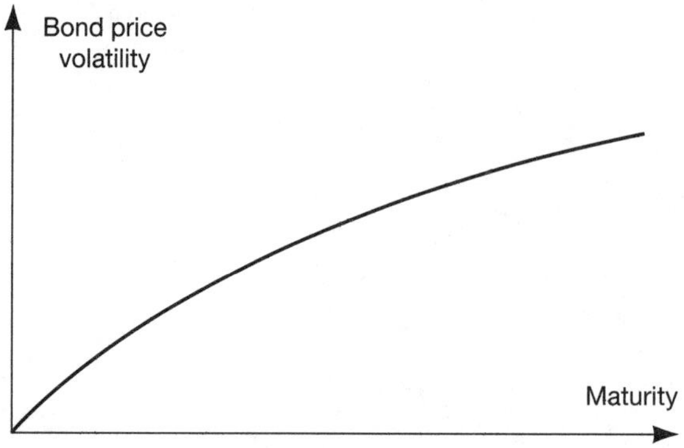

Figure 17.7 Variation of bond price volatility with maturity.

rate starting in three months is greater than the volatility of the three-month forward interest rate starting in two years; this in turn is greater than the volatility of the three-month forward rate starting in five years; and so on.

Mean reversion also has some impact on bond price volatilities. It can be shown that when there is mean reversion, the relationship between volatility and bond maturity tends to have the curvature shown in Figure 17.7.

Fitting the Term Structure

Pioneering work in the development of yield curve models has been done by authors such as Vasicek; Cox, Ingersoll, and Ross; and Brennan and Schwartz. These authors propose models for the short-term interest rate that incorporate mean reversion and involve a number of parameters describing the degree of mean reversion, the reversion level, volatilities, and risk preferences. Typically the parameters are not functions of time and are estimated from data on the current term structure of interest rates and volatilities.

More recently researchers have developed ways of constructing models for r that are automatically consistent with the current term structure of interest rates. The first such model was proposed by Ho and Lee in 1986. This had a flat volatility term structure. (In other words, all interest rates had the same variability.) More sophisticated models have been developed by Heath, Jarrow, and Morton; Black, Derman, and Toy; Black and Karasinski; Hull and White; and Jamshidian. Given the increasing popularity of over-the-counter interest-rate options, this is an area which is likely to see a great deal of research in the future.

SUMMARY

Interest-rate options arise in practice in many different ways. For example, options on treasury bond futures, treasury note futures, and Eurodollar futures are actively traded by exchanges. Many traded bonds include features that are options. The loans and deposit instruments offered by financial institutions often contain hidden options. Mortgage-backed securities contain embedded interest-rate options. A swaption (the option to enter into a swap) is a type of bond option. Interest-rate caps are portfolios of interest-rate options.

Interest-rate options are more difficult to value than stock options, currency options, index options, and most futures options. This is partly because we are dealing with a whole term structure—not a single variable. It is also partly because the behavior of interest rates is relatively complicated. For example, interest rates appear to exhibit a phenomenon known as mean reversion. This means that they have a drift rate that always tends to pull them back toward some central value. Superimposed upon this mean reversion is a volatility.

Bond options are frequently valued using the Black–Scholes model with the stock price being replaced by the bond price less the present value of the coupons that will be paid during the life of the option. When the strike price is the quoted price rather than the cash price that will be paid for the bond on exercise of the option, accrued interest on the exercise date must be added to the strike price. The Black–Scholes model has the disadvantage that bond price volatilities are constant during the life of the option. It also fails to take account of the pull-to-par phenomenon that forces the bond back to its face value at maturity.

Caps are frequently valued by assuming that each element of the cap is an option on a forward interest rate and using Black's model. The appropriate forward-rate volatility to use in the model declines as the maturity of the forward contract increases.

Yield curve models provide a way of valuing all interest-rate derivatives in a consistent way. It can be shown that if there are no arbitrage opportunities open to investors, yield curve models are defined by the behavior of the short-term interest rate together with some information on risk preferences. A number of models of the short-term interest rate have been proposed. Recent advances have led to yield curve models that are automatically consistent with the current term structure of interest rates.

Suggestions for Further Reading

BLACK, F. and M. SCHOLES, "The pricing of options and corporate liabilities," *Journal of Political Economy*, 81 (May–June 1973), 637–659.

BLACK, F., "The pricing of commodity contracts," *Journal of Financial Economics*, 3 (1976), 167–179.

BLACK, F., E. DERMAN, and W. TOY, "A one-factor model of interest rates ands its application to Treasury bond options," *Financial Analysts Journal* (January-February 1990), 33–39.

BLACK, F. and P. KARASINSKI, "Bond and option pricing when short rates are lognormal," *Financial Analysts Journal* (July–August 1991), 52–59.

BRENNAN, M. J., and E. S. SCHWARTZ, "An equilibrium model of bond pricing and a test of market efficiency," *Journal of Financial and Quantitative Analysis*, 17, no.3 (September 1982), 301–329.

COURTADON, G., "The pricing of options on default-free bonds," *Journal of Financial and Quantitative Analysis*, 17 (March 1982), 75–100.

COX, J. C., J. E. INGERSOLL, and S. A. ROSS, "A theory of the term structures of interest rates," *Econometrica*, 53 (1985), 385–407.

HEATH, D., R. JARROW, and A. MORTON, "Bond pricing and the term structure of the interest rates: A new methodology," *Econometrica*, 60 (1992), 77–105.

HO, T. S. Y., and S.-B. LEE, "Term structure movements and pricing interest rate contingent claims," *Journal of Finance*, 41 (December 1986), 1011–1029.

HULL, J., *Options, futures, and other derivative securities*. Englewood Cliffs, NJ: Prentice Hall, 1989.
HULL, J., and A. WHITE, "In the common interest," *RISK*, March 1992, 64–68.
HULL, J., and A. WHITE, "One-factor interest rate models and the valuation of interest rate derivative securities," *Journal of Financial and Quantitative Analysis*, 28 no. 2 (June 1993), 235–254.
HULL, J., and A. WHITE, "Pricing interest-rate derivative securities," *The Review of Financial Studies*, 3 no. 4 (1990), 573–592.
HULL, J., and A. WHITE, "Valuing derivative securities using the explicit finite difference method," *Journal of Financial and Quantitative Analysis*, 25 (March 1990), 87–100.
JAMSHIDIAN, F., "An exact bond option pricing formula," *Journal of Finance*, 44 (March 1989), 205–209.
RENDLEMAN, R., and B. BARTTER, "The pricing of options on debt securities," *Journal of Financial and Quantitative Analysis*, 15 (March 1980), 11–24.
SCHAEFER, S. M., and E. S. SCHWARTZ, "Time-dependent variance and the pricing of bonds," *Journal of Finance*, 42 (December 1987), 1113–1128.
VASICEK, O. A., "An equilibrium characterization of the term structure," *Journal of Financial Economics*, 5 (1977), 177–188.

Quiz

1. A company caps three-month LIBOR at 10 percent per annum. The principal amount is $20 million. On a reset date three-month LIBOR is 12 percent per annum. What payment would this lead to under the cap? When would the payment be made?
2. Explain what mortgage-backed securities are. Explain why mortgage-backed securities are more risky than regular fixed-income instruments such as government bonds.
3. Explain why a swaption can be regarded as a type of bond option.
4. Use the Black–Scholes model to value a one-year European put option on a ten-year bond. Assume that the current value of the bond is $125, the strike price is $110, the one-year interest rate is 10 percent per annum, the bond's price volatility is 8 percent per annum, and the present value of the coupons that will be paid during the life of the option is $10.
5. Explain carefully why the Black–Scholes approach is inappropriate for valuing European bond options when the life of the option is a significant proportion of the life of the bond. What other approaches can be used?
6. Calculate the price of an option that caps the three-month rate starting in 18 months' time at 13 percent (quoted with quarterly compounding) on a principal amount of $1,000. The relevant forward interest rate for the period in question is 12 percent per annum (quoted with quarterly compounding), the 18-month risk-free interest rate (continuously compounded) is 11.5 percent per annum, and the volatility of the forward rate is 12 percent per annum.
7. What are the advantages of yield curve models over the use of the Black and Black–Scholes for valuing caps and bond options?

Questions and Problems

17.1. Suppose that an implied volatility for a nine-month Eurodollar futures option is calculated using Black's model and that this volatility is then used to value an 18-month Eurodollar futures option. Would you expect the resultant price to be too high or too low? Explain.

17.2. Consider an eight-month European put option on a treasury bond that currently has 14.25 years to maturity. The current bond price is $910, the exercise price is $900, and the volatility of the bond price is 10 percent per annum. A coupon of $35 will be paid by the bond in three months. The risk-free interest rate is 8 percent for all maturities up to one year. Use the Black–Scholes model to determine the price of the option. Consider both the case where the strike price corresponds to the cash price of the bond and the case where it corresponds to the quoted price.

17.3. Calculate delta, gamma, and vega in Problem 17.2 when the strike price corresponds to the quoted price. Explain how they can be interpreted.

17.4. Calculate the price of a cap on the three-month LIBOR rate in nine months' time for a principal amount of $1,000. Use Black's model and the following information:

Quoted nine-month Eurodollar futures price = 92
Interest-rate volatility implied by a nine-month Eurodollar option = 15 percent per annum
Current nine-month interest rate with continuous compounding = 7.5 percent per annum
Cap rate = 8 percent per annum

17.5. Calculate delta, gamma, and vega in Problem 17.4. Explain how they can be interpreted.

17.6. Calculate the value of a four-year European call option on a five-year bond using Black's model. The five-year bond price is $105, the price of a four-year bond with the same coupon is $102, the strike price is $100, the four-year risk-free interest rate is 10 percent per annum with continuous compounding, and the volatility of the forward price of the one-year bond whose life starts in four years is 2 percent per annum.

17.7 Does a European interest-rate option always increase in value as the time to maturity increases, with all else being held constant? Explain your answer.

ANSWERS TO QUIZ QUESTIONS

CHAPTER 1

1. When a trader enters into a long futures position, he or she is agreeing to *buy* the underlying asset for a certain price at a certain time in the future. When a trader enters into a short futures position, he or she is agreeing to *sell* the underlying asset for a certain price at a certain time in the future.
2. A company is *hedging* when it has an exposure to the price of an asset and takes a position in futures or options markets to offset the exposure. In a *speculation* the company has no exposure to offset. It is betting on the future movements in the price of the asset. *Arbitrage* involves taking a position in two or more different markets to lock in a profit.
3. In (a) the investor is obligated to buy the asset for \$50. (The investor does not have a choice.) In (b) the investor has the option to buy the asset for \$50. (The investor does not have to exercise the option.)
4. a. The investor is obligated to sell for 50 cents per pound something that is worth 48.20 cents per pound. Gain = (\$0.5000 − \$0.4820) × 50,000 = \$900.
   b. The investor is obligated to sell for 50 cents per pound something that is worth 51.30 cents per pound. Loss = (\$0.5130 − \$0.5000) × 50,000 = \$650.
5. You have sold a put option. You have agreed to buy 100 IBM shares for \$40 per share if the party on the other side of the contract chooses to exercise his or her right to sell for this price. The option will only be exercised when the price of IBM is below \$40. Suppose, for example, that the counterparty exercises when the price is \$30, you have to buy at \$40 shares that are worth

$30. You lose $10 per share or $1,000 in total. If the counterparty exercises when the price is $20, you lose $20 per share or $2,000 in total. The worst that can happen is that the price of IBM declines to zero during the three-month period. This highly unlikely event would cost you $4,000. In return for the possible future losses you receive the price of the option from the purchaser.

6. One strategy would be to buy 200 shares. Another would be to buy 2,000 options (= 20 contracts). If the share price does well, the second strategy will give rise to greater gains. For example, if the share price goes up to $40, you gain [2,000 × ($40 − $30)] − $5,800 = $14,200 from the second strategy and only 200 × ($40 − $29) = $2,200 from the first strategy. However, if the share price does badly, the second strategy gives greater losses. For example, if the share price goes down to $25, the first strategy leads to a loss of 200 × ($29 − $25) = $800, whereas the second strategy leads to a loss of the whole $5,800 investment.
7. You should buy 50 put option contracts with a strike price of $25 and an expiration date in four months. If at the end of four months the stock price proves to be worth less than $25, you can exercise the options and sell the shares for $25 each.

CHAPTER 2

1. The *open interest* of a futures contract at a particular time is the total number of long positions outstanding. (Equivalently, it is the total number of short positions outstanding.) The *trading volume* during a certain period of time is the number of contracts traded during this period.
2. A *commission broker* trades on behalf of a client and charges a commission. A *local* trades on his or her own behalf.
3. There will be a margin call when $1,000 has been lost from the margin account. This will occur when the price of silver increases by 1,000/5,000 = $0.20. The price of silver must, therefore, rise to $5.40 per ounce for there to be a margin call. If the margin call is not met, your broker closes out your position.
4. The total profit is ($20.50 − $18.30) × 1,000 = $2,200. Of this ($19.10 − $18.30) × 1,000 = $800 is realized on a day-by-day basis between September 1993 and December 31, 1993. A further ($20.50 − $19.10) × 1,000 = $1,400 is realized on a day-by-day basis between January 1, 1994 and March 1994. A hedger would be taxed on the whole profit of $2,200 in 1994. A speculator would be taxed on $800 in 1993 and $1,400 in 1994.
5. A *stop order* to sell at $2.00 is an order to sell at the best available price once a price of $2.00 or less is reached. It could be used to limit the losses from an existing long position. A *limit order* to sell at $2.00 is an order to sell at a price of $2.00 or more. It would be used to instruct a broker that a short position should be taken providing it can be done at a price more favorable than $2.00.
6. The margin account administered by the clearinghouse is marked to market daily and the clearinghouse member is required to bring the account back

up to the prescribed level daily. The margin account administered by the broker is also marked to market daily. However, it does not have to be brought up to the initial margin level on a daily basis. It has to be brought up to the initial margin level when the balance in the account falls below the maintenance margin level. The maintenance margin is about 75 percent of the initial margin.

7. In futures markets prices are quoted as the number of U.S. dollars per unit of the foreign currency. Spot and forward rates are quoted in this way for the British currency. For most other currencies, spot and forward rates are quoted as the number of units of the foreign currency per U.S. dollar.

CHAPTER 3

1. a. The rate with continuous compounding is

$$4\ln\left(1 + \frac{0.14}{4}\right) = 0.1376$$

or 13.76 percent per annum.

b. The rate with annual compounding is

$$\left(1 + \frac{0.14}{4}\right)^4 - 1 = 0.1475$$

or 14.75 percent per annum.

2. The investor's broker borrows the shares from another client's account and sells them in the usual way. To close out the position the investor must purchase the shares. The broker then replaces them in the account of the client from whom they were borrowed. The party with the short position must remit to the broker dividends and other income paid on the shares. The broker transfers these funds to the account of the client from whom the shares were borrowed. Occasionally the broker runs out of places from which to borrow the shares. The investor is then short-squeezed and has to close out the position immediately.

3. The forward price is

$$30e^{0.12\times 0.5} = \$31.86$$

4. The futures price is

$$350e^{(0.08-0.04)\times 0.3333} = \$354.7$$

5. Gold is an investment asset. If the futures price is too high, investors will find it profitable to increase their holdings of gold and short futures contracts. If the futures price is too low, they will find it profitable to decrease their holding of gold and go long in the futures market. Copper is a consumption asset. If the futures price is too high, a buy copper and short futures contract works. However, since investors do not in general hold the asset, the sell copper and buy futures strategy is not widely used when the futures price is low. There is, therefore, an upper bound but no lower bound to the futures price.

6. *Convenience yield* measures the extent to which there are benefits obtained from ownership of the physical asset that are not obtained by owners of long futures contracts. The *cost of carry* is the interest cost plus storage cost less the income earned. The futures price, F, and spot price, S, are related by

$$F = Se^{(c-y)T}$$

where c is the cost of carry, y is the convenience yield, and T is the time to maturity of the futures contract.

7. The futures price of a stock index is always less than the expected future value of the index. This follows from the fact that the index has positive systematic risk. For an alternative argument, let μ be the expected return required by investors on the index so that $E(S_T) = Se^{(\mu-q)T}$. Since $\mu > r$ and $F = Se^{(r-q)T}$, it follows that $E(S_T) > F$.

CHAPTER 4

1. A *short hedge* is appropriate when a company owns an asset and expects to sell it in the future. It can also be used when the company does not currently own the asset but expects to do so at some time in the future. A *long hedge* is appropriate when a company knows it will have to purchase an asset in the future. It can also be used to offset the risk from an existing short position.
2. *Basis risk* arises from the hedger's uncertainty as to the difference between the spot price and futures price at the expiration of the hedge.
3. A *perfect hedge* is one that completely eliminates the hedger's risk. A perfect hedge does not always lead to a better outcome than an imperfect hedge. It just leads to a more certain outcome. Consider the situation where a company hedges its exposure to the price of an asset. Suppose the asset's price movements prove to be favorable to the company. A perfect hedge totally neutralizes the company's gain from these favorable price movements. An imperfect hedge, which only partially neutralizes these gains, might well work out better.
4. A minimum variance hedge leads to no hedging at all when the coefficient of correlation between the futures price and the price of the asset being hedged is zero.
5. a. If the company's competitors are not hedging, the treasurer might feel that the company will experience less risk if it does not hedge.
   b. The treasurer might feel that the company's shareholders have diversified the risk away.
   c. If there is a loss on the hedge and a gain from the company's exposure to the underlying asset, the treasurer might feel that he or she will have

difficulty justifying the hedging to other executives within the organization.

6. The optimal hedge ratio is

$$0.8 \times \frac{0.65}{0.81} = 0.642$$

This means that the size of the futures position should be 64.2 percent of the size of the company's exposure in a three-month hedge.

7. The formula for the number of contracts that should be shorted gives

$$1.2 \times \frac{10{,}000{,}000}{270 \times 500} = 88.9$$

Rounding to the nearest whole number, 89 contracts should be shorted. To reduce the beta to 0.6, half of this position, or a short position in 45 contracts, is required.

CHAPTER 5

1. Forward rates (percent per annum with continuous compounding) are

Year 2: 7.0
Year 3: 6.6
Year 4: 6.4
Year 5: 6.5

2. When the term structure is upward sloping, $c > a > b$. When it is downward sloping, $b > a > c$.
3. Suppose the bond has a face value of $100. Its price is obtained by discounting the cash flows at 10.4 percent. The price is

$$\frac{4}{1.052} + \frac{4}{10.52^2} + \frac{104}{1.052^3} = 96.74$$

If the 18-month spot rate is R, we must have

$$\frac{4}{1.05} + \frac{4}{1.05^2} + \frac{104}{(1 + R/2)^3} = 96.74$$

which gives $R = 10.42$ percent.

4. There are 89 days between October 12 and January 9. The cash price of the bond is obtained by adding the accrued interest to the quoted price. It is

$$102.21875 + \frac{89}{182} \times 6 = 105.15$$

5. The cash price of the treasury bill is

$$100 - \tfrac{1}{4} \times 10 = 97.5$$

The annualized continuously compounded return is

$$\frac{365}{90} \ln \frac{100}{97.5} = 10.27\%$$

6. A duration-based hedging scheme assumes that term structure movements are always parallel. In other words, it assumes that interest rates of all maturities always change by the same amount in a given period of time.
7. The value of a contract is 108.46875 × 1,000 = 108,468.75. The number of contracts that should be shorted is

$$\frac{6{,}000{,}000}{108{,}468.75} \times \frac{8.2}{7.6} = 59.7$$

Rounding to the nearest whole number, 60 contracts should be shorted.

CHAPTER 6

1. A has a comparative advantage in fixed-rate markets but wants to borrow floating. B has a comparative advantage in floating-rate markets but wants to borrow fixed. This provides the basis for the swap. There is a 1.4 percent per annum differential between the fixed rates offered to the two companies and a 0.5 percent per annum differential between the floating rates offered to the two companies. The total gain to all parties from the swap is, therefore, 1.4 − 0.5 = 0.9 percent per annum. Since the bank gets 0.1 percent per annum of this, the swap should make each of A and B 0.4 percent per annum better off. This means that it should lead to A borrowing at LIBOR − 0.3 percent and to B borrowing at 13 percent. The appropriate arrangement is, therefore, as shown in the following diagram.

Swap for Quiz 6.1

2. X has a comparative advantage in yen markets but wants to borrow dollars. Y has a comparative advantage in dollar markets but wants to borrow yen. This provides the basis for the swap. There is a 1.5 percent per annum differential between the yen rates and a 0.4 percent per annum differential between the dollar rates. The total gain to all parties from the swap is, therefore, 1.5 − 0.4 = 1.1 percent per annum. Since the bank requires 0.5 percent per annum, this leaves 0.3 percent per annum for each of X and Y. The swap

should lead to X borrowing dollars at 9.6 − 0.3 = 9.3 percent per annum and to Y borrowing yen at 6.5 − 0.3 = 6.2 percent per annum. The appropriate arrangement is, therefore, as shown in the following diagram. All foreign exchange risk is born by the bank.

Swap for Quiz 6.2

3. In four months \$6 million will be received and \$4.8 million will be paid. (We ignore the 360-versus-365-day year issue.) In ten months \$6 million will be received and the LIBOR rate prevailing in four months' time will be paid. The value of fixed-rate bond underlying the swap is

$$6e^{-0.3333\times 0.1} + 106e^{-0.8333\times 0.1} = \$103.33 \text{ million}$$

The value of the floating-rate bond underlying the swap is

$$(100 + 4.8)e^{-0.3333\times 0.1} = \$101.36 \text{ million}$$

The value of the swap to the party paying floating is \$103.33 − \$101.36 = \$1.97 million. The value of the swap to the party paying fixed is − \$1.97 million. These results can also be derived by decomposing the swap into forward contracts. Consider the party paying floating. The first forward contract involves paying \$4.8 million and receiving \$6 million in four months. It has a value of $1.2e^{-0.3333\times 0.1} = \$1.16$ million. To value the second forward contract, we note that the forward interest rate is 10 percent per annum with continuous compounding or 10.254 percent per annum with semiannual compounding. The value of the forward contract is

$$100 \times (0.12 \times 0.5 - 0.10254 \times 0.5)e^{-0.833\times 0.1} = \$0.80 \text{ million}$$

The total value of the forward contract is, therefore, \$1.16 + \$0.80 = \$1.96 million.

4. The term *warehousing swaps* is used to refer to the situation where a financial institution does not enter into two offsetting swaps simultaneously. It enters into one of the swaps and hedges its risk until it finds a counterparty with which it can enter into the other swap.
5. The swap involves exchanging the sterling interest of 20 × 0.14 = \$2.8 million for the dollar interest of 30 × 0.1 = \$3 million. The principal amounts are also exchanged at the end of the life of the swap. The value of the sterling bond underlying the swap is

$$\frac{2.8}{(1.11)^{1/4}} + \frac{22.8}{(1.11)^{5/4}} = \$22.74 \text{ million}$$

The value of the dollar bond underlying the swap is

$$\frac{3}{(1.08)^{1/4}} + \frac{33}{(1.08)^{5/4}} = \$32.92 \text{ million}$$

The value of the swap to the party paying sterling is, therefore,

$$32.92 - 22.74 \times 1.65 = -\$4.60 \text{ million}$$

The value of the swap to the party paying dollars is + \$4.60 million. The results can also be obtained by viewing the swap as a portfolio of forward contracts. The continuously compounded interest rates in sterling and dollars are 10.43 percent per annum and 7.70 percent per annum. The three-month and 15-month forward exchange rates are $1.65e^{-0.25\times0.0273} = 1.6388$ and $1.65e^{-1.25\times0.0273} = 1.5946$. The values of the two forward contracts corresponding to the exchange of interest for the party paying sterling are, therefore,

$$(3 - 2.8 \times 1.6388)e^{-0.077\times0.25} = -\$1.56 \text{ million}$$

$$(3 - 2.8 \times 1.5946)e^{-0.077\times1.25} = -\$1.33 \text{ million}$$

The value of the forward contract corresponding to the exchange of principals is

$$(30 - 20 \times 1.5946)e^{-0.077\times1.25} = -\$1.72 \text{ million}$$

The total value of the swap is − \$1.56 − \$1.33 − \$1.72 = − \$4.61 million.

6. Credit risk arises from the possibility of a default by the counterparty. Market risk arises from movements in market variables such as interest rates and exchange rates. Market risks can be hedged; credit risks cannot be hedged.
7. At the start of the swap both contracts have a value of approximately zero. As time passes it is likely that this will change so that one swap has a positive value to the bank and the other has a negative value to the bank. If the counterparty on the other side of the positive-value swap defaults, the bank still has to honor its contract with the other counterparty. It loses an amount equal to the positive value of the swap.

CHAPTER 7

1. The investor makes a profit if the price of the stock on the expiration date is less than \$37. This is because the gain from exercising the option is in these circumstances greater than \$3. The option will be exercised if the stock price

is less than \$40 at the maturity of the option. The variation of the investor's profit with the stock price is as shown in the following diagram.

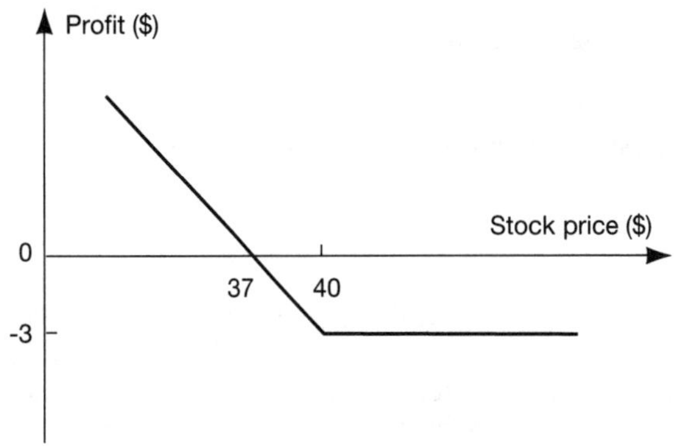

Investor's profit in Quiz 7.1

2. The investor makes a profit if the price of the stock is below \$54 on the expiration date. If the stock price is below \$50, the option will not be exercised and the investor makes a profit of \$4. If the stock price is between \$50 and \$54, the option is exercised and the investor makes a profit between \$0 and \$4. The variation of the investor's profit with the stock price is as shown in the following diagram.

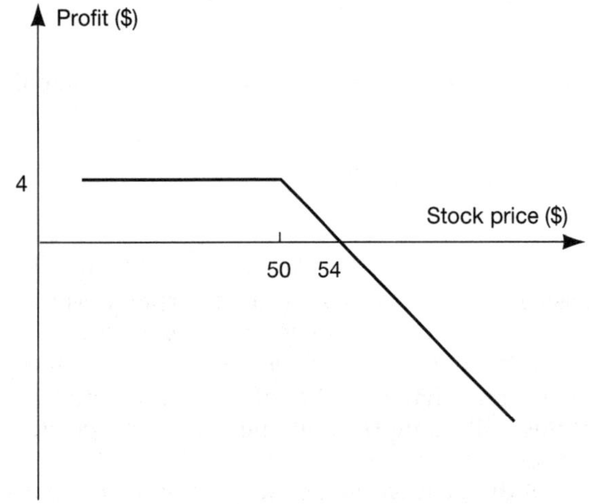

Investor's profit in Quiz 7.2

3. The payoff to the investor is

$$\max(S_T - X, 0) - \max(X - S_T, 0)$$

This is $S_T - X$ in all circumstances. The investor's position is a forward contract with delivery price X.

4. When an investor buys an option, the investor must pay cash up front. There is no possibility of future liabilities and, therefore, no need for a margin account. When an investor sells an option, there are potential future liabilities. To protect against the risk of a default, margins are required.

5. On April 1, options trade with expiration months of April, May, August, and November. On May 30, options trade with expiration months of June, July, August, and November.
6. The strike price is reduced to \$20 and the option gives the holder the right to purchase three times as many shares.
7. In the market maker/order book official system, an individual separate from the market maker keeps a record of limit orders and makes information on these orders available to traders. In the specialist system, a single individual acts as market maker and keeps a record of limit orders. Information on limit orders is not made available to other traders.

CHAPTER 8

1. The six factors affecting stock option prices are the stock price, strike price, risk-free interest rate, volatility, time to maturity, and dividends.
2. The lower bound is

$$28 - 25e^{-0.08 \times 0.3333} = \$3.66$$

3. The lower bound is

$$15e^{-0.06 \times 0.08333} - 12 = \$2.93$$

4. Delaying exercise delays the payment of the strike price. This means that the option holder is able to earn interest on the strike price for a longer period of time. Delaying exercise also provides insurance against the stock price falling below the strike price by the expiration date. Assume that the option holder has an amount of cash X and interest rates are zero. Exercising early means that the option holder's position will be worth S_T at expiration. Delaying exercise means that it will be worth $\max(X, S_T)$ at expiration.
5. An American put when held in conjunction with the underlying stock provides insurance. It guarantees that the stock can be sold for the strike price, X. If the put is exercised early, the insurance ceases. However, the option holder receives the strike price immediately. He or she is able to earn interest on X between the time of the early exercise and the expiration date.
6. If the call is worth \$3, put-call parity shows that the put should be worth

$$3 + 20e^{-0.1 \times 0.25} + e^{-0.1 \times 0.08333} - 19 = 4.50$$

This is greater than \$3. The put is, therefore, undervalued relative to the call. The correct arbitrage strategy is to buy the put, buy the stock, and short the call.
7. When early exercise is not possible, we can argue that two portfolios that are worth the same at time T must be worth the same at earlier times. When early exercise is possible, the argument falls down. Suppose that $P + S > C + Xe^{-rT}$. This does not lead to an arbitrage opportunity. If we buy

the call, short the put, and short the stock, we cannot be sure of the result since we cannot be sure when the put will be exercised.

CHAPTER 9

1. A protective put consists of a long position in a put option combined with a long position in the underlying shares. It is equivalent to a long position in a call option plus a certain amount of cash. This follows from put-call parity:

$$p + S = c + Xe^{-rT} + D$$

2. A bear spread can be created using two call options with the same maturity and different strike prices. The investor shorts the call option with the lower strike price and buys the call option with the higher strike price. A bear spread can also be created using two put options with the same maturity and different strike prices. In this case the investor sells the put option with the lower strike price and buys the put option with the higher strike price.
3. A butterfly spread involves a position in options with three different strike prices (X_1, X_2, and X_3). An investor should purchase a butterfly spread when he or she considers that the price of the underlying stock is likely to stay close to the central strike price, X_2.
4. An investor can create a butterfly spread by buying call options with strike prices of \$15 and \$20, and selling two call options with strike prices of \$17½. The initial investment is $4 + \frac{1}{2} - 2 \times 2 = \$\frac{1}{2}$. The following table shows the variation of profit with the final stock price:

STOCK PRICE S_T	*PROFIT*
$S_T < 15$	$-\frac{1}{2}$
$15 < S_T < 17\frac{1}{2}$	$(S_T - 15) - \frac{1}{2}$
$17\frac{1}{2} < S_T < 20$	$(20 - S_T) - \frac{1}{2}$
$S_T > 20$	$-\frac{1}{2}$

5. A reverse calendar spread is created by buying a short-maturity option and selling a long-maturity option, both with the same strike price.
6. Both a straddle and a strangle are created by combining a call and a put. In a straddle they have the same strike price and expiration date. In a strangle they have different strike prices and the same expiration date.
7. A strangle is created by buying both options. The pattern of profits is as follows:

STOCK PRICE S_T	*PROFIT*
$S_T < 45$	$(45 - S_T) - 5$
$45 < S_T < 50$	-5
$S_T > 50$	$(S_T - 50) - 5$

CHAPTER 10

1. Consider a portfolio consisting of

-1: call option
$+\Delta$: shares

If the stock price rises to \$42, this is worth $42\Delta - 3$. If the stock price falls to \$38, it is worth 38Δ. These are the same when

$$42\Delta - 3 = 38\Delta$$

or $\Delta = 0.75$. The value of the portfolio in one month is \$28.5 for both stock prices. Its value today must be the present value of 28.5 or $28.5e^{-0.08\times 0.08333} = 28.31$. This means that

$$-f + 40\Delta = 28.31$$

where f is the call price. Since $\Delta = 0.75$, the call price is $40 \times 0.75 - 28.31$ or \$1.69. As an alternative approach, we can calculate the probability, p, of an up movement in a risk-neutral world. This must satisfy:

$$42p + 38(1 - p) = 40e^{0.08\times 0.08333}$$

so that

$$4p = 40e^{0.08\times 0.08333} - 38$$

or $p = 0.5669$. The value of the option is then its expected payoff discounted at the risk-free rate or

$$[3 \times 0.5669 + 0 \times 0.4331]e^{-0.08\times 0.08333} = 1.69$$

This agrees with the previous calculation.

2. In the no-arbitrage approach, we set up a riskless portfolio consisting of a position in the option and a position in the stock. By setting the return on the portfolio equal to the risk-free interest rate, we are able to value the option. When we use risk-neutral valuation, we first choose probabilities for the branches of the tree so that the expected return on the stock equals the risk-free interest rate. We then value the option by calculating its expected payoff and discounting this expected payoff at the risk-free interest rate.
3. The delta of a stock option measures the sensitivity of the option price to the price of the stock when small changes are considered. Specifically, it is

the ratio of the change in the price of the stock option to the change in the price of the underlying stock.

4. Consider a portfolio consisting of

-1: put option
$+\Delta$: shares

If the stock price rises to \$55, this is worth 55Δ. If the stock price falls to \$45, it is worth $45\Delta - 5$. These are the same when

$$45\Delta - 5 = 55\Delta$$

or $\Delta = -0.50$. The value of the portfolio in one month is -27.5 for both stock prices. Its value today must be the present value of -27.5 or $-27.5e^{-0.1\times 0.5} = -26.16$. This means that

$$-p + 50\Delta = -26.16$$

where p is the put price. Since $\Delta = -0.50$, the put price is \$1.16. As an alternative approach we can calculate the probability, p, of an up movement in a risk-neutral world. This must satisfy:

$$55p + 45(1 - p) = 50e^{0.1\times 0.5}$$

so that

$$10p = 50e^{0.1\times 0.5} - 45$$

or $p = 0.7564$. The value of the option is then its expected payoff discounted at the risk-free rate or

$$[0 \times 0.7564 + 5 \times 0.2436]e^{-0.1\times 0.5} = 1.16$$

This agrees with the previous calculation.

5. In this case $u = 1.10$, $d = 0.90$, and $r = 0.08$ so that

$$p = \frac{e^{0.08\times 0.5} - 0.90}{1.10 - 0.90} = 0.7041$$

The tree for stock price movements is shown in the following diagram. We can work back from the end of the tree to the beginning as indicated in the diagram to give the value of the option as \$9.61. The option value can also be calculated directly from Equation (10.8):

$$[0.7041^2 \times 21 + 2 \times 0.7041 \times 0.2959 \times 0 + 0.2959^2 \times 0]e^{-0.08} = 9.61$$

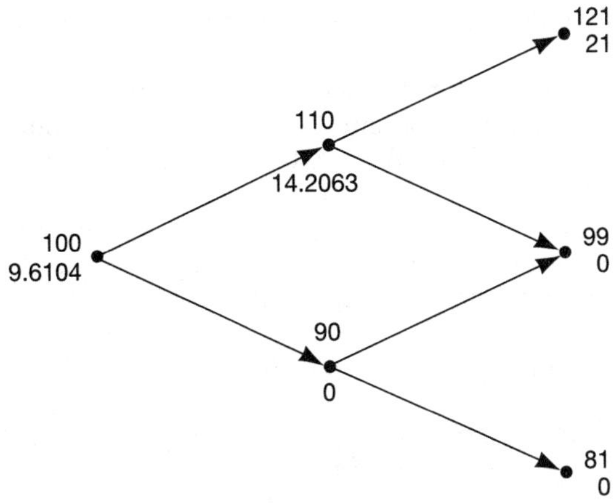

Tree for Quiz 10.5

6. The following diagram shows how we can value the put option using the same tree as in Quiz 5. The value of the option is \$1.92. The option value can also be calculated directly from Equation (10.8):

$$e^{-2\times 0.5\times 0.08}[0.7041^2 \times 0 + 2 \times 0.7041 \times 0.2959 \times 1 + 0.2959^2 \times 19]$$
$$= 1.92$$

The stock price plus the put price is $100 + 1.92 = 101.92$. The present value of the strike price plus the call price is $100e^{-0.08} + 9.61 = 101.92$. These are the same, verifying that put–call parity holds.

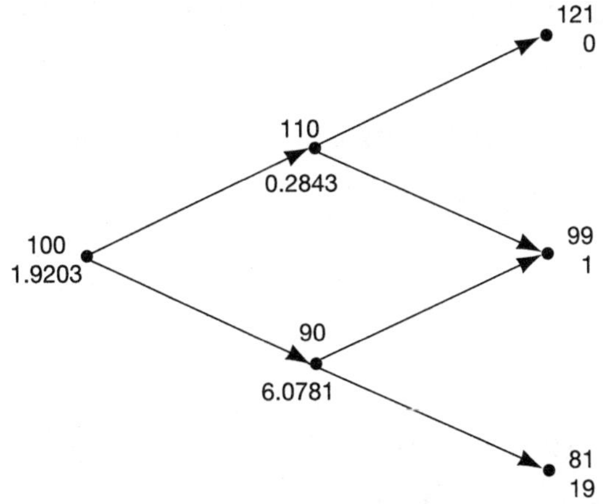

Tree for Quiz 10.6

7. The riskless portfolio consists of a short position in the option and a long position in Δ shares. Since Δ changes during the life of the option, this riskless portfolio must also change.

CHAPTER 11

1. The Black–Scholes option pricing model assumes that the probability distribution of the stock price in one year (or at any other future time) is lognormal.

It assumes that the continuously compounded rate of return on the stock is normally distributed.

2. The standard deviation of the proportional price change in time Δt is $\sigma\sqrt{\Delta t}$ where σ is the volatility. In this problem $\sigma \geqslant 0.3$ and, assuming 250 trading days in one year, $\Delta t = 1/250 = 0.004$ so that $\sigma\sqrt{\Delta t} = 0.3\sqrt{0.004} = 0.019$ or 1.9 percent.
3. Assuming that the expected return from the stock is the risk-free rate, we calculate the expected payoff from the option. We then discount this payoff from the end of the life of the option to the beginning at the risk-free interest rate.
4. In this case $S = 50$, $X = 50$, $r = 0.1$, $\sigma = 0.3$, $T = 0.25$, and

$$d_1 = \frac{\ln(50/50) + (0.1 + 0.09/2)0.25}{0.3\sqrt{0.25}} = 0.2417$$

$$d_2 = d_1 - 0.3\sqrt{0.25} = 0.0917$$

The European put price is

$$50N(-0.0917)e^{-0.1\times 0.25} - 50N(-0.2417)$$

$$= 50 \times 0.4634e^{-0.1\times 0.25} - 50 \times 0.4045 = 2.37$$

or \$2.37.

5. In this case we must subtract the present value of the dividend from the stock price before using Black–Scholes. Hence, the appropriate value of S is

$$S = 50 - 1.50e^{-0.1667\times 0.1} = 48.52$$

As before $X = 50$, $r = 0.1$, $\sigma = 0.3$, and $T = 0.25$. In this case

$$d_1 = \frac{\ln(48.52/50) + (0.1 + 0.09/2)0.25}{0.3\sqrt{0.25}} = 0.0414$$

$$d_2 = d_1 - 0.3\sqrt{0.25} = -0.1086$$

The European put price is

$$50N(0.1086)e^{-0.1\times 0.25} - 48.52N(-0.0414)$$

$$= 50 \times 0.5432e^{-0.1\times 0.25} - 48.52 \times 0.4835 = 3.03$$

or \$3.03.

6. The implied volatility is the volatility that makes the Black–Scholes price of an option equal to its market price. It is calculated by trial and error. We keep testing different volatilities until we find the one that gives the European put option price when it substituted into the Black–Scholes formula.
7. In Black's approximation we calculate the price of a European option expiring at the same time as the American option and the price of a European option

expiring just before the final ex-dividend date. We set the American option price equal to the greater of the two.

CHAPTER 12

1. When the S&P goes down to 240, the value of the portfolio can be expected to be 10 × (240/250) = \$9.6 million. (This assumes that the dividend yield on the portfolio equals the dividend yield on the index.) Buying put options on 10,000,000/250 = 40,000 times the index with a strike of 240, therefore, provides protection against a drop in the value of the portfolio below \$9.6 million. Since each contract is on 100 times the index, a total of 400 contracts would be required.
2. A stock index is analogous to a stock paying a continuous dividend yield, the dividend yield being the dividend yield on the index. A currency is analogous to a stock paying a continuous dividend yield, the dividend yield being the foreign risk-free interest rate.
3. The lower bound is given by Equation (12.1) as

$$300e^{-0.03\times 0.5} - 290e^{-0.08\times 0.5} = 16.90$$

4. The tree of exchange rate movements is shown in the following diagram. In this case $u = 1.02$ and $d = 0.98$. The probability of an up movement is

$$p = \frac{e^{(0.06-0.08)\times 0.08333} - 0.98}{1.02 - 0.98} = 0.4584$$

The tree shows that the value of an option to purchase one unit of the currency is \$0.0067.

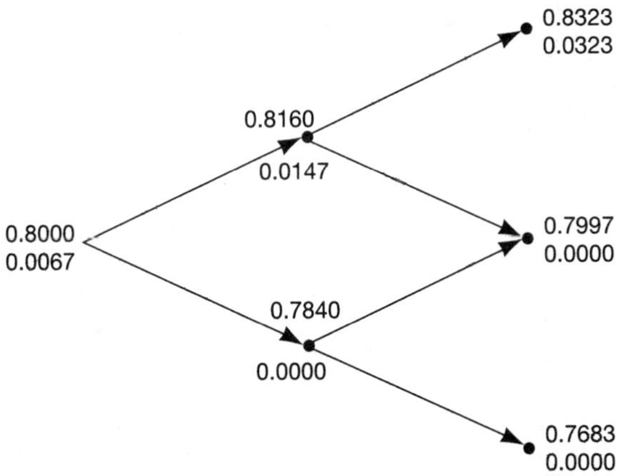

Tree for Quiz 12.4

5. A company that knows it is due to receive a foreign currency at a certain time in the future can buy a put option. This guarantees that the price at which the currency will be sold will be at or above a certain level. A company

that knows it is due to pay a foreign currency a certain time in the future can buy a call option. This guarantees that the price at which the currency will be purchased will be at or below a certain level.

6. In this case, $S = 250$, $X = 250$, $r = 0.10$, $\sigma = 0.18$, $T = 0.25$, $q = 0.03$, and

$$d_1 = \frac{\ln(250/250) + (0.10 - 0.03 + 0.18^2/2)0.25}{0.18\sqrt{0.25}} = 0.2394$$

$$d_2 = d_1 - 0.18\sqrt{0.25} = 0.1494$$

and the call price is

$$250N(0.2394)e^{-0.03\times 0.25} - 250N(0.1494)e^{-0.10\times 0.25}$$

$$= 250 \times 0.5946e^{-0.03\times 0.25} - 250 \times 0.5594e^{-0.10\times 0.25} = 11.14$$

7. In this case, $S = 0.52$, $X = 0.50$, $r = 0.04$, $r_f = 0.08$, $\sigma = 0.12$, $T = 0.6667$, and

$$d_1 = \frac{\ln(0.52/0.50) + (0.04 - 0.08 + 0.12^2/2)0.6667}{0.12\sqrt{0.6667}} = 0.1771$$

$$d_2 = d_1 - 0.12\sqrt{0.6667} = 0.0791$$

and the put price is

$$0.50N(-0.0791)e^{-0.04\times 0.6667} - 0.52N(-0.1771)e^{-0.08\times 0.6667}$$

$$= 0.50 \times 0.4685e^{-0.04\times 0.6667} - 0.52 \times 0.4297e^{-0.08\times 0.6667} = 0.0162$$

CHAPTER 13

1. A call option on yen gives the holder the right to buy yen in the spot market at an exchange rate equal to the strike price. A call option on yen futures gives the holder the right to receive the amount by which the futures price exceeds the strike price. If the yen futures option is exercised, the holder also obtains a long position in the yen futures contract.
2. The main reason is that a bond futures is a more liquid instrument than a bond. The price of a treasury bond futures contract is known immediately from trading on CBOT. The price of a bond can be obtained only by contacting dealers.
3. A futures price behaves like a stock paying a continuous dividend yield at the risk-free interest rate.

4. In this case $u = 1.12$ and $d = 0.92$. The probability of an up movement in a risk-neutral world is

$$\frac{1 - 0.92}{1.12 - 0.92} = 0.4$$

Using risk-neutral valuation, the value of the call is

$$e^{-0.06 \times 0.5}(0.4 \times 6 + 0.6 \times 0) = 2.33$$

5. The put–call parity formula for futures options is the same as the put–call parity formula for stock options except that the stock price is replaced by Fe^{-rT} where F is the current futures, r is the risk-free interest rate, and T is the life of the option.

6. The American futures call option is worth more than the corresponding American option on the underlying asset when the futures price is greater than the spot price prior to the maturity of the futures contract.

7. In this case, $F = 19$, $X = 20$, $r = 0.12$, $\sigma = 0.20$, and $T = 0.4167$. The value of the European put futures option is

$$20N(-d_2)e^{-0.12 \times 0.4167} - 19N(-d_1)e^{-0.12 \times 0.4167}$$

where

$$d_1 = \frac{\ln(19/20) + (0.04/2)0.4167}{0.2\sqrt{0.4167}} = -0.3327$$

$$d_2 = d_1 - 0.2\sqrt{0.4167} = -0.4618$$

This is

$$e^{-0.12 \times 0.4167}[20N(0.4618) - 19N(0.3327)]$$

$$= e^{-0.12 \times 0.4167}(20 \times 0.6778 - 19 \times 0.6303) = 1.50$$

CHAPTER 14

1. A stop-loss scheme can be implemented by arranging to have a covered position when the option is in the money and a naked position when it is out of the money. When using the scheme, the writer of an out-of-the-money call would buy the underlying asset as soon as the price moved above the strike price, X, and sell the underlying asset as soon as the price moved below X. In practice when the price of the underlying equals X, there is no way of knowing whether it will subsequently move above or below X. The asset will, therefore, be bought at $X + \delta$ and sold at $X - \delta$ for some small δ. The cost of hedging depends on the number of times the asset price equals

X. The hedge is, therefore, relatively poor. It will cost nothing if the asset price never reaches X; on the other hand, it will be quite expensive if the asset price equals X many times. In a good hedge the cost of hedging is known in advance to a reasonable level of accuracy.

2. A delta of 0.7 means that when the price of the stock increases by a small amount, the price of the option increases by 70 percent of this amount. Similarly, when the price of the stock decreases by a small amount, the price of the option decreases by 70 percent of this amount. A short position in 1,000 options has a delta of -700 and can be made delta neutral with the purchase of 700 shares.
3. In this case $S = X$, $r = 0.1$, $\sigma = 0.25$, and $T = 0.5$. Also,

$$d_1 = \frac{\ln(S/X) + [(0.1 + 0.25^2)/2]0.5}{0.25\sqrt{0.5}} = 0.3712$$

The delta of the option is $N(d_1)$ or 0.64.
4. A theta of -0.1 means that if Δt years passes with no change in either the stock price or its volatility, the value of the option declines by $0.1\Delta t$. If a trader feels that neither the stock price nor its implied volatility will change, he or she should write an option with as high a negative theta as possible. Relatively short-life at-the-money options have the most negative thetas.
5. The gamma of an option position is the rate of change of the delta of the position with respect to the asset price. For example, a gamma of 0.1 would indicate that when the asset price increases by a certain small amount, delta increases by 0.1 of this amount. When the gamma of an option writer's position is large and negative and the delta is zero, the option writer will lose significant amounts of money if there is a large movement (either an increase or a decrease) in the asset price.
6. To hedge an option position it is necessary to create the opposite option position synthetically. For example, to hedge a long position in a put it is necessary to create a short position in a put synthetically. It follows that the procedure for creating an option position synthetically is the reverse of the procedure for hedging the option position.
7. Portfolio insurance involves creating a put option synthetically. It assumes that as soon as a portfolio's value declines by a small amount the portfolio manager's position is rebalanced by either (a) selling part of the portfolio, or (b) selling some index futures. On October 19, 1987, the market declined so quickly that the sort of rebalancing anticipated in portfolio insurance schemes could not be accomplished.

CHAPTER 15

1. Delta, gamma, and theta can be determined from a single binomial tree. Vega is determined by making a small change to the volatility and recomputing

the option price using a new tree. Rho is calculated by making a small change to the interest rate and recomputing the option price using a new tree.

2. In this case, $S = 60$, $X = 60$, $r = 0.1$, $\sigma = 0.45$, $T = 0.25$, and $\Delta t = 0.0833$. Also

$$u = e^{\sigma\sqrt{\Delta t}} = e^{0.45\sqrt{0.0833}} = 1.1387$$

$$d = \frac{1}{u} = 0.8782$$

$$a = e^{r\Delta t} = e^{0.1\times 0.0833} = 1.0084$$

$$p = \frac{a-d}{u-d} = 0.4998$$

$$1 - p = 0.5002$$

The tree is shown in the following diagram. The calculated price of the option is \$5.16.

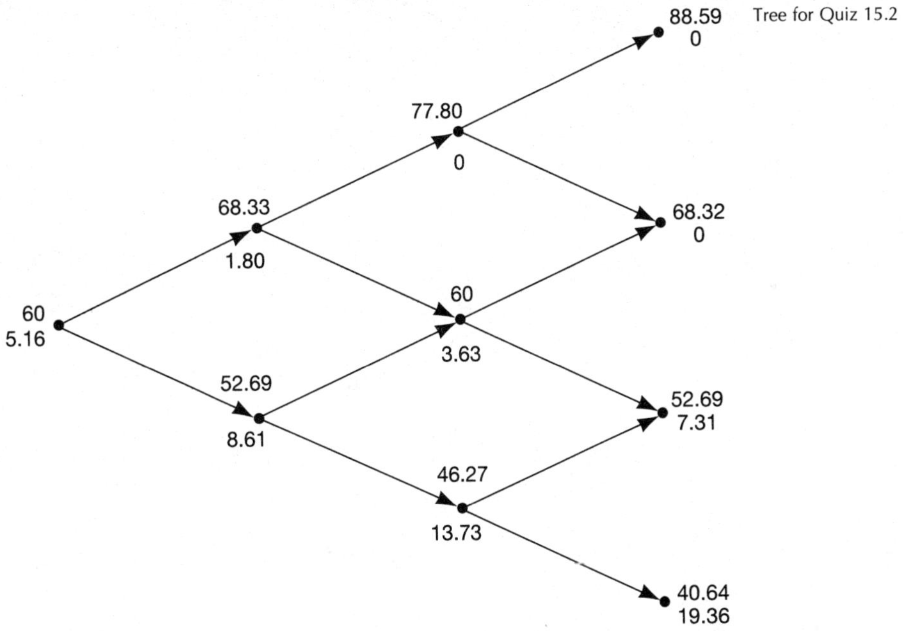

3. The control variate technique is implemented by
   a. Valuing an American option using a binomial tree in the usual way ($=f_A$).
   b. Valuing the European option with the same parameters as the American option using the same tree ($=f_E$).
   c. Valuing the European option using Black–Scholes ($=f_{BS}$).

The price of the American option is estimated as $f_A + f_{BS} - f_E$.

4. In this case $F = 198$, $X = 200$, $r = 0.08$, $\sigma = 0.3$, $T = 0.75$, and $\Delta t = 0.25$. Also

$$u = e^{0.3\sqrt{0.25}} = 1.1618$$

$$d = \frac{1}{u} = 0.8607$$

$$a = 1$$

$$p = \frac{a - d}{u - d} = 0.4626$$

$$1 - p = 0.5373$$

The tree is as shown in the following diagram. The calculated price of the option is 20.3 cents.

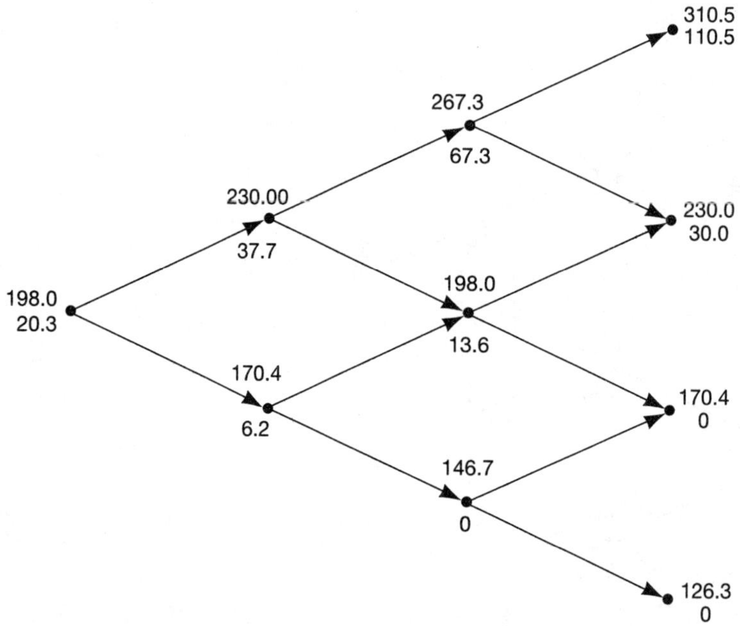

Tree for Quiz 15.4

5. No! This is an example of what is known as a *history-dependent option*. The payoff depends on the path followed by the stock price as well as its final value. The option cannot be valued by starting at the end of the tree and working backward, since the payoff at a final branch depends on the path used to reach it. European options where the payoff depends on the average stock price can be valued using Monte Carlo simulation.
6. Suppose a dividend equal to D is paid during a certain time interval. If S is the stock price at the beginning of the time interval, it will be either $Su - D$ or $Sd - D$ at the end of the time interval. At the end of the next

time interval, it will be one of $(Su - D)u$, $(Su - D)d$, $(Sd - D)u$, and $(Sd - D)d$. Since $(Su - D)d$ does not equal $(Sd - D)u$, the tree does not recombine. If S is equal to the stock price less the present value of future dividends, this problem is avoided.

7. With the usual notation

$$p = \frac{a - d}{u - d}$$

$$1 - p = \frac{u - a}{u - d}$$

If $a < d$ or $a > u$, one of the two probabilities is negative. Usually $d < a < u$. However, a may be less than d when an option on a high-interest currency is being valued and a may be greater than u when σ is very small. The problem can be overcome by modeling the forward price of the asset rather than the asset price itself.

CHAPTER 16

1. When both tails of the stock price distribution are thinner than those of the lognormal distribution, Black–Scholes will tend to overprice options when they are either significantly out of the money or significantly in the money. When the right tail is thinner and the left tail is fatter, Black–Scholes will tend to overprice out-of-the-money calls and in-the-money puts. It will tend to underprice out-of-the-money puts and in-the-money calls.

2. When the stock price is positively correlated with volatility, we tend to get thin left tails and fat right tails. Black–Scholes will tend to underprice out-of-the-money calls and in-the-money puts. It will tend to overprice out-of-the-money puts and in-the-money calls.

3. Jumps tend to make both tails of the stock price distribution fatter than those of the lognormal distribution. This means that Black–Scholes will tend to underprice options that are either significantly in the money or significantly out of the money. These biases are likely to be less pronounced for long options than for short options.

4. The compound option model gives a stock price distribution with thinner right tails and fatter left tails than the lognormal distribution. Black–Scholes tends to overprice out-of-the-money calls and in-the-money puts. It tends to underprice in-the-money calls and out-of-the-money puts. It follows that when Black–Scholes is used, relatively high implied volatilities will be observed for in-the-money calls and out-of-the-money puts. Relatively low implied volatilities will be observed for out-of-the-money calls and in-the-money puts.

5. These biases are the same because of put-call parity. Suppose that p and c are the Black–Scholes prices of a European put and call, and that p^* and c^*

are the put and call prices based on another model. Put–call parity is true for all models. Hence, with the usual notation,

$$c + Xe^{-rT} = p + S$$

$$c^* + Xe^{-rT} = p^* + S$$

so that

$$c - c^* = p - p^*$$

showing that the bias for the call price is the same as the bias for the put price. When the call is in the money, the put is out of the money and vice versa. This explains why the biases for in-the-money call options are usually the same as the biases for out-of-the-money put options.

6. The probability distribution of the stock price at some future time (say, in one month) is not lognormal. Possibly it consists of two lognormal distributions superimposed upon each other and is bimodal. Black–Scholes is clearly inappropriate, since it assumes that the stock price at any future time is lognormal.
7. There are a number of problems in testing an option pricing model empirically. These include the problem of obtaining synchronous data on stock prices and option prices, the problem of estimating the dividends that will be paid on the stock during the option's life, the problem of distinguishing between situations where the market is inefficient and situations where the option pricing model is incorrect, and the problems of estimating stock price volatility.

CHAPTER 17

1. An amount

$$\$20{,}000{,}000 \times 0.02 \times 0.25 = \$100{,}000$$

would be paid out three months later.

2. An investor in a mortgage-backed security has a stake in a portfolio of residential mortgages. The mortgages are insured so that the investor is protected against defaults. The investor receives his or her share of the cash flows (both interest and principal) paid on the mortgages in the portfolio. A mortgage-backed security is more risky than a government bond because the investor's return depends on the extent to which the prepayment options embedded in the mortgages are exercised.
3. A swaption is an option to enter into an interest-rate swap at a certain time in the future with a certain fixed rate being used. An interest-rate swap can be regarded as the exchange of a fixed-rate bond for a floating-rate bond. A swaption is, therefore, the option to exchange a fixed-rate bond for a floating-rate bond. The floating-rate bond will be worth its face value at the beginning of the life of the swap. The swaption is, therefore, an option on a fixed-rate bond with the strike price equal to the face value of the bond.

4. In this case, $B = 125 - 10 = 115$, $X = 110$, $R = 0.1$, $\sigma = 0.08$, and $T = 1.0$.

$$d_1 = \frac{\ln(115/110) + 0.1 + (0.08^2/2)}{0.08} = 1.8456$$

$$d_2 = d_1 - 0.08 = 1.7656$$

The value of the put option is

$$110e^{-0.1}N(-1.7656) - 115N(-1.8456) = 0.12$$

or \$0.12.

5. There are two problems with the Black–Scholes approach when the life of the option is a significant proportion of the life of the underlying bond. One is that the volatility of the bond declines steadily during the life of the option. The other is that the bond price is pulled toward its face value. As the maturity of the bond is approached, this pull becomes stronger. One alternative to Black–Scholes is to regard the option as being written on the forward bond price with the maturity of the forward contract being the same as the maturity of the option. Black's model can then be used. Another more sophisticated alternative (which can also be used for American options) is to construct a yield curve model.

6. In this case $L = 1000$, $\tau = 0.25$, $F = 0.12$, $R_X = 0.13$, $r = 0.115$, $\sigma = 0.12$, and $T = 1.5$.

$$\frac{\tau L}{1 + F\tau} = 242.72$$

$$d_1 = \frac{\ln(0.12/0.13) + 0.12^2 \times 1.5/2}{0.12\sqrt{1.5}} = -0.4711$$

$$d_2 = -0.4711 - 0.12\sqrt{1.5} = -0.6181$$

The value of the option is

$$242.7e^{-0.115\times 1.5}\,[0.12N(-0.4711) - 0.13N(-0.6181)] = 242.7 \times 0.0028 = 0.69$$

or \$0.69.

7. There are two main advantages of yield curve models. First, they enable all interest-rate derivative securities to be valued on a consistent basis. Second, they enable securities other than caps and bond options to be valued. An example of a security that cannot be valued using the Black or Black–Scholes models but can be valued using yield curve models is a long-dated American bond option.

Table for $N(x)$ when $x \leq 0$

This table shows values of $N(x)$ for $x \leq 0$. The table should be used with interpolation. For example,

$$\begin{aligned} N(-0.1234) &= N(-0.12) - 0.34[N(-0.12) - N(-0.13)] \\ &= 0.4522 - 0.34 \times (0.4522 - 0.4483) \\ &= 0.4509 \end{aligned}$$

x	.00	.01	.02	.03	.04	.05	.06	.07	.08	.09
−0.0	0.5000	0.4960	0.4920	0.4880	0.4840	0.4801	0.4761	0.4721	0.4681	0.4641
−0.1	0.4602	0.4562	0.4522	0.4483	0.4443	0.4404	0.4364	0.4325	0.4286	0.4247
−0.2	0.4207	0.4168	0.4129	0.4090	0.4052	0.4013	0.3974	0.3936	0.3897	0.3859
−0.3	0.3821	0.3783	0.3745	0.3707	0.3669	0.3632	0.3594	0.3557	0.3520	0.3483
−0.4	0.3446	0.3409	0.3372	0.3336	0.3300	0.3264	0.3228	0.3192	0.3156	0.3121
−0.5	0.3085	0.3050	0.3015	0.2981	0.2946	0.2912	0.2877	0.2843	0.2810	0.2776
−0.6	0.2743	0.2709	0.2676	0.2643	0.2611	0.2578	0.2546	0.2514	0.2483	0.2451
−0.7	0.2420	0.2389	0.2358	0.2327	0.2296	0.2266	0.2236	0.2206	0.2177	0.2148
−0.8	0.2119	0.2090	0.2061	0.2033	0.2005	0.1977	0.1949	0.1922	0.1894	0.1867
−0.9	0.1841	0.1814	0.1788	0.1762	0.1736	0.1711	0.1685	0.1660	0.1635	0.1611
−1.0	0.1587	0.1562	0.1539	0.1515	0.1492	0.1469	0.1446	0.1423	0.1401	0.1379
−1.1	0.1357	0.1335	0.1314	0.1292	0.1271	0.1251	0.1230	0.1210	0.1190	0.1170
−1.2	0.1151	0.1131	0.1112	0.1093	0.1075	0.1056	0.1038	0.1020	0.1003	0.0985
−1.3	0.0968	0.0951	0.0934	0.0918	0.0901	0.0885	0.0869	0.0853	0.0838	0.0823
−1.4	0.0808	0.0793	0.0778	0.0764	0.0749	0.0735	0.0721	0.0708	0.0694	0.0681
−1.5	0.0668	0.0655	0.0643	0.0630	0.0618	0.0606	0.0594	0.0582	0.0571	0.0559
−1.6	0.0548	0.0537	0.0526	0.0516	0.0505	0.0495	0.0485	0.0475	0.0465	0.0455
−1.7	0.0446	0.0436	0.0427	0.0418	0.0409	0.0401	0.0392	0.0384	0.0375	0.0367
−1.8	0.0359	0.0351	0.0344	0.0336	0.0329	0.0322	0.0314	0.0307	0.0301	0.0294
−1.9	0.0287	0.0281	0.0274	0.0268	0.0262	0.0256	0.0250	0.0244	0.0239	0.0233
−2.0	0.0228	0.0222	0.0217	0.0212	0.0207	0.0202	0.0197	0.0192	0.0188	0.0183
−2.1	0.0179	0.0174	0.0170	0.0166	0.0162	0.0158	0.0154	0.0150	0.0146	0.0143
−2.2	0.0139	0.0136	0.0132	0.0129	0.0125	0.0122	0.0119	0.0116	0.0113	0.0110
−2.3	0.0107	0.0104	0.0102	0.0099	0.0096	0.0094	0.0091	0.0089	0.0087	0.0084
−2.4	0.0082	0.0080	0.0078	0.0075	0.0073	0.0071	0.0069	0.0068	0.0066	0.0064
−2.5	0.0062	0.0060	0.0059	0.0057	0.0055	0.0054	0.0052	0.0051	0.0049	0.0048
−2.6	0.0047	0.0045	0.0044	0.0043	0.0041	0.0040	0.0039	0.0038	0.0037	0.0036
−2.7	0.0035	0.0034	0.0033	0.0032	0.0031	0.0030	0.0029	0.0028	0.0027	0.0026
−2.8	0.0026	0.0025	0.0024	0.0023	0.0023	0.0022	0.0021	0.0021	0.0020	0.0019
−2.9	0.0019	0.0018	0.0018	0.0017	0.0016	0.0016	0.0015	0.0015	0.0014	0.0014
−3.0	0.0014	0.0013	0.0013	0.0012	0.0012	0.0011	0.0011	0.0011	0.0010	0.0010
−3.1	0.0010	0.0009	0.0009	0.0009	0.0008	0.0008	0.0008	0.0008	0.0007	0.0007
−3.2	0.0007	0.0007	0.0006	0.0006	0.0006	0.0006	0.0006	0.0005	0.0005	0.0005
−3.3	0.0005	0.0005	0.0005	0.0004	0.0004	0.0004	0.0004	0.0004	0.0004	0.0003
−3.4	0.0003	0.0003	0.0003	0.0003	0.0003	0.0003	0.0003	0.0003	0.0003	0.0002
−3.5	0.0002	0.0002	0.0002	0.0002	0.0002	0.0002	0.0002	0.0002	0.0002	0.0002
−3.6	0.0002	0.0002	0.0001	0.0001	0.0001	0.0001	0.0001	0.0001	0.0001	0.0001
−3.7	0.0001	0.0001	0.0001	0.0001	0.0001	0.0001	0.0001	0.0001	0.0001	0.0001
−3.8	0.0001	0.0001	0.0001	0.0001	0.0001	0.0001	0.0001	0.0001	0.0001	0.0001
−3.9	0.0000	0.0000	0.0000	0.0000	0.0000	0.0000	0.0000	0.0000	0.0000	0.0000
−4.0	0.0000	0.0000	0.0000	0.0000	0.0000	0.0000	0.0000	0.0000	0.0000	0.0000

Table for $N(x)$ when $x \geq 0$

This table shows values of $N(x)$ for $x \geq 0$. The table should be used with interpolation. For example,

$$\begin{aligned} N(0.6278) &= N(0.62) + 0.78[N(0.63) - N(0.62)] \\ &= 0.7324 + 0.78 \times (0.7357 - 0.7324) \\ &= 0.7350 \end{aligned}$$

x	.00	.01	.02	.03	.04	.05	.06	.07	.08	.09
0.0	0.5000	0.5040	0.5080	0.5120	0.5160	0.5199	0.5239	0.5279	0.5319	0.5359
0.1	0.5398	0.5438	0.5478	0.5517	0.5557	0.5596	0.5636	0.5675	0.5714	0.5753
0.2	0.5793	0.5832	0.5871	0.5910	0.5948	0.5987	0.6026	0.6064	0.6103	0.6141
0.3	0.6179	0.6217	0.6255	0.6293	0.6331	0.6368	0.6406	0.6443	0.6480	0.6517
0.4	0.6554	0.6591	0.6628	0.6664	0.6700	0.6736	0.6772	0.6808	0.6844	0.6879
0.5	0.6915	0.6950	0.6985	0.7019	0.7054	0.7088	0.7123	0.7157	0.7190	0.7224
0.6	0.7257	0.7291	0.7324	0.7357	0.7389	0.7422	0.7454	0.7486	0.7517	0.7549
0.7	0.7580	0.7611	0.7642	0.7673	0.7704	0.7734	0.7764	0.7794	0.7823	0.7852
0.8	0.7881	0.7910	0.7939	0.7967	0.7995	0.8023	0.8051	0.8078	0.8106	0.8133
0.9	0.8159	0.8186	0.8212	0.8238	0.8264	0.8289	0.8315	0.8340	0.8365	0.8389
1.0	0.8413	0.8438	0.8461	0.8485	0.8508	0.8531	0.8554	0.8577	0.8599	0.8621
1.1	0.8643	0.8665	0.8686	0.8708	0.8729	0.8749	0.8770	0.8790	0.8810	0.8830
1.2	0.8849	0.8869	0.8888	0.8907	0.8925	0.8944	0.8962	0.8980	0.8997	0.9015
1.3	0.9032	0.9049	0.9066	0.9082	0.9099	0.9115	0.9131	0.9147	0.9162	0.9177
1.4	0.9192	0.9207	0.9222	0.9236	0.9251	0.9265	0.9279	0.9292	0.9306	0.9319
1.5	0.9332	0.9345	0.9357	0.9370	0.9382	0.9394	0.9406	0.9418	0.9429	0.9441
1.6	0.9452	0.9463	0.9474	0.9484	0.9495	0.9505	0.9515	0.9525	0.9535	0.9545
1.7	0.9554	0.9564	0.9573	0.9582	0.9591	0.9599	0.9608	0.9616	0.9625	0.9633
1.8	0.9641	0.9649	0.9656	0.9664	0.9671	0.9678	0.9686	0.9693	0.9699	0.9706
1.9	0.9713	0.9719	0.9726	0.9732	0.9738	0.9744	0.9750	0.9756	0.9761	0.9767
2.0	0.9772	0.9778	0.9783	0.9788	0.9793	0.9798	0.9803	0.9808	0.9812	0.9817
2.1	0.9821	0.9826	0.9830	0.9834	0.9838	0.9842	0.9846	0.9850	0.9854	0.9857
2.2	0.9861	0.9864	0.9868	0.9871	0.9875	0.9878	0.9881	0.9884	0.9887	0.9890
2.3	0.9893	0.9896	0.9898	0.9901	0.9904	0.9906	0.9909	0.9911	0.9913	0.9916
2.4	0.9918	0.9920	0.9922	0.9925	0.9927	0.9929	0.9931	0.9932	0.9934	0.9936
2.5	0.9938	0.9940	0.9941	0.9943	0.9945	0.9946	0.9948	0.9949	0.9951	0.9952
2.6	0.9953	0.9955	0.9956	0.9957	0.9959	0.9960	0.9961	0.9962	0.9963	0.9964
2.7	0.9965	0.9966	0.9967	0.9968	0.9969	0.9970	0.9971	0.9972	0.9973	0.9974
2.8	0.9974	0.9975	0.9976	0.9977	0.9977	0.9978	0.9979	0.9979	0.9980	0.9981
2.9	0.9981	0.9982	0.9982	0.9983	0.9984	0.9984	0.9985	0.9985	0.9986	0.9986
3.0	0.9986	0.9987	0.9987	0.9988	0.9988	0.9989	0.9989	0.9989	0.9990	0.9990
3.1	0.9990	0.9991	0.9991	0.9991	0.9992	0.9992	0.9992	0.9992	0.9993	0.9993
3.2	0.9993	0.9993	0.9994	0.9994	0.9994	0.9994	0.9994	0.9995	0.9995	0.9995
3.3	0.9995	0.9995	0.9995	0.9996	0.9996	0.9996	0.9996	0.9996	0.9996	0.9997
3.4	0.9997	0.9997	0.9997	0.9997	0.9997	0.9997	0.9997	0.9997	0.9997	0.9998
3.5	0.9998	0.9998	0.9998	0.9998	0.9998	0.9998	0.9998	0.9998	0.9998	0.9998
3.6	0.9998	0.9998	0.9999	0.9999	0.9999	0.9999	0.9999	0.9999	0.9999	0.9999
3.7	0.9999	0.9999	0.9999	0.9999	0.9999	0.9999	0.9999	0.9999	0.9999	0.9999
3.8	0.9999	0.9999	0.9999	0.9999	0.9999	0.9999	0.9999	0.9999	0.9999	0.9999
3.9	1.0000	1.0000	1.0000	1.0000	1.0000	1.0000	1.0000	1.0000	1.0000	1.0000
4.0	1.0000	1.0000	1.0000	1.0000	1.0000	1.0000	1.0000	1.0000	1.0000	1.0000

Major Exchanges Throughout the World Trading Futures and Options With Their Abbreviations

American Stock Exchange	AMEX
Australian Stock Exchange Sydney	AUS
Chicago Board of Trade	CBOT
Chicago Board Options Exchange	CBOE
Chicago Mercantile Exchange	CME
Coffee, Sugar & Cocoa Exchange	CSCE
Commodity Exchange, New York	COMEX
Deutsche Termin Börse	DTB
European Options Exchange	EOE
International Petroleum Exchange	IPE
Financial Instruments Exchange	FINEX
Finnish Options Market	FOM
London Futures and Options Exchange	FOX
London International Financial Futures Exchange	LIFFE
London Metal Exchange	LME
London Traded Options Market	LTOM
Marché à Terme International de France	MATIF
Marché de Options Negóciables de Paris	MONEP
Montreal Exchange	ME
New York Cotton Exchange	NYCE
New York Futures Exchange	NYFE
New York Mercantile Exchange	NYMEX
New York Stock Exchange	NYSE
Osaka Securities Exchange	OSA
Pacific Stock Exchange	PSE
Philadelphia Stock Exchange	PHLX
Rio de Janeiro Stock Exchange	BVRJ
Sao Paulo Mercantile & Futures Exchange	BOVESPA
Singapore Mercantile Exchange	SIMEX
Stockholm Options Market	OM
Swiss Options and Financial Futures Exchange	SOFFEX
Sydney Futures Exchange	SFE
Tokyo International Financial Futures Exchange	TIFFE
Toronto Stock Exchange	TSE
Winnipeg Commodity Exchange	WCE

INDEX